Campden 1914-18

A tribute to the 487 men and women from Campden who served during the Great War, 1914-18.

Paul R. Hughes

ISBN 978-0-9559200-1-1

Published by *Campden People*
The Old Police Station
High Street
Chipping Campden
Gloucestershire
GL55 6HB

Supported by
The National Lottery®
through Awards for All

Printed and bound in Great Britain by Vale Press Ltd.
6 Willersey Business Park, Willersey, Broadway, Worcestershire, WR12 7RR
01386 858900

Contents

Charles Harold Eldred
Charles served as a captain in the Home Guard during the Second World War. In the above photograph he can be seen at the front leading his men.

Foreword

My nephew, Paul R. Hughes, is Head of Design and Technology at Queen Mary's Grammar School in Walsall and has undertaken a considerable amount of research with a view to obtaining a detailed knowledge of the men and women of Campden who served in the Great War. He has visited battlefields and war graves in Belgium, France, Italy, Salonika and Gallipoli regularly over the last fifteen years and has walked the fields where men from Campden fought and died.

I have accompanied him on several of these trips and one particular area near Verdun in France is firmly embedded in my mind. At the Ossuaire de Douaumont the remains of 130,000 men, retrieved from the battlefield at the end of the war, can be seen through a number of small windows. This serves as a potent reminder of the horror of war.

This book identifies 487 men and women who served in the Great War. Not all are true Campdonians but all have a connection with the town. Paul has given many talks on the war and used to run a World War One club at The Bishop's Stortford High School. I remember one occasion when he gave a talk to the Campden and District Historical and Archaeological Society dressed as a uniformed infantryman of the period. A slide show illustrated his walking tour of Gallipoli in Turkey, where he walked in the footsteps of Algernon Hathaway, who was killed in action in August 1915.

I am personally able to recall maimed survivors from the Great War who returned home with serious physical and emotional injuries. These were proud men who served their country with honour and dignity. This book makes me very aware of the sadness and hardships that followed that horrendous conflict.

I will always remember an inscription on a young soldier's headstone, chosen by his mother, that I saw on a visit to the Western Front:

"I often wonder how you died. If only I had heard your last goodbye."

Dennis Hughes
Stoker Mechanic First Class DKX 642537, Royal Navy 1945-48
Campden
April 2008

Dennis Hughes, Royal Navy, 1945

Dennis Hughes, HMS *Consort*, Malta

Joey James, Special Constable, 1939-45
Joey can be seen in the above photograph wearing his three 1914-18 campaign medals.

Acknowledgements

This book has taken over fifteen years to produce and it would not have been possible without the involvement of many people. Everyone in Campden has been magnificent in the way that they have supported, helped and generally shown an interest in the project. The aim of the book was always to remember all people connected with Campden who served in the Great War and families have been very generous in the time that they have spent searching for photographs, documents and medals. They have trusted him with treasured items and it is hoped that all documents loaned to him have been returned promptly and undamaged.

It is not possible to mention by name everyone who has helped with the book but there are some people who deserve special acknowledgement of the time and effort that they have put in during its preparation. Ray White was a meticulous proof reader and made many valuable suggestions for making the text more readable. Judith Ellis, granddaughter of Harry George Ellis, read through each entry as it was being prepared and her thoughts were used to edit the entries to make them as concise, relevant and interesting as possible. Jennifer Bruce and Carol Jackson answered many queries during term time regarding the records held in the archive room in the Old Police Station in Campden. Margaret Fisher provided a similar service for queries relating to Ebrington. Their prompt, efficient replies were very much appreciated.

The members of the *Campden Branch of the Gloucestershire Family History Society* and *Campden and District Historical and Archaeological Society* were always willing to lend a helping hand with any queries and it would not have been possible to complete the project without access to their expertise and local knowledge. The many excellent publications produced by the two societies were also extremely helpful in background research and are highly recommended.

Many Campden families have left the town over the last hundred years and set up home in various countries around the world. In Australia there are relatives of the Biles, Griffiths, Huyshe and Preece families, in Canada relatives of the Ellis, Lynch-Staunton, Plested, Payne, Merriman and Williams families and in USA relatives of the Keen family. Many hours have been spent tracking down these families and again their support and encouragement have been very much appreciated.

The author has visited the battlefields of the Great War regularly each year over the last fifteen years. The last resting places of virtually all of the Campden men have been visited and a special thank you must go to the gardeners of the Commonwealth War Graves Commission (CWGC) who do a magnificent job maintaining the grass and flowers in the cemeteries. The staff of the CWGC at their head office in Maidenhead, and in their offices in Ypres in Belgium and Beaurains in France, have promptly and efficiently provided information of men connected with Campden as and when it has been requested. This process is now made much easier with their searchable website which lists all war dead of the Great War.

Researching the men and women from Campden has also required many hours at various record offices around the country. The staff at Gloucester Record Office have been excellent and are always willing to provide guidance and support when needed. At the National Archives at Kew in London they operate a system where help is provided by information leaflets but when the archivists were asked for more personal assistance they always gave their time freely and with a smile.

It has not always been possible for the author to travel to London and Jonathan Collins, a professional researcher, has been very efficient in carrying out research in relation to the Campden project. His knowledge of the archives held at Kew has meant it has been money well spent. At the Grenadier Guards archive at Wellington Barracks in London Lance Sergeant Tack has promptly copied service papers of the Campden men who served in the Grenadier Guards during the war.

The author has been very fortunate to have access to a number of people who have an excellent knowledge of the Great War. Bob Pike, Paul Reed, Glyn Dutson and Sam Eedle always provided prompt replies to queries and their support has been very much appreciated.

Dennis Hughes, the author's uncle, who kindly agreed to write the foreword, has always shown tremendous interest in this project. He has been a companion on several trips to the battlefields and has walked many fields where Campden men fought and died. To him, and all of the 487 men and women from Campden who served in the war, "*Thank you.*"

Frederick Drinkwater, Oxfordshire and Buckinghamshire Light Infantry
Frederick can be seen in the above photograph with his wife, Martha Mary Drinkwater. This photograph was a very late
addition to the author's collection and was provided by CADHAS from their archives held in the Old Police Station in
Campden.

Introduction

Many years have been spent collecting the information needed to write this book. The author hopes that it is a fitting tribute to the 487 men and women associated with Campden who served their country during the Great War. Some were born in Campden while others moved to the town after the war. Some lived in it for part of their life while others simply found employment in it. Readers will recognise many of the family names but there will be some that lead people to wonder why they have been included. Hopefully, reading each entry will explain how they are connected with Campden.

Many different sources were used to identify the people to include:

- **The *Book of Remembrance* by Josephine Griffiths:** This book records details of sixty-four men from the town who lost their lives during the war and also includes a list of men who served in the various forces.
- **St. James's Church Prayer List**: David James, son of *Jim* James, provided the author with a copy of a prayer list of servicemen produced by the church in 1916. All men listed were either members of the congregation or close friends of members.
- **The *Evesham Journal***: Throughout the winter months of 1914 this local newspaper produced lists of men from each town and village who were in uniform. As the war progressed it published photographs of casualties and letters sent home from the trenches.
- **Commonwealth War Graves Commission**: Family details for most of the country's war dead are held by the CWGC and it is possible to ask them to supply a list of all men and women who have Campden recorded in their details. The author paid for this service and it provided some very interesting results.
- **Church Records**: Many hours were spent looking through church records held at St. James's Church, St. Catharine's Church and Gloucester Record Office and in the archive room in the Old Police Station in Campden. The records of births, deaths and marriages all provided the author with much useful information. A few of the men in this book are only included because they married local girls in one of the churches in the town.
- **School Registers**: The admissions registers for schools in the town provided some interesting background information but very little archive material for Campden Grammar School seems to have survived.
- **Soldiers Died in the Great War**: These volumes were originally published in 1921 but are now available as a fully searchable CD ROM which lists all army casualties of the war. The author searched for all men who were born, lived or enlisted in Campden and this provided some men who would otherwise have not been included in the book.
- **The National Archives**: Using the Internet it is possible to search the National Archives website, using "Campden" as a key word. This enabled the author to find several sets of army pension papers and Royal Navy service papers for men from Campden. All medal index cards and surviving service papers for the Great War are held at Kew. The author spent many hours searching and information about several men from Campden was found, including the service papers for the author's two great-grandfathers, Richard Hughes and Charles Brotheridge.

This is meant to be a reference book and it has not been designed to be read from cover to cover. Every photograph in the author's collection has been included and every effort has been made to enhance the quality of the prints. Some of the photographs were in an extremely poor condition but it was felt that they still needed to be included.

Every effort has been made to ensure that the facts presented are correct but corrections and additional information from family and military historians would be welcome.

The Boys' Brigade, c.1908
The Boys' Brigade was founded in Campden in 1908 by Harry George Ellis. In the above photograph he can be seen standing
on the extreme left-hand side. His son, Gordon, is in the centre with the big bass drum. Arthur Ellis, who served in the RFC
and RAF in the Great War, can be seen kneeling on the left with an "X" on his chest.

Abbreviations

AIF:	Australian Imperial Forces
ANZAC:	Australian and New Zealand Army Corps
ARP:	Air-Raid Precautions
ASC:	Army Service Corps
CB:	Companion of the Order of the Bath
CMG:	Companion of the Order of St. Michael and St. George
CSM:	Company Sergeant-Major
DSO:	Distinguished Service Order
RFA:	Royal Field Artillery
RGA:	Royal Garrison Artillery
MC:	Military Cross
MM:	Military Medal
MSM:	Meritorious Service Medal
NCO:	Non-commissioned Officer
OTC:	Officer Training Corps
RAF:	Royal Air Force
RAMC:	Royal Army Medical Corps
RASC:	Royal Arm Service Corps
RE:	Royal Engineers
RFC:	Royal Flying Corps
RMLI:	Royal Marine Light Infantry
RNAS:	Royal Naval Air Service
RND:	Royal Naval Division
RNR:	Royal Naval Reserve
RNVR:	Royal Naval Volunteer Reserve
TA:	Territorial Army
VC:	Victoria Cross

The Great War

There are many excellent books on the Great War and these can be obtained from any good bookshop. This book is not meant to be a history of the war but a tribute to the men and women from Campden who served in the armed forces, in munitions factories or in hospital as nurses. What follows is a brief overview of the main events that took place before, during and immediately after the war.

Chronology of Events

1914

28 June:	Archduke Franz Ferdinand of Austria-Hungary assassinated at Sarajevo by Gavrilo Princip, a member of a Serbian nationalist organisation, the *Black Hand*.
23 July:	Austria-Hungary sends an ultimatum to Serbia demanding suppression of Slav anti-Austrian activities and demanding Austrian presence at the inquiry into the assassination.
28 July:	Austria-Hungary declares war on Serbia.
1 August:	Germany declares war on Russia.
3 August:	Germany invades Belgium and declares war on France.
4 August:	Britain declares was on Germany at 11.00pm.
14 Aug:	Novelist H. G. Wells calls the conflict "*The War to End All Wars*".
23 August:	The Battle of Mons.
24 August:	The British Expeditionary Force begins the retreat from Mons.
5 Sept:	Basil Neve is killed when HMS *Pathfinder* is torpedoed.
5-9 Sept:	First Battle of the Marne.
October:	First Battle of Ypres begins.
7 Nov:	Richard Tracey is killed in action near Ypres.
25 Dec:	The Christmas truce on the Western Front.

1915

10-12 Mar:	Battle of Neuve Chapelle.
22 Apr:	Second Battle of Ypres begins when the Germans release gas.
25 Apr:	Allied landings at Gallipoli.
7 May:	RMS *Lusitania* sunk by a torpedo from German submarine *U20*.
23 May:	Italy declares war on Germany and Austria.
7 Aug:	Algernon Hathaway is killed in action at Gallipoli.
25 Sept:	The opening day of the Battle of Loos.

1916

16 Feb:	John Dunn dies of illness aged only 16, the youngest Campden casualty.
21 Feb:	The opening day of the Battle of Verdun.
31 May:	The Battle of Jutland begins. This is the largest naval battle of the war.
5 June:	Lord Kitchener dies when HMS *Hampshire* strikes a mine while en route to the Russian port of Arkhangelsk.
1 July:	Battle of the Somme. On the opening day of the battle the British Army suffers almost 60,000 casualties. Almost 20,000 of these are killed.
23 July:	Willie and Charles Brain both die during an attack near High Wood on the Somme.
3 Sept:	The first Allied attacks in Salonika.
15 Sept:	Tanks are used for the first time on the opening day of the Battle of Flers-Courcelette (part of the Battle of the Somme).

1917

8 Mar:	The Russian Revolution begins with riots, strikes and demonstrations in Moscow.
6 Apr:	United States declares war on Germany.

9 Apr:	The opening day of the Battle of Arras.
6 June:	Mines exploded under the German trenches on the Messines Ridge.
31 July:	Third battle of Ypres begins. The village of Passchendaele was eventually taken by the Canadian Army in November.
24 Oct:	Opening day of the Battle of Caporetto.
31 Oct:	Opening day of the Third Battle of Gaza in Palestine.
3 Nov:	The first three American soldiers are killed on the Western Front.
20 Nov:	Opening day of the Battle of Cambrai.

1918

28 Jan:	Lt. Col. John McCrae dies and is buried in Wimereux Cemetery. He wrote the poem *In Flanders Fields*.
21 Mar:	The first day of the German Spring offensive, code-named Operation Michael.
1 Apr:	RFC and RNAS combine to form the Royal Air Force.
15 June:	Opening day of the Battle of Asiago in Italy.
4 Nov:	Armistice on the Italian front.
11 Nov:	Armistice on the Western Front.

1919

28 June:	The Treaty of Versailles, a peace treaty that officially ended the war.

Casualty Figures

The figures below are from *The Fallen: A photographic journey through the war cemeteries and memorials of the Great War, 1914-18* by John Garfield (published by Leo Cooper, 1990).

	Killed or Died of Wounds	Total Casualties
British Empire	908,000	3,190,235
France	1,363,000	6,160,800
Italy	460,000	2,197,000
Russia	1,700,000	9,150,000
United States	115,000	321,350
	4,546,000	**21,019,385**

	Killed or Died of Wounds	Total Casualties
Austria-Hungary	1,200,000	7,020,000
Germany	1,774,000	7,142,000
Turkey	325,000	975,000
Bulgaria	101,000	253,000
	3,400,000	**15,390,000**

The figures below are from The *First World War: A Photographic History,* which was edited with captions by Laurence Stallings. This was published in 1933 by Daily Express Publications, London. The author will leave it to the reader to decide which figures are nearest to the truth.

Country	Known Dead	Seriously Wounded	Otherwise Wounded	Prisoners/ Missing
Russia	2,762,064	1,000,000	3,950,000	2,500,000
France	1,427,800	700,000	2,344,000	453,500
Great Britain	807,451	617,740	1,441,394	64,907
Italy	507,160	500,000	462,196	1,359,000
Belgium	267,000	40,000	100,000	10,000
United States	107,284	43,000	148,000	4,912
Germany	1,611,104	1,600,000	2,183,143	772,522
Turkey	436,924	107,772	300,000	103,731
Bulgaria	101,224	300,000	852,399	10,825

The War Memorial, c.1921
The above photograph was commissioned by Thomas Elsley and was one of several taken on 9 January 1921 when the memorial was unveiled. The photograph was obtained from the CADHAS archives.

Chapter 1

We Will Remember Them

This chapter contains short biographies of 487 men and women associated with Campden who served their country during the Great War.

G v R 1

HE whom this scroll commemorates was numbered among those who, at the call of King and Country, left all that was dear to them, endured hardness, faced danger, and finally passed out of the sight of men by the path of duty and self-sacrifice, giving up their own lives that others might live in freedom. Let those who come after see to it that his name be not forgotten.

Pte. William Edwin Harris
Machine Gun Corps

Hubert Guy Dyke Acland
Captain, Royal Navy

> Born: 8 June 1890
> Died: 6 May 1976

Guy was the second son of Admiral Sir William Alison Dyke Acland and the Hon. Emily Anna Smith, daughter of William Henry Smith and Emily Danvers, Viscountess Hambleden. He fought in the First World War and was mentioned in despatches. He gained the rank of captain in the service of the Royal Navy and was decorated with the Distinguished Service Order in 1920 for distinguished services as a gunnery officer of the First Destroyer Flotilla in the Baltic. He later captained HMS *Halcyon* from 1934-35.

He succeeded to the title of 4th Baronet Acland, of St. Mary Magdalen, Oxford on 4 December 1970 after the death of his brother, William Henry Dyke Acland.

On 21 August 1915 he married Lalage Mary Kathleen Acland, daughter of John Edward Acland and Norah Letitia Nugent Bankes, and they had two children: Major Sir Anthony Guy Acland (1916-1983) and Lieutenant-Colonel James Alison Acland (1919-1993).

The prayer list of servicemen produced by St. James's Church in Campden in 1916 includes Guy, his uncle William Frederick Danvers Smith, Lord Hambleden, and his cousin Dudley Ryder, Lord Sandon.

Ernest Edward Ashwin
Private 21367, Northamptonshire Regiment

> Born: 1879
> Enlisted: 21 July 1915
> Discharged: 20 August 1917

Ernest was baptised at St. James's Church on 8 January 1879. He was the third son of Charles and Lucy Ashwin, who were married in Campden on 10 May 1870. In 1881 his father, Charles, was a shepherd and the family were living in Sheep Street, Campden. In 1891 they had moved to Ebrington and the census records that Ernest had five brothers and sisters: Frank, John, Mary Ann, Flora and Ellen.

Ernest enlisted in the Northamptonshire Regiment on 21 July 1915 and arrived at Salonika in Greece on 24 October 1915. After almost two years' service he was discharged as no longer fit for active service on 20 August 1917 and a Silver War Badge was issued to indicate that he had made his contribution to the war. He was granted a war pension on his discharge from the army.

Harold Douglas Haines Ashwin
Private 9692, 2nd Battalion, South Lancashire Regiment

> Born: 15 June 1893
> Enlisted: 4 December 1911
> Died: 14 November 1914

Harold was born in Campden and was the eldest son of James Henry and Keziah Ashwin. His father, a native of the town, was an agricultural labourer and in 1901 the family were living in Watery Lane. When James married Keziah Merriman at St. James's Church on 7 August 1897 his occupation was recorded as a groom and Keziah was a domestic cook.

After leaving school Harold found employment as an indoor servant but when he was 18 years old he enlisted in the South Lancashire Regiment at Buttevant, County Cork in Ireland on 4 December 1911. He was admitted to hospital on 8 March 1912 with myalgia, muscle pain, but was discharged after three days. A further spell in hospital came in May 1913 when he was suffering from scarlet fever. Several weeks were spent in hospital before he was discharged on 2 July 1913 and appointed to a new position as an officer's servant. During this period leading up to the outbreak of the war he was awarded his third class education certificate.

When the war started in 1914 Harold was with the 2nd Battalion, South Lancashire Regiment at Tidworth in England. They made their way to Southampton and embarked for France on SS *Lapwing*, arriving at Le Havre on 14 August 1914. The battalion saw action during the Battle of Mons on 24 August and battalion diary records that they suffered severely. They then had to endure a long march when the British Expeditionary Force retreated to the River Marne. On 6 September they began the advance north to the River Aisne via the Forest of Crécy. The war diary notes that there were several casualties during wood fighting.

The advance north continued into October and on 16 October they were at Neuve Chapelle, where heavy casualties were sustained during German attacks in the next few days. On 27 October the battalion took part in an unsuccessful assault on German positions.

In November the battalion moved further north to the Ypres sector in Belgium and took over reserve trenches near Hooge. They moved forward to the firing line, near the village of Zandvoorde, on 7 November before being relieved two days later. It was during their next spell in the front line that Harold lost his life. He was killed in action near Zandvoorde, during the First Battle of Ypres, on 14 November 1914 when he was 21 years old. His body was not recovered at the end of the war and as he has no known grave his name is recorded on the Menin Gate Memorial in the centre of Ypres. The *Evesham Journal* published a letter received by Mrs. Ashwin:

"Harold was shot and succumbed to his wounds in a very few minutes. He was buried near the place where he fell by men of his own regiment, although much firing was in progress. He was very well liked by all his comrades and everyone was very sorry to hear of Harold's untimely death."

After he was killed his personal effects (a rosary, a letter and a purse) were returned to his mother in Campden and in the years following the war his mother received Harold's memorial plaque and three campaign medals.

Harold's name is recorded on three memorials in Campden: in St. James's Church, in St. Catharine's Church and in the High Street.

John Ashwin
Private M2-078862, Army Service Corps

Born: 1880

John, the fourth son of Charles and Lucy Ashwin, was born in Campden and baptised at St. James's Church on 25 December 1880. His father, a native of Campden, had married Lucy Benfield in 1870. Charles was employed as a shepherd in 1881 and then as a general agricultural labourer in 1891.

John enlisted in the Army Service Corps during the war and arrived in France on 18 July 1915, when he was 35 years old. He survived the war and was awarded three campaign medals: 1914-15 Star, British War Medal and Victory Medal.

Henry Charles Baker
Private 655, 1st/5th Battalion, Gloucestershire Regiment
Corporal 37356, 1st/5th Battalion, Gloucestershire Regiment

Born: 14 November 1881
Died: 15 June 1918

Henry was the only son of Joseph and Eliza Baker and was baptised at St. James's Church on 19 January 1898 when he was 16 years old. His parents were both born at Kingham in Oxfordshire and his father was employed as a mason's labourer. It is not clear exactly when the family moved to Campden but in 1901 they were living in Watery Lane.

When Henry left school he joined the Volunteer Drum and Fife Band and was a member of "K" Company, 2nd Volunteer Battalion, Gloucestershire Regiment. He soon became the bugler with the Volunteers and when he reached the age of 18 he was sworn in as a man and continued to serve in the company when the Haldane reforms of 1908 saw the Volunteers replaced by the Territorials. He was still a member of "H" Company, 5th Battalion, Gloucestershire Regiment at the outbreak of war in 1914 and was mobilised on 5 August and went to Chelmsford in Essex for final training before the battalion was posted overseas. Lewis Hadley Horne was the Sergeant-Major with the battalion and Henry was appointed his batman.

The battalion arrived in France on 29 March 1915 and they soon made their way north to Ploegsteert in Belgium, where they were given experience of life in the trenches in a quiet sector of the front. In July 1915 the battalion moved south to the northern sector of the Somme battlefield, where they occupied trenches east of Hébuterne. They remained in this sector until May 1916, when they were removed from the line to prepare for their part in the Battle of the Somme. During the battle Henry was badly wounded in five places by shrapnel near the village of Ovillers and a spell recovering in hospital was required.

It is not known when Henry rejoined the battalion but he was with them when they were sent to Italy in November 1917. In June 1918 the battalion occupied a difficult position in the woods around Buco di Cesuna on the Asiago Plateau. They were so under-strength, 466 all ranks, that the brigade commander hesitated to place them in the front line, but there was no other unit readily to hand. The Battle of Asiago began at 3.00am on 15 June 1918 when the Austrians began an artillery barrage that lasted for four hours. This was followed by a massive infantry attack and the 1st/5th Glosters suffered heavy casualties. The forward trenches were breached but a stubborn defence blunted the enemy offensive. The Glosters were steadily pushed back and split into two fighting groups and they had to be very careful not to be encircled by the enemy.

It was during this fighting on the Asiago Plateau that Henry was killed on 15 June 1918. He was 36 years old and had served for over twenty years, as man and boy, with the Glosters. He is buried in Magnaboschi Cemetery on the Asiago Plateau in Italy. The *Evesham Journal* reported his death on 13 July 1918 but stated that he had been killed in action in France.

Henry has his name recorded on two memorials in the town: in St. James's Church and in the High Street.

Thomas Henry Pritchett Barnes
Special Constable

Born: 1873
Died: 11 April 1960

Tom Barnes was born in Brailes in 1873 but spent the greater part of his working life living in Campden with his uncle and aunt, Robert and Annie Guthrie, of Pinkney House. A blacksmith by trade, he quickly became a well-loved Campden character and he was a member of St. James's Church choir. During the First World War he served as a special constable.

Tom died at his home, Pinkney House, on 11 April 1960 aged 87 and he is buried in St. James's churchyard.

Albert Henry Bates

Albert was born in Cleeve Prior on 19 April 1891, the son of Elizabeth Emily Lyne, who was a domestic servant at the Manor House in the village. In 1893 Elizabeth married William Esprey Bates, son of Thomas and Elizabeth Bates of Aston-sub-Edge, and they had three children baptised at St. James's Church in Campden: Thomas in 1896, Hilda Rose Ellen in 1900 and Florence May in 1902. William was employed as an agricultural labourer and during the war he came to Campden when he found work at Old Combe Farm.

The Campden 1918 electoral roll lists Albert as living with his parents at Old Combe Farm and absent on military service. He returned to Campden in the summer of 1919 but by 1922 the family had left the town.

Only one man is listed as "Albert Henry Bates" on the medal index cards at the National Archives in London. Driver T4-252076 Albert Henry Bates enlisted in the Army Service Corps on 13 November 1915 and was discharged owing to sickness on 23 February 1919 without seeing any overseas service during the war.

Alwyn Eli Bates
Gunner TF656745, Royal Field Artillery
Gunner 164650, Royal Field Artillery

Born: 26 December 1897
Died: 1978

Alwyn was born in the Evesham registration district, the son of William Esprey and Elizabeth Emily Bates. During the war he served overseas as a gunner in the Royal Field Artillery. After returning safely at the end of the war he married Emma Victoria James, daughter of Enoch and Fanny James of Watery Lane, Campden, in 1919. They had three children, George Henry, Frances Victoria and Enoch William, who were all baptised at St. Catharine's Church in Campden.

The family home was in Watery Lane and Alwyn lived there until he died in 1978 aged 80 years. His wife also died in 1978 aged 81 years and their ashes were buried in St. James's churchyard on 30 August 1978.

Thomas Henry Bates
Private 7398, Coldstream Guards

Born: July 1889
Enlisted: 8 August 1907
Discharged: 21 November 1914

Thomas was born in Campden and baptised at St. James's Church on 24 August 1890. His father, Joseph Bates, a general labourer, had married Harriet Burson at St. James's on 25 August 1888. In 1891 the family home was in Leysbourne.

After leaving school Thomas found employment as a labourer until he became a regular soldier when he enlisted in the Coldstream Guards on 8 August 1907. He was passed fit for active service and his medical report stated that he was five feet eight inches tall with red hair, grey eyes and a fresh complexion. There was a tattoo of a rose on his left arm and his religion was Church of England.

In 1910 Thomas was stationed at the Tower of London when he slipped while carrying a bucket of water up some steps. He immediately felt pain in his right groin. An operation was recommended but refused. There was an investigation but as Thomas was on duty and sober at the time it was felt that he was in no way to blame.

On 7 August 1911 he married Miriam May Holt in Birmingham. It appears that his father had brought the family to Birmingham as Joseph is recorded as the next of kin on Thomas's pension papers and his address was 6 Weld's Buildings, Highgate Road, Sparkbrook, Birmingham.

Thomas was mobilised on 5 August 1914 and posted to a reserve battalion for home service until he arrived in France on 30 August 1914. He served at the front for only 14 days, arriving back in England on 13 September. The incident in 1910 was still causing him problems and he was discharged from the army on 21 November 1914 as no longer physically fit for active service owing to a hernia.

Allen Benjamin Bathurst
Lieutenant-Colonel, 2nd/5th Battalion, Gloucestershire Regiment

Born: 25 June 1872
Enlisted: 24 October 1891
Discharged: 9 March 1916
Died: 8 October 1947

Benjamin was born in London, the third son of Allen Alexander (later 6th Earl Bathurst) and the Hon. Merial Leicester Bathurst (née Warren) of 3, Grosvenor Crescent. His mother died in July 1872, one month after his birth, and his father then married Evelyn Elizabeth Barnard Hankey.

Benjamin became an officer in 1891 when he joined the 4th Volunteer Battalion, Gloucestershire Regiment after leaving the Royal Agricultural College in Cirencester. He was granted a commission and took up his appointment as 2nd lieutenant on 24 October 1891. He was promoted to lieutenant in 1893, captain in 1895 and then major in 1908.

He retired from the army on 10 May 1913 but soon after the outbreak of war he was appointed a lieutenant-colonel with the 5th Battalion, Gloucestershire Regiment on 30 September 1914. The war had not been in progress many weeks before the necessity for sending Territorial units overseas became obvious. So it was in the early part of September 1914 that the 2nd/5th Battalion of the Gloucestershire Regiment came into being to act as a second line to the 1st/5th already in existence. Benjamin was asked to raise and to command the new unit, designated at the time a home service battalion. In February 1915 the battalion left Gloucester and went to Northampton. This gave the men their first experience of being billeted in a strange borough. While the battalion were there Benjamin met with a riding accident, which resulted in a broken collarbone.

In February 1916 the battalion moved to Salisbury Plain. On detraining at Tidworth Benjamin noted that "*the village was found enveloped in deep snow and a biting wind was blowing*". The battalion was preparing for overseas and he noted: "*I look back on those days at Gloucester, Northampton, Chelmsford, Epping and Salisbury Plain with some sadness, mingled with a pardonable pride, as I knew that the command of the Battalion would have to pass into other hands when the time came for it to go overseas.*"

After eighteen months' home service he retired again on 9 March 1916 and was placed in the Army Reserve. He relinquished his commission in 1921 and was able to keep the rank of lieutenant-colonel to use in civilian life. The 2nd/5th Battalion arrived in France in May 1916.

Benjamin was the Member of Parliament for East Gloucestershire (including Campden) from 1895-1906 and 1910-1918. He was also the Chairman of Governors at Campden Grammar School from 1909-1916. Robert Cook writes that at the school's Speech Day in 1916 "*the war-time atmosphere was completed by the presence of the Chairman, Colonel, the Hon. A. B. Bathurst (in khaki)*".

Benjamin married Augusta Ruby Spencer-Churchill, daughter of Lord Edward Spencer-Churchill, of Northwick Park, Blockley, on 22 April 1902 and they had one son, Peter. Peter became a group-captain in the Royal Air Force and fought during the Second World War.

Henry Edwin Beard
Driver 27223, 12th Brigade, Royal Field Artillery

Born: 1878
Enlisted: 5 November 1902
Discharged: 16 November 1915

Henry was the son of Anthony Edwin Beard and was baptised at St. James's Church in Campden on 23 February 1879. His father was a farmer in the town and had married Annie Marie Franklin, daughter of Thomas and Eliza Franklin, at St. James's Church on 22 February 1870.

After leaving school Edwin found employment as a baker until he became a regular soldier when he enlisted in the Royal Regiment of Artillery on 5 November 1902. His medical examination recorded that he had light brown hair, light blue eyes and a fresh complexion. His religion was Church of England.

The next twelve years were spent on home service until he arrived in France as part of the British Expeditionary Force on 9 September 1914. He remained on the Western Front until 4 November 1915, when he returned to England. He was discharged on 16 November 1915 on completion of his terms of service after 13 years and 12 days in the army.

Richard Beavington
Corporal 2575, Worcestershire Regiment

Born: 31 January 1899
Died: 13 December 1955

Richard was born in Broad Campden on 31 January 1899 and was the youngest son of Richard and Mary Eliza Beavington. After leaving school he gained employment as a farm worker. At the age of 16 in 1915, only a few months after his brother had died on Salisbury Plain with the Gloucestershire Regiment, he enlisted in the Worcestershire Regiment. The greater part of his overseas service was in Mesopotamia and when he was only 17 his battalion was caught up in the fierce fighting at Kut-al-Amarah. It was at this time that he reached the rank of sergeant but because he was under age he had his stripes removed.

Towards the end of the war Richard transferred to the Military Field Police (number P1278). He remained in Mesopotamia (Iraq and Persian Gulf area) after the armistice and became the chief crime prevention officer at the port of Basra.

Richard returned to Campden around 1929 but soon moved to the West Midlands. He found employment with Yeoman's road contractors and married Dora Smith, producing three children, Peter, Gordon and Mary, and adopting a third boy, called Jerry.

During the Second World War Richard again served his country when he joined the Home Guard.

William Thomas Beavington
Private 13721 "B" Company, 8th Battalion, Gloucestershire Regiment

Born: 1897
Died: 26 November 1914

William was the eldest son of Richard and Mary Eliza Beavington of Broad Campden. He went to school in Campden and when war was declared in August 1914 he was working as a farm labourer. Despite being only 17 years old William was one of the first to enlist from Campden, recruited by Sergeant Bill Beckett, who only lived two doors from the Beavington family. Recruiting sergeants received one shilling for each man they persuaded to join the army.

William was one of Kitchener's Army and he went to Salisbury Plain with 8th Battalion, Gloucestershire Regiment for training. The summer of 1914 had been very wet and the rain continued into September and October. The damp conditions were not to his liking and living under canvas while training meant it was very hard to keep warm and dry.

William died of spinal meningitis on 26 November 1914 and is buried in Tidworth Military Cemetery in Wiltshire. His name is recorded on two memorials in Campden: in St James's Church and in the High Street.

William Merrin Beckett
Recruiting Sergeant, Gloucestershire Regiment

Born: 1867
Died: January 1952

Bill was the eldest son of Frederick and Eliza Beckett and was born at Farndon in Nottinghamshire in 1867. After leaving school he found employment as a farm labourer but it was not long before he became a regular soldier when he joined the 1st Battalion, Grenadier Guards as Private 1560 William Beckett. He had previously had an application to join the Royal Marines rejected. He enlisted in London on 5 November 1888 and his attestation papers state that he had previously served with the 4th Battalion, Derbyshire Regiment (The Sherwood Foresters), a militia battalion. The medical examination recorded that he had light brown hair, blue eyes, a fresh complexion and small scars on the front of each knee.

Bill's only period of overseas service was in Bermuda, where he served for twelve months from July 1890 to July 1891. In September 1891 he was promoted to lance corporal and served for the next three years in England before he was transferred to the Army Reserve. He was recalled on 26 December 1899 but was officially discharged as medically unfit for further service on 18 June 1900 after 11 years and 230 days service with the Grenadier Guards. During his time he achieved a certificate for cold shoeing on 31 May 1890.

After leaving the army Bill made his home in Campden. He ran a hairdressing business for many years and during the First World War he was the recruiting sergeant with Colonel Edward Paley at the Campden Recruiting Office, which was located immediately behind the war memorial in the High Street in a shop that became Jackson's Estate Agents.

Bill married twice. He married his first wife, Agnes Annie Simmons, at St James's Church on 10 July 1892 but she died in 1929. He then married Alice Hopkins.

Bill died in January 1952 at East View Hospital in Stow-on-the-Wold aged 84 years and is buried in St. James's churchyard in Campden. He was survived by five children from his first marriage: Lillian, Gladys, Isabelle, Nellie and John. His home in Campden in 1952 was 2, Gainsborough Terrace.

Recruiting Office, 2008

Frederick "Spud" Benfield
Private 23297, Gloucestershire Regiment
Private 177367, Machine Gun Corps

Born: 26 November 1897
Died: 23 August 1973

Frederick was the second son of William Henry and Amy Ellen Knight Benfield of Leysbourne, Campden and was baptised at St. James's Church on 6 February 1898. His father was known as "*Kaiser Bill*" and served in the army during the Boer War and the 1914-18 war.

In 1916 Frederick enlisted in the Gloucestershire Regiment when he was 18 years old but before the end of the war he transferred to the Machine Gun Corps. He was awarded two campaign medals, the British War Medal and the Victory Medal, which indicates that he served overseas in a theatre of war before the armistice was signed. His daughter-in-law, Molly, informed the author that he also served in India before he was discharged from the army.

During the Second World War Frederick volunteered and served as a sergeant in the Royal Engineers in Africa and Italy, where he was employed building bridges and roads. He was awarded five campaign medals including the Africa Star and Italy Star.

The Benfield family: father, son and grandson
Corporal William Henry "Kaiser Bill" Benfield, Army Veterinary Corps
Private 177367 Frederick "Spud" Benfield, Machine Gun Corps
Frederick William Benfield, Home Guard and Royal Navy

His son, Frederick William Benfield, joined the Home Guard at 16 before he enlisted in the Royal Navy. He served on HMS *Frobisher* and was involved in the Normandy landings in June 1944.

After leaving school Frederick worked for the Council as a road repairman and was then employed in the building trade. He was a good footballer and was captain of Campden Football Club. He married Frances Mary Cross in May 1923 and they had five children: Frederick William, Albert Edward, Dorothy Ellen, Mary Louisa and Samuel Arthur.

Frederick died on 23 August 1973 aged 75 and is buried in St. James's churchyard.

Frederick "Stale" Benfield
Driver T2-SR-02584, Motor Transport Company, Army Service Corps

Enlisted: 19 January 1915
Discharged: 4 March 1919
Died: 25 October 1957

Frederick was born in Campden in 1882, the son of Samuel and Mary Ann Benfield, and was baptised at St. James's Church on 25 December 1886. The family home was 11, Sheep Street, Campden. Frederick was born there and he lived there for the greater part of his life.

After leaving school he found employment with his father as a haulier and also joined the Gloucestershire Volunteers. He married Rose Alice Bishop at St. James's Church on 16 April 1906. She was from Temple Guiting and came to Campden in 1909 when she was 19 years old to work as a housemaid for Mrs. Griffiths at Bedfont House. Frederick and Rose enjoyed a long and happy marriage and they had five daughters: Gladys, Frances, Elsie Nora, Doris and Margaret.

Frederick enlisted in Campden on 19 January 1915, witnessed by Sergeant Bill Beckett and Colonel Edward Paley. He joined the Army Service Corps at Aldershot on 25 January 1915 and the next six months were occupied with training in England. He arrived in France on 17 July 1915 and spent the rest of the war on the Western Front, returning to England on 3 February 1919. He was discharged from the army on 4 March 1919 and was awarded a war pension in October 1920 owing to the fact that he was suffering from neuritis. The pension was stopped in January 1921.

After the war Frederick became one of the first members of the British Legion and was the standard bearer for 32 years. He was a member of the town band and during the Second World War he served as a special constable. In his younger days he was a keen footballer and many old scholars of Campden Grammar School will remember him as the caretaker, a job he held for 32 years.

Frederick died on 25 October 1957 aged 74 and is buried in St. James's churchyard.

William Henry "Kaiser Bill" Benfield, senior
Lance Corporal 1818, 2nd Battalion, Gloucestershire Regiment
Corporal SE 19644, Army Veterinary Corps

Born: 1864
Enlisted: 11 August 1916
Discharged: 8 September 1918
Died: 2 March 1941

Bill was born in Campden, the eldest son of Benjamin and Susan Benfield. In 1881 the family were living in Berrington but they later moved to Lower High Street. After leaving school he joined his father as an agricultural labourer. When he was 22 years old he became a regular soldier when he enlisted in the Gloucestershire Regiment on 25 October 1886. He was posted to India in 1887 and served there for seven years, during which time he was promoted to the rank of lance corporal on 11 July 1892. He returned to England on 28 November 1894 and remained on home service until he arrived in South Africa on 3 February 1900 to begin a period of two years serving in the Boer War. When he arrived back in England on 29 July 1902 he was awarded the King's and Queen's South Africa Medals with clasps for Cape Colony, Orange Free State and Transvaal.

Bill ended his period of service with the Gloucestershire Regiment on 24 October 1902 and returned to Campden, where he found employment as a groom. He had married Amy Ellen Knight Day at St. James's Church on 15 April 1895 and two of their sons, Frederick and William Henry, served during the 1914-18 war. The family home was in Leysbourne.

When the First World War started in 1914 he was not a young man but he was an experienced soldier. His knowledge of horses enabled him to enlist in the Army Veterinary Corps on 11 August 1916 aged 52 years and 210 days. He served on the Western Front from 17 November 1916 until 5 June 1918, when he returned to England. He was discharged on 8 September 1918 as no longer medically fit for active service and a Silver War Badge was issued to indicate that he had made his contribution to the war. It was around this time that he was given the nickname "*Kaiser Bill*".

After the war Bill and Amy became the first tenants of 1, Aston Road, a "*Home for Heroes*" built by Gloucestershire County Council for returning servicemen. They remained there for the rest of their lives. Bill died on 2 March 1941 aged 77 years and his wife died six months later on 13 September aged 66 years. They are buried together in St. James's churchyard.

William Henry Benfield, junior
Private S4-042016, 52nd Field Bakery, Army Service Corps
Private A-204067, 9th and 13th Battalions, King's Royal Rifle Corps

Born: 1894
Enlisted: 5 January 1915
Discharged: 9 March 1919
Died: August 1970

Bill was the son of William Henry "*Kaiser Bill*" and Amy Ellen Benfield of Leysbourne, Campden and was baptised at St. James's Church on 26 January 1896. After leaving school he was employed as a baker. On 5 January 1915 he enlisted at Campden Recruiting Office in the Army Service Corps. The witnesses to his enlistment were Sergeant Bill Beckett and Colonel Edward Paley.

Bill joined the Army Service Corps at Aldershot on 6 January 1915 and was employed on home service until he was posted to France on 30 April 1915 to join the 52nd Field Bakery as a "*second class baker*". It is not clear how long he stayed in France but in 1917 he was back in England and was serving with the 9th Battalion, King's Royal Rifle Corps (KRRC), having been transferred. He arrived back at the front with the KRRC on 27 November 1917 and in March 1918 he was gassed. The *Evesham Journal* reported that "*Mrs. W. H. Benfield, Leysbourne, has been officially notified that her son, Pte. W. Benfield, King's Royal Rifles, has been badly gassed and that he is now lying in a hospital at Newport, having been sent home from France*".

After recovering Bill returned to France on 21 June 1918 and continued to serve at the front until he was wounded in the back by shrapnel on 24 August. He was transported back to England and was admitted to the Royal Berkshire Hospital in Reading "*in a serious condition*". He was too weak to have the necessary operation and his parents were sent for. Fortunately he recovered from his wounds and was placed in the Army Reserve on 9 March 1919 before being officially discharged on 31 March 1920.

After the war he married Florence and moved to Birmingham. He was living at 17 Brockley Place, Eliot Street in 1921. They had three children: William, Ernie and Gertrude.

Bill died in August 1976 aged 76 years and his ashes are buried in St. James's churchyard in Campden.

Albert Norman Bennett
Private 18933, 8th Battalion, Gloucestershire
Regiment

Born: 1882
Discharged: 19 February 1919
Died: 28 December 1973

Norman was born in Campden, the fourth son of Thomas and Ann Bennett of Watery Lane, and was baptised at St. James's Church on 25 October 1882. His father, a general agricultural labourer, was a native of the town.

After attending school in Campden Norman went to South Wales to earn a living working in the mines, but he soon returned and found employment as a tree feller and woodcutter with well-known timber merchants in Shipston and Draycott. As with many other working men in those days it was not uncommon for him to walk considerable distances to his place of work.

In the years leading up to the First World War Norman was a member of "H" Company, 5th Battalion, Gloucestershire Regiment, the Territorials. When the war started in 1914 he enlisted in the Gloucestershire Regiment and was posted to the 8th Battalion, arriving in France on 4 August 1915. The battalion were involved in capturing the village of La Boisselle on 3 July 1916 during the Battle of the Somme and when Norman was marching back to Albert he saw Tom Plested's dead body. Tom, a friend from Campden, who was serving with the Machine Gun Corps, was killed by the explosion of a German shell at La Boisselle on 4 July 1916. Norman said that there was not a mark on his body. Tom was buried the next day but at the end of the war his grave had been lost and today he has no known grave.

On 23 July 1916 the battalion were involved in an unsuccessful attack on the German Switch Line between High Wood and Martinpuich. Norman's cousin, George, was serving in the battalion at the time and was killed on that day. Two other Campden men, brothers Willie and Charles Brain, serving in the 10th Battalion, Gloucestershire Regiment, also died in the same attack.

Norman spent the rest of the war in France and Belgium with the battalion and saw action

during the Battle of Messines and the Third Battle of Ypres in 1917. He was wounded but it is not known where or when. He was discharged form the army on 19 February 1919, when he was 37 years old.

Norman had married Emily Louisa Larner before the First World War and they had seven children: Annie, Albert Norman, Prudence, Edwin Ernest, Kathleen, Margaret and Hilda. The family home was in Poppett's Alley but in the 1930's they moved to Watery Lane. Emily died in 1957 and Norman remarried the same year. The last years of Norman's working life were spent quarrying at Strange's in Campden.

Norman died in the Ellen Badger Hospital at Shipston on 28 December 1973 aged 91 years and is buried in St. James's churchyard. His address at the time of his death was 4 Coronation Close, Littleworth, Campden.

Austin Bennett
Gunner 162889, Royal Garrison Artillery

Born: 10 September 1890
Died: 19 September 1965

Austin was born in Campden, the seventh son of Henry and Ann Bennett of Watery Lane, and was baptised at St. James's Church on 25 December 1890. His father was a native of the town and in the early 1900's he was trading as a baker selling bread from his home in the Square.

After leaving school Austin worked as a baker with his father and on 18 November 1914 he married Amy Kate Hughes, daughter of William and Elizabeth Hughes, at St. James's Church. Their first home was at 4 Brick Cottages in Watery Lane, where their children, Anne, Sybil and Gordon, were born. Anne married Wilfred Smith in the Baptist Church, Sybil died in 1917 aged only a few months and Gordon served in the Royal Air Force in India during the Second World War.

During the First World War Austin served as a gunner in France with the Royal Garrison Artillery. After his safe return to Campden his sister bought his share of the bakery business and he turned his hand to many different skills and was classed as a "*handyman*". He always wanted to follow in his brother John's footsteps by joining the police but he never quite achieved the chest measurement, although he did serve as a special constable in Campden.

Austin (left) with his friend Gunner 162888 Archibald James Annandale, RGA, who died on 9 April 1918.

Around 1937 Austin and John bought a field in Hoo Lane and built two houses, one for each family. Austin's house was called "Shernal" and John's was called "Tower View".

Austin's favourite pastime was racing pigeons. George Haysum often took the basket of pigeons to Campden station, where they were placed in the guard's van and taken to their destination before they were released. The empty basket was again collected by George and the pigeons flew back to Austin in Campden.

Austin died in Stratford Hospital on 19 September 1965 aged 75 years and is buried in St. James's churchyard. Amy carried on living on her own in "Shernal" until she was almost 99 years old. She died on 24 December 1989 and her ashes were scattered in the Baptist churchyard in Campden.

Austin and Amy Kate Bennett

Austin Bennett is sitting on the left.

Enoch Mickloth Bennett
Sergeant S4-122575, 69th Field Bakery, Army Service Corps

Born: 17 February 1885
Enlisted: 24 June 1915
Discharged: 26 August 1919
Died: 5 April 1958

Enoch and Ellen Bennett with their son, Harry.

Enoch was born in Campden in 1885, the fifth son of Henry and Ann Bennett of Watery Lane, and was baptised at St. James's Church on 24 May 1885. His father was a native of the town and on the 1901 census his occupation was recorded as a corn miller. In the early 1900's he began trading as a baker and bread was sold from his house in the Square.

After leaving school Enoch was trained in the family business and was able to put these skills to good use during his time in the army. He enlisted in the Army Service Corps at Worcester on 24 June 1915, when he was 30 years old. He joined his unit at Aldershot the next day and a medical examination graded him as "B2". The next month was spent in England before he was posted to the 40th Field Bakery, Army Service Corps, which was part of the Mediterranean Expeditionary Force. He arrived in Egypt on 13 July 1915 as a sergeant but he reverted to private when he was admitted to hospital on 1 October 1915. After failing to recover fully from his illness he returned to England on 7 December 1915 and remained on home service until February 1918, when he was again posted to Egypt. He arrived there with the 69th Field Bakery, Army Service Corps on 2 March and remained there until 12 September, when he returned to England. The next eleven months were spent on home service before he was discharged form the army on 26 August 1919. His grandson Charlie remembers one amusing story of Enoch's time in the army: "*One day Enoch put bread in the oven and the Turks took it out by shelling his oven!*"

The army stated that he was "*perfectly sober, reliable, fairly intelligent and a good baker*". He was awarded an army pension owing to the effects of rheumatism and enteric fever but this was stopped on 16 November 1920.

He married Ellen Thompson at Christ Church in Carlisle on 22 October 1912 and their only child, Henry Lennox, was born on 11 February 1914. After leaving the army Enoch rejoined his family at 14 Tait Street in Carlisle. When he returned to Campden he set up his own business selling bread and cakes from the front room of his small house in Church Street. He then arranged with John Skey, landlord of the Lygon Arms, to rent a building where he had a semi-portable oven installed. In 1931 he bought his own shop in the High Street at auction from Mr. Taylor and his reputation as a baker and confectioner grew rapidly.

Enoch died on 5 April 1958 aged 73 years and is buried in St. James's churchyard. His wife died on 11 February 1966.

Ernest Bennett
Private 26876, Gloucestershire Regiment
Private 26222, "C" Company, 2nd Battalion, Loyal North Lancashire Regiment

Born: 1897
Enlisted: March 1915
Died: 29 July 1918

Ernest was born in Campden, the second son of Noah and Sarah Bennett of Watery Lane, and was baptised at St. James's Church on 9 May 1897. He was a baker by trade and was employed at Broadwell, near Stow-on-the-Wold.

He enlisted in the Gloucestershire Regiment at Stow in March 1915 when he was 18 years old. However, when he was posted overseas in August 1916 he joined the 2nd Battalion, Loyal North Lancashire Regiment in German East Africa. There was mass ill-health in the battalion and Ernest reported sick with fever on three separate occasions.

On 18 January 1917 the battalion landed at Suez in Egypt and later in the year were involved in operations around Gaza in Palestine. After sixteen months in Egypt and Palestine the battalion arrived at Marseille in France on 27 May 1918. Ernest was killed near Beugneux on 29 July during the 1918 Battle of the Marne, which began on 20 July. He was originally buried near to where he fell at Grand Rozoy Wood near Beugneux but after the war isolated graves were opened and their occupants were re-interred in larger cemeteries.

Today Ernest is buried in Raperie Cemetery, Villemontoire, south of Soissons in France. He was 21 years old when he died. His name is recorded on three memorials in Campden: in St. James's Church, in the Baptist Church and in the High Street.

Frederick Bennett

Private 2124, "H" Company, 5th Battalion, Gloucestershire Regiment
Lance Corporal 83429, 116th Company, Royal Defence Corps

Born: 1886
Mobilised: 5 August 1914
Demobilised: 28 February 1919
Died: 25 January 1954

Fred was born in Campden, the son of Thomas and Ann Bennett of Watery Lane, and was baptised at St. James's Church on 24 October 1886. His father, a native of the town, was employed as a general agricultural labourer. Fred enlisted in the 2nd Volunteer Battalion, Gloucestershire Regiment in 1902 and served with them for the next two years.

He joined the town band as a boy and rarely missed a practice or a performance. His instrument was the euphonium and he played it with considerable skill. This was in the heyday of the band and it was one of his biggest disappointments in later life that young men did not come forward to support it.

With the exception of his war service he spent all of his life in Campden. He was a member of the Territorial Army before the war and on 5 August 1914 he was mobilised and went to Chelmsford for training. When the battalion embarked for France Fred remained in England, where he joined the 2nd/5th Battalion, Gloucestershire Regiment and later the Royal Defence Corps. He spent the rest of the war on home service.

A plumber by trade, he was employed for many years by Mr. W. Haines. When his employer retired he obtained a post with the North Cotswold District Council and in this capacity became a familiar and popular figure to council house tenants all over the district.

Fred died very suddenly at his home, 29 Berrington Road, Campden, on 25 January 1954. He was getting ready to go to work and seemed in normal health when he collapsed and died almost immediately. He was 67 years old and is buried in St. James's churchyard. His wife, Martha L. Beatham, a native of Cumberland, whom he married in 1922, survived him. She died on 4 May 1966 and there were no children.

George Edwin Bennett

Private 17656, 8th Battalion, Gloucestershire Regiment

Born: 8 June 1877
Died: 23 July 1916

George was born in Campden and was the second son of Henry and Ann Bennett of Watery Lane. His father was a native of the town and in the early 1900's was trading as a baker selling bread from his home in the Square.

After leaving school George worked on the railways. When the war started in 1914 he enlisted at Campden in the Gloucestershire Regiment. He was posted to the 8th Battalion and arrived in France on 18 August 1915.

The battalion took part in the Battle of the Somme, which started on 1 July 1916. At 7.30am on that morning they moved to positions north of Albert and were in the Tara-Usna line by 10.00am. The British Army suffered almost 60,000 casualties on the opening day of the battle but the 8th Glosters did not attack until 3 July, when they pushed forward into La Boisselle village and consolidated their new position near the ruins of the church. In this action their commanding officer,

Lieutenant-Colonel A. Carton de Wiart, won the Victoria Cross. The battalion held the new positions against German counter-attacks before it withdrew to Albert on 5 July. On 9 July it moved to bivouacs north of Millencourt and the next few days were spent doing physical drill including route marches, bayonet practice and running.

At 9.00pm on 20 July they moved forward again to occupy an old German trench close to Bazentin-le-Petit. The battalion relieved the 10th Battalion, Worcestershire Regiment in the front line at 9.30pm on 22 July and the following day they were involved in an unsuccessful attack on the German Switch Line between High Wood and Martinpuich. The battalion attacked at 12.30am after creeping forward to within 75 yards of the German trenches but they were soon halted by machine gun fire.

It was during this attack on the Switch Line on 23 July that George was killed in action. He was 39 years old and today he is buried in Caterpillar Valley Cemetery, near Longueval, Somme, France. His name is recorded on three memorials in Campden: in St. James's Church, in the Baptist Church and in the High Street.

George never married but he had a partner called Lily and they lived in Poppett's Alley. Four of his brothers, Austin, Enoch, John Ernest and Joseph, also served in the army during the war.

Jack Bennett

Private 43144, 10th Battalion, Royal Warwickshire Regiment
Private 50951, Depot Battalion, Royal Warwickshire Regiment

Born: 12 February 1899
Enlisted: 21 March 1917
Discharged: 31 March 1921
Died: 7 September 1976

Jack was the youngest of three sons of Noah and Sarah Bennett of Watery Lane, Campden who served in the 1914-18 war. He was born at Campden and was baptised at St. James's Church on 9 July 1899.

After leaving school he found employment as a baker but when he reached his 18th birthday he enlisted in the Royal Warwickshire Regiment at Cirencester on 21 March 1917. His uncle, James Trinder, and his two brothers, Richard and Ernest, were already in uniform.

During the war he served on the Western Front with the 10th Battalion and he was not wounded. When the war ended he was discharged on 6 March 1919 after serving for almost two years. He immediately rejoined the

Royal Warwickshire Regiment as he felt that there was no work waiting for him in Campden and served for a further 2 years and 25 days before his final discharge from the army on 31 March 1921. During his second period of service he served in England, Ireland and India.

When he returned to Campden he married Florence Gertrude Collett and they had two children, George Rowland and Dorothy Hilda. Jack found employment as a gardener at Hidcote Manor gardens and the family went to live at Hidcote. He then worked at Lockheed's Garage in Campden before the family moved to Mickleton, where he became a painter and decorator for Mr. J. Moss.

Jack died on 7 September 1976 aged 77 and he is buried in St. Lawrence's churchyard extension in Mickleton. His wife died on 14 November 1973 aged 75 and she is buried with him.

John Edwin Bennett
Trooper 3610, Reserve Household Battalion
Private 30355, Grenadier Guards

Born: 23 March 1881
Enlisted: 10 December 1915
Discharged: 31 March 1920

John was born in Campden, the third son of Thomas and Ann Bennett of Watery Lane, and was baptised at St. James's Church on 31 July 1881. After leaving school he moved to Lancaster, where he married Nancy Wearing on 17 October 1903. They had three children, Thomas, Robert and John Edwin, who were all born in the town, and the family home was in 29 Perth Street.

At the outbreak of war in 1914 John was employed as an *"oil boiler"* at a mill in Lancaster. He enlisted at the Old Town Hall in Lancaster for the duration of the war on 10 December 1915 but was immediately placed into the Army Reserve. He was mobilised on 3 September 1917 and posted to the Reserve Household Battalion as a trooper. While he was employed on home service he was posted to the Grenadier Guards on 29 January 1918 and then on 1 April he arrived in France. On 25 August he was wounded and reported missing in action. The Germans had taken him prisoner and he remained in captivity until after the armistice was signed.

He arrived back in England on 2 December 1918 and continued on home service with the Grenadier Guards until he was placed into Class Z Army Reserve on 19 March 1919. His final discharge came on 31 March 1920.

After the war he continued to live in Lancaster and became known as *"Lancashire Jack"* to friends and family.

John Ernest Bennett

Born: 26 June 1879
Died: 5 July 1942

John was born in Campden and was the third son of Henry and Ann Bennett of Watery Lane. His father, a native of the town, married Ann Southam at St. James's Church on 11 March 1871. In 1905 Henry left Haydon's Mill, where he was a miller and baker, and began trading as a baker and selling bread from his home in the Square.

In 1900, at the age of 21, John joined the Metropolitan Police Force. He served for 25 years in London before he retired from the police in 1925. He then ran a sweet and tobacco shop in Leytonstone before he returned to Campden, where, just before the Second World War, he bought a field in Hoo Lane with his brother Austin and built two houses, one for each family. Austin's house was called "Shernal" and John's was called "Tower View".

Josephine Griffiths includes John in her list of servicemen from Campden but it is not clear whether he left the police to join the army during the First World War as his job was a reserved occupation and made him exempt from being called up.

John married Maud Mary Diamond on 5 October 1901 and they had five children: Austin, Edith, Lillie, Eva and Hilda.

He died on 5 July 1942 aged 63 years and is buried in St. James's churchyard. His wife died on 12 April 1961 aged 83 years and is buried with her husband.

Joseph Bennett
Gunner 98798, Royal Garrison Artillery

Born: 11 February 1882
Enlisted: 10 July 1916
Died: 21 November 1947

Joseph was born in Campden, the fourth son of Henry and Ann Bennett of Watery Lane, and was baptised at St. James's Church on 9 April 1882. His father was a native of the town and in the early 1900's he was trading as a baker, selling bread from his home in the Square.

After leaving school Joseph found employment as a bricklayer and on 30 May 1903 he married Elizabeth Anna Maria Mitchell at St. James's Church. During the First World War he served overseas as a gunner in

Joe Bennett is on the far right.

the Royal Garrison Artillery. On the 1918 electoral roll he is listed as absent on military service and his wife, Bessie, is living in the family home at Silk Mill Yard, Sheep Street. When he returned safely from the war Joseph worked for J. W. Pyment and Sons as a stonemason and builder.

During the Second World War Joseph lost his son Repton when he was killed in an accident in North Africa on 28 June 1943. He landed in North Africa with the First Army in December 1942 and fought in Tunisia. Repton was a lance corporal with the Pioneer Corps when he died and is buried at Medjez-El-Bad Cemetery in Tunisia. He was 28 years old.

Joseph died at his home on 21 November 1947 aged 65 years and is buried in St. James's churchyard in Campden. The funeral service took place at Campden Baptist Church and was conducted by Rev. G. Dudley. His wife died in 1972 and is buried with her husband.

Joseph Edwin Bennett
Sergeant 9203, 2nd Battalion, Gloucestershire Regiment

Born: 1876

Joseph was born in Campden, the second son of Enoch and Ann Bennett, and was baptised at St. James's Church on 26 March 1876. His father, born in Campden in 1844, married Ann Merriman on 14 December 1867 at St. James's Church and was employed as a labourer. He died of epilepsy on 18 March 1879 when Joseph was only 3 years old and after a time Ann married Enoch's brother Thomas.

After leaving school Joseph found employment as an errand boy before he went to Bristol to enlist as Private 3050, Joseph Bennett, in the Gloucestershire Regiment on 15 November 1890, giving his age as 18 years and 7 months. In reality he was only 14 years old. He was passed fit for service and his medical papers state that he was five feet six inches tall with red hair, hazel eyes and a fresh complexion. His religion was Church of England.

He served in England until the battalion arrived in India on 26 February 1892. They remained there until they were posted to Malta in November 1893. After two years in Malta Joseph moved with the battalion to Egypt and they remained there until they returned to England on 31 March 1897. During his time with the battalion he was awarded two good conduct badges and a third class education certificate. He was promoted to lance corporal on 20 January 1896 although he was returned to the rank of private on 27 June 1896.

On 1 April 1897 Joseph was transferred to the Army Reserve. He was recalled on 13 November 1899 when troops were needed for the Boer War in South Arica but was discharged on 26 March 1900 as *"unfit for further service"* without leaving England.

He returned to Campden and found employment as a general labourer. He married Lillian James from Ebrington at St. James's Church on 25 December 1905 and they had three daughters: Hilda Constance, Margaret Ivy and Violet.

Joseph was mobilised at the outbreak of war in August 1914 and arrived in France with the 2nd Battalion, Gloucestershire Regiment on 19 December 1914. The battalion arrived at Le Havre on board SS *City of Chester* after embarking at Southampton. In early 1915 they were in the St. Eloi sector of the Ypres Salient in Belgium. The Second Battle of Ypres began on 22 April 1915 with the Germans using poison gas. The battalion were not directly affected by the gas but they served in the Salient throughout the battle, which lasted until 25 May.

In November 1915 the battalion moved to Salonika in Greece and remained there for the remainder of the war. Joseph was promoted to the rank of sergeant and towards the end of 1918 he was mentioned in despatches. He survived the war and returned to Campden after his official discharge.

Joseph is buried at St. Lawrence's churchyard in Mickleton.

Richard Bennett
Private 5737, 1st/24th Battalion, London Regiment (The Queen's)

Born: 1892
Died: 5 April 1918

Richard was born in Campden, the eldest son of Noah and Sarah Bennett of Watery Lane, and was baptised at St. James's Church on 28 February 1892. After leaving school he served an apprenticeship as a printer before moving to Walworth, London.

Richard enlisted at Whitehall in London and after a period of training in England he was posted to France, where he joined the 1st/24th Battalion, London Regiment. The *Evesham Journal* reported Richard's death:

"Mr. and Mrs. Noah Bennett, of Watery Lane, Campden, have now received from their daughter-in-law the sad news of the death of their eldest son, Richard, aged 26 years. He was a private in the London Regiment in the signallers' section and was killed in action in France on 5 April 1918."

An account of his death was written in a letter from his sergeant:

"He died as bravely as any man could defending his comrades. He was on duty in a front line trench dugout at the phone on April 5, when the enemy attacked our line. He remained at his post trying to get a message through to headquarters, but a cable had been broken by shell fire. Feeling the futility of wasting time he joined his comrades in the firing line, trying to stop the on rush of the Huns. He had not fired many rounds before he was shot through the head by a sniper, who had crawled up to within 40 or 50 yards of our position."

Richard was originally buried in Aveluy Wood, north of Albert in France, but at the end of the war his grave could not be identified. Today his name is recorded on the Arras Memorial. It is also recorded on three memorials in Campden: in St. James's Church, in the Baptist Church and in the High Street. He left a widow and one child at home in London.

Three months after Richard's death his parents received the sad news that their second son, Ernest, had been killed in action in France. 1918 had been an awful year for Sarah Bennett; not only did two of her sons die but she also lost her nephew, James Trinder, killed in action in March 1918.

Ernest Edward Bickley

Private 4489, 2nd/5th Battalion, Gloucestershire Regiment
Private 241489, 2nd/5th Battalion, Gloucestershire Regiment

Born: 30 November 1891
Enlisted: 26 July 1915
Died: September 1966

Ernest was born in Campden , the third son of Edward and Jane Bickley of Westington, and was baptised at St. James's Church on 25 December 1895. His father was an agricultural labourer and by 1901 Jane was a widow. The family also lived in Coldicott's Yard for a time.

Ernest attended school in the town and on 26 July 1915 he enlisted in the Gloucestershire Regiment, giving his home address as Paul's Cottages, Campden. He entered France in 1916 and was posted to the 2nd/5th Battalion, a Territorial unit, and arrived at Albert, with its famous leaning statue of the Virgin Mary on top of the Basilica, on 20 November 1916 at the end of the Battle of the Somme. The winter of 1916/1917 was spent on the Somme Front and in May the tired and under-strength battalion moved to the Arras sector just as the great offensive was coming to a close and were involved only as *"clearing-up troops"*. The next move was north to Belgium, where the battalion was involved in an attack north-east of Wieltje on 22 August during the Third Battle of Ypres. They moved to the Brigade support area on 30 August 1917 on the banks of the canal near Dead End, north of Ypres. A good deal of swimming was indulged in until it was found that broken bottles were poor things to step on bare-footed and that dead horses made unpleasant bath salts.

Ernest returned safely to Campden after two years on the Western Front. He was wounded only once. After the war he married Edith Rogers and had two children: Francis and Dorothy. He died in September 1966 aged 74 years and is buried in St. James's churchyard.

Thomas James Bickley

Private 3278, 2nd/5th Battalion, Gloucestershire Regiment
Private 241137, 2nd Battalion, Gloucestershire Regiment

Born: 18 February 1897
Enlisted: 28 October 1914
Discharged: 14 June 1919
Died: 1 April 1981

Tom was born in Campden and was baptised at St. James's Church on 3 October 1897. He was educated in the town and then found employment as a gardener before he enlisted at Gloucester in the Gloucestershire Regiment on 28 October 1914 when still only 17 years old. He was sent to France in 1916 and served in the 2nd/5th Battalion alongside Jack Taplin, Jerry Howell and his brother Ernest. The winter of 1916/1917 was spent on the Somme front and the wet conditions caused Tom to develop trench foot. He was admitted to Number 3 Stationary Hospital at Rouen in March 1917.

In May the battalion arrived at Arras to take part in the closing stages of the Battle of Arras. This was followed by a move north to Belgium, where they were in action on 22 August 1917 when they attacked the German line north-east of Wieltje during the Third Battle of Ypres (also known as the Battle of Passchendaele). The battalion made a magnificent advance but the losses were great and it was impossible to hold the furthest objectives; they were pushed back, fighting hard. Tom was wounded during this action and was admitted to Number 1 Australian General Hospital at Rouen on 23 August with a shell wound in the right forearm.

After recovering from this Tom was posted to the 2nd Battalion, Gloucestershire Regiment in Salonika in Greece after serving a period of 1 year and 95 days on the Western Front. In September 1918 Tom was wounded in the shoulder by a bullet and was admitted to the 80th General Hospital in Salonika. Mrs. Bickley, who was living in Broad Campden at the time, received a letter, dated 10 February 1919, informing her that Tom was in the 27th Casualty Clearing Station in Salonika and was "*dangerously ill*". Another letter dated 20 February 1919 said that he was "*still dangerously ill*" but when a final letter arrived, dated 28 February 1919, Tom was "*now out of danger*".

Tom returned to England after serving 1 year and 122 days in Salonika and was admitted to St. Luke's War Hospital in Halifax. After his release from hospital he was discharged from the army on 14 June 1919. He applied for a war pension but this was rejected.

After returning to Campden he married Sarah Lizzie Whatcott and they had a daughter called Joan. The wound in his shoulder continued to trouble him throughout his life and his daughter told the author that his shirt had to be washed every day owing to the continual bleeding.

Tom died on 1 April 1981 aged 84 years. He is buried in St. James's churchyard with his wife, who died on 15 April 1992 aged 90 years. Tom was living at "Kenyon" on the corner of Sheep Street when he died.

Sidney James Biggerstaff
Private S-343962, Army Service Corps

Born: 6 January 1896
Enlisted: May 1917
Died: 4 June 1974

Sidney was the son of Charles Edwin Alfred and Alice Biggerstaff. His father was a stonemason and the family home was in Poppett's Alley, Campden. He was the brother of Mabel, Alfred Harry, Gladys and Edward.

Just before his father's death on 31 May 1917 he enlisted, aged 21, in the Army Service Corps (ASC). After a spell in England he was sent to Africa. He embarked on 28 November 1917 but it was January 1918 before he actually set foot there. The next sixteen months were spent in German East Africa. This was not an easy time for Sidney, as he was ill six times and passed a total of fifty-one days in hospitals in Port Amelia, Mwali, Masula and Dar-es-Salaam. In the first, as the *Evesham Journal* reported in 1918, he was suffering from malaria.

When out of hospital he saw service with the ASC at Manspula and Ndanda. At the time of the armistice he was in Dar-es-Salaam, where he was to remain until April 1919, when he eventually returned to England.

Back in Campden, he married Laura Tout, the sister of Arthur Augusta Tout, who won the Military Medal. She was in service with the Noel family, one of whom, Captain Robert Noel, had died in Dar-es-Salaam in February 1918 and was buried there. It was not long before the pair moved to Deacle Place, Evesham, where Sidney remained for the rest of his life. They had one child, a daughter called Vera.

Sidney was employed as a butcher in Mill Street, Evesham. His time as a butcher was only interrupted when he became an air raid warden (ARP) during the Second World War.

He died on 4 June 1974 aged 78 and was cremated at Worcester.

Frank Arthur Biles
Private S2-11107, Number 8 Field Butchery, Army Service Corps
Private 20887, 1st/4th Battalion, Royal Sussex Regiment
Private TR 10-45447, 100th Royal Sussex Training Reserve Battalion
Private 202905, 3rd Battalion, Royal Sussex Regiment

Born: 19 April 1895
Enlisted: 24 August 1914
Discharged: 2 May 1919
Died: 23 April 1931

Frank was born in Weston-sub-Edge. He was the eldest of three sons of William Henry and Lillian Gertrude Biles, who were living in Broadway in 1914. He attended school at Aston-sub-Edge and in Campden before he found employment as a butcher.

When the war started he enlisted at Campden Recruiting Office on 24 August 1914, when he was aged 19 years and 4 months. William Beckett was the recruiting sergeant and Frank's address on enlistment was given as High Street, Broadway. His medical examination recorded that he was five feet eleven inches tall with blue eyes and brown hair.

After a short period of home service he arrived in France with Number 8 Field Butchery, Army Service Corps on 8 October 1914. He was stationed at Rouen in 1915 and on 13 January 1915 he was awarded seven days Field Punishment Number 2 for breaking two windows in his billet. He had to pay for the damage.

On 17 October he was admitted to hospital suffering from tonsillitis and it was not until 29 December that was able to return to duty with the Field Butchery. He was transferred to the Royal Sussex Regiment on 27 June 1916 while he was in France and on 2 December 1916 he returned to England. The next 87 days were spent on home service before he was posted to the

Mediterranean Expeditionary Force; he arrived at Alexandria on HMS *Transylvania* on 16 March 1917. He was posted to 1st/4th Battalion, Royal Sussex Regiment on 7 April but was admitted to Number 26 Casualty Clearing Station with diphtheria on 16 July 1917. He also had time in hospital suffering from malaria and diarrhoea before he embarked at Alexandria on 17 June 1918. He arrived at Taranto in Italy on 22 June en route for France, where he was wounded by a bullet in the left shoulder on 29 July 1918 and was evacuated to the 1st Australian General Hospital at Rouen. A telegram received by his parents stated that he was "*seriously ill and returning to England*". Further treatment followed at The King George Hospital in London where he was admitted on 6 August. After his discharge from hospital on 12 September a period of convalescence followed at Eastbourne until 12 October 1918.

He spent the rest of the war attached to 424 Agricultural Company from 3rd Battalion, Royal Sussex Regiment before he was discharged from the army at Fovant on 2 May 1919.

On returning home he married Florence Score. In 1920 he emigrated to Australia and his wife joined him two months later. They started a home in Queensland at a place called Ravenshoe in the Atherton Tablelands and, once settled, Frank got a job in a sawmill, cutting logs to make homes. On 26 December 1920 Frank Arthur (their only child and known as Arthur) was born. In 1924 the family moved to Bilyana, where the railway line from Townsville to Cairns was being built. Frank worked on the line and Florence did the cooking and washing for the workers. They lived in tents and all the food came from Townsville, 117 miles away.

After a few years Frank moved the family to Upper Murray, where he grew oranges and mandarins until a cyclone washed out all the trees and blew part of the roof off the house. The family then moved back to Bilyana and started a banana farm, building a big hut and calling it a house. Frank dug a well near the house for washing but the water was not good enough to drink and they had to get all drinking water from a creek 250 yards away.

The depression caught up with the family when Frank sent 144 cases of bananas to Townsville by rail and a bill came back, as the sale price did not cover the cost of transporting the fruit. All the banana trees were dug up and tomatoes were planted which ended up being eaten by wildlife.

In 1930 Frank started to become ill; he had pains in his stomach and could not keep his food down, yet refused surgical treatment. When the pain became unbearable, however, he was taken to Townsville Hospital. He died of cancer there on 23 April 1930, when he was 36 years old. He is buried in Townsville Cmetery..

His son, Arthur, served in the army for five years during the Second World War and saw action in the Pacific against the Japanese. After the war he returned to Australia and married Margaret Elizabeth Sparnon. When the author contacted him he was delighted to share his father's life story and much of what he said has been included above.

Frank's two brothers also served in the army during the war. His wife died aged 94 years.

Left to right: William Henry Biles, Frank Arthur Biles, Ada Mary Biles and Percy George Biles.

Percy George Biles
Corporal 15528, 9th Battalion, Gloucestershire Regiment

Born: 30 August 1898
Enlisted: 13 November 1914
Discharged: 8 April 1919
Died: 4 March 1996

Percy was the youngest of three sons of William Henry and Lillian Gertrude Biles who served during the 1914-18 war. He was born in 1898 and attended school in Aston-sub-Edge and Campden. In 1910 the family were living in Lower High Street, Campden, but by 1914 they had moved to Broadway.

When war was declared Percy was only 16 years old but he enlisted in Campden in the Gloucestershire Regiment on 13 November 1914. His two brothers were already in uniform and they all believed that the war would be over by Christmas. The recruiting sergeant, Bill Beckett, did not want him to join but Percy insisted and he was accepted.

Percy had been a scout before the war and was given the job of signaller in the Gloucestershire Regiment. He knew semaphore and Morse code and was equipped with a pair of flags, a coil of wire and a bicycle. He rarely had the chance to ride it as the ground was too rough and muddy and it had to be carried.

Percy went to France on 20 September 1915, when he was just 17 years old and still under age. This fact was reported to the authorities by an uncle in England but before anything could be done Percy was posted to Salonika in Greece with the 9th Battalion, Gloucestershire Regiment. He soon developed dysentery and was admitted to hospital in Malta. After leaving Malta he returned to England, where he was taught to use a machine gun at Maidstone and became an instructor. Percy then volunteered to go to France to instruct American troops in the use of machine guns. When he arrived he did not get to instruct any American troops; instead, he was given his own gun and gun crew and was sent to the front line. When advancing his platoon came under shellfire and the next thing Percy knew was that he could not feel anything. He could not move and was sure that he must be dead. After a long period he eventually struggled free and realised that he had been buried under a huge layer of soil and mud. His gun and all his crew were blown to pieces; he was the only survivor.

Percy was still in France when the armistice was signed and he said that the best bit was being able to stand erect in the trenches without the fear of being shot. He was discharged from the Gloucestershire Regiment on 8 April 1919, when he was still only 20 years old. He had served in the 8th and 9th Battalions for over four years.

Percy was a very good sportsman and he won medals in the army in football and cross-country competitions.

After the war he found employment as a draper's assistant in Rugby and married Mildred "Millie" London (née Lee), a war widow with a little boy, on 30 August 1922. They had two children, Barbara and Judith, who both married in Rugby after the Second World War.

When that war started Percy went out and dug a full-sized trench at the bottom of the garden for the family, although they would never go in it. He served as an air raid warden and later as a NAAFI inspector.

Percy died on 4 March 1996, aged 97 years. His wife, Millie, died several years before him.

William Henry Biles
Private, S4-039076, Army Service Corps
Private S-43932, Gordon Highlanders

Born: 24 June 1896

William was the second of three sons of William Henry and Gertrude Biles, who were living in the High Street in Broadway in 1914. He was educated in Campden, however, and was admitted to St. James's Boys' School in 1905.

At the age of 18 he enlisted in the army and after a period of training in England he arrived in France on 20 July 1915. He served in the Army Service Corps and the Gordon Highlanders before he returned safely to England for his discharge on 16 March 1919. His brothers, Frank Arthur and Percy George, had also done army service.

After demobilisation William became butler to an Oxford professor. On 23 September 1936, when he was 40 years old, he married Hilda Jackson; the wedding certificate recorded his occupation as "farmer". They subsequently ran the Green Dragon pub at Galgate near Lancaster. They had no children.

William died in a nursing home in Lancaster.

William wearing his Gordon Highlanders uniform.

1939-45: William as a corporal

William (left) with his brother, Lance Corporal Percy George Biles, Gloucestershire Regiment.

Raymund Louis Binns
Private 2811, Inns of Court Officers' Training Corps
2nd Lieutenant, 8th Battalion, Yorkshire Regiment

Born: 21 March 1884
Enlisted: 29 January 1915
Died: 10 July 1916

Raymund was the son of Dr. William Binns of "The Cedars", East Burgholt, Suffolk. He entered Stonyhurst College, near Preston, Lancashire in 1897 and quickly showed his talents as an artist and in sport. He was frequently among the winners of drawing prizes and excellent at swimming and hockey.

After leaving Stonyhurst he went to London to work for Paul Woodroffe, an old boy of the college, who was rapidly becoming a very successful illustrator, book designer and stained glass artist. Father John Gerard sent Raymund with a letter of introduction. Attendance at evening classes soon gave him greater facility in draughtsmanship and when Woodroffe moved to Campden in 1905 Raymund gladly went with him. His studio was at Westington in Campden and his team of workers included George Phillipson, Michael Pippet, Gabriel Pippet, Percy Newman and Fred Bennett. Woodroffe described Raymund as "*clean-minded and cheery. A Catholic through and through.*"

The time came when Raymund's artistic ability had outrun the work that Woodroffe could lay before him. In London he was rapidly making a name for himself by the dignity and well-ordered balance of his designs and letterings. The outbreak of the First World War came at a time when his career as a designer was beginning to flourish.

He married Sarah Maud Cartman at the Church of the Sacred Heart in Wimbledon on 23 October 1913. She was the only daughter of the Reverend J. and Mrs. Cartman of Bonby Vicarage, Hull. They had two children, Cyrilla Mary (born in 1914) and John Raymund (born in 1915).

At the outbreak of the war Raymund, though married and successfully embarked on a career as artist, gave up his happy home and congenial work to join the army. "*I feel the times call for something a bit heroic,*" he observed to a near relative. He enlisted as a private in the Inns of Court Officers' Training Corps on 29 January 1915 and three months later he obtained his commission, joining the 3rd (Reserve) Battalion, Yorkshire Regiment as a 2nd lieutenant on 22 April. He was stationed at West Hartlepool. After a period of training in England he was sent to France in 1916 and in May he was attached to the 8th Battalion, Yorkshire Regiment.

The battalion moved to the Somme area on 24 June in preparation for the forthcoming offensive. The Battle of the Somme began at 7.30am on 1 July 1916 and Raymund spent the day moving up to bivouacs in Baizieux Wood, east of Albert. The next day they reached Albert and on 4 July they were employed in digging a communication trench from the old British line to Sausage Redoubt. On 5 July they took part in a successful attack on Horseshoe Trench before they were relieved and returned to bivouacs south of Albert. On 10 July they moved forward again and assembled in Horseshoe Trench ready for an attack on Contalmaison. The advance began at

4.50pm and at about 500 yards from the village heavy machine gun and rifle fire inflicted great casualties. The German wire was found uncut in front of the battalion's first objective but after fierce fighting the battalion fought their way into the village and consolidated their gains, holding on against counter-attacks.

Raymund was killed in this action which captured Contalmaison on 10 July, dying instantly from a bullet through the head as he went forward with a party of bombers. A fellow officer was quoted as saying, "*He was perfectly splendid, the men followed him wherever he went. They carried him back to Bécourt Cemetery outside Albert and gave him a burial any soldier would be proud of. He was the bravest platoon commander I have had.*"

Raymund was 32 years old when he died during the Battle of the Somme and is buried in Bécourt Cemetery in France. He left a wife and two young children at home in 5 Putney Road, Wimbledon. He had sacrificed £800 a year to serve for king and country and his wife had to fight hard for a quick issue of her widow's pension as she had no income to support her and the children. In 1934 Sarah was living at "Wells Cottage" in Broadway.

Raymund has his name recorded on two war memorials in Campden: in St. Catharine's Church and in the High Street. It is also recorded on the memorial in Stonyhurst College.

Charles Birch
Lieutenant, Royal Army Medical Corps

Born: 1880
Died: 19 August 1942

Charles was the son of Frank Birch. It is believed that he was brought up in the Southport area. He had one brother, George, who became a solicitor in Lichfield. Charles qualified as a doctor in 1902 and went on to become the medical officer at Clayesmore School and then a surgeon and physician at Birmingham General Hospital.

During the First World War he obtained a commission in the Royal Army Medical Corps, beginning his overseas service in Egypt on 14 March 1915.

In 1928 he set up in practice at Campden, living at "The Gables" in the High Street. He remained the town's doctor until he died in 1942. He married Enid Johnson on 26 August 1937, when he was 57 and she was 41. Enid was from West Kirby; they met when she brought a group of Guides to Dover's Hill in 1932. They had one son, John, who died after only four days, on 4 April 1938.

Charles died of cancer on 19 August 1942 aged 62 and is buried in St. James's churchyard. The Royal Army Medical Corps cap badge is carved into his headstone. His wife continued to live at "The Gables" until her death in 1989.

Henry Oswald Blake
Labour Corps

Born: 6 July 1881

Harry was the third son of Oswald and Lucy Ann Blake. His father was baptised at St. James's Church in Campden on 12 March 1843 and married Lucy Ann Bickerstaff at the same church on 11 November 1872. Harry was baptised at St. James's Church on 25 December 1881.

He married Ada Athalia Bone, from Croydon, at St. James's on 7 May 1916 while he was on home service a short time after enlisting in the Labour Corps. The 1918 electoral roll gives his home address as Gainsborough Terrace and records him as absent on military service.

William Walter Blakeman
Pioneer 181899, 30th (Great Western Railway) Company, Royal Engineers
Pioneer WR-257523, Royal Engineers

Born: 17 May 1878
Enlisted: 9 December 1915
Mobilised: 14 June 1916
Died: 29 October 1956

William was the only son of Charles and Elizabeth Blakeman of Campden. In 1891 his father was a gardener and the family was living in Sheep Street.

After leaving school William found employment as a builder's labourer before he joined the estate staff of the Noel family when he was 14 years old. A career of sixty years working for the Earl of Gainsborough began by planting trees in the wood at Campden House. At the Royal Show at Shrewsbury in 1949 he received the bronze medal of the Royal Agricultural Society of England for long service. In this he was true to his heritage; Blakemans worked for the Noel family for over three hundred years and after William retired the tradition was continued by his son, Alfred.

William married Martha Gisbourne, a native of Pebworth, on 18 August 1903. They had four children, who were all baptised at St. James's Church in Campden: Alfred Charles, Grace, Angela and Walter James. The family home was "Wood House" in Campden.

During the war William served on the Western Front with the Royal Engineers.

He died on 29 October 1956 aged 78 and is buried in St. James's churchyard with his wife, who died in March 1929 aged 56.

Nathaniel Charles Butler Bloodworth
2nd Lieutenant, 12th Battalion, Gloucestershire Regiment

Born: 22 February 1882
Died: 12 March 1956

Charlie was born in Cheltenham. He was the son of Nathaniel James and Mary Parker "Nelly" Bloodworth of 306 High Street, Cheltenham. His father was a baker and after leaving school Charlie became a baker's assistant.

He married Minnie Ada Brushfield in Cheltenham in 1912 and they went to live in Birmingham, where he had a good job in a bakery. The marriage was short-lived as Minnie died in 1914. His second marriage took place in 1916 at Shipston-on-Stour Registry Office when he married Ada Starkiss from Campden, whose mother was a widow and the licensee of the Plough Inn. It lost its licence in 1919 and Mrs. Starkiss appealed at the Campden Petty Sessions, as she was entirely dependent on the business with no sons and two daughters. Her appeal was rejected and she moved to a cottage in Watery Lane, where she used to sell sweets from a shed in her garden.

Charlie gained his commission as a 2nd lieutenant with the 12th Battalion, Gloucestershire Regiment on 26 April 1917 and arrived in France on 8 June 1917. In September 1917 the

Evesham Journal had a headline "Campden Officer Gassed" and the article said, "*It has now been reported that 2nd Lieutenant N. C. Bloodworth is now lying in hospital badly gassed. He married Miss. Starkiss of The Plough Inn, Campden, on 8 September 1916. We are glad to say he is now progressing favourably.*" The *Gloucestershire Echo* also carried a report on Charlie being gassed and it ended by saying that "*he visited Campden about two years ago with a recruiting party and then made a romantic attachment and eventually married Ada, the younger daughter of the late Mr. William and Mrs. Starkiss of the Plough, Campden on September 8 and then returned to France. He was incapacitated through being gassed which chiefly affected his eyes but he is progressing favourably.*"

Charlie is on the right. Campden Recruiting Office is in the background.

Charlie was back serving with the battalion in September 1918 but in 1919 he was discharged from the army as "*no longer fit for active service*" and issued with a Silver War Badge.

After the war he returned to Campden and was living in Lower High Street in 1922 and employed as a fishmonger.

He died on 12 March 1956 aged 74 years.

William Borsay
Gunner 51677, Royal Horse Artillery

William was born in Blackburn in 1891, the son of Peter and Susannah Borsay of 15 Crawshaw Street, Accrington. His father was born in Bolton and a blacksmith by trade.

William was a regular soldier and was mobilised at the outbreak of war, arriving in France in 1914 as a gunner with the Royal Horse Artillery. He was still serving in the regiment when he married Dorothy Rosalind Plested, daughter of William, at St. James's Church in Campden on 26 August 1919.

Charles James Allen Boulter
Lance Corporal 20347, 2nd Battalion, Gloucestershire Regiment

Born: 25 July 1897
Enlisted: 14 April 1915
Discharged: 1 March 1919
Died: 27 October 1961

Charles was one of three sons of James and Clara Jane Boulter. The family were originally from Ebrington but by 1918 they were living at Rogue's Hill, Campden.

He enlisted in the 2nd Battalion, Gloucestershire Regiment on 14 April 1915, when he was 17 years old, and arrived in France on 20 July. He served on the Western Front until the battalion was sent to Greece, arriving at Salonika on 26 November 1915.

After the armistice was signed they were given orders to proceed to Russia but it was at this time that Charles left the battalion. He arrived back in England at midnight on New Year's Eve. He was discharged from the army on 1 March 1919.

After the war he was confirmed at Blockley Parish Church on 15 March 1920 and found employment as a labourer. He married Gladys Mary Stevens and had three children: Frank, Joan and Mary.

During the Second World War Charles again volunteered to join the army. According to his son, Frank, he put his age up to enlist in the First World War and down to enlist in the Second World War.

Charles died on 27 October 1961 aged 64 and he is buried in Buckland churchyard extension, near Broadway, Worcestershire. His wife died in 1979 aged 69 years.

Frank Robert Boulter
Private 30793, Oxfordshire and Buckinghamshire Light Infantry
Private 208837, Corps of Hussars
Private 39353, 8th Battalion, Gloucestershire Regiment

Born: 1899
Enlisted: 16 March 1917
Died: 12 April 1918

Frank was born in Kelmscott, near Lechlade in Oxfordshire, in 1899. He was the son of James and Clara Jane Boulter, who were living at Rogue's Hill, Campden in 1918. His parents were originally from Ebrington and were married in 1896. Clara Jane died in 1928 and is buried in St. Eadburgha's churchyard, Ebrington.

After leaving school Frank worked on a farm on Westington Hill at Campden. He was only 15 years old when the war started and he waited until he was 18 before he enlisted at Oxford on 16 March 1917. The next year was spent training in England and when he arrived in France on 1 March 1918 he was posted to 8th Battalion, Gloucestershire Regiment. On 1 April 1918 the battalion relieved the Australians in front of Messines in Belgium, south of Ypres, and for the next nine days they held the front line trenches. At 3.30am on 10 April 1918 the enemy put up a very heavy barrage that lasted about five hours. This was followed by a very heavy attack that resulted in the Glosters being flanked and compelled to fall back to a line nearing Stinking Farm. It was during this action on 10 April that Frank was wounded and taken prisoner by the Germans only a month after arriving in France. His wounds were serious and after treatment behind the German lines in Tourcoing he died on 12 April 1918 aged 19.

Frank's grave in Tourcoing Communal Cemetery in France.

He is buried in Tourcoing Communal Cemetery in France and his name is recorded on the memorial in St. James's Church in Campden. It is not recorded on the memorial in Campden High Street.

Frank's brother, Charles, returned safely from the war after serving in France and Salonika with the 2nd Battalion, Gloucestershire Regiment.

Thomas Bourne
Private 21801, 14th Battalion, Gloucestershire Regiment

> Born: 19 April 1878
> Enlisted: 24 July 1915
> Discharged: 1 August 1917
> Died: 20 May 1969

Thomas was born in Burslem, the son of Thomas and Eliza Bourne. He joined the Church Army after leaving school and in 1904 became a commissioned officer. When he married Alice Ann Smallridge at All Saints Church in Roffey, near Horsham in Sussex, on 14 August 1910 his occupation was recorded as *"licensed reader"*.

It is not clear exactly when Thomas and Alice arrived in Broad Campden but records of St. James's Church show that they had a son called Stanley baptised at the church on 18 May 1913 and a daughter called Joyce baptised on 22 November 1914. Thomas was then an *"Evangelist Captain"* in the Church Army.

Thomas enlisted in the army on 24 July 1915 and was posted to the 14th Battalion, Gloucestershire Regiment on Salisbury Plain. The battalion was a *"Bantam"* battalion made up of men who were under regulation size but otherwise fit for service. He was five feet one inch tall with blue eyes, brown hair and a dark complexion. During his time in England he was placed in charge of the battalion recreation room. When the battalion arrived in France on 30 January 1916 Thomas was employed assisting the Army Service Corps loading the rations for the 105th Brigade. In 1917 he became ill and was returned to England, where he was discharged from the army on 1 August 1917 owing to deafness in both ears. The deafness had started at Tidworth in November 1915 and steadily worsened. A Silver War Badge was issued to indicate that he had made his contribution to the war.

Thomas left Campden after the war. He went to live at 9, Red Lane Cottage, Limpsfield, Surrey and returned to the Church Army. He died on 20 May 1969 aged 91 and his obituary appeared in the Church Army quarterly magazine in July 1969. His funeral service was held in the delightful parish church at Limpsfield, near Oxted in Surrey, where Thomas had spent 28 years as a parochial officer in the Church Army.

Alfred Theodore Bower
Private 2073, 5th (Cinque Ports) Battalion, Royal Sussex Regiment
Private 202416, 5th (Cinque Ports) Battalion, Royal Sussex Regiment
2nd Lieutenant, 99 Squadron, Royal Flying Corps

> Born: 1 August 1889
> Enlisted: 11 August 1914
> Died: 31 January 1958

Alfred was born in Wentworth, near Rotherham, the fourth son of George and Mary Jane Bower. His father was a carpenter and joiner by trade; his mother died before the 1901 census was recorded.

Alfred was educated at Rotherham Grammar School and was then employed by a firm of estate agents in Southport in 1908. In 1912 he moved to Rye in Sussex and when he enlisted in the army on 11 August 1914 he gave his occupation as an auctioneer's clerk. He was passed fit for active service and his medical examination reported that he was five feet three inches tall with normal vision and good physical development.

He was posted to the 5th Battalion, Royal Sussex Regiment and was employed on home service until he arrived in France on 18 February 1915. After only 73 days at the front he returned to England on 2 May. He then embarked for France again on 7 March 1916 and served for 257 days on the Western Front before returning to England. He served at the front for a third time when he arrived in France on 3 March 1917 but after 99 days he was back in England on 9 June.

His final time on the Western Front began on 23 July 1917 and lasted only 39 days. He arrived back in England on 31 August and was posted to "D" Company, 4th (Reserve) Battalion, Royal Sussex Regiment at Tunbridge Wells.

On 27 October 1917 he applied for a temporary commission in the regular army and stated that he wished to join the Royal Flying Corps. His application said that he knew how a motor works and was capable of carrying out minor repairs. Captain G. S. Johnson, Royal Army Medical Corps, examined him and found him fit for service as an officer. He was placed in medical category A3 and his weight was nine stone six pounds.

He was appointed to a temporary commission as a 2nd lieutenant with the Royal Flying Corps on 24 July 1918 and he was issued with an allowance of £50 to buy his uniform. He spent the remainder of the war as an observer with 99 Squadron.

After the war he was employed as an assistant estate agent in Chipping Norton until he opened an office of his own in Campden in 1922. He worked in the town until his death in 1958.

Alfred died at the Radcliffe Infirmary, Oxford on 31 January 1958 aged 68 years. He is buried in St. James's churchyard. He was survived by his wife, Dorothy Gladys Bower, and two children. His home in Campden was in Grevel Lane and he was a founder member of the local Masonic Lodge.

Albert Henry Bradley

Private 686, "D" Company, 1st/5th Battalion, Gloucestershire Regiment
Private 245986, Labour Corps

Born: 3 September 1878
Discharged: 15 February 1919

Albert was born in Shipston-on-Stour, the eldest child of Isaac and Elizabeth Bradley, and was baptised at St. James's Church on 24 May 1885 when he was 6 years old. His father was a fishmonger by trade and married Elizabeth Ladbrook in 1877. He died in 1884, aged 38, leaving his wife to bring up their three children, Albert, Rose and Emily. In 1891 Elizabeth was a charwoman living in Lower High Street.

Albert joined "K" Company, 2nd Volunteer Battalion, Gloucestershire Regiment in 1899 and on 1 July 1911 he was awarded the Territorial Efficiency Medal for 12 years' service. At the outbreak of war he was serving as a private in "H" Company, 5th Battalion, Gloucestershire Regiment, the local company of the Territorial Army, and was mobilised on 5 August 1914. He went to Chelmsford in Essex with many other Campden men as part of the newly formed "D" Company and after a period of training they arrived at Boulogne in France on 29 March 1915. Their first experience of life in the front line came at Ploegsteert in Belgium and they remained there until they headed south to Hébuterne in France in July 1915. The battalion saw heavy fighting during the Battle of the Somme, near Ovillers, in July and August 1916 and in November 1917 they were posted to Italy.

It is not clear how long Albert stayed with the battalion after his arrival in France in March 1915. He ended the war as a private in the Labour Corps and was discharged on 15 February 1919, when he was 40 years old. He then returned to his wife and children at the family home in Lower High Street.

Albert had married Mary Ann Fletcher in 1900 and four children were born before he was mobilised in 1914: Albert Edward, Charles Henry, Harry and Amy. Their fifth child, Margaret Annie, was baptised at St. James's Church on 30 July 1916 while he was in France.

Mary Ann died in May 1922 aged 46 years and is buried in St. James's churchyard.

The Territorial Army: "H" Company, 5th Battalion, Gloucestershire Regiment outside the Armoury, Campden.

Charles Thomas Brain
Private 13234, 10th Battalion, Gloucestershire Regiment

Born: 26 July 1896
Enlisted: September 1914
Died: 23 July 1916

Charles was born in Campden, the second son of John and Mary Katharine Brain of Watery Lane, and was baptised at St. James's Church on 6 September 1896. His father was an agricultural labourer. After Mary died he married Emma Cherry on 10 December 1910 at St. James's Church.

At the age of 18 Charles enlisted in the Gloucestershire Regiment in September 1914. The next year was spent training in England before he arrived in France on 4 October 1915. He was posted to the 10th Battalion, which had just suffered heavy casualties during the Battle of Loos, including Tom Smith and William Hedges, who both died on 25 September 1915, the opening day of the battle.

The battalion was still in the coal-mining region of northern France around Lens in June 1916 and the war diary remarks that the chief incident of note was when British miners exploded two mines under the German trenches in front of the battalion's lines. The second of these two mines formed a crater and the battalion occupied the near lip, which was shelled somewhat persistently by the enemy, causing a number of casualties. The end of the month was spent in reserve in preparation for a move south to the Somme.

The battalion arrived at Doullens by train and then marched to billets in Naours, arriving on 6 July. They rested all day in their billets before they marched at night to billets in Pierregot, beginning their gradual move to the front and the Somme battlefield. On the evening of 7 July they marched further forward to Baizieux Wood, where they bivouacked for the night. They arrived at billets in the town of Albert at midnight on 9 July. The next day they moved up to the front line at The Dingle, about one mile north of Fricourt. The ground occupied had only just been won from the Germans and was strewn with corpses, between four and five hundred of which the battalion buried. The next few days the battalion were mainly employed in improving existing defence works and digging fresh communication trenches to Contalmaison, which had just been won from the enemy.

On 14 July the battalion arrived back in Albert, where they spent time bathing and cleaning up before they moved forward to Bécourt Wood. On 19 July trenches were occupied in the vicinity of Shelter Wood, one mile south of Contalmaison, and the next two days were spent providing working parties to dig a new front line in front of Bazetin-le-Petit Wood, which had just been captured from the enemy.

On 21 July the battalion moved up to the front line trenches opposite, and due south of, Martinpuich. That night was spent digging a new front line about 160 yards in front of the trench that had been dug the previous night, just south of the crest of the ridge in front of them. The next day was spent in improving the advanced front line, which was going to form the kicking-off point for the attack that the battalion had been ordered to make early on the morning of 23 July.

At 12.30am on 23 July 1916 they attacked a portion of the new German Switch Line in front of Martinpuich. They failed to take their objective but they did capture Point 17 and from this position it was possible to observe the enemy's line for the first time. During the attack the battalion lost 147 casualties, including Charles and his brother, William. Their bodies were never recovered after the war but their names are recorded on the Thiepval Memorial in France. Charles was 19 years old when he died and his name is recorded on two memorials in Campden: in St. James's Church and in the High Street.

Harold William Brain
Private 23298, 10th Battalion, Gloucestershire Regiment

Born: 29 January 1898
Died: 23 July 1916

Willie was born in Campden, the third son of John and Mary Katharine Brain of Watery Lane, and was baptised at St. James's Church on 10 April 1898.

Willie's brother Charles enlisted in the Gloucestershire Regiment in 1914 but as Willie was younger he had to wait before he could join him in the army. Willie joined the 10th Battalion, Gloucestershire Regiment in France in the coal-mining area around the city of Lens early in 1916. What happened next can be read in the entry for Charles.

Willie died on 23 July 1916 aged 18. His grave could not be located at the end of the war so his name is recorded on the Thiepval Memorial in France. It also appears on two memorials in Campden: in St. James's Church and in the High Street. The Commonwealth War Graves Commission record that Willie's parents were living at Littleworth in Campden when their records were compiled after the war.

The deaths of Charles and Willie Brain are the only example of two brothers from Campden being killed on the same day during the war. Their photographs were published in the *Evesham Journal* on 9 September 1916.

The *Evesham Journal* published this photograph of Willie Brain in 1916 when he was reported as "*missing*". The cap badge does not appear to be that of the Gloucestershire Regiment. Is this Willie?

Robert Brain
Private 1128, "D" Company, 1st/5th Battalion, Gloucestershire Regiment

Born: 12 June 1890
Enlisted 13 November 1909
Discharged: 28 January 1916

Robert was born in Mickleton in 1890 and was the son of Frederick Jonathan and Joyce Brain. His father was employed as a farm labourer.

After leaving school Robert found employment as a groom and was soon living in Lower High Street, Campden. He enlisted in the Territorial Army on 13 November 1909 and joined "H" Company, 5th Battalion, Gloucestershire Regiment. His attestation papers state that he was five feet five inches tall with blue eyes and light brown hair.

When the war started in 1914 he was mobilised on 5th August and went to Chelmsford for final training before the battalion was sent to France. He signed up for overseas service on 2 September 1914 and arrived in France on 29 March 1915 but was soon heading north to the Belgian village of Ploegsteert, where he gained experience of trench warfare in a "*quiet*" part of the Western Front. In November 1915 his initial period of service with the Territorial Army expired and he was sent home for discharge from the 1st/5th Battalion, Gloucestershire Regiment. He was taken ill en route and sent to hospital. Robert declined re-engagement and requested discharge as soon as possible. This was granted and he was discharged from the army on 28 January 1916.

Frank Arthur Brett
Air Mechanic Second Class F27080, Royal Naval Air Service

Frank was born in Folkestone on 9 June 1897, the son of John Henry George and Mary Ann Brett of 32, Rendezvous Road, Folkestone. His father was a clothier, tailor and hatter.

Frank was a member of the Royal Navy Volunteer Reserve when he enlisted in the Royal Naval Air Service on 19 March 1917. He gave his occupation as a motor mechanic and his medical examination found him to be five feet nine inches tall with brown hair, blue eyes and a fresh complexion. The next year was spent on home service at Crystal Palace and then Chingford.

On 1 April 1918 he joined the Royal Air Force when the Royal Naval Air Service and the Royal Flying Corps were amalgamated.

The reason for Frank's inclusion on the 1916 St. James's Church prayer list is not known.

Harry William Bricknell
Private 2436, "D" Company, 1st/5th Battalion, Gloucestershire Regiment
Private 2114, Machine Gun Corps

Born: 9 September 1886
Died: 20 May 1966

Harry was the second son of William Henry "Tadpole" and Sarah Ann Bricknell of Broad Campden. He became a wheelwright and blacksmith in the family business after leaving school. His parents were also the landlords of the Angel public house and later the Baker's Arms, both in Broad Campden. In the years leading up to the war Harry, and his two brothers, Tom and William, were members of the local Territorial Army, "H" Company, 5th Battalion, Gloucestershire Regiment. Their weekends were spent training and each summer there was a camp.

When war was declared Harry volunteered for overseas service. He was mobilised on 5 August 1914 and went to Chelmsford with several other Campden men, including his brother Tom, for initial training before they went to France. The 5th Glosters embarked at Folkestone and arrived at Boulogne on 29 March 1915. The next few days were spent making their way slowly north to the front line at Ploegsteert (known as "*Plugstreet*" to the Tommies) at the extreme southern

Harry and Margaret Bricknell

end of the Ypres Salient. This was a "*quiet*" area and the battalion alternated between time in the front line and time spent resting behind the lines. In July 1915 they made their way down to the Somme area and several months were spent in and around the trenches at Hébuterne.

After going overseas in March 1915 Harry served twenty-one months in the trenches on the Western Front before he was sent back to England suffering with dysentery. Five months were spent in hospital recovering and it was at this time that he married Margaret Elizabeth Cole in Wales. Harry had met his future wife before the war in Broad Campden, where she was in service.

He returned to France in November 1917 and was now a member of the Machine Gun Corps, having

Harry in his blue hospital uniform, 1917.

transferred from the Gloucestershire Regiment. The following month a telegram arrived in Broad Campden giving official notification that Harry was reported missing in action on 14 December 1917. This must have been a worrying time for his parents as the casualty lists grew longer each week in the *Evesham Journal*. It was not long before they received news that he was in fact a prisoner of war in a camp in eastern Germany very close to the border with Poland. Harry spent the last twelve months of the war in the camp, working down a mine. Life was very hard as conditions were poor and food was in short supply.

After being discharged from the army Harry returned to Broad Campden and worked as a wheelwright and blacksmith. He also developed into an expert sign-writer. Three children were born in the post-war years: Margaret Helen Joan, Monica May and Malcolm Thomas. During the Second World War Malcolm served as Flight Sergeant 1606254, Royal Air Force, while Harry was an air raid warden.

Harry died on 20 May 1966 aged 79 and is buried in St. James's churchyard. His wife, Margaret, died on 21 May 1980 aged 89.

Harry is at the back, second from the right.

Thomas Bricknell

Private 2435, "D" Company, 1st/5th Battalion, Gloucestershire Regiment

Born: 11 May 1884
Died: 21 July 1916

Tom was the eldest son of William Henry "Tadpole" and Sarah Ann Bricknell of Broad Campden and became a wheelwright and blacksmith in the family business after leaving school. In the years leading up to the war he was a member of "H" Company, 5th Battalion, Gloucestershire Regiment, the local company of the Territorial Army.

When war was declared Tom signed up for overseas service and was mobilised on 5 August 1914. A period of training took place at Chelmsford in Essex before the battalion made its way to Folkestone for the crossing to France. Tom arrived at Boulogne on 29 March 1915. The next few days were spent moving slowly north to the front line at Ploegsteert at the extreme southern end of the Ypres Salient. In July 1915 the battalion moved down to the Somme area and several months were spent in and around the trenches at Hébuterne. As "*The Big Push*" approached Tom had a period of rest in a safe area several miles behind the front line.

The Battle of the Somme started on Saturday 1 July 1916. The battalion had their orders to attack on this day cancelled at the last minute and it was not until 20 July 1916 that the 5th Glosters were to be involved in a big assault; they were ordered to attack the German trenches east of the village of Ovillers. The only clue as to what happened to Tom comes from a story told to Malcolm Bricknell, Harry's son, in 1948 by Inspector Lewis Ryland of the Cheltenham Police, who was with the battalion at the time. He saw Tom's body destroyed by a shell burst and they never even found his gun. Tom was in charge of a machine gun at the time of his death.

Tom died on 21 July 1916 aged 32 and as he has no known grave his name is recorded on the Thiepval Memorial in France. The *Evesham Journal* reported his death, saying that "*he was killed by a shell as he proceeded up a communication trench*". It also noted that "*he was a pigeon fancier, and before the war broke out he won many prizes in the Evesham district with his brother Harry*".

William Bricknell
"H" Company, 5th Battalion, Gloucestershire Regiment

Born: 15 August 1892
Died: 8 November 1961

William (known as Bill) was born on 15 August 1892, the youngest son of William Henry "Tadpole" Bricknell and his wife, Sarah Ann, of Broad Campden. His father was originally a blacksmith, undertaker and wheelwright, but later became the landlord of the Angel and then the Baker's Arms public houses.

In the years leading up to the war Bill was a member of the local Territorial Army. Campden men were all members of "H" Company, 5th Battalion, Gloucestershire Regiment. Prior to 1908 the unit was called "K" Company, 2nd Volunteer Battalion, Gloucestershire Regiment.

With his two brothers, Harry and Tom, volunteering for overseas service in 1914, Bill remained at home helping to run the family business. He did eventually receive his call-up papers in October 1918 but the war ended before he was in uniform. His daughter said that he would have chosen to join the Royal Air Force. During the Second World War he served in the Home Guard.

Bill married Emma Crowe in London in 1934 and had two children, Eileen and Thomas William.

He died at Hook Norton on 8 November 1961 aged 69 and is buried in St. James's churchyard, Campden.

John Bridge
Private SE 14676, Army Veterinary Corps

Born: 6 October 1876
Died: 1 April 1970

Jack was born in Kingham in Oxfordshire, the son of Cornelius and Sarah Ann Bridge. From a very early age he developed an interest in horses and after leaving school he trained as a groom before finding a job as a coachman.

It is not clear exactly when Jack came to Campden but he was living in Broadwell when he married Ellen Rathbone at St. James's Church on 24 September 1905. They had four children, Gladys Ellen, John William, Sidney and Mabel. Sidney's birth certificate, issued in 1908, shows that he was born at Castle Cary in Somerset. Mabel's birth was registered in Dorset.

When war was declared in 1914 Jack and Ellen were running the Rose and Crown public house in Campden. Jack was 38 years old but he was keen to do his bit and, with his love of horses, he enlisted in the Army Veterinary Corps, although he did not arrive in France until after the start of 1916. In his time at the front he was wounded once when a shell blast threw him against some barbed wire. He spent most of his time looking after wounded horses.

In the years after the war John and Ellen ran the Red Lion public house and as horses remained Jack's main interest he had stables built at the back of the pub. When Jack retired he went to live at "Collett's Cottage", Back Ends, Campden and Sidney took over the running of the Red Lion.

Jack died on 1 April 1970 aged 94; he was living at Badsey at the time of his death. He is buried in St. James's churchyard.

Sid Bridge served in the Warwickshire Yeomanry between the wars and then in the Home Guard during the Second World War.

Wilfred James Bright
Captain, Royal Field Artillery

Born: 11 July 1890
Enlisted: 1916
Discharged: 1 March 1919
Died: 6 March 1978

Wilfred was born in Norwich, the youngest son of Thomas and Edith Ellen Bright. His father was a native of Wem in Shropshire and a Primitive Methodist minister. Thomas and Edith had married in 1887 at Bury St. Edmunds where they later ran a company producing mineral water. Thomas died in 1917 and the company was taken over by Wilfred's brother Frank after he had been discharged from the Royal Air Force.

Wilfred was educated at Bourne College in Birmingham and after a period in Germany he entered Fitzwilliam Hall at Cambridge University in 1910 where he graduated with an MA in History and Modern Foreign Languages in 1913. While he was there he was a member of the Officer Training Corps and a player for Ipswich Town Football Club. After leaving university he became a schoolmaster and taught French and German at Charlton Park in Woolwich. He then taught at a school in Switzerland but had to return to England when the war started in 1914. Back home he joined the staff of Aldenham School, where he became a 2nd lieutenant in their Officer Training Corps. By 1916 he was still at Aldenham and anxious to transfer to the Royal Field Artillery to play a more active part in the war.

He left Aldenham after five terms and joined the Royal Field Artillery as a 2nd lieutenant. A period of training in Edinburgh developed his horse-riding skills before his posting to India to complete his training in Bombay and Karachi. On 14 January 1917 he arrived in Basra in Mesopotamia on board HT *Sofala* and was posted to Number 2 British Depot at Makina. In May he was admitted to hospital but rejoined his unit the following month. On 10 September he was promoted to lieutenant and on 31 July 1918 to captain, which saw him command a section whose job it was to supply front-line gun batteries with artillery shells. Life in Mesopotamia was "*heaven and hell*", too hot during the day and cold at night, which meant that all shells were transported at night.

Wilfred left Mesopotamia on 27 January 1919 and returned to England, where he was discharged from the army on 1 March 1919. He resigned his commission on 19 March 1920. He immediately returned to teaching and found a post at Campden Grammar School, where he met Elizabeth Gertrude Jones, known as "*Betty*". Betty taught Geography and sport at the school and was an excellent hockey player. They married in Cardiff in 1920 and had four children: Peter, Derek, Michael and Graham.

After a year in Campden Wilfred

Wilfred Bright is standing on the right. His brother Frank, Royal Flying Corps, is standing on the left. At the front are Thomas and Edith Ellen Bright, Wilfred's parents. The two girls at the back are, on the left, Dorothy, who married Frank, and Meb, Wilfred's sister.

became Headmaster at West Suffolk County School in Bury St. Edmunds in 1920. In 1927 Matthew Cox retired as Headmaster at Campden Grammar School and Wilfred immediately applied for the vacancy. He was given the post and remained at the school until he retired in 1951. During his time in the town he was a churchwarden, Chief of the Voluntary Fire Brigade, President of Campden's Festival of Britain Committee, a member of the British Legion and an excellent player for the town football team. During the Second World War he was a special constable.

After he retired Wilfred and Betty initially moved to Cleeve Hill but soon settled in Felixstowe. In 1957 Betty died and four years later Wilfred married Ida Mercer.

Wilfred died on 6 March 1978 aged 87 years and is buried in Felixstowe. To commemorate his life a memorial service was held in St. James's Church on 13 April 1978.

Members of Campden Grammar School Staff, c.1919
Back: Miss Anderson, Miss Williams, Miss Ingham, Captain Bright and Miss Jones
Front: Miss Neill, Mr. Cox and Mr. C. Hughes

Edward Brooks
Worcestershire Regiment

In her *Book of Remembrance* Josephine Griffiths lists Edward Brooks as serving in the Worcestershire Regiment during the war. He is also included in the 1916 prayer list produced by St. James's Church. No other record of him in Campden has been traced by the author.

There are two men called Edward Brooks who served overseas in the Worcestershire Regiment during the war: Private149385 Edward Brooks who entered France on 26 May 1915 and Private 27703 Albert Edward Brooks. It is not known whether either of these has connections with Campden.

Charles Foster Brotheridge
Sapper WR 43820, Road and Quarry Troops Depot, Royal Engineers

Enlisted: 18 April 1918
Discharged: 20 December 1918
Died: 19 January 1953

Charles was born in Campden in 1868, the second son of Charles and Elizabeth Brotheridge of Watery Lane, and was baptised at St. James's Church on 30 September 1892. All but eight months of his long life were spent living and working in and around the town. During these eight months he was in the Royal Engineers, having enlisted as a sapper in April 1918. He was 50 years old at the time but his expertise as a steam traction engine driver was extremely valuable in his country's time of need and he was posted to the Road and Quarry Troops Depot.

His medical examination stated that he was five feet nine inches tall and had brown hair. His religion was Church of England and he was told that he would not be placed in a medical category higher than B1 at any point during his service. It was due to this fact that he never served outside England during his time in the Royal Engineers.

When the war ended he was at Aldershot and his discharge papers state that there was *"no misconduct recorded against him during his service"*. He returned to Campden in December 1918 to be with his wife, Keziah, whom he had married on 30 September 1892 at St. James's Church. At the time of his enlistment in the Royal Engineers he was the father of five daughters (May, Florence, Gladys, Doris and Edith) and three sons (Percy Leonard, Fred and Jack). Edith married Charles Hughes and they had four children, including the author's father, Norman.

Charles learnt how to drive a steam traction engine from his father. The family were experts with engines and steam engines and they travelled the area with steam ploughing tackle to work on the land. His father was often seen carrying a red flag through Campden while his sons followed behind, driving large traction engines for steam ploughing. With their specialist knowledge and skill the family were in great demand and used to carry out work over a large area of the Cotswolds and the Vale of Evesham. Charles turned to market gardening later in his life and was still cultivating an acre of land when he retired in 1952.

He died at Cheltenham Hospital on 19 January 1953 aged 85 and is buried with his wife in St. James's churchyard. His wife died on 20 September 1939 aged 65 years.

Frederick John Brotheridge
Private 16018, Coldstream Guards
Private 452, 2nd Guards Brigade Machine Gun Section

Enlisted: 22 April 1915
Discharged: 21 March 1920

Frederick was born in Campden on 6 August 1896, the second son of John Charles and Mary Jane Brotheridge, and was baptised at St. James's Church on 3 November 1896. His father married Mary Jane Plested in 1889 and was employed as a farm labourer.

After leaving school Frederick found employment as a carter and then on 22 April 1915, when he was 18 years old, he enlisted at Campden in the Coldstream Guards, witnessed by Corporal

Beckett and Colonel Paley. He was five feet nine inches tall and his father, who was now living and working at Old Combe Farm, Campden, was named as his next of kin.

Frederick was employed on home service until he arrived at Harfleur in France on 23 August 1916. He was posted to the 2nd Guards Brigade Machine Gun Section and was stationed at base camp in Etaples for further training until 27 September 1916, when he moved up to the front line. He continued to serve on the Western Front until he was granted ten days' leave to England in October 1917. He returned to France on 3 November and was reported missing in action on 27 November. His parents later received official notification that he had been wounded and taken prisoner by the Germans. Frederick spent the last year of the war in a prisoner of war camp at Munster in Germany. He was liberated from the camp in January 1919.

He arrived back in England on 12 January 1919 and was discharged from the army on 21 March 1920 after serving for 4 years and 344 days. During his time in the army he passed qualifications as a first class machine gunner, a Lewis gunner and a bomber.

In 1920 the family were living in High Street, Campden and Frederick became a policeman.

Henry Brotheridge
Royal Buckinghamshire Hussars

Born: 16 October 1898
Died: November 1983

Harry was born in 1898, the third son of John Charles and Mary Jane Brotheridge of Campden. His father was a stock manager on a farm and after leaving school Harry joined his brother Tom as a farm labourer employed by William R. Haines at Top Farm, Westington, Campden.

Harry was only 16 years old when the war started so he continued working on the farm while many Campden men went off to war. He soon developed into an excellent horseman and when he was old enough to enlist he joined the Royal Buckinghamshire Hussars (Buckinghamshire Yeomanry). The war ended before Harry was posted overseas and he was serving with the 11th Hussars when the armistice was signed. His obituary in the *Evesham Journal* states that he served as "*a mounted trumpeter in the Light Infantry*".

He married Bertha Greenway at St. James's Church on 16 July 1924 and they did not have any children. They lived in Park Road before moving to Littleworth and after leaving his job as a farm labourer he worked at Long Marston Army Camp.

Harry died at his home in Littleworth, Campden in November 1983 aged 84 years.

Leonard Brotheridge
Private 29037, Devonshire Regiment

Enlisted: 11 December 1915
Discharged: 25 January 1919
Died: 21 February 1919

Leonard was born in Campden, the son of Charles and Elizabeth Brotheridge, and was baptised at St. James's Church on 30 January 1876. His father, a native of the town, was a well-known engine driver of steam ploughs.

Leonard enlisted in the Devonshire Regiment on 11 December 1915 at Campden with his Watery Lane neighbour, Richard Hughes (the author's great-grandfather), and served in a labour battalion in England. Very little is known about his war service. He never served overseas and was discharged as "*no longer fit for active service*" on 25 January 1919.

Leonard died of pneumonia following influenza, aged 41, at his home in Watery Lane on 21 February 1919, shortly after his official discharge from the army. He is buried with his parents in St. James's churchyard in Campden. He never married.

Mark Brotheridge
Private 26809, Royal Warwickshire Regiment
Private 50689, Royal Berkshire Regiment

Mark was born in Chipping Norton on 15 July 1899 and was the fourth son of Mark and Sarah Ann Brotheridge, who were living in South Littleton near Evesham in 1916 when their son enlisted in the army. His father was born at Campden in 1868 and married Sarah Ann Carter at St. James's Church on 7 November 1890. In 1891 the family were living in Watery Lane. The author's great-grandfather, Charles Foster Brotheridge, was the cousin of Mark senior, who was employed as a signalman with the Great Western Railway while living in Campden.

Mark joined the Royal Warwickshire Regiment on 23 September 1916, when he was 17 years old. He later transferred to the Royal Berkshire Regiment. After a period of service in a theatre of war he was discharged from the army on 23 July 1918 as no longer fit for active service owing to sickness and a Silver War Badge was issued to indicate that he had made his contribution to the war. He returned home to Victoria Terrace in Bretforton and later worked as a gardener at Saintbury rectory.

Thomas William Brotheridge
Private 55230, Machine Gun Corps

Enlisted: 24 June 1916
Discharged: 12 April 1918
Died: 30 October 1953

Thomas was born in July 1892 and was the eldest son of John Charles and Mary Jane Brotheridge of Campden. He was a lifelong farm worker and was a very knowledgeable, capable and industrious employee. He worked for William R. Haines at Top Farm, Westington for about 26 years. His father, John, was a stock manager on a farm.

Thomas married Lucy Helen Chapman at St. Catharine's Church in Campden on 4 June 1914 and their first child, Maria Agnes, was born in June 1915. Lucy was pregnant with their first son, John Edward, when Thomas enlisted in the Worcestershire Regiment on 24 June 1916. During initial training in England he transferred to the Machine Gun Corps before he arrived on the Western Front, where he spent the next two years. He experienced his heaviest fighting at Ypres in Belgium during the Battle of Passchendaele in 1917.

The war ended for Thomas when he was hit in the shoulder by a piece of shrapnel from an exploding shell. He was firing his Vickers machine gun at the time and his loader was killed by the shell. This injury scarred him for life and it resulted in his discharge from the army on 12 April 1918. In the post-war years Lucy and Thomas went to live at Gunn's Cottages in Saintbury after two more children were born, George Henry and Frederick William.

Thomas died on 30 October 1953 aged 61 and is buried in St. James's churchyard. His wife, Lucy, died on 5 February 1942.

Albert William Bruce
Gloucestershire Regiment

Born: 15 November 1876
Died: 29 January 1941

Albert was born in Campden, the eldest son of Charles and Rose Ellen Bruce of Cider Mill Lane, Campden, and was baptised in the Catholic Chapel at Campden House. His father was born in Scotland and was employed as a labourer in the town.

Albert married Maria Anna Catherine Wilkes at St. Catharine's Church in Campden on 15 October 1910 and the family consisted of nine children: Lilian, Alfred, Albert, Charles John (born 1912), William Francis

Albert with his sister, Dorothy.

(born 1915), Winifred Rose (born 1918), Anna Margarita *"Nancy"* (born 1920), Wilfrid Ernest (born 1922) and Agnes Maria (born 1925).

During the First World War Albert served with the Gloucestershire Regiment. His younger brothers, Oscar, Alfred and Charles, all served in the army during the war. Oscar died of wounds in 1918 and Charles died of illness in 1919.

Alfred John Bruce
Private 10105, 2nd Battalion, Gloucestershire Regiment

Born: 12 July 1896
Discharged: May 1919
Died: 2 January 1949

Alfred and Lucy May Hughes

Alfred was the youngest son of Charles and Rose Bruce of Cider Mill Lane, Campden and he was baptised at St. Catharine's Church on 2 August 1896.

During the 1914-18 war he served as a private in the 2nd Battalion, Gloucestershire Regiment and saw service in France, Belgium, Italy, Greece and Russia. His first period of overseas service was on the Western Front and he arrived there on 18 May 1915, joining the battalion as they were coming towards the end of fierce fighting in the Ypres Salient around Sanctuary Wood. A period of rest in Armentières soon followed Alfred's arrival. In November 1915 they were sent to Salonika in Greece and after the armistice was signed he was with the battalion when they were sent to Russia. They disembarked at Batum in Armenia on 8 January 1919 and then moved to Tiflis. They remained in Russia until May, when they returned to Chiseldon in England. It was at this point that Alfred was discharged from the army.

After the war he married Lucy May Hughes (the sister of the author's grandfather, Arthur Charles Hughes) on 12 February 1921 at St. Catharine's Church and they had four surviving children: Cecilia, Les, Cyril and Mick. The family home was at 3, Aston Road in Campden in a house built by the Council for returning servicemen which had originally been occupied by Henry Pope.

Alfred found employment as a builder's labourer with his wife's two brothers, Charles and George. He also was a member of Campden Town Football Club and during the Second World War he was a prominent member of the Home Guard.

Alfred died on 2 January 1949 in a tragic accident on Aston Road when he was knocked off his bicycle by a car. He was 52 years old and is buried in St. James's churchyard.

The *Evesham Journal* reported the death on 3 January:

"*Four witnesses at an Evesham inquest described how a Campden man, cycling along Aston Road towards Campden against a rough wind, rode to his off-side of the road and after apparently seeing a car coming in the opposite direction attempted to swerve back again. The cyclist sustained fatal injuries in a head-on collision with the car, the driver of which had swerved to his off-side of the road to avoid him.*"

Charles John Bruce
Private 7478, Royal Warwickshire Regiment
Private 2240, 1st Battalion, Gloucestershire Regiment

Born: 1882
Died: 3 April 1919

Charles was the second son of Charles and Rose Bruce of Church Cottages, Cider Mill Lane, Campden. The family home was in Cider Mill Lane but in 1891, when Charles was 9 years old, he was living with his grandparents, John and Mary Freeman. His father was born in Scotland and was employed as a general labourer in Campden.

After leaving school Charles found work as a labourer but when he was 18 years old he enlisted in the Royal Warwickshire Regiment at Birmingham on 27 October 1900. His attestation papers record that he was five feet three inches tall and had grey eyes and brown hair; there was a mole on the left side of his chin. He was a Roman Catholic.

During his initial period of service in England he was guilty of two offences: he went absent without leave and lost his clothing and regimental kit. A regimental court martial met in March 1901 and found him guilty and he was sentenced to 28 days in prison. He was released on 25 April 1901 and returned to duty with the regiment.

He served abroad with the Royal Warwickshire Regiment in Malta, Bermuda, Gibraltar and Africa between 1901 and 1907. The final five years of his army service were spent in England and he was discharged on 26 October 1912.

When the 1914-18 war started he was one of the first to enlist, joining the Gloucestershire Regiment on 12 August 1914. He left England on 11 November and joined the 1st Battalion during the final stages of the First Battle of Ypres. The battalion suffered terrible casualties during the battle, with only two officers and 100 men remaining. Charles was one of the men sent to the battalion as reinforcements.

The winter months were spent in trenches in northern France at Festubert, Givenchy, Le Plantin and La Quinque, while periods of rest were spent in Béthune. The trenches were very wet and the weather was very cold and Charles developed frostbite in his toes. Gangrene developed and he returned to England where he was admitted to the 1st Western General Hospital at Fazakerley in Liverpool on 21 January 1915. After an operation to amputate his great toe, and the second and third toes, on both feet he was discharged from the army on 14 June 1915 as no longer fit for active service. A war pension of twenty shillings per annum was awarded.

Charles died on 3 April 1919, aged 37, after a long illness. He is buried in St. James's churchyard and has a Commonwealth War Graves Commission headstone that also bears a memorial inscription to his brother, Oscar, who died in Italy in 1918. His name is recorded on three memorials in Campden: in St. Catharine's Church, in St. James's Church and in the High Street.

George James Bruce
Brigade Major, 109th Infantry Brigade, 36th (Ulster) Division

Born: 3 June 1880
Enlisted: 14 September 1914
Died: 2 October 1918

George was the son of Samuel and Louisa Mary Julia Bruce of Norton Hall, near Campden. He was educated at Winchester and New College, Oxford where he graduated with a BA (Hons) in Physics in 1903. In 1907 he married Hilda Blakiston-Houston and they had four children. The family lived in Ireland, where George was the manager of Comber Upper Distillery, County Down.

In the years leading up to the outbreak of war the British Government had moved slowly and largely reluctantly towards the declaration of Home Rule for Ireland. The Ulster Volunteer Force was set up in Ulster in 1912 as an organisation to resist by force the implementation of Home Rule. George helped establish a County Down Battalion of the Ulster Volunteers. On 14 September 1914 he enlisted in the newly formed 13th Battalion (1st County Down Volunteers),

Royal Irish Rifles and on 24 September 1914 he applied for a commission and was appointed Captain.

George arrived in France with the battalion on 4 October 1915 and on 1 July 1916, the opening day of the Battle of the Somme, they attacked the German lines in front of the Schwaben Redoubt, near Thiepval. They made some notable and much admired advances but at the end of a day of fierce and bloody combat they had fallen back almost to their start lines. George was mentioned in despatches for his conduct on this day.

In May 1917 he was in Belgium and was awarded the Military Cross for distinguished conduct in the field near the Messines Ridge. The award was announced in the *London Gazette* on 4 June 1917. Later that summer he was promoted to Brigade Major with the 109th Infantry Brigade, 36th Division.

The division moved back to Picardy, opposite the Hindenburg Line, to prepare for the Battle of Cambrai. The main attack began on 20 November 1917 on a six-mile front with significant tank support. The Germans then launched a massive counter-attack on 30 November and at the start of December George was awarded a bar to his Military Cross: "*When the situation was obscure after the enemy counter-attack and a heavy bombing fight was in progress, he went forward to reconnoitre. He took command at the threatened point, pushed the enemy back, and established a block. By his quick decision and gallantry he stopped the enemy's progress, which would have endangered the whole position.*"

In late March 1918, during Operation Michael, the Germans' spring offensive, George was awarded a Distinguished Service Order for conspicuous gallantry and devotion to duty during an enemy attack near Brouchy, south of St. Quentin. "*He rallied a company and rode in front of it as it once more advanced and took a village. Next day he galloped to two companies under heavy fire and directed them. When the brigade withdrew he was the last to leave and covered the withdrawal with Lewis gun sections under his personal supervision. Throughout he displayed high qualities as a Staff Captain with total disregard for personal safety.*"

By September the tides had turned and the German army was in retreat. On 2 October, near Dadizeele, east of Ypres, 109th Brigade was pressing up a small hillock in face of stiff opposition. A German barrage opened up and George went forward to see how it was getting on when a shell burst caught him. He died in a dressing station later in the day.

He was 38 years old when he died and was originally buried in Molenhoek Military Cemetery but in the early 1920's his body was exhumed and reburied in Dadizeele New British Cemetery in Belgium. His name is recorded on memorials in Weston-sub-Edge, Mickleton and St. Mary's Church at Comber in Ireland. It is not recorded on any memorials in Campden.

Maye Emily Bruce
Commandant, Norton Hall Voluntary Aid Detachment Hospital

Maye was born in Ireland on 3 May 1879, the eldest daughter of Samuel and Louisa Mary Julia Bruce of Norton Hall near Campden. Her father was the owner of Comber Distillery Group in Ireland and at the time Irish whiskey was as popular in Victorian England as Scotch whisky, hence Samuel would have a significant share of the market. Despite remaining in control of the group for many years he never returned to live in Ireland, preferring to live at Norton Hall or in London according to the social season.

Samuel married Louisa Mary Julia Colthurst in County Cork and they had seven children, two of whom, George and Robert, served in the army during the war. Maye was born before the move to Norton Hall but later, when her father moved to London, she stayed on and ran a VAD hospital there, staffed by volunteer nurses. The *London Gazette* announced in 1918 that she had been awarded an MBE for her work. She never married and the house was sold in 1921. She then bought a farm near Cirencester, where she developed her Quick Return composting method.

Oscar Bruce

Private 2040, 1ˢᵗ/5ᵗʰ Battalion, Gloucestershire Regiment
Lance Corporal 240043, 1ˢᵗ/5ᵗʰ Battalion, Gloucestershire Regiment

Born: 21 March 1888
Died: 19 July 1918

Oscar was born in Campden, the second son of Charles and Rose Bruce of Cider Mill Lane, and was baptised in the Catholic Chapel at Campden House on 15 July 1888. He joined "K" Company, 2ⁿᵈ Volunteer Battalion, Gloucestershire Regiment as a bugle boy at the age of 16 in 1904 and served continuously until the outbreak of war in 1914. He was then mobilised on 5 August 1914 and left for Chelmsford with many other Territorial soldiers from Campden as part of "D" Company, 1ˢᵗ/5ᵗʰ Battalion, Gloucestershire Regiment. They arrived in France on 29 March 1915 and Oscar served on the Western Front until the battalion was posted to Italy in November 1917. The Battle of Asiago began on 15 June 1918 and the battalion occupied a difficult position in the woods around Buco di Cesuna. It is not clear whether he received his fatal wounds during this action but he died of a fractured spine in a dressing station at Dueville in Italy on 19 July 1918, when he was 30 years old. He is buried at Dueville Communal Cemetery Extension in North-East Italy, just south of the Asiago Plateau, and he left a widow and a young son at home in Bourton-on-the-Hill.

Oscar Bruce
Oscar with his wife, Lizzie Edith Taylor, and their son, Gordon.

He had married Lizzie Edith Taylor on 1 July 1911 and their only son, Joseph Gordon Wrinklin, was born soon after. Gordon died on 26 July 1991 aged 79 and is buried in Bourton-on-the-Hill churchyard.

Oscar has his name recorded on the war memorial at Bourton-on-the-Hill and on three memorials in Campden: in St. Catharine's Church, in St. James's Church and in the High Street.

Robert William Vesey Bruce

Major, 17ᵗʰ Lancers (The Duke of Cambridge's Own Lancers)

Born: 23 January 1882

Robert was born in London on 23 January 1882, the son of Samuel and Louisa Mary Julia Bruce of Norton Hall, near Campden. He served in South Africa during the Boer War and was mentioned in despatches. He was awarded the Queen's South Africa campaign medal with four clasps.

At the outbreak of war in 1914 he was immediately mobilised and arrived in France as a captain with the 17ᵗʰ Lancers. The announcement that he was again mentioned in despatches appeared in the *London Gazette* on 11 December 1917 and he ended the war as a major.

In early 1918 Robert was in England and he married Norah Mary Fynvola Egerton, daughter of Major-General Sir William Henry MacKinnon, at Chelsea in London. This was her second marriage as her first husband, Lieutenant-Colonel Arthur George Edward Egerton, 1ˢᵗ Battalion, Coldstream Guards, had been killed in action at Loos in France in 1915.

In the early 1920's Robert and Norah were living at Bentworth Lodge, Alton in Hampshire. Norah died at Wokingham near Reading in 1953 aged 71 years.

Horace Buckland

Born: 8 August 1902

Horace was the second of four sons of William Albert and Kate Elizabeth Buckland of Watery Lane, Campden and was baptised at St. James's Church on 31 May 1903. He was educated in the town and then found employment as a farm labourer. In 1918 the family were living in Sheep Street.

In her *Book of Remembrance* Josephine Griffiths lists Horace as serving in the army during the war. It is possible that Horace was in uniform in 1918 but he did not serve in a theatre of war.

He married Mabel Gertrude Cherry at St. James's Church on 19 February 1927 and their daughter, Leonora, was baptised on 19 February 1928. The family home was in Catbrook, Campden.

William Albert Buckland, senior
Private 23386, 10th Battalion, Gloucestershire Regiment

Born: 1868
Enlisted: 1914
Discharged: 19 May 1916
Died: 1 February 1963

William was born in Blockley, the son of Emmanuel Buckland, who was a horse-dealer. He married Kate Elizabeth Benfield at St. James's Church on 17 August 1898 and they had eight children baptised at St. James's Church between 1900 and 1919: William Albert, Horace, Ernest Emmanuel, Susan, Leonora Kate, Frederick Walter, Elizabeth and Gladys Ethel. The family home was in Watery Lane but by 1918 they had moved to Sheep Street. William was employed as a cowman and later as a gardener in the town.

At the outbreak of war he enlisted in the Gloucestershire Regiment and when he arrived in France on 28 October 1915 he was 46 years old. He was posted to the 10th Battalion as part of a draft of men to reinforce the battalion after they had suffered heavy casualties during the Battle of Loos. His stay on the Western Front lasted only a few months before he was returned to England. He was discharged from the army on 19 May 1916 as no longer fit for active service.

William died at his home in Berrington Road, Campden on 1 February 1963 aged 94 and is buried in St. James's churchyard.

William Albert Buckland, junior

Born: 26 January 1900
Died: March 1956

Bill was born in Campden, the eldest of four sons of William Albert and Kate Elizabeth Buckland, and was baptised at St. James's Church on 15 April 1900. He was educated in the town and towards the end of the war he enlisted in the army and saw service in Ireland.

In the post-war years he worked as a gardener in Bristol until his health began to deteriorate. He then returned to Campden, where he lived at 27, Berrington Road until he died in March 1956 aged 56 years. He is buried in St. James's churchyard in Campden.

William George Bunker
Private 34020, 7th Battalion South Lancashire Regiment

Enlisted: 19 July 1915
Discharged: 9 May 1918
Died: 30 June 1963

Bill was born in Campden on 3 June 1883 and was the son of Edward and Mary Bunker. Edward Bunker was a sergeant in the police force and was stationed at Campden for a number of years. After leaving school Bill became a postman but this was only a temporary job as he soon followed in his father's footsteps, joining the Cheltenham Police Force. He was discharged from the force prior to 1914

owing to a weak chest but this did not stop him from joining the army when war broke out. He initially enlisted in the Welsh Regiment (Private 2069 Bill Bunker, 7th Battalion, Welsh Regiment) at Cardiff on 19 July 1915. His trade on enlistment was recorded as a jeweller's porter.

When Bill arrived in France in July 1916 he had been transferred to the South Lancashire Regiment. He had served almost a year on the Western Front when he received gunshot wounds to both feet that led to his discharge from the army. His battalion was in the trenches south of Ypres facing the Germans who were holding the Messines Ridge. He had been involved in the capture of the ridge and had witnessed the explosion of nineteen mines on the morning of 7 June 1917. It is said that the explosion of these mines was heard in London. It was on this day that he received his wounds.

After treatment in France he was taken back to England, where he spent time at the Royal Herbert Hospital in Woolwich and at Cheltenham Hospital. The wounds left bad scars in the heel of one foot only. Bill was discharged as no longer fit for active service on 9 May 1918.

On returning to Campden he resumed his old job as a postman and then married Mary Ann Benfield at Broadway in 1920. They had two daughters, Jessie and Monica. The family home became "Braithwaite House" in the High Street when Bill became the steward at the British Legion Club, a job that he held until 1947. After he retired he moved to "Job's Cottage", Leysbourne and spent time helping at the Guild.

Bill died on 30 June 1963 aged 80 and his ashes are buried in St. James's churchyard.

Bill Bunker, Royal Welsh Regiment

Bill Bunker, South Lancashire Regiment. Bill is seated second from the right with an "X" marked on his wounded foot.

Arthur Ernest Bunten
Air Mechanic First Class 28184, 52 Squadron, Royal Flying Corps

Born: 5 March 1888
Enlisted: 10 May 1916
Discharged: April 1919
Died: 29 January 1937

Arthur was born in Royston in Hertfordshire, the eldest son of William James and Mary Bunten. After leaving school he joined the Guild of Handicraft as an apprentice cabinetmaker in 1902 just as they were preparing to move to Campden. James Pyment, a senior member of the Guild and experienced cabinetmaker, looked after Arthur in his early days with the Guild and they both became long-serving members of the town band. After the Guild disbanded James Pyment bought the Silk Mill and set up J. W. Pyment and Sons, builders, joiners, cabinetmakers and ecclesiastical woodworkers. Arthur spent many years working with the firm.

Arthur soon became a very well known figure in Campden and he spent the rest of his life in the town apart from when he was away during the war. Fred Coldicott remembers Arthur as *a hell of a nice man, always jolly*".

In the years leading up to the war Arthur was a member of "H" Company, 5th Battalion, Gloucestershire Regiment, the local company of the Territorial Army. In August 1914 he did not sign up for overseas service with the 5th Glosters. Perhaps this was because his wife was pregnant with their second child.

Arthur enlisted in the Royal Flying Corps as an air mechanic second class on 10 May 1916 and arrived in France on 16 November 1916. He remained on the Western Front until 21 January 1919, when he returned to England for his discharge, which came in April. During his time in France he was promoted to the rank of sergeant mechanic in July 1918. The following month he was reduced to the rank of air mechanic third class after a field general court martial had found him guilty of causing danger to the life of an officer through his own negligence. In the remaining months of the war he managed to reach the rank of air mechanic first class.

Arthur returned to Campden in May 1919 where he rejoined his wife, Lucy Edith James, and his three children, Dorothy Mary, Margaret Lucy and Arthur James. A fourth child, Jessie Maud, was born in 1920. The family set up home at Withy Bank in Broad Campden.

Sadly, both Arthur and his wife died young. Lucy died in 1935 and Arthur died on 29 January 1937 aged 48 years. His coffin was draped with a Union Jack flag and a town band cap. The bearers were six members of the town band and Last Post was played at his funeral.

Arthur will be remembered as a skilled cabinetmaker and an expert cornet player.

Harold Darwin Burgess
Private 24524, 1st/4th Battalion, Gloucestershire Regiment

Died: 2 October 1917

Harold was born in Faringdon in 1896, the son of Albert and Katharine Burgess of Church Street, Faringdon. His father was a saddler and harness maker by trade. Harold enlisted in Campden and after a period of home service was posted to France, where he joined the 1st/4th (City of Bristol) Battalion, Gloucestershire Regiment. The battalion had been on the Western Front since March 1915 and Harold was part of a draft of men to bring the battalion back up to full strength.

On 2 October 1917 he died of wounds received during the Third Battle of Ypres aged 20 years. He was evacuated from the battlefield and died at Dunhallows Advanced Dressing Station. Today he is buried in Dunhallows ADS Cemetery. Harold does not have his name recorded on any memorials in Campden.

Henry Burrows
Private 13991, 5th Battalion, Wiltshire Regiment

Born: 1872
Enlisted: 1888
Died: 24 December 1915

Henry was born in Kingcombe, Campden, the second son of John and Elizabeth Burrows. His father, a native of Willersey, married Elizabeth Nightingale in 1864 and was a farmer.

Henry enlisted in a Guards regiment in 1888 when he was 16 years old and served in the Ashanti Expedition on the Gold Coast of East Africa, 7 December 1895 to 17 January 1896. The expedition was sent to East Africa to re-open a roadway to Prempeh's Palace at Kumassi and bring the offending king to account. He then served in South Africa during the Boer War.

At the outbreak of war in 1914 he was mobilised at Swindon and posted to the 5th Battalion, Wiltshire Regiment, which was formed at Devizes in August 1914. The battalion was attached to the 13th (Western) Division and received orders on 6 June 1915 to prepare to be sent to the Mediterranean. The division then began leaving England and soon arrived at Alexandria in Egypt. On 4 July 1915 the 5th Battalion, Wiltshire Regiment arrived at Mudros on the island of Lemnos to prepare for their landing at Cape Helles on the Gallipoli peninsula two days later. At the end of the month they returned to Mudros before going back to Gallipoli in early August 1915, when they landed at ANZAC Cove. They remained on the peninsula until they were evacuated from Suvla Bay on the night of 19-20 December 1915.

Henry died on 24 December 1915 aged 43 years and is buried at Alexandria (Chatby) Military Cemetery in Egypt. It is not clear whether he died of wounds or illness contracted while serving at Gallipoli.

He does not have his name recorded on any memorials in Campden as he was living in Stratford-upon-Avon when he was mobilised in 1914.

Dennis Ronald Butler
Lance Corporal P 3095, Military Mounted Police

Born: 1895
Enlisted: 13 July 1916
Discharged: 11 November 1918

Dennis was born in Campden in 1895, the son of Agnes Butler, who was living in Watery Lane in 1901 and earning a living as a laundress. Agnes was a widow as her husband, George, died on 17 December 1888 aged 32 years.

Dennis served in France with the Military Mounted Police during the war and was awarded the Meritorious Service Medal. His medal index card indicates that he was promoted to the rank of lance corporal and that he received two campaign medals: the British War Medal and the Victory Medal.

On the 1918 electoral roll Dennis is listed as living at Westington and absent on military service.

George Butler
Royal Warwickshire Cycle Corps

George was born in Campden on 17 April 1889, the youngest son of George and Agnes Butler of Watery Lane, Campden, and was baptised at St. Catharine's Church on 12 May 1889. His father married Agnes Godson in 1880 and he died on 17 December 1888, aged 32 years, four months before the birth of his son.

On the 1918 electoral roll George is listed as living at Westington and absent on military service. In her *Book of Remembrance* Josephine Griffiths records that he served in the Royal Warwickshire Cycle Corps during the war.

Henry Benjamin Byrd
Private 29811, 2 Troop, "A" Squadron, 15th Hussars

Born: 23 May 1895
Died: December 1950

Harry was the youngest son of Benjamin Henry and Alice Byrd of the Angel Inn, Broad Campden, and was baptised at St. James's Church on 20 June 1895. He was educated in the town and at the age of 18 he enlisted in the Hussars. During the war he served in France with the 14th Hussars but on his brother Sam's army service papers it states that he was in 2 Troop, "A" Squadron, 15th Hussars. In her *Book of Remembrance* Josephine Griffiths says that he served in the 13th Hussars.

After the war he married Jeannett Elizabeth Beavis of Whitwell, Isle of Wight and they had three children: James, Dorothy and Frank. For a number of years he acted as a newspaper roundsman for Thomas Elsley and then he engaged in market gardening. His last job before his death was working for Sidney Bridge at the Red Lion pub.

Harry died suddenly in December 1950 aged 55 years when he collapsed in the road while walking to Broad Campden. He is buried in St. James's churchyard.

Samuel Byrd
Private 28360, 7th Battalion, Gloucestershire Regiment

Born: 8 October 1885
Enlisted: 22 May 1916
Discharged: 14 April 1917
Died: 20 May 1952

Samuel was born in Broad Campden, the third son of Benjamin Henry and Alice Byrd of Broad Campden, and was baptised at St. James's Church on 21 March 1886. His father was born at Bourton-on-the-Hill and in 1891 was employed as a carpenter.

Samuel attended school in Campden and then found employment as an agricultural labourer before becoming a carter. When Samuel enlisted in the Gloucestershire Regiment at Bristol on 22 May 1916 he was living at the Angel Inn in Broad Campden where his eldest brother, William, was the licensee.

The first three months of his service were spent training in England with the 3rd Battalion, Gloucestershire Regiment before he was posted to Mesopotamia with the 7th Battalion. He arrived there on 5 September 1916 but returned to England on 22 December 1916 after only 108 days overseas service. He had been very badly affected by the heat in Mesopotamia and had become ill and was admitted to the Royal Victoria Hospital at Netley as "*mentally sick*". He failed to recover from his illness and was discharged from the army on 14 April 1917 after being classified as "*no longer physically fit for war service*" at Lord Derby War Hospital in Warrington on 24 March 1917. He left the hospital on 31 March 1917 and returned home to wait for his official discharge papers. Although he had been discharged the papers did not arrive in Broad Campden until 4 September 1918 following letters to the War Office from his sister. A Silver War Badge was issued to indicate that he had made his contribution to the war.

After the war he worked for Captain Churchill at the Northwick Estate and then became a gardener. His marriage to Priscilla did not produce any children and she died on 7 August 1956 aged 70 years.

Samuel died on 20 May 1952 aged 67 years. He was found drowned in the River Cam and is buried in St. James's churchyard in Campden. The *Evesham Journal* reported that "*the body of Mr. Samuel Byrd, a 67 year old jobbing gardener, of The Haven, Catbrook, Campden, was recovered from the River Cam at 10.00am on Tuesday by Mr. William Bayliss, a herdsman on Home Farm*". The following week the coroner's verdict was published and it concluded that "*death was caused by asphyxia by drowning caused by the deceased placing himself in water when the balance of the mind was disturbed*".

William Byrd
Private 24344, 10th Battalion, Royal Berkshire Regiment
Private 94864, 159th Company, Labour Corps

> Born: 1878
> Enlisted: 23 May 1916
> Died: 1 November 1917

William was born in Broad Campden, the eldest son of Benjamin Henry and Alice Byrd of Broad Campden, and was baptised at St. James's Church on 29 September 1878. His father was born at Bourton-on-the-Hill and in 1891 was employed as a carpenter.

In the years leading up to the First World War William became the licensee of the Angel Inn in Broad Campden. In June 1916 Alice Byrd, who was then 65 years old, applied for the absolute exemption of her son William, who was then 38 years old and single. She already had two other sons in the army and she could not manage the business by herself as she was a widow. The tribunal stated that as William had already joined the army about a month ago they could do nothing about the matter.

William and his brother Samuel both enlisted in the army at Bristol on 22 May 1916, Samuel joining the Gloucestershire Regiment and William the Royal Berkshire Regiment despite requesting to join the Royal Artillery. At his medical examination William was found to be five feet five inches tall and to have arthritis in the big toe on his right foot. The first three weeks of his service were spent in England before he arrived in France on 17 June 1916.

In October 1917 he was in Belgium, in the Ypres Salient, and was badly wounded by shrapnel in the side, back and arm during the Third Battle of Ypres (also known as the Battle of Passchendaele). He was evacuated back to a dressing station at Remi Sidings near Poperinge but his condition was considered too serious to move him to a hospital at Rouen. He died of his wounds on 1 November 1917 aged 39 years and today is buried in Lijssenthoek Military Cemetery, Poperinge, Belgium. His name is recorded on two memorials in Campden: in St. James's Church and in the High Street. On 18 October 1918 his mother received her son's personal possessions that included a pipe, mirror, various letters, a photograph and a tobacco pouch. William never married and his mother took over the licence the Angel Inn.

William's army service papers survived the German bombs during the Second World War and can be viewed at Kew in London. They record that his sister Mary was living at 12 Fairfield Road, Leckhampton in 1919 after marrying a man called Quelch.

Frederick James Callaway
Corporal 6560, 3rd Battalion, Worcestershire Regiment

> Born: 1886
> Enlisted: 18 November 1911
> Died: 5 August 1916

Frederick was born in Birkenhead and was the son of James and Sarah Callaway of Worcester. He enlisted as a regular soldier at Worcester when he was only 15 years old and joined the 2nd Battalion, Worcestershire Regiment. He was appointed a drummer in 1906.

He married Frances Emily Griffin of Campden, on 7 April 1913 at St. James's Church. Their son, Frederick Thomas, was baptised at St. James's Church on 1 April 1917.

Frederick arrived in France on 11 September 1914 and joined the 2nd Battalion near the Chemins Des Dames, just north of the River Aisne. He then made his way north to Ypres in Belgium to take part in the heroic defence of Gheluvelt on 22 October 1914 during the First Battle of Ypres. In December he was admitted to hospital in Boulogne suffering from frostbite.

When Frederick was fit to return to the front in July 1915 it appears that he was posted to the 3rd Battalion. On 12 September he was wounded in the head by a bullet at Hooge, east of Ypres and admitted to hospital. A short period of home leave followed in May 1916.

After again being passed fit for active service he rejoined the battalion and on 4 July 1916, four days after the start of the Battle of the Somme, he crossed the River Ancre, a tributary of the

River Somme, and entered trenches just outside the village of Authuille. The battalion supported an attack on the Leipzig Salient on 5 July 1916 and then it was involved in action at Ovillers before it was withdrawn for a period of rest, returning to the front on 31 July.

The August 1916 battalion war diary records very little activity at the start of the month. All it states for five consecutive days is *"in trenches opposite Beaumont Hamel"*. It was on 5 August 1916 that Frederick died. He was *"killed by a shell and death was instantaneous and he was buried in a small cemetery behind the lines"*. There were two men killed and five wounded on that day.

Frederick was 30 years old when he died and he is buried in Knightsbridge Cemetery, Somme, France. The cemetery is situated very near the trench where he was killed and can be seen from the car park of Beaumont Hamel Battlefield Park. Access is difficult and the cemetery is not visited very frequently, a truly peaceful location in the heart of the Somme battlefield.

William Thomas Callaway
Corporal S4-128405, 2nd Field Bakery, Army Service Corps

Born: 1880
Enlisted: 11 September 1915
Discharged: 28 June 1919
Died: June 1957

Tom was born in Claines near Worcester in 1880, the eldest son of James and Sarah Callaway. In 1891 the family were living at the Hare and Hounds pub in Bridgnorth, Shropshire, where his father was the landlord. The 1901 census records that they had moved to Gillam Street, Worcester and his father was employed as a grocer's porter.

After leaving school Tom found employment as a baker and on 13 March 1905 he married Rose Ellen Surman, daughter of Levi Surman, at the Baptist Church in Campden. Their first child, Dorothy May, was baptised at St. James's Church in Campden on 17 June 1906 and two years later their second child, Florence Hilda, was baptised on 14 June 1908. Tom was a baker in Campden and the family home was in Sheep Street.

Tom enlisted in the Army Service Corps on 11 September 1915 after being passed fit for active service at a medical examination in Evesham. He was graded A1 despite a slight stiffness of the index finger on his right hand.

He was posted to the Mediterranean Expeditionary Force as a baker and arrived at Gallipoli on 15 October 1915. After leaving Gallipoli he served on the Western Front for over two years. He was promoted to the rank of corporal before he was discharged on 28 June 1919. At the time of his discharge he was graded B3 and was complaining of weakness and pains in his chest. A war pension was granted and his papers can be viewed at the National Archives in London.

After the war Tom returned to Campden and continued working as a baker with his own shop on the corner of Sheep Street. He died in June 1957 aged 77 years. His wife died in April 1939 aged 59 years. They are both buried in St. James's churchyard.

William John Carter
Worcestershire Regiment

Born: 1894
Died: 1960

William was born in Campden, the son of George and Elizabeth Carter. His father was born with a deformed foot and was employed as a labourer. The family home was at Greystone Cottages in Broad Campden.

During the war William served with the Worcestershire Regiment and after being demobilised he returned to Campden and married Martha Fletcher at St. James's Church on 24 December 1919. He was employed as a gardener and they lived at 18, Berrington Road.

William died at Stratford Hospital in 1960 aged 66 years and is buried in St. James's churchyard. He was survived by his wife.

Edgar Francis Chainey

Corporal 27589, 2nd Battalion, Devonshire Regiment
Private 897072, 34th Battalion, London Regiment

Born: 23 August 1893
Died: 19 December 1972

Edgar was born in Blockley in 1893 and was the son of William Frederick and Sarah Chainey, who were married at Burntwood Church on 20 April 1883. He married Ethel May Plested, sister of George and Tom, in 1913 and their eldest son, Allan Roy, was baptised at St. James's Church in Campden on 18 March 1917. The family home was in Back Ends in 1918.

It is not clear exactly when Edgar enlisted in the Devonshire Regiment but he did not serve overseas until after the start of 1916. While he was on home service he was posted to the 3rd Battalion but after arriving in France he served with the 2nd Battalion and was promoted to corporal. He was then transferred to the 34th Battalion, London Regiment, which was formed at Clacton-on-Sea in June 1918. On 18 June they were posted to the 49th Brigade of the 16th Division and arrived in France on 1 August 1918 and saw action in the final advance in Artois during the last months of the war.

Edgar lost two of his brothers in December 1917. Lionel was serving with the 1st Battalion, Otago Regiment, New Zealand Expeditionary Force and his name is recorded on the New Zealand Memorial at Buttes New British Cemetery near Ypres in Belgium. Charles was a gunner with the Royal Canadian Horse Artillery and died in England. He is buried in the parish cemetery in Blockley.

After the war Edgar and Ethel split up and he moved to Nottingham, where he died on 19 December 1972 aged 79 years.

Charles Henry Chamberlain

Sergeant, 1st Battalion, Royal Berkshire Regiment

Born: 25 March 1884
Died: 5 August 1949

Charles was born in Radstock in Somerset, the son of John Chamberlain. He enlisted in the Royal Berkshire Regiment as a regular soldier before the First World War and served in India. At the outbreak of war in 1914 he was mobilised and left Campden on 14 August 1914. He arrived in France without any further training and after nine months at the front was wounded in the knee by shrapnel at La Bassée on 15 May 1915. He was invalided back to England and while he was convalescing he married Alice Maud Sansom at St. Catharine's Church in Campden on 9 July 1915. The best man was Lance Corporal George Mann, who was also wounded at La Bassée.

After recovering from his wound Charles returned to France and was injured on two further occasions during the war. In early 1918 he received a bullet wound in the leg, which resulted in his admission to hospital in Sunderland, and then a shrapnel wound in his neck saw him admitted to St. James's Hospital in Leeds. He was also gassed on one occasion and this had the greatest long-term effect on him.

Charles was a machine-gunner on the Western Front and after returning from France he was posted to Ireland in 1919.

Charles and Alice had three children: John (born in 1917), Agnes (born in 1920) and Joseph (born in 1923). The family home was in Leysbourne, Campden and later in Twine Cottages, and Charles found employment as a plasterer. At the outbreak of war in 1939 Charles re-enlisted as a sergeant in the Royal Berkshire Regiment and was involved with the training of new recruits. He was invalided out of the army after three years' service. His son John joined the Royal Air Force and was sent to Kenya to train as a Spitfire pilot but during the journey by sea to North Africa it was decided that he should join the crew of a Blenheim bomber. This was a high-

The wedding of Charles Henry Chamberlain and Alice Maud Sansom on 9 July 1915
Back Row: William Sansom, Joseph Arthur Turner, Mary Teresa Turner, Father Henry Leeming
Bilsborrow, Lizzie Sansom and John Sansom.
Front Row: George Mann, Mrs. Mann, Charles Chamberlain, Alice Maud Sansom, unknown and
Granny Mary Sansom.

speed light bomber used extensively during the early days of the Second World War. Joseph, his second son, served in the Royal Army Medical Corps and spent most of the war in the Far East.

Charles died at his home, Twine Cottages, on 5 August 1949 aged 65 years and is buried in St. Catharine's cemetery in Campden. His coffin was draped in a Union Jack, paid for by his friends, not the army, despite three periods of service for the same regiment, and the bearers were friends from the British Legion and the Gainsborough Lodge of the RAOB.

Collett Chamberlain
Private 28379, 3rd Battalion, London Regiment
Private 566263, Labour Corps

Born: 2 March 1894
Enlisted: 25 October 1915
Discharged: 23 February 1919
Died: 19 July 1969

Collett was the younger son of William Collett and Blanche Chamberlain of High Street, Campden. He was born in Stow-on-the-Wold in 1894 and was baptised at St. James's Church in Campden on 3 February 1904 at the same time as his brother Walford. His father was a native of Stow-on-the-Wold and was a printer and stationer by trade. His mother, Blanche, died at the age of 29 in 1896.

Collett was educated in Campden and both he and his elder brother went to the Grammar School.

On 25 October 1915 Collett enlisted in the 3rd Battalion, London Regiment as a private. The battalion was raised in London and he was with it when he first went to France. His medal index card indicates that he did not arrive in a theatre of war until after the start of 1916.

Under the headline "*Campden Soldier III*" the *Evesham Journal* reported in 1917:
"*Information has been received by Mr. W. C. Chamberlain, to the effect that his son, Pte. C. Chamberlain, London Regiment, is lying at 26th General Hospital, Etaples, suffering from pleurisy. Pte. Chamberlain has been wounded once before.*" He also had a spell in hospital with trench fever.

After returning to England to recover Collett was transferred to the Labour Corps. He continued to serve with them until he was discharged owing to "*sickness*" on 23 February 1919 and despite the fact that the war had been over for three months he was issued with a Silver War Badge to indicate that he had made his contribution to the war effort.

Collett died on 19 July 1969 aged 75 years.

Walford Chamberlain
Private 240472, 1st/5th Battalion, Gloucestershire Regiment

> Born: 29 January 1893
> Died: August 1941

Walford was born in Tasmania in 1893 and was the elder son of William Collett and Blanche Emmeline Chamberlain of High Street, Campden. His father was a printer and stationer and a member of "K" Company, 2nd Volunteer Battalion, Gloucestershire Regiment. His mother died in April 1896 when she was only 29 years old and is buried in St. Catharine's cemetery.

At the age of 11 Walford was baptised at St. James's Church with his younger brother, Collett, on 3 February 1904. He attended Campden Grammar School and was also a member of "H" Company, 5th Battalion, Gloucestershire Regiment, the local company of the Territorial Army. During the war Walford served overseas with the Territorial Army but did not enter a theatre of war until after the start of 1916.

After the war he regularly attended St. James's Church and was a chorister for many years. He never married but his fiancée at the time of his death was Miss Grace Lovelady.

Walford died in August 1941 aged 48 years and was buried in St. James's churchyard with full military honours. His coffin was covered in a Union Jack and on top were his army cap, bayonet and medals. The bearers were members of the Home Guard.

Dorothy Amina Chatwin
Voluntary Aid Detachment Nurse

> Born: 9 September 1866
> Died: October 1953

Dorothy was born in Birmingham, the youngest daughter of Alfred Chatwin of Edgbaston and Leamington Spa. After her father retired she lived with her parents at Colwyn Bay in North Wales, where, during the 1914-18 war, she served as a VAD nurse at the Colwyn Bay Hospital.

After the war she and her parents lived at Clarendon Crescent in Leamington Spa but on her father's death in 1926 she and her mother came to live in Broad Campden. Dorothy soon became well known and greatly liked by a wide circle of friends, taking a great deal of interest in the affairs and activities of the town.

In the last four years of her life she began to suffer from heart trouble, the burden of which she bore with great courage, never losing her keen interest in life, and it was this illness that was the cause of her death in October 1953. She was 87 years old.

She was the aunt of Christopher Whitfield of the Malt House in Broad Campden and the sister of Margaret Chatwin, who was well known to audiences of the Birmingham Repertory Theatre for many years as a fine actress of great versatility and power.

David Thomas Cherry
Royal Navy Transport Service

David was born in Bridgend in Wales in 1895 and during the war he served in the Royal Navy Transport Service as a craftsman. He continued to serve until 1926, when he returned to Campden and found employment as a labourer. He is included in the *Book of Remembrance* by Josephine Griffiths and the Campden 1918 electoral roll lists him as living in Littleworth and absent on military service.

He married Rosa Mary Coles in 1920 in Birmingham and they had two children baptised at St. James's Church in Campden: Robert Clifford in 1921 and Vera in 1927. The church records state that David was a "*sailor in the Merchant Service*". In the 1930's the family were living in Broad Campden.

Ernest Cherry
Private 2303, "D" Company, 1st/5th Battalion, Gloucestershire Regiment
Private 45471, 13th Battalion, Devonshire Regiment

Enlisted: 8 July 1914
Discharged: 10 February 1919
Died: 5 October 1937

Ernest was born in Campden on 1 May 1892, the second son of Joseph and Mary Jane Cherry of Watery Lane. In 1901 his father was working as a shepherd on a farm.

When the war started in 1914 Ernest was already a member of the Territorial Army, 5th Battalion, Gloucestershire Regiment, and was mobilised on 5 August. The battalion went to Chelmsford for final training before they arrived in France on 29 March 1915. This was the start of sixteen months' overseas service for Ernest, during which time he was gassed and suffered shellshock. He left the 5th Glosters in July 1916, probably just before they were involved in heavy fighting on the Somme.

When he arrived back in England he was transferred to the 13th Battalion, Devonshire Regiment. This was a "*works*" battalion that included in its ranks the author's great grandfather, Richard Hughes. Ernest spent the rest of the war in England providing labour for all of the necessary jobs to help soldiers live and train before they went overseas. He was discharged from the army, still suffering from the effects of gas, on 10 February 1919.

Ernest married Susanna Bodenham at Birmingham Registry Office on 10 March 1917 while he was serving in the Devonshire Regiment and they had four children: Thomas Henry, Ernest Austin, Evelyn and Joseph. The wedding was blessed at St. Catharine's Church on 12 April 1925 when he returned to Campden.

After the war Ernest worked on the railways as a carman in Birmingham and the family home was in Crab Tree Road. When they left Birmingham the family lived in Aston-sub-Edge before they moved to 6 Catbrook in Campden.

Ernest died on 5 October 1937 aged 45 and is buried in St. Catharine's cemetery. At the time of his death he was still suffering from the effects of the gas that he was exposed to during the war. His mother died the following month and is buried in the same plot as Ernest. His wife, Susannah, died at Northleach Hospital on 13 May 1957 aged 73 years.

Hubert William Cherry
Private 27686, Royal Warwickshire Regiment
Private 55813, Royal Berkshire Regiment

Hubert was born in Campden on 15 September 1897, the son of William and Selina Stribblehill Cherry of Watery Lane, and was baptised at St. James's Church on 11 September 1904. When Hubert was born his father was a farm labourer but in 1901 he was a wharfman at a railway coal depot.

When the war started Hubert enlisted in the Royal Warwickshire Regiment and he served in France, arriving there after his eighteenth birthday. He was wounded twice. The *Evesham Journal* reported on 7 July 1917 that "*Mr. W. Cherry, Park Road, Campden, has received a letter from a Chaplain in France to say that his son is lying ill, suffering from a gunshot wound in the lung. He is, however, progressing favourably and has written home himself to tell his parents not to worry. This is the second time that he has been wounded. He is in the Royal Warwicks*."

After recovering from his wounds he was transferred to the Royal Berkshire Regiment.

When the war ended Hubert married Edith Bachelor and they moved to Leamington Spa, where he found employment at The Regent Hotel.

Leonard Francis Cherry
Private 11787, 13th Battalion, Hampshire Regiment

> Born: 21 May 1890
> Enlisted: 4 September 1914
> Discharged: 29 August 1916

Leonard was born in Cropthorne, Worcestershire but was baptised in the Catholic Chapel at Campden House on 6 July 1890. He was the eldest of six sons of Joseph and Mary Jane Cherry of Watery Lane and his father, a native of Campden, was employed as a shepherd in 1901.

Leonard enlisted in the Hampshire Regiment on 4 September 1914 and after over a year training in England he arrived in Egypt on 5 December 1915. Early in 1916 he was wounded and was brought back to England where he was discharged from the army on 29 August as *"no longer fit for active service due to wounds"*. A Silver War Badge was issued to indicate that he had made his contribution to the war effort.

By 1937 Leonard had left Campden and was living in Birmingham.

Alastair Edward Chisholm
Lieutenant, 3rd Battalion, Royal Scots (Lothian Regiment)

> Died: 25 September 1915

Alastair was born in 1894, the son of Edward Consett and Edith Chisholm. He obtained a commission with the Royal Scots and was a 2nd lieutenant when he arrived in France on 23 June 1915. Three months later he was killed on 25 September in the Ypres Salient in Belgium while attached to the Royal Scots Fusiliers. He was 21 years old and had only just been promoted to the rank of lieutenant. At the end of the war his body could not be found and his name is listed on the Menin Gate in the centre of Ypres. It is also recorded on the memorial in St. Catharine's Church in Campden.

The family must have been members of the congregation in the years leading up to the First World War, for Alastair's brother, Cuthbert Charles Windsor George, was baptised there on 9 May 1910.

Herbert Parker Church
Private 58574, Northamptonshire Regiment
Private 68131, Hertfordshire and Bedfordshire Regiment

> Died: 31 July 1966

Herbert was born in 1882 in Evenley in Northamptonshire, the fourth son of George and Elizabeth Church. His ambition was to become a schoolteacher but his father refused him the opportunity of further education and at the age of 13 he became a servant. In 1901 he was a footman for Joseph Graham, a widowed barrister, in Prince of Wales Terrace, Kensington.

Herbert married Alice Cotterill Elizabeth Keyte at St. James's Church in Campden on 1 November 1911 and they went into service as butler and housekeeper at a number of big houses in Kent and London before they returned to Campden in 1930. They lived at Jasmine Cottage, Sheep Street, which had been enlarged by Joe Warmington in 1927. Rooms were rented to paying guests and sometimes both bedrooms were let, so that Herbert and Alice had to sleep downstairs in the living room.

During the war Herbert enlisted in the Northamptonshire Regiment but did not serve overseas until after the start of 1916. He was transferred to the Hertfordshire and Bedfordshire Regiment before he returned safely from the war.

He died at Jasmine Cottage on 31 July 1966 aged 84 years and is buried in St. James's churchyard. His wife, Alice, died at Evesham in 1968 and is buried with her husband. They did not have any children.

Frederick Walton ("Dick") Clark
Captain, 60 Squadron, Royal Air Force

Born: 28 December 1898
Died: 9 July 1967

Dick was born in the Alcester registration district, the son of John Henry and Nora Elizabeth Clark, who were married at Halford Parish Church in Warwickshire on 4 January 1898. This was his father's second marriage as his first wife died in 1896.

In 1911 a tall red-brick factory was built by his father between Battle Brook and Campden railway station. He had been head gamekeeper for the Earl of Plymouth and, using this experience, he decided to set up in business producing pheasant eggs, dog biscuits and animal medicines. He built Battledene House in 1912 for his family, overlooking the factory and four cottages for workmen. There was a siding and loading platform by the factory and the building had large sliding doors above the railway. A huge wired pen accommodated his pheasants, which produced 2000 eggs a day.

At the outbreak of war in 1914 the factory was in business selling pheasant feed and dog food, milling flour and making dog biscuits. The factory was soon commandeered by the government and the machinery was adapted to make biscuits for the armed forces. Compensation for the requisition was promised but when the fighting was eventually over no money was forthcoming. Consequently the factory was closed and the Clark family left the area.

John Henry Clark died in Kent in April 1926 and is buried in Maidstone.

Dick was educated at Wellingborough School in Northamptonshire. After a period as an officer cadet he enlisted in the Royal Flying Corps and was granted a commission as a 2nd lieutenant on 2 August 1917. He served on the Western Front with 60 Squadron and was gassed, which left him badly traumatised for the rest of his life. In 1919 he was promoted to captain and was posted to Germany as part of the Army of the Rhine. He returned to Cranwell in England in September 1919 and in 1921 he was posted to 39 Squadron, Royal Air Force.

Fred Coldicott remembers seeing Dick in his plane just after the end of the war: "*Dick landed in a single-wing plane near Campden station. He was in the Royal Air Force at the time and his parents lived at Battledene Farm. His father owned the factory which became the Campden Research Station. He stayed the night with his parents and a huge crowd watched him take off the following day. He was a fine-looking young man and could easily be mistaken for the Prince of Wales.*"

After the war Dick found it very hard to settle and was employed in agricultural work in various parts of the country. He married Dilys, a lady from Welshpool, and they had one son, called Phillip.

Dick died on 9 July 1967 aged 61 years.

Herbert Henry Clark
Private 9451, 1st Battalion, Oxfordshire and Buckinghamshire Light Infantry

Died: 20 July 1916

Herbert was born in Teddesley Hall, Penkridge, Staffordshire in 1893, the son of Fred and Julia Clark. His father was the head gardener at Teddesley Gardens in 1901 and then Kiftsgate Lodge in 1913.

Herbert enlisted in the 1st Battalion, Oxfordshire and Buckinghamshire Light Infantry at Chipping Norton as a regular soldier before the First World War and his place of residence was recorded as Campden. At the outbreak of war the battalion was stationed in India but it was quickly dispatched to Mesopotamia to safeguard oil supplies on Abadan Island. The general aim was to advance from the head of the Persian Gulf up the River Tigris towards Baghdad, drawing away Turkish troops from other fronts and hoping to grab Arab support. They arrived at the mouth of the river in late November 1914 and ten months later, on 28 September 1915, the battalion was involved in the capture of Kut-al-Amara, 100 miles from Baghdad. The action took place in extreme conditions. The temperature was high and the troops were suffering from intense thirst.

In December 1915 the Turkish Army counter-attacked and was able to stem the British advance. The British withdrew to the walls of Kut-al-Amara and a siege began that lasted five months. Two relief attempts failed and the remaining troops surrendered on 29 April 1916.

Herbert was amongst those taken prisoner at Kut. He reached captivity at Airon, 125 miles south-east of Ankara, but no news of his whereabouts reached his parents until December 1917, nineteen months after the surrender and fourteen months after he had died there of disease on 20 July 1916 aged 22 years. He is buried in Baghdad (North Gate) Cemetery in Iraq.

Herbert's name is recorded on the memorial in St. Lawrence's Church in Mickleton. The memorial also contains the name of his brother, Lance Corporal 13490, Fred Clark, 10th Battalion, Gloucestershire Regiment, who died at Loos in France on 13 October 1915. Sidney Walter Clark, another brother, served in the Royal Army Medical Corps and survived the war.

Herbert does not have his name recorded on any memorial in Campden.

John Henry Clark

Jack was born in Ipsley, Redditch on 17 December 1892, the son of John Henry and Ann Eliza Clark. His mother died on 17 December 1896 and in January 1898 his father married Nora Elizabeth Walton. His father was a game food manufacturer and came to the Campden area before the war when he built a factory at a railway siding near to Campden station.

In September 1917 the *Evesham Journal* reported that "*Mr. J. H. Clark, of Battledene, Ebrington, received a telegram on Friday saying that his son Lieutenant Jack Clark, who is serving in France, has been severely wounded by gunshot in the knee and hand. Up to the present no further news has, we understand, been received.*"

After the war he married Winifred Scott.

Charles Edgar Clifford
Corporal 18235, 13th Battalion, Gloucestershire Regiment

Charles was born in Stow-on-the-Wold in 1882, the son of Charles and Lucellia Clifford. His father was a stonemason and after leaving school Charles joined him in the trade. He married Dorothy Mary Bruce, daughter of Charles and Rose Ellen Bruce of Campden, on 20 June 1914 at St. Catharine's Church in Campden and they had three children: Ernest Charles, Sybil Maria Magdelena and Bernard Frederick. The family home was in Cider Mill Lane in 1918 and then in Church Cottages in 1922.

When war was declared in 1914 he enlisted in the 13th (Service) Battalion, Gloucestershire Regiment and after a period of home service the battalion arrived at Le Havre in France on 4 March 1916 as the Pioneer Battalion in the 39th Division.

By midsummer 1916 the British Army was preparing for an offensive on the Somme and this required divisions on the quieter sectors further north to mount diversionary raids in an attempt to prevent the Germans from moving troops and artillery south. The 39th Division were ordered to assault, capture and hold the German trenches at the Boar's Head, a salient which projected, snout-like, from the German line a few thousand yards south-east of Richebourg L'Avoue, between Neuve Chapelle and Festubert. The attack took place on the night of 29-30 June 1916, just twenty-seven hours before the *Big Push* on the Somme. It was a disaster and Charles was one of the men listed as wounded during the attack.

John Robert A. Codrington
Lieutenant-Commander, Royal Navy

Enlisted: 15 March 1901
Died: 1 November 1918

John was born in Sheerness in Kent in 1884, the son of Rear Admiral William Codrington and Mary Auber Leach, daughter of Benjamin Auber Leach and Emily Danvers, Viscountess Hambleden. After leaving school he joined the Royal Navy as a midshipman on 15 March 1901 and on 15 June 1904 he was promoted to sub-lieutenant. When he joined HMS *Mercury* at Portsmouth for a course of induction in submarines in June 1907 he was a lieutenant. For his first command he was given submarine *A5* in January 1910, which operated from Portsmouth. The following year he was sent to China as Commanding Officer of *C38* in the Hong Kong Flotilla. He remained in China until he returned to England in November 1914 and was posted to HMS *Maidstone* at Harwich on 1 December 1914, where he joined the 8th Flotilla. He was promoted to lieutenant commander on 31 December 1914 and in March 1915 he moved to Portsmouth to take charge of submarine *V1*. In August 1915 he was posted to Mudros to take charge of *E11* and then in April 1916 *E11* was transferred to Malta. John remained in Malta until December 1916, when the submarine was posted to Brindisi in Italy.

John returned to England in June 1917 and was posted to submarine *K14* in the Firth of Forth in Scotland and it was during this period of his service that his engagement to Mary A. Fraser, daughter of Lord and Lady Saltoun, was announced in *The Times*. They married in London in early 1918 while he was in command of *L5*.

John was serving on HMS *Ambrose*, a depot ship at Plymouth, when he contracted Spanish influenza. He died on 1 November 1918 aged 34 years and is buried in Plymouth Old Cemetery (now called Ford Park Cemetery).

John is listed on the 1916 prayer list produced by St. James's Church in Campden and in 1919 his mother was living in Ilmington.

Charles Arkell Coldicott
Sergeant 856, "D" Squadron, 1st/1st Battalion, Warwickshire Yeomanry

Born: 21 October 1884
Enlisted: 31 March 1902
Died: 19 September 1915

Arkell was the eldest son of Charles and Mary Coldicott of Mickleton Woods Farm. He was educated at Campden Grammar School and then found employment as an ironmonger's apprentice. He enlisted in "D" Squadron, Warwickshire Yeomanry at Shottery in 1902. The Yeomanry was the mounted reserve of the Regular Army and in 1912 Arkell was awarded the Territorial Forces Efficiency Medal.

At the outbreak of war in August 1914 Arkell was employed farming a hill near Stanton and was immediately mobilised and joined the Warwickshire Yeomanry at St. John's in Warwick. On 14 August 1914 they moved to Bury St. Edmunds and then to Newbury Racecourse, where they were inspected by the King. After further training the regiment embarked at Avonmouth on 11 April 1915 to join the force being concentrated in Egypt for the landings at Gallipoli. They had 763 horses on board and sixty miles north-west of the Scillies they were torpedoed, but did not sink. They were towed to Queenstown, County Cork and after only a short delay they arrived at Alexandria on the *Saturnia* on 24 April 1915. A further 357 horses were bought locally for the regiment.

The first landings at Gallipoli were made on 25 April 1915 but the Warwickshire Yeomanry did not see action there until August 1915. On 14 August 1915 the regiment embarked on the *Ascania*, where they received inoculations against cholera. Three days later they arrived at Mudros Harbour on the island of Lemnos and transferred to the slower *Queen Victoria* for the landing at Suvla Bay on the Gallipoli Peninsula.

The Warwickshire Yeomanry, including Arkell and his brother Walford, landed in the small hours of 18 August 1915 at Suvla Bay. They bivouacked on a hill and dug in under the eyes of the Turks. On 20 August they moved out and marched to Lala Baba. The following day they moved on to support an intended advance to Chocolate Hill. The British artillery preparation was inadequate and the attack suffered horrendous casualties. By 5.00pm it had failed and the Warwickshire Yeomanry were called forward from their support positions, having to cross the open ground of the Salt Lake while subjected to shrapnel fire. Arkell had a lucky escape when a piece of shell split his trousers and only grazed his skin, but 170 men of the Warwickshire Yeomanry were killed or wounded. As the troops reached the fields beyond the Salt Lake the order was given to speed up to the double, but casualties continued to mount until the foot of Chocolate Hill was reached. From here the brigade launched an attack on Scimitar Hill but it was repelled by intense fire. The Warwickshire Yeomanry were then withdrawn from the attack and spent the rest of August 1915 in trenches and dugouts under enemy shelling of varying intensity.

In September 1915 Arkell contracted enteric fever and pneumonia and was evacuated to hospital in Alexandria. He had only been in hospital three days when he died on 19 September 1915. He was 30 years old and is buried at Alexandria (Chatby) Military Cemetery in Egypt. He has his name recorded on memorials at Campden Grammar School, Stanton, Mickleton Church and on his parent's grave in Mickleton churchyard. He was the eldest of five brothers who served during the war.

After his death a memorial service for Arkell was held at St. Lawrence Church in Mickleton on 3 October 1915.

Ellen Coldicott

Ellen was born in Weston-sub-Edge in 1875, the third child of William Henry and Elizabeth Ann Coldicott. William married Elizabeth Haines in London in 1868 and in 1881 the family were living at Marfurlong Farm, Ebrington, where William was a farmer with 174 acres, employing three men and two boys. In 1901 the family were living in Lower High Street, Campden, where William was a master butcher.

Ellen was living with her parents in 1901 and was employed as a commercial clerk. At the outbreak of war she was still single and living at home, and the 1918 electoral roll indicates that she was absent on military service. She does not have a medal index card so she must have been employed on home service only.

Francis Holt Coldicott
Corporal 2323, "D" Squadron, 1st/1st Warwickshire Yeomanry
Corporal 310423, Corps of Hussars

Born: 1 August 1890
Discharged: 25 March 1919

Francis was the fourth son of Charles and Mary Coldicott of Mickleton Wood Farm and he joined "D" Squadron, Warwickshire Yeomanry at the outbreak of the war in August 1914. They embarked at Avonmouth on 11 April 1915 and Francis arrived in Egypt on 20 April. He landed on the Gallipoli Peninsula at Suvla Bay on 18 August 1915 and served on the peninsula until they were evacuated to Mudros on 31 October 1915. In 1917 he was in Palestine and he continued to serve until he was discharged in England on 25 March 1919.

Harry Izod Coldicott
Private 241, "B" Squadron, 2nd Australian Light Horse

Born: 31 January 1887
Enlisted: 24 August 1914
Died: 7 June 1917

Harry was the second son of Charles and Mary Coldicott of Mickleton Wood Farm and was educated at Campden Grammar School. He was keenly interested in the training of Boy Scouts and he trained a very smart company of lads from Hidcote Bartrim and Mickleton. In the Spring of 1913 he emigrated to Australia with a group of former Boy Scouts and found employment working in an orchard growing fruit.

At the outbreak of war he was serving with the 15th Australian Light Horse and had previously served in the Warwickshire Yeomanry with his brother Arkell in England. He enlisted in the 4th Australian Light Horse Regiment at Broadmeadows in Victoria on 25 August 1914, when he was 26 years old. He was passed fit for overseas service and his medical report stated that he was five feet six inches tall with yellowish eyes, brown hair and a fair complexion.

He embarked for Egypt at Melbourne on the troopship *Wiltshire* on 18 October 1914, a departure delayed by the outbreak of measles in the unit. They arrived at Alexandria on 8 December 1914 and then settled at Mena and commenced training. They completed their training at Heliopolis, at the apex of the Nile delta, and embarked for the Gallipoli Peninsula. They landed at Gaba Tepe on 20 May 1915 and served on the peninsula until they were moved to rest camps on the island of Imbros on 14 July. After returning to the front on 22 July they were involved in devising ruses to attract Turkish artillery fire and reveal the locations of their guns.

Sickness was rife in the trenches and Harry developed a hernia. He was conveyed, sick and wounded, to Alexandria on the hospital ship *Nevasa* and admitted to Number 3 Auxiliary Hospital at Heliopolis on 19 September. There he contracted influenza and was sent to the ANZAC Convalescent Depot at Helouan, becoming fit for service on 12 November. He rejoined his unit at Heliopolis on 2 January 1916. The *Evesham Journal* reported that Harry "*saw some hard service at Gallipoli and received a wound in the head*". His service papers state that it was in the hand.

He had only been back with his unit for three weeks when he developed mumps and was admitted to Number 4 Auxiliary Hospital at Abbassia. He was discharged on 8 February and at the end of March he embarked with his unit at Alexandria on the troopship *Castrian.* They disembarked at Marseille on 27 March 1916 before moving to the Western Front west of Bailleul. The following month he was found guilty of disobeying orders when he was out of bounds at Strazeele and awarded 21 days' detention by his commanding officer.

Harry was away on leave for two weeks beginning on 25 September 1916. On 12 January 1917 he developed influenza and was admitted to the 3rd New Zealand Field Ambulance before being discharged to duty three days later and rejoining his unit, 2nd ANZAC Light Horse. He was detached from his unit on 16 April 1917 for duty with the New Zealand Division but returned on 22 April.

Harry died of wounds received in action on 7 June 1917, the opening day of the Battle of Messines. The battle was planned as a preliminary to a major British offensive further north, its objective to capture the strategically important ridge that dominated the British lines south of Ypres. The battle started at 3.10am when nineteen mines were exploded under the German trenches. Nine divisions took part in what is often described as the best-planned British operation of the war. The *Evesham Journal* reported details of Harry's death: "*He was one of the patrol going out with the advanced squadron when he was hit by a fragment of a high explosive shell in the right side of his head above the forehead. He never regained consciousness and died without any pain in a field hospital behind the lines the same day. He was with his old friend, Clive Doyle, and enjoying being in action. Everything that could be done was done for him at once by our aid post and he was carried away by our own stretcher bearers.*" This account differs from the one recorded in his service papers, which states that he died of multiple gun shot wounds at the 77th Field Ambulance.

Harry was buried at Westhof Farm Cemetery, near Neuve Eglise in Belgium, on 8 June 1917 by Rev. C. H. Edwards. He was 30 years old and a memorial service was held at Mickleton Church on 24 June 1917. His name is not recorded on the memorial at Campden Grammar School but it is on the memorial at Mickleton Church.

Jack Garfield Coldicott

Private 66449, Royal Army Medical Corps
2nd Lieutenant, 14th Battalion, Gloucestershire Regiment

> Born: 9 October 1897
> Enlisted: 9 September 1915
> Discharged: 30 April 1919

Jack was the youngest son of Charles and Mary Coldicott of Mickleton Wood Farm. He was educated at Worcester Royal Grammar School and then found employment as a bank clerk at the Capital and Counties Bank in Malvern. He enlisted in the Royal Army Medical Corps at Worcester on 9 September 1915 and joined his unit at Bulford Camp. He arrived in France on 12 November 1915 and served with the 11th Field Ambulance on the Western Front until 15 July 1916, when he returned to England suffering from bronchitis. He was admitted to Colchester General Hospital and then transferred to Romford Union Hospital on 20 July 1916 before completing his recovery at Eastbourne Convalescent Hospital. A further period of service in France began on 6 November 1916 but he returned to England eight weeks later on 30 December. He then applied for a commission and he had character testimonials from Mr. F. A. Hilliard, Headmaster of Worcester RGS, and Rev. Edgar Arthure, Vicar of Mickleton.

Jack was discharged from the RAMC on 26 June 1917 to take up his commission with the Gloucestershire Regiment. He embarked for Le Havre as a 2nd lieutenant on 19 August 1917 and joined his unit, 14th Battalion, Gloucestershire Regiment, at the racecourse at Rouen. The following month he was very severely wounded in the right forearm at Cambrai while on patrol duty on 29 September. The bullet caused the fracture of a bone three inches above the wrist. He was admitted to Number 55 Casualty Clearing Station before being evacuated to Number 8 General Hospital at Rouen. On 14 October 1917 he embarked at Le Havre, arriving at Southampton the following day, and was admitted to Number 4 General Hospital, Denmark Hill, London. The wound slowly recovered but there was a permanent loss of power in the arm and he was declared permanently unfit by a medical board and graded C2. He purchased a leather forearm splint in April 1918 and then in June 1918 he was posted to the Infantry Records Office in Warwick.

In October 1918 he returned to the battalion in France, and was attached to Number 2, Infantry Section, General Headquarters. He was soon admitted to a British Red Cross Hospital and then discharged from duty on 1 November 1918.

Jack was promoted to lieutenant on 27 December 1918. In February 1919 he was given special leave so that he could return home as his father had died on 31 January. After returning to his unit he was then struck off the strength of the 3rd Echelon and returned to Chiseldon for demobilisation on 30 April 1919. In September 1919 he relinquished his commission and was able to keep the rank of lieutenant for use in civilian life.

Jack married Katharine May Lissaman on 5 October 1920 and they had three children. Their only son, John Keith, was killed in action in Normandy in 1944. After his wedding Jack returned to work as a bank clerk and worked in banks in Broadway, Cheltenham and Stow-on-the-Wold. His last appointment was the manager of the Oswestry branch. After retiring he moved to Shilton in Oxfordshire and died in May 1985 aged 87 years.

James Walford Coldicott

Lance Corporal 1729, "D" Squadron, 1st/1st Warwickshire Yeomanry

> Born: 23 February 1888
> Enlisted: 10 March 1911
> Discharged: 8 April 1916

Wally was the third of five sons of Charles and Mary Coldicott of Mickleton Wood Farm. He joined the Warwickshire Yeomanry in 1910 and was mobilised for overseas service, with his two brothers, Arkell and Francis, in August 1914 at the outbreak of war. On 14 August 1914 the Warwickshire Yeomanry moved to Bury St. Edmunds and then to Newbury Racecourse, where they were inspected by the King. After further training the regiment embarked at Avonmouth on 11

April 1915 to join the force being concentrated in Egypt for the landings at Gallipoli. They arrived in Egypt on 20 April 1915 and on 18 August 1915 they landed at Suvla Bay on the Gallipoli Peninsula, where Wally was wounded on 21 August 1915. He was evacuated to hospital at Alexandria and later returned to England, where he was discharged from the Yeomanry on 8 April 1916.

He married Ivy Slatter and they had three children: Charles, Roy and Joan. After his father died in 1919 he took over the running of Mickleton Wood Farm. Wally died on 31 January 1981 aged 92 years and is buried in Mickleton Cemetery alongside his wife, who died on 14 April 1977 aged 79 years.

John Nelson Combes
Royal Field Artillery

John was born in Weston-sub-Edge in 1878, the fourth son of Frank and Frances Combes of West End Terrace, Campden. His father was born in Tisbury, near Salisbury, Wiltshire and was a land surveyor and a civil engineer.

After leaving Campden John moved to 64, Round Hill Crescent in Brighton, where he worked as a draper's assistant. He married May Gillam at the Register Office in Brighton on 23 February 1903 and a son, William Edward, was born at their home, 2, Normanton Street, Brighton, on 23 February 1906.

Reginald Cyrus Combes
Gunner 110224, Royal Field Artillery

Reginald was born in Campden in 1887, the fifth son of Frank and Frances Combes of West End Terrace, Campden, and was baptised at St. James's Church on 18 December 1887. His father was born in Tisbury, near Salisbury, Wiltshire and was a land surveyor and a civil engineer. In 1881 the family were living at The Lynches in Weston-sub-Edge but they are listed as living at West End Terrace in Campden on the 1891 and 1901 census returns. The census returns list the following children of Frank and Frances: James Gray, Frank Rogers, Catharine May, Frances Elizabeth, Emily Mary, John Nelson and William Edward. His father died in 1916 aged 76 years and his mother died in 1915 aged 74 years. They are buried in St. James's churchyard.

Reginald served overseas as a gunner in the Royal Field Artillery during the First World War and returned safely.

His father's obituary in the *Evesham Journal* stated that he had three sons serving in the army during the war. The author believes that the third son was Private 14292 William Edward Combes, Coldstream Guards.

John Cook
Royal Garrison Artillery

In her *Book of Remembrance* Josephine Griffiths lists John as serving in the Royal Garrison Artillery during the war. The 1918 electoral roll records that John was living in Back Ends in Campden with his wife, Millicent, and absent on military service.

It appears that John arrived in the town after 1914 and left soon after the end of the war.

George Charles Cooper
1st/5th Battalion, Gloucestershire Regiment

Died: 20 January 1965

George was born in Campden on 29 July 1889, the fourth and youngest son of Henry and Mary Cooper of "Boxhedge", Sheep Street. He was baptised at St. James's Church on 27 July 1890. He went to school in the town. His father was an agricultural machinist and George found employment as a labourer. He soon developed a genuine interest in pigeons and became an active member of Moreton-in-Marsh Pigeon Club for many years. The last job he held before he retired was as caretaker at Campden Grammar School.

He married his first wife, Kate Beasley (not to be confused with Kate Amelia Beasley, who married his brother William in 1913), at St. James's Church on 21 December 1912 and they had three children: George Henry Austen, George Donal and George Reginald. Kate died on 28 July 1923 aged 43 years and is buried in St. James's churchyard in Campden.

During the First World War George served with the 1st/5th Battalion, Gloucestershire Regiment. This was a Territorial battalion that contained several other Campden men. The 1918 electoral roll lists George as living in Twine Cottages and absent on military service.

George died on 20 January 1965 at Stratford-upon-Avon Hospital aged 75 and is buried in St. James's churchyard. His address at the time of his death was 3, The Almshouses, Campden and his obituary in the *Evesham Journal* indicates that his second wife, formerly Miss Gladys Williams, survived him. Gladys died in 1969 aged 75 years.

James Cooper
Private T-359821, 5th Corps Troops, Motor Transport Company, ASC

Born: 15 June 1883
Died: 3 May 1971

Jim was born in Campden, the third of four sons of Henry and Mary Cooper of "Boxhedge", Sheep Street. His father was an agricultural machinist on a farm and in 1901 Jim was living at home with his parents and working as a shepherd.

He married his wife, Bertha Helen Bachelor, in 1916 and they had two sons, Barlow and Eric. He worked as a labourer throughout his life and the family lived at Woodbine Cottage before they moved to "The Bungalow" in Back Ends.

During the war Jim served in the Army Service Corps and documents held by the family indicate that he was stationed at the following places in France and Belgium: Watten, Hazebrouck, Villers-au-Bois, Bihucourt, Achiet-le-Grand, Bapaume, Frémicourt, Doullens, Acheux, Marieux, Bailleul and Poperinge. His commanding officer was Major H. A. Trapp and Jim was included in a muster roll dated 11 November 1918. His medal index card indicates that he did not serve overseas until after the start of 1916.

Jim died on 3 May 1971 aged 87 and is buried in St. James's churchyard.

William Cooper
Royal Engineers

Died: 4 December 1925

William was born in Campden in 1860, the son of James Cooper, a labourer, and his wife Fanny. He was baptised at St. James's Church on 19 May 1861 and after leaving school he found employment as a general labourer. He married Mary Ann Court at St. James's Church on 3 November 1887 and they had four children: James William, Mary Jane, Rose and Alexander.

When war was declared William was 54 years old. It is not known when he enlisted in the Royal Engineers, or whether he served overseas, but he was recorded as absent on military service on the 1918 and 1919 electoral rolls. After the war he became the first tenant of 6, Aston Road, Campden, a house built for returning servicemen. Two of his children, Alexander and Rose, became the tenants of the house after William's death in 1925.

William died on 4 December 1925 aged 65 and is buried in St. James's churchyard. His wife died on 16 April 1948 aged 82 years.

Albert Reginald Corbett

Private 5273, Norfolk Regiment
Private 29516, Norfolk Regiment
Private 41610, 1st Battalion, Essex Regiment

Died: 22 April 1917

Albert was born in Campden in 1889, the son of Michael Henry and Elizabeth Annie Corbett of the Police Station, High Street, Campden. His father was a police constable and he married Elizabeth Ireson, daughter of George and Louisa, at St. James's Church on 3 March 1885. Their first three children, George Henry, William Ireson and Albert, were born in the town and baptised at St. James's Church. The family left Campden in 1891 and their fourth child, Louisa Miriam, was born in Hardwicke near Gloucester in the same year.

At the outbreak of war in 1914 Albert was married and living in Stoke Ferry in Norfolk with his wife, Elsie Florence. He enlisted at Norwich in the Norfolk Regiment but he did not arrive in France until after the start of 1916. It is not clear when Albert was transferred from the Norfolk Regiment but when he lost his life in 1917 he was serving with the 1st Battalion, Essex Regiment.

The 1st Essex arrived in France at Marseille on 29 March 1916 after leaving Gallipoli and then saw heavy fighting during the Battle of the Somme. The Battle of Arras began on 9 April 1917 and the battalion was involved in what was known as the First Battle of the Scarpe from 9-14 April 1917. The battle was initially successful but soon got bogged down and became a very costly affair. Albert was wounded in action during this phase of the battle and was taken prisoner by the Germans. He died in captivity on 22 April 1917 aged 28 years and is buried in Cologne Southern Cemetery in Germany. When the Commonwealth War Graves Commission compiled their information on British casualties in 1921 Albert's wife had moved to Little London, Northwold, Norfolk, only a short distance south-east of Stoke Ferry.

Henry John Dyer Cossins

Royal Field Artillery

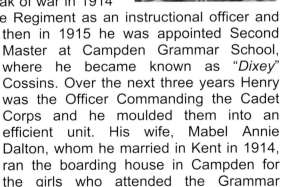

Born: 25 July 1882

Henry was born at 3, Devonshire Villas in Bath, the son of William Brown and Sarah Ann Cossins. After completing his education he became a schoolmaster and joined the staff at Taunton School, where he held the post of Master of the Army Class. He was also the platoon commander of the Officer Training Corps. At the outbreak of war in 1914 he joined a service battalion of the Royal Warwickshire Regiment as an instructional officer and then in 1915 he was appointed Second Master at Campden Grammar School, where he became known as "*Dixey*" Cossins. Over the next three years Henry was the Officer Commanding the Cadet Corps and he moulded them into an efficient unit. His wife, Mabel Annie Dalton, whom he married in Kent in 1914, ran the boarding house in Campden for the girls who attended the Grammar School.

In 1918 Henry left the school to join the Royal Field Artillery. Owing to the great difficulties of catering and to failing health Mabel was unable to continue the boarding house during the absence of her husband on military service.

Campden Grammar School Cadet Corps
Captain Dixey Cossins is seated at the front with his dog.

George William Cother
Private 5812, 1st Battalion, Gloucestershire Regiment

Born: 29 April 1880
Died: 23 August 1916

George was born at Campden Ashes Farm on the Springhill Estate, the second son of George and Elizabeth Cother. On the 1881 census his father was employed as an agricultural labourer and a carter and the family were living at Campden Ashes. The family surname was spelt "*Cothier*" on the 1881 census and on George's birth certificate. By 1891 the family had moved to Brook Lane in Blockley and George senior was a road labourer.

George served in South Africa during the Boer War and was awarded two campaign medals, the Queen's South Africa medal and the King's South Africa medal, with clasps for Transvaal, Cape Colony and Orange Free State. When war was declared in 1914 George was on the Army Reserve list and was called up for active service in August and posted to the 1st Battalion, Gloucestershire Regiment. When he arrived in France on 20 September 1914 the battalion had already been on the Western Front for over a month. He first saw action in October at Langemarck in Belgium during the First Battle of Ypres. Brigadier-General H. J. S. Landon noted that the battalion had "*inflicted great losses on the enemy who had come within 50 yards of their line. Each man fired some 500 rounds and some had the bayonets shot off their rifles. Not a man retired.*"

On 29 October they were involved in heavy fighting at Gheluvelt, on the Menin Road east of Ypres, where they had to withdraw after strong enemy attacks. In November the battalion remained in the Ypres area and casualties increased daily as the fighting continued. The battalion then moved south into France, where the first few months of 1915 were spent in trenches east of Béthune near Neuve Chapelle, Richebourg-St. Vaast, Sailly-Labourse and Cambrin.

The battalion were not involved in the fighting on the opening day of the Battle of the Somme on 1 July 1916 and it was on 16 July that they were sent into action at Contalmaison, where they captured enemy positions north of the village. After a period of rest they were sent forward to a position west of High Wood on 20 August 1916. It was during this time that George was killed in action on 23 August 1916, when he was 36 years old. His body was not recovered at the end of the war and today his name is recorded on the Thiepval Memorial, Somme, France.

The *Evesham Journal* reported George's death on 9 September 1916. "*Mrs. Cother, of Paxford, has received news of the death of her husband, George Cother, of the Gloucestershire Regiment. He was a reservist and was called up in August 1914. His father resides in Blockley, where he has been for many years roadman in the employment of the District Council.*" It is interesting to note that the *Evesham Journal* published a photograph of George but they spelt his surname "*Cotter*".

George married Sarah Ann Peachey at Blockley Parish Church on 22 July 1911 and they had three children: Mary, George and Jesse. His name is not recorded on any memorials in Campden but it is on memorials in Blockley Church, Blockley village and Paxford.

George's younger brother, Private 7899 Joseph Cother, also served in the 1st Battalion, Gloucestershire Regiment. Joe arrived in France with the battalion on 27 August 1914 and was wounded at Langemarck during the First Battle of Ypres. He was discharged from the army on 10 May 1915 as no longer fit for active service and a Silver War Badge was issued to show that he had made his contribution to the war. Both George and Joe were members of what the Kaiser called "*that contemptible little army*".

Sydney James Cotton
Sapper 89593, 91st Field Company, Royal Engineers

Born: 1884
Died: 20 August 1915

Sydney was born in Malta in 1884, the eldest son of Benjamin and Mary Matilda Cotton. His father worked for the Admiralty and in 1901 the family were living at 98 Sibford Grove, West Ham, London. After leaving school Sydney joined the Guild of Handicraft and began an apprenticeship as a cabinetmaker. In 1902 he came to Campden with Charles Ashbee but only stayed with the Guild for eight years and never took up full membership. His nickname was *The Mad Hatter*.

After leaving Campden Sydney returned south to live in Ilford to carry on his work as a cabinetmaker. He then set sail for Canada although when the war started he was back in England. He enlisted in the Royal Engineers at Chelsea in London and after final training in England was sent to the coal-mining region of northern France near to Lens. Final preparations were under way for a big attack in September 1915 on the German trenches around the village of Loos. Sydney never took part in the battle as he was killed on 20 August 1915.

He died aged 30 years and his body was buried in Loos British Cemetery, France in plot 16, row G, grave 14. The Commonwealth War Graves Commission record that his parents were living at 10 Brisbane Road, Ilford, Essex at the time of his death.

Sydney does not have his name recorded on any memorial in Campden but he was a friend and colleague of Charles Ashbee and was in the town, with the Guild, from 1902 until 1906.

James Edward Court
Private 18934, Gloucestershire Regiment
Private 430301, Labour Corps

Born: 1874
Enlisted: 19 January 1915
Discharged: 26 March 1918
Died: December 1941

James was the son of James and Mary Ann Court and was baptised at St. James's Church on 28 June 1874. After leaving school he was employed as a general labourer before he joined his father as a market gardener. In his spare time he was a member of the Town Band and of "H" Company, 5th Battalion, Gloucestershire Regiment, the local company of the Territorial Army (previously "K" Company, 2nd Volunteer Battalion, Gloucestershire Regiment).

Drum and Fife Band, "K" Company, 2nd Volunteer Battalion, 1897
James is at the back on the far right. Harry Baker, who died of wounds in 1918, is on the far left.

When the war started James was still living with his father in Lower High Street, Campden. He enlisted in the Gloucestershire Regiment on 19 January 1915, when he was 40 years old, and was employed on home service only. On 25 July 1917 he was transferred to the Labour Corps before he was discharged on 26 March 1918 as medically unfit for further service after a period of 3 years and 67 days in the army.

In 1922 he married Patience Eleanor Grace Ethel Poole at St. James's Church. They had one son, who died in 1940, and the marriage ended in 1937 when his wife died. James died at Evesham Hospital in December 1941 aged 67 years. He had lived all his life in Campden and is buried in St. James's churchyard.

John Lennox Cox
Private 15549, Number 7 Officer Cadet Battalion, Gordon Highlanders
Lieutenant, 4th Battalion, Scottish Rifles (The Cameronians)

Born: 24 April 1897
Enlisted: 14 January 1916
Died: 19 September 1918

John was born in Buckingham, the only son of Walter Matthew and Margaret Whytock Cox. His father, Matthew, was the headmaster of Campden Grammar School for fourteen years, 1913-1927, and he came to the town from the Blue School in Wells in Somerset.

John began his education at the Royal Latin School in Buckingham and then attended the Blue School in Wells, where his father was a master. At the age of 14 he won the first scholarship at Exeter School and joined the school as a boarder in September 1912. He immediately joined the Officer Training Corps (OTC), rising to the rank of platoon sergeant by the time that he left the school in April 1916. He was an excellent student and was fully involved in the life of the school. He won the Scott Medal for Mathematics 1914-1915 and was also a school prefect and head of house in 1915. On the games field he was an all-round athlete. He was top of the batting averages in 1915 and on 16 June 1915 he scored 157 out of a total of 270 for 3 wickets. The school archives state that he was a *"very sound bat and he uses his wrists well. Most difficult to dislodge and very good on the leg side."* On the rugby field he was a *"greatly improved centre, good in attack and defence. Cuts through cleverly and feeds his wing well. Often makes ground with excellent place kicks."*

In his four years at Exeter School he held many positions of responsibility including Secretary of the Science Club, Cricket Club and Hockey Club and a member of the Library and Reading Room Committee and Games Committee. He was awarded school colours in hockey, cricket and football.

John enlisted in the army on 14 January 1916 in Exeter but was immediately put in the Army Reserve, which enabled him to continue with his education at Exeter School. He was eventually mobilised on 4 September 1916 and was posted to Number 7 Officer Cadet Battalion, Gordon Highlanders at Fermoy in Ireland. While he was at Fermoy he developed tonsillitis and was admitted to hospital. After leaving hospital he remained at Fermoy until he was gazetted to the 4th Battalion, Scottish Rifles as an instructor in physical education and bayonet fighting. He left the camp on 1 July 1918 as a 2nd lieutenant, having gained his commission on 19 December 1916, and embarked for overseas service on 2 July 1918. He arrived at Bralo in Spain, en route for Greece, on 14 July 1918, before arriving at their destination, Salonika, on 18 July.

The next two months were spent gaining experience of life in a theatre of war and John must have a made a favourable impression as he was promoted to lieutenant on 19 August 1918. The Allied army was preparing for a major attack in September and it was during the Second Battle of Doiran that began on 18 September 1918 that John was killed in action. He was attached to the 11th Battalion, Scottish Rifles and on the morning of 19 September 1918 his company attacked. On reaching the enemy wire John asked a soldier his name. *"Sergeant 28396 Gormley,"* was the reply and at that moment John was wounded by a bullet in the right temple and fell into his arms. He died within a few minutes and Sergeant Gormley placed his body in a shell hole in front of the wire. His commanding office wrote: *"We had learnt to know him as a brave and capable officer, popular with both officers and men. He had done brilliantly throughout the battle, leading his men with that bravery and coolness which he had displayed during the whole of the recent operations. He died a glorious death and was actually killed while he was in temporary command."*

John was killed in action on 19 September 1918 aged 21 years and is buried in Doiran Cemetery in Northern Greece. The cemetery was originally called Colonial Hill Military Cemetery Number 2. The news of his death was a devastating blow for his parents in Campden as he was their only child. His mother, Margaret, died on 4 October 1919 and she is buried with her husband in St. James's churchyard in Campden. There is a memorial inscription at the bottom of their headstone for their son.

John has his name recorded on three memorials in Campden: in St. James's Church, in Campden School and in the High Street. It is also on the memorial at Exeter School.

Ernest Geoffrey Crisp

Private 15717, 7th Battalion, Northamptonshire Regiment
2nd Lieutenant, "D" Company, 15th Battalion, Royal Warwickshire Regiment

Born: 20 March 1891
Enlisted: 14 September 1914
Died: 16 December 1915

Ernest is shaking hands with Neville Chamberlain at Codford Camp, Salisbury Plain on 19 November 1915.

Ernest was born in Evesham, the only son of George and Sarah Ellen Crisp of 9 Market Place, Evesham, where they ran the post office. He was educated at Campden Grammar School and then found employment as a bank clerk at the Capital and Counties Bank in Daventry.

Ernest was 23 years old when he enlisted in the Northamptonshire Regiment on 14 September 1914. He had dark brown hair and grey eyes and was five feet nine inches tall. He then applied for a commission in the Royal Warwickshire Regiment on 27 January 1915 and this was accepted on 1 February. He was discharged from the Northamptonshire Regiment on 5 February and then joined the 15th Battalion (2nd City of Birmingham Battalion), Royal Warwickshire Regiment as a 2nd lieutenant on the following day. A period of training in England followed in preparation for being posted to the Western Front.

The battalion embarked at Folkestone and arrived at Boulogne on 21 November 1915. The next month was spent making their way on foot to the Somme battlefield. The weather was wet and daily marches were typically ten miles long. Billets were found in barns and houses in the villages that they passed through. The battalion finally arrived at Suzanne, on the northern banks of the River Somme, at 10.00am on 13 December. Tents were provided in the grounds of the château. The weather was very bright but the roads were extremely muddy. On 14 December the officers and non-commissioned officers of "B" and "D" Company visited the trenches for their first period of instruction. Two men were killed during this time in the front line before they returned to Suzanne at 9.00am on 15 December. Later that day, at 4.00pm, the same group made their way into the trenches for their second period of instruction in the front line. Ernest was a member of an instructional bombing expedition into No Man's Land and was wounded twice. He made it back to his own lines but died of wounds the following day.

Ernest died on 16 December 1915 aged 24 years and is buried in Suzanne Communal Cemetery Extension, Somme, France. He was the Company's bombing officer and died of wounds during his first time in No Man's Land, less than a month after arriving in France. His name is recorded on the war memorial in Campden School and in Evesham Park. There is also a memorial plaque in St. Laurence's Church in Evesham, where he was a regular member of the congregation when he lived there.

His parents received a letter from Ernest's commanding officer that said, "*With more regret than I can express I have to inform you that your dear son was killed in action yesterday. With another officer he went on a bombing expedition and got into the German lines and did excellent work, but whilst doing so he was shot through the shoulder, and whilst returning to our lines he was hit by shrapnel, which smashed his thigh. One other man was killed. I saw your son an hour after he was hit and told him how proud I was of him and his work. He was very weak but in no pain. Two doctors were with him and everything possible was done but the dear fellow died in the afternoon and was buried with full military honours. I have to mourn the loss of one of my best junior officers.*"

Thomas Cross
Somerset Light Infantry

Born: 1872
Died: December 1922

Tom was born in Kempley Green, near Dymock in Gloucestershire, in 1872 and was the eldest son of George and Fanny Cross. In 1901 he was living in Aston-sub-Edge with Eber and Caroline Wright and working as a timber-feller. Later that year he married Ellen Pinchin on 10 October. This was Ellen's second marriage as her first husband, William Henry Franklin, died of dysentery on 4 February 1900 in South Africa during the Boer War while serving with the Royal Warwickshire Regiment.

Tom and Ellen had nine children baptised at St. James's Church in Campden between 1905 and 1915: Albert George, Frances Mary, Thomas, Robert, Katharine, Minnie Louisa, Frederick, Rose Ellen and Wilfrid. Frederick lost his life on 16 August 1944 during the Second World War while serving as Private 5249458 Frederick Cross, 1st Battalion, Worcestershire Regiment, in Normandy, France. He is buried at Banneville-la-Campagne, ten kilometres east of Caen.

During the First World War Tom served in the Somerset Light Infantry. He died in December 1922 aged 50 years and is buried in St. James's churchyard in Campden.

Frederick Cecil Curtis
2nd Lieutenant, Royal Warwickshire Regiment

Born: 14 January 1896
Died: 1979

Fred was the third son of Walter and Eliza Curtis. His father was a cabinetmaker and came to Campden from London with the Guild of Handicraft in 1902. Fred lived in Campden with his parents until the Guild was disbanded in 1908, when the family moved to Ashford in Kent.

Fred was 18 years old when the war started and his elder brother Wally was killed in action in 1914. The *London Gazette* announced that Fred was appointed to the rank of

1939-45: Fred is pictured with his son, Brian.

temporary 2nd lieutenant with the Royal Warwickshire Regiment on 1 May 1918. He arrived in France just after the armistice was signed and remained there for a few months. In May 1919 he was back in England and stationed in Catterick in Yorkshire with the 3rd (Reserve) Battalion.

After the war he married Hilda and they had two children, Pauline and Brian. The family home was in Birmingham and he worked as a wholesale jeweller for a big London firm. During the Second World War he initially joined the Royal Warwickshire Regiment but was soon transferred to the Royal Air Force. He served in British West Africa and then in 1943 was posted to India, where he was employed in an administrative post.

Fred died in Birmingham in 1979 aged 83 years.

Officers of the Royal Warwickshire Regiment.
Fred is fourth from the right of the middle row and has no medal ribbons.

Walter Stuart Curtis
Guardsman 14651, 2nd Battalion Grenadier Guards

Born: 1889
Enlisted: 12 February 1910
Died: 23 September 1914

Walter Stuart (always known as "*Wally*") was one of the seven children of Walter and Eliza Curtis. His father, a cabinetmaker, was with the Guild of Handicraft for twenty years, second in length of service only to Ashbee. The family were originally from London; their connection with Campden began in 1902, when the Guild arrived there. One of Wally's brothers, Charles George, who died at the age of eleven, is buried in the Baptist churchyard. A sister, Gladys, married Reginald Richard Smith and became well known in the town. Walter and Eliza moved to Ashford in Kent, however, when the Guild disbanded in 1908.

Wally was born in London in 1889. In due course he followed his father into the Guild and served his apprenticeship as a cabinetmaker. During his time in Campden he was a member

Wally Curtis, Grenadier Guards

of "K" Company, 2nd Volunteer Battalion, Gloucestershire Regiment, but on 12 February 1910 he enlisted in the Grenadier Guards. He joined his unit at Caterham later that month after being passed fit for the army at a medical examination in Maidstone on 14 February. He was five feet ten inches tall and had brown eyes, dark brown hair, a sallow complexion and an operation scar on his neck. After three years' service in England he was transferred to the Army Reserve on 11 February 1913 and found employment in the motor industry. His conduct in the army was "*fair*" and he was a "*clean and hardworking*" soldier.

When war was declared in 1914 Wally was 25 years old. He was mobilised on 5 August. The Grenadier Guards left Wellington Barracks in London for Southampton on 12 August, arriving at Le Havre the next day. On 23 August they entered Belgium and saw action on a chalk ridge near Harmignies, four miles south-east of Mons. On the 24th the battalion took up positions to cover the British retreat from Mons before undertaking a long march south. After reaching the River Marne the army regrouped and a slow advance north began. It was at this point that Wally joined the battalion in France on 11 September. The Grenadier Guards crossed the River Aisne on 14 September and on the 22nd they took over the front line from the Irish Guards at Chavonne. The next day Wally was dead. His comrade, Private Usherwood, saw him struck in the stomach by a piece of shrapnel which killed him instantly. The local Ashford newspaper reported his death and said that he was "*a good shot and an efficient soldier and many friends in Ashford held him in the highest esteem*".

Wally is buried in Bouilly Crossroads Cemetery in France. His name is recorded on his brother's grave in Campden but it is not on any of the war memorials in the town.

James Butcher Davies
Trooper 1283, Royal Horse Guards

Born: 29 December 1888
Died: 13 May 1915

James was born in Chelsea in London in 1888, the son of John and Emma Paine Davies. In early 1912 in Chelsea he married Florence Ellen Bennett, daughter of Tom and Ann Bennett from Campden. They had two children, John Butcher and Mona. John was baptised at St. Catharine's Church in Campden in 1922 and later married Pauline Mary Kain in Alveston, Derbyshire.

In 1914 James was a regular soldier with the Royal Horse Guards and the family were living in Chelsea. At the outbreak of war he was immediately mobilised and posted to France with one squadron of the Royal Horse Guards to join the Household Cavalry Composite Regiment. He arrived in France on 21 August 1914 and saw action at Mons and during the First Battle of Ypres.

The Second Battle of Ypres started on 22 April 1915 when the Germans opened up on the Allied lines with an intense artillery barrage. As the barrage continued, a yellow-green cloud descended on the Allied lines. For the first time in the history of warfare, poison gas was being used. The Germans had launched shells of chlorine gas onto the British and territorial troops holding the sector. The attack caused several of the defending units to flee their positions, which opened a four-mile-long hole in the Allied lines.

James was killed on 13 May 1915 during the battle, which lasted until 25 May 1915; he was 26 years old. At the end of the war his grave could not be identified and his name is recorded on the Menin Gate Memorial in the centre of Ypres. It does not appear on any memorial in Campden but it is listed in the *Book of Remembrance* compiled by Josephine Griffiths in 1920.

In 1922 his widow, Florence Ellen Davies, was living in Watery Lane, Campden.

Bertrand Ward Devas
Private 2224, Inns of Court Officers' Training Corps
2nd Lieutenant, 10th Battalion, Suffolk Regiment

Born: 7 February 1882
Enlisted: 3 December 1914
Died: 13 November 1916

Bertrand was the third son of Charles Staunton Devas, the distinguished political economist, and of Elizabeth M. S. Devas. The family home was in Kensington in London in 1881 but by 1901 they had moved to Bath. His early education was at Beaumont College in Windsor and he then entered Stonyhurst College in 1898 at the age of 16 years. In his first year at Stonyhurst he gained the Religious Doctrine Prize, the First Year's Philosophy Prize, a Classical Honours Prize and the Stonyhurst Association English Essay Prize. From Stonyhurst he passed to Corpus Christi College, Oxford, where he graduated M.A. In 1907 he was called to the Bar and from 1907 to 1911 he was the assistant editor of the *Dublin Review*, a member of the Universities Catholic Education Board and a Poor Law Guardian for Stepney. At Wapping, where he made his home, he was a devoted and zealous social worker. He was also a member of the committee of the Catholic Truth Society.

On 3 December 1914 he enlisted in London as

a private in the Inns of Court Officers' Training Corps and by the end of the month he had obtained his commission and was posted to the 10th Battalion, Suffolk Regiment as a 2nd lieutenant. His address on enlistment was 5 Pierhead, Wapping Old Stairs, Middlesex and his next of kin was his brother, Gabriel Edward Devas, who was living in East Hendred, Berkshire in 1914.

In September 1915 Bertrand married Elizabeth Helen Ward Fleet, daughter of Mr. J. W. Fleet of Brockenhurst, Hampshire. They had one daughter, Elizabeth, who married Anthony Francis Appleton at St. Catharine's Church in Campden on 9 January 1945.

Bertrand arrived in France on 27 July 1916 and was attached to the 2nd Battalion, Suffolk Regiment in November 1916 when he was killed in action. The battalion were ordered to attack Serre on 13 November 1916, during the closing stages of the Battle of the Somme. They moved into the front line on 12 November 1916 and at 5.00am the next day the first wave floundered forward into No Man's Land, in reality a sea of mud in which movement was barely possible. At Zero Hour, 5.45am, the companies advanced. The mist that hung about the low ground thickened as the smoke from the barrage increased, making direction difficult to maintain. Within a very short time all officers of the leading companies had fallen and owing to a lack of leaders no real progress was made. In spite of the atrocious weather conditions portions of the leading Suffolk companies actually reached the German second line, but all was in vain and the battalion reorganised back in their own front line and remained there for the rest of the day. The attack had failed.

Bertrand was killed in action on 13 November 1916 aged 34 years. He was originally posted missing but his body was found by Reverend Douglas Wood, on 26 May 1917 and given a proper burial. "*The body was found embedded in the rear parapet of the 2nd (possibly 3rd) German line. Only a small portion was visible. It was only the flies settled on it that made me dig and discover it was a body. I identified it by his name on the back of his collar, B. W. Devas, and by a typewritten letter. I buried the body in a cemetery nearby called Luke Copse and his place is number 60 in the row. His brother, Captain Charles Francis Devas, one of the R. C. padres out here has visited it.*"

After the war Bertand's wife moved to Broad Campden and his brother Gabriel and his wife, Vivien, moved to Watery Lane in 1941 after being bombed out of Bath. Their son, Timothy Gordon Devas, died on 13 November 1941 while serving as a lieutenant in the Royal Artillery and his name is recorded on the memorial in St. Catharine's Church in Campden.

Bertrand is buried at Luke Copse Cemetery, Serre, France. His name is not recorded on any memorials in Campden.

Michael Stuart Dewhurst

Private 33304, 17th Officer Cadet Battalion, Gloucestershire Regiment
Officers' Training Corps
2nd Lieutenant, King's Royal Rifle Corps

Born: 18 September 1898
Enlisted: 5 May 1917
Discharged: 20 March 1919

Michael was the son of Doctor John Henry and Ethel Florence Dewhurst of "The Martins" in Campden. He was born in Campden and baptised at St. James's Church on 3 January 1899. He started school in the town in 1905. After leaving St. James's Boys' School he went to Uppingham School where he was in their Officers' Training Corps (OTC) from May 1913 until he left the school as a sergeant on 12 April 1917.

A month later he enlisted as a private in the Gloucestershire Regiment OTC on 22 May 1917 and was immediately posted to an officer training camp at Kinmel Park, Rhyl in Wales. Three months later he obtained his commission and was posted as a 2nd lieutenant in the 6th Battalion, King's Royal Rifle Corps (KRRC).

During final training in November 1917 at Inceborough, Isle of Sheppey Michael received treatment for a hernia problem but this did not prevent him from going overseas with the 18th Battalion, KRRC. They entered France en route for Italy on 13 November 1917 but he was not at the front long as he soon aggravated his hernia. He left the battalion on 22 November 1917 and reported sick at Arquata in Italy. An operation took place at Genoa before he arrived back at

Southampton to be admitted to Mrs. Burns Hospital for Officers at Stoodley Knowle, Torquay on 1 January 1918. After leaving hospital he was granted leave until 8 March 1918, when he was posted to the 6th Battalion, KRRC. A medical examination on 29 April 1918 passed him A1 and ready to return to action.

In the summer of 1918 Michael went to France with the 1st Battalion, KRRC and was wounded at Ayette on 16 August. He was out on patrol when he met a party of Germans. Grenades were thrown and he received a flesh wound when a piece of grenade lodged in the back of his left thigh three inches above the knee. He was initially treated at the 19th Casualty Clearing Station before being admitted to hospital in Rouen. On 22 August he embarked at Le Havre and arrived at Southampton to be admitted to hospital at Edgbaston in Birmingham. The wound healed well and he was granted three weeks' leave before he joined the 5th Battalion, KRRC at Sheerness on 24 October.

Michael spent the last weeks of the war serving in England and was released from his military duties and placed into the Army Reserve on 20 March 1919. He relinquished his commission on 1 September 1921 with the privilege of being able to use the title Lieutenant. He had served a total of four months overseas during the war.

Archibald William John Joseph Douglas-Dick
Lieutenant, 1st Battalion, Scots Guards

Born: 27 October 1889
Died: 11 November 1914

Archie was the only son of Brigadier General Archibald Campbell and Mrs Edith Isabelle Douglas-Dick of Pitkerro House near Dundee, Scotland. He was born in London and his sister, May, married the Hon. Charles Noel in 1912.

After finishing his education Archie became a regular soldier, taking up his commission as 2nd lieutenant with the 1st Battalion, Scots Guards in February 1909. The rank of lieutenant was reached in November 1911.

When war was declared the battalion was at Aldershot. They entrained at Farnborough for Southampton and left for France on board SS *Dunvegan Castle*, arriving at Le Havre on 14 August. Archie's medal index card indicates that he was not with the battalion at this time. He arrived in France on 15 September 1914 in time to see action north of the River Aisne, on the Chemin des Dames, before they made the journey north to Flanders and the battlefields around Ypres.

It was during heavy fighting east of Ypres that Archie lost his life. He went missing on 8 November 1914, but his official date of death is recorded as 11 November, although his body was never found. The battalion was at Veldhoek, five miles east of Ypres, along the Menin Road. There was heavy shelling and the Germans broke into the British trenches. Counter-attacks followed and some lost ground was retaken. It was during these events that Archie died.

George Howley was in the Scots Guards at Ypres in November 1914. He knew Archie and his daughter, Margaret, told the author that he saw Archie wounded and carried him back to an advanced dressing station. It is possible that Archie was buried on the battlefield before further fighting and shelling destroyed his grave. Today Archie has no known grave and his name is recorded on the Menin Gate Memorial at Ypres. He was 25 years old when he died and his name is recorded on the memorial in St. Catharine's Church in Campden and on his parents' headstone in the Catholic cemetery.

The peal of bells in the Catholic church at Broughty Ferry, Forfarshire, Scotland was paid for by his father in memory of his only son.

Archibald Campbell Douglas-Dick
Colonel, Argyll and Sutherland Highlanders
Brigadier General

Born: 24 July 1847
Died: 5 September 1927

Archibald was born in 1847 and was the son of William and Jane Douglas-Dick of Pitkerro, Forfarshire, Scotland. He was educated at Stonyhurst College and then Oscott College before he became a regular soldier.

He married Edith Isabelle Parrott in 1883 and they had eight children. Their only son, Archie, was killed in action at Ypres in 1914 while serving with the Scots Guards.

Archibald commanded the 4th Battalion, Argyll and Sutherland Highlanders in South Africa during the Boer War and was awarded the Queen's South Africa Medal with three clasps: Cape Colony, South Africa 1901 and Orange Free State. In 1900 he was made a *Companion of the Order of the Bath* (CB).

When the First World War started Archibald was 67 years old and the next two years were spent helping to train the new young recruits. In 1916 he was a colonel with the 193rd Infantry Brigade in Montrose and was about to be sent to France. Archibald did not spend much time in France but he was there long enough to command an infantry brigade and be mentioned in despatches. On his return from France in 1917, aged 70 years, he was made a *Companion of the Most Distinguished Order of St. Michael and St. George* (CMG).

After the war Archibald paid for a peal of bells at the Church of our Lady of Good Counsel at Broughty Ferry, Forfarshire, Scotland in memory of his only son, Archie. This was the church where he had been a member of the congregation for many years and where he was responsible for the formation of the Broughty Ferry Catholic Boy Scouts.

In 1912 his daughter, May, married Charles Noel and this was the start of a strong link with Campden in the last years of Archibald's life. Having lived at Pitkerro in Scotland and 34 Ennismore Gardens in London, Archibald and Edith lived at Campden House, a residence of the Noel family, in the 1920's. They were a Roman Catholic family and became regular members of the congregation at St. Catharine's Church.

Archibald suffered a serious illness in 1919 and he never fully recovered. He died at Campden House on 5 September 1927 aged 80 years. He is buried in St. Catharine's cemetery and his headstone bears a memorial inscription to his son, Archie. His wife died on 12 November 1931 aged 68 and is buried with her husband.

Charles Henry James Downer

Born: 27 March 1876
Died: 1962

Charlie was born in London, the son of Thomas Walter and Lydia Downer, and came to Campden in 1902 with the Guild of Handicraft. He and his friend Fred Brown lodged at the Rose and Crown in Lower High Street and felt very homesick during their first few months in the town. He soon settled, however, and established himself as the Gloucestershire Comedian. His jokes and mimicry had convulsed the Guild in London where he was known as the "*Whitechapel Wit*".

Charlie was a blacksmith and a member of the Guild for fourteen years. As the Guild neared collapse some guildsmen left the town while others saw a future in Campden setting up their independent workshops. Charlie and Bill Thornton worked together as blacksmiths and an advertisement in a town guide described them as *"art metalworkers and blacksmiths in ornamental wrought iron work"*.

At the outbreak of war Charlie was 38 years old. He was not called up for service but was employed in England in munitions work. The 1918 electoral roll lists him as living in Sheep Street in Campden and absent on military service.

Charlie married Mary Gwin at Walthamstow Parish Church in London on 30 June 1910. After the war they remained in the town. His wife died in 1952 aged 76 years and Charlie died in January 1962 aged 85 years. He is buried in St. James's churchyard in Campden.

Frederick Drinkwater
Oxfordshire and Buckinghamshire Light Infantry

Born: 28 May 1875
Died: 17 July 1970

Fred was born in Offenham in 1875 and was the fourth son of William and Ann Drinkwater. His father was a native of Offenham and employed as a labourer in the market gardening industry, although on the 1881 census his job was recorded as a *"machinist"*.

After leaving school Fred found employment as a market garden labourer and on 12 December 1896 he married Martha Mary Rose at St. Mary's Church in Childswickham. His residence at the time of the wedding was recorded as Murcot, near Broadway in Worcestershire. Their first son, Frederick Arthur, was born on 8 March 1901 and the family home was in the Silk Mill Cottages in Badsey near Evesham. The family moved to Campden before the First World War and several children were baptised at St. James's Church.

Fred enlisted in the Oxfordshire and Buckinghamshire Light Infantry during the war but did not serve overseas. After the war the family were living in Lower High Street but later moved to 2, Catbrook, where they were living when his wife died in 1942 aged 67 years. She was buried in St. James's churchyard and was survived by a family of one daughter and five sons.

Fred went to live in South Littleton after his wife died. He died at Avonside Hospital in Evesham on 17 July 1970 aged 95 years and is buried in South Littleton churchyard.

Frederick Arthur Drinkwater
Royal Flying Corps

Arthur was born in Badsey on 8 March 1901, the eldest son of Fred and Martha Mary Drinkwater. The family moved to Lower High Street in Campden before the First World War.

Arthur enlisted in the Royal Flying Corps in 1918 but did not see any service overseas before the armistice was signed. He continued to serve in the Royal Air Force after the war and was still listed as absent on military service on the 1926 electoral roll for Campden. During the Second World War he served as a flight sergeant in the Royal Air Force.

After leaving the Royal Air Force Arthur moved to Stoke Mandeville near Aylesbury with his wife, Elsie, and worked at Stoke Mandeville Hospital.

John Gordon Dunn
Boy Second Class J45953, Royal Navy

Born: 17 September 1899
Enlisted: 17 September 1915
Died: 16 February 1916

John was the youngest person from Campden to die serving his country during the 1914-18 war. He was the son of Fred and Helen Dunn of "The Chestnuts", Campden and was baptised at St. James's Church on 12 October 1899. After leaving Campden Grammar School he enlisted at

Chatham in the Royal Navy on 17 September 1915, his sixteenth birthday. The attestation papers record that he was just over five feet tall and had fair hair, grey eyes and a fresh complexion.

A period of two months on the training ship HMS *Mercury* followed John's enlistment before he joined HMS *Impregnable*, another training ship at Devonport, on 2 November 1915 as a boy second class.

John died on 16 February 1916 aged 16 years after suddenly becoming ill. He was rushed to the Royal Naval Hospital at Plymouth and died after three days of "*cerebrospinal meningitis*".

John's body was returned to Campden and he is buried in St. James's churchyard with a private headstone. His coffin was carried by six of his old school friends who were dressed in their army cadet uniform and the service was conducted by Rev. G. E. Hitchcock. His name is recorded on three memorials in the town: in Campden School, in the High Street and in St. James's Church.

In her *Book of Remembrance* Josephine Griffiths records that "*he was a bright, good-looking boy who loved his seafaring life and was always cheery and companionable*".

Henry Joseph Dyde
Able Seaman R/960, Howe Battalion, Royal Naval Volunteer Reserve

Born: 23 March 1898
Enlisted 21 March 1917
Died: 26 October 1917

Harry was born in Campden, the third son of William and Anna Maria Dyde of Lower High Street. After leaving school he was employed by Richard Smith at the George and Dragon public house in High Street, Campden.

Just before his nineteenth birthday Harry enlisted in the Royal Naval Volunteer Reserve on 21 March 1917. His attestation papers state that he was five feet three inches tall, with fair hair, blue eyes and a fresh complexion. In civil life he was last employed as a farm labourer and his religion was Church of England. It is also recorded that he could swim.

Harry joined "A" (Reserve) Battalion on 21 March 1917 and was transferred to the 2nd Reserve Battalion at Blandford on 15 May 1917. After less than three months' training in England he was posted to Howe Battalion on 13 June and began his journey to France. He eventually joined Howe Battalion on 2 August 1917 after a period at the base depot in France.

In November 1917 the *Evesham Journal* reported Harry's death. "*Mrs. William Dyde, Lower High Street, Campden, has received a letter from the Chaplain of the Royal Naval Division to say that her son A. B. Harry Dyde was killed in action by a shell on 26 October 1917*." The division attacked with one brigade at 5.40am on 26 October 1917 and by 7.20am Varlet Farm was captured and by 8.20am Banff House had fallen. Howe Battalion was in reserve and was used to consolidate the gains made by the first wave. It was during this action that Harry died in this area of flat farm land south-east of Poelcappelle during the Third battle of Ypres in Belgium. His grave could not be identified at the end of the war and his name is recorded on the Tyne Cot Memorial near Passendale (formerly Passchendaele) in Belgium. He was 19 years old when he died and his death occurred only three weeks after his elder brother, Jack, had been killed in action with the Royal Warwickshire Regiment on 4 October 1917 only a few miles from the spot where Harry died.

Harry's name is recorded on three memorials in Campden: in St. James's Church, in St. Catharine's Church and in the High Street. It is also recorded on the memorial at Quinton.

John Dyde
Private 9668, 1st Battalion, Royal Warwickshire Regiment

Born: 21 December 1894
Enlisted: 1914
Died: 4 October 1917

John was born in Campden, the second son of William and Anna Maria Dyde of Lower High Street and was baptised at St. Catharine's Church on 22 March 1895. His father was employed as a carter on a farm and his mother's maiden name was James.

John enlisted at Warwick in the Royal Warwickshire Regiment in 1914 and when he arrived in France on 2 May 1915 he was posted to the 1st Battalion. Bill Franklin was serving in the same battalion as John and he wrote home in July 1917:

"Just these few lines thanking you very much for the cigarettes, which I received quite safely in the trenches. I am sorry that I could not see Dick Griffin to share them. Don't expect I will see him for a couple of days so I shared them with Jack Dyde. We are both OK. Don't know how Dick is as yet, he is in another company."

In October 1917 John was in Belgium and the 1st Battalion, Royal Warwickshire Regiment was in support for an attack on German positions northeast of Langemarck during the Third battle of Ypres (also known as the Battle of Passchendaele). Zero Hour was at 6.00am on 4 October. The British artillery put down a very good barrage and the first wave captured Kangaroo Trench. At 1.15pm orders were received that the battalion was to reinforce the Seaforth Highlanders. The battalion arrived at Eagle Trench at about 3.30pm and immediately came under a heavy German artillery barrage but there were very few casualties. Two companies were then sent forward to reinforce the Seaforth's left flank, which was unsupported. The leading companies came into contact with the enemy before reaching 19 Metre Hill and were held up by machine gun fire and rifle fire. Two strong patrols were sent forward and two pillboxes, a machine gun, a German officer and seven men were captured. This enabled the battalion to advance and take up a position on the reverse slope of 19 Metre Hill. Patrols were again sent forward with the object of getting in touch with the troops on their left and right. Connection was made with the 2nd Battalion, East Lancashire Regiment on the right but no connection could be established on the immediate left.

John was killed in action on 4 October 1917 during this operation near Langemarck. He was 22 years old when he died. At the end of the war his grave could not be identified and his name is recorded on the Tyne Cot Memorial near Passendale (formerly Passchendaele) in Belgium. His younger brother, Henry Joseph, also died during the Third Battle of Ypres in October 1917 and has his name recorded on the Tyne Cot Memorial. John's name is recorded on three memorials in Campden: in St. James's Church, in St. Catharine's Church and in the High Street.

Roland Dyer
Private 436504, 7th Battalion, Canadian Expeditionary Force

Born: 26 August 1896
Enlisted: 20 January 1915
Discharged: 6 June 1919
Died: 27 October 1928

Roland was born in Blockley, the second son of Lewis and Ellen Dyer of Draycott. He emigrated to Canada in 1913 and joined his elder brother, who had settled there 18 months prior to the outbreak of the war in 1914. He found employment as a carpenter and his home address was 10916, 72 Avenue, Strathcona, Alberta.

He enlisted in the Canadian Army on 20 January 1915, aged 18 years and 5 months, at Edmonton, and was posted to the 51st Battalion. He was five feet five inches tall with black hair, brown eyes and a dark complexion. The first year of his service was spent in Canada before he embarked at Halifax on 18 April 1916 and arrived at Liverpool on 28 April. Final training took place at Bramshott before he arrived in France on 9 June where he joined the 7th Battalion in the field on 11 June. He was wounded in the left upper arm and knocked unconscious by the explosion of a shell on 13 April 1917 at Vimy Ridge during the Battle of Arras and after being admitted to hospital at Etaples he was invalided back to England on board HS *Stad Antwerpen*. The shell damaged his hearing and he was deaf for a long time after the explosion but the wound in his arm was superficial with no permanent disability. He was admitted to the 4th Northern General Hospital at Lincoln on 19 April 1917 and then in June he was transferred to the Canadian Division Convalescent Hospital at Woodcote Park in Epsom, where he was discharged on 22 June and joined the 1st Canadian Reserve Battalion at Seaford.

Roland rejoined the 7th Battalion in France on 8 December 1917 and on 25 February 1918 he was sentenced to 28 days Field Punishment Number 1 for "*an act to the prejudice of good order and military discipline when he franked one of his own letters*".

On 8 September 1918 he was severely gassed and the seeds were sown that were eventually to cause his premature death. He was evacuated to hospital at Boulogne and in October was posted to a Canadian rest camp in France. In December 1918 he was granted 14 days leave to England and he rejoined his unit in France in January 1919. He remained in France until he returned to England on 15 March. After returning to Canada he was admitted to Manitoba Military Hospital with scabies before he was discharged from the army at Winnipeg in June 1919.

In 1919 Roland married Mary Heaps in Edmonton, Alberta. He had first met Mary in Canada in 1913 and had corresponded with her throughout the war. The effects of being gassed in France soon began to cause Roland problems and he was admitted to a Canadian sanatorium, where he remained for three years. Eventually he returned to Draycott and set up a shop which was soon destroyed by fire. He then bought Barrels Pitch allotments in Campden when the Gainsborough Estate was broken up in 1924 and sold land for building plots. He used one of the plots to build a bungalow for his family and this is where he lived up until he died in 1928.

Roland joined Campden British Legion and was one of the most popular members. In January 1928 he began having problems with his lungs again. There was an improvement during the summer but he did not have sufficient strength to cope with the bad weather of the autumn and he died on 27 October 1928 aged 32 years. The *Evesham Journal* reported that his death was from the continued effects of mustard gas from the war. He is buried in Blockley cemetery but the first part of the funeral service was conducted by Rev. G. E. Hitchcock at St. James's Church in Campden and Campden British Legion provided the men who acted as bearers for the coffin.

Roland was survived by his wife, Mary, and a son, Roland, then aged 4 years. He had been awarded a war pension from the Canadian Government and his wife continued to claim it until she died in 2000 aged 101 years.

George Ebborn
Corporal 161822, Transport Branch, Royal Engineers
Corporal WR201044, Transport Branch, Royal Engineers

Born: 28 December 1859
Discharged: 1 July 1918
Died: 16 February 1951

George was the son of William and Jane Ebborn and was born at Mill End Farm, Newlands, near Coleford in 1859. After leaving school he became a policeman. In 1880 he arrived in Campden as a police constable and remained in the town for the rest of his long life. He married Elizabeth Whatcott at St. James's Church on 29 December 1881 but their time together was very short as she died not long after the birth of their only child, George Stephen. Sadly George's son only lived one month and died on 11 July 1884.

George quickly became one of Campden's best-known residents. He was a member of the Vestry, which was dissolved in 1889, the Town Trust and the Parish Council. In 1927 he was appointed a Justice of the Peace and sat on the local Bench until placed onto the supplementary list in 1944. After leaving the police force he became licensee of the Plough Inn, and later was in business with two of his wife's sisters.

In 1914 he volunteered for the army when he was 54 years old, one of the oldest men from Campden to enlist. He was immediately placed in the Army Reserve and then posted to the Royal Engineers on 10 April 1916. After two months' home service he arrived in France on 29 June and remained on the Western Front until he returned to England on 7 May 1918. His official discharge came in London on 1 July 1918 following a medical examination after 2 years and 83 days in the Royal Engineers. The medical recorded that he was five feet ten inches tall with grey hair, blue/grey eyes and a fresh complexion. He was now over 58 years old and no longer physically fit for active service. His conduct and character throughout his period of service were "*very good*".

George was wounded once and awarded two campaign medals, the British War Medal and Victory Medal, which were buried with him when he died. He was promoted to the rank of corporal during the war but when he attended the funeral of James Josiah Simmons in 1941 he was listed as an "*ex-Colour Sergeant*".

George died at his home in the High Street, after a short illness, on 16 February 1951 aged 91 and is buried, with his wife and son, in St. James's churchyard.

William Edward Eden
Leading Signalman 210203, Royal Navy

Born: 6 November 1884
Enlisted: 1899
Discharged: 18 April 1919
Died: 6 October 1957

Edward joined the Royal Navy at Devonport at the age of 15 in 1899 and when he reached the age of 18 in 1902 he signed on for a period of 12 years. His statement of service gives his place of birth as Campden and his occupation prior to joining the Royal Navy as a schoolboy. In 1902 he was five feet five inches tall with black hair, dark blue eyes and a fresh complexion. His period of 12 years' service expired in November 1914. He chose to remain in the Royal Navy for the duration of the war following a medical that recorded he was still fit for active service. He was now five feet eleven inches tall.

Edward began his naval service as a boy second class on HMS *Black Prince* and was promoted to a boy first class on 14 March 1901. On 6 November 1902 he became a signalman while serving on HMS *Rainbow*, a depot ship based in the Pacific Station. When war was declared in August 1914 he was serving on HMS *Dublin* as a leading signalman and he remained on board this ship until 5 February 1916, when he was transferred to HMS *Vivid,* the Royal Navy barracks in Devonport. Edward continued to serve in the Royal Navy throughout the war and when hostilities ceased he was serving at HMS *Victory,* a depot in Portsmouth. His final posting saw him return to HMS *Vivid* in Devonport on 16 January 1919 but he was then invalided out of the Royal Navy on 18 April 1919 after serving for almost 20 years. His character and conduct throughout his period of service were at all times *"very good"*.

Edward married Florence Hands at St. James's Church on 12 December 1911 while he was home on leave. In 1921 they moved to 1, Station Road in Campden, where they occupied the first council house to be built in the town. In 1923 Edward found employment as a rate collector and a part-time postman and then in 1930 he began a five-year period as a full-time postman. After losing his job as a postman he worked with J. W. Pyment and Sons as a painter and during the Second World War he returned to the Royal Navy and served in the communications branch.

Edward spent the last few years of his life living at the Almshouses and he died on 6 October 1957 aged 72 years. He is buried in St. James's churchyard and his medals were placed in his coffin. His wife, daughter of William Hands, died on 15 March 1953. They did not have any children of their own but they did adopt a son, William Edward, who was born in 1927.

Charles Harold Eldred
Corporal 890, 9th Battalion, Highland Light Infantry
Lieutenant, 9th Battalion, Argyll and Sutherland Highlanders

> Born: 1886
> Enlisted: 17 March 1909
> Discharged: 5 November 1919
> Died: 10 February 1979

Charles was born in Rochester in Kent in 1886, the son of Henry Eldred. When he enlisted in the Highland Light Infantry on 17 March 1909 his occupation in civilian life was recorded as *"HM Customs Officer"*. He joined his unit, 9th (Glasgow Highland) Battalion, Highland Light Infantry, at Glasgow on 16 July 1909 and then spent the next two weeks at Camp Gailes, a Territorial Army camp in Ayrshire in Scotland. He was posted to Stirling in 1910 and then Troon in 1911. He was given an extended period of leave in 1912 and then he spent most of 1913 back at Camp Gailes. He was promoted to lance corporal on 5 August 1914 and then to corporal on 3 November 1914. The battalion entrained for Southampton on 2 November 1914 and then sailed for France on 4 November. They arrived at Le Havre the next day and then travelled to St. Omer, where they were in billets on 7 November. Charles saw his first action at Kemmel in Belgium on 25 November when the battalion occupied the firing line. The trench was found to be very shallow and without communication trenches. No attempt was made to deepen it as the bottom was full of dead French soldiers.

The early months of 1915 were spent in northern France in the Béthune sector and at Beuvry on 25 January 1915 Charles was promoted to acting sergeant. In February 1915 the battalion dug a new communication trench at Cuinchy that they called *"Glasgow Street"*.

Charles ended his service with the Highland Light Infantry on 15 September 1915 when he was commissioned in the field and promoted to 2nd lieutenant and posted to the 9th (Dumbartonshire) Battalion, Argyll and Sutherland Highlanders. The following year the war on the Western Front ended for Charles during the Battle of the Somme when he was hit in the arm by a bullet on 18 September 1916. He was attached to the 1st/4th Battalion, London Regiment, 168th Brigade, 56th Division and they were in the support line trenches at Leuze Wood, north-east of Combles. At 5.50am the division attempted to attack the sunken road that joined Ginchy to Combles but this was quickly checked and the scheduled attack on Bouleaux Wood was postponed. Charles was taken on a stretcher to a casualty clearing station before being admitted to Number 8 General Hospital at Rouen. On 23 September he embarked at Le Havre and arrived at Southampton the following day. He was then admitted to the 1st Southern General Hospital at Edgbaston, Birmingham on 25 September. The next year was spent in and out of hospital and on periods of extended leave as he gradually recovered from his wound. In October 1917 he was posted to the 5th (Reserve) Battalion, Argyll and Sutherland Highlanders at Ripon after a medical board had stated that he was fit for light duties on home service. He was then transferred to Number 116, Territorial Force Depot at Dumbarton in Scotland, where he was the commanding officer. He remained at the depot until he was discharged from the army at Kinross on 5 November 1919. His discharge papers state that his wound was received at Bouleaux Wood and that it was *"severe with some degree of permanence"*.

Charles arrived in Campden after the First World War and lived at the Guild House in Sheep Street. He was employed as a customs inspector of public houses and during the Second World War he was a captain in the Home Guard. He left Campden in the early 1970's and went to live at Winchcombe, where he died on 10 February 1979 aged 92 years.

Arthur George Ellis

Corporal 766712, "D" Company, 28th Battalion (Artists' Rifles), London Regiment
Lieutenant, Royal Flying Corps

Born: 1 May 1899
Enlisted: 17 August 1917
Died: 22 August 1987

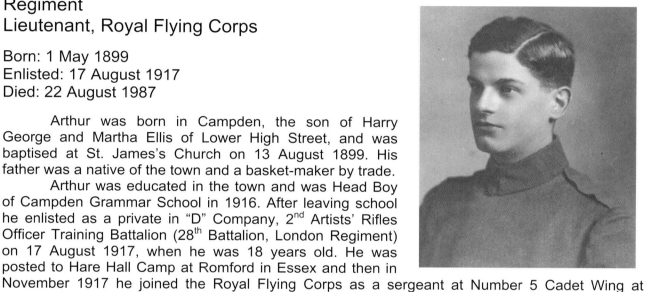

Arthur was born in Campden, the son of Harry George and Martha Ellis of Lower High Street, and was baptised at St. James's Church on 13 August 1899. His father was a native of the town and a basket-maker by trade.

Arthur was educated in the town and was Head Boy of Campden Grammar School in 1916. After leaving school he enlisted as a private in "D" Company, 2nd Artists' Rifles Officer Training Battalion (28th Battalion, London Regiment) on 17 August 1917, when he was 18 years old. He was posted to Hare Hall Camp at Romford in Essex and then in November 1917 he joined the Royal Flying Corps as a sergeant at Number 5 Cadet Wing at Hastings. In 1918 he obtained his commission and by the end of the war he held the rank of lieutenant. Arthur did not serve overseas during the First World War.

In 1918 he was admitted to hospital and this was followed by a period of convalescence in Brighton. He then took a course in land surveying at Southampton University. After he qualified as a land surveyor he went out to Uganda in 1921, where he was always known as George. In 1924 he returned to England on leave and married his first wife, Gloria. They had two children, Jacqueline and Michael, who were both born in Uganda. This marriage ended in divorce when Jacqueline was only 2 years old and Arthur then married his second wife, Millicent Guppy.

Arthur worked in Uganda for 18 years, moving to Ethiopia in 1939. During the Second World War he served as a major in the 5th Battalion, King's African Rifles in Kenya and was awarded six medals for his time in the army in Africa. After the war he became an engineer with the East African Railway Company in Kenya. In 1962 he moved to South Africa and lived there until he died on 22 August 1987 aged 88 years. He was survived by his third wife, Dorothy, who then returned to live at Seaton in Devon. He is buried at Port Shepstone, Natal, South Africa.

Arthur's son, Michael George Rupert Ellis, was a lieutenant with the Grenadier Guards and he died on 26 March 1946 aged 20 years. He is buried in Cologne Southern Cemetery in Germany.

Gordon Ellis
Private 13734, 5th Battalion Canadian Expeditionary Force

Born: 7 November 1894
Enlisted: 17 September 1914
Died: 24 May 1915

Gordon was born in Campden, the third son of Harry George and Ellen Ellis, and was baptised at St. James's Church on 14 April 1895. His mother died on 4 October 1895 aged 33 years; subsequently Harry married his second wife, Martha, and had six more children.

Gordon attended school in the town and the family address was recorded as Lower High Street in the admissions registers. This was where his parents ran their fishmongers and basket-making business. After leaving school Gordon joined his parents in the family business. In 1909 he joined the Boys' Brigade which had been started in Campden by his father and two years later, aged 17 years, he joined "H" Company, 5th Battalion, Gloucestershire Regiment, the local company of the Territorial Army.

At the age of 15 years his brother Roland emigrated to Canada to work as a farm labourer in Saskatchewan with the Walton family from Campden. In March 1913 he returned to England for his sister's wedding and when he went back to Canada in June 1913 Gordon went with him. When Britain declared war on Germany Gordon was one of the first to enlist, joining the Canadian Army at Valcartier on 17 September 1914. He had already been a member of the Saskatchewan Light Horse since June 1913 and was immediately accepted by the authorities. His medical examination recorded that he was six feet tall with black hair, brown eyes and a dark complexion. There was a mole on the left side of his neck and three vaccination scars on his left arm. In her *Book of Remembrance* Josephine Griffiths states that he was a "*fine-looking lad*".

After a short period of training Gordon was posted to the 5th Battalion (Saskatchewan Regiment) Canadian Expeditionary Force and arrived in England with the first Canadian contingent for further training on Salisbury Plain. It was while he was in England that he was able to meet up with friends and family from Campden for one last time. He arrived in France in February 1915 and immediately transferred to a machine gun section. Three months later he was killed in action while manning his machine gun at the Battle of Festubert, which began on 15 May 1915.

Gordon is with two of his sisters, Dora and Mabel. The other man is Tom Summers, Dora's husband.

The *Evesham Journal* reported: "*It is a curious coincidence that he was killed on the sixth anniversary he first put on his Boys' Brigade uniform in Campden. Gordon was working a machine gun at the end of a communication trench which had been taken by the battalion. The trench was taken early in the morning and the enemy were bringing up troops to counter-attack and Gordon was on the gun which was mowing them down. He was struck by a shell, together with two other men, and killed instantly but not disfigured. They were brought out and buried at night near the village of Festubert. Gordon was a universal favourite with all and he died at his post a hero.*"

Gordon died on 24 May 1915 aged 20 years and as his grave could not be identified at the end of the war his name is recorded on the Canadian Memorial at Vimy Ridge in France. The memorial stands on Hill 145 and records the names of 11,285 Canadians who died in France during the war and who have no known grave. His name is recorded on two memorials in Campden: in St. James's Church and in the High Street.

Harry Ellis
Sergeant 2215, Devonshire Regiment
Company Sergeant-Major 265645, "B" Company, 6th Battalion, Devonshire Regiment

Born: 6 December 1889
Died: 9 January 1955

Harry was born in Campden, the eldest son of Harry George and Ellen Ellis of Lower High Street, Campden. He was baptised at St. James's Church on 23 March 1890 and then attended school in the town. His father was a native of Campden and took over his parents' basket-making business in 1902 on the death of his mother, combining this with his fishmonger's shop, which was run by his second wife, Martha.

In 1903, when Harry was 14 years old, he was sent to Lincoln to work as a fishmonger but the attraction of Canada proved too great and in June 1913 he chose to make the long journey with his two brothers, Gordon and Roland, to experience a completely new life style.

At the outbreak of war in 1914 Harry returned from Canada and enlisted in the Devonshire Regiment. He was posted to the 6th Battalion and soon rose to the rank of sergeant. After a short period of training in England the battalion arrived at Karachi in India on 11 November 1914. They stayed in India until January 1916, when they were posted to Mesopotamia for the rest of the war. After hostilities had ceased the battalion was sent to Salonika in Greece and arrived there on 9 December 1918.

On his return to England Harry was discharged from the army. He then returned to Campden and married Muriel "*Madge*" Halliwell at St. James's Church on 13 February 1923. They had one child, Doreen, who was born in 1927 at Blackpool.

After their marriage in 1923 Harry and Madge decided to move to Canada, where Harry found employment as a tracklayer on the railways. They returned to England in 1926 and went to Blackpool, where they lived until 1937. The next move was to 28 Hills View, Barnstaple in Devonshire and this is where the family remained until Harry died on 9 January 1955 aged 65. He is buried in Barnstaple cemetery.

Harry George Ellis
Colour-Sergeant 2662, 1st National Reserve Company, 8th Battalion Worcestershire Regiment

Born: 10 August 1856
Enlisted: 26 October 1914
Discharged: 2 March 1916
Died: 22 December 1938

Harry was born in Campden and was the son of Henry and Hannah Ellis. His father was a basket-maker and after leaving school Harry joined him in the family business. In 1884 he married his first wife, Ellen, and they had seven children. Harry succeeded his father in the business and also carried on as a fishmonger and game dealer in the High Street.

Like his father before him, Harry was a member of the old Campden Volunteers, "K" Company, 2nd Volunteer Battalion, Gloucestershire Regiment. He was a fiercely patriotic man and

in 1897 he represented "K" Company at Queen Victoria's Diamond Jubilee celebrations in London. A *"Certificate of Good Service"* was presented to him on his retirement from the Volunteers. It stated, *"Harry George Ellis, Colour-Sergeant, joined on 14 March 1872 and retired 12 December 1901. He served with credit and was returned efficient for 29 successive years and is also the possessor of the Volunteer Long Service Medal."*

He volunteered for service in South Africa during the Boer War but was not accepted owing to his age and the fact that he was married with a family. He was an excellent drill instructor and in 1908 he started on his own initiative a Boys' Brigade Company in Campden and soon had a membership of forty boys. This proved a great local attraction and they held regular drills, parades and concerts. The value of this excellent training proved its worth in 1914, when many of the boys were old enough to enlist in the army.

At the outbreak of war Harry was listed as a company sergeant-major on the Army Reserve list. He was posted to the 1st National Reserve Company, 8th Battalion, Worcestershire Regiment on 26 October 1914 and was employed as a sergeant instructor training recruits on home service. He was 58 years old and his character and conduct throughout his 1 year and 136 days'

Harry and his daughter Augusta, 1915

service were *"exemplary"*.

After his first wife died on 4 October 1895 Harry married Martha Kate Prince and had a further six children (thirteen in total). He served on the Scuttlebrook Wake committee for many years and was a devout churchman, a great supporter of king and country and an active member of the town bowling club, being a past president and life member. He was on the Town Council for many years and was Mayor of Campden at one point.

Harry died at Barnstaple, while visiting one of his daughters, on 22 December 1938 aged 82 years and is buried in St. James's churchyard. Six former members of the Boys' Brigade carried his coffin at the funeral. The bearers were Frederick Benfield, Gerald Howell, John Howell, George Plested, John Franklin and William Payne. All but John Franklin had served overseas during the First World War.

Harry is seated fourth from the right.

Roland Ellis

Private 887469, 46th Battalion, Canadian Expeditionary Force

Born: 12 March 1891
Enlisted: 4 March 1916
Discharged: 5 March 1919
Died: 11 January 1939

Roland was born in Campden, the second son of Harry George and Ellen Ellis of High Street, Campden, and was baptised at St. James's Church on 17 May 1891. On 22 March 1906, at the age of 15, he emigrated to Canada to join the Walton family from Campden and was employed as a farm labourer. He embarked on Allen Line Steamship *Virginia* at Liverpool and his port of destination was Halifax. In March 1913 he returned to Campden for his sister's wedding and when he returned to Springside, Saskatchewan in Canada in June 1913 his brothers Harry and Gordon went with him.

He enlisted in the Canadian Army at Yorkton, Saskatchewan on 4 March 1916 when he was almost 25 years old. The medical officer passed him fit for overseas service and recorded that he was six feet three inches tall with blue eyes, a dark complexion and black hair. His religion was Church of England. He arrived in England on SS *Olympic* on 19 October 1916 with the 188th Battalion, Canadian Expeditionary Force. He was then admitted to hospital with measles on 17 November 1916. He was discharged from hospital on 30 November 1916 and was immediately sent overseas to France, where he joined the 46th Battalion, Canadian Expeditionary Force. The next nine months were spent on the Western Front, where he was wounded on 22 June 1917 but was able to rejoin his unit seven days later.

Roland's war ended when he was wounded in the neck by shrapnel on 1 September 1917 and admitted to Number 5 Canadian Field Ambulance. He was transferred to Number 23 Casualty Clearing Station and then admitted to Number 13 General Hospital in France on 4 September 1917. The wound, though serious, was not life-threatening and he was invalided back to England and admitted to hospital at Edmonton in London on 9 September 1917. After being discharged from hospital he was posted to the 15th Reserve Battalion at Bramshott on 19 October 1917. In 1918 he was awarded one Good Conduct badge and was promoted to acting lance corporal while

Roland (seated) with his brother Gordon.

he was employed as a drill instructor at Bramshott. On 15 June 1918 he had to have treatment for "*trench mouth*" but was again working as a drill instructor in August 1918.

Roland returned to the rank of private on 15 November 1918 and left Bramshott to go to Kinmel Camp at Bodelwyddan, near Rhyl in North Wales, where he remained until he began his long journey back to Canada on 18 January 1919. He was discharged from the army at Regina on 5 March and was entitled to wear three blue service chevrons.

He married Annie Dimsdale in Springside in Saskatchewan in 1921 and they had three children: Harry Gordon, Roland and Margaret. During the Second World War his son Gordon was a navigator with the Royal Canadian Air Force. When he arrived in England he was transferred to Bomber Command and served with 78 Squadron, based at Breighton, Yorkshire.

Roland died at Trail in British Columbia, Canada, on 11 January 1939 aged 47 years and is buried in Trail Rossland Memorial Cemetery in Canada. He died from a long debilitating disease that was never properly diagnosed.

Frederick Thomas Ellison
Sapper 66136, Royal Engineers

Born: 1879
Enlisted: 18 January 1915
Discharged: 20 March 1919
Died: 1957

Tom Ellison, son of Frederick,
baptised at St. James's in 1903.

Frederick was born in Campden and was the eldest child of Thomas and Kezia Ellison of Middle Row, High Street, Campden. His father died while he was still a boy and Frederick soon learnt the necessary skills to work as a saddler and harness-maker, a job that he carried out in his workshop in the High Street until he retired in 1955.

Frederick married Elizabeth Jane Tanner, a native of Bristol, at St. Paul's Church in Bedminster on 30 April 1901. They had one son, Thomas Henry, who was baptised at St. James's Church on 18 October 1903. The family home for all of their married life was in the High Street in Campden.

In the years leading up to the war Frederick was a captain in the Boys' Brigade and then a sergeant in "H" Company, 5th Battalion, Gloucestershire Regiment.

Five months after war was declared Frederick joined the Royal Engineers in January 1915 and he served throughout the war in Egypt, France, Belgium and at Gallipoli in Turkey. On 11 September 1915 the *Evesham Journal* wrote about his experiences at Gallipoli:

"*Mrs. Ellison, of Campden, has received a long-delayed letter from her husband, Mr. F. T. Ellison, saddler, who, it will be remembered, joined the Royal Engineers in January last. Mr. Ellison, who sailed with the 85th Field Company of the Royal Engineers for the Dardanelles, writes from the base hospital as follows. 'I wrote to you about ten days ago, but fire in the camp destroyed the letter. When we arrived here we stayed for a week on an island before going up to the front. I was with the party that forced a new landing under shellfire. I went into the trenches for two days and nights. Taking things all round, we had a real rough time of it. All the clothing we had was what we stood up in, and nothing more. This is written in hospital after being wounded in the body, right leg and knee. My wounds are not dangerous, and I am pleased to say I am going on all right. I am still very stiff and will not be able to get about for a few days. I had one or two narrow escapes and I think I am one of the lucky ones to come out of it alive. Please remember me to all of my old friends.'*"

Frederick was wounded while serving at Gallipoli in August 1915 and after arriving back in England he was admitted to the Countess of Lytton's Hospital in London.

After the war Frederick returned to Campden and became a founder member of the *Comrades of the Great War*, which developed into the British Legion. He also continued his job as a saddler where, from his workshop, he could watch the stream of life go by and there was an easy exit to the nearest hostelry for a well-deserved pint of cider. He retired in 1955 but unfortunately lost his wife soon afterwards. During the Second World War he served as a special constable.

Frederick died in January 1957 aged 78 years and is buried in St. James's churchyard. His coffin was covered with a Union Jack bearing a wreath of Flanders poppies. His obituary sums him up as "*an unforgettable character, latterly remarkable for his unrestrained remarks on man, nature and human life*".

Thomas Elsley
Royal Flying Corps

Thomas was born at Alcester in 1884, the son of John and Elizabeth Elsley. In 1901 his father was living in High Street, Alcester and trading as an ironmonger. Thomas was then aged 16 and employed by his father as an assistant in the shop.

Thomas came to Campden in the early 1900's and set up his ironmongery business on the top side of the High Street. In 1912 William Horne, who ran a newsagent's and stationer's shop in Cheltenham House, retired and leased his shop to Thomas. Two years later he bought the building. The business grew over the next few years and in 1921 he bought the adjoining property when the Live and Let Live pub closed down. This gave him even greater opportunities to display his goods, which at the time included china, seeds, nails, paint, padlocks and toys. In 1930 he bought a property next door to the Noel Arms Hotel, which was previously Prout's, and relocated all his goods into this new shop.

In 1939 Thomas retired and went to live in Bridport. Two years later he sold the premises to Lewis Keeley and the range of goods sold in the shop expanded further.

Thomas married Ina Risdon in Somerset in 1912 and they had two children, Thomas Escott and Ruth Elworthy, who were both baptised at St. James's Church in Campden. During the First World War he served in the Royal Flying Corps.

He died in 1969 aged 76 years and is buried in Bridport, Dorset. His grandson Bryan was a journalist with the *Evesham Journal* for many years.

William Evans
Private 1263747, 38th Battalion, Canadian Expeditionary Force

Born: June 1884
Enlisted: 28 March 1918
Discharged: 27 March 1919
Died: March 1945

William was born William Evans Warner in Campden in 1884 and was the only son of William Wyatt and Emily Elizabeth Warner of High Street, Campden. His father was a native of the town and a "*teacher of music and a pianoforte tuner*". After leaving school William found employment as a farmer and in 1908 he emigrated to Canada, where he dropped the surname Warner as he felt that it sounded too German, remaining William Evans for the rest of his life. He worked as a teamster in various parts of Western Canada and developed a love of horses.

When the war started in 1914 William was living at Luseland in Saskatchewan and it was not until he was drafted under the Military Services Act, 1917 that he joined the army. He was medically examined at Saskatoon in Saskatchewan on 11 January 1918, when he was 33 years old, and graded A2. He was five feet seven inches tall with brown hair, brown eyes and a dark complexion. Now that he was passed fit to join the army he enlisted in the 1st Depot Battalion, Saskatchewan Regiment, Canadian Army at Regina on 28 March 1918 and was given the service number 258965. The next of kin stated on his army papers was his youngest sister, Beatrice, who was living in Campden and married to William Smith. A short period of training followed in Canada with the 15th Reserve Battalion, where William was issued with a new army number, 1263747.

William arrived in England on board SS *Melita* on 28 April 1918 and he joined the 28th Battalion, Canadian Expeditionary Force for final training before he was posted to France. He entered France on 7 September and was posted to the 38th Battalion. On 29 September he was wounded in the back by shrapnel from an exploding shell and was evacuated back to England after a spell in hospital at Wimereux near Calais. He was admitted to hospital in Manchester on 12 October and was then transferred to Woodcote Park Military General Hospital in Epsom. The war was now over and his stay in hospital ended on 6 January 1919 when the doctors reported that there was "*no evidence of the wound in the back, all bruises had healed and there was no evidence of disability*".

William now joined a large group of Canadian soldiers in England and Wales desperate to return to Canada. The war was over and the men could not understand why it was taking so long to organise their passage home. On 25 January 1919 William was admitted to the Canadian Special Hospital at Whitley, near Bury, after contracting an illness and was discharged after seventeen days on 10 February. He returned to his unit at Seaford but was then sent to Kinmel Camp at Bodewyddan, near Rhyl in North Wales, on 18 March 1919 to wait for his passage home. He finally left Wales a few days later and was discharged from the army on 27 March after arriving back in Canada.

William returned to Luseland and married Winnifred Elizabeth Bulter at Moose Jaw, Saskatchewan on 10 January 1920. They had five children: William, Leroy, Robert, Thomas and David. He continued farming and then ran a Drayline, continuing his love of horses, right up until his death in 1945.

William died of a heart attack in March 1945 aged 60 years and is buried in Luseland. His son William served in the Canadian Air Force from 1941 to 1945 and was with Number 6 Bomber Command near York.

James Farquhar
Lieutenant-Colonel, Royal Field Artillery

Born: 1 December 1875
Died: 31 January 1961

James was born in Brecon in 1875, the son of Lieutenant-Colonel and Mrs. H. R. Farquhar, of Wickham, Hampshire and of Appleshaw, Compton, Winchester.

After completing his education James took up a commission with the Royal Artillery and saw service in the Boer War and afterwards in West Africa. He then served in India but when war was declared in 1914 he returned to serve in France, where he won the Distinguished Service Order (DSO). In June 1915 he went to Gallipoli and then to Palestine, where he won a second DSO. He was also mentioned in despatches six times during the war.

In the post-war years James took a keen interest in the affairs of the Church and was on the Worcester Diocesan Council for many years when he lived at Leigh Lodge near Worcester. He moved to Tithe House, Campden in 1947 and remained in the town for the remainder of his life.

James died on 31 January 1961 aged 85 and is buried in St. James's churchyard. His wife, Frances Benita, died on 18 April 1973 aged 81.

Cecil Ernest Figgitt
Able Seaman J32479, Royal Navy

Born: 17 December 1898
Enlisted: 7 September 1914

Cecil was born in Birmingham, the son of Christopher and Ellen Figgitt. He was baptised in Weston-sub-Edge and attended the village school before his parents moved to Sheep Street in Campden. He finished his education in the town and then enlisted in the Royal Navy on 7 September 1914 as a boy second class when he was only 15 years old. He was five feet three inches tall with blue eyes and had a scar on the back of his head. After an initial period of basic training he was promoted to ordinary seaman in July 1916. He then signed up for twelve years' service with the Royal Navy on 17 December 1916, when he reached 18 years old.

During the 1914-18 war Cecil served on HMS *Powerful*, HMS *Argyll* and HMS *Revenge* and at HMS *Vivid,* a shore base in Devonport. When the war ended Cecil was an able seaman and had been serving on HMS *Revenge* for over two years.

In 1921 he was promoted again and began his service as a petty officer on HMS *Impregnable,* a Royal Navy training ship at Devonport. He then joined the crew of HMS *Maidstone* and was still serving in the Royal Navy in 1929 when details of his service end on his personal papers held at the National Archives in London.

Cecil married Nellie Cowell in Newton Abbot in Devon in 1928 and died in 1971 aged 72 years.

Edgar Fisher
Private 9906, 1st Battalion, Welsh Regiment
Private 250191, 544th Home Service Employment Company, Labour Corps

> Born: 8 May 1888
> Died: 27 June 1918

Edgar was born in Broad Campden, the son of Fanny Fisher, dressmaker, and was baptised at St. James's Church on 9 June 1895, when he was 7 years old.

At the outbreak of war the 1st Battalion, Welsh Regiment were in India but they returned to Wales on 22 December 1914 and were attached to the 84th Brigade of the 28th Division, which was formed in England in December 1914 and January 1915. Edgar enlisted at Cardiff and joined the 1st Battalion, Welsh Regiment and arrived in France with them on 16 January 1915. They landed at Le Havre with the 28th Division and made their way north into Belgium, where they took part in the Second Battle of Ypres during April and May 1915. Later that year the battalion fought at the Battle of Loos in September before it embarked for Egypt at Marseille in October 1915. The battalion arrived at Salonika in Greece with the 28th Division in November 1915 and stayed there for the rest of the war.

It is not clear when Edgar left the battalion but he was invalided back to Great Britain either because of wounds or illness contracted at Salonika. In 1918 he was serving in the 544th Home Service Employment Company, Labour Corps when he was admitted to hospital at Kinmel Camp at Bodelwyddan, near Rhyl, in North Wales. He died in hospital on 28 June 1918 aged 30 years and was buried in St. Margaret's churchyard, Bodelwyddan, Flintshire, North Wales. St. Margaret's Church is also known as "*The Marble Church*" and the military hospital was situated nearby. The churchyard also contains the graves of several Canadian soldiers who died at Kinmel Camp.

The *Evesham Journal* reported Edgar's death under the headline, "*Broad Campden Soldier's Death*". In her *Book of Remembrance* Josephine Griffiths states that Fanny "*had four sons serving in His Majesty's forces at the same time*", Edgar, James, Hubert and John.

Hubert Fisher
Mining Corps

Hubert was born in Broad Campden on 2 August 1885, the son of Fanny Fisher, dressmaker, and was baptised at St. James's Church on 9 June 1895, when he was 9 years old. He entered Campden Mixed Infant School in 1890 and after leaving school found employment as an agricultural labourer. In 1901 he was living with his mother in Kitchen Lane, Broad Campden.

Very little is known about Hubert but he is listed on the 1918 electoral roll as resident in Broad Campden and absent on military service. In her *Book of Remembrance* Josephine Griffiths states that he served with the "*Mining Corps*".

James Ivins Fisher
Private 298, Coldstream Guards
Sergeant-Major 1865, Royal Glamorganshire Yeomanry

> Born: 9 February 1876
> Died: 19 June 1960

James was born in Broad Campden, the son of Fanny Fisher, dressmaker. He entered Campden Mixed Infant School in March 1881. When he was 18 years old he enlisted in the Coldstream Guards as a regular soldier. He served in South Africa during the Boer War and was present at the Battle of Belmont in November 1899. At the end of the war he received the Queen's South Africa Medal with a clasp for Belmont.

After leaving the army James found employment as a groom and on 14 March 1903 he married Kate Keefe, daughter of David Keefe, labourer, at St. John's Parish Church, Tondu, Bridgend, Glamorgan. They had five daughters.

At the outbreak of war in 1914 James was 38 years old and after being mobilised he joined the Royal Glamorganshire Yeomanry, which became a battalion of the Welsh Regiment. He was a squadron sergeant-major and on the photograph he is wearing a Royal Arms cap badge which was worn by a volunteer regiment, the equivalent of the Home Guard.

James lived most of his life in Bridgend and died there on 19 June 1960 aged 84 years.

Fanny Fisher, James's mother, died on 6 October 1931 aged 86 years and is buried in Bridgend.

John Fisher
Glamorgan Yeomanry

Born: 25 February 1879

John was born in Broad Campden, the son of Fanny Fisher, dressmaker, and was baptised at St. James's Church on 9 June 1895, when he was 16 years old. He attended Campden Mixed Infants School from 1885-1887 and on the 1901 census his occupation is recorded as "wheel finisher".

Very little is known about John but in her *Book of Remembrance* Josephine Griffiths lists him as serving in the Glamorganshire Yeomanry during the war. It must be assumed that he was employed on home service only as no medal index card could be found for him at the National Archives in London.

George Fletcher
Private 9555, 2nd Battalion, Gloucestershire Regiment

Born: 30 April 1892

George was born in Campden, the son of Ann Fletcher, a charwoman, of Wyatt's Yard, Back Ends, Campden and was baptised at St. Catharine's Church on 9 October 1892.

He was a regular soldier before the war with the 2nd Battalion, Gloucestershire Regiment and at the outbreak of war in August 1914 they were stationed in Northern China. They arrived back in England on 8 November 1914 and after a months' reorganisation they embarked for France at Southampton on SS *City of Chester*. George arrived in France on 19 December. During the winter months he suffered badly from frostbitten feet and had to be evacuated back to England for treatment in hospital. He returned to France on 21 June 1915 and took part in the Battle of Loos in September 1915, during which the British Army used poison gas for the first time. George was taken ill during the battle with inflammation of the lungs and malaria fever and was sent to base hospital for a week before being admitted to Warncliffe War Hospital in Sheffield. After being discharged from hospital he spent a period of leave at home with his mother in Campden before returning to France.

In 1916 George was again wounded but was able to rejoin his unit after treatment.

Thomas Fletcher
Gloucestershire Regiment

Born: 25 March 1898

Thomas was born in Campden, the son of Ann Fletcher, a charwoman, of Wyatt's Yard, Back Ends, Campden. He was educated in the town and on the 1918 electoral roll his home was recorded as Sheep Street and he was absent on military service.

Thomas Floyd
Private M-337064, Army Service Corps

Born: 1891

Thomas was born in Walthamstow, the son of John and Mary Ann Floyd of 2 Myrtle Road, Walthamstow. His father was a native of Bethnal Green, London and a carpenter and joiner by trade. During the war Thomas enlisted in the Army Service Corps and served overseas in a theatre of war after the start of 1916. He was back in England in 1918 when he married Florence Ellen Plested, daughter of William and Jane Plested, at St. James's Church, Campden on 16 March.

Christopher Jack Forster
Private, London University Officers' Training Corps
Able Seaman LZ/1439, 3rd Reserve Battalion, Royal Naval Division
Lieutenant, Royal Field Artillery, attached 3rd Company, Special Brigade, Royal Engineers

Born: 27 May 1895
Enlisted: 7 October 1914
Died: 21 July 1917

Christopher was born in Campden Vicarage during the time of his father's incumbency and was baptised at St. James's Church on 28 July 1895. His parents were Rev. Francis Samuel and Lola Pauline Forster, who were married at St. James's Church on 6 November 1890. Lola was the daughter of William Higford and Ellen Griffiths of Bedfont House.

Christopher had a defect in his right eye from birth but this did not affect his vision or stop him from joining the army in 1914. He enlisted in the London University Officers' Training Corps on 7 October 1914 and served with them until 14 March 1915. He then transferred to the 3rd Reserve Battalion, Royal Naval Division and served with them at Blandford Camp in England until 13 November 1915. He was granted a commission with the 9th Battalion, Somerset Light Infantry on 17 November 1915 but he did not take up this posting as he had applied for a commission with the Royal Field Artillery. On 26 November 1915 his commission with the Somerset Light Infantry was cancelled and in December he joined the Royal Field Artillery as a 2nd lieutenant and arrived in France just in time to qualify for a 1915 Star campaign medal. After serving on the Western Front for just over a year he was attached to the Royal Engineers on 5 February 1917 but three days later he was admitted to Number 10 Stationary Hospital at St. Omer with severe rheumatic fever. He was transferred to hospital at Boulogne and then embarked at Boulogne on the *Cambria* and arrived back in England on 16 February. He entered a convalescent hospital at 6, Clarendon Terrace in Brighton on 28 February and after a medical examination at Caxton Hall he was graded as "*unfit for service for at least two months*". A further medical examination followed at the 2nd Eastern General Hospital in Brighton on 11 April when he was again graded as "*unfit for active service for six weeks but fit for service at home*". The board recommended twenty-one days' leave.

Christopher reported to Withnoe Camp at Devonport on 2 May 1917 to begin his home service after his leave had finished and on 22 May he was passed fit for active service at the Military Hospital in Devonport. When he returned to France he was attached to the Royal

Engineers and in July 1917 he was in Belgium as the British Army prepared for the start of the Battle of Passchendaele. Christopher died at Remi Sidings Casualty Clearing Station at Lijssenthoek near Poperinge on 21 July 1917 aged 22 years. Lijssenthoek was situated on the main communication line between bases in the rear and the Ypres battlefields. The trains carrying the wounded soldiers stopped and men were carried on stretchers to be treated by the doctors.

He was not married. His name is recorded on the war memorial in St. James's Church in Campden. At the time of their son's death Francis and Lola had left Campden and were living at Frinsbury Cottage, Loose, Maidstone, Kent.

Christopher is buried in Lijssenthoek Cemetery near Poperinge in Belgium. William Byrd is also buried in the same cemetery, making this the only cemetery on the Western Front that contains the graves of more than one man from Campden.

Albert John Franklin
Royal Marines

Born: 3 May 1898
Died: 9 June 1966

Jack was born in Campden, the son of William Henry and Ellen Franklin, and was baptised at St. James's Church on 25 July 1899 at the same time as his younger brother, Leonard. His father was a regular soldier and died during the Boer War in South Africa.

At the outbreak of war in 1914 Jack was only 16 years old. He enlisted in the Royal Marines and returned to Campden safely at the end of the war.

Jack married his first wife, Maria Anna Reddy, at St. Catharine's Church in Campden on 1 March 1928. When Jack died on 9 June 1966 aged 68 years he was survived by his second wife, Mary Plested. He was buried in St. James's churchyard.

Frederick Edward Franklin
Private, Gloucestershire Regiment
Private 267996, Royal Warwickshire
Regiment

Born: 9 January 1888
Discharged: 31 December 1917
Died: 16 November 1958

Fred was born in Blockley, the third son of William Henry and Eliza Franklin. His father was a coachman and groom although he also worked as an agricultural labourer later in life. After leaving Blockley the family moved to Campden and lived in Back Ends, Watery Lane and the High Street.

Fred was educated in the town and then found employment in a variety of jobs including gardener, agricultural labourer, builder's labourer and biscuit-maker at the factory near Campden railway station. At the age of 15 he joined "K" Company, 2nd Volunteer Battalion, Gloucestershire Regiment on 26 August 1903. The Volunteers became the Territorials on 5 August 1908 and Fred continued spending his weekends, and a fortnight each summer, with several other Campden men learning how to march, drill, shoot and act like regular soldiers.

When war was declared in 1914 Fred had been with the Gloucestershire Regiment eleven years. He was mobilised on 5 August and went with the battalion to Chelmsford. He did not sign up for overseas service and remained in England when the battalion arrived in France on 29 March 1915. On 10 April 1916 his time with the Territorial Army expired and he was discharged from the Gloucestershire Regiment. Three months later he enlisted in the Royal Warwickshire Regiment on 21 July 1916. Soon after arriving in France Fred was involved in a raid on a trench that had only recently been occupied by the Germans and they *"found an officer with a shiny pointed helmet and a smart uniform with all buttons polished"*. They jumped on him and took him prisoner.

In January 1917 Fred developed *"trench foot"* after a long period of being in the trenches and was evacuated out of the firing line to recover. He ended up in the same hospital in England as Tom Nobes, a friend from Campden. After leaving hospital he was sent to Cork in Ireland for a period of convalescence. The sea crossing was very rough and they were not allowed below deck.

Fred never fully recovered from his *"trench foot"* and was discharged from the army on 31 December 1917. He was awarded a small pension that was stopped in 1922.

Fred lost two of his very special pals during the war, Frank Merriman, who died of wounds in 1917, and Mark Merriman, who was killed in action in 1918.

After the war Fred was granted a bounty of £25 to start up in market gardening in the council ground on Aston Road in Campden. He was in partnership with his brother Jim and they each had an acre of land. They grew good produce but there were no customers in the depressed market of the 1920's. The brothers soon gave up the ground and looked to other ways of earning a living. When the ground was being worked both brothers were unmarried and living with their parents in Watery Lane.

Fred married Jane *"Ginny"* Harper, from Littledean, in 1926 and they had one son, Clifford, who became a policeman in Birmingham. Fred found work as a builder's labourer and as a postman and the family home was 6 Royal Terrace, Sheep Street, Campden.

Fred died on 16 November 1958 aged 70 and is buried in St. James's churchyard.

James Franklin
Private 635, 5th Battalion, Gloucestershire Regiment
Private 50914, 13th (Works) Battalion, Devonshire Regiment
Lance Corporal 101605, 170th Company, Labour Corps

Born: 3 August 1889
Mobilised: 5 August 1914
Discharged: 5 April 1919
Died: 1950

Jim was born in Campden, the youngest son of William Henry and Eliza Franklin. His father was born in Blockley in 1851 and was a coachman and groom, although in 1901 he was employed as an agricultural labourer. The family home in Campden was recorded as Lane's Yard in the High Street on the 1901 census but they also lived in Back Ends and Watery Lane.

Jim attended school in the town and then found employment as a gardener and builder's labourer. He enlisted in the 2nd Volunteer Battalion, Gloucestershire Regiment on 18 November 1906. When war broke out in 1914 he was still living at home with his parents. He was mobilised on 5 August and was employed on home service until he arrived on the Western Front on 26 February 1917. During his time in France he served as a stretcher-bearer and orderly with a field dressing station.

Jim was discharged from the army on 5 April 1919 after over twelve years of unbroken military service. He returned to Campden where, together with his brother Frederick, he took a £25 bounty and set up with one acre of ground on Aston Road, where they grew vegetables. Life was hard in the depressed market of the 1920's and they struggled to make ends meet. Jim was unable to settle and suffered periods of deep depression owing to his war experiences. He left Campden in the mid-1920's to travel the country, unable to forget the war and lead a settled life.

Jim died in 1950 aged 61, one of the casualties of the war that were not counted, and is buried in Cirencester. He never married.

Jim's brother, William Henry, died of dysentery during the Boer War on 4 February 1900.

Leonard Franklin
Royal Warwickshire Regiment

> Born: 31 May 1899
> Died: 27 January 1967

Leonard was born in Campden, the son of William Henry and Ellen Franklin, and was baptised at St. James's Church on 25 July 1899 at the same time as his younger brother, Jack. His father was a regular soldier and he died of dysentery at De Aar in South Africa during the Boer War on 4 February 1900 aged 27 years. The family were living in an army home in Liverpool at the time but after her husband's death Ellen returned to Campden with her two youngest sons, Leonard and Jack. She was in Lane's Yard in 1901 and "*living on her own means*". Her eldest son, Bill, was placed into an orphanage in Liverpool. On 10 October 1901 she married her second husband, Thomas Cross, at St. James's Church.

During the First World War Leonard enlisted in the Royal Warwickshire Regiment and before he was discharged from the army he served with horses at the Khyber Pass. The 1918 electoral roll lists Leonard as absent on military service and gives his address in Campden as Sheep Street, where his mother and stepfather were living.

After the war he left Campden and married Florence Knott from Medway in Kent. They had one child, a son named Leonard Charles, who joined the Royal Air Force at the outbreak of the Second World War and was stationed at Babbington. The family home was in Piggotts Road in Caversham near Reading and Leonard worked with horses and then became involved in repair and conservation work at the ruins of Reading Abbey. During the Second World War he served the community as a lookout on top of Reading Town Hall.

Leonard died on 27 January 1967 aged 67 years and is buried in Caversham Crematorium. On his death certificate his occupation was recorded as "*corporation fence erector, retired*".

William Henry Franklin
Private 1674, "B" Company, 1st Battalion, Royal Warwickshire Regiment
Private 70753, Machine Gun Corps

> Born: 14 September 1894
> Enlisted: 9 September 1910
> Discharged: 16 September 1918
> Died: 16 November 1963

Bill was born in St. Mary's in Warwick, the son of William Henry and Ellen Franklin, and was baptised at St. James's Church in Campden on 28 October 1894. His father served as a regular soldier with the 2nd Battalion, Royal Warwickshire Regiment and died of dysentery at De Aar in South Africa during the Boer War on 4 February 1900 aged 27 years. His mother, Ellen Pinchin, married her second husband, Thomas Cross, on 10 October 1901.

Bill was only five years old when his father died and at the time was living with his mother in an army home in Liverpool. His mother returned to Campden and Bill spent the next nine years in an orphanage at South-End Institution, Hampton Street, Toxteth, Liverpool. On 7th September 1910 Miss Evelyn Black, Superintendent of the orphanage, wrote the following report on Bill to support his application to join the army:

"*This is to certify that William Franklin, who was an inmate of the above-named institution during a period of nine years, is a youth of good character. He was committed to the care of the trustees by the war department of the British Government. His conduct throughout was very good.*"

Bill enlisted in the Royal Warwickshire Regiment on 9 September 1910 aged 15 years and 361 days. He signed up for twelve years and his mother had to send a letter of consent as he was still under age. The medical examination at Worcester on 13 September 1910 passed him fit to join the army and it stated that he was five feet two inches tall and weighed 95 lbs. He had a sallow complexion, blue eyes, brown hair and a large brown birthmark on his left leg. His pulse rate was 96 and he had a scar on the third finger of his left hand. His religion was Church of England.

The period up to the start of the First World War was spent on home service and he began his army life at Lichfield with the 2nd Battalion as a drummer boy and musician. During this time in England Bill was guilty of two offences:

6 October 1911: "*Smoking while on boy service*"

23 August 1912: "*Dirty bugle on parade*".

For each of these he received a punishment of five days confined to barracks although a report on his military character dated 29 September 1913 stated that he was "*a hard-working, willing man with a strong character*".

When the war started Bill embarked at Southampton on SS *Caldonia* and arrived at Boulogne in France on 22 August 1914 with "B" Company, 1st Battalion, Royal Warwickshire Regiment. He saw his first action near Le Cateau on 26 August 1914, the battalion suffering 47 casualties. After the retreat from Mons the battalion were part of the "*Race to the Sea*" which saw them advance from the River Marne and arrive in Belgium to take part in the First Battle of Ypres. They were in the front line on Christmas day 1914 and the war diary records that there was a "*local truce and the dead in front of the trenches were buried*".

Bill served continuously on the Western Front for the next three years and qualified as a grenadier at the 10th Infantry Grenade School on 12 December 1915. He transferred to the 10th Company, Machine Gun Corps on 2 December 1916 and then during the Third Battle of Ypres (also known as the Battle of Passchendaele) Bill was mentioned in despatches for his excellent conduct in the field. The certificate was dated 7 November 1917 and it was reported in the *London Gazette* on page 13474 on 24 December 1917.

The war on the Western Front ended for Bill on 4 October 1917 when he received gunshot wounds to his chest and shoulder during the Battle of Passchendaele. The *Evesham Journal* reported that there was "*no cause for immediate anxiety*". He was admitted to the 11th Stationary Hospital at Rouen in France on 10 October 1917 before being returned to England, where he received treatment at the 1st Southern General Hospital at Edgbaston in Birmingham. He was then transferred to Birmingham Orthopaedic War Hospital at Northfields on 27 February 1918. The wounds resulted in his discharge from the army on 16 September 1918 as he was no longer fit for active service. He received his Silver War Badge on 18 November 1918 to indicate that he had made his contribution to the war. A war pension was issued.

Bill returned to Campden and married Lucy Elizabeth Warren at St. Catharine's Church on 24 December 1924. They had four children: Maria Teresa, William David, Barbara Anne and Kathleen Maria. He worked as a postman and barber in Campden and many people remember his badly withered left hand due to the effects of mustard gas during the war.

Bill died on 16 November 1963 aged 69 years and is buried in St. Catharine's cemetery in Campden. His wife died on 23 July 1971 aged 71 years and is buried with her husband.

William French
Private T-242998, 7th Battalion, The Queen's (Royal West Surrey) Regiment

Born: 1890
Died: 21 October 1917

William was born in Potters Green near Coventry in 1890, the son of William and Ruth French. In 1901 the family were living at 25 Barnacle Lane, Shilton, Coventry and his father was employed as a waggoner on a farm.

At the outbreak of war in 1914 William was 24 years old and a married man. He enlisted at Coventry in the Royal West Surrey Regiment but did not serve overseas until after the start of

1916. When he arrived on the Western Front he joined the 7th Battalion, which was attached to the 55th Brigade of the 18th (Eastern) Division. The division arrived on the Western Front in May 1915 and in 1916 it was heavily involved in the Battle of the Somme. After the opening days of the battle in July 1916 it fought at Bazentin-le-Petit, Trones Wood and on the Ancre Heights.

On 31 July 1917 the Third Battle of Ypres opened and the battalion was involved in the fighting at Pilckem and it remained in the Ypres Salient throughout the battle, which lasted until November 1917. On 21 October 1917 William was killed in action during the assault up the ridge towards the village of Passchendaele.

William was 27 years old when he died and is buried in Cement House Cemetery near Langemarck in Belgium. In 1922 his wife was living at Lapstone House in Campden and after the death of her husband she remarried. The marriages records of St. James's Church in Campden show that on 20 December 1922 Gertrude Phoebe Emma French married Albert Edward John James, son of Joseph James.

John Joseph Galloway
Private Ply/1035, Royal Marine Artillery

Born: 6 February 1883
Enlisted: 19 August 1915
Died: 12 November 1916

John was born in Oxborough, near Swaffham in Norfolk, the younger of two sons of John and Ann Galloway. His parents married in 1877 and his father was a shepherd. On the 1891 census his mother is recorded as living in Chapel Lodge in Oxborough and listed as a widow and a charwoman. Her husband died in 1886 aged 49 years.

After leaving school John found employment as an agricultural labourer in his home village but then became a butler. He enlisted in the Royal Marine Artillery at Liverpool on 19 August 1915 and gave his year of birth as 1885. He was five feet two inches tall with grey eyes, brown hair and a scar on the calf of his right leg. His religion was Roman Catholic.

The first part of his service was spent with the Plymouth Division at their depot and while he was there he passed a musketry course on 4 November 1915. He embarked on a troopship on 8 February 1916 and landed in France later the same day. After nine months serving on the Western Front he died on 12 November 1916 during the closing stages of the Battle of the Somme. He was 33 years old and is buried in Ancre British Cemetery, two kilometres south of the village of Beaumont-Hamel, Somme, France.

John's name is recorded on the memorial in St. Catharine's Church in Campden. The reason for this is not known but he was working as a butler when he enlisted in 1915. His mother was living at 40, Vaughan Road, Southport at the time of her son's death.

Frederick Arthur Gibbins
Private 4872, 1st/5th Battalion, Gloucestershire Regiment
Private 241705, 11 Platoon, "C" Coy., 13th Bn., Gloucestershire Regiment

Born: 1890
Enlisted: 1916
Died: 9 April 1918

Frederick was born in Todenham, near Moreton-in-Marsh, in 1890, the son of Francis John and Clara Gibbins of Mollington Mill near Banbury. His father was a farmer and postmaster and in 1901 the family were living at Barton-on-the-Heath in Warwickshire.

Frederick was employed in Campden by Herbert Wixey as a grocer's assistant and lodged at 4 Gordon Cottages with Joseph Meadows. Dorothy Stanley (Joseph's daughter) can remember Frederick going away to war and not returning. In her *Book of Remembrance* Josephine Griffiths states that "*he could do anything with animals, especially with horses, and was a keen and expert rider in local sports and pastimes*".

Frederick enlisted in Campden in 1916 and was posted to the 1st/5th Battalion, Gloucestershire Regiment in France. In July 1916 the *Evesham Journal* reported that *"Private Fred Gibbins, who joined the army about four months ago, and was attached to the Devonshire Regiment, has been wounded in France during the big advance, and is now in Rednal Hospital near Birmingham"*. In a letter to a friend in Campden Frederick said, *"I got wounded on 20 July 1916 on a road by the side of a wood. We had it jolly hot for a bit. I caught it by the side of the left eye and the left cuff, my eye is very bloodshot. They don't think it will affect the sight. I have not got up yet, shall be glad when I can do so."*

Fred was attached to the 8th Battalion, Devonshire Regiment when they attacked High Wood on 20 July 1916. After a barrage the battalion started crawling towards their objective 20 minutes before Zero Hour at 3.25am. They had no trouble in taking the track or the corner of the wood after the barrage had lifted.

After recovering from his wounds Frederick returned to France and was posted to 11 Platoon, "C" Company, 13th Battalion, Gloucestershire Regiment. He was reported missing in action on 21 March 1918 when the German army began their Spring offensive but later turned up as a prisoner of war. When Frederick enlisted in the army his only dread on going to the front was the fear that he might be taken prisoner. This premonition was, alas, only too fully verified as he died while in German captivity on 9 April. He may have been one of those of "C" Company wounded by the explosion of a single German shell on the night of 21/22 March (most of the company becoming casualties in that incident) or may have simply been left behind wounded during a rearguard action as the Germans pushed forward on 22-23 March.

He was 27 years old when he died and is buried in La Chapellette British and Indian Cemetery, near Péronne in France. His name is recorded on two memorials in Campden (in St. James's Church and in the High Street) and in the church in Mollington.

In 2005 Frederick's medals were listed for sale on eBay and the author was eventually able to purchase them via another collector.

William Gould
Worcestershire Regiment

Born: 15 June 1873
Died: 3 May 1955

William was born in Weston-sub-Edge, the son of Henry and Dinah Gould, and after leaving school he found employment as an agricultural labourer. When he married Angelina Rose Tallott at St. James's Church in Campden on 30 May 1898 he was living in Camp Hill, Sparkbrook, Birmingham and employed as a carman for the London and North Western Railway Company. The 1901 census lists William and Angelina living in Aston, Birmingham with their first two children, Olive and William. The family soon returned to Campden and three children were baptised at St. James's Church: Harry and William James in 1903 and Maurice in 1905.

William moved to Weston-sub-Edge in late 1905 and four more children were baptised at St. Lawrence's Church: Marjorie Helen, Irene Mary, Florence Rose and Ronald Philip. During the war he enlisted in the Worcestershire Regiment and the 1918 electoral roll lists him as living in Main Street and absent on military service.

William, who was known as *"Weary Willie"*, lived the rest of his life in Weston-sub-Edge and died in May 1955 aged 81 years. He is buried in Weston-sub-Edge churchyard.

William James Gould
Trooper 1991, "D" Squadron, Warwickshire Yeomanry
Private 310138, Corps of Hussars

Discharged: 24 March 1919
Died: 15 May 1950

William was born in Weston-sub-Edge in 1876, the son of Samuel and Sarah Gould, and was baptised at St. Lawrence's Church on 9 January 1876. After leaving school he found employment as an agricultural labourer and a groom. He joined the Warwickshire Yeomanry and was mobilised at the outbreak of war in 1914. The Yeomanry arrived in Egypt on 20 April 1915 and William served with them in Gallipoli, Egypt, Palestine and on the Western Front before he was discharged on 24 March 1919. He was not a Campden man but in 1914 the *Evesham Journal* published a list of men who were serving in the army and it included "*Trooper W. Gould, Warwickshire Yeomanry, Chipping Campden*".

After the war William returned to Weston-sub-Edge and married Louisa Hamilton at St. Lawrence's Church on 15 February 1923. They were both 47 years old when they married and they did not have any children. They lived at the post office in Church Street which was run by Louisa, who was always known as "*Miss Hamilton*". William was known as "*Tired Tim*".

William died on 15 May 1950 aged 74 years and is buried in Weston-sub-Edge.

Hubert Edwin Green
Yeomanry Cyclists

Born: 30 December 1898

Hubert was born in Campden, the son of John and Sarah Annie Green, and was baptised at St. James's Church on 4 December 1901. His father married Sarah Annie Tomes, daughter of Edwin and Mary Tomes of High Street, Campden, in 1896. On the 1901 census Annie Green is listed as living with her son in Twine Cottages in Campden and working as a dressmaker.

Hubert was educated in the town and during the war he served with the Yeomanry Cyclists. On the Campden 1918 electoral roll he was listed as residing in the High Street and absent on military service.

In July 1916 the 2nd/1st Worcestershire Yeomanry and the 2nd/1st Gloucestershire Yeomanry were both converted to cyclist units and joined the 8th Cyclist Brigade, 2nd Cyclist Division. In November 1916 the 2nd Cyclist Division was broken up and the 2nd/1st Gloucestershire Yeomanry amalgamated with the 2nd/1st Worcestershire Yeomanry to form the 12th (Gloucester and Worcester) Yeomanry Cyclist Regiment in the 4th Cyclist Brigade at Ipswich. In March 1917 the 12th Cyclist Regiment was disbanded and the two units resumed their separate identities and continued as cyclists in the 4th Cyclist Brigade.

Richard Green
Sergeant 29692, 91st Siege Battery, Royal Garrison Artillery

Born: 11 October 1887
Enlisted: 19 September 1908
Discharged: 17 September 1918
Died: 30 November 1960

Richard was the son of Richard and Mary Green of 22 Coronation Street, Bengeworth , Evesham. After leaving school he worked as a market gardener but at the age of 20 years and 11 months he enlisted at Worcester in the Royal Garrison Artillery on 19 September 1908. He gave his place of birth as Badsey and his last permanent address as Evesham. The medical examination stated that he had brown eyes and dark brown hair. There was a large scar from his right buttock to his left foot.

Richard signed on for eight years in the army and four years in the reserve and began his first period of overseas service when he arrived in Hong Kong on 1 October 1909. He returned to England in 1913 and married Mary Elizabeth Hawtin. When the war started in 1914 Richard was still in England and he remained on home service until he arrived in France on 25 May 1916. His unit left Folkestone at 6.30pm and arrived at Boulogne at 8.30pm. They remained at Boulogne until 1 June 1916, when they left in lorries heading for Pommier, a village situated behind the British lines at the northern end of the Somme battlefield. During his time in France Richard kept a diary which was given to the author while this book was being written. When the Battle of the Somme started on 1 July 1916 he was at Hébuterne and saw dozens of German prisoners being brought in and a lot of British wounded with very severe injuries. He returned to his battery at Sailly-au-Bois later that day and on 21 July 1916 he had a lucky escape when twenty German artillery shells landed in the village, some landing only twenty yards from him.

Richard and Mary Elizabeth Hawtin, 1913

The next two months were spent in and around the area of Pommier, Sailly-au-Bois and Hébuterne and on 19 September 1916 Richard completed his initial period of eight years' service in the army, but as the war was still in progress he remained in France. His diary states that *"it was a nasty day and we engaged another Hun battery and smashed it up after 18 rounds"*. On 25 September the diary records that Richard *"rose at 7.00am and had two targets to engage. We fired 200 rounds by 11.00am. At 2.00pm we engaged another battery and smashed it up in 30 rounds. We gave them the other 170 rounds for luck."*

Richard is on the left.

On 18 October 1916 Richard was promoted to sergeant and his diary entry for 24 October 1916 states that *"we are continually firing day and night. On average we are firing 50 rounds a day."* As the Battle of the Somme drew to a close Richard had the opportunity to visit Beaumont-Hamel after its capture in November 1916. He saw *"the Hun dugouts and lots of dead Huns"*. The following day saw a fatal accident to Number 2 Gun of his battery. Corporal Clemans, Gunner Ritchie and Gunner Whiting were all killed and are all buried at Mailly Maillet in France.

On 9 April 1917 the 91st Siege Battery had moved north to Arras and Richard went to Point de Jour Farm near Athies, east of Arras, to prepare for the arrival of 13th Corps Heavy Artillery. The following day Richard was involved in the capture of a German battery. He then fired ten rounds of percussion shrapnel, five gas shells and ten rounds of rifle fire at the enemy. For this brave action he was recommended for a Distinguished Conduct Medal.

Richard continued serving on the Western Front until January 1918, when he received a gunshot wound to his left arm which caused a severe compound fracture of the bone. He was admitted to Number 11 Stationary Hospital at Rouen before

Corporal Richard Green, RGA, is sitting second from the right.

returning to England on 7 March. The remaining months of Richard's service were spent in England before he was discharged from the army on 17 September 1918 as no longer fit for service owing to his wounds after serving 9 years and 364 days with the colours. His commanding officer wrote the following character reference for him: "*A thoroughly sober, steady, hardworking and intelligent non-commissioned officer. Honest and reliable.*"

On 8 December 1917 it was announced that Richard was going to be awarded two Belgian medals for distinguished conduct and gallantry in the field when working alongside the Belgian Army: the Belgian Croix de Guerre and the Ordre de Léopold, Chevalier. These medals, together with his two British campaign medals, were presented to Campden British Legion by his family and they were seen hanging in a frame for many years in the club.

After the war Richard settled in Campden and lived at 2, Aston Road in one of the houses built by the Council for returning servicemen. On 1 January 1920 he was enrolled as a member of the "*Comrades of the Great War*" and then became a founder member of the British Legion. He worked as a plasterer and builder and during the Second World War he was a special constable.

Richard died from cancer at Stratford-upon-Avon Hospital on 30 November 1960 aged 73 years and is buried in St. James's churchyard in Campden. His wife died on 17 June 1984 aged 97 years and is buried with her husband. They did not have any surviving children. Mary gave birth to triplets but two died almost immediately. The third, Tommy, died aged 8 years when he fell out of a tree and drowned in a pool of water - a tragic set of circumstances that Richard and Mary never got over.

George Richard Greenall
Private 3076, King's Liverpool Regiment
Private 2322, Gloucestershire Regiment
Private 213373, Labour Corps

Born: 1872
Enlisted: 1887
Discharged: 24 September 1917
Died: September 1935

George was born in Wormington in 1872, the son of George Richard and Mary Greenall. His father was a carpenter and the family were living in Mickleton in 1881 and in Cider Mill Lane in Campden in 1891. In 1887 George ran away from Campden and enlisted in the King's Liverpool Regiment, giving his age as 18 years. He served in India, Bermuda, Egypt and Canada and after 10 years and 178 days in the army, 8 years of which were spent abroad, he returned to England and in June 1897 he transferred to the Army Reserve. He then returned to Campden and married May Pinchin at St. James's Church on 22 July 1899.

At the outbreak of the Boer War in October 1899 he rejoined his regiment and served in South Africa throughout the campaign. He was severely wounded by shell fire but recovered in hospital and was able to rejoin his unit. Poor May – married three months and then alone for nearly three years! In the 1901 census she was living in Lower High Street next to the Red Lion on Sheep Street corner and is listed as living on a war fund. George's brother, Ernest Herman, served in South Africa with the 2nd Battalion, Duke of Cornwall's Light Infantry.

George returned safely from South Africa and was discharged in July 1902. He returned to his wife in Campden and got down to the business of raising a family. They had four children, all baptised at St. James's Church: Florence Gertrude, Ellen Miriam, George Richard and Fanny Bertha.

At the outbreak of the First World War George volunteered for service on 4th August 1914 and after being mobilised he was posted to the 1st Battalion, Gloucestershire Regiment on 18 August. It seems that he could not wait to get back to soldiering despite being over 40 years old. He embarked on SS *Gloucester Castle* at Southampton and arrived in France on 13 August. He remained on the Western Front for 3 years and 38 days before being invalided home in September 1917 after receiving gunshot wounds in the hands. After recovering from his wounds he was transferred to 302nd Company, Labour Corps for a period of home service but was soon discharged from the army as no longer fit for further service.

When George came back from the war he started in the building trade and soon became a skilled stonemason. He was the Campden lamplighter between 1919 and 1921. Fred Bennett took over in January 1922.

George was a man of fine disposition, very intelligent but quiet and unassuming, always ready to help in any good cause, and many young men profited from his sound advice. He was interested in all kinds of sport and won trophies in physical drill, bayonet exercise, football and cricket during his days in the army. He was a fine billiards player, for many years considered to be the best player in Campden, and also a member of the Campden Mummers.

His wife died in August 1933 aged 58 years and this, together with his own failing health, hastened his end. George died at his home in Watery Lane in September 1935 aged 62 years and is buried in St. James's churchyard.

Richard Lewis Griffin
Private 9667, 1st Battalion, Royal Warwickshire Regiment
Private 635806, Labour Corps

Born: 8 January 1888
Enlisted: 1914
Discharged: 5 June 1919
Died: 19 November 1923

Dick was born in Campden, the son of James Richard and Elizabeth Griffin of Back Ends, Campden and was baptised at St. James's Church on 4 September 1889. His father, a native of Campden, was a carpenter and joiner by trade.

Dick went to school in the town and when war was declared in 1914 he enlisted in the Royal Warwickshire Regiment, serving in the same battalion as two of his Campden friends, Bill Franklin and Jack Dyde. After initial training in England he arrived in France on 2 May 1915.

During the war he was wounded on five separate occasions and gassed three times. When the armistice was signed in 1918 Dick had been transferred to the Labour Corps and was being treated in hospital at Cheltenham. After being there for some time he was able to return to Campden and was discharged from the army on 5 June 1919. He continued to suffer greatly and eventually had to return to Cheltenham Hospital, where he passed away from the terrible effects of gas poisoning on 19 November 1923, when he was 35 years old.

Dick is buried in St. James's churchyard and his name is recorded on the war memorial in the High Street on a panel headed "1918", a late addition after his death due to war injuries in 1923. His brother, William Edward Griffin, also served in the war and died in hospital in Bath in 1922 as a consequence of his wartime experiences.

Thomas William Griffin
Private 13422, 9th Bn., Gloucestershire Regiment

Born: 2 December 1882
Enlisted: 28 September 1914
Discharged: 27 March 1919
Died: 22 April 1956

Thomas and Susan with three of their children.

Thomas was born in Campden, the son of James Richard and Elizabeth Griffin of Wyatt's Yard in Back Ends, and was baptised at St. James's Church on 24 February 1884. His father was a native of the town, a carpenter and joiner by trade, and he married Elizabeth Merriman in 1872.

After leaving school Thomas was employed as a farm labourer and this remained his source of income for the rest of his working life. At the outbreak of war in 1914 he enlisted in the Gloucestershire Regiment and while on home service he married Susan Matilda Masters Packer at All Saints Church in Cheltenham on 13 March 1915. His wife was a parlour-maid and the daughter of George Packer, a police sergeant.

Thomas was posted to the 9th Battalion, which was formed at Bristol, on 9 October 1914. The battalion was posted to 78th Brigade, 26 Division and when the men arrived on Salisbury Plain for training they were not fully equipped with their khaki uniforms. After several months of training Thomas arrived in France on 20 September 1915, where the division moved north to Guignemicourt, west of Amiens. The stay on the Western Front only lasted two months before the battalion moved to Salonika in Greece, where it remained until it returned to France in July 1918. In September 1918 the battalion became the Pioneers in the 66th Division.

Thomas served throughout the war with the 9th Glosters and was demobilised from the army after returning to England. He continued working as a farm labourer and had four children: Ethel, Frank, William and Lilian.

During the Second World War he served as a special constable. He died on 22 April 1956 aged 73 years and is buried in Blockley cemetery.

Thomas is sitting at the front in the centre.

William Edward Griffin
Private 27279, "C" Company, 9th Battalion, Worcestershire Regiment

Born: 24 June 1894
Enlisted: 11 December 1915
Discharged: 3 October 1919
Died: 28 April 1922

William was born in Campden, the son of James Richard and Elizabeth Griffin. His father was a carpenter and joiner by trade and the family home was in Back Ends in 1901, in Cider Mill

Lane in 1919 and then at Rose Cottage in Broad Campden in 1922. After leaving school William found employment as a farm labourer and when the war started in 1914 he was living in Blockley.

He enlisted in the Worcestershire Regiment at Blockley on 11 December 1915 aged 21 years and was placed in the Army Reserve to await mobilisation, which came on 3 February 1916. He was then posted to the 12th Battalion, Worcestershire Regiment and a period of 124 days was spent on home service before he left for Mesopotamia on 7 June with the 9th Battalion, Worcestershire Regiment. William spent the next 2 years and 320 days serving in Mesopotamia and arrived back in England after the war had ended on 23 April 1919. He was admitted to the Alexandra Hospital in Cosham in May 1919 and after leaving the hospital he was allowed a period of leave, from 28 June to 7 July, when he returned to Campden.

After rejoining his unit he was posted to Dublin with the 2nd Battalion, Worcestershire Regiment. On 18 July 1919 he was found guilty of "*not complying with an order to have his kit laid out for a company officer's inspection*" and was given seven days confined to barracks as a punishment.

He was discharged from the army on 3 October 1919 after 3 years and 244 days service and was given a war pension that lasted from 18 June 1920 until it was stopped on 27 July 1921.

William died at the Ministry of Pensions Hospital in Bath on 28 April 1922 aged 27 years and is buried in St. James's churchyard in Campden. He died of "*tuberculosis of the spine and cardiac failure*" and the *Evesham Journal* reported that he died of "*war injuries*". His name, and that of his brother Richard, who died in 1923, is recorded on the war memorial in Campden High Street. This was a very sad time for their parents, James and Elizabeth, as all three of their sons returned from the war but two of them died as a direct result of the war in the early 1920's.

William Henry Griffin
Private 33607, 12th Battalion, Gloucestershire Regiment

Born: 1883
Died: 28 June 1918

Harry was born in Campden, the only son of Thomas and Leah Griffin of Gainsborough Terrace, and was baptised at St. James's Church on 28 January 1883. His father was a native of the town and a baker by trade. The family had previously lived in Church Street and Silk Mill Yard. After leaving school Harry joined Harry George Ellis as an apprentice and worked for many years as a basket-maker. He was well known in the district as a football player and a few years before the start of the First World War he moved to Deddington after marrying.

Harry enlisted in the Gloucestershire Regiment in Banbury and when he arrived in France in 1916 he joined the 12th Battalion. He was killed in action in France on 28 June 1918 and the sad news was conveyed to his widow by a letter from his officer and one by his chum. Lieutenant F. J. Benjamin wrote:

"*He was my batman and he had been for sometime past and it is with the deepest regret that I give you the circumstances of his death. He had been with this battalion for close on 16 months and had never missed any action since joining it. On 28 June 1918 Griffin was with me during the attack, but while we were consolidating a machine gun bullet went through his brain.*"

On 28 June 1918 the battalion attacked the German trenches east of the Forêt de Nieppe, south-east of Hazebrouck in Northern France. They moved up from Caudescure village during the night of 27/28 June 1918 and took up positions in the assembly trenches. At Zero Hour, 6.00am, the barrage opened and the troops moved forward under it and at first met little opposition, although some casualties were caused by men pushing forward too close under the barrage. Le Cornet Perdu was captured and patrols were sent forward to River Plate Becque to destroy bridges and observe enemy movements. When nearly all of the objectives for the attack were taken the enemy machine guns became troublesome and the enemy artillery opened with shrapnel shells on our front line and on the area around Caudescure church.

Harry's body could not be identified at the end of the war and his name is recorded on the Ploegsteert Memorial at Hyde Park Corner in Belgium. He was 35 years old when he died and his name is recorded on two memorials in Campden: in St. James's Church and in the High Street.

Guy Desmond Griffiths

Trooper, Royal East Kent Imperial Yeomanry
Private 725, "C" Company, 22nd Battalion, Australian Imperial Forces
Private 725, No. 6 Company, 2nd Pioneer Bn., Australian Imperial Forces

Born: 21 January 1879
Enlisted: 9 February 1915
Discharged: 7 August 1917
Died: 5 April 1949

Guy was the youngest son of William Higford and Ellen Griffiths of Bedfont House, Campden and was baptised in Aston-sub-Edge Church on 11 March 1879. He was educated at Campden Grammar School and during the Boer War he served with the Royal East Kent Imperial Yeomanry. After returning from South Africa he emigrated to Australia and became a farmer. He embarked on White Star Steamship *Ceramic* at Liverpool on 17 December 1913 and his port of destination was Adelaide.

When war broke out in 1914 Guy had no intention of enlisting, but as time went on things began looking black and, following a number of letters from his sister, Josephine, describing the situation, he made the decision to enlist as soon as possible. He sold his equipment, locked up the farmhouse and gave the key to a neighbour after notifying the owner to come and take possession.

Guy went to Melbourne and enlisted in the 22nd Battalion, Australian Imperial Forces on 9 February 1915. He was 36 years old, five feet nine inches tall with blue eyes, dark brown hair and a medium complexion. There was a vaccination scar on his left arm and tattoos on both forearms and at the base of his neck. After some training at Broadmeadows Camp, which consisted mostly of drills and parades, Guy embarked on the troopship *Ulysses* on 8 May 1915. The boat was overcrowded and the weather was very rough. The food was poor and this caused much discontent amongst the troops. When the ship arrived at Colombo they were forbidden leave to go ashore, which had the result that many men got ashore by any means or methods that they could. Several of them were put in prison on board ship when the journey to Egypt continued. A short time after leaving Colombo this rankling discontent, aggravated by the "*still rotten tucker*", broke out into open mutiny. One evening the men were growling and muttering, evidently in a very dangerous mood. Some of the officers tried to pacify them and finally Colonel Crouch appeared on the bridge. He endeavoured to address the men below him, but no sooner had he opened his mouth than growls began swelling into an ominous roar and cries of "*throw the old b****** overboard*" rose in the air. The troops then took possession of the ship. The doors of the prison cells were bashed in or prized off and the men inside liberated. They then entered the canteen and stripped it bare of all the food. During all this confusion, young officers who were notably liked by the men had been going up and down amongst them, trying to quieten them, and their efforts had the desired effect, for towards midnight the men resumed their normal conduct.

Guy arrived at Suez on 10 June 1915 before travelling to Alexandria, where they entrained for Heliopolis. The weather was blazing hot and drills were done in the early morning. Leave was given to the troops at certain times to go into Heliopolis and up to Cairo but these Egyptian places were full of stench, dirt, filth and corruption. The troops soon had trouble there and after they blew up a British general's motorcar in Cairo all leave was stopped.

Just before Guy was sent to Gallipoli the troops were massed in a big parade and addressed by an Australian general. He called his men criminals and hard cases and told them they were not fit to be sent to France as they could not be trusted in a civilised country and that they were going to be sent to Gallipoli. Guy embarked at Alexandria on 30 August 1915 and arrived at Mudros on the island of Lemnos a few days later. From here they embarked on small, fast boats and were taken over to Anzac Cove on the Gallipoli peninsula. They landed at night and after stumbling over a lot of rough ground in the dark they got what sleep they could before dawn. Guy remained at Gallipoli for the next four months until the campaign ended with the evacuation. Before they left they rigged up the trenches with all kinds of devices to keep an occasional rifle popping off long after the men had left. The men moved out of the trenches in small parties and muffled their feet with any rags or bags and on the beach they got aboard small, fast boats which quickly took them over to Lemnos. They did not stay on Lemnos very long but embarked again for

Egypt, where they arrived on 7 January 1916 and where they were posted to Ismailia. While Guy was en route to Egypt he was found guilty of "*when on active service behaving in such a manner as to show wilful defiance of his company commander*". He was awarded ten days' field punishment number two with loss of pay.

On 13 March 1916 Guy was transferred to a pioneer battalion and then on 19 March they embarked at Alexandria before arriving in France at Marseille on 26 March. After a long train journey and several marches they arrived at Armentières and took up their positions in the third line of trenches. In July 1916 they moved south to the Somme and saw heavy fighting at Pozières. Guy's battalion was employed digging a communication trench from the original British front line to the captured German trenches. It was all open land under heavy German artillery fire and the work had to be done at night. On one day when dawn came Guy had a look over the trench into No Man's Land and saw scores of dead bodies lying just where they fell. In his diary Guy described what he saw: "*Of all the God-forsaken desolations ever impressed on a man's mind I think this tract of country that had come under the sweep of my glance was it. The utter desolation of it seemed to penetrate into a man's soul. I could only liken it in my mind to the desolation of the cities of the plain, when God destroyed them.*"

After being relieved from the Pozières sector Guy moved north into to Belgium to the Ypres Salient but as winter approached they returned to the Somme, where everything was water, mud and slime. On 3 November 1916 Guy was found guilty of two military offences: refusing to obey the order of an NCO and insolence and threatening language towards an NCO. He was awarded 21 days' field punishment number 2 and 21 days' loss of pay as a punishment.

The war on the Western Front ended for Guy when his pioneer battalion were trying to build a corduroy road. When he went over to a railway siding to unload a lot of poles he found that he could not lift a little finger. He was completely exhausted and was evacuated back to England, where he was admitted to hospital in London on 20 January 1917 with "*anaemia and debility*". He failed to recover fully and was discharged from the army on 7 August 1917 as "*medically unfit for home or general service*" and a Silver War Badge was issued to indicate that he had made his contribution to the war. His application to be discharged in England was granted and he went to live with his brother Scudamore at 81, Linden Gardens in London.

Guy returned to Australia after the war and in 1919 married Sarah Stonehouse at Frankston in Victoria and they had three children: Desmond Guy, Nelly and Ronald. He continued working as a farmer and the family home was in Carrum Downs, Frankston. Sarah died of pneumonia soon after the birth of her third child and times became very hard for Guy.

He died on 5 April 1949 aged 70 years and is buried in Midlands, Perth, Western Australia.

Heston Fon Griffiths
Private 2109898, Overseas Battalion, Canadian Army Medical Corps

> Born: 5 November 1874
> Enlisted: 28 April 1917
> Discharged: 8 December 1918
> Died: 2 February 1959

Hes was born in Campden, the third son of William Higford and Ellen Griffiths of Bedfont House, High Street, Campden, and was baptised in Buckland on 27 January 1875. His father was a solicitor and he married Ellen Sherborn, a native of Heston in Middlesex, on 14 December 1863.

Hes was a member of "K" Company, 2nd Volunteer Battalion, Gloucestershire Regiment in Campden for a year before he emigrated to Argentina, where he worked as a rancher. He then worked in Patagonia and Mexico before he settled in Canada, where he continued as a rancher and also started farming. On 28 April 1917 he enlisted in the Canadian Army Medical Corps at Calgary in Alberta aged 42 years. He was passed fit for overseas service and his medical papers state that he was five feet ten inches tall with brown eyes, brown hair and a fair complexion but with a swollen right cheek. He was a single man living in Carstairs at the time of his enlistment and his next of kin was his brother Brinton, who was living in Campden.

Hes embarked in Canada on 27 July 1917 with draft number 9 from the Canadian Army Medical Corps Training Depot Number 13. He arrived in England on 6 August 1917 and was transferred to the 21st Reserve Battalion in September. A further transfer saw him join the 31st Battalion, Canadian Expeditionary Force at Bramshott to prepare for service in France. He entered France on 14 December 1917 and after serving throughout the winter months he was "*blown up by a shell*" at the start of February 1918 but no hospital treatment was required and he carried on serving until he was admitted to the 5th Canadian Field Ambulance on 9 February 1918 with bronchitis. He then transferred to 4th Canadian General Hospital at Dannes Camiers on 5 March 1918, where he was treated for bronchitis and trench fever. On 7 March 1918 he was discharged from hospital and posted to base camp at Etaples. After recovering from his illness he joined the Canadian Labour Pool in March 1918 but the following month he returned to England and was posted to the Labour Pool in Shorncliffe.

On 28 April 1918 Hes was present at a medical board hearing at Somerset Barracks at Shorncliffe, where he complained of headache, dizziness and praecordial pain after exertion. After feeling dizzy he said that "*things look black*" and he felt that the cause of his problem was being blown up by a shell in France. The board found that Hes was a "*well nourished, muscular man*". There was a slight tremor of his outstretched hands and his reflexes were slightly exaggerated. His disability was classed as "*neurasthenia*" and he was graded as medical category B2.

The next few months were spent serving in England before he embarked at Liverpool and arrived at Montreal in Canada on 8 October 1918 on board the ship *City of Poona*. He was granted "*leave with subsistence*" until 13 November 1918 but when he reported for duty he complained of "*tightness and discomfort in his chest*" and was given a further period of leave. He was discharged from the army at Calgary on 8 December 1918 as "*being medically unfit for further service although fit for employment in civil life*". His character and conduct were reported as "*very good*" and he left the army to return home to Carstairs to continue as a farmer and rancher.

Hes died in Canada on 2 February 1959 aged 84 years after spending the last few years of his life living in a veterans' home in Academy Road, Winnipeg.

Michael Philip Grove

Private 23611, 8 Platoon, 16 Section, "B" Company, 1st Battalion, Worcestershire Regiment
Gunner 15616, Gun 12, Howitzer Battery, Royal Marine Artillery
Corporal 5244612, Worcestershire Regiment, Territorial Army
Sergeant 5244612, 660 Construction Company, Royal Engineers

Born: 13 October 1899
Died: 23 August 1979

Michael was born in Campden, the second son of William Thomas and Lily Grove of Church Cottages, Campden, and was baptised at St. James's Church on 3 December 1899. His father was a stonemason by trade.

Michael was a member of the Boys' Brigade and educated at Campden Grammar School. He left school when he was 15 years old owing to the outbreak of war and as there was very little work about in Campden he got a job at Evesham International Stores and lodged in Evesham during the week. When one of his friends went to enlist in the army at Norton Barracks Michael joined him. He gave a false age and enlisted in the Worcestershire Regiment.

He was sent to the Worcestershire Training Depot in Davenport for initial army training before he arrived at Le Havre in France on 16 December 1915 with a draft of men to reinforce the 1st Battalion, Worcestershire Regiment. When his mother found out where he was she wrote to the Colonel

Michael (standing) with his brother Bill.

of the Regiment informing him that her son was under age. He was put on a train at Noeux-les-Mines and then boarded a ship at Le Havre.

After returning to England Michael went to work in a munitions factory in Birmingham before he returned to Campden and found employment at the Guild. He was unsettled and as he was almost 18 years old he put his age up a little and enlisted in the Royal Marine Artillery at Bristol on 4 May 1917. They said that he could only be accepted if he signed on for 12 years, although he was told that there was going to be free discharge at the end of the war as they were likely to be over strength for peacetime service. He trained at Eastney Barracks in Portsmouth and after he had volunteered for land service he returned to France. He embarked at Dover and arrived at Calais on 31 May 1918. Apart from a period of leave in January 1919 he remained on the Western Front until 14 June 1919, when he returned to Portsmouth.

After his discharge Michael went to South Wales in search of work but soon returned to Campden and joined the Territorial Army as a corporal with the Worcestershire Regiment. Times were hard in the post-war years and after struggling to find regular work in Campden he joined the Red Star Liner *Lapland* as a steward in 1922 and worked on two trips to New York.

In 1924 he was back in Campden and working for J. W. Pyment and Sons doing masonry and stone-carving. He then married Edith Annie Benfield. They had two children, Robert and Tony, and the family home was at 3, West End Terrace.

As the Second World War approached work was again in short supply. The state was advertising for volunteers to work on the defences in Belgium and in 1940 he went to Clacton for trade tests. He was accepted and was posted to Number 4 Section, 660 General Construction Company, Royal Engineers. He was initially employed in North Scotland before he was issued with tropical kit and sailed from Liverpool for the Middle East. On one occasion he was repairing a marble statue in Egypt when Sir Winston Churchill, who was in the area at the time, came over to have a word with him.

After returning safely to Campden at the end of the war he continued working as a stonemason in partnership with two of his brothers, Robert and Frank.

Michael died on 23 August 1979 aged 79 years and is buried in St. James's churchyard in Campden.

Michael is sitting on the right in his Royal Marine Artillery uniform.

William George Grove
Stoker First Class K27475, Royal Navy

Born: 15 December 1897
Enlisted: 14 July 1915
Discharged: 13 July 1927
Died: 8 March 1988

William was born in Campden in 1897, the son of William Thomas and Lily Grove of Church Cottages, and was baptised at St. James's Church on 6 February 1898. His parents were natives of the town and his father was a stonemason by trade. After leaving school William began an apprenticeship as a plumber but on 14 July 1915 he enlisted in the Royal Navy, giving his date of birth as 15 June 1897 to make it appear that he was actually 18 years old. He was five feet six inches tall and had blue eyes.

William signed on for 12 years with the Royal Navy and began his service as a stoker second class at HMS *Vivid*, the Royal Navy barracks in Devonport. He then transferred to HMS *Devonshire,* where he was promoted to stoker first class on 15 June 1916. During the war he served in most naval stations, including the China Station, and on one occasion in the English Channel his ship was torpedoed and sank. Fortunately for William he was rescued safely. He also served on HMS *Ambuscade* and after the war he received a silver medallion engraved with the ship's name.

When the war ended William was on board HMS *Gibraltar* and in 1920 he served on an escort destroyer on the Prince of Wales' world tour. When he was not at sea his home base was in Devonport and he continued to serve until his 12 years period of service expired on 13 July 1927.

After returning to Campden he completed his apprenticeship as a plumber with Thomas Parsons and then remained in the trade for the rest of his working life.

In 1921, while home on leave from the Royal Navy, he married Frances Lloyd at St. Eadburgha's Church, Ebrington, and they had two children: George and Endine.

After leaving the Royal Navy he returned to Ebrington and remained there for the rest of his life, living in Victoria Terrace, then in Station Road and finally in a bungalow at Church Close.

During the Second World War he joined the Ebrington Home Guard as a sergeant but by the end of the war he had been promoted to 2nd lieutenant.

William died in Moreton Hospital on 8 March 1988 aged 90 years and is buried in St. James's churchyard in Campden with his wife, who died in 1974.

Bill is on the left and his brother Michael is sitting.

William Gilbert Gruer
Private 2591, Leicestershire Regiment
Private 240650, Leicestershire Regiment

> Born: 30 January 1892
> Discharged: 27 March 1919
> Died: 1960

William was born in Exton, Oakham, Rutland, the son of James and Mary Gruer. His father was a carpenter and his mother's maiden name was O'Brien. At the outbreak of war in 1914 William enlisted in the Leicestershire Regiment. He arrived in France on 26 June 1915 and served throughout the war until he was demobilised on 27 March 1919.

After the war he was employed as a gardener at Campden House by the Noel family. He died in Campden in 1960 aged 68 years and after a funeral service at St. Catharine's Church he was buried in Exton.

William's medals, the 1914/15 Star, British War Medal and Victory Medal, were donated to Campden British Legion and were on display for a number of years.

Sidney George Guy
Colour-Sergeant 1974, 1st Battalion, Gloucestershire Regiment
Colour-Sergeant, "K" Company, 2nd Volunteer Bn., Gloucestershire Regiment
Colour-Sergeant, "H" Company, 5th Battalion, Gloucestershire Regiment
Lieutenant-Colonel, 7th Battalion, Cheshire Regiment

Sidney will always be remembered in Campden as "*Sergeant Guy*" with the Volunteers and the Territorial Army in the years between the Boer War and the First World War. He was a "*most interesting character*" who went from drill sergeant to lieutenant-colonel in twenty months.

Sidney was born at Daresbury, near Chippenham, in 1872, the son of John Broom Guy, a certified inspector of reformatory and industrial schools. After becoming a regular soldier on 10 January 1887 he was posted to India, where he served as a colour-sergeant with the 1st Battalion, Gloucestershire Regiment. While he was in India he married Cecilia Vigrass, the 16-year-old daughter of Benjamin Vigrass, at All Saints Cathedral in Allahabad on 19 March 1901. Their first son, Percy Vernon Vigrass, was born at Allahabad on 9 February 1902. Two more children followed soon after and both Barbara May and Norman George Broom were baptised at St. James's Church on 29 March 1905 after Sidney returned to England and settled in Campden. Sidney and Cecilia left Campden before the outbreak of war in 1914 and after being commissioned he joined the Cheshire Regiment. He rapidly rose through the ranks, being promoted to lieutenant-colonel on 11 February 1916 and put in command of the 2nd/7th Battalion (Territorial Force). Very little is known about his wartime service but he entered France on 7 January 1917 and returned home safely at the end of the war.

After leaving Campden Grammar School Percy, Sidney's son, was a pupil at Bristol Cathedral School. He then entered the Royal Military College at Sandhurst to train to become a regular army officer and he became a major on 1 August 1938 with the Green Howards. At the start of the Second World War Percy was with the Green Howards who were billeted in Campden.

Cecil Warner Hall

Cecil was born in Chipping Norton in 1899, the youngest son of Robert William and Myra Hall of New Street, Chipping Norton. His father was the Town Hall keeper and he married Myra Warner in Chipping Norton in 1881. Robert and Myra both died in 1900 and the 1901 census indicates that Cecil and his sister Nellie went to live with their aunt and uncle, John and Priscilla Miles, at Dingle Lodge, which is in the parish of Campden near the road to Moreton-in-Marsh.

In her *Book of Remembrance* Josephine Griffiths lists Cecil as serving during the war but it has not been possible to find out any further information. In 1922 he was listed on the Campden electoral roll and still living at Dingle Lodge.

Thomas Hall
Private 17744, 2nd Battalion, Gloucestershire Regiment

Thomas was born in 1887, the son of David Hall, and after leaving school he found employment as a labourer. When he was 19 years old he married Elizabeth Ellen Johnson at Stretton-on-Fosse Parish Church on 31 May 1906. They moved to Cider Mill Lane in Campden before the war and in 1914 Thomas enlisted in the Gloucestershire Regiment. After a period of training in England he arrived in France on 19 May 1915 and joined the 2nd Battalion in billets two miles south of Poperinge in Belgium. They then marched south into France and spent June 1915 in the Armentières sector. The summer months were spent on the Western Front before they moved to Salonika in Greece in November 1915.

Thomas spent the next few months in Greece but he must have returned to England in early 1917 as his wife gave birth to a daughter on 3 January 1918. Dorothy Annie Hall was born in Campden and baptised at St. James's Church on 27 January 1918. Her birth certificate states that Thomas was a carter before he joined the army.

At the end of the war Thomas was placed into Class Z of the Army Reserve. Class Z was authorised by an Army Order of 3 December 1918. There were fears that Germany would not accept the terms of any peace treaty and therefore the British Government decided it would be wise to be able to quickly recall trained men in the eventuality of the resumption of hostilities. Soldiers who were being demobilised, particularly those who had agreed to serve "*for the duration*", were at first posted to Class Z. They returned to civilian life but with an obligation to return if called upon. The Z Reserve was abolished on 31 March 1920.

Thomas left Campden after being discharged from the army.

Ernest Avery Hancox
Lance Corporal 106266, 1st Canadian Mounted Rifles

Born: 2 July 1884
Enlisted: 29 December 1914

Ernest was born in Evesham, the fourth son of Edmund Owen and Ann Hancox. In 1891 his father was the managing director of a flour mill in Mill Street, Evesham. After his father retired his parents moved to Warminster.

On the 1901 census Ernest was an apprentice market gardener and living at Avon Mill House, Evesham with his eldest brother, John, who was a mill manager. At some point before the outbreak of the war he emigrated to Canada and settled in Glidden in Saskatchewan. He enlisted in the 1st Canadian Mounted Rifles on 29 December 1914 and was passed fit for active service at a medical examination at Saskatoon. He was five feet seven inches tall with blue eyes, fair hair and a fair complexion. His religion was recorded as "*Presbyterian*".

He served in France and Belgium with the Canadian Expeditionary Force during the war and then on 5 December 1919, when he was a lance corporal, he married Vera Ledger, daughter of George Ledger of Broad Campden, at St. James's Church, Campden.

Garnet Joseph Hands
Private 2725, 28th Battalion (2nd Artists' Rifles), London Regiment
Lieutenant, 7th Battalion, East Kent Regiment (The Buffs)
Captain, Royal Engineers

Born: 28 September 1882
Enlisted: 5 September 1914
Discharged: 6 March 1920

Garnet was born in Campden, the second son of Henry Joseph and Rose Ellen Hands of High Street, Campden, and was baptised at St. James's Church on 26 November 1882. His father was a native of the town and ran the chemist's shop until he retired in 1908 and moved to Bournemouth.

When war was declared Garnet was employed as an architect at 22 Carlisle Place, Westminster, London. He enlisted in the Artists' Rifles on 5 September 1914, aged 31 years, but soon applied for a commission and was posted to the East Kent Regiment as a 2nd lieutenant on 7 December 1914. The next few months were spent training in England before he was posted overseas with the 7th Battalion, East Kent Regiment on 3 October 1915. On 21 April 1916 he was promoted to temporary captain but when he was transferred to the Royal Engineers on 12 December 1916 he reverted to the rank of lieutenant. On 17 December 1916 he developed typhoid fever and left his unit. After a period in hospital in France he arrived at Le Havre and boarded a boat that took him to Southampton, where he arrived on 22 January 1917. On 31 January he was passed medically unfit for duty owing to typhoid.

In February he requested permission to return to France and visit his brother, Leslie, who was dangerously ill in hospital in Etaples after being wounded in action. The request was refused and Leslie died of his wounds in March 1917.

The next few months Garnet spent in and out of hospital in Bristol and Bournemouth recovering from typhoid before he was passed fit on 15 September 1917 and ready to return to active service with the Royal Engineers in northern Italy. He was promoted to the rank of captain and remained in Italy until the end of the war. On 9 March 1919 he left his unit and made his way to France, embarking at Le Havre on 14 March 1919. He arrived at Southampton the next day and was immediately granted two weeks' leave by the medical board. A medical assessment at the 5th General Hospital in Leicester found him to be suffering from diphtheria and they refused to give him permission to return to overseas duty. Garnet spent the last few months of his army career in England before he was discharged on 6 March 1920. He was able to retain the title of Captain to use in civilian life.

Garnet's service papers give the following addresses for him in 1919 and 1920:
1919: "Cotswold", Keswick Road, Boscombe, Bournemouth, Hampshire
1920: Argyle Lodge, South Road, Forest Hill, London, SE 23.

Leslie Hickman Hands
Private B23339, 11th Battalion, Royal Fusiliers

Enlisted: January 1916
Died: 4 March 1917

Leslie was born in Campden in 1895, the youngest son of Henry Joseph and Rose Ellen Hands of High Street, Campden, and was baptised at St. James's Church on 2 June 1895. His father was a chemist in the town and when he retired in 1908 the family moved to Bournemouth.

Leslie was educated at Campden Grammar School but at the outbreak of war in 1914 he was living at Portland in Dorset. He enlisted in the Royal Fusiliers at Weymouth in January 1916 and after a period of training in England was posted to France, where he joined the 11th Battalion in the Somme sector.

He received a gunshot wound in the thigh on 17 February 1917 at Boom Ravine and after being evacuated from the battlefield was admitted to Number 6 General Hospital at Rouen. Wounds in the thigh were a big killer during the war owing to blood loss and Leslie succumbed to his wounds on 4 March 1917. He was 21 years old and is buried in St. Sever Cemetery Extension, Rouen, France. His name is recorded on three memorials in Campden: in St. James's Church, in Campden School and in the High Street. At the time of his death in 1917 his mother was a widow and living at "Cotswold", Keswick Road, Boscombe, Bournemouth. She died in 1939 aged 85 years.

Boom Ravine is a system of sunken roads shaped roughly like a T, situated south of the River Ancre between Petit Miraumont and Grandcourt. The Battle of Boom Ravine on 17 February 1917 is among the less well-known engagements on the Western Front. It took place in the depths of winter, three months after the First Battle of the Somme had come to a slithering, slushy and miserable halt in November 1916. It was a short, sharp and, from the British point of view, not very successful battle in ghastly conditions. The British failure and loss of life were, on this occasion, very largely due to treachery. A man, or men, from a British regiment willingly and wilfully gave information to the Germans which allowed them to prepare a vigorous and determined response to the attack.

Philip Norman Hands
Private 2199, East Surrey Regiment
Private 243257, The Queen's Regiment (Royal West Surrey Regiment)
Private 206177, East Surrey Regiment

Born: 1888

Philip was born in Campden, the third son of Henry Joseph and Rose Ellen Hands of High Street, Campden, and was baptised at St. James's Church on 23 September 1888. His father was a native of the town and married Rose Ellen Roberts in 1880. He was a chemist in the town but when he retired in 1908 the family moved to Bournemouth.

At the outbreak of war in 1914 Philip had been a member of the Territorial Army for over four years and when he was posted overseas he arrived in Mesopotamia with the East Surrey Regiment. He soon transferred to the Queen's Regiment before another transfer saw him return to the East Surrey Regiment.

Philip returned safely from the war and was awarded the Territorial Force War Medal, the British War Medal and the Victory Medal. The Territorial Force War Medal was issued to all personnel of the Territorial Force who had completed four years' service by 30th September 1914 and who had served outside of the UK in the period 5th August 1914 to 11th November 1918. Those personnel who had previously qualified for the 1914 Star or the 1915 Star were ineligible. Only 34,000 medals were issued.

Very little is known about Philip's life after the war but the *Evesham Journal* published a photograph in 1978 of the Campden veteran bowls team with a combined aged of 303 years. The team included Harry Warmington, aged 73, and Philip aged 80 years.

Sarah Hands

Born: 1883

Sarah was born in Winderton, near Brailes in Warwickshire, the daughter of William Wincott and Mary Hannah Hands. Her father, a native of Ilmington, married Mary Hannah Jordan in the Driffield district of Yorkshire in 1875. He was a farmer and census returns show that in 1881 he was farming in Tredington and then, in 1891, in Evenlode.

The family moved to Campden before the 1910 electoral roll was recorded and William farmed at Court Piece Farm until he died on 12 April 1919 aged 66 years.

Sarah was still living with her parents when the war started in 1914 and the 1918 electoral roll lists her as living at Court Piece Farm and absent on military service. Nothing is known about her life after the war apart from the fact that her married name was Smedley and that she was still alive when her brother William died in South Africa in 1949.

William Hands
Number 347, Middelburg Kommando, South African Forces

Born: May 1877
Died: 13 June 1949

William was born in Burmington, near Shipston-on-Stour, in Warwickshire, the eldest son of William Wincott and Mary Hannah Hands. His father was a farmer and brought the family to Campden before the war and farmed at Court Piece Farm until he died in April 1919.

William emigrated to South Africa before the start of the war and worked as a farmer. During the war he served in J. L. Hamman's Commando in the 1914 Rebellion from 12 October until 15 December. He then served in the Collins Scouts (16th Intelligence) from 12 January 1915 until 7 August 1915. The South African archives confirm that he was issued with three campaign medals for his service during the war: 1915 Star, British War Medal and Victory Medal.

After the war he continued to work as a farmer at Farm Hartogshoop, Pan, District Middelburg, Transvaal. He married Margaret Jordan and they had a daughter called Marian Ethel.

William died in South Africa on 13 June 1949 aged 72 years. In his will he left £100 per year for his sisters, Sarah and Ethel Marion, and brother John, and £500 went to the Rector of Newbold-on-Stour Church to be used to maintain the graves of the Hands family buried there. The remainder of his estate went to his daughter.

His wife died on 27 August 1948 aged 53 years.

Walter Owen Handy
Stoker First Class K23192, Royal Navy

Born: 4 August 1896
Enlisted: 22 September 1914
Discharged: 20 March 1919

Owen was born in Alderminster in Warwickshire, the second son of Walter and Julia Handy, who were married in 1889. His mother was Julia Harper from Blockley and his father's occupation was recorded as a shepherd on his birth certificate. In 1901 the family were living at Erdington in Birmingham and his father was a general labourer.

After leaving school Owen found employment as a farm labourer and on 22 September 1914, at the age of 18, he enlisted in the Royal Navy at Portsmouth. He was immediately posted to HMS *Pembroke*, a Royal Navy depot at Chatham, as a stoker second class. On 9 June 1915 he was invalided out of service until 25 September 1917, when he was again fit for duty and posted to HMS *Victory*, the Royal Navy barracks at Portsmouth.

He soon transferred to the crew of HMS *Glory* and was promoted to stoker first class on 8 January 1918. When the armistice was signed Owen was again stationed at HMS *Victory* in Portsmouth and was discharged from the Royal Navy on 20 March 1919.

Josephine Griffiths lists Owen in her *Book of Remembrance,* which she compiled in 1920.

James Henry Harley
Private 1872, 3rd Battalion, London Regiment (Royal Fusiliers)

Born: 1895
Died: 13 October 1915

James was born in Paddington, the son of Joseph Henry and Mary Jane Harley of 17, Torquay Street, Harrow Road, Paddington, London. His mother was born in Campden, the eldest daughter of Alfred and Rose Aston of Leysbourne, Campden. After leaving school he joined the staff of the Great Western Railway Company in 1910 as a boy porter at Holborn and at the outbreak of war was employed as office porter at Paddington goods station.

James was mobilised in August 1914 and arrived in France with the 3rd Battalion, London Regiment, a Territorial battalion, on 6 January 1915. The battalion was posted to the 7th Meerut Division, Indian Corps and saw action at Neuve Chapelle, Aubers and Festubert. On 25 September 1915 the Battle of Loos began and the battalion was involved in a subsidiary attack made at Pietre. James was killed in action on 13 October 1915 in the Béthune sector and is buried at Gorre British and Indian Cemetery, east of Béthune in northern France. He was 20 years old.

James was well known and highly popular in Campden, although his name is not recorded on any of the town's memorials. His brother, Robert Alfred Aston Harley, was baptised at St. James's Church on 5 June 1892.

Photograph provided by STEAM, Museum of the Great Western Railway, Swindon.

Francis Joseph Harris

Private 2257, "H" Company, 5th Battalion, Gloucestershire Regiment
Private 242186, 4th (Reserve) Battalion, Gloucestershire Regiment

Born: 1884
Enlisted: 15 June 1914
Mobilised: 5 August 1914

Frank was born in Campden, the son of William and Agnes Mary Harris of Gainsborough Terrace. His father was a shepherd and married Agnes Leadbetter in 1879. He died in 1904, leaving Agnes a widow.

After leaving school Frank found employment as a carter on a farm and for two years, 1908 to 1910, was a member of "H" Company, 5th Battalion, Gloucestershire Regiment, the local company of the Territorial Army. He rejoined the unit on 15 June 1914. At the outbreak of war he was mobilised and the *Evesham Journal* lists him as one of the men who went with the battalion to Chelmsford. However, when the battalion embarked for France he remained in England.

On 30 December 1916 he was reported absent without leave from his unit, the 4th (Reserve) Battalion, Gloucestershire Regiment, at Cheltenham and on 3 January 1917 was posted as a deserter. Fred Coldicott writes in his book, *Memories of an Old Campdonian,* the following account of the incident:

*"Towards the end of the war Dudley Haydon had a young man working for him to help get the harvest in. His name was Frank Harris, who lived in Cider Mill Lane, next to Bob Dickinson and his wife. Frank was really a "penny short of a shilling", the common term for being a little mentally retarded. One day Mr. Haydon said something to Frank, he took offence and said "B****r your corn, I'll go and join the army." Off he went and did just that. About three months later there was a warrant out for Frank; he had deserted the army. One evening old Mother Dickinson heard Frank's voice next door and immediately rushed off and informed the police. The police came up and they knocked at the door. Frank dashed up the stairs and jumped out of the back window. There was no way out at the back so he had to come through a passage into Cider Mill Lane. On seeing him the two policemen ran after him, but the further they went, the further Frank got in front, and eventually made good his escape. About two years later Frank was discharged from the army, came back to Campden and got a regular job with Dudley Haydon."*

The *Evesham Journal* reported the trial of Agnes Mary Harris and George Alfred Griffin, who were both charged with concealing Frank at their home in Cider Mill Lane. Both pleaded not guilty and after considering the evidence the Bench did not deem it sufficient to convict them. Frank returned to his unit and spent the remainder of the war on home service.

After the war Frank returned to Campden and was living with his mother in Littleworth in 1922.

James Arthur Harris
Royal Engineers

Jimmy was born in Tredington in 1888, the son of Alfred and Sarah Elizabeth Harris, and his father was the landlord of the White Lion Inn in Tredington at the time of his birth. During the war he served with the Royal Engineers and is listed on the 1916 St. James's Church prayer list and in the *Book of Remembrance* by Josephine Griffiths.

Thomas Alfred Harris
Royal Garrison Artillery

Born: 1881

Thomas was born in Shipston, the son of Alfred and Sarah Elizabeth Harris. His father was the landlord at the George Hotel in Shipston and then the White Lion Inn at Tredington. After leaving school Thomas became an "*engineer's clerk*".

In 1904 Thomas married Harriet Marshall in the Bromsgrove registration district and they came to Campden when they took over the running of the Eight Bells. In 1921 James Sadler replaced Thomas as the landlord of the pub.

At the outbreak of war Thomas was 33 years old and he enlisted in the Royal Garrison Artillery. While he was on home service he was transferred to a Volunteer regiment, the equivalent of the Home Guard for the Great War. In October 1918 he was at home in Campden when a group photograph of nine local soldiers was taken at the back of the Eight Bells pub.

The Eight Bells, Campden
The photograph was taken in 1918 between 4 October and 4 November as this is when Jack Tomes was home on agricultural leave after being wounded in his left wrist.
Back Row: Thomas Harris (landlord), Ormonde Plested, Lawrence Ladbrook, Tom Nobes and Frank Nobes
Front Row: Unknown, Harry Nobes, Jack Tomes MM and unknown (believed to be Albert Bradley).

119

William "Joyful Billy" Harris

Sergeant, 1st/5th Battalion, Gloucestershire Regiment
Sergeant, Army Service Corps

Born: 1873
Died: 3 February 1951

William was for many years a member of the local Volunteers and later the Territorial Army and joined up at the start of the war in August 1914. He served throughout the war as a sergeant in the Home Forces, initially with the Gloucestershire Regiment and later with the Army Service Corps.

He married Kate Kirby Haines at St. James's Church on 4 June 1900 and they had seven children: Ruby Florence, Dorothy Irene Gwendoline, Cyril Victor, Alexander George, Violet Millicent, Louis and Geoffrey. Ruby became the Mayor of Wolverhampton and Cyril died serving his country during the Second World War. The family home was in Watery Lane and William was employed as a painter and decorator and a builder.

William was a member of St. James's Church choir for over fifty years and a bellringer for thirty years, during seventeen of which he was the foreman ringer. He was a member of the town band for many years.

William died on 3 February 1951 aged 78 years and is buried in St. James's churchyard. His wife, Kate, died on 5 October 1957 aged 83 and is buried with her husband.

William Edwin Harris

Private S4-125938, Army Service Corps
Private 103465, 15th Battalion, Machine Gun Corps

Born: 14 June 1888
Enlisted: 1915
Died: 13 August 1918

William was born in Campden, the second son of Edwin and Jane Harris of Mitchell's Yard, High Street, Campden, and was baptised at St. James's Church on 26 August 1888. His father was a native of the town and employed as a gardener.

After attending school in the town William served an apprenticeship as a baker and before the war started was employed by Mr. Burrows of Broadway. In 1915 he enlisted in the Army Service Corps as a baker but then transferred to the Machine Gun Corps as an officers' cook in 1917. He was taken ill in France with peritonitis and tuberculosis and was sent to England to the Northern General Hospital at Lincoln in June 1918. He failed to recover from his illness and died at Lincoln on 13 August 1918 aged 30 years. His body was sent to Campden on 15 August and then taken to St. James's Church for the night, the funeral taking place the following day. Many discharged soldiers and others home on leave attended it. In the absence of the vicar the service was conducted by the curate, Reginald Bently. The coffin was elm with brass furniture and bore the following inscription, "*Pte. William E. Harris, died August 13th 1918, aged 30 years*".

William is buried in St. James's churchyard with a Commonwealth War Graves Commission military headstone and his name is recorded on two memorials in the town: in St. James's Church and in the High Street. It should be noted that his name on the memorial in the High Street is recorded incorrectly as *W. H. Harris*.

William's two campaign medals and his memorial plaque were sent to his parents in Sheep Street in the early 1920's. In 1999 the author received a phone call from a military shop in Staffordshire offering William's medals and plaque for sale. The deal was done on 1 May 1999 and they are now framed and in the possession of the author.

Frederick Philip Hart
Lieutenant-Commander, Royal Navy

Born: 24 March 1879
Enlisted: 1 March 1896
Discharged: 23 March 1924
Died: 15 May 1971

Fred was born in Harlow in Essex and was the second of three sons of Frederick Thomas and Hester Ann Hart. He was educated at Epping School and given the nickname "*Buskins*". He left school when he was 13 years old and took a job as a potboy at the Cross Keys pub two miles from Epping.

His father died in 1882 when Fred was only 3 years old and in 1883 his mother married Wentworth Huyshe. The family moved to Besom Cottage, Thornwood Common near Epping Forest in 1887 and then in 1893 they moved to Piggott's Farm at Abridge in Essex. The following year Fred and his elder brother William applied to join the Royal Navy. They were both turned down and Fred went to work in an architect's office in St. Albans. During the evenings he attended classes in woodcarving and this is how his two brothers first got introduced to the craft. In 1895 the family moved to Horseshoe Farm, between Epping and Harlow, and Fred became a ploughboy and then a groom in Woodford.

He joined the Royal Navy at Chatham on 3 March 1896 at the age of 16 years. The medical examination passed him fit to serve and noted that he had blue eyes and light brown hair. He was posted to HMS *Northampton* as Boy Second Class 187871 Fred Hart and he served with his brother William, who had joined the Royal Navy on 7 October 1895. In 1897 the brothers both joined HMS *Scylla,* where they fired 4.7-inch guns, and on 29 July 1899 Fred was promoted to the rank of leading seaman. It was while the brothers were serving at HMS *Pembroke,* a Royal Navy depot in Chatham, that William was invalided out of the Royal Navy on 6 November 1899 with "*bad teeth*". Frederick remained in the Royal Navy and was promoted to a petty officer first class on 11 October 1901 while serving on HMS *Wildfire*. He was now trained and qualified to be a gunnery instructor and captain of a gun turret.

In 1902 Fred's brother George moved to Campden with the Guild of Handicraft and Fred stayed with him in the town whenever he had leave. In November 1903 Fred was posted to HMS *Albemarle*, a new battleship, and was again a captain of a gun turret. Further promotion followed and he was given the rank of gunner warrant officer in 1907 and during the next four years he was given the job of training midshipmen on HMS *Eclipse* and HMS *Cornwall*.

Fred was a keen sportsman and he broke his leg during a rugby match in Gibraltar and was on sick leave for nine months. Three months were spent in hospital in Gibraltar before he returned to England and was admitted to hospital in Gosport. A period of three months' convalescence was spent with his brother George in Broad Campden. In 1912, now fully recovered, he became a gunnery officer on Torpedo Boat

Number 14 and then a year was spent on HMS *Dwarf* before he joined the gunnery school at Chatham as an instructor in 1913.

In July 1914 Fred won the Naval Championship for rifle shooting and he used the prize money to go on holiday to Switzerland. The holiday had to be cut short owing to war being declared with Germany. On his return he was posted to HMS *Humber,* which was involved in the bombarding of the right wing of the German army near Nieuport in October-November 1914. In 1915 he joined HMS *Lord Clive* and remained with her until October 1918. In August 1915 the ship was involved in the bombardment of the locks and canals at Zeebrugge. On 7 September 1915 she bombarded Ostend dockyard and later the same month bombarded the gun batteries at Zeebrugge, Middelkerke and Westende. The next few months saw HMS *Lord Clive* continue to bombard the Belgian coast and in September 1916 it was involved in a seven-day bombardment of enemy coastal positions. June 1917 saw another bombardment of Zeebrugge and then August and September 1917 saw further bombardment of Ostend.

In October 1918 HMS *Lord Clive* was withdrawn from her service in the Dover Patrol and all officers were transferred to HMS *Carlisle*, one of the first ships to carry aeroplanes, and it was while Fred was on this ship that the war ended.

Fred was promoted to lieutenant in 1917 and after the end of the war he spent the whole of 1919 at the Royal Naval College. In 1920 he was promoted to captain and given command of a minesweeper, HMS *George Andrew*, which was employed patrolling the west coast of Ireland. The next two years, 1921 and 1922, Fred requested to go on half pay and he spent this prolonged period of leave with his brother George at Attlepin in Campden, where he became a farm labourer. He returned to service in 1923 and joined HMS *Blenheim* but on 23 March 1924 he retired from the Royal Navy as a lieutenant-commander after 28 years' service.

Frederick (left) and his brother William.

After leaving the Royal Navy Fred moved to Campden and bought Trinder House in the High Street. He was Scoutmaster for four years, 1924-28, captain of Campden Cricket Club, 1924-31, and secretary of the Norton Estate War Club. When the Second World War started he volunteered his services if required. In October 1939 he began nine months of service during which he was posted to the Royal Naval Barracks (HMS *Drake*) in Devonport, where he was in charge of the dining hall and every third day he was the commanding officer of the barracks. In July 1940 he again retired from the Royal Navy and returned to Campden.

Fred never married and he spent the rest of his life living at Trinder House, where he built up an amazing collection of antiques and collectables. He died on 15 May 1971 aged 92 years and his body was bequeathed for medical research.

William Thomas Hart
Able Seaman 186164, Royal Navy
Corporal 7031, Lord Loch's Horse
Major, 11th Battalion, Royal Warwickshire Regiment

Born: 7 March 1878
Enlisted: 21 January 1915
Discharged: 20 November 1920
Died: December 1966

William was born in London in 1878, the eldest of three sons of Frederick Thomas and Hester Ann Hart. He was educated at Epping School and given the nickname "*Bags*". His father died in 1882 when William was only 4 years old and his mother married Wentworth Huyshe in 1883.

William enlisted in the Royal Navy on 7 October 1895 when he was 17 years old and he was posted to HMS *Northampton* as a boy second class. His medical examination recorded that he was five feet six inches tall with light brown hair and grey eyes. When he left HMS *Northampton* in April 1896 he held the rank of ordinary seaman. Further promotion followed when he became an able seaman on 28 August 1898 while serving on HMS *Scylla*. He served with his brother Frederick on HMS *Scylla* for over two years and they both fired 4.7-inch guns on board the ship. William was then invalided out of the Royal Navy with "*bad teeth*" on 6 November 1899 and when he applied to rejoin on 11 January 1900 they turned him down. He now turned to the army and volunteered on 22 February 1900 for service in South Africa during the Boer War with the machine gun section of Lord Loch's Horse. He was discharged from Lord Loch's Horse on 9 January 1901 and was awarded the Queen's South Africa Medal with four clasps: Diamond Hill, Johannesburg, Orange Free State and Cape Colony.

After leaving the army William became a woodcarver and joined the Guild of Handicraft in 1907. His mother and stepfather were now living in Campden. He married Dorothy Annie Haydon in 1910 in London and they had one daughter, Margaret, born in 1913, who donated her father's military papers and diaries to the National Army Museum, Chelsea, London, where they can be viewed by appointment.

When the First World War started William applied for a commission on 21 January 1915 and was posted to the 11th (Service) Battalion, Royal Warwickshire Regiment as a captain. His home address at the time was Attlepin in Campden, where he was living with his brother George. William entered France on 31 July 1915 and served for an unbroken period of twenty months on the Western Front. His batman was Private 10441 Andrew Chambers, whose home address was Chadwick End in Birmingham.

The battalion saw action during the Battle of the Somme. On 1 July 1916 they were at Hannescamps, where they provided a defensive flank and fired smoke bombs along the front of the 46th Division's attack at Gommecourt. On 15 July 1916 they suffered 275 casualties during an attack on Pozières and in August 1916 they faced the German Intermediate Line, a trench between Bazentin-le-Petit and High Wood. They attacked at 10.30pm on 12 August 1916 but it was unsuccessful. A period of rest and training followed before they were back in action on the Somme when they attacked Frankfurt Trench near Beaumont-Hamel on 14 November 1916. It is interesting to note that William was writing the battalion's war diary during their time on the Somme.

On 30 March 1917 the war diary records that "*Major W. T. Hart left the battalion for Command Course at Aldershot*". He embarked at Boulogne on 1 April 1917 and arrived at Folkestone later the same day. He attended the senior officers' course at Aldershot and then on 16 June 1917 he was granted special leave on medical grounds. He was then ordered back to France but when he reported for duty he had a note from Dr. Dewhurst from Campden which resulted in his being sent for a full medical examination at the Military Hospital in Warwick. He was found to have heart problems and was sent to the 3rd Southern General Hospital at

11th Bn. Officers, Doullens, France, 1916
Major William Hart, second in command, is seated at the front on the left. 2nd Lt. A. A. Milne, author of *Winnie the Pooh*, is standing at the back on the left.

Oxford. After being discharged from hospital he reported back for duty on 30 July 1917 and was sent to Lichfield as an assistant to the colonel who was in charge of the infantry records.

The rest of the war was spent on home service but he continued to suffer from heart problems and in July 1920 he entered Central Military Hospital for Officers at Brighton. His official discharge from the army came in November 1920 when he left the hospital. William then resigned his commission on 20 November 1920, keeping the title Major to use in civilian life. Owing to the medical problems that he experienced during his military service he was able to claim a war pension all of his life.

After the war he became the Education Officer for Higher Education in the North Gloucestershire Area and President of the British Legion in Campden.

William spent the last few years of his life living with his daughter at Cheltenham. He died in December 1966 aged 88 years and is buried in St. James's churchyard in Campden. His mother and stepfather are both buried in St. Catharine's cemetery in Campden.

"C" Company Officers of the 11th (Service) Battalion, Luggeshall, 1915
William is smoking his pipe at the front on the left. Three of the other officers on the photograph were later killed in action: 2nd Lt. Jenkins, Lt. Baswell and 2nd Lt. Collins.

Albert George Hathaway
Gloucestershire Regiment

Albert was born in Condicote, near Stow-on-the-Wold, in 1880, the third son of George and Charlotte Anne Hathaway. In 1881 the family were living at Condicote, where his father was a farm carpenter. After moving to Campden his father became a wheelwright and census returns show that the family were living in Church Street in 1891 and in Twine Cottages in 1901.

Albert had left home by 1901 and it is possible that he served in South Africa during the Boer War as the medal rolls for that campaign show a Private 4198 A. G. Hathaway, 4th Battalion, Gloucestershire Regiment. In her *Book of Remembrance* Josephine Griffiths lists Albert as serving in the Gloucestershire Regiment during the Great War.

Algernon Hathaway
Lance Corporal 10993, 7th Battalion, Gloucestershire Regiment

Born: 5 May 1888
Died: 7 August 1915

Algernon was born in Campden, the fifth son of George and Charlotte Anne Hathaway, and was baptised at home on the day of his birth. In 1891 his father was employed as a wheelwright and the family were living in Church Street. They later lived in Twine Cottages, Grammar School Cottages and in Sheep Street.

Algernon was a member of the town band and for a short time worked in the Guild of Handicraft. Charles Ashbee wrote, "*Algy has probably never read Shakespeare, but he can sing and he can dance the Morris. He has a fine sense of humour and abounding humanity. There are always small boys about him listening to his stories. No one rode the hobby horse or danced in the High Street so well as Algy.*"

Algernon worked at the post office in Campden for eleven years and was a member of the Morris Men with his brothers Frederick and Dennis and nephew Henry. At the outbreak of war in August 1914 he enlisted in Campden and was posted to the 7th Battalion, Gloucestershire Regiment. After a period of training in England the battalion sailed for Turkey and landed at Y Beach at Gallipoli at 10.30pm on 11 July 1915. Algernon was now a lance corporal. They entered the front line trenches for the first time at Gully Ravine on 20 July 1915 and on 28 July they left the Gallipoli peninsula for a period of rest at Mudros on the island of Lemnos, where they could make final preparations for their forthcoming attack.

The battalion arrived back at Gallipoli on 3 August and landed at Anzac Cove. On 6 August they moved the short distance from Rest Gully to Aghyl Dere. At about 10.00am on 7 August the battalion reinforced the New Zealand battalions on Rhododendron Spur. Captain Vassall and three other ranks were killed. The following day the Battle of Sari Bair began and the battalion received the orders to stand to at 3.00am to form the left of the attacking first line.

Algernon was killed in action on 7 August 1915 as the battalion made its way up Rhododendron Spur. He has no known grave and his name is recorded on the Helles Memorial at Gallipoli in Turkey. He was 26 years old when he died.

Algernon wrote to his mother just two days before he died. "*It is terribly hot out here. We dare not say where we are, but we are in the thick of it. I hope it will be over soon. I hope everything is getting on right at home. I am all right up to the time I post this and I hope that God will spare me to get me through safe. I should not care for foreign life. Give me good old England before any of it. Well if I have the luck to return I shall be able to tell you something. There is such a lot suffering with dysentery. I have had my share but have not been laid up with it yet.*"

Algernon has his name recorded on three memorials in Campden: in St. James's Church, in the Baptist Church and in the High Street. In her *Book of Remembrance* Josephine Griffiths describes him as a "*bright, cheerful lad*".

Frederick Charles Hathaway
Gloucestershire Regiment

Born: 22 March 1884
Died: 10 January 1982

Frederick was born in Campden, the fourth son of George and Charlotte Anne Hathaway, and was baptised at St. James's Church on 28 September 1884. In 1901 the family were living at Twine Cottages and Frederick was employed as a butcher.

He married Selina Augusta Ayres at St. Catharine's Church in Campden on 5 October 1911 and at the time of the wedding was employed as a collector for Prudential Insurance.

At the outbreak of war in 1914 Frederick was 30 years old. Josephine Griffiths states that he served in the Gloucestershire Regiment during the war but this is contradicted by the cap badge that he is wearing in the photograph. The badge is strictly that of the Queen's (Royal West Surrey) Regiment but it was also worn by both the 22nd and 24th Battalions, London Regiment.

Frederick was a member of Campden town band and a post-war photograph shows him wearing the medal ribbons of the British War Medal and Victory Medal. This indicates that he served overseas in a theatre of war after the start of 1916 and according to his daughter he served on the Western Front in France and Belgium.

After the war Frederick and Lena lived in Sheep Street and he was employed as a stonemason and a basket-maker. He was a dancer with the Morris Men and later became the Fool. In 1931 he was the choreographer when a new team had to be trained.

His daughter Marjorie married Thomas Jinks and went to live in Weston-Super-Mare. Frederick died on 10 January 1982 aged 97 years and is buried in Weston-Super-Mare.

Henry Brinton Hathaway
Royal North Devonshire Hussars
Army Cycle Corps

Born: 24 September 1899
Buried: 17 June 1955

Henry was the eldest son of Dennis William and Esther Louise Hathaway of Sheep Street, Campden and was baptised at St. James's Church on 24 September 1899. He had one brother and three sisters, Albert Cyril, Gladys Violet, Rose and Annie Margaret. His father was a basket-maker by trade and the brother of Algernon, Frederick and Albert, who all served during the 1914-18 war.

When the war started in August 1914 Henry was only 14 years old and he had to wait until nearly the end of the war before he could enlist in the army. He served in the Army Cycle Corps and the Royal North Devonshire Hussars but did not serve overseas in a theatre of war.

After the war he married May but they did not have any children. They went to live at Stourport-on-Severn and he was employed at Kidderminster railway station. When his wife died Henry returned to live in Campden.

Henry died in June 1955 aged 55 years. His ashes are buried with his parents in St. James's churchyard.

Thomas William Hawtin
Private 28350, Battalion, Royal Berkshire Regiment

Born: 2 June 1889
Enlisted: 30 June 1916
Discharged: 11 September 1918
Died: 12 April 1952

Thomas was born in Stratford-upon-Avon, the only son of Thomas and Rose Annie Hawtin. He had three sisters, Mary Elizabeth, Margaret and Amy, and the family later moved to Broad Campden. Mary Elizabeth married Richard Green in 1913.

Thomas enlisted in Bristol in the Gloucestershire Regiment on 30 June 1916 but transferred to the Royal Berkshire Regiment before being posted overseas. His attestation papers state that he was five feet eleven inches tall with blue eyes, light brown hair and a fresh complexion. He had four vaccination marks on his left arm.

During his time in France with the 2nd Battalion he was a sniper and a lot of time was spent in No Man's Land waiting for Germans to show their heads above the parapet of their trenches. The wet conditions caused Thomas to develop trench foot and at times his whole body became very swollen, causing him to be carried away on a stretcher. The stretcher-bearers threatened to throw him off the stretcher, as the going was so tough carrying a man over the battlefield. After being evacuated back to England Thomas was admitted to hospital at Lytham St. Anne's near Blackpool and on 11 September 1918 he was discharged from the army as no longer fit for active service owing to sickness. Thomas had served a period of 2 years and 75 days in the army.

He had married Emily Harris on 13 January 1912 at Bourton-on-the-Hill and they had eleven children: George, Charles, Frank, Albert, Percy, Gilbert, Vera, Jean, Dennis, Stanley and Ronald. The family home was initially in Broad Campden but they then moved to Bourton-on-the-Hill, where Thomas worked as a labourer on the Batsford Estate. During the Second World War he was a member of the Home Guard and five of his sons served in the war: Percy was in the Royal Artillery, Charles and Frank both served in the Warwickshire Yeomanry, Albert was in the Grenadier Guards and Gilbert in the Royal Navy. His son Charles lost his life at Al Alamein in North Africa and his name is on the memorial at Bourton-on-the-Hill.

Thomas died on 12 April 1952 aged 62 years and is buried in St. Lawrence's churchyard extension at Bourton-on-the-Hill.

Arthur Henry Haydon
Private M2-082836, Army Service Corps

Born: 4 March 1876
Died: 19 September 1936

Arthur was born in Campden, the eldest son of Robert Henry and Ann Haydon of Church Street, Campden. His father was a miller, baker and farmer. When the war started Arthur enlisted in the Army Service Corps and arrived in France on 16 July 1915. His younger brother, Gilbert, was killed in action on 27 August 1916.

Arthur died on 19 September 1936 aged 60 and is buried in St. James's churchyard.

Dudley Haydon
Private 1316, "D" Squadron, Warwickshire Yeomanry

Born: 1885
Enlisted: 8 October 1906
Died: 27 November 1966

Dudley was born in Campden, the son of Robert Henry and Ann Haydon of Church Street, and was baptised at St. James's Church on 26 April 1885. He was a keen horseman and enlisted in "D" Squadron, Warwickshire Yeomanry on 8 October 1906. The squadron had their headquarters in Stratford-upon-Avon. Owing to his occupation Dudley did not serve overseas during the war and was a member of the Yeomanry Reserve. Three of his brothers served in the army during the war: Gilbert was killed in action in 1916 and Arthur and Ronald returned safely.

The Haydon family had farmed in Campden for generations. Dudley at first farmed with his father and then on his own until he was joined by his own son, Gilbert. He did not retire from farming until 1963.

Dudley's first wife died on 30 December 1925 and then he married Daisy Madeline Rimell at St. James's Church on 7 April 1931. There were four children by the first marriage and two by the second.

Dudley died in the same house in which he was born, on 27 November 1966, aged 81 years and is buried in St. James's churchyard in Campden.

Gilbert Haydon
Private 2781, 1st/5th Battalion, Gloucestershire Regiment

Born: 1888
Died: 27 August 1916

Gilbert was born in Campden, the youngest son of Robert Henry and Ann Haydon of Church Street in Campden. He was baptised at St. James's Church on 26 August 1888 and educated at Campden Grammar School.

When the war started in 1914 he was working at the Capital and Counties Bank in Malvern. Keen to enlist, he made his way to Gloucester to join the 1st/5th Battalion, Gloucestershire Regiment. A period of training followed in Chelmsford before the battalion arrived in France on 29 March 1915. The next few months were spent learning about trench warfare at Ploegsteert in Belgium before the battalion headed south to the Somme, where Gilbert was killed in action in a German trench near Pozières. The Campden Parish magazine said that he was *killed by the explosion of a shell in the trenches. Death was instantaneous.* The Brigade Chaplain sent the following letter to Gilbert's parents:

"I am very sorry indeed to have to tell you that Pte.

Haydon was killed in the German trenches which he helped to capture and hold. I buried him just where he fell early this morning. Please accept our sincere sympathy, and believe me, he did his bit for King and Country."

On 3 August 1918 the *Cheltenham Chronicle and Gloucestershire Graphic* published a watercolour sketch of a memorial that had been erected by the 1st/5th Battalion, Gloucestershire Regiment over a trench taken on 27 August 1916, during the Somme Battle, to commemorate three officers and six men who fell in taking it from the Prussian Guard. Gilbert is one of the six men listed on the memorial. This memorial was returned to England after the war and placed in Prestbury Cemetery in Cheltenham. The original memorial fell into a state of disrepair and has been replaced by a new one.

Gilbert's body was never recovered at the end of the war and his name is listed on the Thiepval Memorial in the heart of the Somme battlefield in France. He was 28 years old when he died and his name is recorded on three memorials in the town: in St. James's Church, in Campden School and in the High Street.

Prestbury Cemetery, Cheltenham, August 2000
Memorial originally erected in France in 1916.

Ronald Haydon

Private: M-286978, 369 Motor Transport Company, Army Service Corps

Born: 1886
Enlisted: 1 February 1917
Discharged: 16 July 1919

Ronald was born in Campden, the fifth son of Robert Henry and Ann Haydon of Church Street, Campden and was baptised at St. James's Church on 23 January 1887. His father was a miller, baker and a farmer and his mother was originally from Maidstone in Kent.

In the years leading up to the First World War Ronald worked as a farmer at Manor Farm, Ruthin, Wales before he enlisted in the Army Service Corps on 24 June 1916. His medical found that he had a *"slight degree of flat feet"* and after being graded medical category B2 he was put into the Army Reserve. He was mobilised on 1st February 1917 and posted to the Army Service Corps in Wrexham. Two days later he joined the 369 Motor Transport Company at Grove Park in London, where he spent the rest of the war. He passed his driving test in London on 5 February 1917 and his army form B195(A) states that he was a *"fair light car driver"*.

During his time with the Army Service Corps Ronald's next of kin was his wife, Hilda, who was living at Mill Cottage in Campden. Ronald's address during his time in London was 15 Rosemont Road, Acton.

On 17 October 1918 Ronald developed flu and entered the 4th London General Hospital, Denmark Hill in London, where he stayed until 19 November. The war was now over and he was retained as a car driver for another seven months before being released from the Army Service Corps at Wellington Dispersal Centre in Crystal Palace on 18 June 1919. He was then officially discharged from the army on 16 July.

He married Hilda Florence Book at the Parish Church in Wimbledon, London in 1909 and two of their children, Barbara Ethel (born 1911) and Ruth Lila (born 1916), were baptised at St. James's Church in Campden.

In 1940 Ronald wrote to the Ministry of Defence for a reference and a statement of his army service. He gave his address as 15 Woodgrange Road, Kenton, London.

His ashes are buried in St. James's churchyard in Campden.

William Hayes
Private 3043, Gloucestershire Yeomanry
Private 235655, Corps of Hussars

Born: 1889

William was born in Honeybourne, the eldest son and second child of Bill and Mary Hayes. His father was a farmer and he married Mary Harris in 1885. The family were living and working at Long Hill Farm, Mickleton in 1901. In 1919 they came to Campden when Bill took over the running of Kingcombe Farm.

At the outbreak of war William was 25 years old and he enlisted in the Gloucestershire Yeomanry on 24 May 1915. After a period of training in England he embarked for Egypt, where he joined the Gloucestershire Yeomanry in 1916. They had recently arrived from Mudros, on the island of Lemnos, after being evacuated from Gallipoli on 31 October 1915 with a strength of only 81 men of all ranks.

In February 1917 the Gloucestershire Yeomanry became part of the Imperial Mounted Division but shortly afterwards the name was changed to the Australian Mounted Division as a result of a protest from Australia. The division was heavily engaged in Egypt and Palestine, from the early probing away from the Suez Canal zone, across the Sinai desert and eventually at the Battles of Gaza and the victorious advance to Jerusalem and into Syria.

William served overseas for three years and returned safely to England in 1919. He joined the Norton Estate War Club and was present at all the annual dinners until the club was disbanded after the 1922 dinner.

George Haysum
Private 69466, Infantry Reserve Depot, Royal Welch Fusiliers

Born: 24 April 1882
Enlisted: 1914
Died: 12 April 1963

George was born in Weobley in Herefordshire in 1882, the son of James Haysum, and he married Mary Maria "*Molly*" Keyte at St. James's Church in Campden on 15 October 1907. Molly and his sister Alice were employed together and it was while visiting his sister that George met his future wife. After the wedding George and Molly moved to Abertillery in South Wales, where George drove a pony and trap delivering groceries to isolated houses and farms. Each Saturday he had to collect all of the money owed by the customers. Not once was he mugged or held up.

In 1914 George joined the army and was sent to India with the Royal Welch Fusiliers. He was awarded the British War Medal and his name was erroneously engraved as "*Hayrum*" around the rim. This was his only medal entitlement, as he did not serve in a theatre of war.

In 1916 Molly received a telegram informing her that her father, William Keyte, was dead and that she should return home immediately. After the funeral Molly, and her sister, May Charlotte, went to Birmingham to work in munitions factories.

At the end the war George returned from India and rented 12 Sheep Street from Garnet Keyte. He then bought from the War Department two horses that had been used in France. He also bought a wagon and commenced his work of bringing up from the railway station goods that had been transported by train. The next step was his successful application for the franchise from the Great Western Railway, not only to transport goods but also passengers between Campden and the station. As time passed the horses were sold and a bus was bought. At this point George did not know how to drive but after a quick lesson from Percy Jones he was soon able to drive competently. The business began to thrive and he bought a lorry and a car that was used as a taxi, his wife Molly taking all of the bookings. High House in Sheep Street was bought and the business went from strength to strength.

Molly died on 7 January 1963 at Cheltenham Hospital and George died at Warwick Hospital on 12 April 1963 aged 80 years.

Arthur Neal Hayward
Private 8335, 1st Battalion, Gloucestershire Regiment

Died: 12 September 1915

Arthur was born in Campden in 1890, the son of Arthur and Agnes Hayward, who were married in Cheltenham in 1893. His father was a bricklayer's labourer by trade and his mother, born Agnes Louisa Neal in 1873, was a native of Campden. In 1901 the family were living at 2, Victoria Place in Cheltenham and Arthur was a pupil at St. James's School.

At the outbreak of war in 1914 Arthur was a regular soldier and arrived at Le Havre in France on board SS *Gloucester Castle* with the 1st Battalion, Gloucestershire Regiment on 13 August 1914. He first saw action at Mons on 24 August and was then involved in the long 200-mile march that saw the British army retreat to the River Marne. On 7 November 1914 the battalion was in Belgium and in action east of Zwartelleen during the First Battle of Ypres. The battalion advanced but after coming under heavy fire from the Germans many men were forced to lie down in the open all day, unable to get back to their own lines. It was during this action that Arthur was reported missing. His photograph appeared in the *Cheltenham Chronicle and Gloucester Gazette* on 30 January 1915 and it was said that nothing had been heard from him since being reported missing. His home address was given as Savoury Court, Duke Street, Cheltenham.

It is not clear when he returned to the battalion but Arthur was killed in action on 12 September 1915. His grave could not be identified at the end of the war and his name is recorded on Le Touret Memorial, near Béthune, France. It is not recorded on any memorials in Campden but it is on the memorial at St. James's School, Merestone Road, Cheltenham.

William Guy Hazelton
Private PS/8427, 7th Battalion, Royal Fusiliers

Born: 18 April 1896
Enlisted: 31 July 1915
Discharged: 1 January 1918

Campden Grammar School Cadet Corps: Sergeant Guy Hazelton is standing behind Dixey Cossins.

Guy was born at 164 Hunter Street in Buckingham, the son of William Cottell Hazelton. His father, a native of Southampton, was a veterinary surgeon and he married Margaret Hannah Gough in 1893.

Guy was educated at Campden Grammar School and was Head Boy in 1913 and 1914. He was given the nickname "*Gaffer Hazelton*" when he became a sergeant in the Cadet Corps. After leaving school he enlisted in the Royal Fusiliers on 31 July 1915. He served overseas with the 7th Battalion but was discharged from the army on 1 January 1918 owing to sickness.

Charles Hedges
Private 7404, 1st Battalion, Gloucestershire Regiment

Died: 8 October 1915

Charles was born in Campden in 1885, the second son of William Henry and Emma Hedges of Westington, and was baptised at St. James's Church on 25 December 1885. His father was employed as a *"cattleman on a farm"* in 1901.

Charles enlisted as a regular soldier before the First World War and at the outbreak of war in August 1914 was on the Army Reserve list. He was immediately mobilised and embarked on SS *Gloucester Castle* at Southampton and arrived at Le Havre in France with the 1st Battalion, Gloucestershire Regiment on 13 August 1914. They made their way into Belgium and saw their first action on 24 August when there was heavy rifle fire from the direction of Mons. Contact was made with German cavalry patrols and the order to retire was received. A 200-mile march south to the River Marne took place over the next few days. On 5 September a supply of shirts, socks and boots was received as a number of men were marching in bare feet following the recent retreat from Mons. The advance to the River Aisne began on 6 October 1914 and the rest of the month was spent holding the line north of the river along the Chemin des Dames. Charles was wounded in the leg during the fighting near the river and had to be returned to England to recover.

After recovering from his wound Charles returned to France and rejoined the battalion as they prepared for their part in the Battle of Loos that was due to start on 25 September 1915. In a letter to Mrs. Blakeman written after the start of the battle Charles said: *"Sorry I have not written before but we have had a little hell here these last few weeks, but all has come out in our favour. We have had some very terrible weather here, to make it worse for us, up to our knees in mud and water. We were wet through and we shall know it later on. You will see in the papers about our success, but it was a strain to us as poor Willie Hedges from the Pike got killed and Tom Smith wounded. I can thank god for bringing me safely through without a scratch. I am sat in a corner of an old barn behind the firing line writing this by candle light. We are having a few days rest here after our big dash, and not before we needed it. I never was in such a mess and so tired in all my life."*

After surviving his part in the opening day of the battle Charles was killed in action during the Battle of Loos on 8 October 1915 when *"he was caught right in the head and was killed outright"*. His parents received news of their son's death when Private James Trinder, of the same regiment, wrote to his aunt in Campden. *"I have very bad news for you, poor Charlie Hedges is killed. I did not see him but I was not too far off at the time. You must break the news to his folks. Fancy! I am the only one from Campden left in this battalion now. I must put up with it a little longer I suppose."*

Charles has no known grave and his name is recorded on the Loos Memorial at Dud Corner Cemetery, France. His name is also recorded on three memorials in Campden: in St. James's Church, in the Baptist Church and in the High Street.

"H" Company, 1st/5th Battalion, Gloucestershire Regiment, Lulworth 1911
Charles is standing in the centre at the back. Norman Bennett is on the right with the mallet.

Ernest Walter Hedges
Private S4-055633, Army Service Corps
Private 41744, Royal Irish Fusiliers

Born: 6 August 1894
Died: 1 March 1971

Ernest was born in Campden in 1894, the youngest of three sons of William and Emma Hedges of Westington, Campden. He was baptised at St. James's Church on 25 December 1894 and attended school in the town. His father, William, was a native of the town and worked as a cowman and an agricultural labourer.

When war was declared Ernest was 20 years old and after enlisting in the Royal Irish Rifles he arrived in France on 22 March 1915. During the war he transferred to the Army Service Corps and on 11 April 1918, during the German advance, was reported missing in action.

After the war he returned to Campden and married Lillian Beatrice and they had three children: Anthony Robert, Dorothy Maria and Margaret Jean.

Ernest died on 1 March 1971 aged 76 and is buried in St. James's churchyard. His wife died on 13 October 1976 aged 73 years.

Harry Hedges
Sergeant 28498, Royal Field Artillery

Born: January 1883

Harry was born in Campden, the eldest son of William and Emma Hedges of Westington, and was baptised at St. James's Church on 25 March 1883. In 1901 he was employed as a farm labourer and his father was a cattleman on a farm. He later became a groom.

On 13 November 1902 Harry enlisted as a gunner in the Royal Field Artillery. He was 19 years and 10 months old and his medical examination recorded that he was five feet six inches tall with blue eyes, brown hair and a fresh complexion. The next three years were spent on home service before he was posted to India. He arrived in India on 9 December 1905 and remained there until he returned to England on 27 October 1910. In 1909 he was admitted to hospital on two occasions: thirty-six days were spent in one in Allahabad suffering from pyrexia and immediately after being discharged in March 1909 he was readmitted to another for a further twenty-five days with debility.

Harry completed his eight years' service with the colours on 13 November 1910 and was transferred to the Army Reserve, where he remained until war was declared in 1914. He was mobilised on 5 August 1914 in Glasgow and was soon promoted to bombardier. In December 1914 he was promoted to corporal and then on 1 May 1915 to sergeant.

The landings at Gallipoli began in April 1915 and it was on 29 June that Harry embarked at Avonmouth to join the Mediterranean Expeditionary Force. He arrived at Gallipoli on 2 August and remained there until 14 October when his term of military service expired. The journey home was via Alexandria in Egypt and he arrived back in England on 22 December.

Harry was discharged from the army on 4 January 1916 after 13 years and 53 days with the Royal Field Artillery.

George Henry Hedges
Gunner 195793, Royal Field Artillery

Born: 22 August 1895
Mobilised: 28 November 1916
Discharged: 29 October 1919
Died: 3 April 1972

Harry was the second of four sons of Fred and Elizabeth Ann Hedges of Paul's Pike, Campden. He was baptised at St. James's Church on 24 November 1895 and after leaving school he found employment as a baker.

During the war he enlisted in the Royal Field Artillery at Cirencester and his initial training was in High Wycombe, in barracks that became an area of houses called Archdale. He arrived in France on 29 March 1917 and was wounded in the left foot on 23 July after being at the front for only four months. The *Evesham Journal* reported: "*Mrs. F. Hedges has received a letter from her son, Gunner G. H. Hedges, RFA, to say that he has been invalided home from France with a wound in the left hand and one in the left foot. He is now in hospital in Scotland and progressing favourably.*" He was admitted to Edinburgh War Hospital on 31 July.

After recovering from his wounds he returned to his unit and served in France and Italy, and then in Germany as part of the Army of Occupation in 1919. He was then discharged and returned to Campden before he moved to High Wycombe. In 1928 he married Elsie Pratt and they had three children, Raymond, Barbara and Marjorie. They lived at Radnage near High Wycombe.

Harry worked as a French polisher in High Wycombe and during the Second World War he was an Air Raid Precautions warden. He died on 3 April 1972 aged 76 and his ashes are buried at Aylesbury Crematorium.

William Charles Hedges
Private 17514, 12 Platoon, "C" Company, 10th Bn., Gloucestershire Regiment

Enlisted: January 1915
Died: 25 September 1915

William was born in Campden in 1893 and baptised at St. James's Church on 27 August 1893. He was the son of Fred and Elizabeth Ann Hedges of Paul's Pike and was raised in the town with his brothers and sisters: Harry, Leonard, Joseph and Nora. After leaving school he worked on the Harrowby Estate at Aston-sub-Edge and later went to Sandon in Staffordshire, where he continued working for the Earl of Harrowby.

In January 1915 he and his cousin, Tom Smith, enlisted in Campden in the Gloucestershire Regiment and were posted to the 10th Battalion. The battalion was formed in Bristol in September 1914 and attached to the 26th Division at Codford on Salisbury Plain. In April 1915 they were at Sand Hill Camp, Sutton Veny on Salisbury Plain. After a spell at Longbridge Deverell near Longleat they crossed the Channel from Southampton to Le Havre on 8 August 1915 and were attached a few days later to the 1st Brigade of 1st Division. They moved to Béthune, where they spent the rest of the month in *"bad"* billets. A short time was spent in the trenches and they sustained their first casualties when two men were wounded during a German bombing raid.

The battalion was very soon in serious action at the Battle of Loos, which started on 25 September 1915. Loos-en-Gohelle was a small mining village just to the north-west of Lens and seven British divisions were to attack across terrain that was in general flat, offering little cover and exposed to German fire from slightly higher positions. The attack began at 6.30am and was

The Hedges family 14 August 1915
Back: William, Nora (who married Jerry Howell), Harry (RFA 1914-18) and Joseph
Front: Leonard, Fred and Bess.

preceded by the release of gas forty minutes earlier. The 10th Glosters were in the centre of the British line, leading the attack in three lines on a long, low ridge towards the village of Hulloch. Gas was being used by the British for the first time and initially caused panic in the German trenches, but the wind changed direction and it was blown back towards the British lines. The battalion fought their way forward and were exposed to continuous machine gun fire but they found gaps in the German wire and entered their trenches. Heavy resistance was met but they managed to advance to the German third defensive line. By now the casualties to the battalion were horrendous and when they regrouped at night only 60 men from the battalion had not become casualties. Amongst the dead were William Hedges and his cousin, Tom Smith, together with two men from Mickleton, Frank Waters and Ernest Wright.

William was 22 years old when he died. His body could not be identified at the end of the war and his name is recorded on the Loos Memorial at Dud Corner Cemetery, near Loos-en-Gohelle in France. The memorial records the names of 20,000 men who died in the area and who have no known graves. The names of two of William's cousins are recorded on the memorial: Tom Smith and Charles Hedges.

After the war his parents moved to 4 Aston Road in a house built by the Council for returning servicemen and their families and William's name was put forward for two memorials in Campden: in St. James's Church and in the High Street. It is also recorded on the memorials in Aston-sub-Edge, Mickleton and Sandon.

William Charles Hedges
Private 43306, Royal Berkshire Regiment
Private 010010, Hampshire Regiment

> Born: 13 August 1893
> Died: 9 June 1980

Charlie was born in Campden in 1893, the only son of Charles and Ida Hedges of Watery Lane. He went to school in the town and then found employment as an agricultural labourer.

During the war he served in France and Belgium and his parents received a telegram stating that he was *"reported missing, presumed dead"* but he eventually turned up alive. After the armistice was signed Charlie was posted to Sudan, Egypt and was still there in March 1920 when he had his photograph taken wearing his uniform and medal ribbons.

After leaving the army Charlie returned to Campden and married Lillian Evelyn Dunn. Lillian was from Bristol and her brother, Clifford Ernest, was killed in action on 30 November 1917. Charlie and Evelyn moved to Broad Campden and lived in a house near the church. They had five children, Sheila, Sybil, Ida, Clifford and John, and a sixth, William Edward Eden, was adopted at birth. Charlie worked for Mr. Badger as a farm worker and the family later went to live at Guns Cottages. After his wife died on 13 August 1954 aged 59 years Charlie went to live with his daughter and son-in-law, John and Ida Wright, at 42 Littleworth, Campden.

Charlie died on 9 June 1980 aged 87 years and is buried in St. James's churchyard.

Charles Thomas Herbert
Private 23436, Wiltshire Regiment
Private 22977, 10th Battalion, Royal Berkshire Regiment
Private 95005, 159th Company, Labour Corps
Private 26402, 2nd/4th Battalion, Duke of Wellington's West Riding Regiment

Born: 21 December 1895
Enlisted: April 1916
Died: 30 August 1918

Charles was born in Blockley, the son of George Alfred and Mary Ann Herbert. His father was an ironmonger's assistant.

He was educated at Campden Grammar School and was a member of the Boy Scouts. In 1915 he helped carry the coffin of Private Benjamin Keen, 2nd Battalion, Gloucestershire Regiment, a fellow Scout, who died of wounds in hospital in England and was buried in Blockley.

In April 1916 Charles made his way to Oxford and enlisted in the Wiltshire Regiment. He was then transferred to the 10th (Labour) Battalion, Royal Berkshire Regiment, which was formed at Portsmouth in May 1916. The battalion arrived in France on 20 June 1916 and in April 1917 it was split into the 158th and 159th Companies of the Labour Corps. Charles joined 159th Company.

A further transfer occurred in 1918 when Charles joined the 2nd/4th Battalion, West Riding Regiment, 62nd (2nd West Riding) Division, and in the summer months the battalions in the division were involved in a series of blows that began to force the enemy into retreat. On 25 August 1918 Mory, south of Arras, was captured and then several determined counter-attacks from the enemy were repulsed at Vaulx-Vraucourt.

Charles was killed in action in this area, south-east of Arras, near Bapaume, on 30 August 1918. He was 23 years old and as his grave could not be found at the end of the war his name is recorded on the Vis-en-Artois Memorial, near Arras in France. His name is also recorded on the Campden Grammar School memorial and on two memorials in Blockley, in the church and on the village green.

Vis-en-Artois Memorial, France

Robert Heron
Lancashire Regiment

Born: 13 March 1877

Robert was born at Grange Fell, Broughton East, near Cartmel in Cumbria, the son of Robert Heron, a gardener by trade, and his wife, Jane. He married Caroline Asenath Bennett, daughter of Enoch and Ann Bennett of Campden, at Christ Church in Lancaster on 1 December 1900. Caroline was baptised at St. James's Church in Campden on 19 May 1872 and was employed as a domestic servant in Lancaster at the time of the marriage. After the wedding they lived at 74 Clarence Street in Lancaster and Robert was employed as a warehouseman and carter. They had two children: Florence Ellen, known as "Nelly", who was baptised at St. James's Church in Campden on 17 September 1905, and Robert, known as "Bob", whose birth was registered in the Lancaster district in 1907. Sadly, Caroline died in 1910 aged 38 years and her death was registered in Lancaster.

At the outbreak of war Robert was 37 years old and in the *Book of Remembrance* by Josephine Griffiths and on the St. James's Church 1916 prayer list Robert is recorded as serving in the Lancashire Regiment. No medal index card for a "*Robert Heron*" was found at the National Archives in London so it must be assumed that he was employed on home service only in the East Lancashire Regiment, South Lancashire Regiment or the Loyal North Lancashire Regiment.

There was a Robert W. Heron who served in the South Lancashire Regiment but he was discharged from the army in 1917 aged 26 years so he could not be the correct man.

Ernest George Hill
Able Seaman 235264, Royal Navy
Private 3626, 8th Battalion, London Regiment (Post Office Rifles)
Private 385165, 8th Battalion, London Regiment (Post Office Rifles)
Private 190683, Royal Engineers

Born: 17 February 1890
Died: 18 April 1949

Ernest was born in Chipping Norton, the son of George and Sarah Hill. His father was a carpenter by trade. After leaving school Ernest found employment as a baker's boy before he enlisted in the Royal Navy at Portsmouth on 14 November 1905. He began his time in the Royal Navy as a boy second class on HMS *Impregnable*, the Royal Navy training ship at Devonport. He then became a boy first class on 22 August 1906 and when he reached the age of 18 years in 1908 he signed on for a further 12 years' service. He was five feet six inches tall with brown hair, hazel eyes and a fresh complexion. After sixteen months serving as an ordinary seaman he was promoted to able seaman on 18 June 1909 while serving on HMS *Hindustan*.

The next three years were spent serving on HMS *Grafton*, HMS *Excellent* and HMS *Liverpool*. When Ernest was not at sea he was based at HMS *Victory* in Portsmouth.

Ernest's career was cut short when he was invalided out of the Royal Navy on 8 August 1912 with a hernia. He then found employment as a postman. At the outbreak of war he enlisted in the 8th Battalion, London Regiment, the Post Office Rifles, and after a period of home service he arrived in France on 28 October 1915. Nine months later the battalion arrived in the Somme sector after a long march from Vimy. They attacked High Wood on 15 September 1916 and then on 7 October they attacked Snag Trench in front of the Butte de Warlencourt.

He transferred to the Royal Engineers during his time in the army before being captured by the Germans and taken to a prisoner of war camp.

In 1922 he was living at West End Terrace in Campden and Ernest and his wife, Ellen, had a daughter baptised at St. Eadburgha's Church in Ebrington on 12 March 1922. They also had a son called Arthur who lived for many years in Berrington Road in Campden.

Augustine Hinks
Private 51875, 38th Company, Royal Army Medical Corps

Born: 25 October 1883
Enlisted: 1 February 1915
Discharged: 18 October 1919
Died: 8 August 1962

Gus is standing on the right-hand side.

Gus was born in Worcester, the son of James Henry and Mary Ann Hinks. His father was a painter and when Gus was born the family were living in Bowling Green Walk in Worcester.

Gus married Frances Mary Hartwell at St. Catharine's Church in Campden in 1907 and they had three children: Cecilia, Raymond and Philip. The honeymoon was spent in Oxford and their home was 3 West End Terrace, Campden.

On 1 February 1915, when he was 31 years old, Gus enlisted in the Royal Army Medical Corps. He arrived in France on 29 July 1915 but must have been posted to Turkey soon afterwards as there is a family legend that Gus was buried alive at Gallipoli. The trauma of this stayed with him for the rest of his life and he was often seen walking around Campden with very shaky hands.

Gus was in India in June 1918 as the family have a postcard that he wrote to his daughter,

Gus is standing in the centre, sorting letters.

Cecilia, who was only 4 years old at the time. He was discharged from the army on 18 October 1919 and the following reference was written by his commanding officer: "*Gus has a good knowledge of general nursing duties. He is a keen, hard working and sober soldier.*"

After the war he returned to Campden and was a member of the Campden fire crew. He also pumped the church organ at St. Catharine's and found employment at Horne's Grocers in Moreton. The family home became 10 Catbrook after they had moved from West End Terrace.

Gus died on 8 August 1962 aged 78 and is buried in St. Catharine's cemetery in Campden. His wife died on 21 November 1966 aged 84 years.

Ben Biggin Holtam
Driver 65410, Royal Field Artillery

Ben was born in Maugersbury, near Stow-on-the-Wold in 1887, the fourth of five children of James Abel and Louisa Biggin Holtam. His father had emigrated to America with some of his brothers and returned to England in about 1875. He then married Louisa and ran the Naunton Inn and then the Farmer's Arms in Maugersbury. Their eldest child, Charlotte, was born in Naunton and their other four children were born in Maugersbury.

James brought the family to Campden in the early 1900's when he became the landlord of the Red Lion public house. His youngest daughter, Minnie May, took over the running of the pub in 1909 and it was she who subsequently sold it after the death of both her parents. Louisa died on

25 April 1911 aged 51 years and her husband died on 9 November 1916 aged 69 years. They are buried together in St. James's churchyard in Campden.

On the 1901 census Ben was 14 years old and employed as an agricultural labourer. When the war started in 1914 he was living in Campden with his father and sister and he enlisted in the Royal Field Artillery. He entered France on 29 October 1915 and the 1918 electoral roll indicates that the family home was the Red Lion and that he was still away serving in the army. At the end of the war Ben returned safely and in 1922 he was living with his sister Minnie in Lower High Street.

Frederick Kerton Holtam
Private M2-102881 Army Service Corps

Frederick was born in Maugersbury in 1885, the third of five children of James Abel and Louisa Biggin Holtam. His father was born in Cheltenham in 1847; he married Louisa after returning from America. In 1881 he was landlord at the Naunton Inn and then on the 1891 and 1901 census returns the family are living at the Farmer's Arms in Maugersbury where James was the landlord.

Frederick was 16 in 1901 and the census records him as a cattleman on a farm. In 1914 he married Edith Newman in the Stow-on-the-Wold registration district and then enlisted in the Army Service Corps. He entered France on 1 October 1915 and returned safely at the end of the war.

There is no evidence to suggest that Frederick went to Campden with his parents when they took over the running of the Red Lion public house.

Harry Hooke
Army Service Corps

Harry was born in St. Pancras in London in 1887, the son of Elizabeth Hooke, and was a witness when his elder brother, Thomas Charles Hooke, married Ellen Francis Smith, sister of Reginald Richard Smith, in December 1919.

Tom Hooke was quite badly crippled, both his legs and one of his arms being affected. He had been a comedian in London and in Campden he formed "Tom Hooke's Jazz Band". Fred Coldicott writes: "*They were a scream, about eight of them in comic dress and all sorts of instruments.*" They helped raise funds for the war memorial in 1919.

In her *Book of Remembrance* Josephine Griffiths lists Harry as serving in the Army Service Corps during the war.

William Edward Hope
Sergeant-Major, Royal Field Artillery

Born: 6 October 1876
Died: 17 December 1956

William was born in Snitterfield, the fourth son of Thomas and Sarah Hope of The Green, Snitterfield. His father was employed as a gardener and farm labourer. After leaving school William found employment as a painter before he joined the army as a regular soldier. He served in South Africa during the Boer War and during the 1914-18 war he was a sergeant-major in the Royal Field Artillery.

He left the army after 19 years' service and married Kate Edith Hedges of Westington, Campden in 1919. Their first child, Kathleen Edith, was baptised at St. James's Church in Campden on 18 January 1920 before the family moved to Sutton Coldfield. He spent the next thirty years employed at the General Electrics Company at Witton in Birmingham before returning to Campden at the end of the Second World War.

William died at his home, 4, The Almshouses, Campden, on 17 December 1956 aged 80 years. He was survived by his wife, who died on 8 March 1970 aged 80 years, and his son, John, who was living in Berrington Road, Campden.

James Willetts Horne
Engine Room Artificer 5th Class M300036, Royal Navy

Born: 9 February 1898
Enlisted: 22 March 1918
Discharged: 19 March 1920
Died: February 1982

Willetts was born in Campden, the eldest son of Lewis Hadley and Muriel Jesse Horne of Leysbourne, Campden, and was baptised at St. James's Church on 12 April 1898. His father was a farmer and coal merchant and during the First World War he served in France with the Gloucestershire Regiment. His mother was the daughter of Julius and Isabelle Neve.

Willetts was educated at Campden Grammar School and at a public school in Horsham in Sussex. During his time as a schoolboy in Campden he was a mascot with "H" Company, 5th Battalion, Gloucestershire Regiment, the local company of the Territorial Army, and went away on some of their annual camps.

When war was declared he was only 16 years old and it was not until he reached the age of 20 that he enlisted in the Royal Navy on 22 March 1918.

The medical examination recorded that he was five feet seven inches tall, with blue eyes and scars on his right wrist and right calf. After being passed fit for service he was posted to HMS *Pembroke*, a depot in Chatham, as an engine room artificer fifth class. He transferred to HMS *Superb* on 22 June 1918 and remained on the ship until he was discharged on 19 March 1920. On 9 February 1919 he was promoted to acting engine room artificer fourth class.

After the war Willetts began an apprenticeship with the Great Western Railway Company in Swindon but soon left the country to spend ten years jute farming in Assam. On his return he found employment with the British Can Company in Acton, London and met his future wife, who was working as the company nurse. The Metal Box Company Limited then bought the company and Willetts became the manager and technical consultant, a post he held for 30 years.

He moved to Chadbury in 1934 to manage the Worcestershire dealings of the Metal Box Company and he retired in 1963.

Willetts married Emily Stephenson and they had four children: Jessie, Ruth Isobel, Robert Peter and Margaret Mabel. He died at his home, The Bungalow, Chadbury, in February 1982 aged 83 years and his ashes are buried in St. James's churchyard in Campden. His wife died on 8 January 1947.

John "*Jack*" Newton Horne
Lance Corporal 30210, 2nd Battalion, Grenadier Guards

Enlisted: 18 October 1917
Discharged: 20 December 1918
Died: 17 March 1986

Jack was born in Campden in 1899, the eldest son of Lewis Hadley and Muriel Jesse Horne of Leysbourne, and was baptised at St. James's Church on 18 November 1899. His father was a farmer and coal merchant and during the First World War he served with the Gloucestershire Regiment. His mother was the daughter of Julius and Isabelle Neve.

After leaving Campden Grammar School Jack enlisted at Worcester in the Grenadier Guards on 18 October 1917 aged 18 years. He was passed fit to serve at his medical examination and his next of kin was his mother, who was then living at "Wellacres" in Blockley. Jack joined the regiment in Caterham and was trained for mounting the guard at Buckingham Palace, St. James's Palace and Marlborough House, a job that Jack was very proud to do.

In March 1918 they were told that a detachment was going to be sent to France to join the 2nd Battalion, Grenadier Guards. Jack arrived in France on 28 April and the detachment travelled to an area 10 kilometres south of Arras by rail in box trucks labelled "*8 chevaux, 40 hommes*". The comradeship was wonderful and there was always a good deal of humour amidst the men.

Jack remembers being close to Adinfer Wood and during the night it was amazing to hear a chorus of nightingales; usually during the night the wood was shelled frequently. After an explosion the birds stopped, but it was not long before they continued their song. In June 1918 the unit was withdrawn to Saulty-aux-Bois and the officer took the men into a field to form up. There was a cow in the field and soon a French peasant came at them with his fists. He was angry because the men were spoiling the grass for his cow. Needless to say, the unit soon withdrew.

In July 1918 Jack was promoted to lance corporal and in August was badly wounded when he was shot through the elbow and lost a thumb. He returned to England on 31 August and four months of treatment followed before he was discharged from the army on 20 December 1918. It was arranged for Jack to be admitted to Farncombe House near Broadway for treatment, a VAD (Voluntary Aid Detachment) Hospital which later became a Group 4 security centre. After the war his arm was useless.

After returning to Campden Jack was a corn and seed merchant and also had a taxi and a bus available for private hire. In 1930 he married Phyllis Boulten in Bretforton and they had one daughter, Joan Frances, who married Rex Brearley in 1956. During the Second World War Jack was a 2nd lieutenant in the Home Guard and was the commanding officer of the 40th Platoon, 2nd Battalion, Home Guard, Gloucestershire Regiment.

Jack died on 17 March 1986 aged 86 years and is buried in St. James's churchyard.

John is standing at the back in the centre, February 1918.

Lewis Hadley Horne
Company Sergeant-Major 602, 1st/5th Battalion, Gloucestershire Regiment
Warrant Officer Second Class 240029, 1st/5th Bn., Gloucestershire Regiment

Enlisted: 27 December 1902
Discharged: 21 January 1919
Died: 3 March 1950

Lewis was born in Campden in 1868, the son of James Newton and Elizabeth Horne of Leysbourne, Campden, and was baptised at St. James's Church on 21 December 1868. He was educated at Campden Grammar School and then employed in a variety of jobs. In 1891 he was an assistant in a corn-trading business and in 1901 a farmer and coal merchant.

His wife was Muriel Jesse Neve, the sister of Basil and Gerald, and they had six children, including two sons who served during the 1914-18 war, John Newton and James Willetts.

In "K" Company, 2nd Volunteer Battalion, Gloucestershire Regiment Lewis was the colour-sergeant. He then became the company sergeant-major in "H" Company, 5th Battalion, Gloucestershire Regiment, the local company of the Territorial Army, with whom he served on the Western Front during the 1914-18 war. He was a good marksman and won several trophies on the rifle range.

Lewis was mobilised on 5 August 1914 and went to Chelmsford for final training before the battalion arrived in France on 29 March 1915. The next few months were spent in the Ploegsteert sector in Belgium before they moved south to the Somme. On 28 May 1916 Lewis was accused of a *"green envelope"* offence and there was a court martial. Only a small sample of *"green envelopes"* were opened, as the men were trusted not to give information that might be helpful to the enemy. Lewis had one of his envelopes opened and an officer was not happy with what he saw. The initial court martial was adjourned to gather further evidence. It met again on 8 June 1916 at Capennes and Lewis was found guilty and reduced to the rank of sergeant.

Before the war Lewis was the Campden correspondent for the *Evesham Journal* for more than twenty years and he continued sending letters from France during the war to keep the people at home informed about what was going on. *"Before going to the trenches last week nearly the whole of the company went to Holy Communion. It was held in a barn, full of stores, and the men sat on bags and sacks over which the chaplain had to climb."* He also added that *"the little New Testaments sent by the vicar and supplied to the men are in constant use"*.

At Christmas in 1915 the *Evesham Journal* printed the following piece about Lewis. *"He is an old Territorial, and although a married man with a family and within a year or two of fifty years of age he had no hesitation about offering his services when the war broke out. The miseries and hardships of trench warfare, up to your knees in water for days, together with death hovering near, have not disheartened him. His initial period of service has expired but knowing that the job must be finished, and that all men are wanted, he has signed on again."*

Lewis served in France until he returned to England on 11 July 1916, where he was posted to the Territorial Force Reserve. The remainder of the war was spent on home service until he was discharged on 21 January 1919. He then returned home and held many public offices during the rest of his life. He was an excellent cricketer and in 1925 was playing for Moreton-in-Marsh. He took an active part in securing the admission of girls into the Grammar School and was a sidesman at St. James's Church and a regular member of the congregation at Broad Campden Church.

Lewis died on 3 March 1950 at his home, "Hillside", Broad Campden, aged 81 and is buried in St. James's churchyard in Campden. His wife died on 13 December 1962 aged 91 years.

George Edward James Horwood
Sergeant 4384, 28 Wing, Royal Flying Corps

Enlisted: 27 March 1915
Discharged: 20 April 1920

Ted was born in Chelsea in London in 1881 and after leaving school found employment as a photographer before later becoming a jeweller. He then joined Charles Ashbee and spent eleven years with the Guild of Handicraft, arriving in Campden in 1902. He married his wife, Jesse, at Benfleet on 1 August 1904 and they had four children, all baptised at St. James's Church in Campden: Jessie May, Annie Lucy, Wilhelmina Daisy and Edward George.

In 1914 Ted was living at the post office in Broad Campden and his occupation was listed as "*shopkeeper at Post Office*" in the Kelly's Directory. He enlisted in the Royal Flying Corps as an air mechanic second class on 27 March 1915 and gained promotion to air mechanic first class on 1 September 1915. Further promotion followed and he reached the rank of sergeant on 27 March 1917 while he was serving in Malta.

Ted served in Malta from 17 September 1915 to 16 August 1917, although he spent six months in 1916 with the Darfur expedition into Central Africa. His final period of service was at Salonika in Greece, where he was awarded the Meritorious Service Medal for "*devotion to duty*". The award was announced in the *London Gazette* on 17 December 1917 and was reported in the *Evesham Journal* under the headline "*Broad Campden Man Decorated*". The report continued: "*His Majesty the King has been graciously pleased to approve of the award of the Meritorious Service Medal to Sergt. G. E. J. Horwood, 4384, RFC. He joined the Royal Flying Corps in March 1915 and has seen service in Egypt and Salonika. He recently returned to England fit and well.*"

After the war ended Ted returned to England, where he was placed into the Royal Air Force Reserve on 3 April 1919 before being officially discharged on 20 April 1920.

Albert John Howell
Company Quartermaster-Sergeant M2-099871, Motor Transport Company, Army Service Corps

Enlisted: 19 May 1915
Discharged: 9 September 1916
Died: 2 December 1918

John was born in Campden in 1877, the only son of Reuben and Eliza Ann Howell of Cider Mill Lane. His father was a mason's labourer and his mother's maiden name was Griffin. In 1891 the family were living in Leysbourne and John was an errand boy aged 13 years. He then left the town and found employment as a motor-driver.

On 14 October 1902 he married Dora Stead in Leominster and they had two children, Honor Elizabeth and Beryl Lena, who were both born in Faringdon. The family returned to Campden before the war and were living in Church Street when John enlisted in the Army Service Corps as a private in Cirencester on 19 May 1915. He joined his unit at Grove Park in London the following day to begin a period of 1 year and 114 days in the army.

In August 1915 John was promoted to corporal while stationed at Bulford Camp and then in October 1915 to company quartermaster-sergeant. He was posted overseas to France as part of the British Expeditionary Force on 22 April 1916 and remained at the front until he returned to England on 3 May 1916 feeling ill and very weak. A medical board reported on 28 June 1916: "*He is very weak. His present condition shows no improvement and his diabetic symptoms are getting worse. There are severe pains in the knees and ankles. This condition is not the result of active service but it has been aggravated by his time at the front.*"

John was discharged from the army on 9 September 1916 and returned to Campden, where he continued to suffer from diabetes. His life came to an end when he died of influenza on 2 December 1918 aged 41 years after being ill for over two years. He is buried in St. James's churchyard with a Commonwealth War Graves Commission headstone and his name is recorded on two memorials in the town: in St. James's Church and in the High Street.

Charles Clapton Howell
Gloucestershire Regiment

Died: December 1949

Charles was born in Campden in 1873, the second son of George Obed and Elizabeth Julia Ann Howell of High Street, Campden, and was baptised at St. James's Church on 31 May 1874. His father married Elizabeth Clapton, daughter of Charlie Clapton of Campden, on 24 October 1871 and was listed as a "*gas stoker*" on the 1881 census. By 1891 Charles was 18 years old and had left the family home which was now in Leysbourne, where George and Elizabeth were living with four of their children: George William, Thomas Henry, Minnie Sophia and Julia Francis. George was now employed as a "*labourer*".

In 1894 Charles married Ellen Sophia Johnson and a daughter called Julia Elizabeth was baptised at St. James's Church on 7 October 1894. At the time of the baptism Charles was employed as a labourer and living with Ellen in Stretton-on-Fosse.

In the years leading up to the war Charles and Ellen were living in Broad Campden and in August 1914 he was 41 years old. He served in the Gloucestershire Regiment but as no medal index card can be found he must have been employed on home service only.

After the war Charles and Ellen continued living in Broad Campden and they died within a few days of each other in December 1949. They were both 76 years old and are buried in St. James's churchyard in Campden.

Frank Lewis Howell
Lance Corporal 9432, 3rd Battalion, South Wales Borderers

Born: 17 April 1887
Died: 9 February 1915

Frank was the eldest son of Eli and Emily Tabitha Howell of Lower High Street, Campden and was baptised at St. James's Church on 14 July 1887. His father was a native of Campden and in 1891 was employed as a farm labourer. In 1901 Eli was a widower and had moved to Church Street with his sons, Frank and Lewis, and was now employed as a Great Western Railway platelayer.

Frank enlisted at Brecon in the 1st Battalion, South Wales Borderers but became ill and could not go to France with the battalion in August 1914. This resulted in his being posted to the 3rd Battalion, who were a home service battalion. Frank never made it to France and died after a long illness on 9 February 1915, when he was 27 years old. He is buried in St. James's churchyard with a Commonwealth War Graves Commission military headstone and his name can be seen on two memorials in the town: in St. James's Church and in the High Street.

Gerald Howell
Private 3555, 2nd/5th Battalion, Gloucestershire Regiment
Private 241174, 2nd/5th Battalion, Gloucestershire Regiment

Born: 5 October 1896
Enlisted: 16 November 1914
Died: 19 November 1960

Jerry was a native of Campden and was the second of four sons of Gerard and Emily Eliza Howell of Lower High Street. He was baptised at St. James's Church on 15 November 1896 and went to school in the town.

Jerry enlisted in the Gloucestershire Regiment on 16 November 1914, when he was just 18 years old. He joined the 2nd/5th Battalion (a Territorial battalion) and served alongside Jack Taplin and Tom Bickley, who were both from Campden. A period of training in England followed before the battalion left Salisbury Plain on 24 May 1916. They arrived at Southampton later that day to board HMS *681*, the ship that was going to transport them to France. They arrived at Le Havre early on the morning of 25 May 1916 and the battalion made their way towards the French village of Laventie. Their first experience of life in front line trenches came on 15 June 1916. Six days later Jerry was wounded on the day that the battalion were due to be relieved. He was involved in a raid on the German trenches that also included Tom Bickley. It was a bombing raid and he was shot by one bullet that went through both legs. He dropped into a shell hole in No Man's Land and stayed there alongside an Australian soldier who was sheltering during the raid. Jerry was evacuated back to England and ended up being admitted to Shorncliffe Military Hospital. Shorncliffe was an Australian hospital and Jerry was the only English person there at the time. When he left the hospital he returned to Campden and had to be met at the station by his father, who had to carry him to their home in Lower High Street. Apparently no farmer offered them a lift.

After recovering from the wound Jerry returned to the battalion and was wounded again by a piece of shrapnel in the thigh. This shrapnel was never removed and in later life it used to move continuously up and down his thigh.

Jerry returned to Campden after the war and married Nora Hedges at St. James's Church on 4 October 1924. Nora lost her brother, William Charles Hedges, during the war, killed in action at Loos in France on 25 September 1915. They lived at 4, Aston Road, Campden in a house built by the Council for returning servicemen and he found employment as a bricklayer. During the Second World War he was a special constable and throughout his time in Campden he was an active member of the British Legion and in 1956 was made a life member.

Jerry died on 19 November 1960 aged 64 years and is buried in St. James's churchyard. Nora died on 26 September 1992 aged 94 years.

The Black Hand Gang
Jerry is standing at the end of the centre row on the right.

John Howell
Private 137237, Machine Gun Corps

Born: 28 December 1898
Died: 16 September 1972

Jack was born in Campden, the third son of Gerard and Emily Eliza Howell of Lower High Street. He was baptised at St. James's Church on 26 February 1899 and went to school in the town.

When the war started in 1914 he was living in the High Street. He initially enlisted in the Gloucestershire Regiment but transferred to the Machine Gun Corps in late 1917 before he went overseas for the first time.

He was part of the Army of Occupation in Germany in 1919, marching from Belgium, across the Rhine and into Germany to the east of Cologne, a total of 204 miles. He was with the 29th Battalion, Machine Gun Corps, a unit in the 29th Division, and after his discharge from the army he returned to Campden with a map of the long march.

After the war Jack found employment as a roadman. He married Louisa Bryan at St. James's Church on 30 June 1934. They did not have any children. During the Second World War he was a special constable.

He died on 16 September 1972 aged 73 and is buried in St. James's churchyard.

Lewis William Howell
Gloucestershire Regiment
Army Service Corps

Born: 22 November 1891
Died: 30 July 1951

Bill was born in Campden, the eldest son of Gerard and Emily Eliza Howell of Lower High Street, Campden. His father, a farm labourer, was a native of the town; he had married Emily Franklin on 24 August 1889. Bill was baptised at St. James's Church, where he was later to be a member of the choir for over fifty years, having joined it as a young boy.

He went to school in the town and then found employment with the Great Western Railway at Campden station, first as a wheel-tapper and then as a platelayer. He married Mary May Caroline Harper and they had one son, Geoffrey, who subsequently had two sons of his own, David and Allen.

Very little is known about Bill's service during the war apart from the fact that he enlisted in the Gloucestershire Regiment before being transferred to the Army Service Corps. His brothers, Jerry and Jack, also joined the army during the war.

Bill died of a heart attack on 30 July 1951 aged 59 and was buried in his cassock in St. James's churchyard. He had been living in Leysbourne, Campden and was survived by his wife, who died on 2 January 1981 aged 85 years.

The Howell Brothers

Back row (left to right): Jerry (Gloucestershire Regiment), Bill (Army Service Corps) and Jack (Machine Gun Corps). Alfred James (Royal Warwickshire Regiment) is standing at the front. Alfred married Mary Howell, the brothers' sister.

George William Howley
Private 7902, 1st Battalion, Scots Guards

Born: 5 September 1893
Discharged: 1 April 1915
Died: 14 December 1948

George Howley was the eldest child of William and Anne Elizabeth Maria Howley of Westington, Campden and was baptised at St. Catharine's Church. After leaving school he became a policeman but at some point before 1914 he became a regular soldier, joining the Scots Guards where he was under the command of Lieutenant Archie Douglas-Dick. When war was declared the battalion was in Aldershot. They left for France from Southampton and arrived in Le Havre on 14 August 1914. George was not with the battalion at this time but eventually joined them in France on 2 September 1914 in time for fighting around the River Marne and River Aisne areas. George was in action north of the River Aisne, on the Chemin des Dames, and then made the long journey north to the Belgian town of Ypres. On 8 November 1914 he came across a wounded Archie Douglas-Dick and carried him back to an advanced dressing station. After returning to the front line George was wounded in the leg near to Veldhoek on the Menin Road. Gangrene set in and his leg had to be amputated.

After recovering in hospital George was officially discharged from the army on 1 April 1915. He returned to Campden and met Elizabeth Gertrude Merriman. They married on 4 February 1922 at St. Catharine's Church and had two daughters, Margaret and Elizabeth.

Life was not easy for George in the years after the war. He found walking very hard as his artificial leg rubbed and his stump constantly ached. Many Campdonians remember him in local pubs massaging his leg between sips of beer.

He received a war pension and also did some tailoring to earn a living. He was an active member of the British Legion and of the Gainsborough Lodge of the Royal Antediluvian Order of Buffaloes (RAOB).

George died on 14 December 1948 aged 55 at Rankswood Military Hospital in Worcester and is buried in St. Catharine's cemetery in Campden.

Michael James Howley
Gloucestershire Regiment
Army Service Corps

Born: 5 March 1897

Michael was born in Campden, the son of William and Anne Elizabeth Maria Howley of Westington, and was baptised at St. Catharine's Church on 28 March 1897. His parents were married at the same church on 9 May 1893. His father was employed as a mason's labourer and his mother was known as Minnie.

During the war Michael enlisted in the Gloucestershire Regiment and then transferred to the Army Service Corps. He appears to have been employed on home service only as no medal index card could be found for him at the National Archives in London.

After the war Michael married and went to live in Broadway. He had a son, who went to work in London.

William Knowle Hudson
Captain, 2nd/7th Battalion, Royal Warwickshire Regiment

Born: 16 May 1892
Enlisted: 13 November 1914
Discharged: 8 September 1919

William was born in Birmingham and arrived in Campden in the 1920's after relinquishing his commission with the Royal Warwickshire Regiment "*on account of ill health caused by wounds*". He was known locally as Captain Hudson and was regularly seen around the town sitting on a stool doing oil paintings which he sold to make ends meet. He was a very good cricketer despite having an artificial leg and Lionel Ellis was always employed as his runner.

During his time in Campden William lived in Lower High Street and then with Lawrence and Gertrude Ladbrook in Berrington Road. When he was not painting he was a regular at the Red Lion.

He was appointed 2nd lieutenant with the 10th Battalion, Royal Warwickshire Regiment on 13 November 1914 when he was 22 years old, and then transferred to the 7th Battalion later the same day. He was promoted to lieutenant on 1 July 1917 and then to acting captain at the end of the month. While he was serving on the Western Front he received a gunshot wound to the left knee which resulted in his leaving his unit on 2 December 1917. He was evacuated to Rouen and admitted to hospital. On 13 February 1918 he embarked at Rouen and two days later arrived at Southampton. The wound received in France caused his left leg to be amputated and a temporary "*peg leg*" was fitted. In December 1918 William was a patient at the King's Lancashire Military Convalescent Hospital in Blackpool, waiting to have an artificial leg fitted, and on 8 January 1919 he was officially promoted to the rank of captain. In April he was still waiting for his artificial leg and had to be transferred to Alder Hay Special Military Surgical Hospital in Liverpool for an operation on his stump. A medical board then examined him on 5 August 1919 and found him "*permanently unfit for any further military service*" and stated that he should "*proceed home and await admission to Roehampton*" where his artificial leg was going to be fitted.

William relinquished his commission on 8 September 1919 but was able to retain the rank of captain to use in civilian life. He returned home to "*Lyndhurst*", Knowle, West Birmingham and then moved to Campden. He never married and left Campden before his death.

Charles Richard Hughes
Adjutant, Salvation Army

Born: 8 November 1870
Died: 10 April 1950

Charles was born in Mickleton, the third of six sons of James and Sarah Hughes. He married Eliza Jones, on 21 January 1901 at Cardiff Registry Office while he was serving as an officer with the Salvation Army. They had two children, Leonard and Claude Charles.

Charles entered training to become a Salvation Army officer from Small Heath, Birmingham in 1896 and served for 25 years as a corps officer at various appointments around the country before he settled in High Wycombe, Buckinghamshire in retirement. His active service saw him command corps in Leeds, Dewsbury, High Wycombe and Balham. At Leeds there was much unemployment and poverty and he ran soup

Charles and Eliza Hughes with their son Claude.

kitchens for many weeks and also distributed milk to the children each day.

In 1917 Charles and Eliza were sent to Kinmel Park Camp at Bodelwyddan, near Rhyl, in Wales to run a Red Shield Hostel where they ran soup kitchens and helped provide for the daily needs of the troops. In 1919 the camp was full of almost 20,000 Canadian troops waiting to be sent home. Conditions were poor and there was a great deal of unrest amongst the men as they became bored with army life now that the war was over. At 9.00pm on 4 March 1919 one thousand troops started a riot. Huts were damaged but the mutineers remembered their debt to the Salvation Army and Charles and Eliza and their quarters were spared. When the riot ended 5 men had been killed and 28 wounded.

Charles was forced to retire from the Salvation Army in 1922 owing to a nervous complaint, neurasthenia, which made it hard for him to do anything other than simple things. After retiring he supplemented his pension by doing gardening jobs and keeping poultry before he moved to High Wycombe in 1924.

He made regular trips to Campden to visit his brother and sister-in-law, Richard and Lucy Hughes, the author's great-grandparents. The two brothers remained extremely close all of their lives despite living in different parts of the country.

Charles died on 10 April 1950 aged 79 years and is buried in High Wycombe.

Donovan George Hughes

Private 34127, Oxfordshire and Buckinghamshire Light Infantry
Private 160684, Machine Gun Corps

Born: 1899
Enlisted: 21 March 1917
Discharged: 27 December 1918
Died: 15 January 1951

Don was born in 1899, the fourth son of William John and Edith Gertrude Hughes of Hidcote Bartrim. His father was born at Admington and employed as a general labourer in 1891, when the family were living at Quinton, and then as a carter on a farm in 1901, when the family were at Admington.

During the war Don enlisted in the Oxfordshire and Buckinghamshire Light Infantry in 1917 but soon transferred to the Machine Gun Corps. He served overseas but was discharged from the army as no longer fit for active service on 27 December 1918. A Silver War Badge was issued to show that he had made his contribution to the war.

After the war he found employment as a gardener and then married Dorothy May Pitcher at St. James's Church in Campden on 26 December 1922. They had two children: Peter Donovan and Roland John. Roland was named after Don's brother, Roland John, who died at Loos in France in 1916. Peter married Sheila Hedges, daughter of Charles

Don died on 15 January 1951 aged 51 years and is buried in St. Lawrence's churchyard in Mickleton.

Richard Hughes
Private 39545, 13th Battalion, Devonshire Regiment
Private 144789, 374 Company, 3rd Labour Battalion, Labour Corps

Born: 2 August 1877
Enlisted: 11 December 1915
Discharged: 18 February 1919
Died: 18 November 1957

Richard was born in Mickleton, the seventh child of James and Sarah Hughes, and was baptised at Mickleton Church on 28 October 1877. After leaving Mickleton School he became a gardener and this remained his trade throughout his working life. On 12 December 1897 he married Lucy Crosswell from Hidcote Bartrim at Mickleton Church. They had seven children: Lucy May, Richard George, Alice Ann, Arthur Charles (the author's grandfather), Gladys Evelyn Annie, Frederick William and Jesse.

Richard moved to Campden around 1905 after working in Mickleton and Weston-sub-Edge and this remained his home for the rest of his life. He had two homes in the town, one in Watery Lane and one in Sheep Street. This was a return to Campden for the author's family as Richard's grandfather, Richard Hughes, married Sarah Beard at St. James's Church in 1828.

When the war started in 1914 Richard was 37 years old and on 11 December 1915 he enlisted in Campden with his Watery Lane neighbour Leonard Brotheridge and both were posted to the Devonshire Regiment. At his medical examination he was found to have flat feet and classed as medical category C3 and placed into the Army Reserve. Nine months later he was mobilised on 14 September 1916 and posted to the 13th Battalion, Devonshire Regiment at Saltash. The battalion was a *"works"* battalion and in April 1917 it became the 3rd Labour Battalion of the Labour Corps and men were given new service numbers. Each labour battalion consisted of 9 officers, 29 non-commissioned officers, 480 privates and 4 batmen. In June 1917 Richard was posted to the Southern Command Labour Centre, which was located at West Farm Camp at Fovant in Hampshire. The establishment of 500 men was intended to supply working parties for both military and civil work. Men from the Labour Corps were involved in a range of civilian tasks including agricultural work, working in munitions factories, rail, canal and dock work, aerodrome work and salvage work.

On 1 June 1918 Richard joined 374 Company at Porton Down, Salisbury, Wiltshire under the command of Major Harbottle and Lieutenant Roberts. They worked on the construction of the Porton Military Railway.

Richard was discharged from the army on 18 February 1919 after serving in England for over two years. He returned to Campden and rejoined his wife and five surviving children and continued making a living as a gardener.

He died on 18 November 1957 aged 80 years and is buried in St. James's churchyard.

Richard and Lucy are seated at the front. At the back, left to right, are their children: Charles, May, George, Alice and Gladys.

Richard George Hughes
Ordinary Seaman J 64065, Royal Navy

Born: 14 August 1900
Enlisted: 22 December 1916
Discharged: 1932
Died: January 1966

George was born in Mickleton in 1900, the elder of two surviving sons of Richard and Lucy Hughes, and was baptised on 9 September 1900 at Mickleton Church. He entered Mickleton School in February 1905 and after leaving school worked with his father as a gardener.

When he was 16 years old he enlisted in the Royal Navy at Devonport on 22 December 1916 and at his medical examination it was recorded that he was five foot four inches tall and had brown hair and an operation scar on his left groin. During the war he served on HMS *Furious* and when he was not at sea he was based on HMS *Impregnable*, a training ship at Devonport, and HMS *Victory*, a navy depot at Portsmouth.

HMS *Furious* was launched in August 1916 but an 18-inch gun turret was removed and replaced by a hangar and flight deck before her first commission. She was completed in July 1917 and during the war she was employed as an aircraft carrier. The first landing was made by Squadron Leader E. H. Dunning, in a Sopwith Pup in August 1917 while George was serving on the ship. With the ship steaming head to wind, the pilot flew past as close as possible, drifted round

the bridge and arrived over the forward flying deck. Here he throttled down and allowed his machine to sink to the deck where, as there was no sort of gear to hold her down, it was grabbed by a party of officers and men while it was still in the air. As this was not a practical method, Dunning gave instructions that for his second attempt the plane was not to be touched until it was on the deck. So with the engine running he tried to land a second time but burst a tyre, and in the high wind the plane slewed over the side before it could be held down and the pilot was drowned.

George was awarded two campaign medals for his service in the Royal Navy during the war, the British War Medal and the Victory Medal. They turned up at "*Q&C Militaria*" in Cheltenham in 2001 and the author was able to purchase his great uncle's medals. George continued to serve in the Royal Navy after the war and eventually retired in 1932 as an able seaman after sixteen years' service.

He then moved to Campden and worked as a painter and decorator with his brother Charles. During the Second World War they both served in the Home Guard. He retired from work in August 1965.

George married his first wife, Winifred Jayne Pay, at Weymouth Registry Office on 2 February 1924 and they had three children: Lawrence, Rita and Doreen. Winifred died in 1930 and George married Edith Keen, who died on 14 April 1952 aged 68 years. He married his third wife, Mary Hall, at St. James's Church in Campden on 15 February 1958 and they went to live in Ebrington.

George died after a short illness at his home, 13 Long Well Bank, Ebrington, in January 1966 aged 65 years and is buried in St. Eadburgha's churchyard.

Roland John Hughes
Private 17658, 1st Battalion, Gloucestershire Regiment

Born: 26 June 1895
Died: 4 June 1916

Roland was born in Admington, Warwickshire, although some official sources state that he was born in Campden, and was the son of William John and Edith Gertrude Hughes. He enlisted in the army at Bristol in late 1914 or early 1915, when he was 19 years old, and arrived in France to join the 1st Battalion, Gloucestershire Regiment on 3 May 1915 in the vicinity of Béthune. Roland and the battalion were involved in the Battle of Aubers, which was a disaster for them. It resulted in the summer months being spent receiving reinforcements and undergoing training for their part in the Battle of Loos in September 1915.

The Battle of Loos began at 6.30am on 25 September 1915 and the 1st Battalion were in reserve. After a wait of over two hours they were ordered forward at 9.05am and, following a change of orders, they spent the rest of the day digging trenches in chalk without entrenching tools. They were relieved at night but had still suffered casualties without attacking the enemy or being attacked. On 5 October they were back in the front line digging trenches and on 8 October there was a strong German counter-attack. A heavy German barrage caused terrible casualties but after it petered out the battalion was able to open fire on the attackers, causing over 400 casualties.

After the end of the Battle of Loos the battalion remained in the Loos sector. May 1916 was particularly quiet and on 2 June the battalion moved to new trenches in the Calonne sector, south-west of Loos-en-Gohelle, and were immediately subjected to shelling and mortar fire from the Germans. Roland was killed in action near Loos on 4 June 1916 aged 20 years. The war diary records that hostile heavy shelling began at 2.30am and continued at intervals until midday. The trenches were "*much knocked about in the centre company*" particularly by a heavy bombardment at 7.00pm. "*Two men were killed.*"

A memorial service was held for Roland in St. Lawrence's Church in Mickleton on 18 June 1916. His name is not recorded on any memorial in Campden but it is on the memorial in St. Lawrence's Church.

Three of Roland's brothers also served in the army during the war: Donovan George, Thomas Edwin and William Eber.

George Stanley Hunt
Bombardier 931002, Royal Field Artillery

Enlisted: 3 June 1915
Discharged: 7 March 1919

George was born in 1894, the son of John Enoch Hunt. He enlisted in the Royal Field Artillery on 3 June 1915 and after a few months of home service was posted overseas. The war ended for George when he was captured by the enemy and taken to a prisoner of war camp. When the camp was liberated at the end of the war he was suffering from sickness caused by the conditions in the camp and was immediately discharged from the army on 7 March 1919.

On 20 June 1919 George married Edith Beatrice Wilkes, daughter of Lewis Wealthy Wilkes, at St. James's Church in Campden.

George Stannard Hunt

George was born in 1882, the son of Thomas Hunt, a general labourer. He married Edith Beatrice Hughes, daughter of William and Elizabeth Hughes of Watery Lane, Campden at St. James's Church on 3 August 1908. At the time of his wedding he was employed as a coach painter and living in Edgbaston.

On the 1918 electoral roll he is listed as living in Broad Campden and absent on military service.

William Hunt
Trooper 1864, "D" Squadron, 1st/1st Warwickshire Yeomanry
Private 164689, 100th Battalion, Machine Gun Corps

Born: 29 July 1893
Enlisted: 23 February 1912
Died: 17 October 1918

William was born at Burleigh Farm, Brinscombe, Gloucestershire, the son of Frederick William and Ada Ellen Hunt. He enlisted in the Warwickshire Yeomanry in Weston-sub-Edge on 23 February 1912 and at the outbreak of war in 1914 was mobilised and went with the regiment to Bury St. Edmunds on 14 August. At the time of his mobilisation he was living and working at Norton Grounds Farm near Mickleton, although "*Soldiers Died in the Great War*" states that his residence was "*Campden*".

On 11 April 1915 William sailed from Avonmouth in the transport *Wayfarer* with 763 horses on board to join the force being concentrated in Egypt for the landings at Gallipoli. Sixty miles north-west of the Scillies they were torpedoed but did not sink and were towed to Queenstown, County Cork. After a short delay they arrived at Alexandria on the *Saturnia* on 24 April 1915. When the Warwickshire Yeomanry were ordered to Gallipoli about one third of the men, including William, were left behind at Chatby Camp in Alexandria to look after the horses. It is possible that he arrived at Gallipoli in a reinforcement draft but he missed the Yeomanry's main involvement on 18 August 1915 when they advanced across the Salt Lake at Suvla. By the end of November the Warwickshire Yeomanry had left Gallipoli and were at Mena Camp in Cairo. In January 1916 they combined with the Gloucestershire and Worcestershire Yeomanry to form the 5th Mounted Brigade and the next few months were spent in operations in the Suez Canal sector. After moving into Palestine they saw action at Beersheba and at Gaza before they distinguished themselves at Huj, where "*a fine charge by squadrons of the Warwickshire and Worcestershire Yeomanry captured 12 guns and broke the resistance of a hostile rearguard, worthy of the best traditions of the cavalry*".

In March 1918 it was announced that the Warwickshire Yeomanry was to be disbanded and to begin a new phase of existence as two companies of the 100th (Warwickshire and South Nottinghamshire) Battalion of the Machine Gun Corps. On 22 May 1918 they boarded HMT *Leasowe Castle* and left Egypt in a convoy on 26 May 1918. One day out to sea they were struck by a torpedo and sank. Most passengers and crew escaped by jumping into the warm water but 110 lives were lost, including eleven Warwickshire men. They returned to Alexandria and re-embarked on HMS *Caledonia* and by the end of August 1918 they were in France. On 17 October 1918 the 100th Battalion, Machine Gun Corps were in action at Le Cateau. Here the Germans had strengthened their defences and were strongly resisting the British advance. It was during this day that William was killed in action. He was 25 years old and was buried in Highland Cemetery near Le Cateau.

William's name is not recorded in Campden but is on the memorials in Aston-sub-Edge and Weston-sub-Edge and in MIckleton Church.

William's sister, Emily Frances Hunt, married Sergeant Arthur Frank Roberts of the Royal Gloucestershire Hussars Yeomanry on 3 August 1916 at Weston-sub-Edge. He was killed in action in Palestine on 30 April 1918.

The entrance to Highland Cemetery near Le Cateau, France.

Reynell Oswald Huyshe

Private, Gloucestershire Regiment
Captain, King's Shropshire Light Infantry
Captain, 8th Battalion, Worcestershire Regiment

Born: 15 December 1894
Enlisted: 1914
Died: 1 December 1939

Ren was the son of Wentworth and Hester Ann Huyshe and was educated at a preparatory day school in London before joining Ratcliffe College in 1907. His obituary published in *The Ratcliffian* states that he "*was a brilliant boy at Ratcliffe, very attractive, a good singer and an actor whose Antonio in The Merchant of Venice of 1910 was long remembered. He was always top of his class, was a good athlete and very popular.*" He left Ratcliffe in 1911 and went to work as a silversmith in the Silk Mill in Campden. His home was with his parents in Pike Cottage. At the outbreak of war in 1914 he enlisted as a private in the Gloucestershire Regiment but joined the King's Shropshire Light Infantry in 1915 after being granted a commission. He arrived in France on 31 August 1917 and was twice wounded in action in the Ypres Salient in Belgium. On one occasion he was buried alive through a shell explosion and was rescued in a state of utter exhaustion. After being wounded a second time he was treated at a base hospital in France before being evacuated to England.

After recovering from his wounds he was posted to Popton Fort, at the mouth of Milford Haven, Pembrokeshire, as Commanding Officer, and was promoted to captain. While he was stationed in Tenby he had the unusual experience of guarding the wreck of an airship that had just crashed. The pilot of the wreck, Horace Leetham, a fellow old boy of Ratcliffe College, was carried away wounded.

Ren ended the war being posted to south-west Ireland, where he was stationed at Clonmel and Fermoy in late 1918 and 1919.

It was while he was on home service in Wales in 1917 that he married Jesse Hilda Louise Rees. She was from Pembroke and they had two children, Ren born in 1918 and Peter in 1928. After his discharge from the army Ren returned to Campden and worked in partnership with George Hart, his stepbrother; the family lived in Station Road. He was a first-class designer and craftsman and delighted especially in making chalices for the Holy Sacrifice. He would put all his soul into such work, regarding it as a vocation. In 1928 he left Campden and went to live in Gravesend, where he held the post of Art Master to the School of Art in Gravesend, a position he held up to the time of his death.

Ren died on 1 December 1939 aged 44 years and is buried in Gravesend in Kent.

Ren with his parents, Hester Ann and Wentworth Huyshe.

Wentworth Roland Huyshe

Corporal 2173, Royal Gloucestershire Hussars Yeomanry
2nd Lieutenant, Worcestershire Regiment
Lieutenant, Worcestershire Hussars Yeomanry

Born: 30 July 1887
Enlisted: 29 August 1914
Discharged: 30 July 1918
Died: 5 November 1971

Wentworth was born in Epping, the son of Wentworth and Hester Ann Huyshe. This was his mother's second marriage as her first husband, William Thomas Hart, died in 1882.

At the outbreak of war Wentworth was already an experienced Territorial Army soldier as he had served for a number of years in the City of London Yeomanry, "*The Rough Riders*". He enlisted in the Royal Gloucestershire Hussars in Bristol on 29 August 1914, when he was 27 years old, and was posted to "D" Squadron as a private. He was promoted to the rank of lance corporal on 31 October 1914 and embarked with the regiment at Avonmouth for Gallipoli on 9 April 1915.

In August 1915 he was promoted to corporal but in October 1915 his service in Gallipoli ended when he contracted malaria. He was evacuated to Mudros on the island of Lemnos for treatment before he embarked for England on 22 November 1915; he arrived on 4 December 1915.

Wentworth was discharged from the Royal Gloucestershire Hussars on 22 November 1916 when he was granted a commission as a 2nd lieutenant in the 6th Battalion, Worcestershire Regiment. He then attended Plymouth Garrison Revolver School for a five-day course in January 1917 and scored a total of 187 points, enough to be awarded a first class certificate for his marksmanship. This was immediately followed by his transfer to the Queen's Own Worcestershire Hussars Yeomanry. He then attended a bomb-throwing instructor's course at the Southern Command Bombing School at Lyndhurst in July 1917 and passed successfully. This was followed by a course on the Hotchkiss machine gun in December 1917 which he again passed with a first class certificate. On 22 May 1918 he was promoted to a lieutenant and on 30 July 1918 he was discharged from the army owing to illness first contracted at Gallipoli in 1915.

After relinquishing his commission he was granted the honorary rank of lieutenant to use in civilian life. On his return to Campden he offered his services to Campden Grammar School Cadet Force and joined them as an officer on 15 August 1918. He remained with them until he left Campden in May 1919 to emigrate to Australia.

Wentworth was living with his parents in "Pike House" in Campden and on 17 May 1919 he married Mary Ann Henrietta Badger at St. James's Church. They had four children, three born in Australia, Cynthia, Olive and Wentworth Frederick, and one born in England, Rowland. Now that

the war was over Wentworth emigrated to Aramac in Queensland and worked as a sheep rancher and stockman. In 1933 the family returned to England and lived at Westington Hill Farm in Campden, where Wentworth set up a riding school. During the Second World War he tried to enrol in the Officers' Emergency Reserve but he was refused. Instead, he was employed by the Royal Air Force as a clerk of works from 13 October 1941 to 8 February 1943, when he resigned his appointment. His conduct throughout was "*exemplary*" and his work "*satisfactory*".

In 1949 he and Mary returned to Australia and their youngest son, Rowland, went with them.

Wentworth died on 5 November 1971 aged 84 years and his ashes are buried in the grave of his son Wentworth Frederick (who died in 1943 aged 20) in Moreton Morrell churchyard in Warwickshire.

Victor William Hyatt
Private 6784, "D" Company, 18th Battalion, Royal Fusiliers

Born: 21 October 1897
Enlisted: 1915
Died: 5 December 1915

Victor was born in Stratford-upon-Avon, the eldest of three children of William and Louisa Ellen Hyatt of Wood Street (previously 18 Albany Place). His father was a saddler.

Victor attended King Edward's School in Stratford from 1905 until 1913 and then continued his education as a boarder at Campden Grammar School. When he was still only 17 years old he enlisted in the Royal Fusiliers in early 1915, joining the 18th (1st Public Schools) Battalion, and in June 1915 he was posted to Clipstone Camp in Nottinghamshire. On 1 July they moved to Wiltshire for intensive training in preparation for action on the Western Front. In August they were at Tidworth and on 14 November they embarked at Folkestone but their arrival at Boulogne was held up by German mines at the entrance to the harbour. After a brief period in a rest camp they moved on foot and by train to the area around Béthune, where they were billeted in the tobacco factory and the Ecole Michelet in the town. They entered trenches for the first time at Vermelles and spent the next few days learning about life in the front line.

In severe weather with hard frost they took over trenches at Le Plantin, north-west of Givenchy on 1 December 1915. When not frozen the trenches were very wet and badly drained. Victor had a quiet day in the front line on 4 December with occasional bursts of machine gun fire and artillery fire from both sides. On 5 December a shelter in a British trench collapsed and two men were killed, one of them Victor Hyatt, a man *"whose bright, energetic disposition won him many friends"*. In a letter to Victor's mother, quoted in the *Stratford Herald*, Private 6783 Ronald Newland wrote, *"It is the greatest*

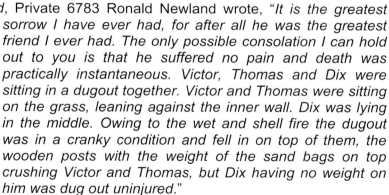

sorrow I have ever had, for after all he was the greatest friend I ever had. The only possible consolation I can hold out to you is that he suffered no pain and death was practically instantaneous. Victor, Thomas and Dix were sitting in a dugout together. Victor and Thomas were sitting on the grass, leaning against the inner wall. Dix was lying in the middle. Owing to the wet and shell fire the dugout was in a cranky condition and fell in on top of them, the wooden posts with the weight of the sand bags on top crushing Victor and Thomas, but Dix having no weight on him was dug out uninjured."

Victor was 18 years old when he died and was originally buried by his comrades in *"a little cemetery at Le Plantin alongside his chum, two crosses marking their resting place."* After the war his grave was moved to Brown's Road Cemetery in Festubert in France.

Victor's name is recorded on the war memorials in Campden School and King Edward's School. It is also recorded on the town war memorial in Stratford and on the wooden panels in Evesham Road cemetery, Stratford. There is an inscription for Victor on his parents' grave in Evesham Road cemetery and his memorial plaque was mounted in their headstone until it was stolen in 2002.

Jim Jackson
18th Hussars

Jim was born in 1889, the son of John Jackson, a farm labourer. In 1912 he was living at The Stables, Abbots Wood, Stow-on-the-Wold and employed as a groom. He married Edith Rickards, a domestic nurse from Worcester, at the Register Office in Worcester on 23 December 1912. They moved to Campden early in 1913 and their first three children, Edward James, William Henry and Clifford, were all baptised at St. James's Church in the town. The church records list his occupation as a groom and a gardener.

During the war Jim served in the 18th Hussars.

The family appear to have left Campden before the end of the war as they are not on the 1918 electoral roll.

Albert Richard James
Gunner 238615, Royal Field Artillery

Born: 21 October 1878
Died: 20 November 1962

Albert was born in Campden, the third son of Jesse and Jane James of Leysbourne, Campden. His father was a carter and an agricultural labourer. In 1901 Albert was living with his mother at Workhouse Bank in Sheep Street.

After leaving school Albert became a ploughboy and a general agricultural labourer like his father. He went on to work as a carter for the Keyte family on Mickleton Hill and then for Gloucestershire County Council.

When the war started in 1914 Albert enlisted in the Worcestershire Regiment but transferred to the Royal Field Artillery before he served overseas. He came home safely at the end of the war but his brother James died of wounds in hospital at Etaples in France in 1917.

In 1920 Albert married Annie May Turvey, who was born in Ebrington in 1894. Annie was a widow as her first husband, Sergeant 171229 John Vass DCM, had been killed in the war. Albert and Annie had four children: Gordon, Alec, Cecil and Irene.

Albert died on 20 November 1962 aged 84 and is buried in St. Eadburgha's churchyard in Ebrington. Annie died in 1972.

Alfred James
Private 266925, Royal Warwickshire Regiment
Private 15-52391, Royal Irish Rifles

Alfred was born in Tidmington in 1890, near Shipston-on-Stour, the seventh son of Jesse and Jane James. His father was a native of Campden who was employed as a carter and agricultural labourer. In 1891 the family were living in Leysbourne, Campden but after Jesse's death they moved to Workhouse Bank in Sheep Street.

Alfred married Mary Ann Howell at St. James's Church on 8 October 1911 and at the time of the wedding was employed as a labourer. At the outbreak of war Alfred was 24 years old and he soon enlisted in the Royal Warwickshire Regiment. After a period of training in England he arrived in France in 1916 and was wounded twice. While he was convalescing in England after being wounded for the second time he was able to have his photograph taken with his wife's three brothers, Gerry, Bill and Jack Howell, who were all serving in the army at the time. On the sleeve of his tunic can be seen two wound stripes.

Alfred was transferred to the Royal Irish Rifles after being passed fit for active service. He returned to France and was wounded for the third time in August 1917, which resulted in his evacuation to a Red Cross hospital in France on 15 August 1917 before being returned to England, where he was admitted to hospital in Cambridge. The *Evesham Journal* published a letter written by Alfred describing how he was wounded: "*Just as we were going over the top a shrapnel shot hit the machine gun I was carrying, and so saved my life, but my neck and shoulders were covered with bits of shrapnel.*" After being transferred to hospital in Liverpool Alfred made a full recovery.

He and Mary moved to Devizes after the war and had three children.

Alfred William James
Sapper 65236, Royal Engineers

Born: 29 June 1879
Died 23 April 1923

Alfred was born in Campden, the eldest son of Joseph and Mary Eliza James of Watery Lane, and was baptised in the Catholic Chapel at Campden House on 17 March 1889, when he was 9 years old. After leaving school he started work as a bricklayer with his father.

When the war started in 1914 Alfred enlisted in the Royal Engineers. He arrived in France on 6 September 1915. He was then posted to Salonika in Greece, where he experienced much fighting. The constant firing of the guns and the blast of the shells affected Alfred very badly and he soon developed "*shellshock*". This eventually caused paralysis of the throat and bad heart problems (bulbar paralysis and cardiac syncope).

Alfred returned home after the war but for the last years of his life he was practically an invalid, experiencing much sorrow and great suffering. With a desire to get strong and well he went to stay with one of his married sisters at 75 King Street in Coventry. Despite the loving care and devoted nursing that he received he died on 23 April 1923 aged 44. He is buried with his parents in St. James's churchyard in Campden. His name, rank and number are recorded on the headstone.

Alfred's name appears on the war memorial in the High Street. It was a late addition and it appears on a column headed 1918. He may have died in 1923 but his death was directly caused by his war experiences.

Cyril Blakeman James
Gunner 150443, "B" Battery, 277 Brigade, Royal Field Artillery

Born: 29 March 1892
Enlisted: 15 February 1916
Discharged: 29 January 1919

Cyril was born in Campden, the son of Joseph and Mary Eliza James of Watery Lane, and was baptised at St. Catharine's Church. His father and eldest brother were bricklayers but Cyril became a baker after leaving school.

He married Edith James on 25 December 1915 at St. James's Church and they lived at 96 Cox Street in Coventry. Two months later Cyril enlisted in the Royal Field Artillery in Coventry on 15 February 1916. He was immediately placed into the Army Reserve and then mobilised on 3 August 1916. The next six months were spent training in England before he arrived on the Western Front on 10 February 1917. In April he was admitted to hospital in France owing to inflammation of the synovial membrane in his knee. After recovering he remained on the Western Front until he returned to England on 28 January 1919, where he was discharged the following day.

During his training in England Cyril was guilty of one offence while his unit was stationed in Hilsea; he arrived back late from leave in January 1917. His punishment was a loss of two days' pay as a consequence.

At the end of the war Cyril returned to his wife in Coventry and by 1926 they had moved to 14 Gresham Street.

Frank H. James
Private 4346, 1st/9th Battalion, London Regiment (Queen Victoria's Rifles)
Private 7511, "A" Company, 1st/23rd Battalion, London Regiment

Born: 1895
Died: 16 September 1916

Frank was born in Campden in 1895, the son of Elizabeth Lucy James. His mother was the daughter of John and Lucy James of Lower High Street, Campden.

At the outbreak of war in 1914 Frank was living at 45 Stadium Street, Chelsea, London with his mother and he enlisted in the 9th Battalion, London Regiment at Davis Street in London. A period of training in England followed before he arrived in France after the start of 1916. When he arrived in the Somme area in August 1916 he had been transferred to the 1st/23rd Battalion, London Regiment (142nd Brigade, 47th Division) and they arrived at Albert on 11 September 1916. The next few days were spent making their way to the front, arriving at Mametz Wood on 14 September and at Bazentin-le-Grand on 15 September.

The Battle of Flers-Courcelette began on 15 September 1916 and the British Army used tanks for the very first time. The battalion attacked east of High Wood at 9.25am on 16 September with their objective being to take Prue Trench. They encountered heavy fire when they passed the Switch Line. Machine gun fire and shells scattered the attack. The attacking companies, "A", "C" and "D", never returned.

Frank was killed in action near High Wood on 16 September 1916 aged 21 years. His body was not found at the end of the war and his name is recorded on the Thiepval Memorial, Somme, France. It is also recorded on 3 memorials in Campden: in St. James's Church, in St. Catharine's Church and in the High Street.

The following letter was received by Frank's mother from the officer commanding "A" Company, 1st/23rd Battalion, London Regiment and it was published in the *Evesham Journal* on 4 November 1916. "*I have to inform you with the deepest regret that your son was killed in action on 16 September. He was a gallant and fearless soldier who died in the execution of his duty. His body was found by a party of the London Regiment who doubtless buried him near to where he fell.*"

George Enoch James
Private 15144, 2nd Battalion, Gloucestershire Regiment

Born: 1893
Enlisted: 8 September 1914
Died: 3 June 1918

George was born in Campden in 1893, the second son of Enoch and Fanny James of Watery Lane, and was baptised at St. James's Church on 24 September 1893. His parents were married at St. James's Church on 6 November 1888 and his father was employed as an agricultural labourer.

When the war started George was 21 years old and he enlisted in the Gloucestershire Regiment in Campden on 8 September 1914. After a period of training in England he arrived in France on 20 January 1915 and was posted to the 2nd Battalion in the Ypres Salient in Belgium. In May, during the Second Battle of Ypres, the battalion held trenches along the eastern edge of Sanctuary Wood when they came under severe bombardment from enemy artillery guns. The next day, 8 May, opened with violent shellfire followed by heavy rifle and machine gun fire. Great damage was done in the front line and at least one platoon of Glosters was cut off. "*It was hell,*" said one officer. At 7.15am on 9 May the enemy attacked and entered the battalion's line. The Germans poured into the trenches and were digging in. Their losses were great as the Glosters shot hard and at least 350 of the enemy were killed. The battlefield was littered with dead and wounded. There were several gallant attempts at counter-attacks but the survivors were ordered to withdraw after dark. This was an awful baptism of fire for George and a period of rest in the vicinity of Armentières followed in June.

George served for eleven months on the Western front before the battalion was sent to Salonika in Greece in November 1915, where he remained until he was granted leave in April 1918. He returned to Campden and soon became very ill and was ordered to Norton Hall VAD Hospital. He died there on 3 June 1918 aged 24 and is buried with a Commonwealth War Graves Commission military headstone in St. James's churchyard in Campden. The illness that he died from was contracted while on active service in Salonika.

His name is recorded on two memorials in the town, in St. James's Church and in the High Street, and his headstone also has a memorial inscription for his brother Harry, who died in France on 23 March 1918.

George Ernest James
Army Service Corps

Born: 1888
Died: 1 February 1939

George was born in Broad Campden, the son of James and Sarah James, and was baptised at St. James's Church on 26 August 1888. He served in the Army Service Corps during the war and returned safely to the town after the armistice was signed.

George never married and he lived the remainder of his short life in Broad Campden. He died on 1 February 1927 aged 38 years and is buried in St. James's churchyard.

Harry James
Private 4873, 2nd/5th Battalion, Gloucestershire Regiment
Private 241706, 2nd/5th Battalion, Gloucestershire Regiment

Born: 1891
Enlisted: 2 March 1916
Died: 23 March 1918

Harry was born in Campden in 1891, the eldest son of Enoch and Fanny James of "The Garden", Watery Lane. His father was an agricultural labourer and his parents were married at St. James's Church on 6 November 1888.

Harry enlisted in the Gloucestershire Regiment in Gloucester on 2 March 1916, when he was 25 years old. After a short period of training in England he arrived in France in August 1916 and was posted to the 2nd/5th Battalion, Gloucestershire Regiment, a Territorial battalion. In April 1917 he was wounded in the arm but soon recovered and rejoined the battalion.

On 18 March 1918 the battalion took over the defences of Holnon Wood, one of the strong points in the Battle Zone, west of St. Quentin. The wood lies on high ground about half a mile west of Holnon village and from its eastern edge views of the ground stretching forward to the German lines could be had. The battalion were 5,000 yards behind the front line and lived in Attilly Huts on the west edge of the wood and worked on defences during the day.

At 4.30am on 21 March 1918 the Germans launched their Spring offensive and a terrific bombardment of high explosives and gas shells rained down on the battery positions and the defences of Holnon Wood. Pieces of shell hurtled through the air, trees came crashing down and the whole place reeked of gas. It was found that every telephone line was down but a message arrived at 4.45am for the battalion to man battle positions. The journey was a matter of several hundred yards through the wood and over an area soaked with gas.

The intense bombardment continued for over four hours but machine gun fire stopped the enemy from capturing the Battle Zone positions in the Glosters' sector. The following day, 22 March, was quite misty until 10.00am but by midday it was clear that the Germans had captured the Battle Zone trenches on the battalion's left and that in a few hours the battalion would be surrounded. At 3.30pm the order to withdraw arrived and "D" Company were ordered to remain in position to give covering fire while the other companies retired. The enemy were now advancing rapidly and casualties were heavy. Harry was reported missing in action near Holnon Wood on 21 March 1918 although the Commonwealth War Graves Commission gave his official date of death as 23 March. He was 27 years old. At the end of the war his body could not be found and his name was recorded on the Pozières Memorial, near Albert, Somme, France.

The *Evesham Journal* reported on 11 May 1918 that "*Harry James has been missing since March 21. His mother has received a letter from his Chaplain confirming the news that he is missing or a prisoner of war.*"

Harry's name is recorded on two memorials in Campden: in St. James's Church and in the High Street. He also has a memorial inscription at the bottom of his brother's headstone in St. James's churchyard. His brother, Private 115144 George Enoch James, died at Norton Hall VAD Hospital on 3 June 1918.

James James
Private 5293, 4th Battalion, Gloucestershire Regiment
Private 9194, 6th Battalion, Oxfordshire and Buckinghamshire Light Infantry

Born: 21 July 1886
Enlisted: 25 October 1904
Died: 2 December 1917

James was born in Burmington in Warwickshire in 1886 and was the son of Jesse and Jane James. In 1891 the family were living in Leysbourne in Campden and his father, who was a native of the town, was employed as a carter and an agricultural labourer. In 1901 Jane was a widow and the family had moved to Workhouse Bank (also known as Gainsborough Terrace). James, who was then 15 years old, was employed as a cowman and an agricultural labourer.

On 25 October 1904 James went to Bristol to enlist in the Gloucestershire Regiment. He was 18 years old and was posted to the 4th Battalion as a private. He was five feet two inches tall with blue eyes, brown hair and a fresh complexion. His religion was Church of England and at the time of his enlistment his mother was living in Watery Lane in Campden.

When the First World War started James was 28 years old and, having been a regular soldier for a number of years, "*he was called from his work in the pleasant fields of Campden to join the colours in the defence of his country*" and posted to the Oxfordshire and Buckinghamshire Light Infantry. He arrived in France on 26 May 1915 with the 2nd Battalion and served on the Western Front for the next two years before he was wounded in action during the Battle of Passchendaele (Third Battle of Ypres) in Belgium while serving with the 6th Battalion. The *Evesham Journal* reported:
"*Mrs. James, Station Road, Campden, has received a letter from the Matron of Number 9, General Hospital, Rouen, to say that her son, Pte. J. James, has been severely wounded in the arm and chest and that his condition is not at all satisfactory. The letter stated that everything was being done that could be done and they hoped the next letter would be more satisfactory. We regret to say, however, that Mrs. James received official intimation a day or two ago to say that her son had since succumbed to his wounds.*"

James was 31 years old when he died on 2 December 1917 and is buried in St. Sever Cemetery Extension in Rouen in France. He has his name recorded on two memorials in Campden: in St. James's Church and in the High Street. Josephine Griffiths includes James in her *Book of Remembrance* but erroneously states that he served in the Army Veterinary Corps.

John Richard James
Private 27223, 9th Battalion, Gloucestershire Regiment

Born: 27 September 1892
Enlisted: 11 December 1915
Discharged: 15 August 1918
Died: 1 June 1956

John was born in Campden, the son of Elizabeth James, and was baptised at St. Catharine's Church on 23 October 1892. His mother was the daughter of John and Lucy James of Lower High Street, Campden. After leaving school he found employment as a farm labourer and when he was 19 years old he married Gertrude James, daughter of Enoch James, at St. Catharine's Church in Campden on 28 July 1912.

At the outbreak of war his younger brother, Frank, enlisted in the army. John enlisted in the Gloucestershire Regiment on 11 December 1915 and after a period of home service he was posted to Salonika in Greece, where he joined the 9th Battalion, which contained a number of other men from Campden. He had not been at the front long when he was wounded and admitted to Number 28 General Hospital in Salonika. After recovering he rejoined his unit.

In 1918 he became sick and returned to England, where he was discharged from the army on 15 August 1918 after serving for a period of 2 years and 247 days in the army. He was no longer fit for active service owing to sickness and a Silver War Badge was issued. He then returned to his wife at the family home in Watery Lane, Campden.

John died on 1 June 1956 aged 63 years and is buried in St. Catharine's cemetery.

Joseph James

Born: 31 December 1885

Joey was born in Campden, the son of Joseph and Mary Eliza James of Watery Lane. His father was a stonemason. After leaving school he joined his father in the trade and they were employed in building the club at Aston-sub-Edge.

On the 1918 Campden electoral roll Joey is listed as absent on military service. He returned safely from the war in the summer of 1919 and was awarded three campaign medals. After leaving home he lived in West End Terrace and during the Second World War he was a special constable.

Joey died in 1969 aged 83 and was survived by his wife, Gertrude. There were no children.

Mark James
Private 3107, Gloucestershire Yeomanry
Private 235695, Corps of Hussars

Born: 6 April 1887

Mark was born in Tidmington near Shipston-on-Stour, the sixth son of Jesse and Jane James. His father was a native of Campden and in 1891 the family were living in Leysbourne. They later moved to Watery Lane.

Mark's father was employed as an agricultural labourer and a horse carter and Mark must have shared his love of horses, as when he enlisted in the army during the war he joined the Gloucestershire Yeomanry. He did not serve overseas until after the start of 1916 and when he joined the unit they were in Egypt. In January 1916 the Gloucestershire Yeomanry combined with those of Warwickshire and Worcestershire to form the 5th Mounted Brigade. It was heavily engaged in Egypt and Palestine, from the early probing away from the Suez Canal zone, across the Sinai desert and eventually at the Battles of Gaza and the victorious advance to Jerusalem and into Syria.

Mark returned safely from the war and married life produced two children, Nora and Fred. It is not known when he died but he is buried at Maxstoke, near Coleshill.

Philip Frederick ("Jim") James

Private S2-018259, Army Service Corps
Private 51324, 2nd/4th Battalion, Devonshire Regiment
Private 45518, 1st/4th Battalion, Duke of Cornwall's Light Infantry

Born: 1895
Discharged: 14 March 1919
Died: 20 April 1967

Jim was born in Broad Campden in 1895, the son of James and Sarah James, and was baptised at St. James's Church on 11 August 1895. His father was a native of Campden and was employed as a *"cattleman on a farm"* in 1901; his mother's maiden name was Merriman.

Jim went to school in Campden. When the war started in 1914 he enlisted in the Army Service Corps and his trade was listed as a baker on his attestation papers. He began a period of four years overseas service when he entered the Balkan theatre of war on 29 June 1915. He was at Gallipoli in Turkey and then in Egypt. During his time abroad he was transferred twice, first to the Devonshire Regiment and then to the Duke of Cornwall's Light Infantry.

After the war ended he returned to England and was discharged at Chiseldon on 14 March 1919 and arrived back at Campden railway station using a military travel pass.

On 7 April 1928 he married Una Anne Elizabeth Matthews at St. James's Church in Campden and they spent their married life living in Broad Campden at "High Barn" and "Wold Cottage", where his parents ran a shop and post office. They had two children and Jim had various jobs before he retired, including a decorator and gardener.

Jim died on 20 April 1967 aged 72 years and is buried in St. James's churchyard. His wife died on 5 February 1990 aged 86 years.

Charles Edward Jarrett

Lance Corporal 690292, 116th Battalion, Canadian Expeditionary Force

Born: 6 May 1888
Enlisted: 21 February 1916
Discharged: 2 April 1919

Charlie was born in Mickleton, the fourth son of John and Mary Ann Jarrett. His father was a gardener and his mother was a dressmaker and then a laundress. The family home was originally in Mickleton but by 1901 they were living in Back Ends, Campden. They then lived in West End Terrace and the High Street. Three of Charlie's brothers, Walter, Harry and Edgar, also served during the First World War.

After leaving school Charlie found employment as a metal-polisher but on 14 December 1905, at the age of 17, he joined the Royal Navy, signing on for a period of 12 years. His medical examination stated that he was five feet seven inches tall with light brown hair, blue eyes and a fair complexion. There was a small scar on his right forearm.

He was posted to HMS *Nelson* as Stoker SS 101807 and served on this ship until 11 May 1906. On 5 October 1906 he was promoted to stoker first class while serving on HMS *Gladiator*.

The next five years saw him serve on a variety of ships, including HMS *King Alfred* and HMS *Essex*, and his conduct was at all times *"very good"*. He was transferred to the Royal Navy Reserve on 15 January 1911 and then discharged on 20 April 1911.

After leaving the Royal Navy Charlie emigrated to Canada and found employment as a lineman. The family home was at 361 Avondale Avenue, Hamilton, Ontario. He enlisted in the Canadian Army in Hamilton on 21 February 1916 aged 27 years and his attestation papers indicate that he was now married and his wife, Kate, was at home in Hamilton. The next eight months were spent training in Canada. He then embarked at Halifax on 13 November 1916 with the 173rd Battalion, Canadian Expeditionary Force and arrived in England on the SS *Olympic* on 20 November 1916. He was then posted to the 2nd Reserve Battalion at Bramshott on 19 January 1917. After final training he was posted to 116th Battalion for overseas service and arrived in France on 17 March 1917. He had been at the front less than a month when he was wounded at Vimy Ridge on 9 April. He was fixing up a trench after the attack and was struck in the arm by shrapnel from an exploding shell. He was admitted to Number 32 Stationary Hospital at Wimereux for treatment before being evacuated back to England, where he entered Wharncliffe War Hospital in Sheffield on 16 April. He was discharged from hospital on 25 May and then went to Bromley in Kent for a period of convalescence.

Charlie recovered from his wound and was again sent to France on 2 September 1917, where he was posted to the 116th Battalion. He was now a lance corporal, having been promoted on 3 August 1917. He was again wounded in action on 8 August 1918 when he was hit in the left leg by a bullet and was immediately admitted to a casualty clearing station for treatment before being admitted to Number 11 Stationary Hospital at Rouen. He was then evacuated back to England, where he entered Birmingham War Hospital on 16 October 1918 and on 27 November 1918 he transferred to the 15th (Duchess of Connaught) Canadian General Hospital at Taplow in Buckinghamshire. A further transfer saw him enter the 5th Canadian General Hospital at Kirkdale in Liverpool on 8 January 1919, where he stayed until he left for Canada on the ship *Araguaya*. He arrived in Canada on 13 February 1919 and then began complaining of not being able to bend his knee properly, of tiredness when walking and of varicose veins. He was admitted to Brant Military Hospital at Burlington on 3 March 1919 and given a full medical examination. The conclusions were that the varicose veins in the right leg were already there prior to enlistment and that they were not aggravated by his military service. His partial loss of function of the left leg was expected to take about six months to recover, as there had been a steady improvement since he was wounded in August 1918. The medical board recommended that Charlie should be discharged from the army as he was now medically unfit for service.

He was discharged at Toronto on 2 April 1919 and returned to his wife in Hamilton.

Edgar Raymond Jarrett
Lance Corporal 19562, Grenadier Guards

Born: 8 May 1892
Enlisted: 21 September 1914
Discharged: 20 September 1926

Edgar was born in Campden, the fifth son of John and Mary Ann Jarrett. His father was born in Mickleton and in 1901 was employed as a gardener and his mother was working from home as a laundress. After leaving Campden Grammar School Edgar found employment as a grocer's assistant for Reginald Hands.

Edgar enlisted at Campden Recruiting Office on 21 September 1914, when he was 22 years old, and joined the Grenadier Guards in Caterham the next day. He was passed fit for active service at his medical examination in Caterham on 2 October 1914 and his records state that he had fair hair, blue/grey eyes and a fair complexion. His religion was Church of England.

After a period of ten months training in England Edgar arrived in France with the 3rd Battalion, Grenadier Guards on 26 July 1915. He was now a lance corporal as he had been promoted in England on 28 June.

On 27 September 1915 he was badly wounded in the chest, which resulted in his being admitted to hospital in France on 3 October. His condition was serious as the wound had damaged his lung. By the time that he was sent back to England on 18 October he had greatly recovered.

The next year was spent in England and it was not until 14 November 1916 that Edgar was posted overseas again. After only thirty-five days abroad Edgar returned to England on 18 December. The rest of the war was spent serving in England and on 7 July 1917 he married Dorothy Hopkins at St. Andrew's Church, Chelsea, London and they set up home in Beaufort Street, London, SW3.

Edgar continued serving as a regular soldier with the Grenadier Guards after the war ended in November 1918 and was discharged from the army on 20 September 1926 after twelve years' service. The post-war years were all spent on home service.

During his time in the army Edgar passed classes of instruction in bayonet fighting and physical education. He also gained his 3rd class and 2nd class certificates of education.

Henry George Dyde Jarrett
Army Cyclist Corps

Born: 1884

Harry was born in Mickleton, the second son of John and Mary Ann Jarrett who were married in 1880. His father was a gardener and in 1891 the family were living in High Street, Campden. On the 1901 census Harry had moved to Worcester, where he was employed as a domestic servant, and his parents were living in Back Ends, Campden.

During the war Harry served in the Army Cyclist Corps and appears to have been employed on home service only. Three of his younger brothers, Walter, Charlie and Edgar, served in the army during the war.

Walter William Jarrett
Gunner 150694, 153rd Siege Battery, Royal Garrison Artillery

Born: 2 August 1886
Enlisted: 15 February 1916
Discharged: 23 October 1919

Walter was born in Mickleton, the third son of John and Mary Ann Jarrett. His father was also born in Mickleton and was a gardener. The family moved to Campden in the early 1890's and in 1901 were living in Back Ends but by 1916 they were in West End Terrace. They also had a spell living in the High Street.

After leaving school Walter found employment as a harness-maker and then when war was declared in 1914 he was an asylum attendant at Parc Gwyllar Asylum in Bridgend, Glamorgan, Wales. He enlisted in the Royal Garrison Artillery on 15 February 1916, when he was 30 years old (although he gave his age as 28 on his attestation papers), and was immediately put into the Army Reserve. His medical examination found him to be medical category "A" despite having slightly contracted toes on his right foot. He had fair hair and blue eyes and his religion was "*Baptist*".

He was mobilised in Cardiff on 31 March 1917 and the next six months were spent training in England before he arrived in France on 19 September. A period of just over twelve months was spent on the Western Front before Walter returned to England on 4 October 1918. This must have been official leave as he was back in France on 18 October. After the armistice was signed he was sent to Germany as part of the Army of Occupation before he returned to England on 26 September 1919. He was discharged from the army on 23 October.

During his time in the Royal Garrison Artillery he passed as a "*Third Class Signaller*" and for his contribution to the war effort he was awarded two campaign medals, the British War Medal and the Victory Medal. Walter received these medals in 1921.

Ernest Charles Jaynes

Born: 1886

Ernest was born in London, the son of John Fowler and Sarah Ellen Jaynes. His father was a mercantile clerk and he died in 1897 aged 42 years. In 1901 the family were living at 47, St. George's Street, St. Pancras, London and Ernest was employed as an errand boy.

After leaving home Ernest became a motor engineer and at the outbreak of war his address was 8, Old Mill Road, Chelston, Torquay. He married Elsie Beatrice Hands, daughter of Jesse and Jane Hands of Broad Campden, at Hampton-in-Arden Parish Church on 23 December 1916. His wife was baptised at St. James's Church in Campden on 25 December 1888.

In her *Book of Remembrance* Josephine Griffiths lists Ernest as serving in the war but he must have enlisted after December 1916 as he was still employed as a "*motor fitter*" when he was married. He is not included on the Campden 1918 electoral roll but in 1919 Ernest and Elsie are living in Gladstone Cottage in Broad Campden. Their daughter, Beatrice Ellen Jaynes, was born in February 1919 and baptised at St. James's Church.

The family appear to have left the town in the 1920's.

Alexander Charles Jeffrey
Gunner 1423, Royal Field Artillery
Saddler 840986, "B" Battery, 165th Brigade, Royal Field Artillery

Born: 1886
Died: 20 October 1918

Alexander was born in Malvern in 1886, the youngest son of William and Annie L. Jeffrey, landlord and landlady of the Lygon Arms in Campden. On the 1901 census Annie was running the Lygon Arms on her own with her daughter, Louisa, working as a barmaid. Her son Robert was living at home and employed as a groom.

After leaving school Alexander found employment as a saddler but later became the landlord of the Lygon Arms. He enlisted in the Royal Field Artillery in Evesham and entered France after the start of 1916. His skills as a saddler were put to good use while working with the horses that were used to pull the artillery guns. In October 1918 he was serving with "B" Battery, 165th Brigade, Royal Field Artillery near Hazebrouck in Northern France when he became ill and was admitted to a casualty clearing station suffering from influenza. His condition worsened and he was transferred to Number 9 Red Cross Hospital on 17 October 1918, unconscious and suffering from pneumonia. He never regained consciousness and died on 20 October 1918 aged 32 years.

Alexander was buried at La Kreule Cemetery, Hazebrouck, France and his name can be found on two memorials in Campden: in St. James's Church and in the High Street. He was not married.

Alexander (seated) and his friend Lewis Smith.

Arthur Adamson Jones
Rifle Brigade

Arthur was born in Campden in 1900, the second son of Frederick Jones, and was baptised at St. James's Church on 19 October 1900. His father, who was Superintendent of Police in the town, had married Mary Jane Georgina Adamson in 1896. Arthur's elder brother, Frederick Henry, was born in Gloucester and served in the Royal Navy during the war.

Arthur was educated at The Crypt School in Gloucester and was a member of the cadet force. He then enlisted in the Rifle Brigade before his 18th birthday and served overseas in a theatre of war before the armistice was signed. After the war he returned to Campden and was living in Catbrook in 1918 and in Cider Mill Lane in 1922. He then left the town.

Arthur's parents both died in 1943 and are buried in St. James's churchyard in Campden.

Frederick Henry Jones
Ordinary Seaman J34547, Royal Navy

Born: 11 January 1898
Enlisted: 9 February 1915
Discharged: 18 July 1917

Fred was born in Gloucester, the eldest son of Frederick and Mary Jane Georgina Jones, who were married in Cheltenham in 1896. His father, a native of Twyning in Gloucestershire, was a police sergeant and at the time of his marriage was stationed at Crescent Place Police Station in Cheltenham. The family moved to Campden in 1899 when Frederick was promoted to superintendent. His father soon became known locally as "Super Jones".

Fred enlisted in the Royal Navy on 9 February 1915, when he was 17 years old, and was posted to HMS *Impregnable*, a Royal Navy training ship at Devonport, as a boy second class. On 20 August 1915 he was transferred to HMS *Ganges*, a training depot at Harwich, and remained there until 20 January 1916. He was promoted to signal boy on 11 November 1915 and then to ordinary seaman on 11 January 1916, the same day that he signed on for a further twelve years' service with the Royal Navy.

After leaving HMS *Ganges* Fred was posted to HMS *Vivid*, the Royal Navy barracks at Devonport, on 21 January 1916 and served there until he was invalided out of the Royal Navy with epilepsy on 18 July 1918. He was then admitted to a hospital in Plymouth for treatment.

Fred's parents remained in Campden and lived at 1, Catbrook. They both died in 1943.

Percy Theodore Jones
Corporal 3899, Army Service Corps

Born: 14 June 1888
Enlisted: 1914
Discharged: 1919
Died: 20 November 1964

Percy was born in Bromley Cross in Lancashire in 1888, the son of Joseph and Ellen Jones. His father was originally from Wales and when Percy was born he was working as a coachman and groom in Bolton. After leaving school Percy was apprenticed to be a motor engineer and in the spring of 1914 he was asked to drive Harold Harwood, a mill owner from Bromley Cross, to Campden. Percy stayed at the Noel Arms while Harold visited his mother, who lived in the Square in what later became The Cotswold House Hotel.

Scuttlebrook Wake was on and Percy met May Charlotte Keyte, his future wife. They became very close but as war was approaching they decided not to get married as he could die and leave her a widow. Percy enlisted in the Army Service Corps at Woolwich in London and arrived in France towards the end of 1914 just in time to become one of what later became known as "*The Old Contemptibles*". He served throughout the war, regularly driving lorries full of ammunition to the front line, and was promoted to the rank of corporal before he was discharged towards the end of 1919, after spending the last few months of his service clearing the battlefields in France.

Percy returned home to Bromley Cross in 1919 to find that his father had spent all of the money sent to him by the War Department and that all of his clothes had been given away. Apparently his father did not expect him to survive the war. This left Percy, now 31 years old, with nothing. He decided to return to Campden, where he married May Charlotte Keyte at St. James's Church on 18 August 1920. They had two children: John Theodore and Mary Elizabeth. Using money that May had made doing war work, they bought property in Sheep Street and then Percy built and opened the Campden Garage. In 1931 the family moved into Landgate Cottage and this is where Percy and May stayed for the rest of their lives.

During the Second World War Percy was an Air Raid Precautions warden and the headquarters was in an office at the garage in Sheep Street. Percy had a paraffin stove and the wardens often cooked sausages during their time on "*duty*". Donald Bragg, the butcher, and Arthur Pyment were two other ARP wardens who worked with Percy.

Percy died at Landgate Cottage on 20 November 1964 aged 76 years and is buried in St. James's churchyard. May died on 19 May 1981 aged 88 years.

Edgar Keeley
Private 1209, 1st/5th Battalion, Gloucestershire Regiment
Lance Corporal 241989, 1st/5th Battalion, Gloucestershire Regiment
Lance Corporal 241989, 1st/6th Battalion, Gloucestershire Regiment

Born: 30 September 1887
Enlisted: 14 February 1910
Discharged: 28 February 1916
Died: 25 November 1960

Edgar was born in Campden, the son of Eliza Keeley of Watery Lane. His mother was a "*gloveress*" and in 1891 she and her three sons were living with her father, James Keeley, who was then aged 69 years and a hedge-cutter.

After being educated in the town Edgar found employment as an agricultural labourer working with horses on a farm. In 1910 he enlisted in the Territorial Army, joining "H" Company, 5th Battalion, Gloucestershire Regiment. On 5 August 1914 he was mobilised and signed up for overseas service. The battalion went to Chelmsford for training before they arrived in France on 29 March 1915. Edgar was with the battalion when they were at Ploegsteert Wood in Belgium but early in 1916 he returned to England and was discharged from the army on 28 February.

Edgar married Edith Davies at Shipston-on-Stour on 28 October 1911 and they had five children: Albert William, Edgar George, Jim, Molly and Joyce. He found employment as a stonemason and bricklayer and worked for a builder in Ledbury. The family home was at 7, Oatley's Crescent in Ledbury.

Edgar died on 25 November 1960 aged 73 years and is buried in Ledbury in Herefordshire. His brother, Thomas Frederick Keeley, also served in the war and it is interesting to note that he married Elma Davies, the sister of Edith, in Ledbury.

Ernest Keeley
Private 28618, 9th Battalion, Gloucestershire Regiment

Born: 28 December 1887
Enlisted: 11 December 1915
Discharged: 12 October 1919
Died: 30 January 1984

Ernest was born in Campden, the second of six sons of Henry and Susannah Keeley of Poppets Alley. His eldest brother, Frederick, was the local coal merchant and after leaving school Ernest worked with him. He married Ida Eleanor Gasside in 1909 and when hostilities broke out in August 1914 there were two young children at home, Frank Henry (baptised in 1909) and Alwyne Rowland (baptised in 1913), and another one on the way. The birth of Lily Eleanor (baptised at St. James's Church on 27 December 1914) delayed Ernest's enlistment in the army, which came in Campden on 11 December 1915. He was immediately placed into the Army Reserve before being mobilised on 31 May 1916 and posted to Salonika in Greece to join the 9th Battalion, Gloucestershire Regiment. It is not clear exactly when Ernest arrived in Salonika but the battalion remained in Greece until it was posted to France on 4 July 1918. At this point the battalion left the 26th Division in Greece and joined the 66th Division in France. On 22 September 1918 they became the pioneer battalion for the division and were involved in the Battle of Cambrai 1918 and the Battle of the Selle. After the armistice was signed the battalion moved through Belgium but did not join the forces that crossed the border into Germany.

Ernest returned to England and was discharged from the army on 12 October 1919. He returned to his family in Watery Lane, Campden and was able to meet his youngest child, Cyril Laurence, who was baptised at St. James's Church on 25 February 1917. He continued working as a coalman until he found employment with J. W. Pyment and Sons as a builder.

During the Second World War Ernest's son, Aircraftman First Class 953264, Alec Victor Keeley, Royal Air Force, was killed in action on 1 December 1942 and is buried at Mosul in Iraq.

Ernest died at Ellen Badger Hospital in Shipston-on-Stour on 30 January 1984 aged 96 years and is buried in St. James's churchyard. At the time of his death he was living at 15, St. Catharine's Square in Campden. His wife died on 8 November 1970 aged 79 years.

George Charles Keeley
Private 202973, "D" Company, 1st/5th Battalion, Gloucestershire Regiment
Private 37851, "B" Company, 12th Battalion, Gloucestershire Regiment

Born: 1885
Mobilised: 5 August 1914
Died: 8 May 1917

George was born in Campden, the eldest son of James Edward and Mary Ann Keeley of Lower High Street, and was baptised at St. James's Church on 25 December 1885. On the 1901 census he is listed as living at home with his parents and working as a teamster on a farm.

At the outbreak of war in 1914 George had already been a member of the Territorial Army, "H" Company, 5th Battalion, Gloucestershire Regiment, for a number of years. He was mobilised on 5 August 1914 and went to Chelmsford for an intense period of training before the battalion was posted to France. When the battalion entered France on 29 March 1915 George was not with it. He remained in England and finally arrived in France in February 1917 with the 12th Battalion, Gloucestershire

Regiment. George was 32 years old and his wife, Mabel Margaret, was at home in High Street, Campden.

On 1 May 1917 the battalion was in billets in Petit Servin in France and the day was spent being instructed on how to throw grenades. 2nd Lieutenant Bradbury was killed, and four other ranks were injured, during the period of instruction.

A long nine-mile march followed on 3 May as they made their way to the front. On 4 May they relieved a Canadian battalion east of Fresnoy, which had been captured from the Germans the day before. The relief was difficult as the front line trench was only a series of connected shell-holes. The enemy shelled the Glosters' trench all day on 5 May and a large number of soldiers could be seen preparing to advance. An SOS signal was put up but the attack never developed. Much work was done to improve the trenches during the ensuing night although the shelling continued throughout. It persisted on 6 May too and enemy planes were very busy overhead, two machines photographing and reconnoitring the British lines. At 6.00pm the Germans put down a very heavy barrage. The next day they again shelled the Glosters' trenches very heavily and the battalion was warned that an attack was expected.

Rain began to fall just after midnight and at 3.45am on 8 May another very heavy barrage started. The thick mist made observation very difficult and soon the Germans commenced attacking in force. The first assault was checked but before long the front line fell. It was recaptured but could not be held as the enemy occupied the high ground on either side. At the end of the day the battalion was relieved; it had suffered 302 casualties, killed, wounded and missing.

George was killed in action near Fresnoy on 8 May 1917 aged 31 years. His body was not recovered at the end of the war and his name was recorded on the Arras Memorial in France. It can also be seen on three memorials in Campden: in St. James's Church, in the Baptist Church and in the High Street.

He married Mabel Margaret Biggerstaff in 1912. She died on 8 April 1957 aged 78 years and is buried in St. James's churchyard in Campden.

Golden Keeley
Private 17584, "A" Company, 9th Battalion, Gloucestershire Regiment
Private 643502, Labour Corps

Born: 5 January 1898
Died: March 1977

Goldie was born in Campden, the sixth son of Henry and Susannah Keeley of Poppets Alley, and was baptised at St. James's Church on 10 April 1898. His father was a native of the town, an agricultural labourer and for many years a member of "K" Company, 2nd Volunteer Battalion, Gloucestershire Regiment. Henry married Susannah Hughes on 5 November 1881. Goldie's eldest brother, Frederick, became the local coal merchant in Campden.

Goldie was 16 years old at the outbreak of war in 1914 and enlisted in the 9th Battalion, Gloucestershire Regiment. The battalion was formed in Bristol in September 1914 and in October 1914 it was attached to the 78th Brigade of the 26th Division. Goldie arrived in France with the battalion on 20 September 1915 and the 26th Division assembly area was at Guignemicourt, west of Amiens. The division's stay in France only lasted until November 1915, when they and Goldie were posted to Salonika in Greece.

Goldie's time in Salonika ended when he was *wounded in the foot, thigh and knee while fighting against the Bulgars on 21 August 1916*. In a letter that he sent to his parents he said that he was *shot down while on observation duty*. He was evacuated from the battlefield and taken to Malta, where he began a period of treatment in hospital.

After being discharged from hospital in Malta he returned to England and transferred to the Labour Corps for the remainder of his time in the army. After the war ended he returned to Campden and worked as a metalworker at the Silk Milk in Sheep Street in the building once occupied by the Guild of Handicraft. He developed into a very skilful and knowledgeable craftsman and went on to write a number of books on metalworking, including one with George Hart.

Goldie was living in Worcester when he died in March 1977 aged 79 years and his ashes are buried in St. James's churchyard in Campden.

Lewis John Keeley
Boy 2nd Class J10045, Royal Navy
Private 2123, Warwickshire Yeomanry
Union Wireless Operator, Royal Navy

Lewis was born in Campden on 11 February 1895, the fourth son of Henry and Susannah Keeley of Poppets Alley, Campden. His father was a native of the town, an agricultural labourer and for many years a member of "K" Company, 2nd Volunteer Battalion, Gloucestershire Regiment. After leaving school Lewis found employment as a haulier before he enlisted in the Royal Navy on 18 October 1910 aged 15 years. He was posted to HMS *Impregnable*, a training ship at Devonport, as a boy second class and then on 3 February 1911 he joined HMS *Ganges*, a training depot at Harwich. In May 1911 he became a boy first class and then in October 1911 he was posted to HMS *Vivid*, the Royal Navy barracks at Devonport.

On 9 December 1911 he joined the crew of HMS *King Alfred* and served on her until 5 November 1912, when he was returned to shore. His service papers held at the National Archives in London reveal that "*this boy was charged with theft of various articles and received 12 cuts with the cane and discharged to shore, SNLR*". SNLR stands for "*Services No Longer Required*".

All must have been forgiven as Lewis signed on for 12 years with the Royal Navy on 11 February 1913, when he reached the age of 18. His medical examination states that he was five feet six inches tall with brown hair, blue eyes and a fresh complexion. There were scars to the back of his left hand and between his eyes.

He was medically discharged from the Royal Navy before the start of the war and on 7 August 1914 he enlisted in the Warwickshire Yeomanry. After just over a month with the regiment he was discharged as medically unfit for active service on 14 September 1914 and given a job working in a records office in Warwick. Very soon after being appointed he was asked to leave on medical grounds. This did not deter Lewis and he rejoined the Royal Navy as a union wireless operator and saw service during the Gallipoli campaign in Turkey. He continued to serve in the Navy until he was compelled to leave owing to epilepsy.

In 1918 he was living in Priestley Road, Sparkbrook, Birmingham when he applied for a Silver War Badge which was issued to discharged soldiers who were no longer able to serve owing to illness or injury caused by their military service. He was told that he was not entitled.

When Thomas Elsley left Campden in 1939 Lewis took over the running of the shop in the High Street that became *Keeley's*. In 1941 he bought the premises and the range of goods sold developed further. An advertisement in a Campden Official Guide states that there was "*a wonderful display of goods in a large showroom, through which you are invited to walk without obligation to purchase*". The list of items sold included hardware, garden requisites, general ironmongery, paints, china and glass. "*What a lovely shop!*"

Near the end of his working life Lewis lived in a house that he had built in Broad Campden. After retiring he left the town.

During the Second World War Lewis lost both of his sons, Donald and Roy, killed in action. Donald, the elder son, died on 24 March 1944. He was 22 years old and serving as a mid-gunner in a Lancaster bomber. He has no known grave and his name is recorded on the Runnymede Memorial in England.

Sub-Lieutenant Roy Keeley, a pilot in the Fleet Air Arm, was killed in action in a flying accident in the Far East on 29 July 1945. His plane overturned when taking off from the aircraft carrier and he was trapped in the cockpit. He died from his injuries two days later. He has no known grave and his name is recorded on the Lee-on-Solent Memorial in England.

Campden's Second World War Memorial
Donald and Roy were not originally included on the memorial.
Their names are now inscribed at the bottom.

Thomas Frederick Keeley
Private 17682, 3rd Battalion, Coldstream Guards

Born: January 1889
Enlisted: 12 December 1915
Discharged: 15 April 1919
Died: 3 February 1939

Thomas was born in Campden, the son of Eliza Keeley, a gloveress, of Watery Lane and was baptised at St. James's Church on 4 April 1892. He attended school in the town and then found employment as a joiner. He enlisted in the Coldstream Guards in Caterham in Surrey on 12 December 1915, when he was 26 years old, and after several months on home service was posted overseas on 10 October 1916. After serving for a period of two months at the front he returned to England before he rejoined his unit overseas on 26 May 1917. On 2 September he received a gunshot wound to the right thigh and hand and after being evacuated to base hospital he was invalided back to England on 18 February 1918, where he was discharged from the army on 15 April 1919.

After the war he married Elma Davies at Ledbury in 1922 and they had three children: Audrey, George and David. He found employment as a joiner, working as a wagoner and labourer on a fruit farm at Putley owned by Captain R. E. Combe and Mr. Heath.

Thomas died after a few days' illness on 3 February 1939 age 50 years and is buried in Putley in Herefordshire.

Thomas Kilby Keeley
Corporal 646, "D" Company, 1st/5th Battalion, Gloucestershire Regiment
Lance Sergeant 238010, 2nd/4th Battalion, Gloucestershire Regiment

Born: 14 January 1888
Died: 19 August 1917

Thomas was born in Campden, the second son of James Edward and Mary Ann Keeley of Lower High Street, and was baptised at St. James's Church on 1 April 1888. His father was a native of the town and in 1901 was employed as a carpenter on a farm.

Thomas was educated in the town and then found employment as a baker's porter, although he later worked for Thomas Parsons as a plumber. When war was declared in 1914 he had already been a member of the Territorial Army for a number of

Chelmsford, March 1915
Thomas is sitting at the front with his wife, Agnes Ellen Sharpe.

years. He was mobilised on 5 August 1914 and went to Chelmsford with the 1st/5th Battalion, Gloucestershire Regiment for final training before they were posted overseas. That was where he married Agnes Ellen Sharpe before the battalion arrived in France on 29 March 1915. The next few months were spent in the Ploegsteert Wood sector, south of Ypres in Belgium. Here they were able to gain experience of life in the front line in a relatively quiet part of the Western Front.

While he was at the front his initial period of service with the Territorial Army expired and he returned to England, where he went to Bristol and enlisted in the 2nd/4th (City of Bristol) Battalion, Gloucestershire Regiment. He returned to France and had served a period of 1 year and 8 months at the front when he was killed during the Battle of Passchendaele in Belgium.

The battalion were in training at Nieuland in France at the start of August 1917. They practised a trench attack on 7 August 1917 and there were church parades on 5 and 12 August. On 15 August they marched to Esquelbecq, where they entrained at 3.00pm and detrained at Hopoutre at 6.30pm, before marching to a camp for the night. The following day they left the camp at 6.20am and marched to a position north-east of Ypres where trench shelters and bivouacs were erected. On 17 August they relieved the 8th Battalion, Royal Irish Regiment in the front line near Wieltje and the battalion diary notes that there was heavy shelling and an artillery duel all day on 18 August.

Thomas's wife received a letter from his captain informing her of her husband's death: "*It is with very deep regret that I have to inform you that your husband, Sergt. Keeley, was killed in action on 19 August 1917. He was a hero to the end and met his death while advancing on a German position. He was a great fellow, loved and esteemed by all his officers and men. To me his loss is very great indeed. I shall never forget the excellent work that he did for me at all times.*" Thomas was the second son that James and Mary Keeley had lost within four months.

Thomas was 29 years old when he died and is buried in New Irish Farm Cemetery, near Ypres, in Belgium. His wife died on 17 November 1965 aged 83 years and is buried in St. James's churchyard in Campden.

Arthur Keen
Sergeant 12713, "A" Company, 9th Battalion, Gloucestershire Regiment

Born: 26 July 1894
Enlisted: 9 September 1914
Discharged: 23 February 1919
Died: 2 October 1982

Arthur was born in Mickleton, the son of John and Annie Mary Keen, who brought the family to Campden in 1898 when they took over the running of the Live and Let Live public house, which closed at the end of the First World War. He began an apprenticeship as a coachbuilder after leaving school. At the outbreak of war in 1914 he enlisted in the Gloucestershire Regiment in Cheltenham and was posted to the 9th Battalion, where he joined Goldie Keeley and Percy Biles, two friends from Campden, and his brother Edgar. He was five feet eight inches tall with light brown hair, blue eyes and a fresh complexion. His religion was Church of England.

The battalion was formed in Bristol in September 1914 and after twelve months' training in England they arrived in France on 20 September 1915 and went to Guignemicourt, the assembly area for the 26th Division. In November 1915 the division, including the 9th Glosters, were posted to Salonika in Greece, where they remained until July 1918. While he was in Greece Arthur was promoted to the rank of lance corporal on 12 August 1916, corporal on 7 December 1917 and then sergeant on 1 April 1918.

The battalion left the 26th Division on 4 July 1918 and returned to France, where they joined the 66th Division. On 22 September they became the pioneer battalion for the division and the last months of the war were spent advancing through France as the Germans retreated. Arthur was wounded in France on 22 October 1918 and after a period in hospital in Rouen was invalided back to Scotland, where he was admitted to Edinburgh War Hospital. The war was over by the time that he was fit to resume his service and he was discharged from the army on 23 February 1919 after serving 4 years and 168 days. He was entitled to wear one gold wound stripe and four blue chevrons for service.

Arthur returned to Campden and was employed as a chauffeur at the Noel Arms Hotel before he emigrated to Canada in 1927. He married Alice Idonia Blay and they had one child, a son called John Edgar. He spent the rest of his working life as a photographer in Canada.

Arthur died on 2 October 1982 aged 88 years and is buried in Alto Rest Memorial Gardens, Red Deer, Alberta, Canada. His father, John Keen, died at the Almshouses in Campden in 1938. As well as being a publican John was also known locally as a shoemaker and shoe-repairer.

Arthur Henry Frederick Keen
Officers' Steward First Class 363448, Royal Navy

Enlisted: 21 March 1905
Died: 27 December 1919

Arthur was born in Campden on 21 January 1885, the third son of Henry and Sarah Keen of Watery Lane. Henry was a carter and agricultural labourer.

After leaving school Arthur became an indoor domestic servant but at the age of 20 he enlisted in the Royal Navy at Devonport as an officers' steward third class on 21 March 1905. His initial period of service was at HMS *Vivid*, the Royal Navy barracks at Devonport, before he joined the crew of HMS *Impregnable* in July 1905. HMS *Impregnable* was the Devonport flagship and a boys' training ship from 1862-1929. Arthur served on her for the next fourteen years, rising to the rank of officers' steward first class in March 1919. Later that year he developed nephritis and was sent to hospital on 3 December but he did not respond to treatment and died on 27 December aged 34. He was buried in St. James's churchyard, Campden with a Commonwealth War Graves Commission headstone and his name appears on two memorials in the town: in St. James's Church and in the High Street.

Arthur's character and conduct throughout his fourteen years with the Royal Navy were recorded as "*very good*".

Charles Walter Keen
Private, 697th Agricultural Labour Company, Labour Corps

Born: 1878
Died: 1 December 1918

Charles was born in 1878, the second son of nine children of George and Elizabeth Keen of Broad Campden, the others being Joseph, John, Richard, George, Mary, Rose Ellen, Elizabeth and Alice. His father was an agricultural labourer; he died in 1891 aged 46 years. In 1881 the family were living at Rogue's Hill Farm, Broad Campden and then at Lapstone Farm in 1891.

After leaving school Charles found employment as a farm labourer. In 1916, aged 37, he enlisted in the Army Service Corps. Very little is known about his military service and no evidence has been found to indicate that he served overseas. What is known is that he died of heart failure, after flu and pneumonia, at North House in Headcorn near Ashford in Kent on 1 December 1918 aged 39 years. His death certificate states that he was a private in 697th Agricultural Labour Company, Labour Corps when he died. The date of his transfer to the Labour Corps and the location of his grave are not known, but his name can be seen on two war memorials in Campden: in St. James's Church and in the High Street. However, the Commonwealth War Graves Commission does not include him in its records.

Edgar Keen
Private, 9th Battalion, Gloucestershire Regiment
Private 6814, XI Corps Cyclist Battalion, Army Cyclist Corps
Private 34140, 2nd/4th Bn., Oxfordshire and Buckinghamshire Light Infantry

Born: 10 April 1896
Enlisted: 7 September 1914
Discharged: 6 March 1919
Died: 4 July 1986

Edgar was born in Mickleton, the eldest son of John and Annie Mary Keen of High Street, Campden. The family moved to Campden in about 1898 when his father became the landlord of the Live and Let Live public house. When his father died in 1938 he was living in the Almshouses and his last occupation was a shoemaker.

Edgar went to school in the town and then worked as an apprentice with Alec Miller, learning sculpture and carving skills. When he was 19 years old he enlisted at Cheltenham in the 9th Battalion, Gloucestershire Regiment on 7 September 1914, a month after war was declared. After several months' training in England he transferred to the Army Cyclist Corps on 16 March 1915. During further training Edgar was found guilty of "*wilfully absenting himself from parade*" on 24 January 1916. Sergeant Cox and Company Sergeant-Major Thompson witnessed this and his punishment was seven days confined to barracks.

Edgar arrived in France with the Army Cyclist Corps on 29 February 1916 and served at the front until he returned to England on 2 June 1917. He was granted leave and ten days were spent at home in Campden before he rejoined his unit on 9 July.

His next period of overseas service started on 19 December 1917 when he returned to France with the Oxfordshire and Buckinghamshire Light Infantry. On 28 March 1918 Edgar was involved in an incident which caused many people to believe that he was wounded in the wrist during the war. Edgar was practising high jumps at the back of his billet. The bar was raised to four feet six inches and he failed to clear it. He fell to the ground and landed on his left wrist. The back of his hand was facing the ground. It was pulled straight and bandaged and he reported to the doctor. The verdict was "*accidental injury*".

Edgar was discharged from the army on 6 March 1919 and returned to Campden to work as a sculptor in wood and stone, a trade he continued for the rest of his life. Examples of his work can be seen throughout the world but the most viewed example of his work in Campden is on the war memorial in the High Street, where he carved the names of the men who did not return.

In 1925 he emigrated to America and lived in several states before he settled in Tucson for the last 30 years of his life. He married twice. His first wife was Stella Sheila Snowden and the second was Hazel Eleanor Baker. He was the father to three children: Helen, Paul and Charmaine.

Edgar died on 4 July 1986 aged 90 and was buried at Sanctuary Point, Tucson, Arizona. His brother, Arthur, served in the Gloucestershire Regiment during the war and his sister Nora married Ormonde Plested, who served in the Canadian Machine Gun Corps.

Frank Stribblehill Keen
Private 4230, 1st Battalion, Gloucestershire Regiment

Born: 15 January 1876
Enlisted: 28 November 1893
Discharged: 28 November 1915

Frank was born in Campden, the son of Joseph and Annie Keen of Westington. His father was a farm labourer in 1876 and a rustic carpenter in 1891. His mother's maiden name was Stribblehill.

After leaving school Frank found employment as a farm labourer and then a baker. When he was almost 18 years old he became a regular soldier when he enlisted at Bristol in the Gloucestershire Regiment on 28 November 1876. This was the start of 22 years' service with the regiment. He was passed fit for active service and his medical examination recorded that he was five feet four inches tall with blue eyes, brown hair and a fresh complexion.

He began army life with a period of home service until he arrived in Malta on 18 March 1894. He then arrived in Cyprus on 8 October 1895, Egypt on 12 November 1896 and India on 6 February 1897. After serving in India for over two years the battalion was sent to the Boer War in South Africa, where Frank arrived on 20 September 1899. He was reported missing in action at Farquhar's Farm on 30 October 1899 but turned up alive and survived the war, being awarded the Queen's South Africa Medal with three clasps: Natal, Orange Free State and Transvaal.

He remained in South Africa until he arrived in Ceylon on 17 December 1900, where he remained until he returned to India on 6 January 1903. This was his final period of overseas service and he arrived back in England on 9 December 1906 after being abroad for over 13 years.

At the outbreak of war in 1914 Frank was mobilised and posted to the 3rd Reserve Battalion. He was now 38 years old and after fifteen months' home service was discharged from the army as no longer physically fit for active service on 28 November 1915. His 22 years' service gained him the Long Service and Good Conduct Medal.

Frank married Agnes Attridge at South Farnborough on 28 September 1910 and a daughter, Gertrude Mary, was born on 19 November 1912.

George Keen
Royal Field Artillery

George was born in Campden in 1891, the son of Henry Keen of Watery Lane, Campden. His father, who was a carter by trade, married Sarah Saddler Phipps in 1878.

At the outbreak of war George was 23 years old and he enlisted in the Royal Field Artillery. He survived the war but no further information could be found.

George Keen
Private, 10224, Royal Warwickshire Regiment

George was born in Broad Campden on 15 June 1891, the youngest son of George Keen. His father, who was an agricultural labourer, married Elizabeth Hancock in 1874. Elizabeth was left a widow in 1891 when her husband died aged 46 years.

At the outbreak of war in 1914 George enlisted in the Royal Warwickshire Regiment and arrived in France on 18 May 1915. After the armistice was signed he was demobilised and placed into the Class Z Reserve.

Class Z Reserve was authorised by an Army Order of 3 December 1918. There were fears that Germany would not accept the terms of any peace treaty and therefore the British Government decided it would be wise to be able to recall trained men quickly in the eventuality of the resumption of hostilities. Soldiers who were being demobilised, particularly those who had agreed to serve for the duration, were at first posted to Class Z. They returned to civilian life, but with an obligation to return if called upon. The Z Reserve was abolished on 31 March 1920.

Charles Edwin Keitley
Private 16024, Coldstream Guards

Born: 14 April 1896
Enlisted: 23 April 1915
Discharged: 27 November 1918

Charles was born in Cardiff in 1896, the eldest son of Charles Edwin and Maria Louisa Keitley of Leysbourne, Campden, and was baptised at St. James's Church on 2 August 1896. His parents were married at St. James's Church on 11 February 1893 and then moved to Wales, where their first three children were born. The family moved back to Campden in 1900 and on the 1901 census they are listed as living in Leysbourne. In 1918 they had moved to Watery Lane.

Charles's father was a stonemason and his mother's maiden name was Plested. His uncle, Richard Keitley, served in South Africa during the Boer War.

Charles enlisted in the Coldstream Guards on 23 April 1915 when he was 19 years old, and arrived in France on 21 December 1915 just in time to be entitled to a 1914/15 Star campaign medal. In 1916 he was wounded in the leg by shrapnel and had to be evacuated back to England, where he was admitted to hospital in London. After recovering he was sent back to France and continued to serve at the front until he developed frostbite in his feet. This again saw him evacuated back to England where he was discharged from the army on 27 November 1918 as no longer fit for active service owing to the condition of his feet. A Silver War Badge was issued to indicate that he had made his contribution to the war.

In 1922 Charles was living in Broad Campden.

Alfred William Keyte
Army Service Corps

Born: 1878
Died: 26 February 1964

Alfred was born in Campden, the second son of Michael and Elizabeth Ann Keyte of Broad Campden. Michael, a farm foreman, married Elizabeth Stanley in 1865 and died in 1892.

After leaving school Alfred became a ploughboy. On the 1901 census he is listed as an agricultural labourer and living at home with his mother in Watery Lane, Campden. By the time that he married Beatrice Jessie Mary Smith, daughter of Charles Smith, at St. James's Church on 1 June 1907, he was employed as an engineer. They had three children baptised at St. James's Church before the outbreak of war in 1914: Hilda Annie, Albert William and George. A fourth child, William Harold, was born in 1926.

During the war Alfred enlisted in the Army Service Corps and was employed on home service. He was posted to Lincolnshire and assigned to duties involved in the maintenance of aircraft. The Campden 1918 electoral roll records him as living in Grammar School Yard and absent on military service.

Alfred died on 26 February 1964 aged 85 years and is buried in St. James's churchyard, Campden.

Frederick Norton Keyte
Private 1633, 2nd/5th Battalion, Gloucestershire Regiment
Private 240142, 2nd/5th Battalion, Gloucestershire Regiment

Born: 30 May 1892
Enlisted: 15 April 1912
Discharged: 4 October 1918

Frederick was born in Kinwarton near Alcester, the eldest son of Frederick William and Ellen Keyte. In 1901 he was living with his grandparents, Frederick and Rose Keyte, in Church Street, Alcester while his father was living and working at Kinwarton Farm. It appears that his father married for a second time in 1896 when he married Louise Mary Ireson, daughter of George and Mary Ireson of Campden. The 1901 census records that they had three daughters: Dorothy, Lilian and Florence.

Frederick enlisted in the 5th Battalion, Gloucestershire Regiment, the local Territorial Army unit, on 15 April 1912. He was mobilised at the outbreak of war but did not enter France until after the start of 1916.

The war had not been in progress many weeks before the necessity for sending Territorial units overseas became obvious. So it was in the early part of September 1914 that the 2nd/5th Battalion of the Gloucestershire Regiment came into being to act as a second line to the 1st/5th already in existence. In February 1915 the battalion left Gloucester and went to Northampton. This gave the men their first experience of being billeted in a strange borough. With their training over, the battalion left Salisbury Plain on 24 May 1916. They arrived at Southampton later that day to board HMS *681*, the ship that was going to transport them to France. They arrived at Le Havre early on the morning of 25 May and the battalion made their way towards the French village of Laventie. Their first experience of life in front line trenches came on 15 June.

Frederick was wounded on the Western Front and after being evacuated back to England he was admitted to hospital. He failed to recover fully and was discharged from the army as "*no longer fit for active service due to wounds*" on 4 October 1918.

His connection with Campden is confirmed by the Soldiers of Gloucestershire Museum, where an archive exists of all the men who served in the regiment. Against the name of Frederick Norton Keyte it states "*associated with Campden*".

William Henry Thomas Keyte
Private 33558, Devonshire Regiment
Private 4870, Gloucestershire Regiment

Born: 1896
Discharged: 23 October 1918
Died: August 1979

Bill was born in Campden in 1896, the second son of William and Charlotte Keyte of Sheep Street, Campden. He was baptised at St. James's Church on 24 December 1899 and after leaving school he worked with his father and brother, Garnet, in the family coal business.

During the First World War Bill enlisted in the Devonshire Regiment but was later transferred to the Gloucestershire Regiment. After being wounded during the Battle of the Somme he was invalided home and eventually discharged from the army on 23 October 1918.

When he returned to Campden he continued working in the family coal business until 1920, when he took up farming and successfully farmed land at "The Sheppey" and "Cross Hands" until he retired in 1965. He was a member of the National Union of Farmers (NFU) and belonged to the Moreton Show Society from its inauguration.

Bill was a trustee of the Thynne and Weymouth Education Trust, a member of the Campden Lodge of Freemasons, vice-president of the Campden Society and a member of the Bowling Club for many years. He was also a member of the Parochial Church Council and a churchwarden for 15 years.

He married Elizabeth Helen Annie Badger at St. James's Church on 6 February 1923 and they had one daughter, Jean. The family home became "The Sheppey" in Campden.

Bill died at Cheltenham Hospital in August 1979 aged 83 and is buried in St. James's churchyard.

The photograph on the left shows Bill wearing his blue hospital uniform.

Charles Langley King
Private 26283, 3rd Battalion, Gloucestershire Regiment

Born: 1895
Died: 3 April 1916

Charles was born in Gloucester in 1895, the second son of William Arthur and Caroline Martha King. His father was a wine and spirit merchant and in 1901 the family were still living in Gloucester, but in the years leading up to the war they moved to "The Villa", Longborough, Moreton-in-Marsh.

Gloucester Cemetery

Charles enlisted in the Gloucestershire Regiment in Bristol and was posted to the 3rd Battalion for his initial training in England. He never made it to France and died at Gravesend on 3 April 1916, when he was 21 years old. He was buried in Gloucester Cemetery and his name was recorded on the war memorials in Longborough and in St. Catharine's Church in Campden. The family must have been Roman Catholic and regular members of the congregation in Campden.

Charles was the brother of Florence Maria, Reginald, Catharine Elizabeth and Amelia Grace.

Seymour Henry Knight
Private 5461, 11th Hussars
Private 46061, Corps of Hussars

Born: 1885

Seymour was born in Luddington near Stratford-upon-Avon, the second son of Henry and Sarah Knight. After leaving school he left home and went to work as a carter on a farm owned by Edwin Hearle at Little Washbourne near Overbury in Gloucestershire.

In 1912 he was living in Laverton, near Broadway, and working as a carter. He married Beatrice Jane Stevens, second daughter of George and Rose Stevens of Laverton, at the Congregational chapel in Broadway on 14 March 1912. His father was employed as a domestic groom at the time.

Seymour became a regular soldier when he enlisted in the 11th (Prince Albert's Own) Hussars before the outbreak of the First World War. He arrived in France on 9 September 1914 and joined the 1st Cavalry Brigade, Cavalry Division. One of the first divisions to move to France, the Cavalry Division remained on the Western Front throughout the war. It took part in most of the major actions where cavalry were used as a mounted mobile force and also many others where the troops were dismounted and effectively served as infantry.

Seymour's connection with Campden is not known but he is listed in the *Book of Remembrance* by Josephine Griffiths.

Guy John Fenton Knowles

Lieutenant, Royal Naval Volunteer Reserve
Captain, Royal Garrison Artillery

Born: 1 July 1879
Discharged: 19 February 1919

Guy was educated at Rugby School and then became a civil engineer. At the outbreak of war in 1914 he was living at Park Lodge, Park Lane, Knightsbridge, London and on 10 August 1914 he obtained a commission as a lieutenant in the Royal Naval Volunteer Reserve. He arrived in France in November 1914 but was then attached to the Ministry of Munitions as a superintendent engineer.

He was eager to return to the front and left the Royal Naval Volunteer Reserve on 15 March 1916 after successfully applying for a commission with the Royal Garrison Artillery the previous month. He was posted to Bexhill Siege School as a lieutenant in April 1916 and then embarked for Greece at Devonport on 9 August 1916. He arrived at Salonika on 20 August 1916 and in April 1917 was promoted to the rank of captain.

Apart from three weeks' leave in England in mid-1918 he spent the remainder of the war in Greece. He was awarded the French Croix de Guerre in July 1917 and the Greek Military Cross in 1918. His distinguished military career also saw him being mentioned in despatches twice, once in 1917 and once in 1918.

Guy returned to England after the armistice and was discharged from the Royal Garrison Artillery on 19 February 1919.

His name was included on the 1916 prayer list produced by St. James's Church in Campden.

Charles Ladbrook

Private 26862, 7th Battalion, Gloucestershire Regiment

Born: 18 September 1896
Enlisted: 1916
Died: 20 November 1987

Charlie was the elder of two sons of Edwin and Fanny Ladbrook, proprietors of the butcher's shop in Lower High Street, Campden. He was baptised at St. James's Church on 15 November 1896 and after leaving school he joined his brother, Lawrence, in helping to run the family business.

In 1916, aged 20, he enlisted in the Gloucestershire Regiment and was posted to 7th Battalion. After initial training in England he saw service in Mesopotamia, Greece and Turkey. He was reported missing in 1916 and after the war he told friends: *"Ah, if you'd been shot at like those Turks had been shooting at me, you'd have been missing for two days."* On 24 January

Charlie is standing in the centre.

1917 he was shot in the ankle but he made a full recovery and rejoined the battalion. When the war ended he was in Russia and it is said that he brought Russian potatoes back to Campden.

While Charlie was serving in the war his parents closed the butcher's shop but the two brothers opened it again when they returned to Campden. During the Second World War it was closed again when Charlie became a postman, usually delivering mail in outlying districts on horseback. As he was a keen huntsman it was accepted that when there was a hunt on the mail would be very late.

He was a real countryman of a vanishing type. He was a rabbiter, rat-catcher, breeder of ferrets, carer for foxhounds and a colt-breaker. H. J. Massingham's classic book, *Wold Without End*, first published in 1932, records many of Charlie's adventures in and around Campden.

Charlie never married. He died in the Ellen Badger Hospital in Shipston, where he had been resident for the last five years of his life, on 20 November 1987 aged 91 years.

Lawrence Ladbrook
Gunner 162898, Royal Field Artillery

Born: 29 December 1897
Died: 10 June 1993

Lawrence was the younger son of Edwin and Fanny Ladbrook, who were the proprietors of the butcher's shop in Lower High Street in Campden. He was baptised at St. James's Church on 4 January 1898 and after leaving school he joined his brother in helping to run the family business.

When the war started Lawrence was only 16 and it would be another two years before he enlisted in the Royal Field Artillery. He saw service on the Western Front and returned safely to Campden after his official discharge. During the war his parents closed the butcher's shop and it was left to Lawrence and his brother

The Warwickshire Yeomanry
Left to right: Lawrence, Sidney Bridge and Bill Hobbs

Charlie to open it again on their return to Campden. The Ladbrook brothers ran the shop for many years and Lawrence was also an experienced pig-killer.

He married Gertrude Nobes at St. James's Church on 10 August 1929 and they had three children, Marjorie, Edwin and Jean. Gertrude's brothers, Frank, Harry, Tom and George, all served in the army during the war.

In the post-war years Lawrence was a member of the Warwickshire Yeomanry with his friend Sid Bridge and during the Second World War he joined the Home Guard.

He died on 10 June 1993, aged 93, and is buried in St. James's churchyard. The author believes that he was the last man from Campden to die who had seen service in the Great War.

Percy Frederick Lane
Company Quartermaster-Sergeant 13773, 9th Bn., Worcestershire Regiment

Died: 26 September 1918

Percy was born in Malvern Link in 1892, the third son of James and Violetta Lane. His father was a railway signalman and at the outbreak of war the family was living at "The Homestead", Droitwich Road, Fernhill Heath. After leaving school Percy joined his father as an employee of the Great Western Railway and when war was declared in August 1914 he was employed as a signalman at Campden station.

Percy enlisted in the Worcestershire Regiment at Evesham and was posted to the 9th Battalion on Salisbury Plain. It moved to Basingstoke in January 1915 and then to Blackdown in Hampshire in February. On 7 June orders were received to prepare to move to the Mediterranean and Percy arrived at Cape Helles on Gallipoli on 4 July. The battalion left the peninsula at the end of the month but after a short period at Mudros it landed at ANZAC Cove in early August 1915. It then moved to the Suvla Bay sector at the end of the month.

The Lane Family, Vicar's Hill, Leigh Court, 1915
Percy is standing in uniform with his parents and thirteen brothers and sisters.

On 31 January 1916 the battalion was at Port Said in Egypt, where it held forward posts in the Suez Canal defences. It then began the move to Mesopotamia in February 1916 to strengthen the force being assembled for the relief of the besieged garrison at Kut-al-Amara.

After over two years serving in Mesopotamia the 9th Battalion, Worcestershire Regiment was moved with the 39th Brigade to the North Persia Force in July 1918.

Percy died in Iran (then called Persia) on 26 September 1918 aged 26 and as he has no known grave his name is recorded on the Tehran Memorial in Tehran War Cemetery. It does not appear on any memorials in Campden.

Arthur Lavender
Chief Engine Room Artificer 158014, Royal Navy

Born: 10 October 1863
Enlisted: 6 November 1890
Discharged: 4 December 1918

Arthur was born in Stokenbridge, Hagley, Worcestershire in 1863, the son of William and Sarah Lavender. After leaving school he became an agricultural spade-maker and in 1885 he married Sarah Elizabeth Freeman in the Kidderminster registration district. The family then moved to Campden and two children, Edith Lavinia and Gwendoline Eleanora, were baptised at St. James's Church. Arthur was now employed as a fitter.

On 6 November 1890 he enlisted in the Royal Navy at Devonport. He was five feet eight inches tall with grey eyes, dark brown hair and a fresh complexion. His Royal Navy service began as an engine room artificer fourth class at HMS *Pembroke,* a Royal Navy depot in Chatham, and he rose through the ranks until he became an officer on 11 March 1904. His conduct throughout his first thirteen years with the Royal Navy was recorded as "*very good*".

On the 1891 census the family home was recorded as 8, Nelson Road, Gillingham and on the 1901 census they had moved to 41, Penhale Road, Portsmouth.

Arthur served in the Royal Navy throughout the war and retired, aged 55, on 4 December 1918 with the rank of engineer lieutenant. In her *Book of Remembrance* Josephine Griffiths records that he served on HMS *Torpedo Boat Number 23* during the war.

Edward William Lawley
The City of London Yeomanry (*"Rough Riders"*)

Edward first appears in Campden on the 1915 electoral roll, where he is listed as living in the High Street. During the war he served in the City of London Yeomanry, although no evidence of his serving overseas has been found when searching the medal index cards at the National Archives in London.

The Rough Riders started their annual summer camp in August 1914 under canvas at a pleasant location at Worthing. On the outbreak of hostilities the whole regiment volunteered for duty and were soon embodied for active service. In January 1915 they set sail for Egypt and did not return home until after the end of the war. They saw action in Gallipoli, Salonika and Palestine and then on the Western Front.

Alfred William Lee
Private 9248, 2nd Battalion, Worcestershire Regiment

Born: 27 May 1888
Enlisted: 15 May 1905
Died: 27 August 1975

Alfred is sitting on the left. He served in India before the Great War.

Alfred was born in Campden, the son of Charles and Emma Elizabeth Lee of Broad Campden. His father was a native of the town and in 1901 was employed as an agricultural labourer.

Alfred was educated and raised in Campden and on 15 May 1905, when he was almost 18 years old, he went to Evesham to enlist in the Worcestershire Regiment. He was five feet three inches tall with grey eyes, brown hair and a fresh complexion. There was a round scar on the inner side of his right knee. He had been employed as a labourer since leaving school.

He signed on for nine years in the army and three years in the Reserve.

When war was declared in 1914 Alfred was in the Army Reserve, after having served in England and India, and was mobilised immediately. He entrained for Southampton and embarked for France, where he arrived at Boulogne on 14 August 1914. The embarkation roll of the 2nd Battalion, Worcestershire Regiment for August 1914 is kept in Worcester Cathedral and Alfred's name is listed.

The battalion saw their first action near the village of Frameries, near Mons in Belgium, on 24 August 1914 when they came under shellfire at daybreak and suffered their first casualties. They were ordered to retire at

Alfred is sitting on the left. He was wounded in the right elbow by shrapnel in 1916.

8.00am and the battalion formed up in fours, sloped arms and moved off as if they were marching back to barracks at Aldershot. The retreat from Mons had begun and it was October 1914 before the battalion were back in Belgium, when they engaged the enemy north of St. Julien on 21 October during the First Battle of Ypres.

On 31 October the battalion took part in the counter-attack at Gheluvelt, east of Ypres. The leading troops were hit by high explosive and shrapnel shells, causing over 100 casualties. The survivors rushed down the slope towards Gheluvelt Château and with the 1st Battalion, South Wales Borderers cleared the enemy from the grounds.

Alfred was wounded in the right elbow by shrapnel from a shell during the battalion's attack on High Wood in July 1916 during the Battle of the Somme. He was invalided back to England and admitted to hospital in Leeds.

After the war he married Sarah Gee at St. James's Church on 22 November 1919. This was Sarah's second marriage; her maiden name was Cotton. They soon moved to Worcester and Alfred found employment as a transport driver. He died on 27 August 1975 aged 87 and is buried in Worcester.

Alfred was awarded a Long Service and Good Conduct Medal for his time in the Worcestershire Regiment and as he served on the Western Front in 1914 he was an "Old Contemptible".

Harry Richard Lee
Regimental Sergeant-Major 9250, Worcestershire Regiment

Born: 1886
Died: 1968

Harry was born in 1886, the son of Charles and Emma Elizabeth Lee of Broad Campden, and was baptised at St. James's Church on 26 September 1886. Soon after leaving school he became a regular soldier when he enlisted in the Worcestershire Regiment. At the outbreak of war in 1914 he was posted to the 4th Battalion, which joined the 29th Division of the British Army in February 1915. This division was formed by bringing together units of the regular army that were on garrison and similar duties around the British Empire when the war began. Training and mobilisation took place in the Midlands, in the area around Warwick, Leamington Spa, Nuneaton and Rugby. The division then embarked at Avonmouth on 16 March 1915 and arrived in Egypt two weeks

later. Harry does not appear to have embarked with the division in March 1915 as his medal index card states that he entered the Balkan theatre of war (Gallipoli in Turkey) on 14 May 1915 as a sergeant.

The division landed at Gallipoli on 25 April 1915 and remained on the Peninsula until they were withdrawn on 2 January 1916. From here they moved to Egypt and then on 29 March 1916 they landed at Marseille and proceeded to the Western Front, where they remained for the rest of the war.

Harry stayed in the army after the war and joined a Territorial battalion of the Worcestershire Regiment and was awarded a Territorial Force Efficiency Medal. Most of his post-war army life was spent at Kidderminster Barracks.

After he retired from the army he went to live at Rock, south-west of Bewdley, with his wife, Nellie Sims. They had no children. He then went to live at Preston and it is believed that he died in 1968 aged 82 years.

Harry and his wife, Nellie Sims.

Harry and his sister Dorothy Annie, who was known as "Daisy".

Harry proudly wearing his medals.

Leonard Charles Frederick Lee
Leading Stoker K13075, Royal Navy

Born: 7 January 1893
Enlisted: 19 October 1911

Leonard was born at Crooked Corner, Barton near Bidford-upon-Avon, the youngest of three sons of Charles and Emma Elizabeth Lee who served in the war. He was educated in Campden and on the 1891 census he is listed as living with his grandmother, Sarah Lee, in Back Ends. After leaving school he found employment as a farm labourer but when he reached the age of 18 he enlisted at Portsmouth in the Royal Navy on 19 October 1911. He was five feet three inches tall, with brown hair, brown eyes and a fair complexion.

He was a stoker second class and began his service with a period of training at HMS *Victory*, a Royal Navy shore base, near Portsmouth. On 12 November 1911 he joined HMS *Renown* before returning to HMS *Victory* on 14 January 1912. He was then posted to HMS *Hindustan* on 2 April 1912 and soon promoted to a stoker first class.

Leonard served on HMS *Hindustan* for just over four years and left the ship to join HMS *Royal Sovereign* on 18 April 1916. She was built at Portsmouth Dockyard and completed in May 1916 at a cost of £2,570,504.

On 1 October 1916 Leonard joined the submarine branch of the Royal Navy and his first posting was to HMS *Dolphin*. He then spent the rest of the war serving on HMS *Vulcan*, HMS *Platypus* and HMS *Dolphin*. These were all submarine depot ships and while he was on HMS *Platypus* he was promoted to the rank of leading stoker in January 1918. After the war ended he rejoined HMS *Dolphin* before returning to HMS *Victory* on 1 January 1919.

Leonard is sitting on the right.

Leonard's statement of service indicates that he was given a free discharge from the Royal Navy on 16 March 1920, although there is evidence that Leonard rejoined the Royal Navy as he was posted to HMS *Victory* on 15 April 1921 and remained there until 9 June 1921. His conduct throughout his period of service was at all times "*very good*".

The crew of Submarine D7. She was almost sunk in error by HMS *Pelican* on 10th February 1918. D7 was scrapped in December 1921. Leonard is somewhere on the photograph.

187

Samuel Brice Leech

2nd Lieutenant, 8th Battalion, East Yorkshire Regiment

Born: 22 June 1898
Discharged: 21 August 1919

Samuel was born in Argentina, the eldest son of a banker in Buenos Aires, but it was in England that he received his education. He attended Buckingham Royal Latin School and The Blue School in Wells before he joined Campden Grammar School as a boarder. He spent eleven years in Campden at the Grammar School and his three younger brothers, William Charles, Albert Alexander and Edgar George, joined him there. Samuel was an outstanding athlete and a very active member of the Cadet Corps. His army service papers indicate that he was in the Cadet Corps from 15 May 1915 until 5 October 1916 and he achieved the rank of sergeant. At the age of 18, with the war in progress for over two years, he joined "B" Company of the Inns of Court Officers' Training Corps as Private 9695 Samuel Leech. In April 1917 he applied for his commission and he became a 2nd lieutenant with the East Yorkshire Regiment on 26 April.

The Battle of Passchendaele started in July 1917 and Samuel was sent to Belgium to join the 8th Battalion in September. The battlefield was a sea of mud and water-filled shell-holes by the time he arrived at the front as

The Leech brothers. Samuel is sitting at the front. William is in uniform at the back on the left. The other two are Edgar George and Albert Alexander.

a young officer. The conditions in which he was expected to lead men were beyond anything that he could have imagined. It was at Zonnebeke, five miles north-east of Ypres, that he received a severe gunshot wound in his chest on 26 September 1917. He had been at the front for less than a month and he would not see any further overseas military service.

After a period of treatment in hospital in France he left Boulogne for Dover on 11 October 1917 and it was not until June 1918 that he was officially passed fit for further military service. The remainder of the war was spent attached to 3rd Battalion, East Yorkshire Regiment on home service. In October 1918 he was an instructor at the NCO School of Instruction in York but another period of treatment further disrupted his military service when he was admitted to Brighton Grove Military Hospital in Newcastle-upon-Tyne,.

After the war Samuel applied to return to Argentina and was discharged from the army on 21st August 1919; this was after he left England on SS Meteor for Argentina on 31 July. He arrived on 20 August and nothing is known about the rest of his life.

Mr. Cox, Headmaster of Campden Grammar School, is sitting at the front. The boys are Sam Leech, William Leech, Edgar Leech, Albert Leech, John L. Haylock and Henry Ashford Mayne. The order is not known.

William Charles Leech
Inns of Court Officers' Training Corps

William was the second of four sons of Mr. S. Leech, a banker, of Buenos Aires, Argentina. He was educated at Campden Grammar School with his three brothers, Samuel Brice, Albert Alexander and Edgar George. He was Head Boy in 1917 and 1918.

When the war started in 1914 William was still at school but he joined the Cadet Force with his brothers. In 1918 he joined the Inns of Court Officers' Training Corps but the war ended before he was commissioned and posted overseas.

William's brother, Albert Alexander, died on 4 January 1975 and is buried in St. James's churchyard.

Campden Grammar School Cadet Force, c. 1918
Back row (left to right): Lce. Cpl. Fisher, Lce. Cpl. Don Ellis, Lce. Cpl Meadows and Lce. Cpl. Cole.
Front row (left to right): Cpl. Treadwell, Sergeant Billy Leech, Captain Dixey Cossins, Sergeant Gus Cotterell and Cpl. Harry Mayne.

Campden Grammar School Cadet Corps, c. 1919

Back row (left to right): Lewis Horne, C. Mall, H. Purser, C. Clennett, E. Organ and G. Cole.
Front row (left to right): Alexander Leech, E. Williams, A. Cooper and S. Pocton.

The six boys on the back row of the photograph are all holding bugles and Alexander Leech is one of three kettle drummers.
The photograph was taken at the back of the Grammar School in the High Street and the graffiti visible in the background were still there when the author visited the site in 2005.

Campden Grammar School Cadet Corps c. 1916

Back row (left to right): Lce. Cpl. Alec Walker, of Berrington Mill, Lce. Cpl. Reid, Cpl. R. Ellis, Sergeant *Gaffer* Hazelton, Cpl. Sammy Leech, Lce. Cpl. Hartwell and Lce. Cpl. Clements.

Seated at the front is 2nd Lieutenant *Dixey* Cossins, officer in charge of the Cadet Force. Dixey joined the school in 1915 and remained in the town until he joined the Royal Field Artillery in 1918.

Cecil William Lock
Private 17792, Coldstream Guards
Private 641382, Labour Corps

Born: 19 December 1893
Enlisted: 13 January 1916
Discharged: 25 February 1919
Died: 5 June 1974

Cecil enlisted in the Coldstream Guards on 13 January 1916 and after a period of training he served in France and Belgium on the Western Front. He was then returned to England and transferred to the Labour Corps before being discharged from the army on 25 February 1919 owing to "*sickness*". He was issued with a Silver War Badge to indicate that he had made his contribution to the war.

Cecil married Mabel Jones, daughter of William and Fanny Jones of Aston-sub-Edge, at St. Lawrence's Church in Weston-sub-Edge in 1932 and then moved to Campden. In his early working life he was a chauffeur and gardener for Captain Webb in Weston-sub-Edge and was later employed in the building trade with J. W. Pyment and Sons. For many years he was a bellringer at St. James's Church and in this sphere he was well known throughout the Cotswold district.

Cecil died on 5 June 1974 aged 80 years and is buried in St. James's churchyard. He was living at 6, West End Terrace, Campden at the time of his death and was survived by his wife and daughter Margaret.

William Nelson Locke
Sergeant 3565, 1st Battalion, Gloucestershire Regiment
Sergeant 1857, "C" Company, 1st/5th Battalion, Gloucestershire Regiment
Regimental Sergeant-Major 240267, "C" Company, 1st/5th Battalion, Gloucestershire Regiment

Born: 21 January 1871
Enlisted: 8 April 1892
Discharged: 9 May 1919
Died: 8 January 1927

William was born in Bristol, the son of Henry and Sarah Annie Locke. His father was an engineer and in 1871 the family were living at 6 Lower Bedford Place, Bristol.

In 1891 William was employed as a valet at the London Inn in Weston-Super-Mare. He then became a regular soldier when he enlisted in the 1st Battalion, Gloucestershire Regiment on 8 April 1892. At his medical he was passed fit to serve and it was recorded that he was five feet five inches tall with blue eyes, brown hair and a fresh complexion.

After a period of home service he arrived in Malta with the 1st Battalion on 1 November 1893 and remained there until October 1895, when the battalion was posted to Egypt. It was then sent to India in February 1897 and to South Africa on 20 September 1899 to serve in the Boer War. He was promoted to the rank of sergeant soon after arriving and then reported missing in action at Farquhar's Farm on 30 October 1899. He was later released from a prisoner of war camp and posted to St. Helena to help guard Boer prisoners. He arrived there on 4 December 1900 and served there until 31 March 1902, when he returned to South Africa.

William had completed over ten years' service abroad when he left South Africa in June 1904. He had risen through the ranks to sergeant and during his time abroad had been awarded two Good Conduct badges and the Queen's South Africa Medal with clasps for Natal, Orange Free State and Transvaal. While he was at Bloemfontein in South Africa in August 1902 he extended his period of service so that he could remain a regular soldier when he arrived back in England.

When William married Mary Watchorn at Holy Trinity Church in Leamington Spa on 15 June 1908 he was serving as a colour-sergeant with the 2nd Battalion. Their first child, a daughter called Hilda Naomi, was born in 1909 and the family then moved to Campden, where two sons, Frederick Horatio and William Nelson Burman, were born and then baptised at St. James's Church. William was now a drill-sergeant with "H" Company, 5th Battalion, Gloucestershire Regiment, the Campden company of the Territorial Army.

He completed 21 years' service with the Gloucestershire Regiment when his terms of engagement expired on 7 April 1913 and the family moved to Gloucester, where he enlisted as a private in the Territorial Army with the Gloucestershire Regiment on 23 May 1913. He was promoted to sergeant on 3 August 1913 and was mobilised at the outbreak of war in 1914.

He went to Chelmsford with "C" Company, 1st/5th Battalion and remained there until they arrived at Boulogne in France on 29 March 1915. The next 2 years and 157 days were spent on the Western Front before he returned to England on 2 September 1917 to spend the rest of the war on home service. He was promoted to company sergeant-major in November 1917 and then regimental sergeant -major in January 1918.

William had completed 27 years in the Gloucestershire Regiment when he was discharged from the army on 9 May 1919. He returned to his wife and four children in Gloucester (Margaret was born in 1915) and was awarded three campaign medals for his service in the Great War (1914/15 Star, British War Medal and Victory Medal) and the Long Service and Good Conduct Medal.

He died in Gloucester on 8 January 1927 aged 55 years.

Geoffrey Lynch-Staunton
2nd Lieutenant, 13th Hussars

Born: 17 July 1896
Enlisted: 11 May 1915
Died: 5 March 1917

Geoffrey was born in Hamilton, Ontario, Canada on 17th July 1896, the first child and son of George Staunton Lynch-Staunton, and his wife, Adelaide (née Dewar). He attended Downside School at Stratton-on-the-Fosse, near Bath before being admitted to Merton College, Oxford. It was while he was being educated in England that he used to visit his great-uncle, Colonel Richard Lynch-Staunton, in Campden. Richard and his wife, Maria Agnes Margaret Lynch-Staunton, lived at the Court House. Several vacations were spent in the town and he attended St. Catharine's Church with his uncle and aunt. His mother and father were at home in Canada.

In early 1915 Geoffrey returned to Canada and was studying at Osgood Hall Law School in Toronto. His studies were cut short when, like many of his fellow students, he enlisted in the Canadian Army. He joined the Canadian Army Service Corps and was attached to the Canadian Remount Depot with the rank of lieutenant.

In December 1915 he applied to join the British Army and was posted to the Warwickshire Yeomanry as a 2nd lieutenant but was then transferred to the 13th Hussars. The Hussars embarked at Devonport on HT *Miltiades* on 29

October 1916 and arrived at Durban in South Africa on 24 November. They continued their journey on HT *Arcadian* and arrived at Basra in Mesopotamia on 1 January 1917 as part of the 7th Cavalry Brigade.

Geoffrey died on 5th March 1917 aged 20 years during his first engagement with the enemy. He fell at Lajj, on the left bank of the River Tigris 29 miles south-east of Baghdad, in a cavalry charge against entrenched Turks. *The 13th Hussars in the Great War* by Sir Mortimer Durand states that Geoffrey *"rode right down into the Turk trench and walked his horse along it over the Turks. They took him prisoner, but his body was found the next day. They had dressed his wounds but decided that he would be a hindrance to carry along, so murdered him and took everything off him."* He was originally buried near Lajj but his grave was lost in later battles and his name is now recorded on the Basra Memorial in Iraq. It is also recorded on the war memorial in St. Catharine's Church in Campden and at Downside School.

In August 2005 the author purchased a diary written in 1916 by Victor Lynch-Staunton, Geoffrey's younger brother, who was still at school at the time. The diary records the military career of Geoffrey and how Victor saw the war progressing.

Richard Cormick Lynch-Staunton
Colonel, 4th Battalion, Connaught Rangers

Born: 1846
Died: 17 September 1922

Richard was the youngest son of George Staunton and Sarah Jane Lynch-Staunton of Clydagh. He married Marion Agnes Margaret Duncan at the Roman Catholic Chapel, St. James's Square, Cheltenham, on 10 January 1871, when he was 24 years old, and his profession was recorded as *"Gentleman"* on the marriage certificate. Richard and Marion had two children, Frances Juanita (*Dorothy*), who married Paul Woodroffe in 1907, and Bertram, who became a priest. At the time of the wedding Richard was living at 23 Landsdown Road in Cheltenham.

Richard was an officer with a militia battalion of the Connaught Rangers for many years but did not see any active service in either the Boer War or the First World War although he could be seen in uniform around Campden. In the British Army List of July 1872 he is listed as a captain with both the Galway Militia and the Connaught Rangers. On 10 December 1887 he became a major with the 4th Militia Battalion, Connaught Rangers and by 1890 he was listed as a lieutenant-colonel. The final listing for Richard in the Army Lists records him as an honorary colonel attached to the Yorkshire and Lancashire Regiment in 1901.

At the time of the First World War he was living in Campden at the Court House and was a regular member of the congregation at St. Catharine's Catholic Church. His brother, Frances Hardwick Lynch-Staunton, had a grandson, Geoffrey, who was educated in England in the years leading up to the war. Geoffrey regularly used to visit his great uncle in Campden and when he joined the army Richard was named as his next of kin. Geoffrey was killed in action in 1917 and his name is recorded on the memorial in St. Catharine's Church.

Richard died in Campden on 17 September 1922 aged 76 years and is buried in St. Catharine's cemetery. His wife, Marion, died on 2 October 1928 aged 82 years and is buried with her husband. Richard and Marion both have memorial stained glass windows in St. Catharine's Church that were designed by their son-in-law, Paul Woodroffe.

James Maclean
Royal Flying Corps

In her *Book of Remembrance* Josephine Griffiths lists James as serving in the Royal Flying Corps during the war. The Campden 1918 electoral roll lists him as living in Sheep Street with his wife, Edith Frances Maclean. There is no trace of him in Campden before or after the war.

Thomas Lawrence Malins
Private 24431, Gloucestershire Regiment
Private 414937, Labour Corps
Private 49755, South Lancashire Regiment

Born: 1888

Lawrence is wearing his 1914-18 medals.

Lawrence was born in Birmingham, the son of Thomas and Hannah Malins of West Side Story Lane, Balsall Heath. His father was born in Ilmington and was a carpenter by trade, although he later became an undertaker and innkeeper. In 1902 Thomas and Hannah moved to Campden from Stratford-upon-Avon and took over the licence of the Volunteer Inn from Charles Aston. They ran the pub until Thomas died from heart failure on 2 September 1923.

During the war Lawrence enlisted in the Gloucestershire Regiment and was first posted overseas after the start of 1916. He was soon transferred to the Labour Corps and then to the South Lancashire Regiment before returning safely to England. He was listed on the Campden 1918 electoral roll as absent on military service but must have left the town soon after the war as he is not listed in 1922.

John Maurice McGrale
Private 10143, 4th Battalion, King's Liverpool Regiment
Private 435562, 571 Agricultural Company, Labour Corps

Born: 3 November 1895
Enlisted: 24 June 1912
Discharged: 31 March 1920
Died: 28 May 1967

John was born on 3 November 1895, the son of Patrick (*Paddy*) and Ellen McGrale of 121 Portland Street, Liverpool. After leaving school he worked as a labourer but at the age of 16 he enlisted at Southport in the King's Liverpool Regiment on 24 June 1912. His medical examination stated that he had a bald patch on the right side of his head and that there was a mole three inches below his left nipple. He was a Roman Catholic and had brown hair and grey eyes. The next three years were spent on home service with the 3rd Battalion and in August 1912 and June 1913 he was guilty of absence without leave and on each occasion he was fined one day's pay.

When the war started he was mobilised at Seaforth on 8 August 1914 and the next sixteen months were spent in England. He was fined six days' pay for being absent without leave for five days in August 1915. On 15 December 1915 John arrived in France with the 4th Battalion, King's Liverpool Regiment and was soon attached to the 98th Brigade Machine Gun Corps. He was wounded twice. He had a finger blown off and received face and head wounds which resulted in plates being inserted. He was admitted to hospital in Rouen in France in July 1916 and after being discharged arrived back in England on 7 July 1916, where he was posted to the 3rd Battalion for further home service. On 23 April 1917 he was transferred to the King's Own Shropshire Light Infantry and then on 29 October he joined the Labour Corps and was posted to 571 Agricultural Company. He was employed in Campden assembling tractors and showing local farmers how to drive them. It was at this time that he met his future wife, Gladys Eliza Rose Beckett, while he was lodging with her father, William Beckett.

John spent the rest of the war in England serving in various agricultural companies. On 20 June 1918 he was found guilty of "*neglect of duty*" by being away from the mess room during parade hours and was punished by being confined to barracks for two days. His final discharge came on 31 March 1920 after having been put into the Army Reserve on 18 April 1919. His character was recorded as "*very good*" on his discharge papers. He had served for 7 years and 282 days, of which just over 3 years were spent on the reserve list.

He married Gladys Beckett at St. Catharine's Church in Campden on 7 December 1919 and they had three children: John Cecil, Helen and Marjorie. In 1920 the family home was in the High Street in Campden.

John died on 28 May 1967 aged 71 years and is buried in St. Catharine's cemetery.

William Ernest Donald Patrick Matthews
Corporal 27558, 1st Battalion, Manchester Regiment

Born: 4 June 1886
Died: 28 March 1947

William was born at the barracks in Barnard Castle, Durham, the eldest son of George and Margaret Jane Matthews. His father was a regular soldier and at the time of his son's birth he was a colour-sergeant with the 3rd Battalion, Durham Light Infantry. On the 1901 census George was 46 years old and listed as an "*army pensioner*". The family were living at 2 Park Square, Mossley Road, Ashton-under-Lyne and William, who was then 16 years old, was a regular soldier serving at Ashton Barracks with the 6th Battalion, Manchester Regiment. He joined the regiment as a boy soldier and was a drummer in the band.

William was one of eight children of George and Margaret listed on the 1901 census and his eldest brother, Charles Henry, who was then only 14 years old, was also a boy soldier with the Manchester Regiment at Ashton Barracks. When war was declared in 1914 William was a corporal and he served overseas with the 1st Battalion, Manchester Regiment after 1916, returning safely at the end of the war.

He married Agnes Mary Elizabeth Bruce, daughter of Charles and Rose Bruce of Campden, before the war and they had three children:

William and his wife, Agnes, with three of their four children.

Dorothy Margaret Rose, Vera Marie Irene and Ruby Veronica. Dorothy was baptised at St. Catharine's Church in Campden on 1 October 1911.

William died on 28 March 1947 aged 60 years and is buried in St. James's churchyard in Campden. His wife died on 11 November 1958 aged 74 years.

Arthur Frank Meadows

Born: 14 November 1889

Arthur was born in Draycott, the son of Charles Henry and Emma Meadows. His father was a farm labourer and his mother's maiden name was Sharpe.

Arthur lived in Draycott until he married Mary Ann Richardson from Broad Campden at St. James's Church in Campden on 26 January 1915. The family home was at Greystones in Broad Campden and four children were baptised at St. James's Church between 1915 and 1928: Arthur Ernest Henry, Elsie, Algernon Albert and George Edward.

The wedding certificate states that Arthur was a motor engineer by trade and the 1918 electoral roll lists him as absent on military service. On 24 January 1920 the *Evesham Journal* reported that he returned home on 15 December 1919 after over two years away in the army.

Joseph Stanley Meadows
Gunner 107082, Royal Garrison Artillery

Born: 2 July 1890
Died: 10 January 1965

Joe was born in Leicestershire, the son of Andrew Miles and Emma Meadows. In 1908, at the age of 18, he left Leicestershire and came to Campden, finding employment as a butcher with Jack Coldicott. He quickly became very well known, not only in Campden, but also in the surrounding villages, at which he used to call with the delivery van.

He married Gertrude Josephine Harwood in 1911 and they had three children: Joseph Miles, Dorothy Mary and Thomas Francis. The family home was 4 Gordon Cottages, Sheep Street.

During the war he served in France and Belgium with the Royal Garrison Artillery, rising to the rank of lance bombardier before being discharged. On 6 April 1916 he lost his younger brother, Thomas Miles Meadows, who was serving with the Northamptonshire Regiment. Thomas was 23 years old when he died and is buried in Berks Cemetery Extension, near Ploegsteert, in Belgium.

After the war Joe returned to his job as a butcher and he helped to found the Campden branch of the British Legion in 1921. He was service secretary from 1924-63, and served as treasurer for many years. He was the first branch member to receive the gold medal for special services.

He had to give up his Legion work in 1962 owing to failing health and as a token of their appreciation the Legion members presented him with a television set which gave him a great deal of pleasure in the last years of his life. He retired from his job as a butcher with Donald Bragg in 1962.

A keen churchman, Joe was a sidesman at St. James's Church and a member of the Parochial Church Council for many years, also serving as chairman of the churchyard committee.

During the Second World War his two sons joined the army; Joseph Miles was a captain in the Royal Engineers and Thomas was in the Catering Corps.

Joe died on 10 January 1965 aged 74 and is buried in St. James's churchyard.

Albert Edward Merriman
Private 13423, 9th Battalion, Gloucestershire Regiment

> Born: 1880
> Enlisted: 28 September 1914
> Discharged: 11 November 1914

Albert was born in Campden, the son of George and Elizabeth Merriman of Broad Campden. He was a labourer by trade and married Mary Elizabeth Peachey at St. James's Church on 2 March 1901 and by the outbreak of war in 1914 they had two sons: Albert Edward and Harry.

In the years leading up to the war Albert was a member of "H" Company, 5th Battalion, Gloucestershire Regiment, the local company of the Territorial Army. When war was declared the family were living in Blockley and he went to Gloucester to enlist for the duration on 28 September 1914. His pension papers held at the National Archives in London reveal that he was five feet seven inches tall with dark brown hair, blue eyes and a fresh complexion. He was posted to the 9th Battalion, Gloucestershire Regiment at Bristol on 1 October 1914 but was discharged as medically unfit for active service on 11 November 1914 after less than two months' home service. Two of his brothers, Frederick and Francis, served in the army during the war.

Francis William Merriman
Private 7335, 2nd Bn., Worcestershire Regiment

> Born: 9 September 1884
> Died: 12 April 1917

Francis and Julia Maria Merriman.

Francis was born in Campden, the third son of George and Elizabeth Merriman. His father was a general labourer and the family home was in Broad Campden in 1891 and in Sheep Street in 1901. After leaving school Francis was employed as a farm labourer and then as a postman in the town.

When the war started he was in the Army Reserve and was immediately mobilised, arriving in France on 26 September 1914, where he joined the 2nd Battalion, Worcestershire Regiment just north of the River Aisne at Soupir near Soissons. They arrived at Poperinge in Belgium on 19 October 1914 and at 9.30am on 21 October they engaged the enemy at St. Julien during the First Battle of Ypres. They were relieved on 24 October after driving back several attacks by the enemy, totally exhausted from lack of sleep. Later the same day they were ordered forward again and with fixed bayonets they entered Polygon Wood and forced the enemy to retreat. The surviving members of the battalion were then involved in the heroic action at Gheluvelt, where they advanced from Black Watch Corner at Polygon Wood at 2.00pm on 31 October and charged with fixed bayonets towards Gheluvelt. Together with the 1st Battalion, South Wales Borderers they rushed down the slope and cleared the enemy from the grounds of Gheluvelt Château.

In December they moved south into France, where the war diary records that their trenches were *"flooded and in parts waist deep in water and mud"*. The beginning of 1915 saw the battalion in the area around Richebourg-St. Vaast, Festubert, Cuinchy and Béthune. Francis fell into a shell-hole and injured his thigh during his first few months on the Western Front but after treatment he was able to continue his service.

Funeral Procession, 17 April 1917.

During the Battle of the Somme the battalion was involved in an attack on High Wood on 15 July 1916. Men were fighting in the wood and holding off strong counter-attacks during a general withdrawal. The war diary of the 100th Brigade recorded that the *"Worcesters are standing firm"*. Another attack took place on Tea Trench near Delville Wood on 24 July and after assembling at Fricourt they marched to a rest area *"with drums beating"*. On 11 September they took over reserve trenches at Foncquevillers and then entered the front line on 20 September. It was while Francis was in trenches at Foncquevillers that he was buried by a shell and sustained another injury to his leg. He was evacuated to England and admitted to Suffolk Hall Hospital in Cheltenham on 19 March 1917. He did not make satisfactory progress and his leg had to be amputated. Francis never recovered and after collapsing suddenly he died on 12 April 1917 aged 32 years.

The funeral took place in Campden on 17 April and the coffin was borne from St. Catharine's Church, where it had been overnight, by four postman colleagues and by four soldiers from the VAD Hospital at Norton Hall. It was covered by a Union Jack and escorted by a detachment of cadets from the Grammar School under Captain Cossins. Father Bilsborrow conducted the service and a soldier from Norton Barracks in Worcester sounded Last Post.

Francis is buried in St. James's churchyard in Campden with a Commonwealth War Graves Military headstone. He left a wife and three young children, William (born 1910), Richard (born 1911) and Thomas (born 1914). He had married Julia Marie Higgins at St. Catharine's Church on 19 October 1909.

Francis has his name recorded on three war memorials in Campden: in St. James's Church, in the High Street and in St. Catharine's Church.

St. James's churchyard, 17 April 1917. Francis being buried.

Frederick Charles Merriman
Private 647, 5th Battalion, Gloucestershire Regiment

>Born: 12 December 1874
>Enlisted: 11 October 1892
>Discharged: 31 March 1916

Frederick was born in Campden, the second son of George and Elizabeth Merriman of Watery Lane. His parents were both born in the town and in 1881 George was employed as an agricultural labourer. The 1891 census lists the family living in Broad Campden and his father's occupation as a general labourer.

After leaving school Frederick found employment as an agricultural labourer. On 11 October 1892 he enlisted in "K" Company, 2nd Volunteer Battalion, Gloucestershire Regiment. He served with the Volunteers until 4 April 1908, when they became "H" Company, 5th Battalion, Gloucestershire Regiment. He continued to serve as a member of the new Territorial Army up to the outbreak of war in 1914 and was present at the annual training camp each year.

Frederick was mobilised for the war on 5 August 1914 and was employed on home service until he was discharged from the 2nd/5th Battalion on 31 March 1916 at Park House Camp in Salisbury as no longer fit for active service. This brought to an end over 23 years of loyal service with the Volunteers and Territorials for which he was awarded a Territorial Efficiency Medal.

During his time in the army during the war he was guilty of several offences including:
1. On 28 December 1915 he was late on fatigue parade and was confined to barracks for one day as punishment.
2. On 28 January 1916 he was late on early morning parade and was confined to barracks for three days.
3. On 19 February 1916 he was absent from afternoon parade and was confined to barracks.

Frederick married Ellen Fletcher, daughter of Alfred and Ellen Fletcher, at St. Eadburgha's Church in Ebrington on 29 March 1897 and by 1901 they had two children, Fanny and George, and were living in Hidcote Boyce with his wife's parents. They then moved to Ebrington and seven more children were baptised at St. Eadburgha's Church between 1903 and 1922: Doris May, Josephine Alice, Florence May, Gertrude Emily, Francis Gilbert, Percival Arthur and Ernest Leslie.

Frederick is buried in St. Eadburgha's churchyard in Ebrington.

Mark Ernest Louis Merriman
Lance Corporal 241992, 1st/6th Battalion, Gloucestershire Regiment

>Born: 30 September 1888
>Died: 16 June 1918

Mark was born in Campden, the second son of William and Anna Maria Merriman of Watery Lane, and was baptised in the Catholic Chapel at Campden House on 4 November 1888. His father was a native of the town and employed as a farm labourer.

An enameller by trade, Mark was an employee of Bill Mark and served his apprenticeship with the Guild of Handicraft at the Silk Mill in Campden. His name can still be seen engraved on a window in Bill Mark's old workshop. He was with the Guild for five years. Mark served in the local Volunteers and Territorials as a bugler for about fifteen years and was always very popular in the regiment and respected in the town.

He married Frances Beatrice Harwood before the First World War and they had three children, Wilfred Mark, Robert and Margaret Mary. The family home was in West End Terrace in Campden. At the outbreak of the war he was called up but his initial period of service with the Gloucestershire Regiment expired before he went overseas and he returned home in April 1916. He was then called up under the National Service Act in June 1916 and in November 1917 he arrived in Italy with the 1st/6th Battalion, Gloucestershire Regiment.

The Austrian offensive began on the Asiago Plateau at 3.00am on 15 June 1918 when a powerful bombardment fell along the whole of the front. Roads and tracks were shelled with particular severity. Within three minutes all telephone communication forward of headquarters was destroyed as all lines were aerial. At 9.30am information was received that the enemy had broken through the divisional front and that the situation was serious. The battalion was ordered forward to Casa Magnaboschi, arriving at 1.00pm. Some ground was gained in the thick pine forests and all positions gained were held during the night.

At 2.00am on 16 June orders were received stating that the attack would be renewed that morning and at 8.30am the whole line advanced, forcing the Germans back. On reaching their front line they took a considerable number of prisoners and a large amount of booty. Patrols were sent forward which recaptured outpost positions on Hill 972 and Cunico Hill.

Mark was killed in action on 16 June 1918 and his platoon officer, 2nd Lieutenant Pendlebury, wrote to his wife. "*Poor Mark was one of my boys. I was only three yards from him when a bullet caught him in the head and he died instantaneously. He suffered no pain. He was really one of the best N.C.O.'s in my platoon and I shall cherish his memory for ever.*"

Mark is buried in Boscan Cemetery, near Asiago in Italy, and his name is recorded on three memorials in Campden: in St. James's Church, in St. Catharine's Church and in the High Street. After the war his widow married Garnet Keyte.

William Leo ("Wilfred") Merriman
Sergeant T-30106, Canadian Army Service Corps, First Canadian Division Train

Born: 25 July 1891
Enlisted: 19 September 1914
Discharged: 23 April 1919
Died: 4 June 1942

Wilfred was born in Campden just after the 1891 census was compiled, the third son of William and Anna Maria Margaret Merriman of Watery Lane. His father was a native of the town and employed as an agricultural labourer. As a lad Wilfred worked at Campden House for a while and then in the office at the Guild.

He left Campden in 1908 and emigrated to Canada, where he went to an agricultural college before working as a farmer. At the outbreak of war in 1914 he was one of the first to enlist, joining the Canadian Army Service Corps at Ottawa on 19 September 1914, when he was 23 years old. He was medically examined at Valcartier Camp and passed fit for overseas service. He was five feet two inches tall with blue eyes, brown hair, a dark complexion and a scar on his left shin. His father was recorded as his next of kin and the family address was Paltimore, Quebec.

Wilfred arrived in England on 21 October 1914, a member of the First Canadian Division, the first contingent of Canadian soldiers sent overseas during the war. They were given the nickname "*The Old Originals*". While they were in England Wilfred was absent without a pass and was punished with a loss of four days' pay and seven days confined to camp. They then arrived in

Wilfred is standing under the horse's ears, fourth from the right. The men are at a training camp on Salisbury Plain.

France on 11 February 1915 and the following month Wilfred was promoted to acting-corporal. He continued to rise through the ranks and was promoted to corporal on 24 August 1916 and then sergeant on 9 May 1917.

Wilfred served on the Western Front until he returned to England on 2 March 1919. He was present at all of the major battles that the Canadian Expeditionary Force fought in, including Festubert, Givenchy, St. Eloi, Mount Sorrel, Somme, Vimy Ridge, Hill 70, Passchendaele and Amiens. In late 1918 he was awarded the Military Medal for distinguished service in the field on 2 November 1918 after it was recommended on 9 November 1918 in the 1st Division Corps Order Number 5647. The award was announced in the *London Gazette* on 3 July 1919.

Wilfred is standing in the second row from the front, the sixth man from the left.

In March 1916 William was hit in the left eye by the branch of a tree while on convoy duty. He did not report sick at the time but his vision had been poor ever since and on 8 April 1919 he was seen by a doctor at Bramshott. The report states that his vision was good at the time of enlistment and that the defective vision was considered to be permanent.

Wilfred's journey back to Canada began when he embarked at Southampton on SS *Olympic*. After arriving back in Canada he was discharged from the army on 23 April 1919 and returned home to 98 Holland Avenue, Ottawa. He had served in the Canadian Army for 4 years and 201 days and had not been in hospital once.

After the war he married Lucy Agnes Montgomery Bayne at Merivale United Church in Ottawa, Canada and they had eight children: Nora Elizabeth, William James, Adelaide Lucy, David Edgar, Margaret Rose, Mark Bayne, Lillian Louise and Edythe Josephine.

William died in Ottawa Civic Hospital on 4 June 1942 aged 50 and is buried in Merivale Cemetery, Ottawa.

John Midgley

Jack was educated at Campden Grammar School. He lost his life during the war and his name is recorded on the memorial which is located in the main hall of Campden School in Cider Mill Lane. Despite

finding a photograph of Jack it has not been possible to trace his regiment or date of death. No person of his name appears on any census return or electoral roll so it must be assumed that he was a boarder at the school.

Campden School War Memorial
Jack's name is third from the top of the right-hand column.

The photograph on the right shows Jack sitting on the left. His friends Drewett and Reid are also on the photograph but the order is not known.

Walter James Miles
Private 1383, Royal Warwickshire Regiment
Private 23252, Royal Warwickshire Regiment
Private 268396, Royal Warwickshire Regiment

Born: 26 June 1891
Enlisted: 29 May 1913
Discharged: 7 March 1918

Walter was born in Campden, the third son of George and Annie Miles. His father was a cattleman on a farm and in 1901 the family were living in Aston in Birmingham. After leaving school Walter became an annealer and then at the age of 21 years he became a regular soldier when he enlisted in the Royal Warwickshire Regiment in Birmingham on 29 May 1913.

He had been a soldier for just over a year when the war started and he arrived in France on 11 November 1914 to join either the 1st Battalion or 2nd Battalion, Royal Warwickshire Regiment, who were already serving on the Western Front, just in time to qualify for a 1914 Star campaign medal. The next five months were spent on the Western Front before he was returned to England on 15 April. He was sent back to France on 30 September 1915 and after another four months' service he again returned to England. The rest of 1916 was spent in England before he embarked for France on 11 January 1917 but yet again his stay at the front was short-lived as he was back in England on 6 March.

Walter's final period of service in France started on 8 September 1917. Two months later he returned to England for the final time on 13 November. He was discharged from the army on 7 March 1918 as no longer physically fit for war service and a Silver War Badge was issued. Army Form B.2067 describes Walter at the time of his discharge as five feet nine inches tall with grey eyes, brown hair, a fair complexion and a scar on the left side of his head.

Walter's parents came to Campden in 1888 at the earliest (their second son, Thomas, was born in 1887 in Oxfordshire), and left the town in 1900 at the latest (their daughter, Sarah, was born in 1900 in Oxfordshire).

Wilfred Joseph Miles
Private G25340, Coldstream Guards
Private 6483, 5th Reserve Battalion, Guards Machine Gun Regiment

Born: 1892
Enlisted: 15 December 1915
Discharged: 6 January 1919

Wilfred was born in Shipton Oliffe in 1892, the son of Edwin and Julia Miles. After leaving school he trained as a policeman and in 1915 was stationed in Campden. He married Eva Tapscott, daughter of John Henry Tapscott, at Lympstone Parish Church, Exmouth, Devon on 16 December 1915 and their first child, a son called Wilfred John Miles, was baptised at St. James's Church in Campden on 30 July 1916. The family settled in Campden and on the 1918 electoral roll Wilfred is listed as living in High Street, Campden and absent on military service.

Wilfred enlisted in the Coldstream Guards on 16 December 1915, the day before he was married, and was immediately placed into the Army Reserve. He was five feet nine inches tall with brown hair, blue eyes and a fresh complexion. He continued as a policeman in Campden until he was mobilised on 20 April 1918. The following day he joined his unit at Caterham and the next seven months were spent on home service. On 14 May 1918 he was transferred to the 5th Reserve Battalion, Guards Machine Gun Regiment and on 6 January 1919 he was discharged from the army and returned to his wife and family, who were then living at Newport Cottage, Chedworth, Gloucestershire.

Charles Philip Scott Morris
Private 435766, 31st Bn. (Alberta Regiment), Canadian Expeditionary Force

Born: 4 July 1886
Enlisted: 3 October 1915
Died: 6 June 1916

Philip was born in Campden on 4 July 1886, the eldest son of Doctor Charles Edward and Elizabeth Emma Morris of Cotswold House, Campden. His father, the town doctor, was a native of the town and held a commission in "K" Company, 2nd Volunteer Battalion, Gloucestershire Regiment.

During his time at school Philip was a member of the Army Cadet Force and after leaving school he joined the Warwickshire Yeomanry. At the outbreak of war in 1914 he was in Canada and had been serving in the 15th (South Alberta) Light Horse since 1911. He enlisted in the Canadian Army at Calgary on 3 October 1915 and was passed fit for overseas service at a medical examination the following day. He was 5 feet ten inches tall with light brown hair, blue eyes and a medium complexion. He gave his age as 24 years when he was actually 28 and his next of kin was his sister, Mary Eleanor Scott Morris, who was living in Bennington near Stevenage.

Philip arrived in England on 6 November 1915 and was posted to the 50th Battalion at Bramshott. He transferred to the 9th Reserve Battalion in February 1916 and then to the 31st Battalion for service on the Western Front. He arrived in France on 17 March and was killed in action near Ypres in Belgium on 6 June. He was 30 years old and as he has no known grave his name is recorded on the Menin Gate Memorial in the centre of Ypres. It is also recorded on two memorials in Campden: in St. James's Church and in the High Street.

He was not married and he was employed in Canada as a clerk.

Frank Morris
Royal Field Artillery

Born: 1900

Frank was born in Hagley near Stourbridge, the son of John Albert and Alice Maud Morris. His father was a railway platelayer and in 1901 the family was living in Stourbridge Road, Hagley. In 1917 his elder brother Ernest married Edith Alice Tout in Campden and then set up home in Sheep Street. The Campden 1918 electoral roll lists Frank's two elder brothers, Ernest and John, as resident in Sheep Street.

In her *Book of Remembrance* Josephine Griffiths lists Frank as serving in the Royal Field Artillery during the war.

John Samuel Morris
Worcestershire Regiment

Born: 1887

John was born at Hagley near Stourbridge, the son of John Albert Morris, who was a railway platelayer. His father married Alice Maud Ravenhall in 1883 and in 1901 the family was living in Stourbridge Road, Hagley.

John's younger brother Ernest married Edith Alice Tout at St. James's Church in Campden on 8 July 1917. Ernest was a railway signalman and at the time of the wedding was living in Blockley. After the wedding Ernest and Edith lived in Sheep Street, Campden.

The Campden 1918 electoral roll lists John living in Sheep Street with his brother and absent on military service. In her *Book of Remembrance* Josephine Griffiths states that John served in the Worcestershire Regiment.

Harold George Moseley
Private 28688, "Z" Company, 2nd Battalion, Hampshire Regiment

Born: 1899
Died: 5 September 1918

Harold was born in Pershore, the son of Thomas and Lucy Moseley. His parents began their married life in Wyre Piddle before they moved to Pershore in March 1899. In 1920 they moved to Campden and ran a bootmaker's shop in the High Street before returning to Pershore in 1931.

Harold enlisted in the Hampshire Regiment in Pershore and when he arrived in France in 1918 he was posted to "Z" Company, 2nd Battalion to be with his elder brother, Len. He wrote regular letters to his parents at home in Pershore and on 5 May 1918, the day before his brother was wounded, he wrote, "*We had our letters from you when we came off piquet duty in a village near by. We had to stop soldiers entering houses that had been evacuated by the French people and stealing things. Today we have been mending holes in the ground. I have not heard the cuckoo yet but the other birds are singing beautifully despite the guns. I can hear them now.*"

Harold was with Len when his brother was wounded on 5 May 1918. After hearing the news that he had succumbed to his wounds he borrowed a bicycle and went to Ebblinghem to visit his grave. He told his parents, "*I had great difficulty finding the English Cemetery. There is a neat wooden cross over the head of his grave with strips of aluminium inscribed with his name and regiment.*"

Harold was fatally wounded during the advance in Flanders in September 1918 and was evacuated to hospital near St. Omer. He died on 5 September aged 19 and is buried in Longuenesse Souvenir Cemetery, near St. Omer, France. His name is recorded on the war memorial in Pershore Abbey but it is not on any memorial in Campden as his parents only came to the town after the death of two of their sons in the war.

Leonard Thomas Moseley
Private 13181, "Z" Company, 2nd Battalion, Hampshire Regiment

Born: 1895
Died: 6 May 1918

Len was born in Wyre Piddle, the son of Thomas and Lucy Moseley. His parents began their married life at Wyre Piddle before they moved to Pershore in March 1899. In 1920 they moved to Campden and ran a bootmaker's shop in the High Street before returning to Pershore in 1931.

At the outbreak of war Len enlisted at Worcester in the Hampshire Regiment and after a period of training in England he arrived in France on 21 September 1915. In 1918 he was joined in France by his younger brother, Harold, in "Z" Company, 2nd Battalion, Hampshire Regiment. Harold wrote home to his parents in May 1918 informing them that Len had been wounded. He was hit in the left leg and slightly wounded in the right arm. "*You see it was rather dark when the shell burst and I could not see very well. A stretcher came almost at once and he was taken back to the dressing station before I was aware of what had happened. He was very brave about it and thought more about leaving me than of his wounds. We had only been in the line about four hours when it happened.*"

Harry (seated) and Len Moseley

Len died of wounds on 6 May 1918 aged 22 years and is buried in Ebblinghem Military Cemetery, west of Hazebrouck in Northern France. In a letter to his parents dated 2 June 1918 Harold said, "*I am very much shocked and surprised to hear that poor Len died and so soon after he was wounded. I had no idea he was hurt dangerously as he was quite conscious when I last saw him and did not seem worrying at all. Perhaps he is better off after all. We shall all see him again is one consolation. You will be very glad to know he went to Holy Communion with me the day before he died. I shall always remember him as a fine soldier and I miss him very much. He had a decent burial and a service read over him. He also had the Last Post blown and rifle volleys were fired over his grave."*

Len's name is recorded on the war memorial in Pershore Abbey. He does not have his name on any memorial in Campden as his parents only came to Campden in 1920 after the death of two of their sons in the war.

"Z" Company, 2nd Battalion, Hampshire Regiment
Len and Harry are both on this photograph somewhere.

Basil Hoveden Neve
Chief Engine Room Artificer 270424, Royal Navy

Born: 28 June 1875
Enlisted: 17 April 1901
Died: 5 September 1914

Basil was born in Wood Green in London, the youngest son of Julius Robert and Isabelle Emma Neve, and was baptised at St. James's Church in Campden on 30 March 1892, when he was 16 years old. His parents were married at Faversham in Kent on 8 March 1870 and when they came to Campden Julius was a postmaster and a draper in the High Street.

Basil was educated at Campden Grammar School and then began an apprenticeship with the Great Western Railway Company at their engineering works in Wolverhampton. He volunteered to join the St. John Ambulance Company during the Boer War in South Africa and was posted to the Imperial Yeomanry Hospital staff. After returning safely from South Africa he enlisted in the Royal Navy at Chatham on 17 April 1901. His medical passed him fit to serve but noted that he had blue eyes and scars on his wrist and knee. Basil began his service with the Royal Navy as an engine room artificer 4th class at HMS *Pembroke*, a depot in Chatham. He was then promoted to engine room artificer 3rd class on 3 August 1908 while he was on HMS *Bedford*. Further promotions followed and on 14 April 1913 he became an engine room artificer 1st class while serving on HMS *Yarmouth*.

Basil joined the crew of HMS *Pathfinder* as a chief engine room artificer in July 1914. She was a light cruiser and was launched in 1904. After her initial naval service, which saw her in the Atlantic Fleet and the Channel Fleet, she joined the 4th Destroyer

The Neve Family
Back row (left to right): Basil, Dorothy and Higham
Centre row (left to right): Margaret Horne, Isabelle Neve, Julius Neve, Muriel Jesse Horne (wife of Lewis Hadley Horne) and Lewis Hickman Horne
Front row (left to right): Jack Horne and two grand-daughters of Julius and Isabelle.

Flotilla and was stationed at Portsmouth. In October 1913 she joined the 8th Destroyer Flotilla and when Basil joined the crew she was patrolling off Northern Ireland. When the war started she was stationed in the Firth of Forth and on 5 September 1914 she was torpedoed off St. Abbs Head by a German submarine, *U21*, with the loss of 259 lives, including Basil, who was the first Campden man to die serving his country during the war. HMS *Pathfinder* was the third naval casualty of the war.

Basil in his Boer War uniform.

The *Evesham Journal* reported Basil's death: "*We regret to announce that the first victim of the war in Campden is Basil Hoveden Neve who lost his life in the destruction of HMS Pathfinder off St. Abbs Head in the North Sea on Saturday. He sailed on the cruiser HMS Bedford with Prince Louis of Battenburg to the United States and with King Edward VII on a visit to Kiel. He was lent to HMS Pathfinder for the Great Review at Spithead and with war breaking out he remained with her. At the time of the disaster he was ranked as third engineer on board and was well on his way to more promotion.*"

Basil was 39 years old when he died and his name is recorded on the Chatham Naval Memorial. It is also recorded on three memorials in Campden: in St. James's Church, in Campden School and in the High Street. There is also a brass plaque in St. James's Church that was paid for by the family.

Basil had married Helen Rolandson Ley at Govan, Lanark, Scotland on 11 April 1912 and when he died she was living at 80 Rainham Road in Chatham. There were no children.

Gerald Alfred Neve
Private 628080, 47th Battalion, Canadian Expeditionary Force

Born: 18 March 1874
Enlisted: 29 June 1915
Discharged: 20 June 1919
Died: 24 May 1965

Gerald was born in Maidenhead in Berkshire in 1874, the second son of Julius Robert and Isabelle Neve. His father was a postmaster and draper in Campden and Gerald was educated at Campden Grammar School. After leaving school he became a farmer and then he served with the Worcestershire Yeomanry in South Africa during the Boer War. He returned safely from the war and then married Blanche Carrie Louisa Bates on 9 August 1902. Their first child, Ruby Isabelle, was born on 12 June 1903.

The family emigrated to Canada and set up home at 1611 Hearst Avenue, Berkeley, Calgary. Gerald continued to work as a farmer. He joined the local Militia and served with the British Columbia Horse. On 29 June 1915 he enlisted in the Canadian Army at Vermont aged 41 years. He was passed fit for overseas service and his medical report states that he was five feet nine inches tall with blue eyes, brown hair and a dark complexion. There were also three vaccination marks on his left arm.

After a period of training in Canada he arrived in England on 23 November 1915 and the next nine months were spent preparing to be posted to France. Gerald embarked for France with the 47th Battalion, Canadian Expeditionary Force on 10 August 1916. After serving at the front for three months he was buried by the explosion of a shell and suffered a sprained back and right foot in early November 1916. This resulted in his being admitted to Number 1 Canadian General Hospital at Etaples before being evacuated to England, where further treatment began on 14 November at 2nd Western General Hospital in Manchester. He was then discharged from hospital and posted to Shoreham. His ankle continued to give him trouble and he was admitted to a Canadian convalescence hospital at Woodcote Park in Epsom on 18 January 1917.

After being passed fit for further service Gerald was sent to Seaford and seconded to the British Columbia Regiment before joining the 1st Reserve Battalion. On 30 May 1917 he was admitted to hospital again with a sprained right ankle but had recovered sufficiently to be sent to France to join the 47th Battalion on 19 June. After a few months at the front he was transferred to the Canadian Labour Pool in France on 11 March 1918. Gerald was now medical category B1 and almost 44 years old. He remained in France until after the end of the war and returned to England on 9 May 1919. He left England on 6 June 1919 and returned home to Canada, where he was discharged from the army in Vancouver on 20 June 1919. After he had returned home to his wife and child the family moved to 1917 Francesco Street in Berkeley.

Gerald died at Shaughnessy Hospital in Vancouver on 24 May 1965 aged 91 years.

David W. Newman

Private, Gloucestershire Regiment
Private 26218, 3rd Battalion, Loyal North Lancashire Regiment
Private 170400, Royal Army Medical Corps

Born: 15 November 1896
Enlisted: 9 February 1916
Discharged: 13 November 1919

David was born in Campden, the fourth son of Henry and Ellen Annie Newman of Leysbourne, and was baptised at St. James's Church on 22 June 1900. At the age of 19 he enlisted in the Gloucestershire Regiment on 9 February 1916. The next six months were spent on home service and before he served overseas he transferred to the 3rd Battalion, Loyal North Lancashire Regiment on 8 July. On 19 August he left England and served in East Africa until 26 December 1916 when he was posted to Egypt. During his time in Egypt he was guilty of two military offences. On 5 September 1917 he was given two days confined to barracks for being *"untidy on parade"* and on 13 September he was given a further five days for the same offence.

His service in Egypt ended on 17 May 1918 when he set sail for France, where he stayed until 12 September 1918, when he was given leave. He spent a fortnight in England and then returned to France. In May 1919 he was again given more leave but after reporting back four days late he was given a punishment of four days confined to barracks.

The war was now over and David ended his overseas military service in the Royal Army Medical Corps, arriving back in England on 17 October 1919. He was then discharged on 13 November 1919 after 3 years and 278 days in the army.

After returning to Campden he married Elsie and they had two daughters, Enid and Brenda, who both married American soldiers. When their daughters emigrated David and Elsie went with them. The last years of David's life were spent in Germany.

Frederick Joseph Newman

Sergeant 2288, 8th Battalion, Gloucestershire Regiment

Born: 10 September 1881
Enlisted: 17 August 1914
Discharged: 17 October 1915
Died: 26 April 1941

Frederick was born in the Leighton Buzzard registration district, the son of Frederick Newman. Soon after leaving school he joined the army and served in South Africa during the Boer War. At the end of the war he returned to England, where his parents were living in Taunton. The 1901 census shows that Lizzie Sansom, his future wife, attended a covent school there together with her elder sister, Lucy.

Frederick and Lizzie were married at St. Catharine's Church in Campden on 3 May 1908 and they had five children: Charles Frederick, James Jesse Sansom, Frederick Joseph, William Charles and George Edward Albert. When George was baptised in Campden on 4 April 1915 Frederick's occupation was recorded as *"stud groom"*. Twenty-five days later Frederick was baptised at the same church as a *"convert"*.

At the outbreak of war in 1914 Frederick was 33 years old and an experienced soldier. He enlisted in the Gloucestershire Regiment on 17 August 1914 and joined the 8th Battalion at Bristol in September 1914. The battalion was posted to the 57th Brigade of the 19th (Western) Division and the next few months were spent training on Salisbury Plain. Frederick arrived in France with the rank of sergeant on 18 July 1915 and after only a short period of service on the Western Front he was evacuated back to England, having been badly gassed at the front. He was discharged from the army as *"no longer fit for active service"* on 17 October 1915.

After leaving the army Frederick returned to his wife and family. Sadly, Lizzie died at East Reach Hospital in Taunton on 10 November 1916, leaving Frederick, who was still suffering from the effects of gas, to look after five young children. Two yeas later he married Vera Annetta Martyn in Hammersmith, London on 23 November 1918 and they had seven children, a boy and six girls. The family home was in Taunton, where Frederick lived for the rest of his life.

In 1929 Frederick was working at Sweethay Farm, Trull, Taunton as a groom. The effects of the gas were still troubling him and it was not easy for him to find regular work. When he died on 26 April 1943 aged 61 years his occupation was recorded as *"army pensioner"*. He is buried with his second wife in Wellington Road Cemetery in Taunton. His first wife is buried in the Catholic Cemetery nearby.

Henry Newman

Private, King's Own Hussars
Private 40899, 14th Battalion, Worcestershire Regiment
Private 573662, Labour Corps

Henry was born in Campden in 1889, the eldest son of Henry and Ellen Annie Newman of Leysbourne, and was baptised at St. James's Church on 28 September 1890. After leaving school he found employment as a butcher.

At the outbreak of war in 1914 he was living at 36 Bedworth Road in Bedford and he enlisted in the King's Own Hussars on 10 December 1915 aged 26 years. He was immediately posted to the Army Reserve but had to wait until 14 February 1916 before he was mobilised. The initial part of his army career was spent on home service at the Southern Cavalry Depot. He then embarked at Southampton on 6 December 1916 and arrived at Rouen three days later, where he joined the 46th Infantry Base Depot and was transferred to the 3rd Battalion, Worcestershire Regiment. On 12 December he was posted to the 14th Battalion and the next few months were spent at the front.

On 30 June 1917 he was wounded in both eyes and admitted to Number 47 General Hospital at Le Treport in France. The matron of the hospital wrote to his mother saying that *"he is quite helpless at present"*. After being discharged from hospital he rejoined his unit on 15 August 1917 and the next five months were spent serving on the Western Front before he was given two weeks' leave beginning on 13 January 1918, when he returned to England. He rejoined the 14th Battalion on 2 February and in March he was gassed, which resulted in his spending the next two months in hospital in Boulogne and Rouen. In July he was in England and on 22 July 1918 he transferred to the Labour Corps. The remainder of his army service was spent in England and he was discharged on 25 July 1919.

Robert James Newman

Driver T3-031342, Transport Company, Army Service Corps

Born: 1 April 1890
Enlisted: 9 December 1914
Discharged: 2 July 1919
Died: 15 February 1975

Robert was born in Campden on 1 April 1890, the second son of Henry and Ellen Annie Newman of Leysbourne, and was baptised at St. James's Church on 28 September 1890. His father was a native of the town and employed as an agricultural labourer.

When Robert enlisted in the Army Service Corps on 9 December 1914 he was 24 years old. A reference written by Lewis Hadley Horne enabled him to be put in charge of two horses in a transport company. His medical examination found that he had flat feet.

After a period of twelve months' service in England he was sent to Devonport on 8 December 1915 to embark for Egypt on HMS *Minnewaska*. He arrived at Port Said on 22 December and was immediately posted to 219 Company, Army Service Corps, 31st Division. His stay in Egypt was short as he embarked at Port Said on 19 February 1916 en route for Basra where he arrived on 16 March. The next four months were spent in Mesopotamia until he developed dysentery in July and was admitted to hospital in Basra. He was sent back to India on board HMS *Dongola* and HMS *Vita* and spent the next five months in hospital before he was fit enough to join an Army Service Corps unit in the Indian Expeditionary Force.

Robert left hospital at Secunderabad in India on 28 December 1916 and was able to carry out his duties until he was again admitted to hospital in Makina on 22 April 1917. He was discharged from hospital on 30 April and was posted to 104 Battery, Royal Garrison Artillery at Makina on 26 May. A further period of eight days in hospital followed in September 1917.

The remainder of the war was spent in India and he began his journey home on 21 March 1919. He finally reached England on 4 June and his discharge from the army came on 2 July 1919.

After the war Robert married Hannah Hedges and they had one daughter, Mavis Edith, who married Ronald George Sadler in 1948. The family home was at 4, Gainsborough Terrace, Campden and he was employed as a general labourer. During the Second World War he was a member of the Home Guard.

Robert died on 15 February 1975 aged 84 and is buried in St. James's churchyard in Campden.

Albert Edward Nicholls
Private 238837, Army Cyclist Corps
Private 86440, 17th Battalion, King's Liverpool Regiment

Born: 1898
Died: 7 November 1917

Albert was born in Ebrington, the eldest son of Albert and Emily Nicholls. His father was the son of George and Maria Nicholls of Campden and was baptised at St. James's Church in Campden on 26 August 1866. In 1881 Albert senior was living with his mother in Leysbourne and employed as an agricultural labourer. He later moved to Ebrington and became a wheelwright and undertaker by trade.

At the outbreak of war in 1914 Albert junior was 16 years old and living with his parents in Ebrington. He enlisted at Cirencester in the Army Cyclist Corps but when he was posted to France he transferred to the 17th Battalion, King's Liverpool Regiment. This battalion had originally been formed in Liverpool on 29 August 1914 by Lord Derby in the old watch factory at Prescot and probably has the distinction of being the first of the "*Pals*" battalions to be formed.

Albert joined the battalion on the Western Front as part of a draft of men to reinforce the unit following the casualties suffered on the Somme in 1916. He was killed in action near Kemmel, south of Ypres, on 7 November 1917 towards the end of the Third Battle of Ypres in Belgium. Two other members of the battalion were killed in action on this day though Chris McCarthy states in his book, *The Day by Day Account*, that "*nothing of significance happened on this day*".

Albert was 19 years old when he died and is buried in Kemmel Château Military Cemetery. His name is recorded on the war memorial in Ebrington and at the foot of his parents' headstone in St. James's churchyard in Campden. It is not recorded on any memorials in Campden.

Frank Nobes
Private 51792, Gloucestershire Regiment
Private 43319, 1st Battalion, Worcestershire Regiment

Born: 1 July 1898
Enlisted: 25 May 1918
Discharged: 14 February 1919

Frank was born in Campden, the fourth son of Thomas and Emma Nobes of Silk Mill Yard, Sheep Street. His father was a native of the town and a stonemason by trade.

Frank enlisted in the Gloucestershire Regiment on 25 May 1918, when he was 20 years old, but was transferred to the 1st Battalion, Worcestershire Regiment before he served overseas. He was discharged from the army on 14 February 1919 and returned to Campden, where he worked as a farmer, chauffeur and market gardener and was specially known locally for his sprouts. He was an extremely hard worker and his only recreation was his visit to the British Legion, of which he had been a member throughout its existence.

Frank married Kathleen Griffin at St. James's Church on 17 July 1927 and they had two daughters, Marjorie and Kathleen, and a son, Frank. The family home was at 8, Aston Road, Campden in a "*Home for Heroes*" finished in 1921 by the Council for returning servicemen. The original tenant of the house was Reginald Smith.

Frank died suddenly while feeding his livestock at his home on 27 November 1957 aged 59 and he is buried in St. James's churchyard. His coffin was draped in the Union Jack and was carried by members of the British Legion: Sam Sadler, Ernest Hedges, Charles Stanley and Oliver Lowe.

His obituary was published in the *Evesham Journal* and the details of his army service conflict with the dates on his official discharge certificate. The obituary states that he enlisted "*at the age of 18 and did service in France before he was 19*". This suggests he arrived in France in 1916 rather than 1918.

George Nobes
Private 24369, 10th Battalion, Gloucestershire Regiment

> Born: 5 January 1896
> Enlisted: 25 August 1915
> Discharged: 12 July 1919

George was born in Campden, the third son of Thomas and Emma Nobes of Silk Mill Yard, Sheep Street. His father was a stonemason by trade.

George attended school in the town and then found employment as a butcher. He enlisted in the Gloucestershire Regiment on 25 August 1915 aged 19 years and 7 months and was posted to the 11th Battalion for training in England. He arrived in France on 8 December 1915 as part of a draft of recruits used to reinforce the 10th Battalion after they suffered heavy casualties during the Battle of Loos in September. He spent the next few months gaining experience of life at the front and saw his first major action during the Battle of the Somme when the battalion attacked the German Switch Line near Martinpuich on 23 July 1916 and High Wood on 9 September 1916.

George received a gunshot wound in the left thigh that resulted in a fractured femur. He was dangerously ill for a while and was admitted to hospital in France. He was evacuated back to England and after a lengthy spell in hospital he was posted to the 8th Battalion, Gloucestershire Regiment for home service. The wound still troubled George and he was admitted to hospital in Bristol at the start of April 1919. He was discharged from hospital and granted leave until 16 May, during which time he returned to Campden. After rejoining his unit he was given a full medical examination at the Special Military Surgical Hospital at Southmead on 22 June and classed as "*no longer fit for military service*". He was then discharged from the army on 12 July 1919 and a Silver War Badge was issued to indicate that he had made his contribution to the war.

After returning to Campden he became the landlord of the Baker's Arms in Broad Campden and his marriage produced one son, called Sidney.

Henry Sadler Nobes
Private 13510, 10th Battalion, Gloucestershire Regiment

> Born: 9 March 1891
> Enlisted: 4 August 1914
> Discharged: 9 July 1919
> Died: 18 December 1935

Harry was born in Campden on 9 March 1891, the second son of Thomas and Emma Nobes of Silk Mill Yard, Sheep Street, and was baptised at St. James's Church on 26 April 1891.

When the war started Harry was one of the first (if not the first) to enlist in Campden. He enlisted in Campden Recruiting Office on 4 August 1914, the day that war was declared. He was 23 years old and after a period of training in England he arrived in France on 9 August 1915 with the 10th Battalion, Gloucestershire Regiment. The battalion suffered heavy casualties on 25 September during the opening day of the Battle of Loos. This was an awful day for Harry as William Hedges and Tom Smith, both from Campden, were killed in action. The British Army used poison gas for the first time in this attack and the battalion advanced across flat ground just south of the Vermelles-Hulloch road.

In December 1915 Harry's brother George joined the battalion with a draft of men needed to bring them up to strength following the action at Loos. It is not clear how long the two brothers served together but the battalion next saw major action during the Battle of the Somme when they attacked the German Switch Line near Martinpuich on 23 July 1916 and High Wood on 9 September 1916.

Harry continued to serve in the battalion on the Western Front throughout the war and after the armistice was signed he entered Germany with the 1st Battalion, Gloucestershire Regiment as part of the Army of Occupation. After returning to England he was discharged on 9 July 1919 after serving for almost five years with the regiment.

Harry married Florence Edith Elizabeth Stowe at St. James's Church on 7 June 1924 and they had two children. He found employment as a plumber's labourer with Mr. W. Haines and was also a member of Campden Fire Brigade. He died at his home in Lower High Street after several months of bad health on 18 December 1935 aged 44 and is buried in St. James's churchyard. His wife died on 8 November 1975 aged 76 years.

Thomas Nobes

Private 29841, 15th Battalion, Gloucestershire Regiment
Private 33071, "B" Company, Oxfordshire and Buckinghamshire Light Infantry
Private 550633, 599th Agricultural Company, Labour Corps

Born: 29 April 1888
Enlisted: 11 December 1915
Discharged: 5 April 1919

Thomas was born in Campden, the eldest son of Thomas and Emma Nobes of Silk Mill Yard, Sheep Street, and was baptised at St. James's Church on 24 June 1888. His father was a native of the town and a stonemason by trade.

Thomas enlisted in Campden on 11 December 1915, when he was 27 years old, and was immediately placed into the Army Reserve. He was mobilised on 22 June 1916 and posted to the 15th (Reserve) Battalion, Gloucestershire Regiment for training. In September 1916 a considerable reorganisation of the reserve infantry battalions took place owing to the introduction of conscription and he was transferred to the 3rd (Reserve) Battalion, Oxfordshire and Buckinghamshire Light Infantry. He embarked at Southampton on 28 September and arrived in France the next day. He spent the next two weeks at a base depot before being posted to the front, where he joined the 6th Battalion during the Battle of the Somme.

Tom photographed in 1918 at the Eight Bells, Campden.

On 22 January 1917 Thomas received a gunshot wound to his right thigh and was evacuated to hospital in Rouen, where he was admitted on 24 January. He returned to England on 31 January and was admitted to St. John VAD Hospital in Cheltenham for further treatment. The next 159 days were spent in hospital before he was finally discharged on 18 June. He was then granted leave when he returned home to Campden.

In March 1918 Thomas was at Oxford, serving with the 3rd (Reserve) Battalion. He was then transferred to the 440th Agricultural Company, Labour Corps on 9 April 1918 and then to the 599th Agricultural Company before he was discharged from the army on 5 April 1919.

After leaving the army Thomas returned to Campden to be with his wife, Ellen, and his two sons, Reginald and Frederick. He found employment as a bricklayer and a labourer before moving to Scotland, where he is buried.

The Eight Bells, Campden c.1918
Back row (left to right): Thomas Harris, landlord, Harriet Harris, landlady, Ormonde Plested, Lawrence Ladbrook, Tom Nobes, Maggie Richmond, barmaid, and Frank Nobes
Front row (left to right): Unknown, Harry Nobes, Jack Tomes and Albert Bradley (to be confirmed).
Another version of this photograph, without Harriet and Maggie, can be seen in the entry for Thomas Harris earlier in the book.

Wilfrid Edgar Harry Nobes
Private 18734, 11th Battalion (1st South Down), Royal Sussex Regiment

Died: 3 April 1918

Wilfrid was born in Hanworth in Middlesex, the son of William and Emily Nobes of Lime Villas, Staines Road, Hanworth. His parents were both natives of Campden and his father was the son of Thomas and Mary Nobes, who were living near St. James's Church in 1891. William married his wife, Emily, around 1895 and their first three children, Frank, Wilfred and Thomas, were all born in Hanworth.

Wilfrid enlisted in the army in Staines and served in France with the 11th Battalion, Royal Sussex Regiment. He died on 3 April 1918 aged 19 and is buried in Roisel Communal Cemetery Extension, 9 miles east of Peronne, in France. He does not have his name recorded on any memorials in Campden.

Wilfrid was the cousin of Thomas, George, Frank and Harry, whose father was his uncle, Thomas Nobes.

The inscription at the bottom of Wilfrid's headstone, chosen by his parents, reads: "*Father, in thy gracious keeping, leave we now thy servant sleeping.*"

Arthur Edward Joseph Noel, 4th Earl of Gainsborough
Major, 1st/5th Battalion, Gloucestershire Regiment

Born: 39 June 1884
Died: 27 August 1927

Arthur was the eldest son of Charles William Francis and Mary Noel, Earl and Countess of Gainsborough, of Exton Park, Oakham, Rutland and Campden House, Gloucestershire. He was educated at Downside College, near Bath, and then entered Exeter College, Oxford in October 1905 but was in poor health throughout his time there and eventually left in the autumn of 1906 without taking a degree. After Oxford he became an honorary diplomat, a recognised non-paid profession for young aristocrats in those days, and worked as an attaché for the Diplomatic Service in Norway, Sweden and Washington between 1908 and 1914.

Arthur joined "K" Company, 2nd Volunteer Battalion, Gloucestershire Regiment in 1903 as a second lieutenant and at the outbreak of war in 1914 he had become Officer Commanding "H" Company, 5th Battalion, Gloucestershire Regiment, the Campden Company of the Territorial Army. He was mobilised on 5 August 1914 and went to Chelmsford with the battalion for final training before they were posted to France. He entered France on 29 March 1915 with the rank of major, second in command of the battalion, and served in the trenches around Ploegsteert Wood in Belgium. After being badly gassed in 1915 he was invalided back to England and allocated to other duties. His war record was distinguished and culminated in the award of an OBE in 1919.

Arthur married Alice Mary Eyre, eldest daughter of Edward Eyre, of 1, Belgrave Square, London and Blakesware, Widford, Hertfordshire, on 10 November 1915. In 1926 Arthur became the 4th Earl of Gainsborough when his father died on 17 April 1926. He had only held the title for sixteen months when he died of pneumonia, complicated by a kidney infection, on 27 August 1927 aged 43 years. He is buried in the Catholic Cemetery at Exton Park, Oakham and was survived by three children: Anthony Gerard Edward, the 5th Earl of Gainsborough, Maureen and Gerard.

Arthur and Alice Mary Eyre, 1915.

Charles Hubert Francis Noel

2nd Lieutenant, "D" Company, 1st/5th Battalion, Gloucestershire Regiment
Major, Coldstream Guards

Born: 22 October 1885
Discharged: 1921
Died: 26 April 1947

Charles was the second son of Charles William Francis and Mary Noel, Earl and Countess of Gainsborough, of Exton Park, Oakham and Campden House, Gloucestershire. His mother was the aunt of Maurice Dease, who was awarded the Victoria Cross at Mons in 1914.

Charles was educated at Roper's Preparatory School near Brighton before he completed his education at Dresden in Germany and then at Tours in France. He married May Douglas-Dick, daughter of Brigadier General Archibald Campbell Douglas-Dick, of Pitkerro, Forfarshire, at The Oratory, Brompton, London, on 31 January 1912. They had six children: Archibald, David, Andrew, Douglas, Jane and Carol.

In the years leading up to the war Charles was a second lieutenant with "H" Company, 5th Battalion, Gloucestershire Regiment, the Campden Company of the Territorial Army. He was mobilised on 5 August 1914 and went to Chelmsford with the battalion for final training before they were posted to France. He entered France on 3 February 1915, six weeks before the rest of the battalion. On 5 May he transferred to the Coldstream Guards and was promoted to lieutenant on 27 August. He was then appointed to the rank of temporary captain on 1 October 1915.

Charles is standing on the left in Chelmsford in Essex, 1915.

Charles remained on the Western Front during the war and in 1918 he was based at Le Havre in France, where he was overseeing the coming and going of soldiers, the wounded, equipment and ammunition. In 1918 he was awarded an OBE and then in 1921 he retired from the army with the rank of major. He lived at Campden House until 1927, when he moved to Pitkerro House, Forfarshire, Scotland. In 1936 he moved to Moreland, Cleish, Kinross-shire.

During the Second World War Charles joined the Royal Engineers at Derby as a captain (temporary major) in 1939. He then moved to Newcastle and completed his period of service in 1942. He was the County Colonel Commandant for Angus Army Cadet Force from 1943 until 1946.

Charles died on 26 April 1947 aged 61 and is buried in Murroes churchyard, near Dundee in Scotland.

Robert Edmund Thomas More Noel
Captain, 6th Battalion, Royal Fusiliers, attached to 1st Battalion, Nigerian Regiment

Born: 10 April 1888
Enlisted: April 1910
Died: 2 February 1918

Robert was the third and youngest son of the Earl and Countess of Gainsborough, of Exton Park, Oakham and Campden House, Gloucestershire, and was born in 1888. After receiving his early education at Ladycross he entered Downside College at Stratton-on-the-Fosse, near Bath, in April 1901 and left in July 1907. He was a bright and cheerful boy and throughout his life was always popular with those he came into contact with. At school he was a keen tennis player, a good forward at hockey and a very useful member of the choir. He also took part in theatrical productions at Downside. After leaving Downside he went to Trinity College, Cambridge and was secretary of the Fisher Society in 1909. He was then gazetted second lieutenant in the Royal Fusiliers in April 1910, promoted lieutenant on 15 July 1912 and captain on 2 February 1915.

Christmas 1913

In January 1914 he was seconded from his regiment to join the Nigerian Police, his headquarters being in Lagos, where he held the position of Assistant Commissioner with the local rank of captain. On the outbreak of war Captain Noel, who was a good scholar of German, was appointed Provost-Marshal in Lagos. In 1915 he was attached to the Nigerian Regiment, then operating in the Cameroons, until a bad attack of fever caused him to be sent home on sick leave. In June 1916, after returning to Lagos, he was ordered up country to put an end to local risings and carried out this mission with distinction. In July 1917 he proceeded with a draft to reinforce the Nigerian Regiment in German East Africa, and after helping to clear that country of the enemy he died at Massassi on 2 February 1918 of a fever, "*dysentery and concomitant malaria*", contracted during the campaign. He was 29 years old and is buried in Dar-es-Salaam Military Cemetery, Tanzania, East Africa.

A requiem mass was sung for him at Exton Church on 12 February 1918. He always said that when he reached the age of 30 he would become a Benedictine monk or a Catholic chaplain to the Forces. He loved the Church and everything to do with its services and ceremonials.

Robert has his name recorded on three memorials in Campden: in St. James's Church, in St. Catharine's Church and in the High Street. He is also included on memorials at Downside and at Exton.

Captain Noel, November 1915.

Frederick James Osborn
Private 814266, Royal Canadian
Regiment

Born: 27 July 1896
Enlisted: 12 February 1916
Died: 1 April 1917

Fred was born in London, the son of Herbert and Elizabeth Osborn. His father was a woodcarver and together with his brother, William, moved to Campden in 1902 to work with Charles Ashbee at the Guild of Handicraft. The family lived in Watery Lane and Fred was educated at Campden Grammar School. After the disbanding of the Guild the family moved back to London, where Fred soon became ill and was advised to move to a location free from smog. He had kept in touch with an old school friend, William *"Wilfred"* Leo Merriman, who had emigrated to Canada, and in 1913 Fred decided to join him. He was employed as a labourer on farms in the Poltimore area, sixty miles north of Ottawa, and in 1914 was joined by his parents and brothers, Harry and Bert.

Fred enlisted in the Canadian Army at Ottawa on 12 February 1916, when he was 19 years old. He was five feet seven inches tall with

blue eyes, light brown hair and a fair complexion. During his time at Valcartier Camp he was admitted to hospital with measles on 2 July 1916 but was discharged six days later after it was diagnosed as influenza. After seven months' training in Canada he was posted to the 136th Overseas Battalion, Canadian Expeditionary Force and embarked for England at Halifax on HMT *Southland*, a White Star Liner, on 26 September 1916. The *Southland* was a German boat captured by the British. While carrying troops through the Mediterranean to the Dardanelles she was torpedoed by a German submarine but was able to reach port, where she was repaired. The food on the journey to England was good and Fred wrote home saying, *"We got eggs and bacon for breakfast and for dinner, fowl and boiled bacon. The chicken I got was great and I had two helpings. We got pudding after and apples."*

They arrived at Liverpool on 6 October 1916. Fred was transferred to the 36th Battalion and posted to West Sandling Camp in Kent. In December 1916 he wrote home, *"Well mother, I expect to leave for France tomorrow and I am going to join the Royal Canadian Regiment. You see they asked for 45 volunteers for a draft for the RCR and I volunteered. That was at 1.00pm and we had a medical examination, kit inspection, close crop hair cut and new stuff this afternoon and are ready to leave tomorrow. So I guess I will eat my Christmas dinner in France. Don't worry about me darling mother or call me a fool as I would have been drafted after Xmas anyway. Perhaps I may be foolish but God knows I'm no coward and I'll stick to it to the last."*

Fred arrived in France on 23 December 1916 and on 1 April 1917 he died of wounds received at 9.00am when he was accidentally shot in the right hip when a rifle was fired in his dug-out near Vimy Ridge in France. His death was officially recorded as *"accidental"*. He was 20 years old and was buried in Ecoivres Military Cemetery.

Fred's brother Harry got a job in Ottawa during the war as a machinist in a factory making shell cases and soon his parents and brother Bert joined him in Ottawa. Bert was an accomplished engraver and he engraved many of the Mothers' Silver Crosses that were sent to the families in Canada of men killed in the war.

Bert died in 1925 and Fred's parents were ageing. His father was unable to work and as he had no pension an application was made for a survivor's pension on behalf of their son Fred. In 1932 they finally began to receive a war pension. Harry secretly supplemented their groceries and rent payments. He was *"keeping the faith"* with Fred as he was always conscious of the fact that he had not passed the medical for military service and so had not served his country as had Fred. He did his part working in arms factories and looking after his parents as Fred had requested.

Fred does not have his name recorded on any memorials in Campden. In 2002 the author visited Fred's grave and was able to send photographs to Norah Goodman, daughter of Harry. In her thank-you letter she wrote, *"I suppose you are the very first person to have paid a visit there purposely to visit him in all the years he has lain there. His father and mother would be so pleased to think that somebody has taken the trouble to do so."*

Alec William Osborne
Private 1298, 10th Battalion, Royal Fusiliers
Private G25182, 1st Garrison Battalion, East Kent Regiment

Born: 1896
Enlisted: 19 January 1915
Discharged: 1 August 1917

Alec was born in Campden, the second son of Francis Bazley and Mary Ann Osborne, and was baptised at St. James's Church on 1 August 1896. The family came to the town when his father became headmaster of Campden Grammar School in 1889. In 1913 Mr. Osborne left Campden and set up his own school at Malvern House in Blockley.

After leaving school Alec found employment as a bank clerk and on 1 January 1915 he enlisted in the Royal Fusiliers to join his brother, who had enlisted in August 1914. He joined the regiment in Colchester on 23 January 1915 and after a period of home service arrived in France on 30 July 1915, where he was posted to the 10th (*Stockbrokers'*) Battalion.

On the night of 4 May 1916 the battalion was at Monchy-au-Bois, south-west of Arras, when the Germans made a surprise attack. Alec's brother was wounded but refused to leave his men. Raywood was then wounded a second time and while he was being carried away by the stretcher-bearers he was hit for a third time by a shell splinter in the chest. Alec was in a trench behind his brother at the time and went to see what had happened. The wound was fatal and Raywood died later that night.

Alec continued to serve at the front until he received a gunshot wound in the neck on 11 July 1916 that resulted in his being returned to England on 25 July. After leaving hospital he was transferred to the 1st Garrison Battalion, East Kent Regiment, *The Buffs*, in which he was employed on home service until his discharge on 1 August 1917 after 2 years and 194 days in the army.

Francis Raywood Osborne
Sergeant 781, 10th Battalion, Royal Fusiliers

Born: 5 April 1890
Enlisted: August 1914
Died: 4 May 1916

Raywood was born at Campden Grammar School, the eldest son of Francis Bazley and Mary Ann Osborne, and was baptised at St. James's Church on 1 June 1890. He was educated at Campden Grammar School, where his father was headmaster, and then at Christ's Hospital in Horsham. In 1906 he obtained a clerkship in the Capital and Counties Bank in Gloucester before he moved successively to branches in Shrewsbury, Ludlow, Lydney and finally to Head Office in Threadneedle Street in London. He was a member of the Institute of Bankers.

At the outbreak of war Raywood enlisted in the 10th Battalion (*Stockbrokers' Battalion*), Royal Fusiliers in London and in September 1914 he was gazetted to a commission in the Army Service Corps. This he declined as it was a non-fighting unit. In 1915 he was again offered a commission but this time in his own battalion, which he again refused as it entailed a longer stay in England.

Raywood arrived in France as a sergeant on 13 October 1915. On the night of 4 May 1916 he was in charge of his platoon at Monchy-au-Bois, south-west of Arras, when the Germans made a surprise attack. Though wounded, he refused to leave his men. He was wounded a second time and was being carried away by the stretcher-bearers when he was hit for a third time by a shell splinter. His wounds were fatal and he died soon afterwards.

The *Evesham Journal* reported his death: "*There is much sympathy in Blockley, Campden and Evesham with Mr. and Mrs. F. B. Osborne, of Malvern House, Blockley whose elder son, Sgt. F. Raywood Osborne, was killed in action in France on Thursday. The deceased was a man of great promise and he had many friends in the district who will mourn his loss. He was the nephew of Mrs. Crisp, of Evesham Post Office, who lost her only son in the war (2nd Lieutenant Ernest Geoffrey Crisp).*"

Raywood's brother, Alec William Osborne, was in a trench behind him and went to see what had happened to his brother and found that the shell had hit him in the chest. He was later buried alongside five of his comrades in Berles-au-Bois Churchyard Extension in France. He was 26 years old when he died and his name is recorded on three memorials in Campden (in St. James's Church, in Campden School and in the High Street) and on two memorials in Blockley (in Blockley Church and on the village green).

Alan Thomas Paley
Colonel, Rifle Brigade

Born: 1 May 1876
Enlisted: 17 March 1897
Retired: 15 June 1925
Died: 4 September 1950

Superintendent Alan Paley, Gloucestershire Special Constabulary, c. 1939-45

Alan was the son of Colonel Edward Groves and Georgina Hyde Paley of Cotswold House, Campden. He was educated at Eton and the Royal Military College, Sandhurst, before being gazetted to the Rifle Brigade on 17 March 1897, joining the 3rd Battalion then stationed at Umbala. He served in South Africa during the Boer War as a lieutenant and was present at the defence of Ladysmith. On 18 January 1902 he was promoted to captain and then he was Adjutant to the battalion from 1905-07, after which he commenced a long tour of staff duty which included Officer Commanding a company of Gentlemen Cadets at Sandhurst from 1907-11.

During the First World War he entered France on 10 September 1914 and on 1 November he was promoted to major with the 18th Infantry Brigade. In 1915 he was awarded the Distinguished Service Order for distinguished service in the field and this was announced in the *London Gazette* on 23 June 1915. The following year he became a brevet colonel with the 21st Division and on 18 October 1917 he was promoted to temporary colonel when he took on the role of Assistant Commandant at the Royal Military College at Sandhurst. He was mentioned in despatches six times during the war and made a CMG in 1918. The Most Distinguished Order of Saint Michael and Saint George is a British order of chivalry founded in 1818, the sixth most senior in the British honours system, and is used to honour individuals who have rendered important services in relation to Commonwealth or foreign nations. People are appointed to the Order rather than awarded it.

In 1919 the 1st Battalion, Rifle Brigade left England under the command of Colonel Paley and headed for Mesopotamia, where they served during the Arab rebellion. He commanded a brigade in Mosul before they left Mesopotamia in January 1921 and went to Cawnpore in India. Under Alan's command the battalion, made up of a large number of inexperienced young men, began to return to the pre-war standard of 1914.

Alan finished his command in India in 1923, sailing for England in June to take over a Territorial brigade in Birmingham. Commanding a Territorial Brigade never appealed to him and he retired from the army on 15 June 1925 and took command of the London Rifle Brigade with all his customary enthusiasm. In 1930 he handed over the Brigade to Ted Kewley, his late second-in-command in Mesopotamia, and settled down to a country existence at his home, Coxwell House, in Cirencester. He was a member of the local hunt and very keen on shooting. During the Second World War he became a superintendent of the Gloucestershire Special Constabulary.

Alan died on 4 September 1950 aged 74 years.

Edward Groves Paley
Colonel, Recruiting Officer

Edward was born in London in 1850, the son of Thomas Paley, and after leaving school he became a regular soldier. He was a captain in 1881 and in 1891 he was a major serving with the 8th Hussars.

He married Georgina Hyde Clarke on 17 April 1873 at Frimley Parish Church in Surrey when he was a lieutenant and their first son, Alan Thomas, was born on 1 May 1876. The 1891 census lists the family living at Hill House, Lakenham near Norwich.

In 1914 Edward was 64 years old and living with his wife at Cotswold House in Campden. He retired from the army with the rank of colonel and during the war was employed as the recruiting officer in Campden. He was also a Justice of the Peace during his time in the town.

Thomas Parsons
Private 2434, 2nd/5th Battalion, Gloucestershire Regiment

Born: 1867
Enlisted: 4 August 1914
Discharged: 14 March 1916
Died: August 1929

Thomas was born in Gloucester, the son of James Parsons, who was a plumber by trade. He married Elizabeth Ann Trowell in Gloucester in 1889 and they came to Campden soon afterwards and set up home in Weighbridge House, Leysbourne. Their first child, Victor James, was baptised at St. James's Church in Campden on 27 April 1890.

Thomas started a plumbing and house-decorating business in the town and when his son came of age he took him into partnership. His obituary published in the *Evesham Journal* said, "*By his unassuming and courteous manner and his unfailing willingness to oblige he built up his business and gained the confidence and esteem of the town and district.*" He was a devoted churchman and in his younger days was a bellringer.

He was a member of "K" Company, 2nd Volunteer Battalion, Gloucestershire Regiment and was one of the best shots in the company. He won several silver cups for musketry and by the outbreak of war in 1914 he had reached the rank of sergeant with "H" Company, 5th Battalion, Gloucestershire Regiment, the Territorial Army.

Thomas enlisted for the duration of the war in Campden on 4 August 1914, when he was 47 years old. The next 565 days were spent on home service before he was discharged in Gateshead on 14 March 1916 as no longer fit for active service owing to his advancing age and failing health.

Thomas died in August 1929 aged 62 and is buried in St. James's churchyard in Campden. He was survived by his widow and son.

Charles Payne
Air Mechanic Second Class F47247, Royal Naval Air Service

Born: 18 April 1901
Enlisted: 21 January 1918
Died: 16 November 1973

Charles was born in Campden, the fifth and youngest son of William and Matilda Payne of Flag Close, Campden. He was baptised at St. James's Church on 26 May 1901 and after leaving school he found employment as a farm labourer. His father was a general labourer and his mother died in 1916. The family had moved to Watery Lane by 1914.

Charles enlisted in the Royal Naval Air Service (RNAS) on 21 January 1918 when he was still only 16 years old. He was attached to HMS *President* on 21 March 1918 while he did his initial training. On 31 March 1918 the Royal Naval Air Service and the Royal Flying Corps amalgamated to form the Royal Air Force and this brought to an end his time at HMS *President*. For the remaining months of the war Charles served in the RAF. When the war ended he remained in the RAF and on 17 April 1919, a day before he was 18 years old, he signed on for a further twelve years' service. This was the start of a very distinguished career which saw him serve as a wing commander during the Second World War.

Charles married Freda Badham and they had three children: Pauline, John and Peter. They can be seen together in the photograph on the right.

Charles died on 16 November 1973 aged 72 and is buried in St. James's churchyard. His wife died at the age of 94 on 30 October 1999.

Charles Bernard Payne
Machine Gun Corps
London Regiment

Born: 15 September 1899

Charles was born in Campden, the youngest of five sons of Thomas and Sarah Payne who served in the war, and was baptised at St. Catharine's Church in Campden on 22 October 1899.

Charles enlisted in the Machine Gun Corps before he was 18 years old and soon arrived in France to serve on the Western Front. When his parents realised where he was they contacted the authorities and informed them that he was under age and he was promptly returned to Campden.

When he reached the age of 18 Charles rejoined the army and was transferred to the London Regiment. He was again posted to France and then returned home safely at the end of the war.

He married Ethel May Rose Mumford at St. Catharine's Church in Campden on 21 October 1922 and they had three children baptised at the church in the 1920's: Kathleen Alice, Thomas George and Margarita Eileen.

Elick Payne
Able Seaman 220201, Royal Navy

Born: 24 January 1887
Enlisted: 4 April 1902
Discharged: 22 April 1919
Died: 26 January 1936

Elick was born in Mickleton, the second son of William and Matilda Payne of Flag Close, Campden. He had seven brothers and sisters: John, Charles, William, George, Dora, Dorcas and Mabel. His father was a general labourer.

On 4 April 1902, at the age of 15, he enlisted in the Royal

Elick and Florence Elizabeth Street

Elick and Florence Elizabeth Street. Photograph taken in 1919 at Bewdley Street in Evesham.

Navy at Devonport as a boy second class and was posted to HMS *Impregnable*, a training ship at Devonport. The next seventeen years were spent serving on a number of different ships before he was demobilised on 22 April 1919.

On 7 June 1910 Elick passed examinations to become a petty officer but he decided to remain an able seaman. During the war he served on HMS *Blake*, HMS *Defiance*, HMS *Conqueror* and HMS *Dolphin*. He finished his naval career in April 1919 on HMS *Colleen*. When he was not at sea he was stationed at HMS *Vivid*, the Royal Navy barracks in Devonport.

After the war Elick married Florence Elizabeth Street and left Campden to live in Evesham, where he found employment as an electrician. His wife had three brothers who served in the war; Sidney was killed in action, Bill was blinded in both eyes and George returned safely.

Elick died on 26 January 1936 aged 49 and he is buried in Waterside Cemetery in Evesham. His wife died in 1952 aged 60 years.

Elick and Florence Elizabeth Street

Frederick R. Payne
Private 9568, 1st Battalion, Gloucestershire Regiment
Gunner 42513, 11 Siege Battery, Royal Garrison Artillery

Born: June 1893
Died: 30 May 1918

Frederick was born in Campden, the second son of Thomas and Sarah Payne, and was baptised at St. Catharine's Church on 22 March 1895. His father was an agricultural labourer and the family were living at Westington in 1901 and then at 2 Debden Cottages in Watery Lane. After the war they lived at 7, Aston Road in a house built by the Council for returning servicemen.

After leaving school Frederick found employment in the town as a stained glass worker until he became a regular soldier when he enlisted in the Gloucestershire Regiment on 1 January 1912. He was passed fit for active service and his medical examination revealed that he was five feet eight inches tall with dark brown eyes, black hair and a sallow complexion.

Army life began with a period of home service with the Depot Battalion in Bristol. He was then posted to the 1st Battalion in Portsmouth and remained on home service until he was discharged from the army on 18 July 1914 after having been found guilty of theft. On 28 April 1914 a court of enquiry had found him guilty of stealing goods from a comrade and given him 56 days in prison. This was later commuted to 56 days' detention.

At the outbreak of war Frederick enlisted in the Royal Garrison Artillery at Portsmouth and served under the name *Frederick James*. He was immediately sent to China, where he served for two years before he was posted to the Western Front. While he was serving on the Somme battlefield in May 1918 he was exposed to mustard gas and was immediately evacuated to hospital but died twenty minutes after being admitted.

Frederick died on 30 May 1918 aged 25 and is buried in Crouy Cemetery, near Amiens, France. The *Evesham Journal* reported: "*He was admitted to hospital a few days ago suffering from gas poisoning and although everything possible was done for him he never recovered. His eyes and chest were very bad.*"

Frederick's name is recorded on three memorials in Campden: in St. James's Church, in St. Catharine's Church and in the High Street. He was one of five sons of Thomas and Sarah who served during the war.

George Payne
Aircraftman Second Grade F48572, Royal Naval Air Service
Royal Air Force

Born: 11 January 1899
Enlisted: 30 January 1918
Died: 2 March 1942

George was born in Campden on 11 January 1899, the fourth son of William and Matilda Payne of Flag Close, Campden, and was baptised at St. James's Church on 5 March 1899. His father was a platelayer with the Great Western Railway.

After leaving school George found employment as a farm labourer. Then on 30 January 1918 he enlisted in the Royal Naval Air Service as an aircraftman second grade and was attached to HMS *President II* for his initial period of training. He was five feet four inches tall with brown hair, grey eyes, a fresh complexion and a scar under his chin. Three months later, on 1 April 1918, he was transferred into the Royal Air Force after the amalgamation of the Royal Naval Air Force and the Royal Flying Corps.

After returning safely from the war he emigrated to Canada and settled in Springside, Saskatchewan, where he worked as a farmer. He married a Swedish girl, Anna Christina Landine, and they had eight children: Willard, Dorcas, Lorraine, Ethel, Alan, Mabel, James and Stewart. His brother, John, also emigrated to Canada after the war and worked as a farmer at Bear River, Nova Scotia.

George died on 2 March 1942 aged 43 and is buried in Springside in Canada.

John Payne
Boy Second Class 220187, Royal Navy
Private 7327, 2nd Battalion, Worcestershire Regiment

Born: 2 January 1885
Enlisted: 1902
Died: 7 November 1957

John was born in Mickleton in 1885, the son of William and Matilda Payne. He lived in Campden with his parents at Flag Close until he left his job as a groom and enlisted in the Royal Navy on 4 April 1902. He was posted to HMS *Impregnable*, a training ship at Devonport, as a boy second class and his medical examination recorded that he was five feet two inches tall with brown hair and brown eyes. After only six months' service he was invalided out of the Royal Navy on 3 October 1902. He immediately enlisted in the Worcestershire Regiment and arrived in South Africa at the time of the cease-fire marking the end of the Boer War. Following this he served in India and Ceylon. After serving nine years in the army he returned to England and was placed into the Army Reserve. He then married Catharine Rebecca Gray, a native of Ebrington, on 23 November 1911 and moved to Ebrington. Their first two children, John Charles and Mary Elizabeth, were born before the start of the First World War.

At the outbreak of war in 1914 he was recalled to duty and disembarked in France on 12 August. He saw action at

Mons and was wounded at Verneuil in France during the retreat from Mons and was invalided back to England. He was discharged from the army as no longer fit for active service and issued with a Silver War Badge. His daughter Catharine told the author in 1999 that he *"always suffered a great deal from his war injuries"*. Her middle name was the village where her father got wounded.

After the war John and Catharine had three more children, Catharine Verneuil, Joan Matilda and Henry James, all born in England before the family emigrated to Canada under the provision of the Soldiers Settlement Act. He settled on a farm near Bear River and soon gained a wide reputation as a farmer, game-fancier and trapper, taking many prizes and trophies at the annual Digby Exhibition. During the Second World War he served with the reserves in Canada.

John died on 7 November 1957 aged 72 and is buried in Bear River Cemetery in Nova Scotia. The funeral service was conducted by Rev. H. Y. MacLean at St. John's Church in Bear River.

John is seated on the ground on the right. The photograph was taken in Aldershot.

Lewis George Payne
Private 240457, 1st/5th Battalion,
Gloucestershire Regiment
Private 7657877, Royal Army Pay Corps

Born: 26 November 1896

Lewis was born in Campden, the fourth son of Thomas and Sarah Payne, and was baptised at St. Catharine's Church on 6 December 1896. In the years leading up to the war he was a member of "H" Company, 5th Battalion, Gloucestershire Regiment, the local company of the Territorial Army. He was mobilised on 5 August 1914 and went with the battalion to Chelmsford for final training before they were posted to France. When the battalion embarked for France in March 1915 Lewis remained behind in England. He joined the battalion at the front in 1916 but was soon wounded in the knee. After a period in hospital in France he returned to England, where he transferred to the Royal Army Pay Corps. He was then discharged in 1917 as no longer fit for active service and a Silver War Badge was issued. The Silver War Badge, first authorised in September 1916, was awarded to all those who retired or were discharged owing to sickness or injuries sustained in the conflict.

Lewis was awarded three medals: Territorial Force War Medal, British War Medal and Victory Medal. The Territorial Force War Medal was awarded to Territorial Force members who joined up before 30 September 1914 and served overseas between August 1914 and November 1918 but were not eligible for the 1914 or 1914/15 Stars.

After returning to Campden he married Amy Maunders at St. Catharine's Church on 24 March 1923.

Thomas Payne
Railway Labour Battalion, Royal Engineers

Born: 1862
Died: 11 June 1934

Thomas was born in Stratford-upon-Avon in 1862, the son of John and Emma Payne. His father was an agricultural labourer from Broad Marston and his mother was a charwoman from Fenny Compton in Warwickshire. In 1881 the family were living in Poppets Alley in Campden.

After leaving school Thomas found employment as a general labourer and in 1885 he married Sarah Cherry. Their first child, William, was born in 1886 and he was one of five sons to serve in the army during the 1914-18 war. In 1891 the family were living at Broad Entry, Lower High Street, Campden but in 1901 they had moved to Westington and Thomas had become an agricultural labourer with his eldest son on a farm.

Thomas enlisted in the Grenadier Guards during the 1890's and fought in South Africa during the Boer War. He was discharged after seven years' service. At the age of 52 he enlisted in the Royal Engineers at the outbreak of war in 1914. He was posted to a Railway Labour Battalion but was soon discharged as no longer fit for service without leaving England.

On 23 October 1915 the *Evesham Journal* published photographs of the five sons of Thomas and Sarah who were serving in the army under the heading "*Patriotic Campden Family*". Their third son, Thomas Henry, was killed in 1916 and their second son, Frederick, died in hospital in 1918.

On 16 June 1917 the *Evesham Journal* reported on the five sons: "*The father, Thomas Payne, is an old soldier and joined the Royal Engineers at the outbreak of the war, but has since been discharged. The eldest son, William, is serving in France with the Machine Gun Corps. The second son, Frederick, is with his regiment, the Royal Garrison Artillery, in China. The third son, Thomas, has given his life. The fourth, Private Lewis Payne, of the Glosters, was wounded in France last year, and is now getting his discharge and Charles, the youngest son, who will not be 18 years of age until next September, has seen action in France with the Machine Gun Corps, but his parents have him at home and out of the army on account of his age.*"

PATRIOTIC CAMPDEN FAMILY.

PTE. W. PAYNE.

PTE. F. PAYNE.

PTE. T. PAYNE.

PTE. L. PAYNE.

PTE. C. PAYNE.

After the war Thomas and Sarah lived at 7 Aston Road, Campden in a house built by the Council for returning servicemen. Sarah died at the house aged 83 in 1948.

Thomas died on 11 June 1934 at East View, Stow-on-the-Wold aged 72 years. He is buried in St. James's churchyard and his death certificate recorded his occupation as "*Army Pensioner*".

Thomas Henry Payne
Lance Sergeant 19563, 1st Battalion, Grenadier Guards

Enlisted: 21 September 1914
Died: 10 September 1916

Thomas was born in Campden in 1895, the third son of Thomas and Sarah Payne of Debden Cottages, Watery Lane. After leaving school he found employment as a footman and in 1914 was working at Swinbourne Castle, Northumberland. When war was declared he enlisted in Campden in the Grenadier Guards on 21 September 1914. The attestation papers record that he was five feet nine inches tall with a fair complexion, brown eyes and dark hair. His religion was Roman Catholic and he was passed fit for the army at a medical in Caterham on 2 October 1914.

Thomas spent the next year training in England and was promoted to lance corporal on 10 May 1915. He arrived in France with the Grenadier Guards on 13 October 1915 and in March 1916 he was promoted to corporal. This was followed by further promotion to lance sergeant on 29 May 1916.

The battalion arrived on the Somme in August 1916 and two days were spent in trenches at Beaumont-Hamel before the battalion was moved forward to reserve positions at Bernafay Wood. On 10 September one company was sent forward to Arrow Head Copse to support the 4th Battalion, Grenadier Guards. It was on this day that Thomas went missing in action in this area south-west of the village of Guillemont. The *Evesham Journal* reported: *"Mr. And Mrs. Payne, of Park Road, Campden, have now received official intimation that their third son, Lance Sergeant T. H. Payne, of the Grenadier Guards, who was reported missing in action on 10 September 1916, was killed on that date. Lance Sergeant Payne enlisted in September 1914 and served twelve months in France before making the great sacrifice."*

It was on 5 June 1917 that Thomas and Sarah Payne received official notification that their son was dead. He was 21 years old when he died and is buried in Guillemont Road Cemetery, Somme, France. His name is recorded on three memorials in Campden: in St. James's Church, in St. Catharine's Church and in the High Street.

William Charles Payne
Machine Gun Corps

Born: 1886
Died: 3 July 1967

William was born in Campden, the eldest of five sons of Thomas and Sarah Payne who served in the war. After leaving school he found employment as a milk boy on a farm and just before the outbreak of war he married Florence Ashwin at St. Catharine's Church in Campden on 25 April 1914.

Little is known about William in the war but in June 1917 the *Evesham Journal* reported that he was serving in France with the Machine Gun Corps. In early 1918 he was wounded and evacuated back to England, where he was admitted to hospital in Weymouth.

William died on 3 July 1967 aged 81 years.

William Spencer Payne
Air Mechanic First Class F6440, Royal Naval Air Service

Born: 4 September 1896
Enlisted: 12 July 1915
Died: 11 December 1967

Bill was born in Campden, the third son of William and Matilda Payne. He was baptised at St. James's Church on 1 November 1896 and after leaving school he found employment as a farm labourer.

Bill enlisted in the Royal Naval Air Service on 12 July 1915 as an air mechanic second class when he was 18 years old. His attestation papers record that he had brown hair and grey eyes and his parents had moved to Watery Lane, Campden. He was immediately attached to HMS *President II* to begin his initial training in England. On 1 July 1917 he was posted to Caldale, where he remained until he was transferred to Airship *Icarus* on 1 October 1917.

He was promoted to air mechanic first class on 1 January 1918 and on 19 March was transferred to HMS *Daedalus* and posted to Portsmouth. On 1st April Bill joined the Royal Air Force after the amalgamation of the Royal Flying Corps and Royal Naval Air Service and the remaining months of the war were spent stationed at Cardington in Bedfordshire and at Scapa Flow.

After the war Bill married Florence Mabel Maker at St. Eadburgha's Church in Ebrington in 1920 and it was at this point that he left Campden and made his home in Ebrington. He found employment as a plumber with Thomas Parsons in Campden before he set up his own plumbing business.

Bill was an outstanding local footballer, playing for Campden, Ebrington and Brailes, but he will be best remembered for playing Ned Larkin in "The Archers", a role that he played from 1956 until his death in 1967. The show was recorded in Birmingham and Bill had to catch a train to make the journey. He died suddenly on a train on 11 December 1967, when he was 71 years old, and his ashes are buried in St. Eadburgha's churchyard in Ebrington.

Bill and Florence had four children, Harold, Hazel, Viola and Brenda, and the family home was at Tower View, Hidcote Road, Ebrington. Florence died on 31 March 1975, when she was 77 years old.

Bill served throughout the Second World War as a corporal in the Royal Air Force working with barrage balloons in England.

Albert Percival John Phillips
Driver T/36838, Army Service Corps

Born: 8 November 1892
Enlisted: 6 April 1915
Discharged: 5 June 1921
Died: 17 August 1983

Albert was born in Westcote near Stow-on-the-Wold, the eldest son of Alfred Phillips. His father, who was employed as a groom, married Annie Castle in 1892. In 1908 the family moved to Donnington, where his father worked at Broadwell Manor. After leaving school Albert found employment as a farm labourer.

At the outbreak of war Albert and his younger brother Robert were employed in a shop in Croydon. When they both decided to join the army Albert enlisted in the Army Service Corps on 6 April 1915. After a period of training in England he arrived in France on 9 September 1915. He was five feet four inches tall with blue eyes, brown hair and a fresh complexion.

While this book was being prepared Paul Phillips, Albert's grandson, was able to tell the author stories that he recalled about his grandfather's time in the army. One day he was riding a horse that was leading a team of horses pulling a water bowser up to the front. As they approached a railway line the sergeant told him to take a good gallop at it. Needless to say, the bowser stayed on one side of the track and the horse team with Albert went over to the other.

Albert served on the Western Front for over two years and saw action at Ypres, St. Julien, Albert, Cambrai and St. Quentin. He had great respect for the Australian troops after they suffered horrendous casualties at Pozières and was very impressed with the tanks that he served alongside at Cambrai.

In late 1917 Albert was posted to Egypt and from there to Palestine, where he contracted malaria. After returning to England he was placed into the Army Reserve in April 1921 after serving for 4 years and 157 days in the army. A letter was then received notifying him that he was being mobilised and had to join the Royal Army Service Corps at Aldershot on 11 April 1921. He served for a further two months before being returned to the Army Reserve on 5 June. His character reference stated he was *very good, accustomed to horses and honest and sober*".

Albert is on the right at the very front of the group, without the cigarette.

He married Elsie James in Stow-on-the-Wold on 4 June 1921 and after leaving the army he became a market gardener. He worked the land that he bought in Paxford Road, Campden, where in 1928 the family moved into a bungalow that he had built by J. W. Pyment and Sons.

During the Second World War he served in the Home Guard from 28 May 1940 until 31 December 1944.

Albert died on 17 August 1983 aged 90 and is buried in St. James's churchyard in Campden.

Michael Augustine Pippet
Private 3097, 21ˢᵗ and 23ʳᵈ Battalions, Royal Fusiliers

Enlisted: 15 September 1914
Discharged: 13 July 1917

Michael was born in Solihull in 1885, the fourth son of Joseph Aloysius and Juliet Pippet of Lode Lane, Solihull. His father was an ecclesiastical artist and four of his sons, including Michael, followed in their father's footsteps by becoming artists, designers and craftsmen. The Catholic Church of Saint Augustine in Solihull contains several examples of work by the Pippet family.

Michael and his brother Gabriel came to Campden before the war to work with Paul Woodroffe at his studio in Westington to develop as designers and craftsmen. Woodroffe was an illustrator, book designer and stained glass artist and his team included Raymund Binns, George Phillipson, Percy Newman and Fred Bennett. While they were in Campden the Pippet brothers lodged at Blakeman Cottage with Bill and Dedamia Thornton. Michael became the godfather of their daughter Mary and Gabriel the godfather of their daughter Edith.

In 1911 Michael took part as an actor in a Guild play, "*Fair Maid of the West*", with Arthur Pyment, Charlie Downer and Ren Huyshe. A photograph of Michael in the cast can be seen on page 18 of *Alec Miller* by Jane Wilgress.

When the war started Michael enlisted in the army on 15 September 1914. His medical examination recorded that he was five feet six inches tall with blue eyes, brown hair and a fresh complexion. His religion was Roman Catholic. He joined the Royal Fusiliers in Birmingham and after an initial period of training in England he arrived in France on 14 November 1915 with the 21ˢᵗ Battalion. The next few months were spent gaining experience of trench warfare in quiet parts of the line and on 29 April 1916 he was transferred to the 23ʳᵈ (*1ˢᵗ Sportsmen's*) Battalion.

The battalion received orders detailing their involvement in the Battle of the Somme, *The Big Push*. On 20 July 1916 they entrained at Dieval for Longpré and from there they marched to Morlancourt. They arrived at Bernafay Wood on 24 July and there they made the final preparations for an attack at Delville Wood. At 6.10am on 27 July a severe barrage was laid down on Delville Wood. At 7.10am the 23ʳᵈ Battalion, Royal Fusiliers advanced, following the lift in the barrage. By 9.00am they had reached their objective and held a line about 50 yards inside the wood. The regimental historian, H. C. O'Neill, records the battalion suffered 288 casualties and the survivors came out of the wood smoking German cigars.

Michael was badly wounded during the attack when a bullet hit him in the jaw. He was evacuated to hospital and arrived back in England on 19 November, where he was admitted to Tankerton Hospital in Whitstable. While he was there he acknowledged the return of his personal effects, which included a sketch book, a Roman Catholic prayer book, a pipe and a spray of dried flowers.

Michael was discharged from the army on 13 July 1917 as no longer physically fit for war service after 2 years and 302 days in the Royal Fusiliers. His military conduct and character were "*very good*" throughout his time in the army. He returned to his home in Streetbrook Road, Solihull but soon moved to Southampton, where he was living at *Craigmore*, Highclere Road, Bassett in 1920. In 1934 he was a member of the Ordnance Survey Golfing Society.

Cecil Ernest Pitcher
Hampshire Regiment

Born: 24 April 1900
Enlisted: 1918
Died: January 1973

Cecil was born in Bourton-on-the-Hill, the second son of William and Annie Maria Pitcher. His father was a native of Moreton-in-Marsh and employed as a postman. In 1901 the family were living in Back Ends, Campden but by 1918 they had moved to a house in Lower High Street.

Cecil was educated in Campden and was only 14 years old when the war started. In 1916 his brother Charles reached the age of 18 and enlisted in the Royal Garrison Artillery. When Cecil reached the age of 18 in April 1918 he enlisted in the Hampshire Regiment but the war ended before he was able to serve overseas.

After the war he married Isabelle May and they had two children baptised in Weston-sub-Edge: Douglas John and Doris May.

Cecil died in January 1973 aged 72 and is buried in St. James's churchyard in Campden.

Charles William Pitcher
Gunner 121347, Royal Garrison Artillery

Born: 13 January 1898
Enlisted: 25 January 1916
Discharged: 25 July 1919
Died: 19 February 1975

Charles was born in Bourton-on-the-Hill, the eldest son of William and Annie Maria Pitcher. In 1901 his father was a postman in Campden and the family were living in Back Ends. By 1918 they had moved to a house in Lower High Street.

Charles went to school in Campden and then became a market gardener. On 25 January 1916 he enlisted in the Royal Garrison Artillery and he served overseas before the war ended. On 25 July 1919 he was discharged as no longer fit for active service and was awarded a Silver War Badge to indicate that he had made his contribution to the war.

After the war he returned to Campden and continued working as a market gardener. He married Gladys Irene Emily Hill at St. James's Church on 3 April 1926.

Charles died on 19 February 1975 aged 77 and is buried in St. James's churchyard.

Felix Henry Pitcher
Private 51431, Gloucestershire Regiment
Private 20863, Dorset Regiment
Private 30299, Hampshire Regiment

Born: 8 January 1898
Enlisted: 1916
Died: 7 July 1939

Felix was born in Campden, the eldest son of Henry and Joyce Irons Pitcher. His father was a native of Moreton-in-Marsh and a postman like his elder brother William, Felix's uncle. In 1918 the family were living in Lower High Street, Campden.

Felix was baptised at St. James's Church on 10 April 1898. The church records indicate that five other children of Henry and Joyce were also baptised there: Allan Edward, Phyllis Annie, Elsie Mary, Olive and Eric Mons. Eric's middle name is the name of the town in Belgium where the British army first saw action with the Germans in August 1914.

Felix enlisted in the Gloucestershire Regiment in 1916 when he was 18 years old. He served overseas in France and Belgium and ended the war as part of the Army of Occupation in Germany in 1919 before he was discharged. During the war he was transferred twice, first to the Dorset Regiment and then to the Hampshire Regiment.

After the war he returned to Campden and married Elsie Robins. He worked as a cabinetmaker and an upholsterer and the family home was in the Square in Campden.

Felix died suddenly of a cerebral haemorrhage at his home on 7 July 1939 when he was 41 years old. He is buried in St. James's churchyard.

George Plested
Private 46065, 2nd Battalion, Essex regiment

Born: 17 April 1899
Enlisted: 30 January 1917
Discharged: 9 May 1919
Died: 11 November 1985

George was baptised at St. James's Church in Campden on 27 August 1899. He was the son of Ezra John and Jane Plested, who were married at St. James's on 23 August 1890. John was a stonemason by trade and they were living in Watery Lane in 1901. John and Jane had nine children, who were all baptised at St. James's Church: George, Tom, Maud, Ethel, Mary, Alfred ("*Tim*"), Wilfred ("*Bill*"), Harry and Edgar. George and Tom both attended Campden Mixed Infants School and were regular members of the Boys' Brigade which was founded in the town by Harry George Ellis.

When war was declared in 1914 George was only 15 and was working as a farm labourer on Westington Hill. In 1915 his elder brother Tom enlisted as a private in the Gloucestershire Regiment and in 1916 was transferred to the Machine Gun Corps while serving in France. The Battle of the Somme started on 1 July 1916 and Tom was involved in the capture of La Boisselle. On 4 July he was killed by the explosion of a shell while manning his machine gun.

Despite being only 17 years and 9 months old George made his way to Cirencester to enlist in the army. His medical examination papers record that he was five foot eight inches tall and that he was fit to join the army. He was made to wait until his eighteenth birthday before being called up for active service at Bristol, where he was posted to the 47th Training Battalion, Essex Regiment as a private. The next eleven months were spent training in England and his service papers state that on 26 October 1917 he committed an offence while on parade and was confined to barracks for three days.

George embarked at Dover on 5 April 1918 and arrived in Calais later that day. He joined his unit, 2nd Battalion Essex Regiment, four days later. This was a difficult time for the British Army as the Germans had launched a major offensive on 21 March and had captured a lot of ground and British casualties were high. The situation was "*touch and go*" at times but the summer of 1918 saw it stabilised.

On 3 May George was admitted to Field Ambulance Number 12 before being sent to Number 30 Casualty Clearing Station. He was fit to rejoin his unit at Robecq in France on 21 May. Two months later he was admitted to Number 11 Field Ambulance on 18 July before he was transferred to Number 4 Canadian Casualty Clearing Station and then Number 30 Casualty Clearing Station. A period at a recuperation camp followed before he rejoined the battalion on 22 August.

Throughout the latter part of August the battalion (12th Brigade, 4th Division) had been involved in pushing the Germans back to the Drocourt-Quéant Line ("*Wotanstellung*"). This trench was part of the Hindenburg Line and was located halfway between Arras and Cambrai. On the night of 1 September the 2nd Essex pushed on, taking more German trenches with little difficulty, but they were then halted by withering machine gun fire which kept them pinned down for several hours. It was probably a bullet from one of these German machine guns that hit George in the arm.

The war in France ended for him on 2 September when he received this gunshot wound in his right arm. He was first treated at Number 12 Field Ambulance before being evacuated to hospital in Etaples. On 6 September he returned to England on the ship *Stad Antwerpen* and was admitted to Barnet War Hospital later that day. Three months were spent in hospital before he was granted a furlough to recover at Westington Hill Farm in Campden. The war ended while George was in hospital.

On 16 December he was ready to return to duty and was posted to the 3rd Battalion, Essex Regiment. The next four months were spent in England before he was sent to the dispersal centre at Fovant for his final discharge from the army on 9 May 1919. He had served overseas for five months and was awarded two campaign medals.

After the war George married Alice Ann Hughes (sister of the author's grandfather and daughter of Richard and Lucy Hughes) at St. James's Church on 2 January 1924 and they had six children: Norman, Jane, Ann, Mary, John and Jennifer. The family home was at "The Marleys", Aston Road, Campden. Until he retired George was a very skilled builder and stonemason and the only interruption to his work came during the Second World War, when he served as an air raid warden in Campden.

George died on 11 November 1985 aged 86 and is buried in St. James's churchyard. His wife died in 31 May 1982 aged 80 years.

Ormonde William Plested
Private 434010, 4th Battalion, Canadian Machine Gun Corps

Born: 30 May 1888
Enlisted: 30 December 1914
Discharged: 20 June 1919
Died: October 1953

Ormonde was born in Campden, the only son of William and Jane Plested of Silk Mill Yard, Sheep Street, and was baptised at St. James's Church on 22 July 1888. His father was a stonemason by trade and Ormonde followed in the family profession for a short while after leaving school. On 27 May 1911 he emigrated to Alberta in Canada and found employment as a farmer and then as a surveyor for the North-West Territories. He embarked for Canada at Liverpool on a White Star Dominion steamship, *Megantic*, and the port of destination was Quebec.

He enlisted in the Canadian Expeditionary Force at Calgary in Alberta on 30 December 1914, when he was 26 years old. He was five feet ten inches tall with grey eyes, dark hair and a fair complexion. There was a scar on his left shin. He was immediately posted to the 50th Battalion and after a period of training in Canada he embarked on SS *Orduna* on 27 October 1915 and arrived in England on 6 November. He was then transferred to the 10th Canadian Infantry Brigade Machine Gun Corps at Bramshott, where he received final training before being sent to France.

He arrived at Le Havre in France on 11 August 1916 and on 30 December he was awarded a Good Conduct Badge. A second Good Conduct Badge was awarded on 8 October 1917. The following month Ormonde left the unit for a period of training at Abbeville, returning to duty on 24 January 1918. On 19 March his unit was absorbed into the 4th Battalion Canadian Machine Gun Corps and on 19 September he was appointed to the rank of acting corporal.

The following month he was granted fourteen days' leave, which was spent in England. After returning from his leave he remained in France until he returned to England on 7 May 1919. He then embarked at Southampton on HMT *Olympic* on 6 June 1919 and arrived at Halifax in Canada on 12 June. He was discharged from the Canadian Army at Toronto on 20 June 1919 and resumed farming.

Ormonde returned to Campden in 1926 when his mother died and married Nora Keen, eldest daughter of John and Annie Keen, at St. James's Church on 28 February 1927. They had four children: Patrick, Hazel, Noreen and Judith. He worked as a gardener, first at Cotswold House and then at Westington Mill. He joined the Campden Morris Men as the "*Fool*", a role he held for 21 years, and was very popular with the crowds, especially the children, and was a member of the Scuttlebrook Wake Committee. During the Second World War he served as a special constable.

Ormonde died at his home, 10, Station Road, Campden, in October 1953 aged 65 and is buried in St. James's churchyard.

Tom Plested
Private 24643, Gloucestershire Regiment
Private 7974, Machine Gun Corps

Born: 31 December 1896
Died: 4 July 1916

Tom is on the left and George on the right.

Tom was born in Campden, the second son of Ezra John and Jane Plested. He was educated in the town and joined the Boys' Brigade with his brother George when it was formed by Harry Ellis in 1908. After leaving school he found employment as a farm labourer before he enlisted in Campden in the Gloucestershire Regiment at the outbreak of war in 1914. In late 1915 he was transferred to the Machine Gun Corps and posted to the 56th Brigade Machine Gun Company in Grantham. They disembarked in France on 9 February 1916 and five days later they joined the 56th Brigade, 19th Division. On 4 July Tom was in action at La Boisselle during the Battle of the Somme when he was killed. A letter sent to his mother from Lieutenant Turner gave details of Tom's death: "*He died at his gun; the guns had been sent up to help the infantry to hold the village of La Boisselle, which had been splendidly taken, when the enemy began to shell the village. A shrapnel shell burst near your son's gun, killing him and another man instantaneously.*"

Norman Bennett, who was serving in the area with the 8th Battalion, Gloucestershire Regiment, saw Tom's body and remembered that there was not a mark on it. The blast from the shell had killed him. He attended the funeral the next day but the grave was lost during later fighting in the area. Tom's name is today recorded on the Thiepval Memorial in France as he has no known grave. He was 19 years old.

The Boys' Brigade founded by Harry G. Ellis in 1908. George and Tom Plested are together on the second row from the back. Tom is fifth from the right.

In her *Book of Remembrance* Josephine Griffiths says that "*when a lad he handled catapult and gun with unerring aim. He is spoken of with pride, as being an affectionate and dutiful son, as well as being an expert gunner.*"

Tom's name is recorded on two memorials in Campden: in St. James's Church and in the High Street.

William Plunkett
Corporal M2-121030, 780th Motor Transport Company, Army Service Corps

Born: 1885

William was born in 1885 in Bethnal Green, London, the son of Charles and Phyllis Daisy Plunkett. His father was a French polisher and the family moved to Campden in 1902 with the Guild of Handicraft. It does not appear that William joined the Guild, as his jobs before enlisting in the army were as a fitter, a fishmonger and a groom. In his spare time he served in "K" Company, 2nd Volunteer Battalion, Gloucestershire Regiment.

On 24 December 1908 he married Bertha James at St. James's Church. Two daughters, Bertha Edna and Irene Dorothy, were baptised at the same church before the family moved to 5 Raglan Street in Coventry at some point before war was declared in 1914.

William enlisted in the Army Service Corps in Leamington Spa on 13 September 1915 aged 30years. When his initial training in England was completed he left Devonport for overseas service on 20 September 1916 after being posted to 780th Motor Transport Company. He arrived in Salonika, in Greece, on 2 October and it was here that he was to spend the rest of the war. He was promoted to corporal in December 1917 and much of his time in Greece was spent with a motor machine gun section. A period of three months was spent in hospital in 1918 before he was transferred to 887th Motor Transport Company. William remained in Salonika until 11 March 1919, when he embarked for England on board HMT *Seeang Bee*. His discharge from the army came later that month when he arrived back in England.

His army service papers indicate that he was guilty of two military offences during his training in England in 1916. They were "*absent from tattoo on 29 July 1916 to reveille on 30 July 1916*" and "*replying in an improper manner to an NCO*". For each offence he received a punishment of three days confined to barracks.

Army service papers can be very harsh in their appraisal of men. A report on William's character required an answer to the question, "*Is he intelligent?*" The entry says, "*No*".

Walter William Poole
Private 1748, "D" Squadron, Warwickshire Yeomanry

Born: 1870
Enlisted: 20 March 1911

Walter was born in Grafton in Warwickshire, the son of Elizabeth Poole, who was a widow by 1891. After leaving school he found employment as a groom. He was living in West End Terrace in Campden when he enlisted in the Warwickshire Yeomanry on 20 March 1911 as a dismounted member of "D" Squadron, who had their headquarters in Stratford-upon-Avon. When war started in 1914 he was 44 years old and he did not go overseas with the regiment. He spent the first years of the war on home service and by 1918 was back in Campden, living in West End Terrace.

Henry Pope
Lance Corporal, Motor Transport Company, Army Service Corps

Born: 30 July 1871
Died: August 1945

Henry was born in Tewkesbury, the son of James and Elizabeth Pope of Church Street, Tewkesbury. After leaving school he found employment as a painter before enlisting in the army and serving in South Africa during the Boer War. He returned safely to England and on 21 April 1908 he married Lily Louisa Thornbury in Tewkesbury and they had four children: Dorothy

Henry Pope is standing second from the right.

Elizabeth, Harry, Edith and Dennis Arthur. The first three were born in Tewkesbury and the fourth, Dennis, was baptised at St. James's Church in Campden on 10 September 1916.

Henry brought the family to Campden in 1913, after the birth of Edith, and their home was in Sheep Street next door to the Benfield family.

He was 43 years old when the war started in 1914 but he was an experienced soldier and he enlisted in the Motor Transport Company of the Army Service Corps and served overseas.

At the end of the war he returned to Campden and continued working as a painter and decorator. The family home was now in Lower High Street opposite St. Catharine's Church, but they soon moved to 3, Aston Road, one of the houses built by the Council for returning soldiers.

He spent the last years of his life living in Alcester before he died in August 1945 aged 74 years. He is buried in Alcester.

Henry is standing third from the left in front of the passenger door of the lorry.

Alfred James Potter
Private 290916, 1st/6th Battalion, Welsh Regiment
Private 75758, Northumberland Fusiliers

Born: 5 April 1886
Enlisted: 2 August 1916
Discharged: 23 June 1919

Fred was the third and youngest son of Alfred James and Rhoda Ann Potter of Wold's End Farm, Campden. He enlisted in the army on 2nd August 1916, when he was 30 years old. After a period of training in England he was posted to France, where he joined the 1st/6th (Glamorgan) Battalion, Welsh Regiment, which was the

Pioneer Battalion for the 1st Division. He was then transferred to the Northumberland Fusiliers and on 27 May 1918 he was wounded by a bullet in the throat and taken prisoner by the Germans. Fred was initially reported "*missing in action*" but in August 1918 he was able to write to his wife informing her that he was in a prisoner of war camp at Heuberg in Germany. He had been very weak with loss of blood in the days after being captured and was now suffering from a paralysed arm.

After the armistice was signed he was released from the camp and returned to England, where he was discharged from the army on 23 June 1919 as no longer fit for active service owing to his wounds and a Silver War Badge was issued.

Fred worked as a gardener after leaving the army and he had two children by his first wife: Arthur and Freda. After serving as a sergeant in the Home Guard during the Second World War he lived in Broad Campden with his second wife.

Leonard Levi Potter
Farrier Sergeant 66646, Royal Field Artillery

Born: 7 June 1884
Enlisted: January 1915
Died: 21 April 1972

Leonard was the second of three sons of Alfred James and Rhoda Ann Potter of Wold's End Farm, Campden. After leaving school he became a policeman in the Worcestershire Police before he went to Canada, where he was a mounted policeman and then a farmer.

In January 1915 he enlisted in the Royal Field Artillery and after a period of training in England he was posted to France in February 1916. On 21 July and 24 August 1917 he was mentioned in despatches for his gallant conduct at the front. He was wounded in action in August 1917 and in November he was home on leave granted specially by the general as reward for his distinguished conduct in the field. Later that month he received recognition of his gallantry when he was presented with an inscribed parchment from the commanding officer of the division.

After returning to the front he was again wounded when his horse was shot from beneath him and he was thrown into a shell hole full of water, where he stayed for two days until he was found. Rheumatic fever developed and he was sent back to England and admitted to hospital in Cardiff.

Leonard married Bertha Jane Clements and they had seven children: Alfred John, Leonard Levi, Albert Edward, Grace, Evelyn, Helen and Agnes Leah. He worked as a farmer until he bought the Lygon Arms in 1942.

Leonard died on 21 April 1972 aged 87 and was cremated in Cheltenham.

Thomas Heinrich Potter

Born: 17 November 1877

Thomas was born in Alstone, near Winchcombe, the eldest of three sons of Alfred James and Rhoda Ann Potter. His father, a native of Bishop's Cleeve, was an agricultural labourer and the family were living in Alstone in 1881 and in Birlingham, near Pershore, in 1891. When the family moved to Campden they lived and worked at Wold's End Farm.

After leaving school Thomas became an agricultural labourer with his father. He then moved to Wolverhampton and became a carter. On 24 February 1906 he married Martha Lloyd at Tettenhall Parish Church, Staffordshire and a daughter called Phyllis was born on 15 January 1912 at the family home, 31 Lowe Street, Wolverhampton. Thomas was employed as a "brewer's drayman" at the time of his daughter's birth.

At the outbreak of war Thomas was 36 years old and he joined his two younger brothers in the army. In October 1917 the *Evesham Journal* reported that he was in hospital in Leeds.

Harry Powell
Metropolitan Police

Born: 1890
Died: 20 December 1954

Harry married Catherine Mabel Hughes, daughter of William and Elizabeth Hughes of Campden, at Lillington Parish Church, Leamington Spa on 1 June 1914. Their first son, Rodney, was baptised at St. James's Church in Campden on 17 January 1915.

After leaving school Harry had become a policeman and during the war he served in the Metropolitan Police in London. When Harry and Catherine moved to Campden after the war they lived at "The Croft" in Westington.

Harry served for many years on the committee of the Campden branch of the British Legion and during the Second World War his second son Norman Henry Powell died on 28 April 1944 aged 26 years. Norman was a sergeant in the Royal Air Force Volunteer Reserve and is buried in St. James's churchyard in Campden.

Harry died on 20 December 1954 aged 64 and is buried in St. James's churchyard. His wife died on 14 July 1969 aged 80 years.

Francis George Preece
Lance Corporal 28667, 13th Battalion, Gloucestershire Regiment

Enlisted: 1 June 1916
Died: 22 March 1918

Francis was born at Malvern Link in Worcestershire in 1885, the son of James William and Annie Preece. His father's working life was spent as the manager of gasworks in Upton-upon-Severn, Leigh Sinton and Pershore.

In his youth Francis was a champion cyclist and a wonderful sportsman. He married Ada Rolls at Naunton Beauchamp on 6 February 1907 and they had five children, all born before Francis joined the army. The family moved to Campden when Francis took the job of manager of Campden Gasworks and as this was a reserved occupation he did not volunteer when war was declared in 1914. He finally enlisted in Campden on 1 June 1916 after his brother was badly wounded in

France. After a period of training in England he was sent to France in December 1916 and posted to the 14th Battalion, Gloucestershire Regiment.

In February 1918 the battalion was at Langemarck in Belgium, where Francis was involved in a raid on Gravel Farm. The party left Taube Farm at 6.30pm on 4 February and split into two equal groups. The battalion bombers and men carrying Bangalore torpedoes were attached to each. They arrived at Gravel Farm at 7.00pm and it was found to consist of three buildings. Bombs were thrown in and Bangalore torpedoes were used. The report on the raid stated that "*the leading of the raid and the behaviour of all ranks appear to have been excellent*".

Francis was awarded the Distinguished Conduct Medal (DCM) for his part in the raid. His citation reads: "*For conspicuous gallantry and devotion to duty. When in charge of a party of bombers during a raid, carrying some Bangalore Torpedoes to cut the enemy wire, he joined the attacking party and inserted a spare torpedo in a shelter full of the enemy and blew them up. His conduct was excellent throughout.*"

Francis and Ada Preece

On 24 January 1918 Francis wrote to the *Evesham Journal*: "*I have had great pleasure reading your paper out here in the front line trenches. We had a very good time out here at Christmas. We happened to be out of the trenches, so we all settled down for a good time. We partook of all the usual Christmas pudding, beer and turkey. On Boxing Day there was a Brigade Cross Country Race. The ground was covered with snow, and of course not being very far from the line the ground was very rough, but I managed to get through the lot. Nearly 200 started, I got home with ease, being presented with a medal and winning a silver bugle from my battalion. I used to do a good deal of running in peace time round Worcestershire and Essex. We don't mean to let the Germans have their own way. I for one should be glad to see it all over, especially after leaving a wife and five children, but I would sooner fight on than give in to the Germans. Everything is done to make us as comfortable as possible. We get well fed so we cannot grumble a lot.*"

The 14th Battalion was disbanded in February 1918 and Francis transferred to the 13th Battalion, Gloucestershire Regiment along with 14 officers and 250 men. On 22 March 1918 he died in hospital after being wounded by a shell. The *Evesham Journal* reported his death under the headline "*Campden Gas Manager Killed*". A letter was sent to his wife from his commanding officer: "*I am very sorry to have to inform you that your husband has died in hospital of wounds received in action. He was wounded by a shell and succumbed a few days later, though we were able to send him off to hospital within half an hour of being hit. He was a first class soldier, and was liked and respected by all ranks. I am pleased to forward you the official announcement of the award of the DCM for his gallantry while serving with me. Please accept our deep sympathy with you in your great loss.*" A memorial service was held at the church in Naunton Beauchamp and Francis has a memorial inscription at the foot of his wife's parents' grave in Naunton Beauchamp churchyard.

Francis's grave was lost during the confusion that occurred as a result of the German Spring Offensive that began on 21 March 1918 and his name is today recorded on the Pozières Memorial, near Albert, in the Somme region of France. He was 32 years old and "*was of a genial disposition, and was greatly liked by everyone with whom he made contact*".

Francis does not have his name on any memorials in Campden but it is recorded as "*Francis J. Preece*" on the memorial in Pershore Abbey. After the war his wife remarried and went to live in Pinvin.

Francis in his days as a runner

Arthur Sidney Pyment
Sergeant Air Mechanic 4780, 101 Squadron, Royal Air Force

Born: 15 April 1896
Enlisted: 24 April 1915
Died: 10 March 1945

Arthur was born in Royston in Hertfordshire, the son of James William and Emily Pyment. He came to Campden when his parents moved to the town with the Guild of Handicraft in 1902. After leaving Campden Grammar School Arthur joined the Guild as an apprentice carpenter and cabinetmaker.

When war was declared in August 1914 Arthur's elder brother, Harry, was mobilised. Arthur then enlisted in the Royal Flying Corps in April 1915 as an air mechanic second class, one month after his brother had arrived in France. A very short period of initial training took place in England before he arrived in France in May 1915.

He served on the Western Front for over two years and he had risen to the rank of sergeant mechanic by the time he left France for the last time in May 1918. His time overseas was spent with 3 Squadron in 1916 and 1917 and then with 101 Squadron in 1918.

The last few months of Arthur's military service were in England and he was discharged from the RAF on 19 March 1919. When he returned to Campden he joined his brother and father working in the family business, J. W. Pyment and Sons, builders, cabinetmakers and ecclesiastical woodworkers.

Arthur Pyment is standing on the left. His brother Harry is standing behind him. Both brothers attended Campden Grammar School.

He became a special constable, a role he held for twenty years, 1919 to 1939. When the Second World War started Arthur became an air raid warden and was the senior warden for the Sheep Street District.

Arthur died on 10 March 1945 aged 48 and he is buried in St. James's churchyard. He left a widow, Nancy, and two children at the family home, "Hollymount" in Campden. Nancy died in 1986 aged 82 years.

The Pyment Family, 1914
Left to right: Arthur, Emily, James, two Belgian refugees, Harry and Ethel Harris.
Corporal Harry Pyment, Gloucestershire Regiment is about to go to Chelmsford for final training before embarking for France.

Harold George Pyment
Sergeant 1063, "D" Company, 1st/5th Battalion, Gloucestershire Regiment
Sergeant Air Mechanic 335383, 36 Wing, Royal Flying Corps

Mobilised: 5 August 1914
Discharged: 28 February 1919
Died: 11 June 1978

Harold was born in Bow in London in 1893, the eldest son of James William and Emily Pyment. He arrived in Campden as a young boy aged 9 when his parents moved to the town with the Guild of Handicraft in 1902. His father was a cabinetmaker and a senior member of the Guild. When the Guild disbanded and many of the craftsmen left Campden, James bought the Silk Mill in Sheep Street and set up the family business, J. W. Pyment and Sons.

After leaving Campden Grammar School Harold joined his father at the Guild as an apprentice carpenter and cabinetmaker. In his spare time he was a regular member of "H" Company, 5th Battalion, Gloucestershire Regiment, the local company of the Territorial Army. They trained every weekend and went away on annual camp every summer. A lot of time was spent on the rifle range in Broad Campden in fields opposite the Baker's Arms.

When war was declared in August 1914 Harold immediately volunteered for overseas service with the 5th Glosters and was mobilised on 5 August. Initial training took place in Chelmsford in Essex before they arrived in France on 29 March 1915. The next few months were spent in a "quiet" area of the Western Front, in and around the village of Ploegsteert ("Plugstreet" to the soldiers). This was located at the extreme southern end of the Ypres Salient. Casualties here were very light and all of the Campden men with Harold in the Glosters moved south to the Somme in July 1915. Harold became "time expired" on 12 November 1915 when the initial period of service that he signed up for in 1909 had expired and he returned to England.

Harold married Ethel Harris at St. Mark's Church, Harlesden, London on 5 June 1916. His wife was originally from Topsham in Devon and she moved to Campden in 1911 as a telegraph clerk at the Post Office, but when the war started she moved to a London branch. Two weeks later he enlisted in the Royal Flying Corps as an air mechanic second class, no doubt influenced by his brother Arthur and other Campden men who had transferred to the RFC from the Glosters, including Harry and Joe Warmington.

Harold served for nearly three years with the RFC before he was finally discharged

Harold and Ethel Pyment. Harold is wearing his RFC uniform.

Corporal Harold Pyment, Gloucestershire Regiment, is standing at the back in entrance to the bell tent.

on 28 February 1919. He rose to the rank of sergeant mechanic in April 1918 and his overseas service was on the Western Front with 36 Wing, RFC.

When he returned to Campden in 1920 he joined his brother and father working in the family business, J. W. Pyment and Sons, builders, cabinetmakers and ecclesiastical woodworkers.

During the Second World War Harold was Head Warden in charge of ARP services in Campden and his wife, Ethel, worked in the services canteen at Bedfont House. He served for twenty-five years on the Campden Bench as a Justice of the Peace, the last being as chairman.

Harold died at the Royal Berkshire Hospital in Reading on 11 June 1978 aged 84 and is buried in St. James's churchyard. His son, Desmond, saw service during the Second World War and then became an architect.

Corporal Harold Pyment, Gloucestershire Regiment, is on the left of the photograph.

"H" Company, 5th Battalion, Gloucestershire Regiment
Harold can be seen in the centre of the photograph (the tallest man).
The photograph was taken by J. W. Hack, Suffolk Road, Cheltenham.

George Gilbert Radband
Private 18971, 1st Battalion, Leicestershire Regiment

Born: 1 December 1884
Died: 22 March 1918

George was born in Campden on 1 December 1884, the second son of John and Sarah Jane (*Fanny*) Radband, who were married at St. James's Church on 6 February 1883. His parents were both natives of the town and their first four children were all born in Campden: Francis Frederick, George Gilbert, Henry Alexander and Nellie Dorothy. His father was a police constable and his wife's maiden name was Hayward. In 1892 the family moved to Eastwood in Nottinghamshire and their fifth child, William Ewart, was born the same year.

After leaving school George found employment with two of his brothers as a coalminer. In 1914 he was still living in Eastwood when he enlisted in the Leicestershire Regiment. After a period of home service he joined the 1st Battalion, Leicestershire Regiment in France on 22 December 1915 just in time to be eligible for a 1915 Star campaign medal.

At 6.20am on 15 September 1916 the battalion advanced from Ginchy during the Battle of the Somme but immediately faced uncut wire and machine gun fire forced them to take shelter in shell holes. They were relieved two days later and remained in the Somme sector until they entrained at Pont-Remy for Béthune on 29 October 1916.

In 1917 the battalion did not see action during the Third Battle of Ypres but they attacked with the support of tanks at Ribecourt-la-Tour in November 1917 during the Battle of Cambrai. Four months later the Germans launched their Spring offensive on 21 March 1918 and the battalion was in the trenches near Hermies, south-west of Cambrai. The Germans advanced in numbers and the British Army were in retreat. George died on 22 March 1918 and is buried in Grévillers British Cemetery near Bapaume. Casualty clearing stations were located near to the cemetery but in late March 1918 the Germans captured Grévillers.

George was 33 years old when he died and his name is not recorded on any memorials in Campden.

William Ethelbert Richardson
Private 670, Royal Warwickshire Regiment
Captain, Royal Warwickshire Regiment

Born: 1895

William was born in the registration district of Prescot in Lancashire in 1895 and was the eldest son of Rev. James and Louisa C. E. Richardson. In 1901 the family were living at the Vicarage in Aston Magna and James was a Church of England clergyman.

William was educated at Campden Grammar School and when the war started he enlisted as a private in the Royal Warwickshire Regiment. After a period of training in England he arrived in France on 21 November 1915 and was invalided home in September 1916 after being wounded in action during the Battle of the Somme.

He obtained a commission and returned to France as a second lieutenant. He was awarded the Military Cross for gallantry while attached to the 14th Battalion, Royal Warwickshire Regiment. The citation was published in the *London Gazette* on 1 February 1919: "*This officer was in charge of the counter-attack company during the fighting at Gouzeaucourt on 27 September 1918, and when the enemy had forced their way into our left he got his men up with amazing speed under heavy fire, and choosing the most important point, led an attack, which was successful. His cool gallantry at a critical moment inspired confidence in all ranks.*"

William reached the rank of captain before he was discharged from the army.

Leonard Faulkner Richmond

Born: 17 December 1887

Leonard was born in Ullenhall, near Wootten Wawen, on 17 December 1887, the son of William Henry and Mary Jane Richmond. His father was a farm labourer at the time of his birth but then became a roadman.

Leonard married Marion Withers at St. James's Church on 7 December 1915. Prior to the wedding he had been working as a pipe-fitter in South Farnborough in Hampshire.

The 1918 electoral roll states that Leonard was living at Church Cottages in Campden but absent due to military service.

Albert Roberts
Private 26155, 7th Battalion, Gloucestershire Regiment

Died: 3 February 1917

Albert was born at Cow Honeybourne in 1897, the third son of William and Elizabeth Roberts. His father married Elizabeth Payne in 1887 and their first child, a boy called Thomas, was born in 1890. William was employed as an agricultural labourer in 1891 and then as a coal merchant in 1901.

Albert enlisted in the Gloucestershire Regiment in Campden and after a period of home service was posted to the 7th Battalion in Mesopotamia. The battalion had been evacuated from Cape Helles on the Gallipoli peninsula on the night of 8-9 January 1916 and after a short period manning the Suez Canal defences they arrived in Mesopotamia in February 1916, part of 39th Brigade, 13th (Western) Division. The division was involved in attempts to relieve the siege at Kut-al-Amara, which lies on the River Tigris at its confluence with the Shatt-al-Hai, 500 miles upstream from the port of Basra. After these efforts failed and Kut fell, the British force in the theatre was built up and reorganised. The division then took part in the following, more successful, operations: The Battle of Kut-al-Amara, December 1916-February 1917, and the capture of the Hai Salient, 25 January - 5 February 1917.

Albert died on 3 February 1917 and as he has no known grave his name is recorded on the Basra Memorial in Iraq. His name is not recorded on any memorials in Campden but it is does appear on the memorial in Honeybourne.

Frederick Gordon Roberts
Corporal 106554, "D" Battery, 11th Brigade, Royal Field Artillery

Born: 1889
Died: 24 September 1917

Frederick was the fourth and youngest son of Francis Edward and Annie Elizabeth Roberts of High Street, Campden. He was born in the town and baptised at St. James's Church on 27 July 1890 at the same time as two of his brothers, Douglas Ewart and Russell Edward. His father was a native of Campden and a draper and outfitter by trade, proprietor of "Roberts and Company", located in Commercial House in the High Street, selling a range of clothes, boots, shoes and haberdashery. His mother was originally from London.

Frederick was educated at Campden Grammar School but as soon as he was old enough to enlist in the army he joined the Royal Engineers and became a wireless operator and was drafted to India. He eventually bought himself out of the army and took up a position as a telegraphist on the railway for the Indian Government.

When war was declared in 1914 Frederick was keen to enlist but it took a while to be released from his position in India. When he was freed he wanted to join the Royal Flying Corps but his request was refused and he eventually joined the Royal Field Artillery and served in France and Belgium. After he had been abroad for over a year he was promoted to corporal in 1917.

Frederick died of wounds on 24 September 1917 aged 28 and is buried in Bleuet Farm Cemetery, Elverdinge near Ypres in Belgium. The dugout that he was in was destroyed by a gas shell and despite treatment in a field dressing station he died of the effects of the gas. The news of his death was conveyed to his parents in a letter from his major, who reported that he was a most intelligent non-commissioned officer, and he had reported his gallantry in action to the brigadier.

Frederick has his name recorded on three memorials in Campden: in Campden School, in St. James's Church and in the High Street.

Christopher Jack Robson
Private 9440, 2nd Battalion, Coldstream Guards

Died: 14 July 1916

Chris was born in Scorton, near Catterick, in North Yorkshire and was a very good friend of Charles Robert Ashbee. He was not a member of the Guild of Handicraft but is mentioned in the Ashbee Journals which are held at King's College, Cambridge.

At the outbreak of war he was mobilised in Darlington and arrived in France on 12 August 1914 with the 2nd Battalion, Coldstream Guards. The battalion saw action at Mons and Ypres in 1914. They then joined the newly formed Guards Division in France in August 1915 and in September 1915 they fought at the Battle of Loos. In July 1916 the division were in Belgium in the Ypres Salient and it was here that Chris was hit by a stray shell. He was evacuated to Essex Farm Advanced Dressing Station but died of his wounds on 14 July.

Chris is buried in Essex Farm Cemetery, near Boesinghe, north of Ypres in Belgium. During the Second Battle of Ypres in 1915 the dressing station was manned by officers and men from the Canadian Army Medical Corps. One of the officers was Captain John McCrae, an amateur Canadian poet who, after the death of a friend, and coming out of the dressing station one morning to see the ever growing number of wooden crosses, was moved to write the now immortal poem, *In Flanders Fields*.

Francis John Rogers
Able Seaman BZ 3006, Drake Battalion, Royal Naval Volunteer Reserve

Born: 13 October 1898
Enlisted: 24 July 1915
Died: September 1971

Frank was born in Upper Heyford in Oxfordshire on 13 October 1898, the son of Charles and Annie Ada Rogers, who were living at Paul's Pike in Campden in the years leading up to the First World War.

He enlisted in the Royal Naval Volunteer Reserve on 24 July 1915, when he was 16 years old, and his attestation papers record that he was five feet two inches tall with black eyes, black

Frank and Elizabeth Rogers enjoying a day out.

hair and a dark complexion. His religion was Church of England and his occupation in civil life had been a farm labourer. The next of kin was his mother and her address was "*The Grounds, Honeybourne*".

Frank was posted to the 1st Battalion in July 1915 and then attended a signal school in August. In October he was posted to Blandford and then in February 1916 he was drafted from the 2nd Reserve Battalion to Drake Battalion as a signaller for service in the Mediterranean Expeditionary Force. He disembarked from SS *Olympic* at Mudros, on the island of Lemnos, on 28 February 1916 and remained on the island until it was discovered that he was 17 years old and under age. He embarked on HT *Minominee* at Mudros on 1 June 1916 and disembarked at Marseille in France on 7 June and was posted to the base depot at Etaples. He then returned to Blandford in England, where he was demobilised owing to his age on 30 August.

He was remobilised on 7 December 1916, now aged 18, and posted to "A" Reserve Battalion. The next few months were spent on home service before he was sent to a course of instruction at Tidworth on 1 October 1917. In February 1918 he was drafted to Drake Battalion, British Expeditionary Force in France and embarked at Folkestone on 5 February 1918, arriving at Boulogne the next day. The following month Frank was badly gassed and his mother received a telegram dated 14 March 1918 stating that her son was "*dangerously ill and may be visited*". He was admitted to Number 3 General Hospital at le Tréport in France on 13 March. A further telegram was sent on 24 March informing Mrs. Rogers that her son was "*now no longer seriously ill*".

Frank was evacuated back to England and admitted to Queen Mary's Military Hospital at Whalley in Lancashire on 5 April 1918. After leaving hospital Frank was given furlough and he returned home to The Grove Cottages, Honeybourne. In October he was again fit for active service and he entrained with a draft from 2nd Reserve Battalion for the Drake Battalion in France. He arrived at L-Base Depot in Calais on 16 October 1918 but was soon found to have "*flat feet*" and classified medical category B1 and posted back to England, where he arrived before the armistice was signed.

After the war Frank married Elizabeth Ellen Benfield at St. James's Church in Campden on 26 September 1931 and they had two children: Francis Albert (*Bert*) and John. The family home was at the corner of Sheep Street near the Red Lion and Frank had a number of jobs during his working life, including tile-maker, milk roundsman, worker at the brickworks in Blockley, gardener at Seymour House and gardener at the Research Centre. He was an excellent footballer and together with his two brothers, Jim and Fred, he played for Ebrington Football Club.

As a result of the gassing in 1918 he remained very "*chesty*" throughout his life. He died of cancer of the lungs in September 1970 aged 71 and is buried in St. James's churchyard in Campden. He never claimed a war pension but the Royal Marines contributed to the cost of his funeral.

ARP Wardens, 1939-45: Frank's brother Jim is standing at the end of the row on the right.

Donald George Shefford Russell

Corporal 202916, 3rd/8th Battalion, Worcestershire Regiment
Lance Sergeant 202916, 7th Battalion, Worcestershire Regiment
2nd Lieutenant, 7th Battalion, Worcestershire Regiment

Born: 18 April 1894
Enlisted: 12 December 1915
Discharged: 1919

Donald was born in Langley Road, Tooting in London, the son of Sydney Bolton and Elizabeth Russell. He was educated at Campden Grammar School and when he enlisted at Worcester in the 7th Battalion, Worcestershire Regiment on 12 December 1915 his home address was the Lygon Arms, Broadway. His occupation was a hotel manager. He was immediately placed into the Army Reserve until he was mobilised on 2 February 1916 and posted to the 3rd/8th Battalion. He was promoted to lance corporal on 19 August 1916 and on 1 September he returned to the 7th Battalion, where he was promoted to lance sergeant the following day.

In 1917 he joined Number 13 Officer Cadet Battalion at Newmarket and was soon admitted to hospital with measles. He was discharged from hospital on 6 March 1917 and returned to his officer training. On 9 November it was reported that he was "*on the heavy side but has the right qualities and will make a good instructor*".

Donald was commissioned on 30 April 1918 and posted to the 7th Battalion, Worcestershire Regiment as a second lieutenant. He arrived in France on 22 June 1918 and in August was wounded at Locon in Belgium. His discharge from the army came in 1919.

Sydney Gordon Russell

Lance Corporal 2600. "B" Company, 1st/8th Battalion, Worcestershire Regiment
Sergeant 240568, 1st/8th Battalion, Worcestershire Regiment
2nd Lieutenant, 1st Battalion, Worcestershire Regiment

Born: 20 May 1892
Enlisted: 22 September 1914
Discharged: 15 January 1919
Died: 7 October 1980

Gordon was born in Cricklewood in London, the eldest son of Sydney Bolton and Elizabeth Russell. He was educated at Campden Grammar School and then became a designer of furniture. When the war started he went to Worcester and enlisted in the Worcestershire Regiment on 22 September 1914, when he was 22 years old. The autumn of 1914 was spent in billets in Worcester with no khaki uniform or rifles. At Christmas he was sent to Maldon in Essex with a draft for the 1st/8th Battalion and after more home service they embarked at Folkestone on SS *Invicta* on 31 March 1915 and arrived at Boulogne the following day. The battalion then headed north into Belgium and gained their first experience of life in the trenches at Ploegsteert Wood, where on 21 July 1915 Gordon was promoted to lance corporal. In September 1915 the battalion returned to France and took part in the Battle of Loos, which began on 25 September.

The battalion saw action during the Battle of the Somme in July 1916. Gordon was now a sergeant and on 19 July the battalion came under attack from a new type of gas shell while digging a communication trench near Pozières. Only eighteen men were not affected by the gas and later the whole battalion had to be moved away for treatment.

As 1916 drew to a close Gordon was a company quartermaster-sergeant and also a sergeant instructor in bombing. In January 1917 he was offered a commission and returned to England for training as an officer at Lichfield, where he joined Number 8 Officer Cadet Battalion. He was appointed a second lieutenant on 27 June with the 1st Battalion, Worcestershire Regiment but remained on home service until he returned to Belgium on 21 August, where he saw action during the Third Battle of Ypres.

On 13 February 1918 Gordon's post was rushed by a storming party of Germans and during the battalion's counter-attack he was awarded the Military Cross. The *London Gazette* published the citation on 19 April: *"For conspicuous gallantry and devotion to duty. When two of his platoon posts had been raided and occupied by the enemy, he at once went forward to eject the enemy. Finding that the latter were about fifty strong, he returned, collected more men from other posts, and, working round from the rear of the raided posts, succeeded in reoccupying them from the right flank. Having reorganised and supervised the evacuation of the wounded he went round the whole of his company's front to ascertain whether the whole of the front was intact. It was due to his rapid grasp of the situation, and great skill and coolness that the line was re-established by daylight."*

In late February 1918 Gordon was ordered to train a battle platoon to be used as a raiding party. This platoon, under the leadership of Gordon, was rushed to the Somme Canal sector on the 22 March 1918; the day after the Germans launched their Spring offensive. On the morning of 23 March Gordon was shot through the left arm from a range of only twenty yards during a scrap with the enemy in a churchyard at Peronne. He was evacuated back to England and admitted to hospital in Wandsworth in London. After being discharged from hospital he was sent to a convalescence camp in Eastbourne during the summer of 1918 and the doctors told him that he had been very lucky not to lose his arm.

Gordon spent the remainder of his time in the army on home service with the 5th Battalion, Worcestershire Regiment and was discharged on 15 January 1919. He then married Constance Elizabeth Jane Vere Denning, always known as Toni, in 1921 and they had four children: Michael, Robert, Oliver and Kate.

The family home was at Kingcombe, Campden in a house that Gordon had built after he bought the plot of land. They moved to Kingcombe in 1926 and in the same year Gordon became the managing director of Gordon Russell Limited, a position he held until 1940. He then became a director, chairman and partner in Russell and Sons Limited. His reputation as a designer of furniture continued to grow and he was knighted in 1955.

Gordon died at Kingcombe on 7 October 1980 aged 88 and is buried in St. James's churchyard.

The author has close family connections with Sir Gordon Russell as his great aunt, Margaret Jelfs, was his housekeeper at Kingcombe for many years.

William Masson Russell

Private M2-269997, 3rd Auxiliary Petrol Company, 315 Motor Transport Company, Army Service Corps

Died: 25 July 1918

William was born in Hurlswynd, Ceres, Fife (Cupar, Fife) in Scotland in 1880, the son of William and Janet Russell. The family were employed at Norton Hall by Samuel Bruce and both William and his father were employed as grooms. William junior was also the chauffeur.

At the outset of the war Norton Hall became a Red Cross hospital under the command of May Bruce, the eldest daughter, as her parents had returned to Ireland and her two brothers were in the army. When conscription came towards the end of 1915 William appeared before the Mickleton tribunal, May Bruce putting the case for exemption on his behalf. His work was essential for the functioning of the hospital as wounded men arrived by rail at all hours and he went to meet the trains and bring them to the hospital by car. Exemption must have been refused as he was called up soon afterwards. He enlisted in Campden and was posted to the 3rd Auxiliary Petrol Company, Army Service Corps.

This unit was officially formed on 9 March 1915 but its origins are on 12 August 1914, when eight petrol lorries arrived at Boulogne. At first the unit was accommodated in a yard at the railway station in Le Havre. In March 1915 a new unit, 315 Motor Transport Company, was formed and it consisted of 63 petrol lorries. The unit was responsible for local issues of petrol and oil and for the repair of Red Cross vehicles. In July 1915 it was transferred to Etaples and this is where William joined it.

The work for the unit increased dramatically after the start of a massive German offensive that began on 21 March 1918. There were 100,000 men in local camps and more lorries were needed to transport men to the front and to bring back wounded men to the hospitals.

As part of a new air offensive the Germans began to bomb Etaples regularly and many casualties resulted. 315 Motor Transport Company had the foresight to dig seventy-five yards of trench, seven feet deep, for shelter. Their depot was next to the railway station and they had to hide their vehicles three miles away in woods beside the road to Boulogne.

William died at Etaples on 25 July 1918 aged 39 years. The unit diary records that on 24 July *"damage was done to buildings of the company by hostile aircraft and there were two casualties"*. However, the *Evesham Journal* reported that he had been killed instantly by a shell.

William is buried in Etaples Military Cemetery in France and he has his name recorded on war memorials in Mickleton and Weston-sub-Edge. It does not appear on any memorials in Campden.

Dudley Ryder, 6th Earl of Harrowby

Major, Royal Field Artillery

Born: 11 October 1892
Discharged: 4 February 1919
Died: 7 May 1987

The 6th Earl was born on 11 October 1892, the son of John Herbert Dudley Ryder, the 5th Earl of Harrowby, and the Hon. Mabel Danvers Smith, and was educated at Eton and Christ's College, Oxford. He was known as Viscount Sandon from 1900 until 1956, when his father died and he became the 6th Earl of Harrowby.

At the outbreak of war he was granted a commission as a second lieutenant and posted to the 6th Staffordshire Battery, Royal Field Artillery (RFA). On 27 February 1915 he arrived in France with the 3rd North Midland Brigade, RFA and remained at the front until he was wounded at Sanctuary Wood near Ypres on 27 September 1915. This resulted in his evacuation back to England and after treatment he was posted to an artillery training school at Ripon Camp.

He returned to France on 12 May 1916 and the next five months were spent serving at the front until he was again invalided back to England on 23 October. After a full recovery he embarked for France on 31 July 1917 and spent the rest of the war on the Western Front. On 1st October 1917 he was promoted to captain and then on 1st October 1918 to major.

After the armistice was signed the 6th Earl remained in France and served as part of the Army of Occupation in Germany from December 1918 to January 1919. He then returned to England, where he was discharged from the army on 4 February. His horse, "*Christ Church*", served with him throughout the war. He said, "*A dog may be a wonderfully loyal child, but a horse is a colleague.*"

After the war the 6th Earl received a doctorate from the University of Oxford and was the official historian of the Battle of Cambrai. He married Lady Helena Blanche Coventry, daughter of George William Coventry, Viscount Deerhurst, on 31 January 1922 and they had three children: Dudley Danvers Granville, John Stuart Terrick Dudley and Frances Virginia Susan.

He was elected to the House of Commons for Shrewsbury in 1922, a seat he held until 1923 and again from 1924 to 1929, and was Parliamentary Private Secretary to the Secretary of State for Air, Sir Samuel Hoare, between 1922 and 1923. He was also a member of the Commission on Historical Manuscripts from 1935 to 1966 and the author of *Geography of Everyday Things* and *England at Worship*. In 1956 he succeeded his father in the earldom and entered the House of Lords.

The 6th Earl lived at Burnt Norton near Campden and was listed on the 1916 prayer list for servicemen produced by St. James's Church, Campden.

He died on 7 May 1987 aged 94 and is buried at Sandon, Staffordshire.

John Philip Sansom
Lance Corporal, Gloucestershire Regiment

Died: 18 February 1965

John was born in Ebrington in 1884, the younger of two sons of James and Maria Theresa Sansom of Ebrington Hill Farm. He moved to Campden with his mother after his father died in 1889 aged 45 years. In 1901 the family were living in Cider Mill Lane and he was employed as a printer's boy. He later became a postman in the town.

In 1918 the family were living in Leysbourne and John was listed as absent on military service on the electoral roll. He returned safely from the war and on 10 October 1925 he married Edith Ann Roberts at St. Catharine's Church in Campden. Their first son, James Peter Sansom, was baptised at the same church on 30 October 1929.

John died on 18 February 1965 aged 80 and is buried in St. Catharine's cemetery in Campden.

William Rimell Sansom
Private 2305, 2nd/5th Bn., Gloucestershire Regiment

Enlisted: 24 July 1914
Discharged: 17 February 1915

William was born in Ebrington in 1881, the elder of two sons of James and Maria Theresa Sansom of Ebrington Hill Farm. His father was a farmer with 100 acres and in 1881 he employed three men and two boys. After her husband's death in 1889 Maria brought the family to Campden. They were living at Middle Row, High Street in 1891 and in Cider Mill Lane in 1901.

After leaving school William found employment as a

cowman on a farm and later as a labourer for J. W. Pyment and Sons. He was a member of "H" Company, 5th Battalion, Gloucestershire Regiment, the local company of the Territorial Army, and his pension papers held at the National Archives in London show that he enlisted in Campden on 24 July 1914, witnessed by 2nd Lieutenant Charles Noel. After 197 days' home service he was discharged from the 2nd/5th Battalion as medically unfit for active service on 17 February 1915. He then returned home to his wife, Mary, in Cider Mill Lane.

Ernest Harry Shadbolt
Private 306579, Royal Warwickshire Regiment

Born: 25 November 1896
Died: 14 September 1968

Harry was a native of Chipping Norton but he was employed as a railway guard at Campden station for the greater part of his working life. He was the fifth son of John and Emma Shadbolt and the family were living in Spring Street, Chipping Norton in 1901. His father was employed as a builder's carter.

When the war started in 1914 Harry was still only 17 years old. He enlisted in the Royal Warwickshire Regiment and his medal index card indicates that he did not serve overseas until after the start of 1916. He saw service in Italy and France and after the war he joined the staff of the Great Western Railway. When he retired in February 1962 he was the guard at Honeybourne station. He had put in 42 years' service and was presented with a gold watch. After his retirement he was very busy in the garden. In his younger days he played football for Campden and was an active member of the British Legion.

Harry married Gladys Violet Hathaway, daughter of Dennis William and Esther Louise, in 1921 and they lived at 5, Catbrook in Campden. Tragically, they were both killed in a road accident near Toddington on 14 September 1968 only a short time after leaving home for a holiday in South Wales. They had been married for 47 years and spent all of their married life in Campden and were survived by seven sons and two daughters.

Harry was 71 when he died and is buried with his wife in St. James's churchyard. Their son, Dennis John, died in 1984 and is buried with them.

Lewis Sharpe
Leading Stoker K6233, Royal Navy

Born: 15 February 1899
Enlisted: 20 April 1910

Lewis was born in Campden, the third son of John George and Sarah Ann Sharpe, and was baptised at St. James's Church in March 1889. After attending school in Campden Lewis became a bricklayer before he enlisted in the Royal Navy as a stoker at Devonport in 1910. He was five feet nine inches tall with brown hair and blue eyes. He began his period of service at HMS *Vivid*, the Royal Navy barracks at Devonport. He then joined the crew of HMS *Hannibal* on 10 August 1910 and was promoted to stoker first class in March 1911. Further promotion followed in August 1913 when he became a leading stoker and he then served on HMS *Indus* until he transferred to HMS *Ocean* at the outbreak of war. He then joined HMS *Shaitan* in December 1914 and from June 1916 until August 1918 he served on HMS *Berwick*.

When the armistice was signed Lewis was stationed at HMS *Vivid* and in the middle of his initial period of twelve years' service that he signed up for in 1910. He continued to serve in the Royal Navy throughout the 1920's and was promoted to the rank of mechanic in 1927. When he retired from the Royal Navy he went to live on Dartmoor.

Robert James Sharpe
Devonshire Regiment

Robert was born in Campden in 1880, the son of John George and Sarah Ann Sharpe. His father was a gardener and later a domestic servant. His mother was a dressmaker. The family home was in a cottage near St. James's Church in Campden in 1891.

After leaving school Robert became a carpenter and in 1899 he married Bertha Earle Wheeler, a native of Upper Slaughter, in the Stow registration district. Their first child, a daughter called Gertrude Agnes, was born the following year and on the 1901 census the family are recorded as living in Lower Slaughter.

In her *Book of Remembrance* Josephine Griffiths lists Robert as serving in the Devonshire Regiment during the war but a search of the medal index cards at the National Archives reveals that he must have been employed on home service only. Only those soldiers who served in a theatre of war have a medal index card listing the medals that they were awarded. Soldiers employed on home service in the war did not receive any medals.

Joseph Charles Mardel Shepard
Lieutenant, 2nd Battalion, Essex Regiment

Born: 1892
Enlisted: 7 March 1913

Charles was born in Kingsthorpe near Northampton, the second son of Thomas and Marie Shepard. His father was a native of Northampton and a farmer and leather merchant by trade. When Charles was 21 years old he was granted a commission as a second lieutenant in the Essex Regiment on 7 March 1913. At the outbreak of war in August 1914 he was posted to the 3rd (Reserve) Battalion, Essex Regiment. He then embarked for France on 12 September 1914 and landed at St. Nazaire two days later.

He joined the 2nd Battalion, Essex Regiment at Sainte Marguerite near Missy-sur-Aisne, east of Soissons, on 28 September 1914. The battalion was relieved from the front on 1 October 1914 and then began its journey north to Hazebrouck. The end of the month was spent in the trenches around Armentières and Ploegsteert Wood.

Charles was evacuated to hospital in France on 7 December 1914 and then arrived back in England on 17 December. After recovering he was promoted to lieutenant on 2 February 1915 and then in April he was posted to the 9th Battalion, Essex Regiment. On 25 May 1915 the battalion landed in Boulogne but Charles was back in England before it saw action in the 1916 Battle of the Somme.

In April 1916 he was posted to the 3rd (Reserve) Battalion, Essex Regiment for home service and then in January 1918 he was attached to the 2nd (Garrison) Battalion, Northamptonshire Regiment. He spent the remainder of the war in England.

Charles is listed by Josephine Griffiths in her *Book of Remembrance* and on a list of Campden servicemen published by the *Evesham Journal* in 1914.

Roland Henry Shenton
Private 88651, Royal Army Medical Corps

Born: 1890
Enlisted: 3 April 1915
Discharged: 31 August 1918
Died: 10 March 1956

Roland was born in Tipton in 1890, the son of John Henry and Clara Shenton of Victoria Boulevard, Tipton, and educated at Dudley Grammar School. At the outbreak of war in 1914 he was working as a civil servant and on 3 April 1915 he enlisted in the Royal Army Medical Corps.

He was badly gassed in France and when he was discharged from the army on 31 August 1918 he was completely blind. Although his sight was never fully restored, he was able to return to his post as executive officer in charge of the finance section at the Smethwick office of the Ministry of Labour, but in 1945 he lost his sight completely and had to retire. He entered Birmingham Eye Hospital and despite treatment it was thought that he would never see again. Together with his wife he went to live in Broadway, where they stayed for two years with Miss Hunt at St. Patrick's Tea Rooms.

After two years with practically no sight he came under the care of Dr. Kenneth Forsyth at the Birmingham Eye Hospital and he gradually got back a little sight, enough to find his way around the house and to read the newspaper. He then moved to Stanton, where he lived for four years before moving to Grevel Lane in Campden in 1953. While in Campden he joined the British Legion and received great help from St. Dunstan's.

Roland died on 10 March 1956 aged 65 and is buried in St. James's churchyard in Campden. His wife, Martha Gladys Sofia Shenton, died on 21 September 1994 and is buried with her husband.

John Shere
Private 40866, Royal Warwickshire Regiment

Born: 16 September 1899
Died: 28 October 1978

John was born at Green Farm, Hardwicke, near Gloucester, the elder of two sons of Jack and Eliza Shere. His parents moved to White's Farm in the parish of Weston-sub-Edge in 1901 and after leaving school John became a farmer. He was one of three children. His brother, Charles William Leslie, was born in 1905 and his sister, Gertrude Mabel, in 1902.

When the war started John was only 14 years old and as it entered its final stages he enlisted in the Gloucestershire Regiment, although he transferred to the Royal Warwickshire Regiment before embarking for France in 1918. He served at the front for six months and saw action during the final advance of the British Army as they pushed the Germans back through France towards the German border. He was gassed but this did not have any effect on his health in later life.

After being discharged from the army in 1919 he returned to White's Farm and joined the Norton Estate War Club in Aston-sub-Edge. He attended the annual dinner in 1919 but was marked as "*abroad*" on the register for 1920. He became disillusioned with farming in England and the decision was made to emigrate to America. His family escorted him to Honeybourne station and after saying their goodbyes never saw him again although letters were exchanged on a regular basis.

John worked as a wheat farmer in America and married Maggie Moore at Coeur d'Alene in Idaho in May 1930. They had one child, a daughter called Pat, and the family home was first at Hay and then Lacrosse, both in the state of Washington. After leaving his job as a corn farmer John bought a bus company and drove the bus taking children to and from school.

He died on 28 October 1978 aged 79 and is buried in Lacrosse in America. His parents are buried together in St. Lawrence's churchyard in Weston-sub-Edge.

James William Simmons
Private 240154, "D" Company, 1st/5th Battalion, Gloucestershire Regiment

Born: 21 December 1894
Discharged: 5 April 1919
Died: 22 August 1958

James is holding the axe on the left of the photograph taken by J. W. Hack, Suffolk Road, Cheltenham, while the Glosters were training in England.

James and his wife.

James is pictured here with his wife in 1919 after the end of the war. He is wearing four service chevrons on his right sleeve and the ribbon for his 1914/15 star campaign medal on his chest.

James was born in Broad Campden, the son of Josiah and Sarah Ann Simmons, and was baptised at St. James's Church on 11 November 1894. His father was a regular soldier serving in the 17th Lancers.

James was educated in the town. After leaving school he became a butcher's boy and a member of "H" Company, 5th Battalion, Gloucestershire Regiment, the local company of the Territorial Army. When the war started in 1914 he was 20 years old and he quickly signed up for overseas service with the Glosters. He was mobilised on 5 August and a period of training took place at Chelmsford in Essex. The battalion embarked at Folkestone and arrived in Boulogne on 29 March 1915. James spent the next three years on the Western Front, serving in France and Belgium with the 1st/5th Glosters. He was badly gassed on one occasion and suffered with a weak chest for the rest of his life. His discharge from the army came on 5 April 1919 after serving throughout the war with the Gloucestershire Regiment.

After the war he became a groom. He married twice and had seven daughters and one son. He soon left Campden after his first marriage and went to live in Birmingham.

When James died on 22 August 1958 aged 63 he was living in Castle Bromwich. He is buried in the family grave in Castle Bromwich churchyard.

Josiah James Simmons
Trooper 3614, 17th Lancers

Born: 23 November 1871
Enlisted: 1891
Died: 1 November 1941

Josiah and Sarah Ann Simmons
Josiah is proudly wearing his two Boer War medals.

Josiah was born in Campden, the son of James Simmons, and he enlisted in the 17th Lancers in 1891 when he was 19 years old. The first few years of his military service were spent in England, which enabled him to marry Sarah Ann Tracey on 20 October 1894. They had one son, James William, who served in the Gloucestershire Regiment during the 1914-18 war.

Josiah served in South Africa during the Boer War with the 17th Lancers and took part in the charge at Diamond Hill. His two campaign medals have six clasps: Johannesburg, Diamond Hill, Wittenbergen, Cape Colony, 1901 and 1902. After returning to England he continued to serve in the army until he was discharged on 3 September 1913 after twelve years with the 17th Lancers.

At the outbreak of the war in 1914 he rejoined his old regiment and was sent to the Cavalry Reserve Depot at The Curragh. He did not serve overseas and was eventually discharged in May 1917 as *"physically unfit for further war service"* after receiving a badly fractured wrist when he was thrown from an officer's horse.

After the war Josiah was a very active man. He was heavily involved in the work of the British Legion and dedicated a lot of his time to raising funds for ex-servicemen and local hospitals. He took a great deal of interest in the war memorial and he kept the surrounding grass in good condition until 1939.

After working with horses as a regular soldier Josiah found employment as a groom, although he later worked as a gardener for the Sharpley family in the High Street. He was also a special constable until he reached the age limit and enjoyed a day's hunting with the North Cotswold Hunt.

Josiah died at his home on 1 November 1941 aged 69 after he had spent the last year of his life confined to the house. He is buried in St. James's churchyard.

Julian Hamilton Cassan Simpson
Sergeant 567, "G" Company, 1st Battalion, Australian Naval and Military Expeditionary Force
Captain, 1st Battalion, Grenadier Guards

Born: 1894

Julian was born in Australia, the son of George Hamilton Cassan and Lillian Simpson. His father died in 1898 and his mother then married John A. Thompson in Woollahra, Sydney in 1902. The family home was at 52, Maclery Street, Sydney, New South Wales.

On 19 August 1914 Julian embarked at Sydney on board HMAT *Berrima* and headed for the North-West Pacific. He was a sergeant in "G" Company, 1st Battalion, Australian Naval and Military Expeditionary Force and his unit was designated a *"tropical unit"*.

Nothing is known about the next four years but on 11 June 1918 he was a captain when he was posted to the 4th Battalion, Grenadier Guards in France. In August 1918 he transferred to the 2nd Battalion and on 2 September he was slightly wounded by shellfire. On 11 September he took part in a raid on part of the Hindenburg Line with his commanding officer, Lord Gort, and then on

27 September he was involved in another attack at the Canal du Nord, near Flesquières, for which Lord Gort was awarded the Victoria Cross.

In October he was again wounded by shellfire and while he was attached to the 1st Battalion, Grenadier Guards he was awarded the Military Cross for gallantry in face of the enemy. A bar to his Military Cross was awarded soon afterwards and it was announced in the *London Gazette* on 1 February 1919.

It has not been possible to identify Julian's connection with Campden but he was listed on the prayer list produced by St. James's Church in 1916.

William Sinclair
Sergeant SE-11844, 38th Mobile Veterinary Section, Army Veterinary Corps

> Born: 1884
> Died: 19 January 1919

William was the son of William and Johanna Sinclair of 88 Langton Road, Wavertree, Liverpool. When the war started in 1914 he enlisted in the Army Veterinary Corps and was posted to the 38th Mobile Veterinary Section, which was part of 26th Division. Embarkation for France began in September 1915 and by the end of the month the division were concentrated west of Amiens. However, they were destined not to stay on the Western Front as orders came through in November 1915 sending them to Salonika in Greece, where they remained for the rest of the war. The division left France via Marseille and after arriving at Salonika the units began to move from Lembet to Happy Valley Camp in December 1915.

The division was involved in a number of actions in Greece and forward units crossed the Serbian-Bulgarian border on 25 September 1918. Hostilities with Bulgaria ceased two days later. The division then advanced towards Adrianople as the war with Turkey was still under way. However, this soon came to an end and they ended the war as part of the Army of the Danube and then the occupation of Bulgaria.

William died of influenza in Greece on 19 January 1919 aged 34 and is buried in Bralo British Cemetery, 185 kilometres from Athens. The cemetery began in October 1917 when the 49th Stationary Hospital was transferred to Bralo. It contains the graves of 102 soldiers; a large proportion of them died of the influenza epidemic of 1918.

William does not have his name recorded on any memorials in Campden but his wife, Gladys Emily Sinclair, was living in Leysbourne in the post-war years.

Charles Harland Skey
Private 3588, 19th (2nd Public Schools') Battalion, Royal Fusiliers
Captain, "C" Company, 1st Battalion, The Black Watch (Royal Highlanders)

> Born: November 1891
> Enlisted: 15 September 1914
> Died: 18 August 1916

Harland was born in Margate in Kent, the son of Lieutenant-Colonel Edward Oscar and Maud Emmeline Skey. His father was born in Campden, the son of John Skey, landlord of the Lygon Arms. After leaving school Harland gained a place at Queen's College, Cambridge, where he gained college colours for football and cricket. He graduated B.A. and became a schoolmaster.

He enlisted in the 2nd Public Schools' Battalion of the Royal Fusiliers in Westminster on 15 September 1914, when he was 22 years old. After obtaining a commission he was discharged from the Royal Fusiliers on 18 September. A period of home service followed before he entered France in 1915. He was promoted to the rank of temporary captain on 17 March 1916 and was then transferred to the 1st Battalion, The Black Watch on 18 June 1916 as they prepared for their part in the Battle of the Somme.

The battalion arrived in Doullens from Béthune on 6 July and from there they marched to billets in Naours. They arrived in the front line at Contalmaison on 11 July and fought off a German counter-attack the following day. A period of rest followed in Albert before they moved up to support trenches at Bazentin-le-Petit, where the battalion was involved in an unsuccessful attack on Intermediate Trench, north of the village and west of High Wood, on 18 August. The battalion advanced at 4.15am but the men became disorganised owing to shellfire. Small parties penetrated 70 yards beyond the trench but were forced back.

Harland was initially reported missing but it was later confirmed that he had been killed in action while leading "C" Company in the attack on Intermediate Trench. Private 8216, David Menzies, 9 Platoon, "C" Company, 1st Battalion, The Black Watch, reported: *"He got into the German trench well ahead of his company and was killed instantly by a shell just as he was coming out of a dugout. He was buried close by."*

Harland's battlefield grave could not be found at the end of the war and his name is recorded on the Thiepval Memorial, Somme, France. He was 24 years old when he died and he does not have his name recorded on any memorial in Campden. At the time of his death his parents were living at 1 Craythorne, Cliftonville, Margate, Kent and his father was the headmaster of Cliftonville College.

Cyril Oscar Skey
Major, 8th (Service) Battalion, Royal Fusiliers

Born: 1894

Cyril was born in Margate in Kent, the son of Lieutenant-Colonel Edward Oscar and Maud Emmeline Skey. At the outbreak of war he enlisted in the 18th (1st Public Schools') Battalion, Royal Fusiliers, which was formed in Epsom in September 1914. The battalion was posted to the 33rd Division in June 1915 and final training before being posted to France took place at Clipstone Camp, Nottinghamshire in July and at Bulford, Salisbury Plain in August.

Cyril arrived in France as a lieutenant on 13 November and after the 18th Battalion was disbanded on 24 April 1916 he was transferred to the 9th Battalion, Royal Fusiliers. He was awarded the Distinguished Service Order during the Battle of the Somme and the award was announced in the *London Gazette* on 26 September 1916. The following citation accompanied the announcement: *"For conspicuous gallantry in action. He led his company with great dash in the attack, and entered an enemy trench immediately our barrage lifted, thereby completely surprising the enemy. During the following day he did fine work under shell fire."*

In 1918 he was promoted to captain and awarded the Military Cross. The citation appeared in the *London Gazette* on 16 July: *"For conspicuous gallantry and devotion to duty. When left with one officer only, he reorganised the remnants of the battalion and by his good example and leadership succeeded in rallying the men, who had been much shaken, and held on to his position for 48 hours."*

Further promotion followed when he became a major and was appointed second-in-command of the 8th (Service) Battalion, Royal Fusiliers. When the war ended he remained in the army as a regular soldier.

Edward Oscar Skey
Lieutenant-Colonel, 2nd/4th Battalion, East Kent Regiment (*The Buffs*)

Born: 1863
Enlisted: May 1898
Discharged: 24 May 1921
Died: 1931

Edward was born in Campden, the son of John George and Esther Skey. His father was the landlord of the Lygon Arms and also employed as an undertaker.

Edward enlisted as a second lieutenant in the 1st Volunteer Battalion, East Kent Regiment on 11 May 1898 and was promoted to full lieutenant on 11 January 1899. He continued to rise through the ranks and became a captain in 1901 and then a major in 1909 when he was second-in-command of the 4th Battalion, East Kent Regiment. In 1912 Edward was posted to India with the battalion and on 19 April 1914 he was promoted to temporary lieutenant-colonel when he was given command of the 2nd/4th Battalion.

In July 1915 he was given the job of organising and training the 71st Provisional Battalion, which consisted of men from the 2nd/4th and 2nd/5th Battalions of the East Kent Regiment and

Edward Oscar Skey, East Kent Regiment
The author was told that this was Harland Skey. Edward and Gordon both served in The Buffs but Gordon was only 19 in 1914.

the 2nd/5th Battalion, Wiltshire Regiment. After nine months the 71st Provisional Battalion was absorbed into the 69th Battalion. Edward was recommended for leave and was then transferred to the Territorial Force Reserve in May 1916.

The reason for being given leave was that he was the owner and headmaster of Cliftonville College in Margate, a large school for boys, and thirteen masters had left to join the army. His wife had recently died and all of his three sons were serving in the army. Two of them were in France by 1916. The period of leave was granted from 29 April 1916 to 29 June 1916. It was at this time that he was informed that his rank was reverting to major. Apparently Edward did not know that the rank of lieutenant-colonel was only temporary! When he retired from the army on 24 May 1921, owing to reaching the upper age limit, he was allowed to keep the rank of lieutenant-colonel for use in civilian life.

Edward married Maud Emmeline Morine, in Kent in 1886 and the sons, Charles Harland, Cyril Oscar and Leslie Gordon, were all born in Margate. The family home was at 1 Craythorne in Cliftonville but they also used Luton House in Selling near Faversham in Kent during the school vacations.

Edward died in 1931, fifteen years after the death of his wife.

Leslie Gordon Skey
2nd Lieutenant, 2nd/4th Battalion, East Kent Regiment
Captain, 71st Punjabis, Indian Army

Born: 9 August 1895
Enlisted: 18 August 1911

Gordon was born in Margate, the youngest of three sons of Lieutenant-Colonel Edward Oscar and Maud Emmeline Skey and grandson of John Skey, landlord of the Lygon Arms in Campden. He was educated at Cliftonville College, Margate in Kent, where his father was headmaster.

Gordon enlisted as a trooper in the 1st/4th East Kent Regiment (The Buffs) on 18 August 1911, when he was 16 years old. At the start of the war he applied for a commission and joined the 2nd/4th Battalion, East Kent Regiment as a second lieutenant on 17 November 1914. His medical examination in 1914 graded him as "A1" and stated that he was five feet eleven inches tall with good hearing and sound teeth.

Gordon was promoted to lieutenant on 1 June 1916 and then on 24 October 1917 he embarked at Devonport en route to India as he had been seconded to the Indian Army Reserve of Officers as a newly promoted captain. He disembarked at Bombay on 21 January 1918 and served with the 71st Punjabis (Punjab Christian Battalion) until 11 February 1919, when he reverted to the rank of lieutenant with the East Kent Regiment.

The 1st/4th East Kent Regiment were mobilised for service on the North-West Frontier in August 1919 and Gordon was posted to the battalion and given the rank of temporary captain while he commanded a company. The North-West Frontier is an area of barren mountains dissected by fertile valleys and the region is historically and strategically important owing to the passes leading to India. The men arrived at Quetta on 23 August 1919 for service in the field and Gordon was awarded the General Service Medal with a "*South Persia*" clasp for this period of his army career. Quetta is the capital of the province of Baluchistan in Pakistan and is known as the "*Fruit Garden of Pakistan*". It is located in a river valley near the Afghanistan border. In 1919 Britain sent forces to Persia to secure future oil supplies and the Anglo-Persian Agreement was signed in that year.

Gordon embarked at Bombay on SS *Nevasa* on 25 October 1919 to return to England, where he reverted to the rank of lieutenant. He continued to serve with the East Kent Regiment before being transferred to the Army Reserve on 3 November 1920. He relinquished his commission on 30 September 1921, retaining the rank of lieutenant for use in civilian life, and farmed in the inter-war years.

During the Second World War he enlisted in the Royal Artillery Territorial Army on 12 April 1939 aged 43 and saw service with 306th Anti-Aircraft Battery as Private 1474956 Gordon Skey.

Charles Slatter
Private 2338, "D" Squadron, Warwickshire Yeomanry
Private 310433, Corps of Hussars

Born: 1892
Discharged: 3 May 1919

Charles was born in Ashton-under-Hill near Evesham, the eldest son of Charles and Elizabeth Esther Jane Slatter, who were married in the Tewkesbury registration district in 1890. His father was a farmer and in 1901 the family were living and working in Clopton near Lower Quinton in the Campden Rural District.

In the years leading up to the war Charles and his younger brother, Raymond, enlisted in the Warwickshire Yeomanry. He was mobilised at the outbreak of war and on 14 August 1914 the battalion moved to Bury St. Edmunds. On 11 April 1915 they sailed from Avonmouth in the transport *Wayfarer* to join the force being concentrated in Egypt for landings at Gallipoli. They were torpedoed 60 miles north-west of the Scillies but did not sink and were towed to Ireland. After a short delay they arrived in Alexandria on the *Saturnia* on 24 April.

Charles remained with the battalion throughout the war and served in Gallipoli, Egypt and Palestine. "D" Squadron, Warwickshire Yeomanry contained many local men including Reg Smith, Arkell Coldicott and William Hunt, and more details of the battalion can be found in their entries in this book.

In January 1916 the Warwickshire Yeomanry combined with those of Gloucestershire and Worcestershire to form the 5th Mounted Brigade. It was heavily engaged in Egypt and Palestine, from the early probing away from the Suez Canal zone, across the Sinai desert and eventually at the Battles of Gaza and the victorious advance to Jerusalem and into Syria.

Charles returned safely from the war and was discharged from the army on 3 May 1919. He was included on the 1918 electoral roll for Campden, as he owned land in the town, and was marked absent on military service.

Albert Frederick Walter Smith
Private 19029, 8th Battalion, Gloucestershire Regiment
Private 224979, Labour Corps

Born: 14 March 1880
Enlisted: 26 January 1915

Frederick was born in Aston-sub-Edge, the third son of William and Sarah Ann Smith. His father was an agricultural labourer and in 1881 the family were living in Mickleton, but by 1884 they had moved to White's House in Weston-sub-Edge.

The 1901 census lists Frederick as a cowman on a farm and living in Saintbury with his wife, Lena, and son, Ernest. Before the outbreak of war the family returned to Aston-sub-Edge, where Frederick was employed by the Earl of Harrowby on the Norton Estate.

On 26 January 1915 he enlisted in the Gloucestershire Regiment and served on the Western Front for three years and seven months, where he saw action on the Somme and at Hill 60 near Ypres in Belgium. He was transferred to the Labour Corps before returning safely home after being discharged from the army.

After the war he joined the Norton Estate War Club in Aston-sub-Edge and attended each annual dinner until the club was disbanded in 1923.

Arthur Henry Smith
Army Service Corps

Born: 1876

Arthur was born in Campden, the son of Charles and Mary Ann Smith. His father was a shepherd and the family home was in the High Street. After leaving school Arthur found employment as a ploughboy and then as an agricultural labourer. During the war he served in the Army Service Corps and the Campden 1918 electoral roll lists him as living in Lower High Street and absent on military service.

Fred Smith
Sapper 352001, Transport Branch, Royal Engineers

Born: 1878
Enlisted: 8 February 1915
Discharged: 20 July 1918
Died: December 1959

Fred, known as *"Flago"*, was born in Campden, the son of Thomas William and Sarah Smith of the Square, High Street, Campden, and was baptised at St. James's Church on 29 September 1878. After leaving school he became a stonemason and married Bertha Keeley, daughter of Frederick and Jane Keeley of Aston-sub-Edge, on 3 December 1904. They had five children, who were baptised at St. James's Church: Miriam, Frank, Stella Cicely, Wilfred and Helena. The family home was in Back Ends.

During the war Fred was employed on home service with the Royal Engineers for a period of 3 years and 163 days before he was discharged in London as *"no longer physically fit for active service"*. His discharge papers held in the National Archives in London state that he was five feet five inches tall with grey eyes, light brown hair and a fresh complexion. His character and conduct were *"very good"* throughout his time with the Royal Engineers.

Bertha died on 20 October 1954 aged 78 only two days before Fred's brother, Lewis, died. Fred died in December 1959 aged 81 and is buried in St. James's churchyard.

Frederick William Smith
Private 42569, 2nd Battalion, Worcestershire Regiment
Private 642556, Labour Corps

Born: 18 November 1889
Enlisted 4 January 1915
Died: 7 November 1970

Frederick was born in Tysoe, the eldest son of Thomas George and Sarah Elizabeth Smith. His father was a general labourer and in 1901 the family were living in Westington in Campden.

After leaving school Frederick became a farm worker and he lived in Longlands Cottages while he worked on the land between Campden and Mickleton. At the outbreak of war in 1914 he was 24 years old and his parents had moved to Paul's Pike. On 4 January 1915 he enlisted in the Worcestershire Regiment and the next eighteen months were spent training in England before he arrived in France in August 1916. He had been at the front for only four months when he was severely wounded in his right hand, which resulted in the amputation of a number of fingers. He was evacuated back to England and admitted to the Auxiliary Military Hospital in Birkenhead. After he was discharged from hospital he transferred to the Labour Corps and spent the remainder of the war on home service.

When Frederick was discharged from the army he was unable to continue as a farm worker owing to his wounded right hand. In the early 1920's he returned to Campden with his wife, Hannah Lilian Smith, and worked for Commander Fred Hart, who had just retired from the Royal Navy. Frederick worked as the gardener at "Trinder House", Hannah did the cleaning and they lived in Clifton Cottage in the High Street. He was a member of the Campden branch of the British Legion and a member of the Norton Estate War Club until it disbanded in 1923.

Hannah died in August 1960 aged 74 years. Fred then moved to the Almshouses and remained there until he died in Cheltenham Hospital on 7 November 1970. He was 80 years old and is buried in St. James's churchyard in Campden.

In her *Book of Remembrance* Josephine Griffiths suggests that Frederick served in the Gloucestershire Regiment during the war.

George Arthur Smith
Private S4-058687, Army Service Corps
Private 40469, King's Shropshire Light Infantry

Born: 10 November 1887
Discharged: 15 March 1919
Died: 17 March 1974

George was born in Campden, the second son of George and Eliza Smith, and was baptised at St. James's Church on 22 January 1888. His father was an agricultural labourer and the family home was at Broad Entry, Lower High Street, Campden in 1891 and then at Paul's Pike in 1901. His parents married in 1885 and his mother's maiden name was Toft. Eliza died in December 1910 aged 60 and is buried in St. James's churchyard in Campden.

George married Mary Paget in Tenbury Wells on 28 October 1911 and they had three children: Evelyn, Kathleen Winifred and Iris. Evelyn and Kathleen were both baptised at St. James's Church in Campden and George's occupation was recorded as a baker in the church records. The family home was in Flag Close in Campden.

At the outbreak of war George enlisted in the Army Service Corps and after a period of home service he arrived in France on 10 March 1915. He then transferred to the King's Shropshire Light Infantry and on 21 September 1918 was admitted to Number 22 General Hospital in France suffering from a gunshot wound. Evacuation back to England followed and he was admitted to hospital in Northumberland. After being discharged from hospital George remained in the army until he was demobilised on 15 March 1919.

In the photograph George is wearing on the sleeve of his tunic a chevron that was awarded for long service and good conduct over a period of two years. This indicates that he spent at least two years in the Army Service Corps.

After returning to Campden George and Mary soon moved to Church Street, Hampton, Evesham, where George was employed at Izod's Bakery in Bridge Street. He later became a market gardener.

George died in Evesham General Hospital on 17 March 1974 aged 86 years.

George Edward Smith
Royal Field Artillery

Born: 1895

George was born in Campden, the second son of Thomas George and Sarah Elizabeth Smith, and was baptised at St. James's Church on 25 December 1895. His father was a general labourer in 1889 when their first son Frederick was born and then a shepherd in 1895. The family home was in Westington in 1901 and then at the time of the war in Paul's Pike.

During the war George served in the Royal Field Artillery and is listed as absent on military service on the Mickleton 1918 electoral roll.

Hiram Smith
Able Seaman 182784, Royal Navy

Born: 23 August 1878
Enlisted: 14 August 1895
Discharged: 4 August 1919

Hiram was born in Campden, the son of Isaac and Alice Smith, and was baptised at St. James's Church on 30 October 1881, when he was 4 years old. After leaving school he became a plumber but when he was 17 years old he enlisted in the Royal Navy at Devonport on 14 August 1895. He was five feet six inches tall with light brown hair, blue eyes and a fair complexion. When he reached the age of 18 on 23 August 1896 he signed on for 12 years with the Royal Navy.

He began his period of 12 years' service as a boy second class on HMS *Impregnable*, a Royal Navy training ship at Devonport. While serving on HMS *Lion* in 1895 he was promoted to boy first class and then while on home service in 1896 at HMS *Vivid*, the Royal Navy barracks, he was promoted to ordinary seaman. Further promotion followed in 1898 when he became an able seaman.

Hiram's period of service came to an end on 22 August 1908 and he was then posted to the Royal Navy Reserve. His conduct throughout was "*very good*". He remained in the reserve until he was mobilised on 2 August 1914 when war was declared and posted to HMS *Amphitrite* as an able seaman. In June 1915 he returned to the Royal Navy barracks at Devonport and remained there until he was posted to HMS *Mechanician* in January 1918. In February he returned to barracks before he joined the crew of HMS *Caesar* in April and was still serving on the ship when the armistice was signed.

In March 1919 Hiram was transferred to HMS *Theseus* and on 13 May he returned to barracks. He was discharged from the Royal Navy on 4 August 1919.

Lewis Smith
Private S-290218, Army Service Corps
Private 42062, Gloucestershire Regiment

Born: 19 April 1888
Died: 22 October 1954

Lewis was born in Campden, the son of Thomas William and Sarah Smith. His father, a native of the town, was recorded as a "*shoemaker and caretaker*" on the 1891 census. In 1917 Thomas, who was the town crier and caretaker of the Town Hall, accidentally fell down the stairway in the Town Hall and broke his neck. He left a widow, five sons and six daughters.

Lewis was baptised at St. James's Church on 26 August 1888 and then educated in the town. After leaving school both Lewis and his elder brother Frank went to London to train as butchers. Frank remained in London after serving his apprenticeship.

When the war started in 1914 Lewis enlisted in the Army Service Corps but did not serve overseas until after the start of 1916. When his turn came to face the enemy he was posted to Salonika in Greece, where he remained until at least March 1918, when a photograph of him was taken in uniform. Lewis also served in the Gloucestershire Regiment during the war but it is not clear when this transfer took place.

After the war he returned to Campden and continued his work as a butcher in his shop in the High Street. He married Violet Newbury and their son, Robert, took over the running of the shop after Lewis died.

Lewis died on 22 October 1954 aged 66 and is buried in St. James's churchyard.

Owen Smith
Corporal 3628, 1st/8th Battalion, London Regiment (Post Office Rifles)
Corporal 371429, 1st/8th Battalion, London Regiment (Post Office Rifles)

Born: 6 January 1885
Enlisted: April 1915
Died: 7 October 1916

Owen was born at Campden, the fourth son of Thomas William and Sarah Smith of the Square, High Street, Campden, and was baptised at St. James's Church on 26 August 1888. His father was a native of the town and a shoemaker by trade.

After attending school in the town Owen became a postman and by 1914 he was secretary of Campden Town Band. He enlisted at Moreton-in-Marsh in April 1915 and after a period of training in England he arrived in France with the 1st/8th Battalion, London Regiment (140th Brigade, 47th Division) on 28 October 1915. When the Battle of the Somme started on 1 July 1916 the battalion was in the Arras area. It began the march south from Vimy, near Arras, on 21 July and was involved in an attack on High Wood on 15 September and then on the trenches in front of Flers on 18 September. These two attacks cost the battalion 300 casualties.

A period of rest followed in Albert before the battalion was again ordered forward for another attack, which was to take place on 7 October 1916. The objective was Snag Trench in front of the Butte de Warlencourt. The two companies involved in the attack were almost entirely wiped out. There were 411 casualties, including Owen, and only seven survivors.

Owen was killed during the latter stages of the Battle of the Somme aged 31 years. His body was not found at the end of the war and his name is recorded on the Thiepval Memorial, Somme, France. It also appears on two memorials in Campden: in St. James's Church and in the High Street.

Reginald Richard Smith

Private 2666, "D" Squadron, 1st/1st Warwickshire Yeomanry
Private 164940, 100th Battalion, Machine Gun Corps

Born: 10 July 1891
Died: 6 January 1981

Reg was born in Oldberrow, Worcestershire and was the only son of Richard and Mary Jane Smith. His parents were married in Alcester in September 1888 and at the time of the First World War they were running the George and Dragon pub in Campden. His sister, Ellen Frances, married Thomas Charles Hooke, an entertainer from London, in December 1919 and they ran a bicycle shop in the High Street in Campden.

Reg did not like pub life and emigrated to New Zealand and it is unlikely that he would have returned to Campden if war had not been declared. He enlisted at Warwick in the Warwickshire Yeomanry and after a period of training in England was posted overseas and arrived in Egypt in September 1915. The Warwickshire Yeomanry landed at Suvla Bay at Gallipoli on 18 August 1915 and after four months serving on the peninsula they returned to Egypt.

In December 1915 Reg was at Mena Camp in

Cairo when the orders to evacuate Gallipoli were issued and in January 1916 the Warwickshire Yeomanry combined with those of the Gloucestershire and Worcestershire to form the 5th Mounted Brigade. Early in January 1916 they moved by train from Cairo to Salhia and in March crossed the desert to camp at Ballah, where they carried out escort and patrol duties for some weeks. April brought a further advance to Hamisah and on 19 April they had their first contact with the Turks, when a troop was surrounded and one man killed, but they managed to hold off the enemy and the advance continued to a new railway east of Katia. During August they saw action during the Battle of Rumani at Hod-Abu-Adi and Seifanlya. In September they had three days' leave in Port Said as preparations were being made for a further advance through Eastern Egypt into Palestine. After the Turks had evacuated the "*most important strategic point in Eastern Egypt*" there followed a victory at Rafah on 9 January 1917 which opened the way for the advance into Palestine. The next few months saw the Yeomanry advance north through Palestine and on 8 November 1917 Reg took part in the cavalry charge at Huj. The Turks were in full retreat and the pursuit began during which the Warwickshire Yeomanry distinguished themselves. "*A fine charge by squadrons of the Warwickshire and Worcestershire Yeomanry captured 12 guns and broke the resistance of a hostile rearguard.*" In the words of General Shea, it was "*worthy of the best traditions of the British Cavalry*".

In March 1918 it was announced that the Warwickshire Yeomanry was to be disbanded and form two companies of the 100th (Warwickshire and South Nottinghamshire) Battalion of the Machine Gun Corps for service on the Western Front. On 22 May they embarked on HMT *Leasow Castle* and left Egypt four days later. One day out to sea, 27 May, they were struck by a torpedo and sank. Reg survived by jumping into the warm sea and was picked up by an escorting Japanese destroyer. After their return to Alexandria the journey continued on HMS *Caledonia* and after a brief period of leave in England they arrived at Etaples on 25 August and their tour of duty in France began. They saw action at the Battle of Epehy in September 1918 and at Le Cateau in October as the British Army pushed the Germans back until hostilities ceased on the Western Front on 11 November.

Reg was discharged from the army in 1919 and returned to Campden, where he lived at 8, Aston Road in a house built by the Council for returning servicemen. The house had an acre of land and he used it to start his market gardening business. In 1926 he married Gladys Emily Curtis, whose father, Walter Curtis, came to Campden in 1902 with the Guild of Handicraft as a cabinetmaker. Reg and Gladys had three children: Richard, Rosemary and John.

As his business grew Reg bought more land and built Berrington Orchards in Station Road, and they moved there in 1934. This became the family home and business for many years.

On his retirement Reg and Gladys moved to "The Orchard" in Back Ends, where they had many happy years. Gladys died in April 1980 and Reg in January 1981 aged 89 years. They are both buried in St. James's churchyard, Campden.

During the Second World War Reg was an air raid warden in Campden and was then instrumental in reviving Scuttlebrook Wake. He was its chairman for 26 years.

Tom Smith
Private 17510, "C" Company, 10th Battalion, Gloucestershire Regiment

Born: 1895
Enlisted: January 1915
Died: 25 September 1915

Tom was baptised at St. James's Church on 24 March 1895 and was the third son of George and Eliza Smith of Paul's Pike. After leaving school he was employed as a farm labourer on Mr. Keyte's farm at Kingcombe, Campden.

In January 1915 Tom and his cousin, William Hedges, enlisted in Campden in the Gloucestershire Regiment and they were posted to the 10th Battalion for final training on Salisbury Plain before they were sent to France. At 7.00am on 8 August 1915 the battalion left Number 6 Camp at Sutton Veny and three trains carried them to Southampton. At 5.00pm they left Southampton and arrived at Le Havre the next day, where they disembarked at 7.00am. After waiting on the quayside for an hour they marched to a rest camp. The day was very hot and the roads were very difficult to march on with heavily loaded packs and new boots. At 12.30am on 11 August they boarded a train at Le Havre "*Gare des Marchandises*" and arrived at Saint Omer at 7.30am. There was a shortage of water on the journey and the men were travelling forty to a covered truck. On 19 August they went into the trenches for the first time and the next few days were spent gaining experience of life in the front line.

The battalion was very soon in serious action at the Battle of Loos which started on 25 September. Loos-en-Gohelle was a small mining village just to the north-west of Lens and seven British divisions were to attack across terrain that was in general flat, offering little cover and exposed to German fire from slightly higher positions. The attack began at 6.30am and was preceded by the release of gas forty minutes earlier. The 10th Glosters were in the centre of the British line, leading the attack in three lines on a long, low ridge towards the village of Hulloch. Gas was being used by the British for the first time and initially caused panic in the German trenches, but the wind changed direction and it was blown back towards the British lines. The battalion fought their way forward and were exposed to continuous machine gun fire but they found gaps in the German wire and entered their trenches. Heavy resistance was met but they managed to advance to the German third defensive line. By now the casualties to the battalion were horrendous and when they regrouped at night only 60 men from it had not become casualties. Tom was reported missing at the end of the day and the *Evesham Journal* reported that "*no news has been received of him by his father since September 14*". Another report in the same edition of the Journal stated that "*Willie Hedges from the Pike got killed and Tom Smith wounded*".

Tom was killed, in fact, on the first day of the battle. He was 20 years old. As his body could not be identified at the end of the battle he has no known grave and his name is recorded on the Loos Memorial at Dud Corner Cemetery, near Loos-en-Gohelle. It is also recorded on memorials in Campden (in St. James's Church and in the High Street), Aston-sub-Edge and Mickleton.

William Smith
Private 6512, Royal Defence Corps

Born: 1873
Enlisted: 23 March 1915
Discharged: 13 August 1918
Died: August 1951

William was born in Campden, the son of John and Elizabeth Smith, and was baptised at St. James's Church on 31 August 1873. He married Beatrice Warner, daughter of William Wyatt Warner, at St. James's Church on 28 June 1905 and their only son, William Evans Smith, was baptised on 16 December 1906. The family home was in Watery Lane and he worked with his father as a builder for many years. When his father retired he went to work for J. W. Pyment and Sons.

During the war William was employed on home service with the Royal Defence Corps for a period of 3 years and 144 days before he was discharged in London on 13 August 1918 as no longer physically fit for active service. His discharge papers held at the National Archives state that he was five feet five inches tall with brown eyes, dark brown hair and a fresh complexion.

The Royal Defence Corps was a corps of the British Army formed in August 1917 and disbanded in 1936. It was initially formed by converting the (home service) Garrison battalions of line infantry regiments. Garrison battalions were composed of soldiers either too old or medically unfit for active front-line service. The role of the regiment was to provide troops for security and guard duties inside the United Kingdom, guarding important locations such as ports or bridges. It also provided independent companies for guarding prisoner-of-war camps. The regiment was never intended to be employed on overseas service.

After the war William joined the British Legion and was a member of St. James's Church Choir for forty years. He died in August 1951 aged 78 and is buried in St. James's churchyard. He was survived by his wife, who died in 1956 aged 81 years.

William Allen Smith
Royal Warwickshire Regiment
Army Service Corps

Born: 1885

William was born in Campden, the eldest son of George and Eliza Smith, and was baptised at St. James's Church on 30 August 1885. His father was an agricultural labourer and married Eliza Toft on 4 April 1885 at St. James's Church in Campden. The family home was in Broad Entry, Campden in 1891 and then at Paul's Pike in 1901.

William was one of three sons of George and Eliza to serve in the army during the war. Tom was killed in action in 1915 and George returned safely at the end of the war. His cousin, William Hedges, was killed in action in 1915 and in October 1915 the *Evesham Journal* published a letter that William wrote to his father from St. Andrew's Soldiers' Home in Aldershot following the Battle of Loos, where his cousin and brother both lost their lives. It should be noted that Tom was originally reported missing in action: *"Oh, how sorry I am to hear the sad news. I send my deepest sympathy to Aunt Bess and Uncle Fred. It's a terrible blow for them. I hope our Tom is not wounded much, but all we can do is to hope for the best. I have seen from the papers that they are getting very heavy fighting in France. I wonder when it will all come to an end. It's awful to see the young chaps here who have been crippled and knocked useless. Why do you keep wishing that I will not go out? I think I should be a coward if I stopped in England when my own brothers and relations are falling trying to keep back a foe that is anxious to serve this home of ours the same as they have France and other places. I feel it's the duty of every British man who is fit to give his services and so I feel we all must do our bit, trusting God will bring us comfort in our hour of need."*

William served in France with the Army Service Corps during the war. He also served in the Royal Warwickshire Regiment but it has not been possible to find out when or why he was transferred.

William Frederick Danvers Smith, Lord Hambleden
Lieutenant-Colonel, 1st Royal Devonshire Yeomanry

Born: 12 August 1868
Died: 16 June 1928

Lord Hambleden was the son of the Rt. Hon. William Henry Smith and Emily Danvers, Viscountess Hambleden. During the war he arrived in Gallipoli in October 1915 as a lieutenant-colonel with the 1st Royal Devonshire Yeomanry and in 1922 he was made Honorary Colonel of the Royal Devonshire Yeomanry Artillery.

In 1913 he became the 2nd Viscount Hambleden, of Hambleden in the County of Buckingham, following the death of his mother. The title was first created in 1891 for his mother, in honour of her deceased husband.

In 1891 he succeeded his father as Member of Parliament for the Strand constituency, holding the seat until January 1910. He became involved in the management of the family business, W. H. Smith's, which was founded by his grandfather, William Henry Smith, and when he died in 1928 he owned the whole of the business.

Lord Hambleden married Esther Georgiana Caroline Gore, daughter of Sir Arthur Saunders William Charles Fox Gore, the 5th Earl of Arran, on 26 July 1894 and they had five children: Edith Mabel Emily, William Henry, James Frederick Arthur, David John and Margaret Esther Lucie. When he died on 16 June 1928 aged 59 his eldest son, William Henry, became the 3rd Viscount Hambleden.

Lord Hambleden is included on the prayer list of servicemen produced by St. James's Church, Campden in 1916. His connection with the area is through his sister, Mabel Danvers Smith, who married John Herbert Dudley Ryder, the 5th Earl of Harrowby.

Norman Verdina Somerville
Stoker First Class K34701, Royal Navy

Born: 3 September 1896
Enlisted: 24 June 1916
Discharged: 4 February 1919

Norman was born in Huddersfield on 3 September 1896, the son of John George and Florence Somerville. His parents took over the running of the gasworks in Campden in the years leading up to the war and Norman stated his occupation as a "*gasworks foreman*" on his Royal Navy enlistment papers.

At the age of 20 he enlisted in the Royal Navy as a stoker second class in June 1916 and he began his period of service at HMS *Victory*, a Royal Navy depot near Portsmouth. He was promoted to the rank of stoker first class in September 1916 and in June 1917 he was posted to HMS *Tartar*. HMS *Tartar* was built in 1907 and was the fastest ship of her day. In September 1914 she joined 6th Flotilla and was part of the Dover Patrol for most of the war. In November 1918 she was stationed at Blyth with the 11th Submarine Flotilla and was decommissioned in 1921.

In November 1917 Norman was transferred to HMS *Titania*, a submarine depot ship, and he remained with her until he was discharged from the Royal Navy on 4 February 1919.

Norman was listed as absent on the 1918 electoral roll for Campden owing to his service with the Royal Navy. His residence was listed as the High Street and his parents were still working at the gasworks.

James Stanbridge
Lance Corporal, "B" Company, 15th (Reserve) Bn., Gloucestershire Regiment
Corporal 33343, 2nd Battalion, Royal Berkshire Regiment

Born: 15 May 1884
Died: 11 July 1961

James was born in Dorking in Surrey, an only child, and in 1901, at the age of 16, he was employed as a footman for Herbert Swift, a retired barrister, in Paddington, London. On 26 December 1908 he married Mary Ann Gillman in Ipswich and their only child, a daughter called Rose, was born in 1913. He then found employment as a gardener with Rev. Hitchcock and came to Campden with him when he became the vicar of St. James's Church.

At the outbreak of war he enlisted in the Gloucestershire Regiment and was posted to the 15th Reserve Battalion. After a period of home service he was transferred to the Royal Berkshire Regiment and was

sent to France. In August 1917 he was serving with the 2nd Battalion in Belgium during the Third Battle of Ypres when he was wounded. This was reported in the Reading Mercury on 11 August 1917.

James was evacuated back to England and admitted to hospital at Longleat House in Westminster, London. His wife had originally been notified that James had been killed in action and was extremely relieved when she received a second telegram stating that he was in hospital in England. His daughter Rose remembers going to visit her father in hospital: "*I was put on the bed and told to mind Daddy's bad leg.*"

During his time on the Western Front James received two citations for bravery in the field and this resulted in the award of the Military Medal. In September 1981 his daughter donated James's three medals, Military Medal, British War Medal and Victory Medal, to The Royal Gloucestershire, Berkshire and Wiltshire Regiment Museum

in Salisbury, where they can be viewed.

James recovered from his wounds and spent the last period of his army service in Ireland before he was discharged. After leaving the army he returned to Campden and continued working as a gardener at the Vicarage. When Rev. Hitchcock retired and moved to Saintbury James went with him. A few years later James moved to Essex.

His daughter Rose informed the author that her father "*never spoke about his*

Room 14, Number 7 Squad, Tidworth 1916
James is seated in the middle row second from the left. He is wearing his Gloucestershire Regiment uniform.

Lce. Cpl. James Stanbridge, Gloucestershire Regiment, is seated on the right.

experiences in the trenches in the 1914-18 war. He said it was too awful. He very seldom joined in any ex-servicemen's parades. I think he just wanted to forget the horrors of the trenches."

In 1942, during the Second World War, Rose joined the Air Training Service and ended the war as a sergeant. This made James very proud as he ended the 1914-18 war as a corporal.

James died on 11 July 1961 aged 77 and is buried in Weymouth.

Alfred Louis Standbrook
Pioneer 161928, Railway Troops Depot, Royal Engineers

> Born: 1892
> Enlisted: 15 April 1916
> Discharged: 3 October 1916
> Died: 14 January 1949

Alfred was born in Campden, the son of Alfred Joseph and Annie Catharine Standbrook of Lower High Street, and was baptised at St. Catharine's Church on 28 August 1892. He enlisted in the Royal Engineers on 15 April 1916 and his attestation papers state that he was five feet four inches tall with blue eyes and hair that was turning grey. He was a labourer by trade.

After a short period on home service he was posted to France on 17 May 1916, where he remained for four months before he arrived back in England on 16 September. The following month he was discharged from the army at Aldershot as no longer physically fit for active service after a period of 172 days with the Royal Engineers. His conduct and character throughout were very good.

Alfred died at Radcliffe Hospital in Oxford on 14 January 1949 aged 56 and is buried in St. Catharine's cemetery in Campden.

Frederick Eli Stembridge
Pioneer 181815, 30th Railway Labour Battalion, Royal Engineers

> Born: 1876
> Enlisted: 19 November 1915
> Discharged: 15 July 1918

When the war started in 1914 Fred was living in Watery Lane, Campden with his pregnant wife, Louisa. Their daughter, Gwendoline Dorothy, was born on 2 December 1914.

On 19 November 1915 Fred enlisted in Campden, where he was recruited by Colonel Paley and Sergeant Bill Beckett. On his attestation form he gave his age as 36, although he was actually 39 years old. He was immediately put into the Army Reserve before being mobilised on 14 June 1916 and posted to the 30th Railway Labour Battalion, Royal Engineers. After a period of initial training in England he left for Egypt as part of the Egyptian Expeditionary Force on 14 July 1916. The next twenty-two months were spent building and maintaining railways in Egypt.

Fred arrived back in England on 22 May 1918 and almost immediately he became ill and was admitted to 3rd Southern General Hospital in Oxford. He left hospital on 28 June and was sent home to Campden to await his discharge from the army, which came on 15 July owing to "sickness". His service papers state that he was "no longer physically fit for war service due to malaria and old trachoma".

The last unit that Fred served with was 270th Railway Labour Company and the officer commanding the unit said that Fred was "reliable and intelligent".

James Cornelius Stevens
Flight Sub-Lieutenant, Royal Naval Air Service

> Born: 25 September 1891
> Enlisted: 20 June 1906

Con was born at 2, Ryland Cottages, Ryland Street, Ladywood, Birmingham, the son of Cornelius and Annie Elizabeth Stevens. At the time of his birth his father was a schoolmaster on board the industrial training ship Clio, which was moored off Bangor, North Wales.

After leaving school Con found employment as a warehouse boy before he enlisted in the Royal Navy at Portsmouth on 20 June 1906 when he was 14 years old. He was five feet four inches tall with light brown hair, grey eyes and a fresh complexion. He began his service as a boy second class at HMS *Ganges,* a base and training depot at Harwich, before joining HMS *Impregnable*, a training ship at Devonport, on 20 October 1906. Promotion to boy first class came in February 1907 and on 15 September 1908 he signed on for 12 years' service with the Royal Navy and his medical examination recorded that he had grown to five feet eight inches tall and now had blue eyes and a fair complexion.

Further promotion followed and he became an able seaman on 1 October 1908 while serving on HMS *Prince of Wales*. He held this rank for the next four years and on 6 September 1910 he passed the examinations required for him to apply for the rank of petty officer.

In 1912 he was sent to Farnborough for an airship course and then joined the Royal Naval Air Service as an able seaman on 1 January 1913. He was promoted to leading seaman on 25 February 1913 and then while he was attached to HMS *Pembroke,* a depot at Chatham, he became a petty officer mechanic on 1 July 1914.

At the outbreak of the war Con was still attached to HMS *Pembroke* and he remained there until he transferred to HMS *President*, the accounting base for the RNAS, on 1 April 1915. By 1917 he had been promoted to a flight sub-lieutenant and while home on leave he married Dorcas Mary Payne, known as Dora, daughter of William and Matilda Payne of

Father and son: Con and Barry Stevens, Royal Air Force, 1939-45

Flag Close, Campden. Their eldest son, Barry Osborne Cornelius Stevens, was baptised at St. James's Church on 23 December 1917 and the family home was in Lower High Street, Campden.

After leaving school Barry successfully passed through the Royal Air Force College at Cranwell and was granted a permanent commission as a pilot officer on 17 December 1938. His father was still serving with the Royal Air Force when the Second World War started. He was a squadron leader but was soon promoted to wing commander. This was announced in the *London Gazette* on 1 July 1941.

Harry Stilwell
Lance Corporal 13259, 26th Field Company, Royal Engineers

Born: 1884

Harry was born in Godalming in Surrey, the eldest son of Harry and Ellen Stilwell. After leaving school he joined his father as a bricklayer and at the time of his marriage in 1913 he was living at 87, Brighton Road, Busbridge. He married Emma Gillman at Busbridge Parish Church on 3 September 1913.

After his marriage he became a regular soldier. At the outbreak of war he was mobilised and arrived in France with the 26th Field Company, Royal Engineers on 17 August 1914. He remained on the Western Front throughout the war. His field company was attached to the 1st Division and was involved in all of the major battles on the Western Front.

On 13 January 1918 his son, Frederick Harold Stilwell, was baptised at St. James's Church in Campden and the family home was at Busbridge, Godalming, Surrey.

Bert Howard Sullivan
Private 4226, Worcestershire Regiment
Private 437608, Royal Army Medical Corps

Enlisted: 27 May 1915
Discharged: 1 August 1919

In Campden British Legion there is a framed discharge certificate that was issued to Bert. He enlisted in the Worcestershire Regiment on 27 May 1915 and entered a theatre of war after the start of 1916. After being transferred to the Royal Army Medical Corps he returned to England to be discharged from the army as no longer fit for active service aged 24 years and 2 months. A Silver War Badge was issued to indicate that he had made his contribution to the war.

Denys Keith Sworder
Lieutenant, Royal Flying Corps

Born: 20 February 1884
Enlisted: 21 January 1916
Died: 11 August 1964

Denys was born in Barham Court, near Canterbury in Kent, the fifth son of Edward Robert Sworder. His father married Eliza Shepherd in 1877 and the 1891 census records that the family were living in White Hill House, White Hill, Luton. In 1901 they had moved to Bedford St. Peter.

On 7 November 1905 Denys embarked at Liverpool on board a ship called *Ivernia* and his port of destination was Boston, USA. He soon joined his two brothers, Ronald and Kenneth, in California; they had both emigrated in 1902. In 1910 Denys was living with Ronald in Armona, California and was employed as a labourer on a fruit farm.

At the outbreak of war Denys returned to England and obtained a commission in the Royal Flying Corps on 21 January 1916. He joined 4 Squadron in France on 15 September 1916 and for the next eight months he served on the Western Front, where he flew B.E.2c two-seater aircraft engaged on reconnaissance, ground attack and artillery observation duties. He was shot down three times. The third occasion was on 24 March 1917, when he was severely wounded. A medical report states that *"when flying in France he was hit by a bullet on the outer surface of the right ankle. It passed through, fracturing the lower end of the right fibula. After being wounded he crashed to the ground and was unconscious for 3 to 4 days."* Denys crashed at Ervillers in France and his observer, Air Mechanic 2nd Class 61782, James Boon, from Cleethorpes, was killed in the incident.

The next three weeks were spent in a Red Cross hospital at le Touquet in France before he embarked on HS *Laufranc* at Le Havre on 17 April 1917. He arrived at Poole the following day after his hospital ship had been torpedoed and was admitted to Cornelia Hospital. In June 1917 he was admitted to a Royal Flying Corps convalescent hospital and his condition was monitored each month by a medical board. In March 1918 a doctor reported: *"The right ankle is still stiff after 2 or 3 miles walking but there is practically no deformity or disability except that he complains that the toes cannot be flexed or extended as readily as before. The effects of the concussion have practically disappeared."*

Denys was, however, suffering headaches after flying for over two hours or after flying over 4000 feet. He had by now flown over 330 hours but was graded as having a 25% flying disability and *"unfit for high or prolonged flights"*. He was not fit for active service abroad. The remainder of the war was spent on home service as a flying officer at Number 1 School of Navigation and Bomb Dropping at Stonehenge on Salisbury Plain and at the training depot at Stamford.

It was while he was stationed at the training depot in Stamford that he married Jeannette Huyshe, daughter of Wentworth and Hester Ann Huyshe of Campden, at Willesden Roman Catholic Church on 20 December 1917. They had two children, who were baptised at St. Catharine's Church in Campden before the family left the town in 1923. They embarked at Southampton on 30 January 1923 on a Cunard steamship called *Mauretania* and after arriving in New York they made the journey to California where they again lived with Ronald, who was now living in Visalia. By 1930 the family had their own home in Hanford, California and Denys was employed as a farm labourer. He then managed a motel in King City, California before returning to Fresno, where he lived until his death on 11 August 1964 aged 80 years.

John George Mansell Taplin
Sergeant 2285, 1st/5th Battalion, Gloucestershire Regiment
Sergeant 240473, 2nd/5th Battalion, Gloucestershire Regiment

Born: 15 September 1896

Jack was born in Campden, the eldest son of George Mansell and Sarah Taplin of Sheep Street, and was baptised at St. James's Church on 10 January 1897. His father, a carpenter by trade, was born in Blockley.

Jack was educated in the town and then joined his father as a carpenter. He was a member of "H" Company, 5th Battalion, Gloucestershire Regiment, the local company of the Territorial Army, and on 5 August 1914 he was mobilised. The battalion went to Chelmsford in Essex for training as they prepared to be posted to France and all of the Campden men joined "D" Company, 1st/5th Battalion.

When the battalion embarked for France on 29 March 1915 Jack stayed behind in England and was posted to 2nd/5th Battalion, Gloucestershire Regiment, where he joined Gerry Howell and Tom Bickley, two friends from Campden. A period of training in England followed before the battalion left Salisbury Plain on 24 May 1916. They arrived at Southampton later that day to board HMS *681*, the ship that was going to transport them to France. They arrived at Le Havre early on the morning of 25 May and the battalion made their way towards the French village of Laventie. Their first experience of life in front line trenches came on 15 June.

In 1917 Jack was wounded and from hospital he sent a cheerful letter to his mother: *"I have been wounded in the forehead by a rifle grenade, and am now having a fine time of it, and I could do with being here for the duration of the war."*

The *Evesham Journal* reported in 1918 that *"Mrs. George Taplin, of Campden, has received the news that her eldest son, Sergeant John Taplin, of the Territorials, who is serving in France, has been promoted to Sergeant, and that he has been awarded the Military Medal."* The Military Medal was awarded for most conspicuous gallantry and devotion to duty in action and the award was announced in the *London Gazette* on 11 February 1918. The report went on to say that his mother had also received a field postcard stating, *"He has been wounded and admitted to hospital. This makes the third time that Sergt. Taplin has been wounded."*

After leaving the army Jack returned to Campden but in the 1920's he left the town and went to live in West London. His parents moved to 5, Aston Road, Campden, a house built by the Council for returning soldiers. His sister, Norah Angelina, a VAD nurse during the war, continued to live in the house after her parents had both died until her death in 1988. The house then became known as "Taplins", a bed and breakfast establishment.

Miriam Dora Taplin
Voluntary Aid Detachment (VAD) Nurse

Born: 30 June 1899

Miriam was the youngest daughter of George and Sarah Taplin of Sheep Street, Campden. She was baptised at St. James's Church on 4 December 1901 and attended school in the town. During the war she worked as a nurse at Norton Hall VAD Hospital near Mickleton with her sister Norah.

In 1909 the Voluntary Aid Detachment was formed to provide medical assistance in time of war. VAD hospitals opened in most large towns in the country and volunteers worked as assistant nurses, ambulance drivers and cooks. In 1915 volunteers over 23 years old who had more than three months' experience were allowed to work overseas in theatres of war. Katharine Furse was the Commander-in-Chief of the organisation during the 1914-18 war.

Norah Angelina Taplin
Voluntary Aid Detachment (VAD) Nurse

Born: 30 January 1898
Died: December 1988

Norah was the eldest daughter of George and Sarah Taplin of Sheep Street Campden and during the war she was a nurse at Norton Hall VAD Hospital near Mickleton. After the war she lived with her parents at 5, Aston Road in Campden in a house built by the Council for returning soldiers. She continued to live on her own in the house after her parents died until her death in 1988. She was 90 years old.

Norah's mother, Sarah, was the daughter of Polly Waine, an old Campden character. Polly's father, William Bayliss, fought at the Battle of Waterloo. He was born in 1792 and as a young man enlisted at Worcester in the 39th Regiment of Foot. After the Battle of Waterloo he was sent to India until November 1836. William was discharged from the army when he was 46 years old after twenty-four years' service.

William Randolph Victor Taplin

Born: 24 January 1901

Bill was the youngest son of George Mansell and Sarah Taplin of Lower High Street. He was baptised at St. James's Church on 4 December 1901 and went to school in the town. His father was a carpenter by trade and Bill became a bricklayer after leaving school.

Bill was too young to join his brother in France during the war but he did enlist in the army, serving in Ireland during the post-war years. He was still serving in the army in 1922 as he was listed as absent on the electoral roll.

After the war Bill lived with his parents at 5, Aston Road in Campden in a house built by the Council for returning servicemen. He married Lilian Winifred Reynolds and they had three children: Martin, John and Judith.

Bill died in Ireland in the early 1980's.

Edward Charles Taylor
Royal Navy

Charles was born in Campden on 1 August 1899, the third son of Reuben and Eliza Gertrude Taylor of Watery Lane, and was baptised at St. James's Church on 14 July 1912, when he was 12 years old. His father, an agricultural carter and a native of Honeybourne, married Eliza Clayton, a native of Campden, in 1890. The 1910 and 1914 electoral rolls list Reuben and Eliza living in Lower High Street.

Charles enlisted in the Royal Navy during the war and the 1918, 1922 and 1926 electoral rolls list him as resident in Broad Entry, Campden and absent serving in the Royal Navy.

William Thomas Thornton
Private, Royal Engineers

Born: 5 March 1871
Died: 28 February 1948

Bill was born on 5 March 1871 and after leaving school he served an apprenticeship as a blacksmith in London. He came to Campden in 1902 when Charles Ashbee arrived with the Guild of Handicraft. He served a total of fourteen years with the Guild. When the Guild disbanded he continued working as an ornamental blacksmith in Campden and was in partnership with Charlie Downer until the Second World War.

He married Dedamia Catherine Maria Laker in the registration district of Cuckfield in Sussex in 1899 and they had four daughters: Dedamia Catharine Maria, Elsie Lillian Maria, Edith Annie and Maria Agnes. The first three were baptised together at St. Catharine's Catholic Church in Campden on 24 December 1909.

The family home in Campden changed several times and Bill lived in Westington, Blakeman Cottage in Lower High Street by the Catholic Church, High Street by Cutts' Garage, Elm Tree House in the High Street and at 5, Sheep Street, where he was living when he died.

When the war started in 1914 Bill was 43 years old and, together with Charlie Downer, he worked in a munitions factory. He later enlisted in the Royal Engineers and served in France.

Bill died on 28 February 1948 aged 76 and is buried in St. Catharine's cemetery. His wife died on 2 January 1933 aged 59 years.

John Tomes
Sergeant 6/3489, 1st Battalion, Canterbury Regiment, New Zealand Expeditionary Force
Private 810286, Vital Points Guard
Aircraftman First Class 432130, Royal New Zealand Air Force

Born: 4 October 1893
Enlisted: 5 June 1915
Discharged: 2 March 1919

Jack was born in Campden, the son of John and Alice Tomes. He emigrated to New Zealand before the outbreak of war in 1914 and found employment as a labourer with a gold-mining company. He was living at Hutchinson Avenue, New Lynn in Auckland when he enlisted in the Canterbury Regiment following a medical examination which passed him fit for overseas service on 5 June 1915. He was five feet eleven inches tall with dark brown hair, brown eyes and a dark complexion.

Jack was posted for service on 24 August 1915 and after four months of training he embarked for Egypt and disembarked at Suez on 20 December 1915. He joined the 1st Battalion, Canterbury Regiment at Ismailia on 9 January 1916 and on 6 April they embarked for France at Port Said. On 16 September he was wounded in action and admitted to a casualty clearing station before being evacuated to Number 3 General Hospital at le Tréport. After being discharged from hospital he was posted to a base depot until he rejoined his unit at the front on 19 October. He served at the front until he was accidentally wounded on 17 August 1917 and was admitted to hospital at Rouen. He rejoined his unit on 25 October in Belgium and was promoted to sergeant on 26 November.

The battalion was in trenches east of Ypres in the area of Polderhoek and Jack was awarded the Military Medal for *"acts of gallantry in the field"* in operations opposite Polderhoek between 27 November and 5 December. The citation reads: *"For conspicuous gallantry and devotion to duty. On 3 December 1917, about mid-day, during the attack on the château, this N.C.O. was in command of a section of the attacking troops. Soon after the attack commenced his Platoon Commander became a casualty and this N.C.O. immediately assumed command of the Platoon and led it forward under heavy hostile rifle and machine gun fire, showing great coolness and brilliant leadership. He continuously sent in valuable situation reports to his Company Commander. His splendid behaviour throughout the whole operation was an example to all his company."*

Sergeant Jack Tomes, Campden, 1918
He is wearing two wound stripes and his
Military Medal ribbon.

Following the award of the Military Medal Jack was granted leave to Paris on 5 January 1918. He returned from leave on 14 January and was again wounded when he was hit in the left wrist by a bullet on 27 March during the German Spring offensive. He was admitted to hospital in France before he was invalided back to England on 31 March and admitted to hospital at Walton-on-Thames. On 29 April he was transferred to a New Zealand convalescent hospital at Hornchurch and while he was there he was reprimanded on 24 June for *"neglecting to obey hospital orders by leaving letters lying in his bed during an inspection"*.

Jack was able to return to his home town on 4 October 1918 when he was granted *"agricultural leave at Campden"* until 4 November. It was during this period that he met up with several other Campden soldiers and a group photograph was taken at the Eight Bells pub. After leaving Campden he embarked for New Zealand on 19 December and was discharged from the army on 2 March 1919 after serving with the New Zealand army for 3 years and 191 days.

Jack returned home to Auckland and when the Second World War started he was still single but had moved to 138, Grey's Avenue in Auckland and was employed as a bushman. He enlisted in the Vital Points Guard on 11 July 1940, when he was 46 years old, and on 20 July was placed into an area pool. He then enlisted in the Royal New Zealand Air Force at Waipapakauri on 29 March 1943 and served for a period of 1 year and 213 days in New Zealand before he was discharged on 28 October 1944. His conduct through this period of service, carrying out general duties with the works section, was *"very good"*.

Jack married Marjory Maureen Phillips on 25 August 1943 at Auckland and after the war they continued living in Auckland.

Albert Edward Tooke
Devonshire Regiment

Albert was born in Ormesby near Middlesbrough in 1881, the eldest son of Albert Edward and Mary E. Tooke. In 1891 the family were living in Thornaby, not far from Ormesby, and his father, a native of Norfolk, was employed as a general labourer. Albert married Mary Eaton at Lymm Parish Church, Cheshire, on 8 February 1908 and at the time of the wedding was working as a gentleman's servant in St. George's, Hanover Square in London. His father's profession was also recorded as a gentleman's servant on the wedding certificate.

In 1914 Albert was living in Station Road, Campden and working as a laundryman. His son, Harold, was born in 1914 and baptised at St. James's Church on 19 July 1914.

During the war Albert enlisted in the army and was posted to the Devonshire Regiment, where he appears to have been employed on home service only.

Augustus Arthur Tout
Sergeant 10683, 8th Battalion, Devonshire Regiment

Born: 3 January 1882
Discharged: 22 May 1919
Died: 4 February 1969

Augustus was born in Devon and lived in the county until the outbreak of the war in 1914, when he volunteered to join the Devonshire Regiment. He was posted to the 8th Battalion and arrived in France on 25 July 1915. The battalion was involved in heavy fighting during the Battle of the Somme and he was awarded the Military Medal for gallant service at the front. This was announced in the *London Gazette* on 1 September 1916.

Augustus was promoted to sergeant in 1916 and ended the war in Mesopotamia. He was wounded three times during the war, once in the leg, once in the arm and once in the neck. He qualified as a Lewis gunner and was once court-martialled by a young officer new to the front for being "*asleep at his post*". The case was dismissed and Augustus was not punished.

Augustus returned to England from Mesopotamia in 1919 and was discharged from the army on 25 July 1919 when he was 37 years old. He then lived in Sheep Street in Campden but in 1920 he left the town and married Rose Loveday. They had three sons: Sidney, Walter (killed in action in 1944) and Harold. Two of his sisters married Campden men: Laura Tout married Sidney Biggerstaff and Beatrice Tout married Reginald Williams.

After leaving Campden he worked on the railway at Nailsworth until he was 60 years old and the family home was at 6, Sunnybrook in Sharpness. He died on 4 February 1969 aged 87 and is buried in Berkeley Cemetery near Sharpness.

Archibald Edgar Tracey
Private 2465, Royal Warwickshire Regiment

Born: 19 July 1889
Enlisted: 3 September 1914
Discharged: 15 May 1916
Died: 26 March 1965

Archie was born in Broad Campden, the son of William Henry and Ann Tracey, and was baptised at St. James's Church on 4 September 1892. His brother William died in South Africa during the Boer War and he lost two other brothers, Harry and Richard, during the 1914-18 war.

Archie moved to Birmingham before the outbreak of war and married Evangeline Bowerman in 1914. He enlisted in the Royal Warwickshire Regiment and embarked at Southampton on 22 March 1915 as part of 143rd Brigade, 48th (South Midland) Division. They arrived at Le Havre and boarded a train which took them north to Cassel, where they then marched to billets.

Archie spent the next month in the Armentières sector before he was seriously wounded on 4 April 1915 and admitted to a French hospital. He was evacuated back to England but failed to recover fully from his wounds and was discharged from the army as no longer fit for active service on 15 May 1916. A Silver War Badge was issued.

After his first wife died he moved back to Campden and married Lily Gowens, an old sweetheart from his early days in the town, and they lived in the Almshouses. Archie died on 26 March 1965 and is buried in St. James's churchyard.

George Tracey
Sergeant, 9891, Portsmouth Division, Royal Marines

Born: 25 November 1868
Enlisted: 25 May 1889
Discharged: 17 March 1919

George was born in Campden, the eldest son of William Henry Tracey, and was baptised at St. James's Church on 25 December 1868. His father had married Ann Lee at St. James's Church on 8 December 1866.

After leaving school George found employment as a labourer but soon progressed to become an engineer. On 25 May 1889, when he was 20 years old, he enlisted at Cirencester in the Royal Marines. He was five feet seven inches tall with light brown hair, blue eyes and a fresh complexion. There was a scar on the back of his right leg and his religion was Church of England. After a period of home service he joined the crew of HMS *Warspite* on 23 December 1890 and served on her until he returned to England on 25 June 1893. He was then posted to the Plymouth Division and remained with them at their depot until he was sent to Gosport on 31 May 1899.

George returned to the Portsmouth Division on 20 June 1899 and when he embarked on HMS *Duke of Wellington* on 4 November 1902 he had been promoted to the rank of corporal. He was transferred to HMS *Fire Queen* in October 1903 and then returned to England in December 1904. Further promotion followed on 1 August 1908 when he became a sergeant and he remained on home service until the outbreak of war in 1914.

When Great Britain declared war on Germany George was 45 years old and was serving on HMS *Hermione*. He returned to the Portsmouth Division depot on 1 April 1915 and then on 23 April 1915 he embarked on RMS *Arlanza,* which saw wartime service as an armed merchant cruiser. George left the ship on 24 November 1915 and returned to the Portsmouth Division at their base in Deal where he spent the rest of the war. George was discharged from the Royal Marines on 17 March 1919 after almost 30 years' service. His conduct and character were at all times "*very good*".

During his time with the Royal Marines he qualified as a marksman in 1902, passed a swimming test on 31 January 1899, graded able to swim, and achieved a second class education certificate in 1890. He was also awarded a Long Service and Good Conduct Medal in August 1904

After being demobilised George returned to his wife, Caroline, who was living in Queen Street, Avonmouth, Bristol.

Harry Tracey
Private 9579, 1st Battalion, Worcestershire Regiment

Born: 7 September 1883
Enlisted: 31 October 1905
Died: 13 March 1915

Harry was born in Broad Campden, the fifth son of William Henry and Ann Tracey. His brother William died of dysentery in 1899 in South Africa during the Boer War and his brother Richard was killed in action in 1914.

Harry's name on the memorial at le Touret in France.

Harry went to school in Campden and then found employment as a labourer before he enlisted in the Royal Artillery. He only served for 99 days before he returned home to help support his parents. He then enlisted in the Worcestershire Regiment in Worcester on 31 October 1905, when he was 22 years old. His attestation papers state that he had blue eyes and light brown hair and his religion was Church of England. A period of home service followed before he was posted to India, where he arrived on 5 December 1906. After almost six years in India he returned to England on 23 October 1912 and was then posted to the Army Reserve on 31 October. While he was in the Reserve he emigrated to Australia but he returned to England when war was declared in August 1914. He was mobilised on 5 August 1914 and posted to 1ˢᵗ Battalion on 30 December but he did not join the battalion in France until 12 January 1915.

The battalion took part in the Battle of Neuve Chapelle, 10-12 March 1915, the British Army's first major offensive of the year. During the German counter-attack of 12 March the battalion held positions between Mauquissart and Neuve Chapelle. They stopped the German advance by rapid rifle fire and then charged with the bayonet and after much hand-to-hand fighting drove the enemy back. An account of this is written in *The Worcestershire Regiment in the Great War* by Captain Stacke: "*The Worcesters had their tails up with a vengeance. They chased the Germans up and down that muddy field like terriers after rats. They pursued them with the bayonet round the trees.*" German records state that "*they suffered very severely and left six hundred dead in No Man's Land*".

On the evening of 12 March 1915 the battalion received orders that they were to make a night attack. Arrangements for the attack were finalised at 11.00pm and the battalion remained lying on the ground, waiting for the orders to advance, until 3.00am of 13 March. It was then that the attack was cancelled and the battalion were ordered to march back to Brigade Reserve on Rue Tilleloy, where they arrived at 4.45am. At 1.00pm orders were received stating that the battalion was to march to billets near Red Barn.

Harry was killed in action in the fields around Neuve Chapelle on 13 March 1915. He was one of 370 casualties that the battalion suffered during the fighting in the area from 10-13 March.

His body was never recovered after the war and his name is recorded on Le Touret Memorial, near Béthune, France. He was 31 years old when he died and his name appears on two memorials in Campden: in St. James's Church and in the High Street.

James Tracey
Private 33107, Royal Defence Corps

Born: 1864
Enlisted: 23 March 1915
Discharged: 26 March 1919

James was born in Broad Campden in 1864, the son of Thomas and Ann Tracey, and was baptised at St. James's Church in Campden on 28 December 1869 when he was 5 years old. After leaving school he found employment as an indoor farm servant with Charles Hopkins at Kingcombe Farm.

His father had married Eliza Esprey, a widow, on 5 June 1864 after the death of James's mother earlier in the same year. He died in 1890 aged 75 and the 1891 census lists James living with his step-mother, Eliza Tracey, in Broad Campden and working as a shepherd..

At the outbreak of war James was 50 years old but this did not stop him from enlisting on 23 March 1915. He was posted to the Royal Defence Corps and spent the next three years on home service before he was discharged on 26 March 1919 owing to sickness.

Joseph Frederick Tracey
Pioneer 117902, Royal Engineers
Private 294752, Labour Corps

Discharged: 17 April 1919
Died: 18 September 1950

Joseph was born in 1875 in Campden, the third son of William Henry and Ann Tracey of Broad Campden. His father, a native of Campden, was employed as a general labourer in 1881, a carter in 1891 and as an ordinary agricultural labourer in 1901.

Joseph was educated in Campden and then found employment as a baker's assistant. His eldest brother, William, died of dysentery in South Africa during the Boer War. Two of his younger brothers, Richard and Harry, lost their lives in the 1914-18 war.

Joseph enlisted in the Royal Engineers in 1914, arriving in France on 2 September 1915, but towards the end of the war he transferred to the Labour Corps. On the 1918 electoral roll he was recorded as living in Watery Lane but absent on military service. After the war he lived in Twine Cottage in Back Ends and found employment at Featherstone Quarries. During the Second World War he was a member of the Home Guard.

He married Emma Cotton from Birmingham and they had a daughter, Josephine, who, after marrying Cyril Buggins, lived in Dover's View, Weston-sub-Edge for many years.

Joseph died on 18 September 1950 aged 75 and is buried in St. James's churchyard in Campden.

Richard Tracey
Private 9593, 3rd Battalion, Worcestershire Regiment

Born: 6 October 1885
Died: 7 November 1914

Richard was born in Broad Campden, the sixth son of William Henry and Ann Tracey, and was baptised at St. James's Church on 8 November 1885. His elder brother William died of dysentery during the Boer War and his brother Harry was killed in action in 1915.

Richard enlisted at Worcester in the Worcestershire Regiment and arrived in France with the 3rd Battalion on 25 August 1914, when he was 28 years old. The battalion were already in action at Mons and Richard joined them during the retreat. The British Army regrouped at the River Marne and an advance to the River Aisne began on 6 September 1914. The battalion crossed the river on 14 September and took up positions in Vailly-sur-Aisne. They moved forward to the firing line the next day and suffered 28 casualties. An enemy attack was repulsed on 20 September but there were 80 casualties.

In October the battalion moved north and on 12 October they took part in an attack at Richebourg St. Vaast, when they came under fire from houses situated along the banks of the Oise. There was a steady advance over the next few days and they bivouacked on the eastern side of the Bois de Biez near Neuve Chapelle on 16 October. The enemy attacked on 21 October and broke the battalion's line. "*A strange dim battle ensued,*" records Captain Stacke in *The Worcestershire Regiment in the Great War.* "*Parties of the enemy would loom out of the mist to be bayoneted or shot at close quarters.*" The lost trenches were retaken before dark.

At the start of November the battalion moved north in buses to the Belgian village of Neuve Eglise. They then advanced via Le Romarin to positions just west of Ploegsteert and the next day took over front line positions on the eastern side of Ploegsteert Wood. Richard was killed on 7 November 1914 when "C" Company's trenches were overrun during an attack by the Germans. The survivors fell back into Ploegsteert Wood and the enemy were checked on the edge of the wood after a counter-attack.

Richard's body was never recovered after the war and his name is listed on the Menin Gate Memorial in Ypres. He was 29 years old when he died and his name is recorded on two memorials in Campden: in St. James's Church and in the High Street.

Harry Joseph Tracy
Trooper 4300, 2nd Life Guards, Household Cavalry

Born: 20 April 1900
Died: 10 July 1974

Harry was born in Horsebridge in Sussex, the fifth of seven children of William Henry and Mary Ann Tracy. William was born in Campden in 1859 and married Mary Ann James in 1887. Their first three children were born in the town but after the birth of their third son, Wilfred Henry, in 1892 they left the town.

After leaving school Harry found employment as a storekeeper but as soon as he was old enough he enlisted in the Household Cavalry and was posted to the 2nd Life Guards as a trooper. He served in France before the end of the war and returned safely. The home address recorded on his attestation papers was 285 St. Leonard's Road, Windsor.

After the war he joined the Metropolitan Police and on 15 December 1928 he married Dorothy Ethel Langworthy. They had two children: Peter Edward and Ella Dorothy.

Harry died on 10 July 1974 aged 74 and is buried in Leicester.

James Basil Tracy
Bombardier 51574, "C" Battery, 150th Brigade, Royal Field Artillery

Born: 9 June 1890
Died: 7 September 1917

James was born in Campden, the second of seven children of William Henry and Mary Ann Tracy, and was baptised in the Catholic Chapel at Campden House on 23 November 1890. William, a native of the town and the youngest of eight children of James and Elizabeth Tracy, married Mary Ann James in 1887. Their first three children, Reginald Hubert, James Basil and Wilfred Henry, were born in the town. The family then left Campden and when James enlisted at Slough in the Royal Field Artillery his home address was listed as 285 St. Leonard's Road, Windsor. He arrived in France on 27 September 1914 but was back in England in 1916 when he married Kathleen Veale and they set up home at 16 Westmoreland Street, Pimlico in London.

James returned to his unit and served in Belgium during the Third Battle of Ypres in 1917. He died of wounds on 7 September 1917 aged 27 and is buried in Mendinghem Military Cemetery, near Proven. Mendinghem, like Dozinghem and Bandaghem, were the popular names given by the troops to groups of casualty clearing stations posted to this area during the First World War.

James does not have his name recorded on any memorials in Campden.

Reginald Hubert Tracy
Private 14289, 2nd Battalion, Grenadier Guards

Born: 15 June 1888
Enlisted: 9 March 1909
Died: 17 March 1915

Hubert was born in Campden, the eldest of seven children of William Henry and Mary Ann Tracy, and was baptised in the Catholic Chapel at Campden House on 15 July 1888. After attending school in the town Hubert found employment as a bricklayer's labourer until he became a regular soldier when he enlisted in the Grenadier Guards at Slough on 9 March 1909, when he was 20 years old. His medical examination on 10 March passed him fit for the army and recorded that he had brown hair, brown eyes and a fresh complexion. He was five feet nine inches tall and Roman Catholic.

He joined his unit at Caterham on 13 March 1909 and a period of three years' home service began. On 24 December 1909 he married Annie Elizabeth Dobson at the registry office in Windsor. His parents were living at 2 Beasley's Cottages in Windsor at the time of the wedding.

Hubert's initial period of service came to an end when he was transferred to the Army Reserve on 9 March 1912. Two years later, when the war started, he was mobilised at Wellington Barracks in London on 5 August 1914 and they entrained at Nine Elms for Southampton on 12 August, arriving at Le Havre in France the following day. The next few days were spent travelling and they arrived in the outskirts of Mons in Belgium on 23 August. The battalion took up positions on the reverse slope of a hill above a railway line. Bullets and shells whistling all around, a railwayman was noted walking along the line with complete disregard of what was going on around him and carrying out his normal duties. The long march south to the River Marne followed the battalion's first action of the war and on 21 October they were back in Belgium when they dug in 400 yards east of the Zonnebeke-Langemarck road during the First Battle of Ypres. The enemy attempted an attack during which they shouted out, "Don't fire, we are the Coldstream." Despite the exactitude of the Germans, who were careful to use the correct term "Coldstream", as opposed to the more likely term from someone outside the regiment, "Coldstreams", the battalion was not fooled.

After the end of the First Battle of Ypres the battalion moved south into France to the Béthune sector and on 7 February 1915 they took over the trenches near Cuinchy.

Hubert died of nephritis and heart failure in Doberitz Prisoner of War Camp, 19 kilometres east of Berlin on 17 March 1915 aged 26 years. He is buried in Berlin South-Western Cemetery, Brandenburg, Germany. It is not known when or where he was taken prisoner.

His wife was living at 41 Arthur Street in Windsor at the time of Hubert's death and it is interesting to note that *Soldiers Died in the Great War* records his name as "*Hubert Tranter*" in their records. It is not on any of the war memorials in Campden as the family left the town after their third son was born in 1892.

Wilfred Henry Tracy

Born: 22 August 1892

Wilfred was born in Campden, the son of William Henry and Mary Ann Tracy, and was baptised at St. Catharine's Church on 18 September 1892. His parents were both natives of the town but the family left it soon after the birth of Wilfred, their third son, and went to live at Bridgend in Wales. The 1901 census lists the family living in Caterham in Surrey, where his father was employed as a carpenter.

At the time of the outbreak of war the family were living in Windsor. Wilfred served in the army during the war but it has not been possible to trace what regiment he was with. He was last heard of in Australia in 1920.

William Thomas Travill
Company Sergeant-Major 18699, "B" Company, 9th Battalion, Northumberland Fusiliers

William was the son of George Travill, a private soldier in the Northamptonshire Regiment, and on 13 January 1908 he married Louisa Mayo at the registry office in Northampton. The wedding certificate states that he was 28 years old, a French polisher by trade and living at 55, Earl Street in Northampton.

It is not clear when William moved to Campden but when war was declared in 1914 he was the sergeant-instructor with "H" Company, 5th Battalion, Gloucestershire Regiment, the local company of the Territorial Army. He was mobilised on 5 August 1914 and went to Chelmsford with the battalion for final training before they were posted overseas. However, when the battalion embarked for France in March 1915 he remained in England and was attached to the Northumberland Fusiliers at Harsley Camp.

On 21 June 1915 William married Edith May Plested at St. James's Church in Campden. He returned to duty a few days after the wedding and arrived in France on 15 July. After serving on the Western Front for almost a year William was awarded the Military Cross during the Battle of the Somme. At 12.45am on 5 July 1916 the 9th Battalion, Northumberland Fusiliers crept to within 100 yards of the enemy under cover of rain and darkness. They secured Quadrilateral Trench and Shelter Alley, located south of Contalmaison near Mametz Wood. The enemy machine gun fire prevented further gains and the battalion had to withdraw. The citation was published in the *London Gazette* on 25 August 1916: *"For conspicuous gallantry in action. He displayed great courage and coolness during the withdrawal of his company, which had lost most of its officers through heavy rifle and shell fire. He was largely responsible for the steady withdrawal."* He was presented with the medal by the King at Buckingham Palace on Wednesday 12 September 1917.

He returned to Campden after the war and his son, William Lawrence, was baptised at St. James's Church on 14 September 1919. In 1920 William was charged with committing bigamy and left Campden. Edith May remarried and went to live in Chipping Norton.

James Trinder
Private 15143, 1st Battalion, Gloucestershire Regiment
Private, 202782, 2nd Battalion, Royal Scots Fusiliers

Born: 23 August 1882
Died: 22 March 1918

James was born in Broad Campden, the son of Mary Trinder, a domestic servant, who was living with her parents, William and Elizabeth Trinder, at Sedgecombe Cottages in Broad Campden at the time of the birth.

James enlisted in the Gloucestershire Regiment in Campden in 1914 and arrived in France on 10 February 1915 with a draft of men to reinforce the 1st Battalion in the Béthune sector. He joined the same company as Charles Hedges, a friend from Campden. The battalion saw action during the Battle of Loos, which started on 25 September 1915, and on 8 October Charles was killed. James wrote to his parents, William Henry and Emma Hedges of Westington, informing them of their son's death. A few days later James was wounded in action.

After recovering from his wounds he rejoined the battalion and in late July 1916 he was again wounded in action near Contalmaison during the Battle of the Somme. He was evacuated back to England and admitted to a hospital in Bethnal Green in London, where he wrote to his aunt in Campden:

"Just a few lines to let you know I am still alive. I expect you will be surprised to know I am back in the dear old country again and very pleased of it. I would rather be anywhere than where I came from. It was like hell on earth, but thank God I got through, so you need not worry as I am going on alright. I have two wounds, one in the thick of the right leg and one in the left hand. I'll bet a good many will remember the Somme for the rest of their lives."

After recovering from his wounds James was transferred to the 2nd Battalion, Royal Scots Fusiliers and returned to France. On 21 March 1918 the battalion was near Savy, west of St. Quentin when the Germans launched *"Operation Michael"*, their Spring offensive. A heavy artillery bombardment began at 4.40am and the infantry began to attack at 7.00am. Savy was eventually taken by the Germans at 1.00pm after heavy fighting. The German advance was rapid and James's position was overrun by the enemy.

James died on 22 March 1918 and was originally buried by the Germans in St. Quentin-Roupy Road German Cemetery in L'Epine de Dallon near St. Quentin along with 231 other British soldiers. These graves were lost during further fighting in the area later in the war and James is today remembered on a special memorial in Savy Cemetery. He was 35 years old when he died and his name is recorded on two memorials in Campden: in St. James's Church and in the High Street.

Frederick Raymond Trinder

Born: 1900

Frederick was born in Cheltenham, the son of Raymond and Florence Trinder. On 13 November 1920 he married Irene Valentine Jacques at St. James's Church in Campden and on the marriage certificate his occupation was recorded as an indoor servant.

Frederick is listed in the *Book of Remembrance* by Josephine Griffiths, which suggests that he enlisted towards the end of the war and was only employed on home service.

Charles William Turner
Private 6473, 1st Battalion, Gloucestershire Regiment
Private 38742, Suffolk Regiment

Born: 1884
Died: 7 November 1957

William, the son of Charles William Turner, married Ada Merriman at St. James's Church on 19 October 1912. They had nine children (Alfred, John, Philip, Peter, William, Ethel, Bertha, Annie and May) and he was employed as a labourer for J. W. Pyment and Sons.

When the war started in 1914 the family were living in Hull's Cottages in Broad Campden and William enlisted in the Gloucestershire Regiment. He arrived in France on 31 August 1914 and was posted to the 1st Battalion. Everard Wyrall, in his history of the Gloucestershire Regiment, records that "*while at Rozoy on 5 September 1914 the battalion's strength was brought up to just above war establishment by the arrival of some 100 men*" (including William). The following weeks saw the battalion move north from the River Marne to the River Aisne and by 20 October they were in Poperinge in Belgium. The battalion took over positions in the front line at Langemarck during the First Battle of Ypres and they inflicted great losses on the enemy, who had come within 50 yards of their trenches. Each man fired some 500 rounds and some even had the bayonets shot off their rifles.

After further action in November during the closing days of the First Battle of Ypres the battalion moved south into France to take over trenches in the sector east of Béthune.

It is not known how long William stayed with the Glosters as he transferred to the Suffolk Regiment before the end of the war, but he was still in the army in 1918 as he is recorded as absent on military service on the electoral roll. His son, John, informed the author that his father lost a finger during the war.

William died on 7 November 1957 aged 75 and is buried in St. James's churchyard in Campden.

Harry Turner
Guardsman 29469, 3rd Battalion, Grenadier Guards

Born: 1897
Enlisted: 28 February 1917
Died: 15 April 1918

Harry was born in Worcester, the second son of Alfred and Elizabeth Turner. In 1901 the family were living in Livingstone Street, Worcester and his father was employed as a railway engine driver.

Harry found employment as a railway porter at Campden station in 1914 and then on 28 February 1917 he went to Cirencester, where he enlisted in the Grenadier Guards. He joined his unit at Caterham on 2 March 1917 and the next nine months were spent training in England. After 305 days on home service he arrived in France on 30 December 1917 and joined the 3rd Battalion. His service papers state that after 107 days on the Western Front he died of wounds on 15 April

1918 aged 20 years. The *Evesham Journal* report contradicts this: "*It may be of interest to Campden readers to know that Private Harry Turner, who was employed as a porter at Campden station for nearly two years, has been killed in action in France on April 14. Mrs. Potter of Wold's End has received a letter from his mother informing her of his death which was instantaneous. The chaplain of the regiment has written to his mother and she has also received an official notification from the War Office.*"

Harry is buried in Doullens Communal Cemetery Extension Number 1 in France and does not have his name recorded on any memorials in Campden. At the time of his death his parents were living in Mere Green, Droitwich.

Joseph Arthur Turner
Driver, Army Service Corps

Born: 25 January 1882
Died: 18 December 1939

Joseph was born at Exton in Rutland, the son of John and Mary Turner. After leaving school he found employment as a driver and in 1902 he married Mary Teresa Sansom, a native of Ebrington, and had five children: Constance, Raymond William, Reginald Joseph, Agnes and Lucy. His son Ray became the licensee of the Volunteer pub in Campden and Lucy married Arthur Bunten.

Joseph was a member of "H" Company, 5th Battalion, Gloucestershire

Joseph and Mary Turner, 1917
The children (left to right): Constance, Raymond, baby Lucy, Reg and Agnes.

Regiment, the local company of the Territorial Army, but early in the war he transferred to the Army Service Corps as a driver. He was posted to Burnham-on-Crouch in Essex and employed as a driver for an officer of the Gloucestershire Regiment. He did not serve overseas.

After the war he returned home to Gainsborough Terrace, Campden and became the proprietor of the Cotswold Garage in Park Road.

Joseph was an expert shot and on 18 December 1939 he was killed in a shooting accident at Court Piece Farm in Campden. He was carrying the loaded gun when he tripped and fell to the ground, causing the gun to fire. He was 57 and is buried in St. Catharine's cemetery. His wife died on 26 March 1952.

Henry Harry Vincent Tyack
Private M-281265, No. 10 Motor Transport Company, Army Service Corps

Born: 21 August 1897
Enlisted: 2 March 1916
Discharged: 11 January 1918
Died: 13 January 1933

Henry, known as "*Teddy*", was born in Pebworth, the eldest child of Henry Harry and Jane Tyack. His father, a native of Cornwall and a baker by trade, married Jane Ball from Pebworth in 1896.

From boyhood Teddy always took a keen interest in machines and motor cars, and after leaving school he was apprenticed to Mr. J. V. Crowhurst, Motor Engineer, of Moreton-in-Marsh.

Teddy enlisted in the Army Service Corps on 2 March 1916 when he was 18 years old, and was immediately placed into the Army Reserve. His attestation papers record that the family were living in Ivy House, Broad Campden and that he was five feet four inches tall with dark brown hair, blue eyes and a fresh complexion. His pre-war trade was a "*motor driver*".

Teddy was mobilised on 29 December 1916 and posted to Number 10 Motor

Transport Company, Army Service Corps. After a few months' home service he was about to be drafted out to France when he was taken ill with spinal meningitis, which left its mark and no doubt partly had the effect of bringing about his untimely death in 1933. He was discharged from the army on 11 January 1918 without serving overseas and a Silver War Badge was issued to indicate that he had made his contribution to the war. His colonel wrote the following character reference: "*He is sober, honest, reliable, intelligent and well conducted. He is a competent motor driver and performed his duties satisfactorily.*"

After the war Teddy set up in Moreton-in-Marsh as a "*Taxi Proprietor*" and then in 1920 he married Sarah Ann Dring Gillett, second daughter of George Gillett, and they had four children: Gerald Vincent, Jean Catherine Mary, Juliet Josephine and Sheila Georgina. Ably supported by his wife, the business gradually grew and in 1921 he bought small premises at the north end of the High Street. In 1924 he bought the Old Crown Inn premises, standing in the centre of the town, and started the Curfew Garage. The business grew and he bought the adjoining

Henry Harry Vincent Tyack with his wife and four children.

property, erecting a fully equipped and modern car showroom. He was a man of great enterprise and soon opened Trooper's Lodge filling station near Bourton-on-the-Hill. This was followed by the purchase of Chapel House filling station at Chipping Norton.

Teddy died suddenly of pneumonia following influenza on 13 January 1933 aged 35 years. He is buried in St. David's Church cemetery in Moreton-in-Marsh. His wife died on 12 May 1982 aged 83 years.

His son, Gerald, was educated at Campden Grammar School and then served as a corporal in the Royal Air Force during the Second World War. He became known locally as the owner of the Wellington Aviation Museum in Moreton-in-Marsh and was awarded the MBE in December 1998.

Alfred Veale
Lance Corporal 865494, 181st Battalion, Canadian Expeditionary Force

Born: 24 May 1887
Enlisted: 25 February 1916
Discharged: 27 March 1919

Alfred was born in Campden, the second son of Charles and Emma Jane Veale of "Boxhedge", Sheep Street, and was baptised at St. James's Church on 26 June 1887. His father was employed as an agricultural labourer and in 1901 Alfred was also working on a farm as a "*teamster*". In the years leading up to the time that Alfred left Campden he was a member of "H" Company, 5th Battalion, Gloucestershire Regiment with his brother Charles.

Alfred emigrated to Canada before the start of the war and in 1914 he was married and living in Brandon, Manitoba, and working as a postman. His wife, Ethel, gave birth to their first child, Ethel May, at the start of 1914 and their second child, Mamie, was born in 1915. He then enlisted in the Canadian Expeditionary Force (CEF) on 25 February 1916, when he was 28 years old. His medical examination recorded that he was five feet eight inches tall with light brown hair, blue eyes and a fair complexion. His religion was Church of England and there was a tattoo mark on his left forearm that said *"Ethel"*.

Alfred embarked at Halifax on HMT *Grampian* on 16 April 1917 and arrived in England at Liverpool on 29 April, where he was seconded to the 18th Reserve Battalion, CEF, and promoted to the rank of acting corporal. He only held this rank for a month but it was during this time that his photograph was taken wearing his stripes and the glasses that were needed for his defective vision. The remainder of 1917 was spent in training camps in Shorncliffe, Dibgate and Seaford. On 17 November 1917 he was employed as an instructor and later that month he was promoted to lance corporal with pay. Alfred then developed a hernia problem and was admitted to Number 11 Canadian General Hospital, Moore Barracks, Shorncliffe on 15 January 1918, where he stayed until 21 February. He was then admitted to the Canadian Convalescent Hospital, Monks Horton, Kent but the hernia failed to heal and he was sent to Number 4 Canadian General Hospital, Basingstoke, where he remained until 2 April.

The next five months were spent with the Canadian Labour Pool doing manual work in England to assist the training of troops before they were sent to France. Alfred's defective vision and recent hernia problem delayed his own overseas posting, which did not come until 10 September 1918. He remained in France until the end of December, when he returned to England. A medical board examined Alfred at Witley in Surrey on 23 January 1919 and commented on his defective vision by saying that he was *"wearing rather powerful glasses"*. They also commented that he was a *"well developed and well nourished man"*. They graded him as B1 and fit for further military service.

In February 1919 he was sent to Kinmel Park Camp at Bodelwyddan, near Rhyl, in Wales to prepare for his return to Canada. Conditions in the camp were poor and the 20,000 Canadian troops became bored with army life now that the war was over. They were keen to go home to be with their families and could not understand why there was such a delay in being allowed to leave England. At 9.00pm on 4 March 1919 one thousand troops started a riot and by the time it ended 5 men had been killed and 28 wounded.

Alfred left England on HMT *Celtic* on 10 March 1919 and was discharged from the army in Brandon in Canada on 27 March.

Charles Thomas Veale
Private 779, "D" Company, 1st/5th Battalion Gloucestershire Regiment

> Born: 16 May 1889
> Mobilised: 5 August 1914
> Discharged: 2 March 1916

Charles was born in Campden, the second son of Charles and Emma Jane Veale of "Boxhedge", Sheep Street, and was baptised at St. James's Church on 30 June 1889. His father was born at Cow Honeybourne and was employed as an agricultural labourer. His mother's maiden name was Ray. In 1901 the family had moved to Cider Mill Lane, although the 1901 census indicates that Charles, who was then aged 12, was living with his grandmother, Caroline Ray, in Watery Lane.

Charles went to school in Campden and then joined "H" Company, 5th Battalion, Gloucestershire Regiment, the local company of the Territorial Army. He was mobilised on 5 August 1914 and went to Chelmsford with several other Campden men for final training before they were posted to France. The battalion arrived in France on 29 March 1915 and then made the journey north to Ploegsteert, a Belgian village at the southern end of the Ypres Salient. This was a *"quiet"* sector of the Western Front and the battalion gained experience in trench warfare. In July they moved south to the Somme area and Charles spent the next seven months in trenches at Hébuterne and resting in Sailly-au-Bois, Bus-les-Artois and Bayencourt.

Charles left the battalion in February 1916 and returned to England, where he was discharged on 2 March 1916. He was awarded three campaign medals for his service in the war: 1914/15 Star, British War Medal and Victory Medal. The location of these medals was unknown until the author saw two of them advertised for sale on eBay. The 1915 Star is still missing but the other two medals now have a very safe home alongside other Campden medals owned by the author.

George Veale
Private 9567, 2nd Battalion, Gloucestershire Regiment
Private 270361, 576th Home Service Company, Labour Corps

Born: 29 November 1892
Enlisted: 1 January 1912
Discharged: 23 May 1919
Died: 2 April 1976

George was born in Campden, the fourth son of Charles and Emma Jane Veale, and was baptised at St. James's Church on 2 April 1893. His parents married in 1882 and in 1891 the family were living in "Boxhedge", Sheep Street, Campden, but by 1901 they had moved to Cider Mill Lane. His father was an agricultural labourer.

George enlisted in the Gloucestershire Regiment as a regular soldier on 1 January 1912 after a period working as a domestic servant. He was five feet six inches tall with blue eyes and dark brown hair. The first part of his military service was spent in England before he was posted to Peking in China on 3 September 1913, where he was part of the British Legation Guard. When the war broke out in 1914 George was still in China serving with the 2nd Battalion, Gloucestershire Regiment. They were then ordered to India and embarked on SS *Arcadia* at Ching-Wang-Tao. While they were at sea off Shanghai they received orders stating that they were to proceed to England, where they arrived at Southampton on 8 November 1914. The next month was spent in camps near Winchester before they embarked at Southampton on SS *City of Chester* on 18 December and sailed for France.

George and his wife, Rosina Dorothea Davis.

They arrived at Le Havre the following day and then entrained for Aire-sur-la-Lys. On the 21 December they were billeted in the French Army barracks at Château Moine and the year ended with the battalion digging defensive works at Boesghem and Pecqueur in Northern France west of Armentières.

The battalion was in Belgium when the Germans began the Second Battle of Ypres on 22 April 1915. On 8 May the battalion's trenches along the eastern edge of Sanctuary Wood came under a severe bombardment. At 7.15am the following day the enemy attacked and broke through into the trenches. Casualties were great but the battalion fought hard and at least 350 of the enemy were killed. The battalion war diary speaks of "*the trenches and the ground being littered with dead and wounded*".

The battalion was relieved from the front line on 18 May 1915 and a period of rest was spent in a camp near Vlamertinghe, west of Ypres. In June they moved south into France and were employed in the Armentières sector. In July the war on the Western Front ended for George when he was wounded in the knee by the explosion of a shell that landed near him in a trench. He was admitted to hospital at Wimereux in France before being invalided back to England, where he was treated at Reading War Hospital. He was later transferred to hospital in Gravesend and he met his future wife, Rosina Dorothea Davis, while convalescing in the area. They were married at St. George's Church in Gravesend on 30 June 1917.

After recovering from his wound George was transferred to the Labour Corps and spent the rest of the war serving in England in a home service company until he was discharged from the army on 23 May 1919. During his time with the Labour Corps he was guilty of two military offences. On 7 May 1918 he was awarded four days confined to barracks, with two days loss of pay, for failing to rejoin his unit on completion of a cooking course and remaining absent until 10.45pm on 8 May 1918. Three months later, on 8 August 1918, he was awarded the same punishment for being absent without leave from 1.00am until 9.30pm.

George never returned to Campden after leaving the army, although he was a frequent visitor to the town as he was best of mates with Jack, Gerald and Bill Howell before the war. Home was now in Maidstone, where he was employed for a while at Tillings and Stevens Motor Works. On leaving the company he had a couple of other jobs before going to work at Fremlins Brewery as a stationary engine operator for the cooling plant, a job that he held until he retired. Despite being employed at a brewery he was semi-teetotal.

George was an excellent sportsman, playing both football and cricket for the firms that he worked for, and was much respected by all his employers for his character, honesty and work. He was a very keen gardener but his life was really his family, sport and gardening, in that order. George's family consisted of his wife and two daughters, Rosa May and Edna, and his home was at 33, Whitmore Street in Maidstone.

George died on 2 April 1976 aged 83 and was cremated at Charing Crematorium, Ashford, Kent.

George is standing in the centre of the photograph.

Joseph Alexander Walker
Royal Flying Corps

Born: 26 March 1897

Alec was born in Campden, the son of Joseph and Elizabeth Walker of Berrington Mill. His father, a native of Long Compton, was a farmer and miller by trade, and came to Campden before the 1881 census was compiled. Alec's mother was from Marchington, near Uttoxeter in Staffordshire, and her maiden name was Deaville.

Alec was educated at Campden Grammar School and during the war he served in the Royal Flying Corps. The 1918 electoral roll lists him as absent on military service.

Campden Grammar School Cadet Corps
Lance Corporal Alec Walker is standing at the end of the row, either on the right or on the left. The names written on the back of the photograph suggest that he is on the left but this is to be confirmed.

Fred Coldicott mentions Alec in his book *Memories of an Old Campdonian* when he wanted to build his own wireless:

"When it came to soldering some of the connections we had to get Alec Walker to do that for us. He was the son of the late "Sloshy" Walker from Berrington Mill, but was living with his mother next door to Jess Taylor's photographic shop near the Lygon Arms. He was very clever and talented with anything to do with the wireless or electrics. I remember he built a very powerful wireless once, took it up to Dover's Hill to test it and you could hear it quite plainly down in Campden. I think one of the large radio companies gave him a job in their laboratories and he left Campden."

William Alfred Walton
Private 4222, 8th Battalion (Post Office Rifles), London Regiment
Private 44058, 1st Battalion, Royal Irish Rifles
Private 27802, 1st Battalion (Royal Canadians), Leinster Regiment

Born: 6 April 1885
Died: 23 October 1918

William was born in Campden, the only son of Alfred and Phoebe Elizabeth Walton of Infant School House, High Street, and was baptised at St. James's Church on 24 May 1885. His father was born in Weston-sub-Edge and was a coal agent and a Wesleyan preacher.

After attending school in the town William found employment as a baker but in 1903, when he was 18 years old, he emigrated to Canada with his parents. A few years were spent in Canada before he returned to England and worked as a postman in Campden. At the outbreak of war he enlisted in the Post Office Rifles in London and during his initial period of training in England he returned to Campden to marry Elsie May Collett, the eldest daughter of Harry Collett, at St. James's Church on 11 February 1915. Their only child, a daughter called Dorothy May, was born on 3 September 1916 and was baptised at St. James's Church in 1917.

William was posted to France at the start of 1916 and served on the Western Front for the next twelve months, where he saw action in the Battle of the Somme, before he returned to England for leave. He then transferred to the 1st Battalion, Leinster Regiment and joined the Egyptian Expeditionary Force in September 1917. The 27th Division, which included the 1st Leinsters, was concentrated around Rafa and after leaving Egypt they entered Palestine, where William served throughout General Allenby's great and victorious advance. He then contracted malaria and was admitted to hospital in Gaza, where he died on 23 October 1918 aged 33 after failing to recover from the illness. He is buried in Gaza War Cemetery in Palestine and his name is recorded on two memorials in Campden: in St. James's Church and in the High Street.

Cyril Warmington
Lance Corporal 10914, 5th Battalion, Oxfordshire and Buckinghamshire Light Infantry

Born: 1894
Died: 30 July 1915

Cyril was born in Lichfield in 1894 and was the youngest of four sons of Henry George and Mary Elizabeth Warmington. He was the cousin of Joe and Harry Warmington and went to school in Campden. After leaving school he returned to Lichfield.

He enlisted in the 5th Battalion, Oxfordshire and Buckinghamshire Light Infantry at the outbreak of the war. The battalion was formed in Oxford in August 1914 and was posted to the 42nd Brigade of the 14th Division. While he was training at Aldershot Cyril wrote the following in a letter home: "*This war cannot last forever and the sooner peace is declared and England begins to settle down again the better for us all I say. When one comes to think about it, it seems as if the world has gone mad. Everyone wanting to kill everyone else. Even when peace is declared there won't be any friendliness between the Germans and us. Still if we hadn't declared war in helping Belgium, Germany would have fought first one country and then another until they were masters of the world. So I suppose it is best to smash them instead. Better to be English than naturalised Germans."*

When training in England was complete the battalion made their way to Dover and crossed to France on SS *Invicta*. They arrived at Boulogne on 20 May 1915 and then moved north to the Ypres Salient. A period of trench instruction followed near Kemmel and the battalion war diary notes that *"the smell of decaying bodies is strong and many are unearthed during digging"*.

In June 1915 Cyril was in trenches near Railway Wood, three miles east of Ypres. The battalion took part in their first attack here and suffered over 120 casualties. The next few weeks were spent in the front line at Railway Wood, in reserve trenches in front of Ypres and resting in Vlamertinghe, a village four miles west of Ypres.

Cyril had only been at the front for just over two months when he was killed in action in a dugout near Hooge. The Germans attacked at Hooge on 30 July 1915 using flamethrowers for the first time. Cyril's battalion were immediately north of Hooge and it was in the fighting on this day that he died. He was 20 years old.

As he has no known grave his name is recorded on the Menin Gate Memorial in the centre of Ypres. At the time of his death his parents were living at 71 Mason Road, Edgbaston, Birmingham.

John Joseph Warmington
Sergeant 16430, 17 Squadron, Royal Flying Corps

Born: 10 April 1888
Enlisted: 16 December 1915
Discharged: 12 June 1919
Died: 22 May 1964

Joe was born in Badsey and was the eldest son of William John and Rose Anne Warmington. He was baptised at St. James's Church on 27 May 1888 but the family did not come to Campden until 1904. After leaving school Joe worked for his father as a bricklayer and carpenter before he started a business with Stanley Keeley. They did bicycle repairs, carpentry and cabinetmaking.

Joe served for several years as a pre-war soldier with "H" Company, 5th Battalion, Gloucestershire Regiment, the local company of the Territorial Army, but when war was declared in August 1914 he did not sign up to serve overseas with the battalion like his younger brother, Harry. Instead he enlisted in the Royal Flying Corps as an air mechanic

"K" Company, 2nd Volunteer Battalion, Gloucestershire Regiment
Joe is seated on the left and Joseph Williams is smoking a pipe. The photograph was taken at Lulworth during the battalion's annual camp in 1907.

second class on 16 December 1915. He was promoted to air mechanic first class in England three months before he married Florence Turvey on 24 December 1916 at Montrose in Scotland. More promotion followed as Joe continued to serve in England. On 1 April 1918 the Royal Flying Corps were renamed the Royal Air Force and Joe was now a sergeant mechanic.

On 14 August 1918 Joe was posted to France, where he remained until 5 April 1919, when he returned to England with flu. He went straight to University Hospital in Southampton and after recovering he was discharged from the RAF on 12 June 1919.

After the war Joe and Florence had one child, William Allan, who was born in 1922. They lived in Broad Campden for a few years before they moved to Westington Corner in 1927. Joe was now working on his own as a builder and cabinetmaker.

During the Second World War Joe helped organise the fire-watching service in Campden and he was involved with servicemen's welfare through Toc H and the soldiers' canteen.

Joe died on 22 May 1964 aged 76 and he is buried at St. James's churchyard.

William Henry Warmington
Private 1564, "D" Company, 1st/5th Battalion, Gloucestershire Regiment
     Enlisted: 18 March 1912
     Discharged: 27 June 1916
Corporal Air Mechanic 34200, Royal Air Force
     Enlisted: 27 June 1916
     Discharged: 15 March 1919

     Born: 2 August 1895
     Died: 12 May 1979

Harry was born in Badsey, the second son of William John and Rose Anne Warmington, and he came to Campden in 1904 when the family moved to Sheep Street. After leaving Campden Grammar School he became a silversmith and, together with his brother Joe, he was a member of "H" Company, 5th Battalion, Gloucestershire Regiment.

Harry joined the Territorials on 18 March 1912 and when war was declared in 1914 he was immediately mobilised. After training in Chelmsford he arrived in Boulogne on 29 March 1915 and served with the 5th Glosters in Belgium at Ploegsteert and in France at Hébuterne on the Somme. The battalion was about to be involved in very heavy fighting in July 1916 at Ovillers when Harry applied for a transfer to join his brother in the Royal Flying Corps.

Harry enlisted in the Royal Flying Corps on 27 June 1916 as an air mechanic second class. While serving in England he was promoted to air mechanic first class in March 1917. Embarkation to France was on 28 March 1918 but by August he was back in England as he married Elizabeth Salmon from Clifford Chambers on 5 August 1918.

He was discharged from the Royal Air Force on 15 March 1919 and he returned to Campden, where he and his wife lived with his parents in Sheep Street until 1926. They then had a number of homes in Campden, including Little Broadwell, Landgate Cottage and Clifton Cottage.

In post-war years Harry developed into an expert silversmith, goldsmith and engraver. George Hart described him as "*one of the finest silver and goldsmiths in the country*". He was the metalwork instructor at the Campden School of Arts and Crafts for twenty years and continued to work at the Silk Mill in Campden until he was 70 years old.

He was a very keen member and former president of Campden Bowls Club, to which he belonged for fifty years, and he also represented the County. He was an active member of the British Legion and in 1935 he joined the Campden Lodge of Freemasons and was its Master in 1946.

During the Second World War he worked as a supervisor at the Lockhead Brake Factory at Cutt's Garage in Campden. He was also a special constable.

Harry died on 12 May 1979 aged 83 at 4, the Almshouses, Campden and was cremated in Cheltenham. His wife died in the early 1970's.

Walter Weale

Born: 1880

Walter was born in Bledington, near Stow-on-the-Wold, the son of William and Rosina Weale. After leaving school he became a carpenter and wheelwright. He married Elizabeth Ann Grace Tomes in 1905 and in 1906 he began a period of three years' service with the Guild of Handicraft as a joiner. The family home was at Hulland House, Station Road, Campden and a son called Walter Raymond was born in 1911.

Walter was a trombone player in the town band and the Campden 1918 electoral roll indicates that he was absent on military service.

Elizabeth Weale died on 25 May 1958 aged 75 and is buried in St. James's churchyard. Her son, Walter Raymond, died on 7 December 1983 aged 71 and is buried with his mother.

Richard Lancelot Weaver
Duke of Cornwall's Light Infantry

Born: 12 March 1900
Died: 1966

Lancelot was born in Broad Campden on 12 March 1900, the son of George Henry and Mary Weaver. He was baptised at St. James's Church on 14 June 1903 and his father's occupation was stated as a general labourer.

At the age of 18 Lancelot enlisted in the Duke of Cornwall's Light Infantry in 1918 but the war ended before he saw overseas service.

Lancelot never married and he lived with his mother in Broad Campden at 1, Halls Cottages with the Godson and Clews families as their neighbours. When his mother died Lancelot became ill. He went to live in a home in Stow and it was here that he spent the last years of his life.

Arthur John Webb
Army Service Corps

Born: 1885

Jackie was born in Campden, the second son of John George Webb of "Boxhedge", Sheep Street. His father, a postman by trade, married Ellen Willis at St. James's Church on 1 October 1883. After leaving school Jackie became a baker's assistant and a member of the town band, in which he played the tenor horn.

He joined "H" Company, 5th Battalion, Gloucestershire Regiment, the local company of the Territorial Army. He was mobilised on 5 August 1914 and went with the battalion to Chelmsford. It is not known whether he went to France with the battalion in March 1915 but by the end of 1916 he had been transferred to the Army Service Corps, where it is believed he was employed as a baker.

The Campden 1918 electoral roll lists Jackie as living in Sheep Street with his wife, Alice Mary Webb, and

Campden Town Band
Back row (L-R): Fred Hathaway and Arthur Bunten
Front row (L-R): Fred Bennet, Charlie Downer and Jackie Webb

absent on military service. In 1922 they are living in Watery Lane and in 1926 Lower High Street. He was employed by J. W. Pyment and Sons as a labourer and worked in a gang that included Fred Coldicott, Ernest Hedges, Charlie Pitcher and Frank Bennett. The family then left Campden and opened a baker's and confectionery shop in Bromyard in Herefordshire.

Frank Webb
Gloucestershire Regiment

Born: 1878

Frank was born in Campden, the son of John Webb, engine-driver, of Sheep Street. His father, a native of Moreton-in-Marsh, married Hannah Merriman in 1870. After leaving school Frank was employed as a farm labourer and on 16 June 1900 he married Frances May Benfield, daughter of Benjamin Benfield, at St. James's Church. The family home was initially in Littleworth and they had four children baptised at the church before the outbreak of war in 1914: Albert, John Ernest, Frances Elizabeth and Fanny.

In 1904 the family were living in Snowshill and then in 1910 they were back in Campden living in Watery Lane. During the war Frank served in the Gloucestershire Regiment.

Fred Webb
Lance Corporal 12817, 1st Battalion, Northamptonshire Regiment

Born 1891
Died: 11 January 1916

Fred Webb in his 16th Lancers uniform, c.1912

Fred was born in Campden, the third son of John George and Ellen Webb of "Boxhedge", Sheep Street, Campden, and was baptised at St. James's Church on 17 May 1891. His father married Ellen Willis, a native of Willersey, at St. James's Church on 1 October 1883 and on the 1901 census they had six children listed: Arthur, Fred, Elsie, Edith, Norah and Dora. John was employed in the town as a postman.

The family left Campden in the years leading up to the First World War and moved to 13, West Street, Weedon, Northamptonshire. It was around this time that Fred became a regular soldier when he joined the 16th Lancers.

At the outbreak of war in 1914 Fred was in the Army Reserve and he was mobilised in Northampton. He arrived in France on 26 May 1915, where he joined the 1st Battalion, Northamptonshire Regiment. The battalion had been on the Western Front since the start of the war and Fred was with a draft of men needed to reinforce the unit. In September and October 1915 the battalion fought in the Battle of Loos and the subsequent action at the Hohenzollern Redoubt. Fred survived his first action and was promoted to lance corporal.

He was killed in action near Loos in France on 11 January 1916 aged 24 and as his grave could not be found at the end of the war his name is recorded on the Loos Memorial at Dud Corner Cemetery, near Loos-en-Gohelle, France. It is not recorded on any memorials in Campden.

Leonard Webb

Leonard was born in Todenham in 1899, the eldest son of Harry Ezekiel Webb. His father, a native of Moreton-in-Marsh and a railway platelayer by trade, married Mary Ann Boulton in 1898. The family does not appear to have any obvious connection with Campden but Leonard was listed on the 1916 list of servicemen produced by St. James's Church.

Roland Webb

Roland is listed on the prayer list produced by St. James's Church in 1916 but it has not been possible to find anybody with this name connected with Campden.

Arthur Conrad Robert Welsh

2nd Lieutenant, 1st/5th Battalion, Gloucestershire Regiment
2nd Lieutenant, 1st Battalion, South Wales Borderers
Captain, 2nd/119th Infantry, The Mooltan Regiment, Indian Army

Born: 14 July 1891

Robert was born in Russia, the eldest son of William Henry and Anna Golighty Welsh of Seymour House, Campden. He was educated at Clifton College in Bristol, where he was a member of the Officers' Training Corps for four years. In the years leading up to the war he worked as a rubber planter in Ceylon and served for two years in the Ceylon Planters' Rifle Corps.

He returned to England at the outbreak of war and joined "D" Company, 1st/5th Battalion, Gloucestershire Regiment, a Territorial battalion, as a private. He was soon granted a commission and on 9 November 1914 he became a second lieutenant.

Robert arrived in France on 18 July 1915 and served with the battalion on the Western Front until he returned to England for a period of leave that began on 26 November 1915. After returning to France he was granted a permanent commission with the Regular Army and posted to the 1st Battalion, South Wales Borderers on 4 February 1916. Five months later he won the Military Cross for bravery in face of the enemy while leading a party of bombers in an attack on Munster Alley, east of Pozières on 25 July 1916 during the Battle of the Somme. He led the party with great dash, refusing to return to his own trenches despite being wounded. His wound resulted in his evacuation back to England, where he was admitted to hospital.

After recovering he embarked for Salonika, where he joined the 7th Battalion, South Wales Borderers on 11 December 1916. He remained in Greece until he embarked for India on 17 September 1917. His application for an appointment to a commission in the Indian Army was successful following a medical examination that took place at Salonika. Brigadier General Cooke wrote a supporting reference: "*I consider him in every way suitable. He has a slight hesitation in his speech which does not affect his efficiency. An excellent young officer who knows all about bombing. I can certify that he is an officer who, by reason of his social status and military efficiency, is fit to command Indian troops.*"

Robert was seconded from the South Wales Borderers and joined the 2nd/119th Infantry, The Mooltan Regiment as a company commander on 5 November 1917. His permanent appointment to the Indian Army took place on 17 October 1918 and he was promoted to captain on 9 August 1919.

He served in the Afghan War in 1919 and was wounded for a second time.

Ralph Henry Wellesley Welsh

Captain, Squadron Officer, 16th Cavalry, Indian Army

Born: 24 July 1893
Enlisted: 24 August 1912
Discharged: 19 November 1922

Ralph was born in India, the second son of William Henry and Anna Golighty Welsh of Seymour House, Campden. He was granted a commission on 24 August 1912 and after a period on the Indian Army unattached list he was posted to the 1st Battalion, Connaught Rangers. His commanding officer wrote a very positive report on him dated 12 January 1913: "*He has only been attached to the battalion for about three months but from my short experience of him I consider him a promising young officer.*"

Ralph was appointed to the Indian Army on 12 October 1913 and on 24 November 1914 he was promoted to lieutenant and posted to the 16th Cavalry. He was stationed at Lucknow in India and his 1914 end of year report stated that he was "*a steady, keen, reliable and hard working young officer, who is learning his work and shows great promise*".

When Ralph's regiment went on service in 1915 he was left to run the depot at Lucknow as the commanding officer had recently died. In 1916 Ralph officiated as the adjutant with the 16th

Cavalry from May until October. He was promoted to captain on 24 August 1916 and finished the year as a squadron commander who was very popular with the men.

In 1917 Ralph was stationed at Delhi and was a squadron commander with the 10th (Bengal) Lancers on field service in India. His annual report written on 1 January 1918 stated that he was "*a very sound and capable young officer*".

Ralph remained in India for the duration of the 1914-18 war and he continued to serve there until he was granted six months' leave on 19 January 1922. After returning to his unit he relinquished his commission on 19 November 1922.

Thomas Vaughan Welsh
2nd Lieutenant, Squadron Officer, 12th Cavalry, Indian Army

Enlisted: 31 January 1918

Thomas was born in India in 1899, the third son of William Henry and Anna Golighty Welsh. His father was born in London in 1854 and his mother was born in Gibraltar in 1861.

His father was employed in the Indian Civil Service and in 1901 the family were living at The Fields, Weeley, Essex. They moved to Seymour House in Campden in the years leading up to the war and Fred Coldicott remembered William: "*We all called him Yabu. He had a lovely large sledge that we used to borrow. He was a huge man with a beard and had travelled the world quite a bit as an explorer. Out at the back of his house he had a large stuffed alligator. When Yabu Welsh left Seymour House it was sold and turned into a boarding house for the girls at the Grammar School.*"

Thomas became a second lieutenant when he was granted a commission on 31 January 1918. He was then appointed to the Indian Army on 6 February 1918 where he was attached to the 12th Cavalry as a squadron officer. He was promoted to lieutenant on 31 January 1919 and in October 1919 he was an acting captain.

During the war Thomas was employed in India and did not serve in a theatre of war.

John William Whalley
Army

Died: June 1967

Bill was born in Bradford in 1888, the third son of Harry Whalley, a clothing club clerk, and his wife, Susan. When Bill married Annie Louisa Smith at the register office in Bradford on 12 November 1912 he was living at 7, St. John's Square, Bradford and employed as a silk-finisher. They had a son, Claude Victor, born in 1913, and a daughter, Muriel, born in 1916.

The family moved to Campden during the war and the 1918 electoral roll lists Bill as living in Cider Mill Lane and absent on military service. After enlisting in the army he served overseas in a theatre of war.

After the war the family moved to Gainsborough Terrace and both Claude and Muriel were baptised at St. James's Church on 28 June 1923. Bill worked as a market gardener.

He died in June 1967 and is buried in St. James's churchyard in Campden.

Frederick Mark Whatcott
Private, Duke of Cornwall's Light Infantry

Born: 11 December 1899
Died: May 1976

Mark was born at Campden Ashes on 11 December 1899, the second son of George and Sarah Ann Whatcott, and was baptised at St. James's Church on 25 December 1900. On the 1901 census his father was a "*cowman on a farm*".

When the war started Mark was only 14 years old and he had to wait until almost the end of the war before he could enlist in the army. In 1918 he was posted to the Duke of Cornwall's Light Infantry and served in Russia and Turkey after the armistice had been signed.

After the war he returned to Campden and found employment as a labourer and then as a gardener for two Campden vicars, working first for Rev. Green and then Canon O'Loughlin in the vicarage garden. He married Lillian Dorothy Howell on 11 December 1926 at St. James's Church and they lived in Watery Lane. During the Second World War he worked at Featherstone Quarry and then did market garden work for Sears Limited. When he retired he was working at Long Marston Army Camp.

Mark died in May 1976 aged 76 and his ashes are buried in St. James's churchyard.

In the photograph on the right Mark is standing on the right. In the photograph at the top of this page he is wearing his regimental cap badge on his lapel.

Joseph George Whatcott
Private, 2nd/5th Battalion, Gloucestershire Regiment
Gunner 225766, 464 Battery, 179th Brigade, Royal Field Artillery

Born: 4 June 1896
Died: 17 February 1919

In the photograph above Joseph is standing on the back row with a cigarette in his mouth. In the photograph on the right he is sitting on the left, again with a cigarette in his mouth.

Joseph was born in Campden, the eldest son of George and Sarah Ann Whatcott of Westington, and was baptised at St. James's Church on 5 July 1896. His father was a "cowman on a farm" in 1901 and the family were living at Campden Ashes.

At the outbreak of war Joseph was 18 years old and he enlisted in the Gloucestershire Regiment but transferred to the Royal Field Artillery in May 1916 before he served overseas. He arrived in France in 1917 and served at the front for twelve months before the war ended. He then returned to England to be demobilised from the army. On his journey home he caught a cold and when he reached Campden on 8 February 1919 he went straight to bed. Despite several visits from the doctor Joseph died of double pneumonia following influenza on 17 February 1919. He was 22 years old and is buried in St. James's churchyard with a Commonwealth War Graves Commission military headstone. The bearers of the coffin were four soldiers from Campden and the funeral was conducted by Rev. R. A. Bentley.

Harry Edgar Wheatcroft
Telegraphist J43973, Royal Navy
Lieutenant-Commander, Royal Navy

Born: 7 August 1899
Enlisted: 15 September 1915
Discharged: 1955
Died: 7 March 1968

Harry with his daughter, Barbara, 1937.

Harry was born in Ebrington, the second son of William and Sarah Wheatcroft. He was one of the first pupils to win a free scholarship to Campden Grammar School and after completing his education he found employment as a market gardener. When he was 16 years old he enlisted in the Royal Navy on 15 September 1915 and was posted to HMS *Impregnable,* a training ship at Devonport*,* as a boy second class. He was promoted to boy telegraphist on 26 February 1916 while serving at HMS *Ganges* at Harwich and then to ordinary telegraphist on 7 February 1917. Later that year he became a telegraphist and he ended the war as a leading telegraphist serving on HMS *Southampton*.

Harry remained in the Royal Navy after the end of the war and on 16 June 1926 he was promoted to acting petty officer telegraphist while serving on HMS *Maidstone*, a supply ship for submarines. Further promotion followed on 16 June 1927 when he was made a petty officer

Above: Harry and his daughter, Barbara, on her wedding day at St. James's Church in Campden.

Left: Harry is standing on the right.

HMS *Ganges*, Royal Navy Training Depot at Harwich, 1916
Harry is standing fourth from the left in the back row.

telegraphist while he was based at HMS *Vivid,* the Royal Navy barracks at Devonport.

In the years between the wars Harry married Molly Nobes and served in Ceylon and Malta before he joined HMS *Nelson* in 1935, which was stationed at a shore base at Portsmouth. In 1936 he was an officer at the Spithead Review.

At the beginning of the Second World War Harry joined HMS *Courageous,* an aircraft carrier, and was amongst those who were saved after the ship was torpedoed and sunk by a German submarine on 17 September 1939. Two torpedoes struck the ship on her port side and she capsized and sank in 15 minutes with the loss of 518 of her crew, including her captain. She was the first British combatant ship to be lost in the war. Harry was granted leave after his rescue and returned home to Campden to see his wife and two children, Dennis and Barbara.

He was then posted to a Royal Navy station at Simonstown in South Africa, where his duties were to get ships around the Cape as they headed towards the Suez Canal in preparation for the offensive in North Africa.

Harry returned to England in 1946 as a lieutenant-commander, was posted to Gateshead and finally to the Admiralty Signal and Radar Establishment (ASRE) based at Risley, Lancashire. He retired from the Royal Navy in 1955 after 40 years' service.

He died in Ashton-under-Lyne Hospital on 7 March 1968 aged 68 and is buried with his wife and parents in St. Eadburgha's churchyard in Ebrington.

HMS *Ganges*
Harwich, 1916

Harry is somewhere on this photograph.

Lewis Wealthy Wilkes
Gloucestershire Regiment

Born: 1867
Died: 13 August 1930

Lewis was born in Campden, the son of George and Julia Wilkes of High Street, Campden. His father married Julia Tracey in 1863.

On 8 February 1896 Lewis married Alma Louisa Maria Hathaway, daughter of George and Ann Hathaway, at St. Catharine's Church in Campden. Their first child, Edith Beatrice, was born on 18 November 1896.

Lewis enlisted in the Gloucestershire Regiment during the war and was employed on home service only before returning to Broad Campden in 1919. He died on 13 August 1930 aged 63 and is buried in St. Catharine's cemetery.

Frank Williams
Private 4834, 1st/5th Battalion, Gloucestershire Regiment

Born: 1888
Enlisted: 29 February 1916
Died: 17 August 1916

Frank was born in Campden in 1888, the fifth and youngest son of Joseph and Lucy Williams of Watery Lane, and was baptised at St. James's Church on 23 January 1889. His father was employed as a mason's labourer in 1891 and then as a shepherd on a farm in 1901.

After leaving school Frank found employment as an agricultural engine driver. Then on 29 February 1916 he enlisted in the Gloucestershire Regiment at Bristol and spent the next five months preparing for overseas service at Weston-Super-Mare and on Salisbury Plain. He was sent to France at the end of July 1916 with a draft of men to reinforce the 1st/5th Battalion, Gloucestershire Regiment after they sustained casualties in the Ovillers sector on 21-23 July 1916 during the Battle of the Somme. Frank joined the battalion while they were in billets in villages west of the front line trenches. They moved forward on 13 August and occupied reserve trenches near the brickworks in Albert. On 16 August "A" and "D" Companies attacked Skyline Trench located south of Thiepval. The attack failed and Frank was wounded. He was evacuated back to a field hospital but died the next day. He was 29 years old and is buried in Varennes Cemetery, Somme, France. His name is recorded on two memorials in Campden: in St. James's Church and in the High Street.

Frank's elder brother Charles named one of his sons Thiepval as a tribute to his brother.

Joseph Williams
Royal Warwickshire Regiment

Enlisted: 1916
Died: 2 December 1934

Joseph was born in Campden in 1878, the third son of Joseph and Lucy Williams. His father married Lucy Brotheridge in 1870 and in 1891 the family were living at Manton's Yard in Campden. By 1901 they had moved to Watery Lane.

Joseph was a member of "K" Company, 2nd Volunteer Battalion, Gloucestershire Regiment for a number of years. In 1916, when he was 38 years old, he enlisted in the Royal Warwickshire Regiment and was posted to France after only a very short period of training. The news that he had been seriously wounded only three months after enlisting was received by his mother shortly after she heard that Frank, her fifth son, had died of wounds in August 1916. He was admitted to a hospital in France for treatment.

Joseph lived all his life in Campden apart from his time in the army and was employed as a labourer. He married Rose Ellen Gertrude Smith at St. James's Church on 30 August 1924 and they lived at Paul's Pike.

Joseph died on 2 December 1934 aged 56 and is buried in St. James's churchyard.

Reginald George Williams

Lance Corporal 13779, 9th Battalion, Worcestershire Regiment
Lance Corporal P11852, Military Foot Police

Born: 17 July 1895
Enlisted: 8 August 1914
Discharged: 18 August 1919
Died: 18 May 1971

Reginald was born "*Richard George Williams*" in Blockley, the son of Elizabeth Annie Keen Williams, and was baptised at St. Catharine's Church on 16 May 1896 as "*Reginald George Williams*". After leaving school he found employment as a farm labourer and then at the outbreak of war he enlisted in the Worcestershire Regiment on 8 August 1914 aged 18 years. The next ten months were spent training in England before he was sent overseas with the 9th Battalion and arrived at Gallipoli in Turkey on 22 June 1915. He served on the peninsula until 29 September, when he was invalided back to England suffering from dysentery and enteric fever and was admitted to the 2nd Southern General Hospital in Bristol on 24 January 1916. After recovering from his illness he was discharged from hospital on 14 February and transferred to the 3rd Battalion in France, where he saw action during the Battle of the Somme. On 18 August the battalion took over the front line at the Leipzig Salient, north of Authuille Wood and at 4.10pm on 24 August they went forward with the 1st

3rd Battalion, Worcestershire Regiment, 1914
Reginald is standing in the centre at the back.

Battalion, Wiltshire Regiment to attack Hindenburg Trench. They advanced under a smoke screen and there was hard fighting with bomb and bayonet. The German position was taken and held despite a tremendous bombardment from the German artillery. The battalion suffered 234 casualties during this action.

Reginald was wounded when he was hit by an explosive bullet in his back. He was evacuated back to England and admitted to the 3rd General Hospital in Bedford on 31 August. Further treatment followed when he was transferred to Bencote Hospital on 5 October 1916 and from there he was sent to a convalescent hospital at Butterfront Camp in Ireland on 4 November.

Lance Corporal Reginald Williams is seated second from the left.

After recovering from his wound he was placed into medical category C3 and transferred to the Military Foot Police. He began his service with this unit in late 1917 and remained with them until the end of the war. He served in Clonmel and other Southern Ireland locations.

Reginald was discharged from the army on 18 August 1919 and returned to Campden, where he found employment as a market gardener. On 18 April 1923 he married Beatrice Dora Tout at Bengeworth Church in Evesham. They decided to emigrate to Canada and lived for one year in Tompkins in Saskatchewan where Reginald worked as a farm labourer. In 1924 they moved to Winnipeg, Manitoba, where they remained for the rest of their lives. They had three children, all born in Canada: Douglas Walter Richard, Reginald Sidney and Dick. Reginald started work for T. Eaton Company Limited as a deliveryman on 2 June 1924. This was the start of 36 years with the company and he was presented with a *"beautiful living room chair"* on his retirement in July 1960. Reginald was a very keen breeder of dogs and he operated boarding kennels in Winnipeg from 1929 to 1960.

At the start of the Second World War he tried to enlist in the Canadian Army on 15 August 1940 but he was found to be medically unfit owing to a slightly deformed spine and a very tender scar from his war wound.

Reginald died on 18 May 1971 aged 75 and is buried in St. James's Cemetery, Portage Avenue, Winnipeg, Manitoba, Canada.

Richard Henry Williams
Sergeant 13778, 11th Battalion, Royal Welch Fusiliers

Died: 10 July 1918

Richard was born in Campden, the son of Richard and Margaret Williams of Watery Lane, Campden. His father Richard, a general labourer, married Margaret Dyde, a native of Lower Quinton, in 1873.

At the outbreak of war in 1914 Richard enlisted at Ogmore Vale, Glamorgan, Wales in the 11th (Service) Battalion, Royal Welsh Fusiliers. The battalion was formed in Wrexham in September 1914 and posted to 67th Brigade, 22nd Division. In April 1915 the division was based in Maidstone for training and on 5 September 1915 Richard and the division arrived in France, but after only a very short period on the Western Front they were posted to Salonika. They travelled to Marseille by train and embarked for Greece on 27 October.

Richard was killed in action in Greece on 10 July 1918 aged 28 years. He is buried in Sarigol Cemetery, near Salonika in Northern Greece and his name is recorded on two memorials in Campden: in St. James's Church and in the High Street. He was survived by his wife, Mrs M. F. Williams (formerly Sharp), a native of Kent.

Sidney Thomas Williams
Lance Corporal 6073, 1st King's Dragoon Guards
Lance Corporal D/19579, Corps of Dragoons

Born: 24 April 1886
Enlisted: 1904
Discharged: 1920
Died: 12 August 1963

Sidney was born at Exton in Rutland, the son of Richard and Sarah Williams of Broad Campden, and was baptised at St. Catharine's Church on 16 June 1892, the same day as Walter Richard Williams. Sidney's sister, Elizabeth Annie Keen Williams, was the mother of Walter Richard and Reginald George Williams.

After leaving school Sidney became a regular soldier when he joined "A" Squadron, 1st King's Dragoon Guards in 1904. After a period of home service he was posted to India. When he returned from India he was placed on the Army Reserve list and in 1912 he emigrated to Canada, where he worked on a farm north of Elkhorn in Manitoba. According to relatives living in Canada he arrived in Elkhorn in the middle of January and had to travel miles to the farm dressed in a bowler hat and a coat with a velvet collar.

At the outbreak of war in August 1914 he received a telegram advising him to report to his regiment at Lucknow in India. The Canadian Pacific Railway Company prepared his ticket for the entire journey and it was close to six feet in length. However, on reaching England he was told that his regiment were returning for service on the Western Front. Sidney arrived in France on 30 October and waited to join up with the battalion that was due to land at Marseille on 7 November 1914. The next four years were spent on the Western Front until he was posted back to India with the battalion in August 1918.

The 1st King's Dragoon Guards saw action in the 3rd Afghanistan War in 1919 and Sidney was awarded the Afghanistan Bar on his 1908 Indian General Service Medal.

In 1920 he returned to Campden and married Mary Ellen Bricknell at St. James's Church on 9 February. They emigrated to Canada and settled in Elkhorn, where he worked as a labourer until 1923, when he purchased his own farm five miles north of Elkhorn in the Burbank District. They both farmed until they retired into the town of Elkhorn in 1960.

On a visit to England in the summer of 1963 Sidney had a heart attack and died on 12 August 1963. He was 77 years old and was buried in St. James's churchyard in Campden.

Walter Richard Williams
Private Ply. 2947(S), 54th Sharp Shooters Squad, 1st Battalion, Royal Marine Light Infantry

Born: 12 November 1886
Enlisted: 21 December 1915
Died: 27 March 1918

Walter was born in Bretforton, the son of Elizabeth Annie Keen Williams of Broad Campden, and was baptised at St. Catharine's Church in Campden on 16 June 1892. After leaving school he was employed as a carter. On 21 December 1915 he enlisted in Campden and was immediately placed in the Army Reserve. He was mobilised on 9 April 1917 and posted to the

Royal Marine Light Infantry. He joined his unit in Deal on 11 April and his medical examination passed him fit for overseas service, recording that he was five feet eleven inches tall. His training at Deal ended on 20 September when he was posted to HMS *Victory*, a depot at Portsmouth, where he stayed until 10 December 1917. On 7 November he had attended and passed a musketry course at Blandford.

Walter arrived in France at the end of December as a member of 54th S. S. Squad, 1st Battalion, Royal Marine Light Infantry, which was part of the Royal Naval Division. He had only been at the front for about three months when the Germans launched their Spring offensive on 21 March 1918. A huge infantry attack followed an intense artillery bombardment. There was confusion amongst the British units as the Germans advanced and many men were taken prisoner. Walter was wounded during the opening stages of the offensive and was taken prisoner. The Germans treated his serious head wounds at a field dressing station near Cambrai but he died of them on 27 March. He is buried in Cambrai East Military Cemetery in France. He was 31 years old and not married.

Walter's name is recorded on two memorials in Campden: in St. James's Church and in the High Street.

54th Sharp Shooters Squadron, Royal Marine Light Infantry, Deal, May 1917
Walter is standing on the left-hand side of the photograph in front of the window.

Alfred Withers

Private 59483, Devonshire Regiment
Private 105450, 61st Labour Company, Labour Corps

Born: 7 December 1877
Enlisted: 11 December 1915
Discharged: 4 April 1919
Died: 17 November 1922

Alfred was the second son of Richard and Ann Withers of Campden. His father was a blacksmith and the family home was in the High Street in 1881 and in Sheep Street in 1891. After attending school in the town Alfred became an errand boy before he found employment as a gardener.

When he married Florence Ellen Sallis in Cheltenham on 26 September 1902 he was employed as a gardener at Raynes Park, Wimbledon, London. They had three children: Dorothy Anne (born in 1904 in Wimbledon), Ada Adelaide (born in 1907 in Mickleton) and Douglas Thomas Richard (born in 1914 in Flax Bourton).

The family were living at Lawn Cottage in Flax Bourton, near Bristol, when the war started in 1914. Alfred enlisted in the Infantry Labour Company of the Devonshire Regiment at Backwell, near Flax Bourton, on 11 December 1915, when he was 37 years old. His medical examination classed him as B2 and he was immediately placed into the Army Reserve.

After being mobilised he joined his unit at Weston-Super-Mare and arrived in France on 26 March 1917, where he joined the 61st Labour Company of the Labour Corps in May 1917. He remained on the Western Front for two years and ten days before he arrived back in England on 4 April 1919. He was discharged from the army the same day and returned to his wife and young family in Flax Bourton, where he continued working as a gardener.

Alfred died on 17 November 1922 aged 44 and is buried in Flax Bourton churchyard. He was gassed twice during the war and it is believed that this ultimately caused his death. After her husband's death Florence returned to Cheltenham with the children and she remained there until she died on 21 August 1960.

Alfred is seated second from the left in the photograph.

Charles William Withers

Born: 1879
Died: 11 August 1934

Charlie was born in Campden, the second son of Richard and Ann Withers, who were living in the High Street in 1881, and was baptised at St. James's Church on 29 June 1879. His father was a blacksmith and on the 1891 census Charlie is listed as living with his uncle, James Henry Withers, near St. James's Church and working as a blacksmith's assistant.

In her *Book of Remembrance* Josephine Griffiths lists Charlie as serving in the war. No regiment is recorded against his name, which suggests that he may have been employed in munitions work.

Charlie died on 11 August 1934 aged 55 only five months after the death of his father and is buried in St. James's churchyard in Campden. Fred Coldicott writes: "*It came as a shock to all the inhabitants of Campden, for he seemed such a strong, healthy man who never had an illness. Unfortunately he was a bachelor, and the last to carry on the family trade. Every day for as long as I can remember, at exactly 10.00am, he would take his bread and cheese down to the Eight Bells, have just one pint of beer and go straight back to work. He never even took his leather apron off. As far as I know his only hobby was bell-ringing. He had been a regular bell-ringer for thirty-six years.*"

Ernest H. Withers
Private 1215, "D" Company, 1st/5th Battalion, Gloucestershire Regiment

Born: 14 May 1892
Enlisted: 1912
Discharged: 12 March 1919
Died: 2 August 1930

Ernest was the eldest son of James Henry and Ellen Withers of Campden. His father was a shoeing and general blacksmith and the family home was near St. James's Church.

Ernest went to school in the town and then joined "H" Company, 5th Battalion, Gloucestershire Regiment, the local company of the Territorial Army. When the war started in 1914 he signed up for overseas service and was mobilised on 5th August. A period of training followed at Chelmsford before the battalion arrived at Boulogne on 29 March 1915. The next three years were spent on the Western Front, where the battalion served mainly in the Ypres Salient and on the Somme. In June 1918 the 5th Glosters were involved in heavy fighting in northern Italy on the Asiago Plateau.

Ernest served throughout the war in the Gloucestershire Regiment and was officially discharged on 12 March 1919. During the war his army number changed three times. It started as 1215, then became 5487 and ended up as 37302 at the end of the war.

After the war Ernest was a bellringer at St. James's Church up until 1923.

He died of a brain tumour at Hampton Workhouse Union Infirmary in Evesham on 2 August 1930. He is buried in Bengeworth Cemetery, Evesham and on his death certificate his occupation was recorded as a builder's labourer. He never married.

Frank Withers

Private 16494, "E" Company, 12th Battalion, Gloucestershire Regiment

Born: 6 August 1894
Enlisted: 7 December 1914
Discharged: 10 July 1916

Frank was the second son of James Henry and Ellen Withers and was baptised at St. James's Church on 16 September 1894. His father was a shoeing and general blacksmith and the family home was in a cottage close to St. James's Church. Frank went to school in the town and was the brother of Elsie, Ernest and Richard.

During the war he enlisted in the Gloucestershire Regiment on 7 December 1914 as a private. After a long period of initial training in England he became ill and was eventually discharged on 10 July 1916 owing to "*sickness*" without serving overseas. A Silver War Badge was issued to indicate that he had made his contribution to the war effort.

After the war he married Alice and they went to live in Birmingham. They did not have any children.

James Henry Withers

Born: 28 November 1876
Died: 1941

Harry was born in Campden, the eldest son of Richard and Ann Withers of Sheep Street. After leaving school he was employed as a baker's boy, and later a carter's boy, before he left Campden to be a coachman for the vicar at Monkton Coombe near Bath. In 1911 he became the verger at St. James's Church in Campden and in 1913 he joined the Choral Society.

In 1916 Harry married Alice Ethel Keech in Blackheath in Kent and their daughter, Barbara Joan, was born at 33, Edward's Road, Erdington, Birmingham on 2 July 1918. Harry was working in Birmingham as a brass caster on "*war work*" in a munitions factory at the time of the birth. The family returned to Campden after the war.

Harry died in 1941 aged 64 and the following tribute to him was written by the vicar of St. James's Church: "*He played the organ each Sunday morning at Holy Communion and as a bellringer he was welcome in the towers of neighbouring churches and here in Campden he was made Master of the Tower. Until the war silenced our bells, night after night he rang the curfew bell to remind our people that night was falling.*" He is buried in St. James's churchyard.

Richard Withers
Private 26452, 10th Battalion, Gloucestershire Regiment
Private M-410662, Army Service Corps

Born: 29 June 1896
Enlisted: 1 December 1915
Discharged: 11 October 1919
Died: 17 July 1962

Richard was the third son of James Henry and Ellen Withers of Campden. He was baptised at St. James's Church on 30 August 1896 and attended school in the town. His father was a blacksmith and the family home was in Church Street.

When the war started Richard enlisted in Campden in the Gloucestershire Regiment on 1 December 1915. He was immediately placed into the Army Reserve before being mobilised on 24 January 1916. After a period of home service with the 3rd (Reserve) Battalion he was posted to France on 23 July 1916, where he joined the 10th Battalion as part of a draft of men to reinforce the battalion after they had suffered heavy casualties in fighting near High Wood during the Battle of the Somme. He remained at the front until he returned to England on 6 October 1916.

The next three months were spent on home service before he embarked for Salonika in Greece on 25 January 1917, where he joined the 9th Battalion in the Mediterranean Expeditionary Force. The battalion remained in Salonika until July 1918 and it is likely that this is when Richard returned to England, where he was transferred to the Army Service Corps to begin another period of home service that ended when he was discharged on 11 October 1919.

After the war he found employment as a carpenter and joiner and in the years leading up to his retirement he was working for the Midlands Electricity Board.

Richard never married. He died on 17 July 1962 aged 66 and is buried in Bengeworth Cemetery in Evesham, Worcestershire. He was found drowned in the River Avon in Evesham and the report in the *Evesham Journal* stated that an "*open verdict*" was recorded at the inquest.

Minnie Eleanor K. Wixey
French Red Cross Nurse

Minnie was the fourth child of Herbert and Annie Wixey. She was born in Campden in 1872 and was baptised at St. James's Church on 29 September 1872. Her father owned and ran Wixey's Stores, which was established in 1863. A newspaper advertisement described Herbert Wixey as a "*high class family grocer, an export tea blender and a provision merchant*". He was a pillar of the local business society, a Sunday School teacher and involved in most of the local committees and activities. Herbert's son Frank took over the business in 1915 and sold to Joseph Burton & Company in March 1920.

Minnie became a schoolteacher after leaving school but by 1901 she was employed as a servant for Charles Hayman at 105 Crouch Hill, Crouch End, Christchurch in Middlesex. During the war she volunteered as a nurse with the French Red Cross and arrived in France in September 1914. Her rank is recorded as a "*masseuse*" on her medal index card and the fact that she did not get issued with a 1914 Star medal indicates that she did not treat British soldiers.

Steven Wright
Army Service Corps

Steve was born in Mickleton in 1897, the fourth son of William Wright. His father, a native of Quinton, was a farm labourer and married Sarah Annie Stephens in 1887. William and Sarah had five sons who served in the war, two of whom lost their lives: Ernest in 1915 and Frank in 1918.

Steve was only 17 years old when the war started. In November 1915 the *Evesham Journal* listed him as a Campden man who had recently enlisted in the Army Service Corps. He returned safely from the war and together with his wife, May, lived in Mickleton for the rest of his life. They did not have any children.

Frederick James Yates

Private 24366, Gloucestershire Regiment
Private 416125, Labour Corps
Private 58295, King's Royal Rifle Corps

Born: 1896
Died: 4 March 1985

Frederick was born in Campden in 1896, the son of Richard and Mary Jane Yates of West End Terrace, and was baptised at St. James's Church on 18 October 1896. His father was a native of the town and a carpenter and joiner by trade.

After leaving school Frederick found employment as a builder's labourer but when the war started he enlisted in the Gloucestershire Regiment. He did not serve overseas until after the start of 1916 and by the end of the war he had also served in the Labour Corps and the King's Royal Rifle Corps. He saw action during the Battle of the Somme in 1916 and returned home safely at the end of the war.

After the war he married Emily Keyte, daughter of Thomas and Fanny Keyte of Blockley, and they had three children: Michael, Philip and Mary. Emily lost her brother, Thomas Keyte, during the war. He was killed in action on 31 July 1917 on the opening day of the Battle of Passchendaele while serving with the 1st Battalion, Worcestershire Regiment. He was 21 years old and as he has no known grave his name is recorded on the Menin Gate Memorial in Ypres.

Frederick and Emily lived in West End Terrace and Frederick worked as a market gardener in Mickleton. During the Second World War their son Michael was in the Home Guard.

Frederick died on 4 March 1985 aged 88 and his ashes are buried in Wellesbourne Crematorium.

Private 21631 James Albert Court, 15th Battalion, Cheshire Regiment
James was born in Weston-sub-Edge in 1890. He was killed in action on 24
March 1918 when he was "*blown up by a shell*". As he has no known grave
his name is recorded on the Pozières Memorial in France.

James Albert Court
James is standing second from the right on the back row. The caption for the photograph
was "*105th Infantry Brigade Headquarters*".

Chapter 2

Photograph Gallery

This chapter contains the photographs in the author's collection that were not used in chapter 1.

The Home Guard
The group of men includes the Home Guard units from Campden, Ebrington, Paxford, Blockley and Mickleton. Many of the men on this photograph saw service during the Great War. Included in this book are Jack Horne (third from the right on the front row) and Charlie Ladbrook (fourth from the left on the second row). George Hughes and Alf Bruce are also on the photograph.

Photograph Gallery

The following section contains photographs that were not included in the previous chapter, which concerned itself with the men and women from Campden who served in the war. All of the photographs were either taken in the town or include people associated with the town, the author or the neighbouring parishes. The author hopes that anyone seeing these photographs for the first time will find the images as exciting as he did.

Richard Beavington
Richard is holding the pony.

Richard Beavington
In the above photograph Richard is standing on the right.
Location: Basra, Mesopotamia.

Percy George Biles
Percy is identified by the arrow second from the right of this group of men from the 9th Battalion, Gloucestershire Regiment. The original caption for the photograph reads: "Ready for the night-entrenching".

Enoch Mickloth Bennett
In the photograph below Enoch is standing fourth from the left on the back row. The caption reads: "On the banks of the Suez Canal with the 69th Field Bakery, ASC".

Charles Birch
In the photograph on the left Charlie is standing with his wife, Enid. They were married at St. James's Church in 1937 and their home was "The Gables" in High Street, Campden.

In the photograph on the right Charlie is wearing his Royal Army Medical Corps officer's uniform. He was a lieutenant and served in Egypt during the war.

Harry William Bricknell
The two photographs on the left show Harry wearing his Gloucestershire Regiment uniform. He entered France in March 1915 and served for 21 months on the Western Front before returning to England with dysentery. The war ended for Harry when he was captured by the Germans and taken to a prisoner of war camp in Germany.

Captain Wilfred James Bright, Royal Field Artillery: the wedding of Wilfred and Betty
Wilfred married Elizabeth "*Betty*" Jones in Cardiff in 1920. They met each other when they were both teaching in Campden. Wilfred's brother Frank is shown wearing his uniform and their mother, Edith Ellen, is sitting to the right of the bride. .

319

Alfred John Bruce
Alfred is sitting next to his wife, Lucy May
Hughes. Dorothy Bruce and Charles Hughes
are at the back.

Alfred John Bruce
Alfred is standing second from the left. He can be seen wearing his
Gloucestershire Regiment cap badge and his medal ribbons.

Alfred John Bruce
In the photograph above Alfred is standing on the back row second from the left. The
photograph on the left shows a group of Campden volunteers. The caption written on the
back suggests that Alfred is on the photograph.

Ernest Cherry
The photograph on the left
shows Ernest and Susanna
Cherry. Ernest married
Susanna Bodenham at
Birmingham Registry Office in
1917. The wedding was later
blessed at St. Catharine's
Church in Campden in 1925.
During the war Ernest entered
France in March 1915 with the
Gloucestershire Regiment.
After serving on the Western
Front for sixteen months he
returned to England and was
transferred to the Devonshire
Regiment.

Ernest George Crisp

The photograph above was taken at Codford Camp, Salisbury Plain on 19 November 1915. Ernest is standing on the right at the front.

The Lygon Arms, Campden, 1908
Left to right: James Franklin, Fred Franklin, William Henry Franklin, unknown, unknown and unknown. James and Fred were brothers and are pictured with their father.

John Tracey Crosswell
John was the son of Millicent Crosswell, sister of the author's great-grandmother, Lucy Crosswell. He was killed in action near the Canal du Nord in France in October 1918 while serving as a private in the Royal Warwickshire Regiment. John is seated in the photograph on the left.

John Crosswell
John was born in 1893 and was the brother of Lucy Crosswell, who married Richard Hughes, the author's great-grandfather. During the war he served in the 164th Battalion, Canadian Expeditionary Force. He arrived in France in September 1917.
John's photograph on the right was taken shortly after he enlisted.

Thomas Bassett Crosswell
Thomas was born in 1893, the son of George and Rose Crosswell. He was living at Hidcote Bartrim in 1899 and entered school in Mickleton the same year. His twin brother John served during the war and his sister Lucy married Richard Hughes, the author's great-grandfather.
Thomas enlisted in the Canadian Machine Gun Corps at Toronto in September 1915 and arrived in France in June 1916. He was discharged from the army in March 1919.
After the war he returned to England and found employment as a gardener. He died in December 1952 aged 59 in Stratford-upon-Avon Hospital and is buried with his wife, Emily, in Stratford Cemetery.

Thomas Bassett Crosswell

Thomas Bassett Crosswell

Private 436504 Roland Dyer, Canadian Expeditionary Force
In the photograph above Roland is seated at the front on the right. The photograph below was taken in Canada in 1915. Roland is standing in uniform with the Sirrett family, who were originally from Blockley.

George Ebborn
Left to right: George, Harry George Ellis and William Izod.
George volunteered in August 1914, when he was 54 years old. He spent two years on the Western Front with the Royal Engineers and was wounded once.

Arthur George Ellis

Arthur was educated at Campden Grammar School and was Head Boy in 1916. In the photograph on the left he is pictured wearing the uniform of the school's cadet force. In 1917 he enlisted in the 28th Battalion, London Regiment (2nd Artists' Rifles) as a private but three months later he joined the Royal Flying Corps. He obtained a commission and ended the war as a lieutenant in the Royal Air Force. The other two photographs show him wearing the uniform of the Royal Flying Corps (later Royal Air Force).

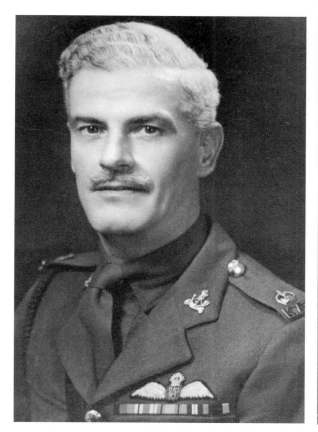

Major Arthur George Ellis, King's African Rifles
Arthur is wearing his RAF flying wings and 1939-45 medal ribbons.

Private 887469 Roland Ellis, Canadian Expeditionary Force
Roland is sitting on the chair on the left of the photograph.

Roland Ellis
Roland is standing second from the left
in the photograph above.

William Evans
William is pictured on the right
with his wife, Elizabeth.

Richard Green
In the photograph above Richard
is standing at the end of the row
on the left.

Michael Philip Grove (left)
Michael served on the Western
Front with the Worcestershire
Regiment and then the Royal
Marine Light Infantry.

William Hart (right)
Left to right: George Hart and
William Hart.
The two brothers are wearing their
Boer War uniforms.

William Thomas Hart
The photograph on the left shows William sitting third from the right at the front. The group of men are officers of the 11th (Service) Battalion, Royal Warwickshire Regiment. William is seen here as a captain but was soon promoted to the rank of major.

The Hart-Huyshe Family 1899
William Hart is the sailor on the left of the photograph and his brother, Frederick Hart, is also in uniform on the right. Wentworth Huyshe, who married Hester Ann Hart, is standing at the front with his arm on the shoulder of his son, Wentworth. Reynell Huyshe is the young boy directly below Frederick Hart.

Lewis Hadley Horne
In the photograph above Lewis is standing on the right. In the photograph in the top right hand corner of this page Lewis is with his wife at Blockley station.

Charles Richard Hughes
Salvation Army

George Hughes
The photographs above and to the right show George in his Royal Navy uniform. He served for sixteen years, 1916-1932.

Richard Hughes
The two photographs above show the author's great-grandfather in uniform, wearing a Devonshire Regiment cap badge.

Thomas Hughes
Sergeant, Royal Warwickshire Regiment.
Thomas and Richard were brothers.

The 8th Battalion, Worcestershire Regiment, 1920's
After the end of the war these men from Campden were members of the Territorial Army. The unit was commanded by Reynell Huyshe.
Back row (left to right): Reynell Huyshe, Sam Hope, Ned Merriman, Jack Ashwin, Jim Payne and Joe Hedges.
Front row (left to right): unknown, unknown, unknown, unknown and Albert Veale.

Reynell Oswald Huyshe, 1918
The above photograph was a postcard sent to his wife on 14 August 1918. Reynell is seated in the centre at the front of the group.

Thomas and Ellen Hughes
Thomas married Ellen Huband in Birmingham in 1899. They had five children: Thomas James, Eric Gerald, Lilian Rosa, Nellie May and Beatrice Ann.

Reynell Oswald Huyshe
In the above photograph Reynell is standing with his wife, Jessie Hilda Lousie Rees. They married in 1917.

In the photograph on the left Reynell is standing at the back on the left.

Private S2-018259 Philip Frederick "Jim" James, Army Service Corps
In the photograph above Jim is standing third from the right smoking a cigarette.
During the war he served in Gallipoli and Egypt.

David Jelfs, Middlesex Regiment
Killed in action in Greece in 1918.
Brother of Harry and Ruby.

Stoker Harry Thomas Jelfs, Royal Navy
Harry was the brother of the author's
grandmother, Ruby Violet Jelfs. Ruby
married Fred Rogers, brother of Frank.

Stoker Harry Thomas Jelfs, Royal Navy
Back: Edith and Harry (husband and wife)
Front: Harry and Matilda Jelfs (Harry's parents).
Harry and Matilda are buried in Mickleton.

Wentworth Roland Huyshe
1887-1971

William Henry Thomas Keyte
Private 4870 Bill Keyte,
Gloucestershire Regiment is
somewhere on this group
photograph.
Bill originally served in the
Devonshire Regiment before
being transferred. He was
finally discharged from the
army on 23 October 1918.

'A' COMPANY 9th SERVICE BATTALION GLOUCESTER REGIMENT.

Sergeant 12713 Arthur Keen, 9th Battalion, Gloucestershire Regiment
Arthur is on the second row from the back. He is below the man who is thirteenth from the left on the back row.

Bill Keyte, 1896-1979
In the photograph on the far left Bill can be seen wearing his blue hospital uniform.

In the photograph on the left Bill is seated on the right. He is wearing his Devonshire Regiment cap badge.

Percy Frederick Lane
Percy was employed at Campden station in 1914.
Photograph was supplied by STEAM: The Museum of the Great Western Railway, Swindon.

Lawrence Ladbrook
Lawrence served as a gunner in the Royal Field Artillery during the war. In the photograph on the left he is standing third from the left in the kitchen, waiting for food.

Gunner Lawrence Ladbrook, Royal Field Artillery
Lawrence is seated on a chair fifth from the left.

Gunner Lawrence Ladbrook, Royal Field Artillery
Lawrence is second from the left in the photograph above.

Basil Hoveden Neve, G. W. R. Ambulance Contingent, Boer War
Basil is seated on the floor at the end of the row on the right.

Elick Payne, Royal Navy
Elick is pictured on the right.

Captain Charles Hubert Francis Noel, Coldstream Guards
Charles is standing at the end of the second row on the right.

The Noel Brothers, Campden House
Left to right: Charles, Arthur and Robert.

Elick Payne, HMS _Conqueror_, 1915
Left to right: Elick, E. May and P. Donald.

Elick Payne, HMS _Vivid_
Elick is seated.

Harry Payne
Australian Imperial Forces

John Payne: John is third from the left on the second row from the back.

Elick Payne
HMS _Janus_, China Station

James Stanbridge
James is seated on the front row fourth from the right. The photograph was taken on 22 March 1918 and the men are the occupants of Hut 6, East Camp, Irish Command Depot, Tipperary.

Jim Rogers
Jim was the son of Charles and Annie Ada Rogers. He was the brother of Frank and Ruby.

Frederick Mark Whatcott, Duke of Cornwall's Light Infantry
Above: Mark is standing second from the right on the back row.
Below: Mark is standing on the left.

Harry Henry Vincent Tyack
Teddy served as a private in Number 10 Motor Transport Company, Army Service Corps.

Harry Edgar Wheatcroft, Royal Navy
Harry joined the Royal Navy in 1915 and served in both world wars.

The Bruce Family
Charles and Rose Ellen Bruce are seated with four of their children. Left to right: Dorothy, Albert, Alfred and Oscar.

The Bruce Family
Seated (left to right): Charles, Dorothy and Rose Ellen.
Standing (left to right): Lucy May, Charlie Clifford and Alfred.

A. G. Wood (right)
Educated at Campden Grammar School.
The writing on the the back of the photograph reads:
"*1st Bn. Worcestershire Regiment, British West Indies, Turks Island.*"

Walter Matthew Cox (left)
Mr. Cox is seated with three students. His son, John Lennox Cox, was killed in action in 1918.

Campden Grammar School, c.1906

All students are listed from left to right.
Back row: Harry Pyment, Gordon Russell, Donald Russell, Rosborough and Randall.
Second Row: William E. Richardson, F. Bates, Walford Chamberlain, Edgar Jarrett, Joe Simmons, and S. Stokes.
Third Row: H. Harrison, Henderson, Rosborough, Alec Osborne, Collett Chamberlain and R. Slatter.
Front Row: Arthur Pyment, Leslie Hands, Loss, H. Sheppard, V. Jordan, Alec Walker, Billy Badger and Willets Horne.

Norton Hall VAD Hospital
The above photograph shows a group of wounded men in front of Norton Hall. Maye Bruce is in the centre at the back with her head turned. The photograph on the right shows two soldiers wearing their blue hospital uniforms at Norton Hall. The man on the left is in the Machine Gun Corps and the man on the right the King's Royal Rifle Corps. Neither man is believed to be connected with Campden.

Wounded soldiers in Campden: There are various regiments and some Belgian soldiers.

The Guild of Handicraft (Six members of the Guild on this photograph are included in this book.)
Front row (left to right): Walter Edwards, Alec Miller, Bert Humphries, Mickey Moran, Arthur Bunten, Jack Cameron, Mark Merriman, Stanley Keeley and Golden Keeley. **Middle row** (L-R)): Bill Thornton, Edward Toy, Bill Scurr, Webster, J. T. Webster, Arthur Naylor, unknown, Bill Wride and Charlie Daniels. **Back row** (L-R): Arthur Cameron, unknown, George Hart, unknown, George Vickery, Walter Curtis, Will Hart, Tom Jellife, Wally Curtis, Alf Smith, William Wall, John Angus, Keyte, Herbert Osborn, unknown, Fleetwood Varley, Bill Mark, unknown and Jim Pyment.

Joseph Edwin Bennett: Joseph is standing on the far left of the photograph.

Brotheridge Sisters
Gladys Brotheridge is standing on the left and her sister, May, is standing on the right. The identity of two people in the centre of the photograph is unknown.
Gladys and May were the daughters of Charles Foster and Keziah Brotheridge. Charles served in the Royal Engineers in 1918.

Thomas James Bickley: Tom is believed to be on this photograph.

Tom Bickley: Tom is fourth from the right, facing the camera.

Tom Bickley: Tom is on the right, holding a shovel.

Major Arthur George Ellis, 5th Battalion, King's African Rifles (standing on the far right of the photograph)
Arthur, known as George in Africa, served in the Royal Flying Corps and Royal Air Force during the First World War.

William Hedges: William is second from the right on the second row.

Elick Payne: Elick is standing on the far right, 1911.

Francis Merriman: Francis is facing the camera on the right-hand side.

L-R: Dorcas Payne, Elick Payne and Mabel Payne

Tom Smith: Tom is facing the camera, sixth from the right.

Joe Whatcott: Joe is believed to be on this photograph.

Veterans of the war proudly wear their medals in High Street, Campden. Is this an Armistice Day parade?

Gloucestershire Regiment parading in the Square, Campden.

H Company, 5th Battalion, Gloucestershire Regiment, August 1914
The company are about to march off to war. Corporal Joyful Billy Harris is standing at the front of the group of men.

10th Battalion, Gloucestershire Regiment, Ferncliff, 1915
William Hedges and Tom Smith could be on this photograph.

A parade in the Square, Campden, occasion unknown.

Jim James
Jim served at Gallipoli and in Egypt in the ASC. In the photograph on the left he is standing on the right.

Bill Benfield
The photograph on the right appeared in the *Cheltenham Chronicle and Gloucestershire Graphic* on 17 June 1916. Bill, son of *Kaiser Bill*, is seated in the middle row on the right.

The Grammar School, CAMPDEN.

With a view to completing the

Roll of Honour

the Headmaster earnestly requests that the Names of

Old Boys

who have been or are serving their Country, may be sent to him at once.

W. MATTHEW COX,
Headmaster.
6641

Campden Grammar School
The advertisement appeared in the *Evesham Journal* and the Roll of Honour board is located in the main hall in Campden School in Cider Mill Lane.

2ⁿᵈ Lt. Charlie Bloodworth, Gloucestershire Regiment
"Five Gloucesters on Service Abroad" was the caption in the local paper.

Roland Dyer: Roland is standing at the end on the right.

Jim **James**, ASC (right)

Unidentified Photographs

While researching this book the author was very fortunate to be lent many photographs from friends, relatives of people included in the book and residents of Campden. The photographs included here are ones where it has not been possible to identify the soldiers pictured. Where information is known it is included in the caption.

The author believes that the soldiers in the photographs are either Campden men, relatives of Campden residents or friends of the men and women included in this book.

Oxford University
Officer Training Corps

Worcestershire Regiment
Photograph owned by David James.

The photograph was owned by Cissie Pither. The lady at the back is believed to be a Crosswell.

The Queen's
22nd County of London Battalion
Original owned by George Veale.

Original photograph was owned by Lawrence Ladbrook.

Original owned by Cissie Pither. A Hughes/Bruce/Crosswell relative?

A soldier's wedding at St. James's Church in Campden.

Original owned by George Veale.   Original owned by George Veale.   Original owned by Cissie Pither.

Recruits in the Square in Campden, August 1914
Sam Byrd, Enoch Bennett, James Trinder and George James are in the group but the names of the other men are not known.
Joe Chamberlain can be seen on the left, watching the parade.

Royal Field Artillery
All five men are wearing the "Imperial Service" badges.

Gloucestershire Regiment
The original was owned by Cissie Pither.

Gloucestershire Regiment
Members of the Gloucestershire
Regiment in High Street,
Campden.
At the front of the men are
members of the Grammar School
Cadet Force band.
The children watching the parade
include Charlie Grove, Sid Smith
and Bill Coldicott. Frank Morrey is
standing in the shop doorway with
dark hair and a waistcoat. All other
people on the photograph are
unknown.

**The Cotswold
House**
A group of people
watch soldiers
parading in the
Square in
Campden.

Chapter 3

Campden's War Memorials

This chapter gives details of the six war memorials in Campden that record the names of those who lost their lives while serving their country during the Great War.

The Home Guard, 1939-45
Captain Horsefield is at the front of the men as they march to the Square. Reverend O'Loughlin is standing in front of the war memorial. Many veterans of the Great War served in the Home Guard during the Second World War.

Campden's War Memorials

There are six separate memorials in Campden that record the names of those men who died during the war. The first man from the town to die was Basil Hovenden Neve, who lost his life when his ship was torpedoed on 5 September 1914. His name is recorded on four separate memorials in the town and on a brass plaque dedicated to his memory in St. James's Church. The last man to die to have his name recorded on a memorial in the town was Richard Lewis Griffin who died on 19 November 1923. He was one of eight men who died after the signing of the armistice to have their names recorded.

The number of names recorded on the separate memorials varies considerably. In her *Book of Remembrance* Josephine Griffiths lists sixty-four men who died, while the Baptist Church memorial records just six names. When you put all of the names on the memorials together you have seventy-six separate men. Twenty-four of these have their names on four separate memorials while thirteen men have their names recorded on only one.

During the course of researching this book a further thirty-four men who died during, or as a direct result of, the war were found. Each had a connection with the town but their names were not included on any of the town's memorials. George Cother, Percy Lane and Francis Preece were all listed by Josephine Griffiths in her nominal roll of servicemen but no indication of their deaths was recorded.

Many of the men included on the town's memorials did not spend all of their lives in Campden and as a consequence their names can be found on a number of memorials in the surrounding area. William Charles Hedges has his name recorded in Aston-sub-Edge and Mickleton and at Sandon in Staffordshire. Oscar Bruce's name is recorded at Bourton-on-the-Hill.

In St. James's churchyard there are nine official war graves maintained by the church on behalf of the Commonwealth War Graves Commission. Eight of these have the standard military headstones while John Dunn, the youngest person from Campden to die while serving king and country, has a private headstone. In September 1925 Rev. Hitchcock received a letter from the Commonwealth War Graves Commission confirming that five shillings per annum for each grave would be paid to Campden Parochial Church Council. Maintenance required the graves to be kept *"clear of all weeds, stones, loose soil and rubbish, to mow the turf from time to time as occasion shall require and to fill up, level and re-turf all holes and bare patches"*.

In April 1970 the regional director of the Commonwealth War Graves Commission wrote to the vicar informing him that as the grave of John Dunn was privately owned it was to be deleted from the agreement and that the next annual payment, due on 2 September 1970, would be five shillings per year for each of the eight remaining war graves located in St. James's churchyard.

The author wrote to the Commonwealth War Graves Commission in April 1994 and was told: *"Please be advised that there are 10 war graves in the churchyard of which 8 graves are maintained on the Commission's behalf by Chipping Campden Parochial Church Council. Payment of 25p per grave per annum is payable on a triennial basis in advance in September and the next payment is due in 1995. I understand that the churchyard is likely to be closed to further burials when the maintenance of the churchyard will become the responsibility of the local authority."*

The tenth grave mentioned in this letter is that of Norman Henry Powell, son of Harry, who died in April 1944 while serving in the Royal Air Force. At the time of the letter quoted above the Commission stated that *"the other two war graves, J. G. Dunn and N. H. Powell, are according to our records maintained by relatives"*.

The Memorial in the High Street

The memorial in the High Street records the names of sixty-two men who died between 1914 and 1923. After the war a war memorial committee was formed with Harry Ellis as the chairman and Wentworth Huyshe the honorary secretary. There was much debate about the form that the memorial should take and who should be commissioned to design it. Agreement was reached that Frederick L. Griggs would be the designer and after its completion it was unveiled on Sunday 9 January 1921 by Major-General Sir Reginald Stephens KCB, Head of Staff College at Camberley. Lord Haig had been invited to unveil the memorial but he was too busy with other appointments.

The names on the memorial were carved by Edgar Keen, an ex-soldier and townsman. Fred Coldicott writes: "*It was very interesting when we came down the street from school to stand and watch Edgar Keen carving the names and dates of those unfortunate men who had lost their lives during the war on the new war memorial. I often wondered what his thoughts were because he had known them all.*"

The original memorial erected by the town. It was replaced by the stone memorial unveiled in 1921.

Parade of ex-servicemen, 9 January 1921, on the day of the unveiling of the war memorial.

The Unveiling of the War Memorial, 1921

The war memorial was unveiled by Major General Sir Reginald Stephens KCB on 9 January 1921. In the photograph above the names of the fallen are covered by Union Jack flags. You can also see the sign for the recruiting office in the background.

The photograph on the left shows the memorial immediately after being unveiled.

The three photographs on this page were taken by Thomas Elsley of Campden. The memorial was designed by Frederick Griggs (1876-1938), who also designed memorials for Weston-sub-Edge, Willersey, Blockley and Snowshill.

The unveiling of the war memorial, January 1921

The War Memorial, 2008

1914
B.H.NEVE
R.TRACY
H.D.ASHWIN
W.BEAVINGTON
1915
F. HOWELL
H.TRACY
G.ELLIS

1915
A.HATHAWAY
W.C.HEDGES
T.SMITH
C.HEDGES
1916
J.G.DUNN
F.R.OSBORNE
C.P.S.MORRIS

1916
T.PLESTED
T.BRICKNELL
W.H.BRAIN
G.E.BENNETT
C.T.BRAIN
R.L.BINNS
F.J.CALLAWAY
F.WILLIAMS

1916
G.HAYDON
T.H.PAYNE
F.JAMES
O.SMITH
1917
L.H.HANDS
F.W.MERRIMAN
C.C.KEELEY

The names on the war memorial are carved on eight separate panels.

1917
T.KEELEY
F.G.ROBERTS
J.DYDE
J.H.DYDE
W.BYRD
J.JAMES
1918
R.T.M.NOEL

1918
F.A.GIBBINS
H.JAMES
J.TRINDER
W.R.WILLIAMS
R.BENNETT
F.R.PAYNE
G.E.JAMES
H.C.BAKER
R.L.GRIFFIN

1918
E.M.MERRIMAN
E.FISHER
W.H.GRIFFIN
R.H.WILLIAMS
O.BRUCE
E.BENNETT
W.H.HARRIS
J.L.COX
A.W.JAMES

1918
A.C.JEFFREY
W.A.WALTON
W.C.KEEN
J.H.HOWELL
1919
J.G.WHATCOTT
C.J.BRUCE
A.H.F.KEEN
W.E.GRIFFIN

The three panels headed 1918 have names at the bottom that were added after the memorial was unveiled. R. L. Griffin and A. W. James both died in 1923 and W. E. Griffin died in 1922. It should also be noted that W.H. Harris should be W. E. Harris as his middle name was Edwin.

The War Memorial, 2008

St. James's Church
Above: Plaque for Basil Neve
Right: Boer War and Basil Neve plaques

St. James's Church

Inside St. James's Church there is a memorial that records the names of sixty men who gave their lives in the war. The names and the dates of death are recorded in four columns on oak panels. Situated below the memorial for the First World War is another set of panels commemorating the men who died in the Second World War. Also in the church is a window, the east window of the chancel, which is a memorial to those who served in the Great War. It was commissioned in 1923 and designed by the distinguished water-colourist and stained glass window artist Henry A. Payne at Amberley, Stroud. It was then dedicated by the bishop of the diocese, Dr. Headlam, on Thursday 24 September 1925. The theme of the window is *"victory through sacrifice"* and at the bottom of the window is the following inscription: *"In memory of those who fell, in thankfulness to God for peace and in thankfulness for those who came back, 1914-18. And us they trusted; we the tasks inherit; the unfinished task for which their lives were spent."* This text was taken from a poem by C. A. A. Allingham called *The Trust*.

St. James's Church: Memorial with 60 names on oak panels.

St. James's Church: East Window of the Chancel.

St. James's Church also contains two memorial brass plaques. One is dedicated to the memory of Basil Neve, the first man from Campden to die in the war, and the second records the names of Alfred Benfield, William Henry Franklin and William Tracey, who all died during the Boer War in South Africa.

Book of Remembrance

In 1920 Josephine Griffiths compiled her *Book of Remembrance*, which includes details of sixty-four men from the town who died in the war. There is also a nominal list of 333 men who served and against their names is recorded their regiment, ship or squadron number where this was known. The original book is held at St. James's Church in a glass-fronted display case and it can be viewed by appointment.

The accuracy of the information contained within the book was dependent upon the information provided by friends and family. In most cases it was correct but there are several examples of people

assuming that Campden men served in the Gloucestershire Regiment just because they lived in the county.

In 1923 the book was updated, with a section called "An Aftermath", following the deaths of Richard Griffin, William Griffin and Alfred James. The end of the Second World War saw further additions, with sections listing the fallen, prisoners of war and all the men and women who served in His Majesty's Forces.

Josephine Griffiths records the following events on 11 November 1918 in the book: "And suddenly the bells pealed out, which during the war had been silent; and like magic the streets were bright with the flags and people were laughing and crying at the same time. At 3.00pm all hurried to the Parish Church for a great Thanksgiving Service. There where the men of Campden in the fighting line had been daily remembered before the Altar. The wounded men from Norton Hall V.A.D. Hospital had chairs in the Nave; and in spite of crutches, pain and suffering, their joy was indescribable. This wonderful day ended with a bonfire in the Square and the singing of the National Anthem with patriotic enthusiasm. But hush! Amid all the gladness, there were broken hearts and tearful eyes, and deep mourning."

Campden Grammar School

The memorial was originally located in the Grammar School in the High Street and it records the names of twelve former pupils of the school who died. The author believes that an error was made when the names for the memorial were being compiled. Charles Arkell Coldicott and his brother Harry Izod Coldicott both died during the war and were both pupils of the school. The names on the memorial read "Arkell Coldicott" and "Charles Coldicott". Should this be C. A. Coldicott and H. I. Coldicott?

The memorial is now located in the main hall of Campden School in Cider Mill Lane and when the author last visited the school in 2007 the memorial had recently been cleaned.

Campden Grammar School

The 3 photographs were taken in Campden School, Cider Mill Lane, Campden in 2007. Two memorials are located side by side. The one on the left records the former pupils of the school who served in South Africa during the Boer War. The one on the right records the names of those who lost their lives during the two world wars.

St. Catharine's Church

The memorial inside St. Catharine's Church records the names of seventeen men who died during the First World War. Five of the men do not have their names recorded on any other memorial in the town: Alistair Chisholm, Archibald Douglas-Dick, John Galloway, Charles King and Geoffrey Lynch-Staunton.

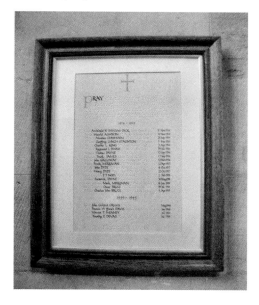

St. Catharine's Church
The framed memorial with the fallen of both world wars.

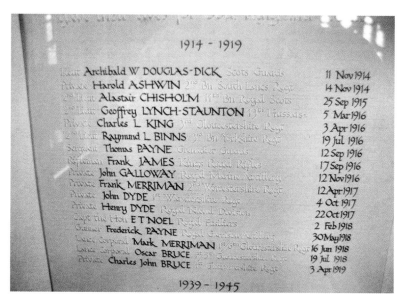

St. Catharine's Church
The fallen of the First World War. The rank and regiment for each man are written in red and do not show up clearly in black and white.

Baptist Church

The memorial inside the Baptist Church takes the form of an oak chair and the back rest records the names of six men who died during the war.

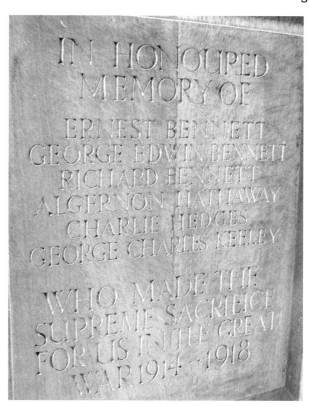

The Names on the War Memorials

In Campden there are six separate memorials for the men who gave their lives during the First World War. Each memorial has a different number and combination of names. When all of the names are listed alphabetically it can be seen that the total number of names recorded is seventy-six. Some of these names appear only once in the town while others appear as many as four times. There are also a further thirty-four men who have connections with the town but whose names did not get included on any of the memorials.

The Memorials

Baptist Church (BC): 6 names

Book of Remembrance (JG): 64 names

Campden School (CS): 12 names

High Street (HS): 62 names

St. Catharine's Church (SC): 17 names

St. James's Church (SJ): 60 names

The table below is a summary of all of the names to be found on the memorials in Campden.

	Surname	First Name	Died	BC	JG	CS	HS	SC	SJ	Total
1	ASHWIN	Harold	14-11-14		■		■	■	■	4
2	BAKER	Henry	15-6-18		■		■		■	3
3	BEAVINGTON	William	26-11-14		■		■		■	3
4	BENNETT	Ernest	29-7-18	■	■		■		■	4
5	BENNETT	George	23-7-16	■	■		■		■	4
6	BENNETT	Richard	5-4-18	■	■		■		■	4
7	BINNS	Raymund	19-7-16		■		■	■		3
8	BOULTER	Frank	12-4-18		■				■	2
9	BRAIN	Charles	23-7-16		■		■		■	3
10	BRAIN	William	23-7-16		■		■		■	3
11	BRICKNELL	Thomas	21-7-16		■		■		■	3
12	BRUCE	Charles	3-4-19		■		■	■	■	4
13	BRUCE	Oscar	19-7-18		■		■	■	■	4
14	BYRD	William	1-11-17		■		■		■	3
15	CALLAWAY	Frederick	5-8-16		■		■		■	3
16	CHISHOLM	Alistair	25-9-15					■		1
17	COLDICOTT	Arkell	19-9-15			■				1
18	COLDICOTT	Harry	7-6-17			■				1
19	COX	John	19-9-18		■		■		■	3
20	CRISP	Ernest	16-12-15			■				1
21	DAVIES	James	13-5-15		■					1
22	DOUGLAS-DICK	Archibald	11-11-14					■		1
23	DUNN	John	16-2-16		■		■	■	■	4
24	DYDE	Henry	26-10-17		■	■	■		■	4
25	DYDE	John	4-10-17		■	■	■		■	4
26	ELLIS	Gordon	24-5-15		■		■		■	3
27	FISHER	Edgar	27-6-18		■		■		■	3
28	FORSTER	Christopher	21-7-17		■				■	2
29	GALLOWAY	John	12-11-16					■		1
30	GIBBINS	Arthur	9-4-18		■		■		■	3
31	GRIFFIN	Richard	19-11-23		■		■			2
	Surname	First Name	Died	BC	JG	CS	HS	SC	SJ	Total

	Surname	First Name	Died	BC	JG	CS	HS	SC	SJ	Total
32	GRIFFIN	William E.	28-4-22				■			1
33	GRIFFIN	William H.	28-6-18		■		■		■	3
34	HANDS	Leslie	4-3-17		■	■	■		■	4
35	HARRIS	William	13-8-18		■		■		■	3
36	HATHAWAY	Algernon	7-8-15	■	■		■		■	4
37	HAYDON	Gilbert	27-8-16		■	■	■		■	4
38	HEDGES	Charles	8-10-15	■	■		■		■	4
39	HEDGES	William	25-9-15		■		■		■	3
40	HERBERT	Charles	30-8-18			■				1
41	HOWELL	Albert	2-12-18		■		■		■	3
42	HOWELL	Frank	9-2-15		■		■		■	3
43	HYATT	Victor	5-12-15			■				1
44	JAMES	Alfred	23-4-23		■			■		2
45	JAMES	Frank	16-9-16		■	■	■		■	4
46	JAMES	George	3-6-18		■		■		■	3
47	JAMES	Harry	23-3-18		■		■		■	3
48	JAMES	James	2-12-17		■		■		■	3
49	JEFFREY	Alexander	20-10-18		■		■		■	3
50	KEELEY	George	8-5-17	■	■		■		■	4
51	KEELEY	Thomas	19-8-17		■		■		■	3
52	KEEN	Arthur	27-12-19		■		■		■	3
53	KEEN	Charles	1-12-18		■		■		■	3
54	KING	Charles	3-4-16					■		1
55	LYNCH-STAUNTON	Geoffrey	5-3-17					■		1
56	MERRIMAN	Francis	12-4-17		■	■	■		■	4
57	MERRIMAN	Mark	16-6-18		■	■	■		■	4
58	MIDGLEY	John	unknown			■				1
59	MORRIS	Charles	6-6-16		■		■		■	3
60	NEVE	Basil	5-9-14		■	■	■		■	4
61	NOEL	Robert	2-2-18		■	■	■		■	4
62	OSBORNE	Raywood	4-5-16		■	■	■		■	4
63	PAYNE	Frederick	30-5-18		■	■	■		■	4
64	PAYNE	Thomas	10-9-16		■	■	■		■	4
65	PLESTED	Tom	4-7-16		■		■		■	3
66	ROBERTS	Frederick	24-9-17		■	■	■		■	4
67	SMITH	Owen	7-10-16		■		■		■	3
68	SMITH	Tom	25-9-15		■		■		■	3
69	TRACEY	Harry	13-3-15		■		■		■	3
70	TRACEY	Richard	7-11-14		■		■		■	3
71	TRINDER	James	22-3-18		■		■		■	3
72	WALTON	William	23-10-18		■		■		■	3
73	WHATCOTT	Joseph	17-2-19		■		■		■	3
74	WILLIAMS	Frank	17-8-16		■		■		■	3
75	WILLIAMS	Richard	10-7-18		■		■		■	3
76	WILLIAMS	Walter	27-3-18		■		■		■	3
	Surname	**First Name**	**Died**	**BC**	**JG**	**CS**	**HS**	**SC**	**SJ**	**Total**
				6	64	12	62	17	60	

Some interesting points to note when using the table:

- The memorial in the school does not list Harry Izod Coldicott. Harry attended the school but the memorial records *Charles Coldicott* and *Arkell Coldicott*.
- Charles and William Brain were brothers and they both died on the same day in 1916.
- John Dunn was only 16 years old when he died.
- Harry and Richard Tracey were brothers. Their brother William died during the Boer War.
- Raywood Osborne and John Cox were both sons of Grammar School headmasters.

Campden's War Dead: Cemeteries and Memorials

Every soldier, sailor or airman who died during the war has a memorial maintained by the Commonwealth War Graves Commission. This memorial either takes the form of a headstone above a known grave or a name on one of the commission's memorials to the missing. The table below gives details of the location of the grave or memorial where you can find the men recorded on the town's six war memorials.

	Surname	First Name	Cemetery or Memorial	Country
1	ASHWIN	Harold	Menin Gate Memorial, Ypres	Belgium
2	BAKER	Henry	Magnaboschi Cemetery, Asiago Plateau	Italy
3	BEAVINGTON	William	Tidworth Cemetery, Wiltshire	England
4	BENNETT	Ernest	Raperie Cemetery, Villemontoire	France
5	BENNETT	George	Caterpillar Valley Cemetery, Somme	France
6	BENNETT	Richard	Arras Memorial	France
7	BINNS	Raymund	Bécourt Cemetery, Somme	France
8	BOULTER	Frank	Toucoing Communal Cemetery	France
9	BRAIN	Charles	Thiepval Memorial, Somme	France
10	BRAIN	William	Thiepval Memorial, Somme	France
11	BRICKNELL	Thomas	Thiepval Memorial , Somme	France
12	BRUCE	Charles	St. James's Churchyard, Campden	England
13	BRUCE	Oscar	Dueville Communal Cemetery Extension	Italy
14	BYRD	William	Lijssenthoek Cemetery, Poperinge	Belgium
15	CALLAWAY	Frederick	Knightsbridge Cemetery, Somme	France
16	CHISHOLM	Alistair	Menin Gate Memorial, Ypres	Belgium
17	COLDICOTT	Arkell	Alexandria (Chatby) Cemetery	Egypt
18	COLDICOTT	Harry	Westhof Farm Cemetery, Neuve Eglise	Belgium
19	COX	John	Doiran Cemetery, near Salonika	Greece
20	CRISP	Ernest	Suzanne Communal Cemetery Extension	France
21	DAVIES	James	Menin Gate Memorial, Ypres	Belgium
22	DOUGLAS-DICK	Archibald	Menin Gate Memorial, Ypres	Belgium
23	DUNN	John	St. James's Churchyard, Campden	England
24	DYDE	Henry	Tyne Cot Memorial, Passchendaele	Belgium
25	DYDE	John	Tyne Cot Memorial, Passchendaele	Belgium
26	ELLIS	Gordon	Vimy Memorial, Vimy Ridge, near Arras	France
27	FISHER	Edgar	St. Margaret's Churchyard, Bodelwyddan	Wales
28	FORSTER	Christopher	Lijssenthoek Cemetery, Poperinge	Belgium
29	GALLOWAY	John	Ancre Cemetery, Somme	France
30	GIBBINS	Arthur	La Chapellette Cemetery, Peronne	France
31	GRIFFIN	Richard	St. James's Churchyard, Campden	England
32	GRIFFIN	William E.	St. James's Churchyard, Campden	England
33	GRIFFIN	William H.	Ploegsteert Memorial	Belgium
34	HANDS	Leslie	St. Sever Cemetery Extension, Rouen	France
35	HARRIS	William	St. James's Churchyard, Campden	England
36	HATHAWAY	Algernon	Helles Memorial, Gallipoli	Turkey
37	HAYDON	Gilbert	Thiepval Memorial, Somme	France
38	HEDGES	Charles	Loos Memorial, Dud Corner Cemetery	France
39	HEDGES	William	Loos Memorial, Dud Corner Cemetery	France
40	HERBERT	Charles	Vis-en-Artois Memorial, near Arras	France
41	HOWELL	Albert	St. James's Churchyard, Campden	England
42	HOWELL	Frank	St. James's Churchyard, Campden	England
43	HYATT	Victor	Brown's Road Cemetery, Festubert	France
44	JAMES	Alfred	St. James's Churchyard, Campden	England
45	JAMES	Frank	Thiepval Memorial, Somme	France
46	JAMES	George	St. James's Churchyard, Campden	England
47	JAMES	Harry	Pozières Memorial, Somme	France
48	JAMES	James	St. Sever Cemetery Extension, Rouen	France
	Surname	First Name	Cemetery or Memorial	Country

	Surname	First Name	Cemetery or Memorial	Country
49	JEFFREY	Alexander	La Kreule Cemetery, Hazebrouck	France
50	KEELEY	George	Arras Memorial	France
51	KEELEY	Thomas	New Irish Farm Cemetery, near Ypres	Belgium
52	KEEN	Arthur	St. James's Churchyard, Campden	England
53	KEEN	Charles	He died in Kent. Place of burial unknown.	England
54	KING	Charles	Gloucester Cemetery	England
55	LYNCH-STAUNTON	Geoffrey	Basra Memorial, Mesopotamia	Iraq
56	MERRIMAN	Francis	St. James's Churchyard, Campden	England
57	MERRIMAN	Mark	Boscon Cemetery, Asiago Plateau	Italy
58	MIDGLEY	John	Unknown	Unknown
59	MORRIS	Charles	Menin Gate Memorial, Ypres	Belgium
60	NEVE	Basil	Chatham Naval Memorial	England
61	NOEL	Robert	Dar-es-Salaam Cemetery, Tanzania	Africa
62	OSBORNE	Raywood	Berles-au-Bois Churchyard Extension	France
63	PAYNE	Frederick	Crouy Cemetery, near Amiens	France
64	PAYNE	Thomas	Guillemont Road Cemetery, Somme	France
65	PLESTED	Tom	Thiepval Memorial, Somme	France
66	ROBERTS	Frederick	Bleuet Farm Cemetery, Elverdinge	Belgium
67	SMITH	Owen	Thiepval Memorial, Somme	France
68	SMITH	Tom	Loos Memorial, Dud Corner Cemetery	France
69	TRACEY	Harry	Le Touret Memorial, near Béthune	France
70	TRACEY	Richard	Menin Gate Memorial, Ypres	Belgium
71	TRINDER	James	Savy Cemetery, near St. Quentin	France
72	WALTON	William	Gaza War Cemetery	Palestine
73	WHATCOTT	Joseph	St. James's Churchyard, Campden	England
74	WILLIAMS	Frank	Varennes Cemetery, Somme	France
75	WILLIAMS	Richard	Sarigol Cemetery, near Salonika	Greece
76	WILLIAMS	Walter	Cambrai East Cemetery	France
	Surname	**First Name**	**Cemetery or Memorial**	**Country**

The men from Campden are buried in eleven countries and, as most readers would expect, the majority lost their lives fighting on the Western Front in France and Belgium. The men buried in Great Britain died as a result of wounds received in action or from illness contracted during training. The table below shows how many men have their memorial in each country. The second table shows the number of men with a known grave and the number on memorials for the missing.

	Country	Number of men commemorated
1	France	34
2	England	16
3	Belgium	14
4	Italy	3
5	Greece	2
6	Africa	1
7	Egypt	1
8	Iraq	1
9	Palestine	1
10	Turkey	1
11	Wales	1
12	Unknown (John Midgley)	1
		Total Number of Men: 76

Number of men buried in known graves	47
Number of men recorded on memorials for the missing (no known grave)	28
Unknown (John Midgley)	1

Campden's War Dead: Not Commemorated in the Town

The table below records details of thirty-four men who died during the war and who had connections with the town. Francis Preece and Percy Lane appear in the *Book of Remembrance* written by Josephine Griffiths alongside the names of other men from the town who served during the war. No mention is made of the fact that they both died in 1918. The other thirty-two men listed below do not have their names recorded on any memorials in the town.

	Surname	Name	Died	Connection with Campden
1	BRUCE	George	2-10-18	Parents owned Norton Hall.
2	BUBB	Manley	22-8-16	Some sources state that he was born in Campden.
3	BURGESS	Harold	2-10-17	He enlisted in Campden.
4	BURROWS	Henry	24-12-15	Son of John Burrows of Kingcombe. Born in Campden
5	CLARK	Herbert	20-7-16	Lived in Campden. Father worked at Kiftsgate.
6	CORBETT	Albert	22-4-17	Baptised at St. James's in 1889. Born in Campden.
7	COTHER	George	23-7-16	Born and enlisted in Campden. A Blockley man.
8	COTTON	Sidney	20-8-15	A member of Ashbee's Guild of Handicraft.
9	CURTIS	Walter	23-9-14	Name on brother's headstone in Baptist churchyard.
10	DEVAS	Bertrand	13-11-16	Wife moved to Broad Campden after the war.
11	FRENCH	William	21-10-17	Wife was living at Lapstone Cottage in 1922.
12	HAYWARD	Arthur	12-5-15	Born in Campden.
13	HUGHES	Roland	4-6-16	Some official sources state "*born in Campden*".
14	HUNT	William	17-10-18	Living in Campden in 1912 when he enlisted.
15	LANE	Percy	26-9-18	Employed at Campden station in 1914.
16	MOSELEY	Harold	5-9-18	Parents ran a shop in Campden after the war.
17	MOSELEY	Leonard	6-5-18	Parents ran a shop in Campden after the war.
18	NICHOLLS	Albert	7-11-17	Names inscribed on parents' headstone in Campden.
19	NOBES	Wilfrid	3-4-18	Cousin of Frank, Thomas and Harry Nobes.
20	OSBORN	Frederick	1-4-17	Educated in the town.
21	PREECE	Francis	22-3-18	Manager of gasworks in Campden.
22	RADBAND	George	22-3-18	Born, baptised and educated in Campden.
23	ROBERTS	Albert	3-2-17	Born and enlisted in Campden.
24	ROBSON	Christopher	14-7-16	A member of the Guild of Handicraft.
25	RUSSELL	William	25-7-18	Groom at Norton Hall. Enlisted and lived in Campden.
26	SINCLAIR	William	19-1-19	Wife lived in Leysbourne, Campden after the war.
27	SKEY	Harland	18-8-16	Grandson of John Skey, landlord of the Lygon Arms.
28	TRACY	James	7-9-17	Born in Campden.
29	TRACY	Reginald	17-3-15	Born in Campden.
30	TURNER	Harry	14-4-18	A porter at Campden railway station.
31	WARMINGTON	Cyril	30-7-15	Educated in Campden. Cousin of Joe and Harry.
32	WATERS	Steven	24-4-18	Some sources state that he lived in Campden.
33	WEBB	Fred	11-1-16	Born in Campden.
34	WITHERS	Alfred	17-11-22	Born and educated in Campden.

Interesting points to note when using the table:

- George Bruce's name is recorded on memorials in Weston-sub-Edge and Mickleton.
- STEAM, the museum of the Great Western Railway in Swindon, has in its archives basic details about Harry Turner and Percy Lane, who were both employed at Campden station.
- Cyril Warmington's name is recorded on the war memorial in Lichfield.
- Alfred Withers died in 1922 as a result of his service during the war.
- The memorial in Pershore Abbey records the names of Francis Preece, Harold Moseley and Leonard Moseley.
- Bertrand Devas was an old boy of Stonyhurst College. Raymund Binns and Paul Woodroffe also attended the college in Lancashire.

Additional Names: Cemeteries and Memorials

The table below records the cemeteries and memorials for the thirty-four additional names. Only Alfred Withers has a grave that is not maintained by the Commonwealth War Graves Commission. He died in 1922 and does not have a headstone.

	Surname	First Name	Cemetery or Memorial	Country
1	BRUCE	George	Dadizeele New British Cemetery	Belgium
2	BUBB	Manley	Thiepval Memorial, Somme	France
3	BURGESS	Harold	Dunhallow ADS Cemetery, Ypres	Belgium
4	BURROWS	Henry	Alexandria (Chatby) Cemetery	Egypt
5	CLARK	Herbert	Baghdad (North Gate) War Cemetery	Iraq
6	CORBETT	Albert	Cologne Southern Cemetery	Germany
7	COTHER	George	Thiepval Memorial, Somme	France
8	COTTON	Sidney	Loos British Cemetery, Loos-en-Gohelle	France
9	CURTIS	Walter	Bouilly Cross Roads Cemetery, Marne	France
10	DEVAS	Bertrand	Luke Copse Cemetery, Serre, Somme	France
11	FRENCH	William	Cement House Cemetery, Langemarck	Belgium
12	HAYWARD	Arthur	Le Touret Memorial, Béthune	France
13	HUGHES	Roland	Loos British Cemetery, Loos-en-Gohelle	France
14	HUNT	William	Highlands Cemetery, Le Cateau	France
15	LANE	Percy	Tehran Memorial	Iran
16	MOSELEY	Harold	Longuenesse Souvenir Cemetery, St. Omer	France
17	MOSELEY	Leonard	Ebblinghem Cemetery	France
18	NICHOLLS	Albert	Kemmel Château Military Cemetery	Belgium
19	NOBES	Wilfrid	Roisel Communal Cemetery Extension	France
20	OSBORN	Frederick	Ecoivres Cemetery	France
21	PREECE	Francis	Pozières Memorial, Somme	France
22	RADBAND	George	Grévillers Cemetery, near Bapaume	France
23	ROBERTS	Albert	Basra Memorial, Mesopotamia	Iraq
24	ROBSON	Christopher	Essex Farm Cemetery, near Ypres	Belgium
25	RUSSELL	William	Etaples Cemetery	France
26	SINCLAIR	William	Bralo British Cemetery	Greece
27	SKEY	Harland	Thiepval Memorial, Somme	France
28	TRACY	James	Mendinghem Cemetery	Belgium
29	TRACY	Reginald	Berlin South Western Cemetery, Brandenburg	Germany
30	TURNER	Harry	Doullens Communal Cemetery Extension, Somme	France
31	WARMINGTON	Cyril	Menin Gate Memorial, Ypres	Belgium
32	WATERS	Steven	Pozières Memorial, Somme	France
33	WEBB	Fred	Loos Memorial, Dud Corner Cemetery	France
34	WITHERS	Alfred	Flax Bourton Churchyard, near Bristol	England
	Surname	**First Name**	**Cemetery or Memorial**	**Country**

	Country	Number of men commemorated
1	France	19
2	Belgium	7
3	Germany	2
4	England	2
5	Egypt	1
6	Greece	1
7	Iran	1
8	Iraq	1
		Total Number of Men: 34

Number of men buried in known graves	24
Number of men recorded on memorials for the missing (no known grave)	10

Campden's War Dead: Year of Death

The table below gives details of the number of men from Campden who died in each year of the war. The Battle of Loos began in September 1915 and then the Battle of the Somme began in July 1916. The number of casualties in 1916 will not surprise most readers but over thirty per cent of the town's casualties came in 1918.

Year of Death	Campden's War Memorials	Additional Names	Total
1914	5	1	6
1915	12	5	17
1916	17	8	25
1917	12	7	19
1918	23	11	34
1919	3	1	4
1920	0	0	0
1921	0	0	0
1922	1	1	2
1923	2	0	2
Unknown	1	0	1
	76	**34**	**110**

Campden's War Dead: Two or More Men

Some cemeteries and memorials have two or more men from Campden. Twelve men recorded on the memorials in the town are buried in St. James's churchyard. Ten men who are recorded in this book lost their lives during the Battle of the Somme in 1916 and have no known grave. Their names are recorded on the Thiepval Memorial in France.

Cemetery/Memorial	Campden's Memorials	Additional Names	Total
St. James's Churchyard, Campden	12	0	12
Thiepval Memorial, France	7	3	10
Menin Gate Memorial, Ypres	6	1	7
Loos Memorial, France	3	1	4
Pozières Memorial, France	1	2	3
Alexandria (Chatby) Cemetery, Egypt	1	1	2
Arras Memorial, France	2	0	2
Le Touret Memorial, France	1	1	2
Basra Memorial, Iraq	1	1	2
Lijssenthoek Cemetery, Belgium	2	0	2
Loos Cemetery, France	0	2	2
St. Sever Cemetery Extension, France	2	0	2
Tyne Cot Memorial, Belgium	2	0	2

Battlefield visitors to the Ypres Salient in Belgium are able to visit eleven men included in this book. Seven have their names recorded on the Menin Gate Memorial, where each night at 8.00pm Last Post is played under the memorial. Anyone who has not experienced this short ceremony is strongly recommended to make the effort. You will not be disappointed. The cemetery at Lijssenthoek, which contains the graves of William Byrd and Christopher Forster, is located near to Poperinge, where Talbot House has provided a base for the author for numerous battlefield tours.

Chapter 4

"H" Company

This chapter provides a short history of "H" Company, 5th Battalion, Gloucestershire Regiment, the local company of the Territorial Army.

The Home Guard, 1939-45
The Home Guard regularly used the same rifle range at Broad Campden that "H" Company, 5th Battalion, Gloucestershire Regiment used in the years leading up to the Great War. In this photograph Lawrence Ladbrook is at the front on the left. Also on the photograph are Gordon Bennett, Fred Nobes, Frederick "*Spud*" Benfield, Pat Moran, Sandy "*Sunny*" Harris and Edward Tomes.

"H" Company

When war was declared in August 1914 forty-two men from Campden were mobilised with "H" Company, 5th Battalion, Gloucestershire Regiment, the local company of the Territorial Army. On 15 August they had the opportunity to volunteer for overseas service. The majority responded and after a period of training in Chelmsford they arrived in France on 29 March 1915. This section provides the reader with a brief history of the battalion from the days when they were *Volunteers* to their service during the war.

The Territorial Army provided an opportunity for working men from Campden to learn the routines of being a soldier. They paraded and drilled every weekend and there was also an annual camp every summer. Men and boys of all ages joined and left the company. The company was the nearest thing that Campden had to a *Pals* unit as no other battalion from any regiment had so many men from the town serving in its ranks during the war. Five men from the town lost their lives while serving with the unit: Henry Charles Baker, Thomas Bricknell, Oscar Bruce, Gilbert Haydon and Frank Williams.

After the war the Campden company of the Territorial Army was part of the 8th Battalion, Worcestershire Regiment.

Chronology of Events

1859: The city of Gloucester formed a rifle corps. Other rifle corps were also formed in all convenient centres around the county.

1860: These rifle corps were combined to form the 2nd Gloucestershire Rifle Battalion. The 1st Gloucestershire Rifle Battalion was in Bristol. The strength of the volunteer organisation lay in the fact that the administration unit was the company. Each company commander had to raise, clothe, equip, train and provide a drill-hall, headquarters and rifle range.

1860: The Moreton and Campden (North Cotswold) Rifle Volunteers was formed as part of the 16th Gloucestershire Rifle Corps.

1880: The 16th Corps were renamed "K" Company, North Cotswold Rifle Volunteers, 2nd Gloucestershire Volunteer Rifles.

1881: Under Lord Cardwell's scheme the unit name changed to "K" Company, 2nd Volunteer Battalion, Gloucestershire Regiment.

1908: Lord Haldane's Territorial Force Act came into operation on 5 April 1908. The 2nd Volunteer Battalion, Gloucestershire Regiment became the 5th Battalion, Gloucestershire Regiment. The new battalion was part of the South Midland Brigade, South Midland Division and Lt. Col. A. B. Bathurst was its first commanding officer. It was divided up into the eight companies:

"A" Company: Gloucester
"B" Company: Gloucester
"C" Company: Stroud
"D" Company: Tewkesbury
"E" Company: Cheltenham
"F" Company: Cheltenham
"G" Company: Dursley
"H" Company: North Cotswold (Moreton-in-Marsh and Campden).

1908: The annual camp took place from 2 August to 16 August. Location unknown.

1909: The annual camp took place from 6 August to 14 August. Location unknown.

1910: The annual camp took place from 10 September to 17 September at Beaulieu on Salisbury Plain.

1911: The annual camp took place from 6 August to 13 August at Lulworth.

1912: The annual camp took place from 4 August to 18 August on Salisbury Plain.

1913: The annual camp took place from 3 September to 17 September at Shorncliffe.

1914

2 Aug: The battalion set off for its annual camp at Marlow-on-Thames.

3 Aug: Germany invaded Belgium and the battalion was sent home as war was inevitable.

4 Aug:	At 7.30pm the orders were given to mobilise.
5 Aug:	The battalion was mobilised and posted to the Isle of Wight, its first war station.
6 Aug:	The battalion left Portsmouth by steam packet at 4.00am for Ryde. On arrival a train took it to Newport. After a long march to Albany Barracks, Parkhurst tea and stew were served but the quality of the rations was poor.
9 Aug:	The battalion was relieved by the 3rd Battalion, Hampshire Regiment and moved to Swindon, where the South Midland Division was concentrating.
15 Aug:	The battalion paraded in Swindon Park and a call was made for volunteers for overseas service, a call to which all the officers and 90% of the men responded.
16 Aug:	The battalion left for Hockcliffe, Bedfordshire.
19 Aug:	The men left Hockcliffe for Chelmsford (an eighty-mile march), where it was intended that the battalion should be stationed for the double purpose of guarding the East Coast and of training in preparation for overseas service.
24 Aug:	The battalion arrived in Chelmsford.
2 Sept:	The South Midland Brigade was inspected by General Sir Ian Hamilton.
14 Oct:	The South Midland Division was inspected by the King at Hylands Park, near Chelmsford.

1915

The battalion was formerly made up of eight companies. All of the officers and most of the men had been born and bred in Gloucestershire and constituted the *"flower of the County"*. By the start of 1915 the battalion had been organised into a four-company system, drafted to full strength, trained and disciplined. "H" Company was now part of the new "D" Company and the battalion's new title was 1st/5th Battalion, Gloucestershire Regiment. When it arrived in France the battalion formed part of 145th (South Midland) Brigade, 48th Division (South Midland Territorial Division).

The first three months of the year were spent based in Chelmsford and there were regular long route marches and plenty of drill, training and inspections.

13 Mar:	A period of *"severe training"* begins.
29 Mar:	The battalion, under the command of Lt. Col. J. H. Collett, left Chelmsford at 5.30am for the Front. It arrived at Folkestone at 9.00pm and embarked on RMS *Invicta* for France, where it arrived at Boulogne.
30 Mar:	The battalion marched to a station and entrained in cattle trucks. After arriving at Cassel the men marched to Steenvoorde in Belgium.
7 Apr:	The battalion marched to Ploegsteert (called *Plugstreet* by the troops), where it experienced life in the trenches for the first time. The headquarters were in a brewery on the edge of the wood.
5 Jun:	A member of the battalion describes his journey to the front line: *"Through the wood where bullets came zipping from all sides. Out of the wood and a mad scamper over two open fields and into the front trench, bathed in sweat."*
July:	The battalion moved south into France and arrived in the Hébuterne sector at the northern end of the Somme battlefield, where it remained until July 1916.

1916

21 Jul:	The battalion suffered 121 casualties in an attack near Ovillers during the Battle of the Somme. Tom Bricknell was killed in action.
23 Jul:	The battalion suffered 114 casualties in another attack near Ovillers.
17 Aug:	Frank Williams died of wounds and was buried in Varennes Cemetery.
27 Aug:	The battalion suffered 156 casualties in another attack near Ovillers. Gilbert Haydon was killed in action.
Sep-Dec:	Somme battlefield area.

1917

Jan-Jul:	Southern Somme sector. The Hindenburg line area between Arras and St. Quentin.
Jul-Oct:	The Ypres Salient in Belgium to take part in the Third Battle of Ypres (The Battle of Passchendaele).

1 Nov:	The battalion was posted to trenches at Vimy Ridge in France.
24 Nov:	The battalion entrained at Tinques and Aubigny for an unknown destination, although most of the men knew they were going to Italy.
27 Nov:	The men passed through the Mont Cenis Tunnel and arrived in Turin at 11.00am. At 6.00pm the battalion arrived in Milan, where the station was packed with cheering Milanese.

1918

June:	The battalion was heavily involved in fighting on the Asiago Plateau.
15 Jun:	Henry Baker was killed in action and was buried in Magnaboschi Cemetery.
19 Jul:	Oscar Bruce died of wounds and was buried in Dueville Cemetery Extension.
11 Nov:	The armistice was signed.

Photograph Gallery

"K" Company, 2nd Volunteer Battalion, Gloucestershire Regiment
Robert Coldicott is standing at the far left-hand edge of the photograph. Joseph Williams is the right-hand man of the two standing in front of the left-hand bay window, to the left of the main door. The photograph was taken in the Square in Campden.

The Drum and Fife Band of K Company, 2nd Volunteer Battalion, Gloucestershire Regiment, 1897
This photograph appeared in the *Evesham Journal* in 1937. It stated that the photograph was 40 years old.
Left to right: James Keeley, Harry Baker. William Taylor, George James (drummer), Alfred Smith, Louis Harris (drummer), Edgar Keeley, William Aston (with the big bass drum in the centre), Charles Veale, Edwin Harris, Frederick Howell, James Court, William Bunker, Algy Hathaway, Frederick Benfield, William Collett Chamberlain (beard) and Charles Bruce.

"K" Company, 2nd Volunteer Battalion, Gloucestershire Regiment.

"K" Company. Which is Alf Bruce?   Annual Camp at Lulworth, August 1911. Norman Bennett is holding the mallet.

5th Battalion, Gloucestershire Regiment
Harold Pyment is the tall man holding the horse. It looks like Tom Bricknell standing on his right-hand side. The photograph was taken after mobilisation.

Annual Camp at Beaulieu, 1910
Arthur Bunten is standing at the back behind Norman Bennett. The following are standing (left to right): Bill Bricknell, George William Plested, unknown, Norman Bennett, Harry Ellis and Tom Bricknell. James Simmons is kneeling with Norman's hand on his shoulder. The three seated on the ground are (L-R): Stan Keeley, Willetts Horne (holding the "H" Company flag) and Harry Bricknell. Joe Warmongton has his hand on Harry Bricknell's back.

Annual Camp at Beaulieu, 1910
Joyful Billy Harris can just be seen standing fifth from the left. Norman Bennett is to the right of centre with his tunic open and right hand on his hip. Harry Bricknell is seated on the ground in the centre to the left of Norman with top tunic button undone.

5th Battalion, Gloucestershire Regiment, England, 1915
Joyful Billy Harris is seated on the ground in the right-hand corner. Harold Pyment and Tom Bricknell can also be seen.

The Territorials in the Square, Campden
Joe Warmington can be seen at the end of the third rank of four men.

Norman Bennett is standing at the back on the left.
Fred Merriman is at the front on the right.

5th Battalion, Gloucestershire Regiment, 1915
The photograph below was taken during final training in England by J. W. Hack of Chelmsford. Harold Pyment can be clearly seen as the tallest man in the group.

"H" Company, 5ᵗʰ Battalion, Gloucestershire Regiment, Chelmsford (August 1914-March 1915)
Back row (left to right): unknown, unknown, Harold Pyment, Fred Bennett, unknown, Walford Chamberlain, unknown, Tom Bricknell, Jackie Webb, Fred Franklin and Joyful Billy Harris.
Front row (left to right): unknown, unknown, Albert Bradley, unknown, unknown, Harry Bricknell and James Simmons.
It is likely that two of the unknown men on the front row are Thomas Keeley and his brother, George Keeley. One of the sergeants on the left of the photograph could be William Travill. All men in the photograph are believed to be from Campden.

Harold Pyment is the tall man second from the left and Joyful Billy Harris is second from the right of the front rank.

"H" Company, 5ᵗʰ Battalion, Gloucestershire Regiment, August 1914
The company are marching to war after being mobilised. Captain Noel is at the front and Harold Pyment is the NCO in the centre.

"K" Company Armoury, the Square, Campden.

Soldiers billeted at 21 Park Avenue, Chelmsford, October 1914.

A group of men loading belts with bullets for the machine guns, Chelmsford.

2nd Volunteer Battalion, Gloucestershire Regiment, West Lulworth, 1907.

The Volunteer Inn, c.1921
Lawrence Malins is wearing his two 1914-18 campaign medals. During the war he served in the Gloucestershire Regiment, the Labour Corps and the South Lancashire Regiment. His parents, Thomas and Hannah, arrived in Campden in 1902 and took over the running of the pub.
Thomas died in the pub on 2 September 1923 aged 66.

Chapter 5

The German Field Gun

This chapter records the events in the town following the arrival of the German field gun.

Private 2575 Gerald Martin Minett, 1ˢᵗ/1ˢᵗ Warwickshire Yeomanry
Gerald was from Aston-sub-Edge and served with several local men in the Warwickshire Yeomanry during the Great War. After the war he was a member of the Norton Estate War Club.

The German Field Gun

In 1919 the War Office offered the town a German field gun and the Parish Council agreed that it should be accepted. George Ebborn said: "*It was a trophy of the war captured by our brave British soldiers. It was in itself evidence of their valour and although I am not particularly enamoured by anything German I am sincerely proud of the great and glorious achievements of our soldiers and sailors of all branches of our King's service.*" George Howley said that from a soldier's point of view he thought that the gun should be accepted although Tom Ellison said: "*Personally I don't want to see another German gun.*"

A committee was formed and, together with the local branch of the Comrades of the Great War, a suitable site for the gun was found. The gun arrived in the town in February 1920 and a concrete base was prepared for it next to the Market Hall. It was ceremoniously installed in March 1920 and handed over into the care of the Parish Council. The ceremony was abruptly cut short by torrential rain and this proved ominous, for it soon became apparent that the presence of a German field gun in the centre of Campden was an emotive and divisive issue. For the children it was an excellent toy for playing soldiers around, and for some it was a symbol of triumph, but for many it was a terrible reminder of the horrors of the war they had been through.

Two weeks after installation the annual parish meeting was asked whether the gun could be moved to a less prominent site, but it was explained that the site had been chosen in full consultation with ex-servicemen. A month later, during the night of 24 May 1920, the gun was removed from its base and dumped in the middle of the cart-wash opposite the Almshouses. Undeterred, the Parish Council replaced it next to the Market Hall but this time the tail and the wheels were bedded firmly in cement, or so it was thought. But before the cement set a child was sent to go and quietly scratch it out. Then on the Saturday night, shortly before midnight, a group of young people gathered around the gun. Speeches were made opposing its continued presence and it was claimed that sealed orders had been given, which were to be opened at the church, to remove the gun to a hitherto unknown destination. Meanwhile, a police constable, hearing the disturbance, came out to investigate. He was told to return to the police station and know nothing, which he did. The sealed orders were opened at the church; they said that the gun should be dragged to the Coneygree and run into the brook. The gate of the Coneygree was reached with considerable difficulty. The gun was hauled up to the top of the bank, where the lynch pins were removed, and from there it was allowed to run down to the brook, its wheels dropping off as it reached the water.

The Parish Council realised that the cost of retrieving the gun for the second time could not be justified and the subsequent offer by Lord Sandon from Burnt Norton to remove it to his grounds was gratefully accepted, as was his gift of two guineas to the Campden War Memorial Fund.

The Market Hall
The German field gun arrived in the town in February 1920 and a concrete base was prepared for it next to the Market Hall. It was ceremoniously installed in March 1920 and handed over into the care of the Parish Council. The concrete slab is clearly visible on the grass bank to the right of the Market Hall.

The German Field Gun
The gun after being dumped in the cart-wash opposite the Almshouses, 25 May 1920.

The Warwickshire Yeomanry, Christmas 1914
Several men from Campden served in the Warwickshire Yeomanry during the Great War. Gerald Martin Minett is standing on the back row fifth from the left. He was born at Stanley Pontlarge, near Gretton, Gloucestershire. When he enlisted in 1914 he was living and working at Middle Norton Farm, Aston-sub-Edge.

The Warwickshire Yeomanry, c.1914
Several men from Campden and the local area around the town served in the Warwickshire Yeomanry during the Great War. Gerald Martin Minett, 1895-1978, is on the back row second from the left. He enlisted on 29 October 1914 and arrived in Egypt in September 1915. After the war he married Muriel Elizabeth Horne at St. James's Church.

Chapter 6

Homes for Heroes

This chapter records details of the eight houses built by the Council for returning servicemen and their families.

Private 310700 Edwin Smith, Warwickshire Yeomanry
Edwin was from Aston-sub-Edge and served with several local men in the Yeomanry during the Great War. His eldest son, Edwin William Smith, was killed in action while serving on HMS *Repulse* in 1941.

Homes for Heroes

In 1919 Gloucestershire County Council, with a government grant, built eight semi-detached houses for returning ex-servicemen and their families on Aston Road, each with an acre of land attached as a smallholding. The houses were finished in 1921 and details of the first tenants can be seen below. Today in 2008 the houses are still there but all have had extensions built. None of the present-day owners is a descendant of the original tenants but it seems very appropriate that number 4 is called *Poppy Bank* and number 5 *Taplins*.

The Tenants

The original tenants' names are in bold. To find out more about the families living in these houses the reader should refer to Chapter 1, where biographies of 487 men and women who served in the war can be found.

Number 1:   **William Henry ("*Kaiser Bill*") and Amy Ellen Benfield**

Number 2:   **Richard and Mary Elizabeth Green**

Number 3:   **Henry and Lily Louise Pope**. After Henry Pope left the town the house was occupied by Alfred John and Lucy May Bruce.

Number 4:   **Fred and Elizabeth Hedges**. Jerry Howell married Nora Hedges, daughter of Fred and Bess, in 1924. After the wedding Jerry and Nora lived with Fred and Bess. Today in 2008 the house is a bed-and-breakfast establishment called *Poppy Bank*.

Number 5:   **George and Sarah Taplin**. Four of their children served during the war. Their daughter Nora continued living in the house until she died in 1988. At the time of writing this book the house is a bed-and-breakfast establishment called *Taplins*.

Number 6:   **William and Mary Ann Cooper.** After the death of William the house was occupied by two of his children, Alexander and Rose.

Number 7:   **Thomas and Sarah Payne**. Thomas died at Stow-on-the-Wold in 1934. Sarah remained in the house until she died in 1948 aged 83 years. Winifred Monica Payne, their daughter, also lived in the house with her husband, Leonard Arthur Powell, and their daughter, Dorothy. Cyril Hobbs was the next tenant.

Number 8:   **Reginald Richard and Gladys Emily Smith**. After Reg moved to Station Road in Campden Frank and Catharine Nobes became the tenants of the house.

4, Aston Road, Campden
Fred and Bess Hedges were the original tenants.

5, Aston Road, Campden
George and Sarah Taplin were the original tenants.

Gloucestershire County Council, Smallholdings, Campden, 1921
Eight houses were built on Aston Road in Campden. The photograph shows a group of men employed building the houses.
Front Row (L-R): Bob Grove, W. Coldicott, J. Payne, Tom Grove, Joe Harwood, Mike Grove, Enoch Bennett, J. Keitley, George Nobes, J. James and unknown.
Middle Row (L-R): W. Bennett, E. Buckland, A. James, A. Cross, Dick Green, G. Mayo and George Plested.
Back Row (L-R): The foreman, Mr. Bates, Fred Smith, Jim Harris, Happy Sadler (from Stow) and Joe Bennett.

The photograph on the left shows a group of men and boys employed building the houses on Aston Road.

Frank Bennett is standing at the back fourth from the left.

Noah Bennett is standing at the back fifth from the left. Noah was the father of Ernest and Richard, who both lost their lives during the war.

Jim Harris is standing on the left.

Homes for Heroes: Aston Road, Campden, 2008

The entrance to 3, Aston Road, Campden, 2008

Maye Emily Bruce, 1879-1964
Maye ran the VAD hospital at Norton Hall during the war.

Norton Hall VAD Hospital, c. 1914-18
The photographs above were provided by Andrew Davenport. He is interested in the work that Maye Bruce did in developing her Quick Return compost method.

Epilogue

The details of 487 men and women who served in the 1914-18 war are included in this book. Listed below are a further thirteen men whose names were listed in the 1916 St. James's Church prayer list, the *Book of Remembrance* by Josephine Griffiths or in the *Evesham Journal*. Despite extensive research by the author no details of any of these men could be found. If anyone reading this book has information relating to these men, or anyone else remembered in this book, the author would be very pleased to hear from them. This new information will be included in *Campden 1914-18 Archive,* held by the author.

- Charles BURNETT

- Reginald CAIRNS

- Arthur William CHERRY

- William HAYLOCK

- Arthur JONES, Royal Fusiliers

- H. B. LEWIS

- The Hon. William LITTLETON

- Cyril SHEADMAN

- John SMITH, Royal Air Force

- Frank THORNE

- William James TURNER

- E. E. WEST, Worcestershire Regiment

- Thomas WHEELER

In the words of Laurence Binyon in his poem *For The Fallen* that was first published in *The Times* in September 1914:

*"**At the going down of the sun and in the morning, we will remember them.**"*

Postscript

The book was about to be sent to the publishers for printing when Stan Nicholls made an enquiry at the archive room in the Old Police Station in Campden. His grandfather served in the war and lived in the town for the greater part of his life. The author was contacted and what follows are the details of Bill Nicholls, Stan's grandfather. This now means that this book contains short biographies of 488 men and women who served their country during the 1914-18 war.

William Nicholls
Army Service Corps

Born: 15 September 1882
Discharged: February 1919
Died: 14 December 1971

Bill was born in Upper Quinton. He was one of four children of Josiah and Rosanna Nicholls. By 1901 he was employed as an assistant baker in Fladbury, where he first met his future wife, Mary Stanford. In 1906 he married Mary and moved to Campden, where their first son, Charlie, was born in 1907 at 3, West End Terrace. Charlie was then baptised at St. James's Church on 6 October 1907.

During his time in Campden Bill was employed at Gabb's bakery. Just before he left the town a second child, a daughter called Winifred, was born. She was baptised at St. James's Church on 2 May 1909. After the family had left the town two further children were born: Stanford in Bourton-on-the-Water in 1909 and then Rose in Northleach in 1913.

When the hostilities broke out in 1914 Bill was still living in Northleach. He enlisted in the Army Service Corps and served on the Western Front throughout the war, where he was employed as a cook and baker. The food was delivered by Bill to the front line trenches using a horse and cart.

In February 1919 he returned home after being granted a compassionate discharge from the army as his wife, Mary, had died a month earlier from the Spanish influenza pandemic sweeping the country. She was already buried by the time that Bill arrived home and he found his four children being looked after by various families in Northleach.

He then returned to Campden with the four children and again found employment at Gabb's bakery. They lived in Poppets Alley and then in Sheep Street, opposite what is now the Cotswold Garage. In the 1920's they moved into a brand-new house, 9, Catbrook. Bill lived in this house until going into hospital in 1971, where he died on 14 December when he was 89 years old. He was buried in St. James's churchyard in Campden.